CU00762971

LEFTISM REINVENTED

STEPHANIE L. MUDGE

LEFTISM REINVENTED

Western Parties from Socialism
to Neoliberalism

Harvard University Press

Cambridge, Massachusetts, and London, England   2018

Copyright © 2018 by the President and Fellows of Harvard College
All rights reserved
Printed in the United States of America

Second printing

Library of Congress Cataloging-in-Publication Data

Names: Mudge, Stephanie L., 1973– author.
Title: Leftism reinvented : Western parties from socialism to neoliberalism /
    Stephanie L. Mudge.
Description: Cambridge, Massachusetts : Harvard University Press, 2018. |
    Includes bibliographical references and index.
Identifiers: LCCN 2017047891 | ISBN 9780674971813 (hardcover : alk. paper)
Subjects: LCSH: Liberalism—Western countries. | Liberalism—Economic aspects—
    Western countries. | Right and left (Political science)—Western countries. |
    Political parties—Western countries.
Classification: LCC JC574 .M84 2018 | DDC 324.2 / 17091821—dc23
    LC record available at https://lccn.loc.gov/2017047891

For Dave, Leighton, and Julian

Contents

List of Tables and Figures

Preface

On New Year's Eve, 1999, the citizens of Western democracies celebrated the coming of the new millennium in a moment marked by the triumph of markets and the dominance of center-left governments. The former had been in the making for decades, but the latter was a novelty. Center-left parties held the reins of government in only a handful of Western countries in 1990, but the 1992 election of William Jefferson Clinton as the forty-second president of the United States was the first of a series of turnarounds. By the year 2000 center-left parties had come to power in many Western countries, including the vast majority of the fifteen nations that made up the European Union (EU) at that time. With Clinton and the British prime minister Tony Blair in the lead, a new cadre of center-left political elites declared the arrival of a new era of "third way"—or, later, "progressive"—leftism.[1]

The event prompted a decidedly mixed reaction. Where some saw a "magical return of social democracy," others saw a leftish brand of free market politics that was social democratic in name only.[2] In 1997 the British scholar Colin Crouch, for instance, described Blair's New Labour government as the culmination of neoliberalism's "new hegemony."[3] For Crouch and others third wayism was mere capitulation, or a case of the left gone right—different in degree, but not in kind, from the free market conservatism of Ronald Reagan and Margaret Thatcher.

Analytically speaking, it was a puzzling state of affairs. At what point is a historically left party no longer left—and if it is not left, then what is it? The unavoidability of the left-right binary in Western politics, and thus also in political analysis, renders answers to such questions forever contestable. The fact that third wayers themselves blurred the left-right distinction only complicates matters. Indeed, at the center of third way rhetoric was the claim that "old" left-right oppositions were no longer meaningful in a globalized world—and that, if social democracy (or, in the United States, liberalism) was to be saved, it had to "modernize." In the famous phrasing of the great British sociologist Anthony Giddens, the task of the twenty-first-century center-lefts was to take their politics in a "radical" direction that was "beyond left and right."[4] And yet, at the same time, third wayers insisted that they remained defenders of social justice and opportunity and stood opposed to naked free market ideology—and thus were not to be confused with their market-loving, inequality-embracing, neoconservative counterparts. How, then, does one assess third wayers' claims to a radical departure from the left-right binary, versus counterarguments—usually from the left—that third wayism was mere rhetorical cover for a soft version of right-wing neo-liberalism, without taking sides in a fundamentally political fray?

Originally, this book grew out of a long-standing fascination (some might say obsession) with this perplexing political moment. The third way period is often explained, still, in terms similar to third wayers': due to economic or political reasons or both, center-left parties *had* to reinvent themselves in a market-friendly way. But standards of proof for these claims are fuzzy. First of all, the "market" has no stable constituency. Second, third way–era center-left political leaders proactively advanced the very same economic globalization that, they claimed, rendered politicians helpless. Third, while the third way center-lefts were electorally successful in the short term, they did not transform their parties into long-term, "natural" parties of government—the professed goal, for instance, of Tony Blair.[5] From the 1990s forward even the most successful social democratic party in Western history, the Swedish Social Democratic Party (SAP), saw its electoral strength seriously erode.

This erosion is critically important for the future of democratic polities. The term "left" means many things in Western contexts, but all those meanings have a shared origin in claims to representation of the underrepresented in service of equality.[6] For this historical reason left parties bear a unique responsibility to speak for poor, disadvantaged, and disenfranchised groups—and are, by extension, important barriers to the descent of democracy into plutocracy. Here we should take note that in the 1980s and 1990s, as third wayism took shape, economic inequality accelerated, voting and political engagement declined, and many people who should have been, in theory, left voters turned to extreme parties. Manifestly, third wayism was not a politics of civic reinvigoration. One can reasonably question whether it gave meaningful voice to insecure, financially anxious, and downwardly mobile people. Everyone should be worried about the answer to this question.

Here we get to the crux of my obsession with the third ways: insofar as left parties are checks on plutocracy, they are also lynchpins of democracy writ large. Without left parties, in other words, democracy is in trouble. Indeed, standard theories in historical political economy—in particular, those of Karl Polanyi—are quite clear on what we should expect of a world in which there is no longer any democratically imposed limit on the expansion of market society: the rise of an unpredictable populist and extremist politics marked by protection-seeking rebellions against the march toward *homo economicus,* grounded in a volatile mix of class politics, ethno-racial and nationalist resentments, and basic human responses to disruption, risk, uncertainty, anxiety, and boundless competition. Around the turn of the twentieth century the French sociologist Emile Durkheim used the term "anomie" to refer to this state of affairs; by the time of Polanyi's *The Great Transformation* (1944), the fate of the whole Western political order hung in the balance. There is now good reason to see the 1990s as the eve of a new Polanyian moment that is very much with us still.

To my mind, if we are to grasp these troubling times, the story of the third ways requires a careful, analytical, historical retelling. This retelling needs to be clear-eyed about the self-justifications of third way spokespersons, but, at the same time, it should avoid the "logic of the trial"— in the phrasing of the sociologist Pierre Bourdieu—in which the more or less explicit question is where, or with whom, blame lies.[7] Third wayers need to be situated and historicized, not frozen in time or rendered one-dimensional. If the aim is to shore up left representation not for parties' sake but for democracy's sake, then we need to grasp the forces that shape how left parties "see," informing political debates rather than feeding the divorce of politics and reason.

To this end I adopt a historical, cross-national, and biographical approach focused on parties and their spokespeople. Essential here is the juxtaposition of third way leftism, and the people who gave it form and substance, with the leftisms (and spokespersons) who came before it. Another important step is a rejection of the notion that there is a clear, hard distinction between parties and electorates—a way of thinking that tends to reduce questions about parties to an irresolvable binary in which parties drive electorates, or electorates drive parties. Rather, I take it as given that parties and electorates *constitute* each other.

Starting from this premise, my analysis centers on left parties' cultural *infrastructure*—that is, the organizations, social relations, persons, and devices through which parties organize how people see and understand the world. Instead of asking whether party change is "top-down" or "bottom-up," I ask how left parties have shaped the very meaning of what it is to be an American "liberal," or to be "Labour" in Britain, or to be a "social democrat" in Sweden or Germany. I also ask why a strikingly uniform cross-national identifier—"progressive"—has now supplanted all of these terms. To ask these questions is to acknowledge that, like the umbrella terms "left" and "right," monikers like "liberal" or "social democratic" do not have the same meaning, or describe the same kinds of people, across times and places. There is also variation in such terms' territorial reach, and indeed whether they travel across national boundaries at all. Perhaps most importantly, political identifiers have little practical meaning in the absence of political and civic organizations—especially, but not only, political parties—through which people come to understand themselves as political in the first place. Analyzing leftism's reinventions requires linking the category "left" to parties and then moving inside parties to understand the social and infrastructural bases of the making of political meanings.

And so, to understand Western leftism's reinventions, I focus on four parties: the German Social Democratic Party (SPD), the Swedish Social Democratic Party (SAP), the British Labour Party, and the American Democratic Party. I punctuate a long historical view, ranging from the late 1800s to the early 2000s, with emphases on three moments: the 1920s–1930s, the 1950s–1960s, and the 1980s-1990s. Via an analysis of programmatic language, I identify a distinctive leftism in each moment: *socialist, economistic* (or Keynesian), and *neoliberalized* (or third way). Noting cross-national variations (for instance, that the Democratic Party was never socialist), I show that the twentieth century's three leftisms were not only rhetorically distinctive; they were also rooted in unique relationships between parties, experts, and expertise. Stated differently, leftisms were both rhetorically and *infrastructurally* distinctive. To show this I focus on the trajectories, experiences, and worldviews of party spokespeople, or *party experts*—and, in particular, of ministers of finance in Sweden and (West) Germany, chancellors of the exchequer in the United Kingdom, presidential economic advisers in the United States, and the networks around them. I thus treat experts and expertise (and, by extension, culture) as crucial to representative politics and indispensable to the analysis of party-political change.

Approached in this way, one can see what was special about the expert and infrastructural bases of twentieth-century leftisms. One can see, for instance, that the Keynesian economists who formulated center-left rhetoric in the 1960s were nothing like the socialist journalists and agitators of the 1920s. One can also see the specificities of the transnationalized, finance-oriented economists (TFEs), think tank–based policy specialists ("wonks"), and strategic experts ("spin doctors") who spoke for third wayism in the 1990s. And, from here, we can ask about the institutional conditions that made different party experts possible, how certain experts displaced others over time, and for whom, or for what, different party experts spoke. In the case of the party experts of the third way, for instance, TFEs spoke for markets, policy specialists spoke for what works, and strategists spoke for what wins—but it is by no means clear that any of them gave effective "voice to the voiceless," in Bourdieu's words.[8]

All that said, I do *not* offer any simple, competing hypothesis to existing accounts of party change—including arguments that electorates, economic events, or party elites drive what parties do. I try to work with these accounts, not against them. But I do reject the notion that parties are like pinballs, pushed around by the forces of external events. I also reject the notion that parties are internally uniform units. In my way of thinking parties are more like prisms than pinballs: what parties do expresses the relationships, perceptions, institutional situations, and action-orientations of people inside of them. Infrastructural differences, in other words, shape how parties *refract*. If we want to understand party change in a way that gets at the crucial problem of representation, and not just whether parties win elections or pursue a particular policy, the analysis of parties must be capable of grasping the dynamics of refraction.

In my emphasis on party experts some will perhaps recognize an old problematic in the sociology of knowledge: the political role of the intellectual. But, in the case of party experts, in a way this problematic is beside the point. By definition, party experts communicate in, through, and on behalf of parties, and so there can be no question that they play a political role. The key questions, to my mind, are how any particular person becomes a party expert, why party experts see things in certain ways, and what the representational consequences of party experts' worldviews are. Answers to these questions lead, in turn, to an overarching question, the answer to which is central to the future of democratic societies: whether left parties are capable of grasping the concerns and daily realities of the people they represent, organizing and channeling people's interests, and building definite political agendas on those bases. The concern my analysis raises, and which I sincerely hope will be taken up, is whether twenty-first-century left parties have the capacity to effectively represent those most in need of representation.

This book has been very long in the making, undergoing its own reinventions along the way. Certain people have been especially crucial to its circuitous trajectory. These include, first, my mentors in the sociology program at the University of California, Berkeley: Neil Fligstein, Margaret Weir, and Sam Lucas. Each of them shaped my intellectual formation in ways that defy tidy summary. As an indefatigable scholar, unwavering friend, supplier of housing to mendicant end-stage graduate students (thanks also to the kindness of Heather Haveman), and enduring professional advocate, Neil Fligstein deserves special recognition. Other members of Berkeley's illustrious sociology faculty also, knowingly or not, exerted a great deal of influence on my thinking. In no particular order, these include Jerome Karabel, Ann Swidler, Mike Hout, Claude Fischer, Loïc Wacquant, Marion Fourcade, and Martín Sánchez-Jankowski. All taught me things about how to be a sociologist that made this book possible.

These pages would not exist without friends made in graduate school and its aftermath. Also in no particular order, fellow Berkeleyites who have kept me (relatively) sane include Ryan Centner, Tony Chen, Isaac Martin, Sarah Quinn, Damon Mayrl, Nick Wilson, Emily Beller, Shelly Malhotra, Caroline Hanley, Melissa Wilde, Jane Gingrich, Beth Berman, Lisa Stampnitzky, Tom Medvetz, Barry Eidlin, Libby Anker, and Greggor Mattson. As a Fulbright fellow doing research abroad in and around Brussels I encountered yet more PhDers who each, in their way, helped me get through—especially Khalisha Banks, Leah Boston, and Kristien Michelson. In San Francisco and thereabouts, Sarah Brydon, Cornelia Sterl, and sundry climbing friends kept me grounded, not to mention housed, fed, and watered. The same is true of my half-brother, Gregory Mudge, and his kids, Emily and Christopher.

After graduate school I had the stupendously good fortune of going to the European University Institute (EUI) in Florence, Italy, on a Max Weber Program postdoctoral fellowship, followed by another postdoctoral year at the Max Planck Institute for the Study of Societies (MPIfG) in Cologne, Germany. The core concerns of this book were developed in these years, thanks in no small part to the people I encountered. These include Brigitte LeNormand, Ted Sandstra, Rubén Ruiz-Rufino, Umut Aydin, Mate Tokić, Jan-Hinrik Meyer-Sahling, Thomas Hintermaier, Helen Callaghan, Anne Rasmussen, Giesela Rühl, Rinku Lamba, Francesco Maiani, Anna Lo Prete, Matei Demetrescu, Giammario Impulitti, Kurtuluş Gemici, and Gabriel Abend. At the EUI I was privileged to have the mentorship of Sven Steinmo and, informally, of the late, great Peter Mair—whose work has been critical to my thinking about political parties and who is sorely missed. I also had the special pleasure of briefly crossing paths with Ann Orloff and with Perry Anderson, with lasting consequences. In particular, Perry Anderson's work on Western Marxism fundamentally reoriented my thinking about leftism's historical arc and the significance of the intellectual-party relationship therein.[9] At the EUI I was also fortunate to make the acquaintance of Antoine Vauchez, who became a coauthor, collaborator, and friend. Last but not least, I benefited immeasurably from spending time at the MPIfG under the directorship of Wolfgang Streeck and Jens Beckert.

After the MPIfG I became an assistant professor at the University of California, Davis. I am deeply grateful for the support of my colleagues, students, and the broader UC-Davis community. I would especially like to thank Fred Block for his unwavering support and uncanny ability to provide incisive, lightning-fast feedback on even the draftiest of chapters. Vicki Smith has been a special source of guidance and professional inspiration. John R. Hall was an invaluable reader in the book's final stages and remains a particularly engaging conversation partner for the politics-obsessed. Tom Beamish, Ming-Cheng Lo, Patrick Carroll, David Kyle, Eddy U, and Ryan Finnigan have all been important sounding boards at some stage. Bill McCarthy shepherded me through a crucial period in my time at Davis. Two graduate students, Brian Veazey and Phyllis Jeffrey, provided indispensable research assistance; they and many others—including Zeke Baker, Dustin Mabry, and Christopher Lawrence—have also been sources of very stimulating conversation. Kate Miller and Christoph Gumb helped with some translations. Jenny Kaminer helped as a confidant, friend, and partner in ladies' nights. Michael McQuarrie, now at the London School of Economics, enriched my intellectual development at Davis tremendously and continues to do so from afar. Michael also deserves thanks for introducing me to Josh Pacewicz, who became a steadfast advocate during even my darkest days of book-writing despair. Josh's sociological wisdom informs a great deal of the analysis to follow.

This project has benefited from various sources of financial support that include, beyond the institutions already mentioned, the Hellman Family Foundation and the Sheffield Political Economy Research Institute (SPERI). Thanks to the Hellman Foundation I was able to connect with journalists, experts, and sundry political professionals, meddle in think tank archives in Washington, D.C., and travel to London, Brussels, and Berlin. I am also grateful for a wonderful year spent with SPERI, headed by Tony Payne and Colin Hay, in 2013–2014, which afforded time to develop my analysis and to deepen my familiarity with British politics. Last but not least, I owe many thanks to three Harvard University Press editors—Michael Aronson, John Kulka, and Andrew Kinney—for shepherding this book through to publication, to several anonymous reviewers for their helpful comments, suggestions, and critical feedback, and to Mary Ribesky and the staff at Westchester Publishing Services for their highly competent editorial support. All errors in the pages to follow are my own.

During the roughly ten years spent writing and rewriting (and rewriting) this book I lost some family members and gained others. Inexplicably, all saw fit to support my sociological adventures. My late mother, Susan Mudge, made everything possible for me; I would have liked to put this book in her hands, but a loving remembrance of her in these pages will have to suffice. My father, James Mudge, has been, and remains, a steady and beloved source of support. He may recognize himself, a little, in the account of the grounded-in-reality economist theoreticians that I give in the pages to follow. So too might John Hansen, a second father who, along with the unstoppable Judy Hansen, has fundamentally shaped how I see the world. Jenny and Dave Ware provided me with food, housing, excellent company, transportation, boundless goodwill, sage last-minute editorial advice, and the joy of getting to know their two lovely girls, Charlotte and Julia. The fabulous Mariam Erenburg, hostess of NYC escapes, fellow lover of margaritas, and provider of Beastie Boys tickets, also provided editorial advice. More importantly, Mar is to thank for a friendship that is more precious than she perhaps understands. Thanks are also due to a second big sister, Camilla Japec, who is a true inspiration, and to Phil Georgatos, for his steadfast friendship for more years than I'd like to count.

I assume that my beautiful and talented sister, Jennifer Mudge, understands that, despite frequent threats to feature her name in a "disacknowledgments" section, her unflagging faith in me has seen me through, well, everything. Jennifer is also to thank for having had the good sense to bring my brother-in-law, Guy Jones, plus the whole Jones clan, into my life, and for giving me the gift of being an auntie to her now shockingly grown-up children, Aidan and Justine Mannan. A very special acknowledgment also goes to Julia and Al McCourt, Clare and Scott Macaulay, and little Alice—who have welcomed me into their family with open arms, thus enriching my existence beyond measure. Last but certainly not least, I want to thank my partner in-all-things, David McCourt, for being a brilliant scholar, the love of my life, and a wonderful father to our two sons, Leighton and Julian—who are, by far, my greatest achievements. This book is for the three of them.

Abbreviations

AAA	Agricultural Adjustment Administration (United States)
AAPC	American Association of Political Consultants
ABF	Workers' Educational Association/Arbetarnas Bildningsförbund (Sweden)
ADA	Americans for Democratic Action
ADAV	General German Workingmen's Association/Allgemeiner Deutscher Arbeiterverein (1863–1875)
ADGB	General German Trade Union Confederation/Allgemeiner Deutscher Gewerkschaftsbund, formerly the General Commission of German Trade Unions/Generalkommission der Gewerkschaften Deutschlands (prewar Germany)
AEA	American Economic Association
AER	*American Economic Review*
AFL	American Federation of Labor (later AFL-CIO)
AHA	American Historical Association
ASA	American Statistical Association
ASSA	American Social Science Association
BAE	Bureau of Agricultural Economics, Department of Agriculture (United States)
BEW	Bureau of Economic Warfare, formerly the Economic Defense Board (EDB) (United States)
BIS	Bank for International Settlements
BOB	Bureau of the Budget (United States)
BYC	British Youth Council
CAB	Civil Aeronautics Board (United States)

CAP	Center for American Progress (United States)
CBO	Congressional Budget Office (United States)
CDF	Conservative Democratic Forum (United States)
CDM	Coalition for a Democratic Majority (United States)
CDU	Christian Democratic Union of Germany/Christlich Demokratische Union Deutschlands (1945–)
CEA	Council of Economic Advisers (United States)
CED	Committee for Economic Development (United States)
CEPR	Centre for Economic Policy Research (United Kingdom)
CIO	Congress of Industrial Organizations (later AFL-CIO) (United States)
CIPU	Counter-Inflation Publicity Unit (United Kingdom)
CLPD	Campaign for Labour Party Democracy (United Kingdom)
CPE	Committee on Party Effectiveness (United States)
DAC	Democratic Advisory Council (United States)
DDR	German Democratic Republic/Deutsche Demokratische Republik
DEA	Department of Economic Affairs (United Kingdom)
DGB	Confederation of German Trade Unions/Deutsche Gewerkschaftsbund ([West] Germany)
DIW Berlin	German Institute for Economic Research/Deutsches Institut für Wirtschaftsforschung, formerly the Institute for Business Cycle Research Research/Institut für Konjunkturforschung
DLC	Democratic Leadership Council (United States)
DNC	Democratic National Committee (United States)
DNVP	German National People's Party/Deutschnationale Volkspartei (1918–1933)
DPC	Domestic Policy Council (United States)
DYG	The Younger Old Men/Den Yngre Gubbarna (Sweden)
ECB	European Central Bank
ED	*Ekonomisk Debatt* (Sweden)
EEA	European Economic Association
EEC	European Economic Community
EFO	Edgren-Faxén-Odhner model (Sweden)
EFTA	European Free Trade Association

EITC	Earned Income Tax Credit
EMI	European Monetary Institute
EOP	Executive Office of the President (United States)
EP	European Parliament
EU	European Union
FDP	Free Democratic Party/Freie Demokratische Partei (1948–, [West] Germany)
FEE	Foundation for Economic Education (United States)
FEPS	Foundation for European Progressive Studies (Belgium)
FERA	Federal Emergency Relief Administration (United States)
FES	Friedrich Ebert Foundation/Friedrich-Ebert-Stiftung (interwar & [West] Germany)
FNS	Friedrich Naumann Stiftung ([West] Germany)
GES	Government Economic Service (United Kingdom)
GOP	Grand Old Party (1854–, Republican Party) (United States)
HWWA	Hamburg Institute of International Economics/ Hamburgischen Welt-Wirtschafts Archiv ([West] Germany)
IBRD	International Bank of Reconstruction and Development
IDU	International Democrat Union
IEA	Institute of Economic Affairs (United Kingdom)
IFO-Institut	Ifo Institute for Economic Research, University of Munich/Ifo Leibniz-Institut für Wirtschaftsforschung an der Universität München ([West] Germany)
IfW	Kiel Institut für Weltwirtschaft/Kiel Institute for the World Economy ([West] Germany)
IIES	Stockholm Institute for International Economic Studies (Sweden)
IIR	Institute for Industrial Research (Germany)
ILP	Independent Labour Party (1893–1975, United Kingdom)
IMF	International Monetary Fund
IPPR	Institute for Public Policy Research (United Kingdom)
JEC	Joint Economic Committee (United States)
KAS	Konrad Adenauer Stiftung ([West] Germany)

KI	National Institute of Economic Research/ Konjunkturinstitutet (Sweden)
KPD	Communist Party of Germany/Kommunistische Partei Deutschlands (1918–1933, 1946–1956)
LI	Liberal International
LO	National Trade Union Confederation/Landsorganisationen (Sweden)
LRC	Labour Representation Committee (United Kingdom)
LRD	Labour Research Department, formerly the Fabian Research Department (United Kingdom)
LSE	London School of Economics and Political Science
MIT	Massachusetts Institute of Technology (United States)
MP	Member of Parliament
MPS	Mont Pèlerin Society
MT	*Marxism Today* (United Kingdom)
MTFS	Medium Term Financial Strategy (United Kingdom)
NAFTA	North American Free Trade Agreement
NBER	National Bureau of Economic Research (United States)
NEA	National Education Association (United States)
NEC	National Executive Committee (Labour Party, United Kingdom)
NEC (US)	National Economic Council (United States)
NEDC	National Economic Development Council (United Kingdom)
NF	National Economics Society/Nationalekonomiska Föreningen (Sweden)
NFRB	New Fabian Research Bureau (United Kingdom)
NLRA	National Labor Relations Act (United States)
NRA	National Recovery Administration (United States)
NRPB	National Resources Planning Board (United States)
NWLB	National War Labor Board (United States)
OECD	Organization for Economic Cooperation and Development, formerly the Organization for European Economic Cooperation (OEEC)
OMB	Office of Management and Budget (United States)
OMOV	One-Member-One-Vote (United Kingdom)
OPA	Office of Price Administration (United States)
OPEC	Organization of Petroleum Exporting Countries

PDS	Party of Democratic Socialism/Partei des Demokratischen Sozialismus (1989–2007, [East] Germany]
PLP	Parliamentary Labour Party (United Kingdom)
PPE	Philosophy, Politics, and Economics (degree program—Oxford University)
PPI	Progressive Policy Institute (United States)
PWA	Public Works Administration (United States)
RAF	Red Army Faction (West Germany)
RNC	Republican National Committee (United States)
RWI	RWI-Leibniz Institute for Economic Research/RWI–Leibniz-Institut für Wirtschaftsforschung, formerly the Rheinisch-Westfälisches Institut für Wirtschaftsforschung ([West] Germany)
SACO	Central Organization of Professional Employees/Sveriges Akademikers Central Organisation (Sweden)
SAF	Employers Association/Svenska Arbetsgivareföreningen (Sweden)
SAP	Social Democratic Workers' Party of Sweden/Sveriges Socialdemokratiska Arbetareparti (Also: Social Democrats/Socialdemokraterna) (1889–)
SAPD	Socialist Workers' Party of Germany/Sozialistische Arbeiterpartei Deutschlands (1875-1891)
SDAP	Social Democratic Workers' Party/Sozialdemokratische Arbeiterpartei (Germany, 1869-1875)
SDF	Social Democratic Federation, formerly the Democratic Federation, or DF (1881–1911, United Kingdom)
SDP	Social Democratic Party (1981–1988, United Kingdom)
SEB	Swedish Central Bank/Sveriges Riksbank
SNS	Center for Business and Policy Studies (Sweden)
SOU	Government Official Investigation/Statens Offentliga Utredningar (Sweden)
SPD	Social Democratic Party of Germany/Sozialdemokratische Partei Deutschlands (1891-1933; [West] Germany 1946-)
SPÖ	Austrian Social Democratic Party/Sozialdemokratische Partei Österreichs, formerly the Austrian Social Democratic Workers' Party/Sozialdemokratische Arbeiterpartei Österreichs (SDAPÖ) (1889–1934, 1945–)

SSA	Social Science Association, formerly the National Association for the Promotion of Social Science (United Kingdom)
SSU	Social Democratic Youth Organisation/Sveriges Socialdemokratiska Ungdomsförbund (Sweden)
SVR	Council of Economic Experts/Sachverständigenrat ([West] Germany)
TCO	Confederation of Professional Employees/Tjänstemännens Centralorganisation (Sweden)
TERA	Temporary Emergency Relief Administration (United States)
TEU	Treaty on European Union, or the Maastricht Treaty (1992)
TFE	Transnationalized, finance-oriented economist
TNEC	Temporary National Economic Committee (United States)
TUC	Trades Union Congress (United Kingdom)
UC	Unemployment Committee (interwar Sweden)
UCL	University College London
UDA	Union for Democratic Action (United States)
UNCTAD	United Nations Conference on Trade and Development
VfS	Association for Social Policy/Verein für Sozialpolitik ([West] Germany)
WASG	Electoral Alternative for Labor and Social Justice/Arbeit und soziale Gerechtigkeit—Die Wahlalternative (2005–2007, Germany)
WPA	Works Progress Administration (United States)
WPB	War Production Board (United States)
WSI	Institute of Economics and Social Sciences/Wirtschafts- und Sozialwissenschaftliches Institut (formerly the Economic-Scientific Institute, or Wirtschafts-Wissenschaftliches Institut [WWI]) (Weimar and [West] Germany)
WTB	Woytinsky-Tarnow-Baade episode (interwar Germany)
WZB	Social Science Center/Wissenschaftszentrum Berlin für Sozialforschung ([West] Germany)

LEFTISM REINVENTED

CHAPTER ONE

Analyzing Leftism's Reinventions

> No social study that does not come back to the problems of
> biography, of history and of their intersections . . . has
> completed its intellectual journey.
>
> —C. Wright Mills, 1959

L ANGUAGE is the means of representative politics, but the represented do not control its production. Analyzing representation
thus requires an understanding of the production, and the *producers*, of political language. Starting from these premises, and taking
heed of C. Wright Mills's sociological injunction to attend to the intersection of history and biography, the present account of Western leftism's
twentieth-century reinventions centers on singularly significant sites of
political language production: the political party and, within it, the party
expert.

Broadly speaking, Western left parties entered the twentieth-century
socialist and departed in the market-friendly, or neoliberalized, form of
the "third way." The implications of left parties' wide arc from capitalism's critics to markets' advocates are much debated in historical scholarship, but those debates sometimes overlook that there was also a
leftism in between: after socialism and before third wayism there was
Keynesianism, or what I call *economistic* leftism. In short, the language
of twentieth-century leftism was not once but twice reinvented: in the first
half economistic leftism displaced its socialist predecessor; in the second
half economistic leftism gave way to neoliberalized leftisms of various
sorts (third way, third road, new middle). I seek to explain these two reinventions via a historical, biographically centered analysis of four parties: the American Democrats, the German Social Democrats (SPD), the
Swedish Social Democrats (SAP), and the British Labour Party.

I take up this explanatory project with the full acknowledgment that "left" means something very different on either side of the Atlantic. If we date Western leftism's birth to the French Revolution, the category "left" is well over two centuries old and is distinctively European. By the early 1900s Western leftism's meaning and practice was hitched to a specific, and relatively new, organization: the mass party, grounded in socialism and linked with organized labor. This novel political organization, which Max Weber termed an "ideological" mass party, was forged in the later decades of the 1800s and thence acquired considerable power.[1] In the United States, however, the party system is older and has a history of systemic "realignments"; shifting axes of differentiation have not always hinged on a left-right distinction.[2] And, as noted in a long line of scholarship dating, at least, to Werner Sombart's *Why Is There No Socialism in the United States?* (1906), the national-level American political scene has never featured a major ideological mass party of the socialist variety.

By the 1920s Americans were well familiar with mass parties of a non-ideological kind. Weber described early twentieth-century Republican and Democratic parties as "patronage" organizations, "merely interested in putting their leader into the top position so that he can turn over state offices to his following."[3] But, even as Weber wrote, American partisan institutions were being displaced by the rise of Progressive Era voluntary and professional associations and, with them, a new "progressive" politics. These new forces intersected with both of the great American parties, especially on the Republican side; progressivism at that time was neither "right" nor "left."[4] By the late 1930s, as progressive forces injected a new expert professionalism into American political institutions, organized labor gained political influence, and the Democratic New Deal coalition coalesced, the Democratic Party *became* "left" in the public imagination—despite the fact that it had never been socialist or a formal representative of organized labor. And so there was a certain convergence of European and American leftisms. There is therefore good reason to include the American Democratic Party alongside that of European socialist, social democratic, and laborite parties in a study of Western leftism—so long as we also keep in mind that this comparison only makes sense *after* the Democrats became left.

All of the four parties analyzed in this book have been, in their own ways, crucial to the meaning and transformation of Western leftism. First, all were major electoral contenders in their respective countries for the whole of the twentieth century. The SPD, the original socialist-ideological mass party, was an influential model for mass party formation well beyond Germany from the late nineteenth century; the SPD's shift from socialist to economistic leftism, which coalesced in the 1950s, was important precisely for this reason. The SAP, meanwhile, was the most electorally successful Western social democratic party in the twentieth century, making Sweden a central reference point in cross-national discussions of the possibilities for social democratic politics. The British Labour Party's highly labor-driven origins make it a particularly important case for the study of the labor-left party relationship and, despite Britain's reputation for political conservatism, the Labour Party's stated policy commitments also remained comparatively radical well into the late twentieth century. The American Democratic Party played a notable part in the definition of Western center-leftism from the New Deal period forward, which is notable especially in light of its peculiar organizational and nonsocialist history. And, last but not least, the Democratic and Labour parties were both leading protagonists in the making of third way leftism, at home and transnationally, at century's end. All are thus useful entry points into the general explanatory problem of leftism's variable meanings over time—that is: how and why left parties moved from socialist, to economistic, to neoliberalized leftism.

There are also reasons for my attention to a specific kind of left party—of the mainstream, or center-left, sort. To the extent I take non-mainstream left parties into account—for instance, communist parties that proliferated in the 1910s and 1920s, green parties in the 1980s, or left protest parties that emerged around the turn of the twenty-first century—I do so by placing them in relation to their mainstream brethren (from which, one should note, smaller communist, green, and left parties often emerged).[5] Mainstream parties of the center and center-right—liberal, conservative, and Christian democratic parties; the U.S. Republican Party—also appear in my account insofar as leftism's reinventions had to do, in whole or in part, with turns of events on the right. Newer parties of the extreme right, which became increasingly prominent in the 1990s, are also considered in relation to goings-on with center-leftism.

But, because my explanatory focus is on how center-left parties spoke, this analysis centers on the contests, collaborations, and social relations that shaped interpretive, or *refraction,* processes in and among mainstream parties of the left. In this sense the present work dovetails with recent scholarship in the political science of parties that emphasizes (in the political scientist Daniel DiSalvo's words) that parties' internal factional struggles are "engines of change" and should be analyzed as such.[6]

This does not mean that I consider non-center-left parties monolithic or unimportant or that I understand center-left parties as hard-bounded entities—far from it. Center-left parties are built on complex social relations that, in turn, occupy but one location in a much broader field of activity. But center-left parties, and the social relations that make them up, also have a special place in Western political history. Originating in Europe in the late nineteenth century, they drove the making of modern party systems not only as forces of democratization but also as innovators of a new organizational technology: the mass party.[7] Key to the ideological mass party form was a triple orientation: first, toward *knowledge production, education, socialization,* and *truth-claiming;* second, toward *representation, agitation,* and *mobilization;* and third, toward *office-* or *power-seeking.* Each orientation, in its own way, expressed the historical moment. Ideological mass parties of the left were educators and knowledge producers when there was no mass education; they agitated and mobilized in a world of severely limited voting rights; they provided a means to political careers for the nonwealthy in an age in which aristocratic avocational politicians, with no need for a regular salary, were the rule rather than the exception.[8] As such the mass party of the left shaped the formation of parties, politicians, political identities, and the boundaries of politics itself. They are major reasons that one can say, in the words of the political scientist Peter Mair, that "above all else, the twentieth century has been the century of the mass party."[9]

Beyond left parties' historical role in the making of mass politics, there are also normative and practical reasons for focusing on parties of the mainstream left. Left parties were built on claims to equal representation in political life, and have always claimed to speak for disempowered and nonprivileged groups. The practical truth of this claim matters a great deal. Normatively, one can argue that democracy is not particularly meaningful if the nonprivileged lack effective representation. Practically, the history of populism and populist movements suggests that underrepresentation of the nonprivileged puts democratic political orders at risk of serious instability. And so how left parties speak, and for whom, has major implications for the representativeness and longevity of democracy as a whole.

My approach to the study of center-left parties is comparative, historical, and biographical. I narrow the general task of analyzing mainstream leftism by punctuating a long-term, four-party analysis with emphases on three time periods: the 1920s–1930s, 1950s–1960s, and 1980s–1990s. I construct my explanatory puzzle, leftism's reinventions, not by measuring policies in these periods but by tracking changes in *political language*—that is, changes in the most basic stuff of representative politics. Embracing the time-tested sociological principle that historical analysis should be able to tell the "big" story *and* that of actors on the ground, I account for changes in political language via an analysis of *both* large-scale institutional transformations *and* the trajectories, positions, and self-accounts of actors who speak for parties: *party experts*. Party experts are social actors in party networks who orient their activities toward the production of ideas, rhetoric, and programmatic agendas in political life in the effort to shape how both electorates and politicians view and understand the world. For reasons explained further below, I focus especially on European ministers of finance and their advisory networks and, in the case of the American Democratic Party, on economic advisory networks centered on presidential candidates.

My focus on experts arises from a theoretical perspective that takes parties as internally contested networks of social relations that do much more than seek votes, policies, and offices. Parties also seek to naturalize themselves by shaping how we understand the world and our place in it. In this effort, experts play a special role. Party experts may have all sorts of backgrounds—they may be academics, politicians, journalists, trade union researchers, backroom strategists, clergy, financiers, and so forth; for present purposes their distinguishing feature is in their action-orientation: they strive to formulate the language by which parties characterize the world, define programmatic priorities, and communicate with publics. In so doing, party experts become *intermediaries* between represented groups and elected or office-seeking representatives.

Party experts are, in other words, spokespersons in a double sense: for parties and for those whom parties claim to represent. The extent to which party experts are able to perform this double task is key to parties' capacity to shape people's worldviews, cultivate constituencies' sense of being meaningfully represented, link everyday concerns to policies or policy agendas, and thus organize political life—or, in the terminology adopted herein, parties' *capacity to intermediate*.[10] For this reason, understanding who party experts are, what makes them possible, and how they see things is especially important.

Left party experts may be of many sorts, but, as I will show in the analysis to follow, the role of economists inside left parties, and the arc of left parties' relationship with professional economics more generally, has a special significance. This relationship was *weak or nonexistent* in the age of socialist leftism, but at midcentury the left party–economics relationship was *strong and interdependent*. I will show that, for all of the parties considered here, around 1960 some of the most prominent left party experts were credentialed economists who were distinctively hybrid: they had one foot in left parties and the other in academic economics professions. I call these historically specific experts *economist theoreticians*. Thanks to their scientific credibility and their institutional in-betweenness, economist theoreticians were able to wear many hats— as strategists and speechwriters, public communicators, and (sometimes) intermediaries between party leadership and a key constituency: organized labor. Their in-betweenness also fostered and reinforced a certain way of seeing the world and their role in it: for economist theoreticians, economic management was of a piece with political consensus-building; their task as economists-in-politics was to keep sound scientific advising grounded in the demands of domestic politics. I call this way of seeing things the *Keynesian ethic*.

The economist theoretician was not like left party experts before or after him. In Western European countries, before the economist theoretician there was the socialist *party theoretician*—a journalist and "agitator" who was deeply party-dependent, and was no academic. I will show that, in the 1920s, the party theoretician tended to be at odds with union leaders and credentialed economists alike, who appeared to the party theoretician as intraparty challengers. If we then skip to the 1990s, past the time of the Keynesian ethic-bearing economist theoretician, we find that there were still plenty of left party–affiliated economists, but they were distinctive *kinds* of economists. The 1990s center-left economist was internationalized, credentialed but not necessarily professionally grounded in the academic world, and had close linkages with domestic and international financial institutions. I call this brand of party expert a *TFE:* the transnational, finance-oriented economist. Like the economist theoretician, TFEs saw things in ways that accorded with their institutional locations, viewing themselves as interpreters, guardians, and (sometimes) saviors of markets.

TFEs were not "neoliberals," but as spokespeople for markets they were bearers of a *neoliberal ethic*. Insofar as TFEs spoke for markets, and not any particular group (trade union or otherwise), they did not perform the domestically grounded strategic and intermediary work that their predecessors did. I will show that the TFE offered more proscription than prescription when it came to problems of representation, coalition-building, and political strategy. This created problems, especially as center-left electoral coalitions fractured and vote margins declined. The arrival of the TFE on the scene fueled left parties' turn to new experts, especially of a strategic sort, who did the work of linking the defense and advocacy of markets to the representation of, and communication with, constituents, with an eye to winning elections.

The economics–left party relationship in the 1990s was thus important, but circumscribed, relative to the 1960s. The influence of TFEs was mediated by growing ranks of policy specialists (sometimes termed "wonks," indigenous to the worlds of nonprofit research, especially think tanks) and strategic experts (sometimes termed "spin doctors," with ties to professional media outlets, consultancies, polling and public opinion research outfits, and so forth). TFEs spoke for markets; specialists spoke for what works; and strategists spoke for what wins. But, as new extreme parties gained appeal, it was by no means clear that TFEs, strategists, and specialists spoke for constituents—traditional or otherwise.

The pages to follow fill out this story, showing how changing party-expert relationships drove the programmatic vocabularies of left parties and, by extension, leftism's reinventions. As the reader will have gathered, I approach this task using a specific analytical strategy. Much research on party politics focuses on big transformations in parties and

electorates; states and governing institutions; organized labor and social movements; or business, capital, and finance. I consider big transformations too, but I look at them from the *inside out* by situating the
biographical trajectories, proximate struggles, and professional ethics
of party experts within broader historical currents. This *refraction* approach is grounded in a conception of parties as prisms rather than pinballs.[11] Via a refraction approach one can see how big transformations
and destabilizing events (for example, the Great Depression, social protest, oil price shocks, or the 1994–1995 Mexican peso crisis) generated
new problems, intensified interpretive struggles, and drew in new kinds
of experts who struggled to define how parties spoke. This book gives
an account of leftism's reinventions with emphasis on this inside-out,
or refraction, story.

One of the advantages of my approach is that, by compelling the analyst to focus on the orientations, situations, and positions of historical
actors, everything becomes relational. The hard distinctions that often
guide political research—between states and markets, parties and electorates, interests and ideas, or the national and the international—look
more fluid from the inside out than from a bird's-eye view. One can see
how social dynamics and relationships inside parties shape, or refract,
events and forces beyond them. A result is that, while I recognize that
the party-electorate relationship is important, I am able to treat the significance and meaning of electoral "demand" as an interpretive question,
determined by forces internal to parties. While I recognize parties as
nationally centered organizational animals, I am also able to avoid an
analysis that is overly nationally bound. My account's center of gravity
begins in Germany, the United Kingdom, and Sweden, attending to the
transnationalism of radical and exiled journalists at mass left parties'
birth; it then moves toward the United States and ends with particular
emphasis on transatlantic political and professional elites in the globalizing and financialized setting of the late twentieth century. This aligns
my analysis with a growing acknowledgment in historical sociology that
the boundaries between the national and the trans- or international are
variable, and variably important, for understanding historical change.[12]

The remainder of this chapter lays out the framework of the book.
In the first section I provide a brief history of Western leftisms in the
twentieth century, which expressed the century's three dominant "isms":

socialism, Keynesianism, and neoliberalism. The second section turns to the problem of analyzing hegemonic political ideologies, or "isms," highlighting the indispensability of political parties to the endeavor. I make the case for a refraction approach that treats parties as internally contested social terrains in which social actors' orientations intersect with, and respond to, neighboring fields—economic, political, cultural, bureaucratic. The third section elaborates the historical, comparative, and biographical epistemological concerns that are consistent with a refraction perspective. In the fourth section I present major arguments of the book and contrast them with alternatives. The fifth, and concluding, section offers a brief overview of the chapters to follow.

WESTERN PARTIES, LEFTISM, AND THE ANALYSIS OF POLITICAL IDEOLOGY

Early 1900s left parties in Western Europe painted a picture of the world with a Marxist brush.[13] Born as mass organizations grounded in socialism and organized labor, left parties told publics a tale of the inexorable but disruptive development of industrial capitalism, the making of the working class, the inevitability of class struggle, and progress toward a socialist future. Advocating not only for basic protections—eight-hour workdays, weekends, child labor laws—but also for the "socialization" of ownership of the means of production, theirs was a specifically *socialist leftism.*

By the 1960s mainstream left parties' geographical reach included the American Democrats, who, alongside their European peers, offered an altogether different leftism. Left parties now framed the world in technocratic, *economistic* terms, assuring publics that they possessed the know-how to intervene in economies precisely, scientifically, and as necessary. For economistic leftism the aim was not socialism so much as full employment; the means was not socialization but scientific economics. In this confident era left parties argued that social problems can and should be resolved with policies that even out distributive inequalities, expand safety nets for the poor, and enhance people's quality of life, regardless of their income or employment status. They recognized the importance of stable prices and currencies, but saw these as manageable via a combination of scientific know-how and cooperative bargaining.

Leftism changed, again, by the 1990s. Left parties' confident assertions of managerial control of the economy gave way to declarations of necessary adaptation to the market. In this era of *neoliberalized leftism,* left parties' rhetoric and policy pursuits became more difficult to distinguish from what, historically speaking, people thought of as politically "right." Surprisingly enough, none other than the most successful social democratic party in the West—the Swedish Social Democratic Party (SAP)—was one of neoliberalized leftism's most important innovators. In an open break with the past, the incoming SAP government of 1982 prioritized containing inflation over keeping unemployment low and pursued financial liberalization with the explicit aim of increasing profits relative to wages. By the 1990s it was clear that the SAP's change of heart was neither temporary nor idiosyncratic. In the United States, the Clinton administration upended the legacy of New Deal liberalism with a "New Democrat" agenda that emphasized work-centric welfare reform, balanced budgets, market-led growth, and smaller government. In Britain a rebranded "New Labour" party abandoned its famous commitment to the common ownership of the means of production and distanced itself from unions. Upon taking office, New Labour empowered the Bank of England as part of a broader effort to depoliticize economic policy-making, summarily ending Labour's long-standing efforts to rein in the powers of British finance.

And then there was Germany. Once the most influential party of the mass socialist left and the standard bearer of Marxist orthodoxy, the German Social Democratic Party (SPD) returned to government in 1998 and, within a year, enthusiastically embraced the Blairite "Third Way." The SPD-led government thence set off in pursuit of more restricted, work–conditional labor market and social insurance reforms and defended the low inflation, money-centered orthodoxies of a newly integrated Europe. These kinds of policies and positions were, by century's end, widespread in the West and were all the more remarkable for their embrace by the political left.

In this brief overview of the twentieth century's three Western leftisms readers may recognize themes that are symptomatic of the period's dominant "isms": socialism, Keynesianism, and neoliberalism. In this sense, leftism's reinventions are merely specific cases of more general political worldviews. And yet the making and remaking of leftism cannot be accounted for by simply chalking them up to ideologies out there.

Rather, the analysis of leftism's reinventions requires thinking about where political ideologies come from, how they manifest in the lives and activities of social actors, and how they intersect with politics and parties. I turn to this in the next section.

ON THE STUDY OF "ISMS"

The suffix "-ism" tends to appear when a worldview of temporally and socially situated people about the means and ends of government becomes a widespread basis on which political power is exercised. An "ism," in other words, is a political ideology.[14] A geographically and politically far-reaching "ism" is a hegemonic ideology—that is, a governing *doxa* or common sense, or what the French social thinker Michel Foucault described as a logic of the art of government.[15]

The three "isms" that feature in the overview of leftisms just given— socialism, Keynesianism, and neoliberalism—are all essentially the same *kind* of analytical object: a political ideology with some original association with the orientations of historically and socially situated people. An implication of this understanding of political ideology is that its analysis is never strictly in the province of political sociology—that is, the sociology of power-seeking and political institutions. It is also, unavoidably, an object of the sociology of knowledge.

Indeed, the sociology of knowledge has always taken ideology as a sociopolitical effect. Karl Mannheim described the major ideologies of nineteenth- and early twentieth-century Germany in these terms: "bureaucratic conservatism" reflected the perspective of Prussian state administrators; "conservative historicism" expressed the viewpoint of German academic historians and dominant bourgeois state leadership; "liberal-democratic bourgeois thought" (or what we might now understand as "old" liberalism) was the standpoint of the new industrial-era bourgeoisie; and so forth.[16] Mannheim took for granted that ideologies expressed the sociostructural locations of their progenitors and that one must therefore locate the origins, background, and positions of the ideolog*ists*.

Here Mannheim drew heavily from Karl Marx and Max Weber, both of whom grappled with the major ideology born of the eighteenth century: liberalism. For Marx, liberalism originated in the misrecognized interests of nonreflexive academics and professionals (the "ideologists").[17] Weber also located liberalism's bases in "the 'liberal' professions," marked by possession of "sought-after expertise or privileged education."[18] Foucault later stressed that the figures who articulated eighteenth-century liberalism were bearers of a hybrid form of expertise: they were grounded in both political economy and public law. Foucault proposed that this duality constituted proof of liberalism's twofold practical nature: liberal governmentality imposed a principle of limitation on the jurisdiction of the state that derived from the truth-telling, or "veridiction," of the market.[19]

In all of this there is a basic assertion that "isms" have definite historical, intellectual, and professional origins to which the study of political ideology must attend.[20] This realization, creditable to Marx, emerged from a kind of exasperation with liberal professionals' lack of reflexivity—that is, their failure to recognize the connection between their position in the world and their interpretation of it.[21] Marx arguably overcorrected for this problem by brushing off actors' self-understandings as misrecognition or false consciousness, arguing that one could explain the liberal views of "ideologists" by simply uncovering their class location and their relationship to class-based political movements.[22] Marx thus laid an important foundation for the sociology of knowledge by linking ideology to social position, but he dismissed the possibility that there was explanatory value in first-person accounts.[23]

Since Marx's time a more full-fledged sociology of knowledge took shape, even as new "isms" arose: Keynesianism, neoconservatism, neoliberalism. All had intellectual and professional origins; none was reducible to class interests. Alongside the formation of new political ideologies, however, sociological thinking on their origins and nature also shifted. Recent work stresses the relational insight that political ideologies are better thought of as strategic orientations and expressions of contested relations rather than essential categories.[24] The sociologists Neil Gross, Thomas Medvetz, and Rupert Russell, for example, explain American neoconservatism as the contested end product of struggles between free market libertarians, New York City–based anticommunist Jewish intellectuals, and "fusionist" conservative intellectuals.[25] Historical analyses of neoliberalism's origins tell a similar story of a political ideology borne of relationality and contestation.[26]

Updates notwithstanding, the sociology of knowledge's basic position stands: political ideologies are situated viewpoints that can and should be traced to situated people. But this is only a starting point. From here, the study of "isms" encounters a whole series of problems: how do we conceptualize any given "ism" in a way that facilitates explanatory analysis? If we reject Marx's dismissal of first-person accounts, then how do we then deal with disjunctures between what people say and what they do? And how do we account for the processes by which political ideology becomes *hegemonic,* or a widespread basis on which political power is exercised?

Three Problems, Three Remedies

The trouble with the analysis of "isms" can be broken down into three distinct problems: conceptualization, consent, and the relationship between ideology and power.[27] Drawing from sociological thinkers including Marx, Weber, Gramsci, and Bourdieu (with a healthy dash of Durkheim), here I address each problem in turn.

Conceptualization. The task of conceptualization has long been a primary concern of social theory. Classical statements highlighted the necessity of the historicization of the object as a preliminary to any attempt at sociological explanation.[28] To this end, a growing body of recent work mobilizes relational thinking to conceptualize various contested objects, including race, the state, the European Union (EU) and its associated institutions, money, terrorism expertise, think tanks, and political ideology.[29] In all cases, a relational approach to conceptualization eschews essentialism, anthropomorphism, and tendencies to attribute causal primacy to the sheer force of ideas, remaining mindful that worldviews always originate with people, that those people are variably positioned and unequally resourced, and that institution building is at once a historical and a contested social process.

In this way of thinking socialism, Keynesianism, and neoliberalism are not singular, essential things but rather contested historical effects of social relations over time. This is not to deny that there is such a thing as a distinctive worldview, or ideology, with intrinsic characteristics: it is true that social democracy is built on the "primacy of politics,"

to get around

— Isms

Keynesianism involves a balancing act between political and economic demands, and neoliberalism elevates markets over politics.[30] But these ways of seeing the world were not born fully formed and then simply installed into the operations of governing institutions. They were developed by historically situated people whose experiences and social situations shaped how they saw things and became central to the exercise of power via definite institutional pathways. For instance: socialism's early formation was inseparable from networks of radical journalists and pamphleteers; its development was always heavily dependent on parties and party-political networks; and its twentieth-century trajectory was hitched to the fate of Soviet Russia. A similar story can be told of Keynesianism—which, as Timothy Mitchell has eloquently shown, had everything to do with the statistical construction of the world as a system of economies in the 1930s amid the breakdown of colonial empire—or, finally, of neoliberalism, which was born at the margins of academe and politics, partly in *reaction* to Keynes, Keynesianism, and the figure of the interventionist Keynesian economist.[31]

The task of conceptualizing an ideology is thus a deeply historical undertaking. So, also, is the task of understanding how an ideology and its bearers become effective. As we move away from the origin stories of socialism, Keynesianism, and neoliberalism and toward their relationship to politics, one finds many pathways, variations, and exceptions—and, by extension, that ideologies are not singular things and cannot be treated as such. It is in the nature of any form of hegemony that one cannot "explain" it as a whole or treat it as a singular X or Y variable; it is simply not a "forcing cause" sort of phenomenon.[32] What one needs is a way of keeping ideology grounded, linked to people, and situated with respect to centers of politics, power, and policy-making—or, in the phrasing of the sociologists Gil Eyal and Larissa Buchholz, understanding the processes by which bearers of knowledge and expertise acquire a capacity for intervention.[33]

It is precisely for this reason—namely, the need to make a distinction between the *production* of ideology and the *acquisition* of capacities for political intervention—that the concept of field comes in handy.[34] The notion of field is roughly analogous to a "game," in the nonrational-choice sense of the term. Putting the field concept to work requires, however, shifting gears from ideologies to people, events, and processes in which ways of thinking (categories of vision and division, in Bourdieu's terms; ethics, in Weber's terms) and doing present themselves.[35] One can then trace those people, events, and processes in place and time, locate them in field struggles (say, over political power, or academic prestige, or state resources), and situate them within intra- and cross-field dynamics—the "spaces between fields"[36]—in order to explain historical change. In the process we can investigate what makes a certain kind of actor, bearing a certain way of understanding the world, possible, likely, and politically consequential. The ultimate aim is to grasp how certain kinds of historical figures acquire a capacity to make their way of seeing things into a more general principle or logic of action—a question that lies, always, at the crux of the move from ideology to hegemony.

Where does relationality come in, exactly—and why is it necessary? Relationality involves seeing social phenomena in terms of social relations and authority struggles therein, rather than as stable essences. In a relational way of thinking political ideologies are born not of consensus but of contestation, expressing the perspective of the victors of struggles over truth and meaning. The products of those essentially cultural struggles—which include not only ways of seeing the world and one's role in it (an *ethic*, one might say) but also distinctive historical types of ethical actors—come into play. Relationality allows one to see that class-based conceptions of political ideology—that is, the notion that political ideologies are expressions of class interests—are never the whole truth, and that they have the troubling property of imputing motives to actors regardless of their positions, capacities, and self-conceptions.

The effort to keep political ideology grounded, however, tends to run into a difficulty with which the Italian political thinker Antonio Gramsci was well familiar: the problem of consent.

Consent. To illustrate the problem of consent in the case of neoliberalism one can point to the self-described "left of center" economist John Williamson, coiner of the phrase "Washington consensus," who is sometimes categorized as neoliberal despite his unfamiliarity with the term and, once he looked into it, his aversion to it.[37] Williamson's case brings to the fore the trouble with otherwise persuasive accounts of neoliberalism as a class project. For David Harvey, for instance, "advocates of the neoliberal way" are clearly identifiable, ideologically unified, and strategically placed in "positions of considerable influence in education . . . , in the media, in corporate boardrooms and financial institutions."[38] But can one say that John Williamson is a "neoliberal"? We can only ask this question if we first ignore the answer he has already provided.

The problem of consent is written all over studies of third way politics. Bill Clinton and his third way peers in other countries (Tony Blair of the British Labour Party, Gerhard Schröder of the German Social Democratic Party, Göran Persson of the Swedish Social Democrats, and others) are indispensable to any historical account of the turn to markets in the later twentieth century—but, unless we are willing to ignore third wayers' self-conceptions, one cannot say that they are *neoliberals.* Third wayers may have cast themselves as "beyond left and right," but they still saw themselves as defenders of social justice and right parties as their main competition. Terming third wayism "neoliberal" works as superficial description, but does not *explain* it.

The result is an inability to ask helpful analytical questions about how a worldview becomes hegemonic. Some accounts seem to render third wayism an ideological vacuum, emphasizing left parties' disorientation in a world dominated by the right or casting self-understood left-of-center progressives (like Bill Clinton or Barack Obama) as bearers of "soft" neoliberalism.[39] These accounts give at best a fuzzy sense of what, exactly, goes into the making of a "neoliberal" party or political actor. The result is a tendency to present what should be a puzzle (namely, why people who oppose neoliberalism, or have never heard of it, might nevertheless act on the world in ways that conform with neoliberal thinking) as a fact ("third wayers are neoliberal, even if they say they're not").

My suggestion, then, is that we take the history, biography, and positionality of people seriously as a means to analysis and explanation. Like Foucault's dually positioned liberal thinkers grounded in both political economy and public law, the *trajectories and social positions* of the bearers of third way politics can tell us something about the institutional arrangements that rendered market-friendly ways of seeing things sensible. Attention to biography and positionality allows one to identify differences in the ethics and practical orientations of historical actors in a way that does not simply take self-accounts at face value but also avoids the substitution of labeling for explanation.

By approaching things in this way the long-standing premises of the sociology of knowledge—that is, explaining ideologies with reference to the social situations of their progenitors and enactors—comes back into play. By contextualizing people in their worlds and tracing their trajectories through time, the analyst is forced to see their multiplicity and changeability, not to mention the necessities and probabilities of their worlds.[40] By extension, one can see how social actors might become two apparently contradictory things at once (for example, "neoliberal" *and* "left"). In the process one can preempt what Pierre Bourdieu called the "logic of the trial."[41] Indeed, for Bourdieu, sociology's "purpose is not to 'pick' on others, to reduce them, to accuse them, to castigate them." Its purpose is "to understand, to account for . . . to *necessitate the world*."[42]

This is key for my categories

The political ideology–hegemony transition: The centrality of parties. So far, I have suggested that the problem of grasping the transition from political ideology to *hegemony*—that is, a form of power that involves both public authority (consent) *and* the authority to govern (force)—is partially resolved by conceptualizing "isms" in a field-theoretic, relational way and by attending to history and biography. To this I will add two points. The first is that the analysis of how political ideologies become hegemonic *must deal with political parties.* The second is that, to do this, parties should *also* be conceptualized in a relational way, as "fielded" entities that are organized by a triumvirate of actor-orientations: truth-claiming or knowledge production, representation, and power- (or office-) seeking. By extension, parties are constitutionally linked with a variety of fields—political, cultural, economic, and bureaucratic (that is, governments)—and, as such, change over time in ways that *refract* (as opposed to either "reflecting" or "articulating") goings-on in worlds beyond parties.

On the first point, that hegemony cannot be studied without placing parties front and center, my claim is neither that parties should be the only objects of analysis nor that they have been completely overlooked. But as one moves from existing literatures on socialism, to Keynesianism, to neoliberalism, the reader is tracked away from explicit concerns

with the political party. The literature on socialism and social democracy, past and present, remains party-centric.[43] But historiographical
and social scientific work on Keynesianism moves away from parties,
focusing heavily on states, professional economics, and expert bearers
of "social knowledge."[44] Research on neoliberalism takes us even further from parties, attending to intellectuals, economists, think tanks,
business interests, international financial institutions, urban political
economy, states and governing institutions.[45] Recently, there has been a
noteworthy turn to civil society, civic culture, and local partisan dynamics
in research on neoliberalism in the United States, but parties are not the
central objects of analysis in this work, either.[46] And yet one cannot
understand political ideologies' importation into governing institutions
without attending to political parties.

As the social thinkers Karl Mannheim and Antonio Gramsci well understood, parties are vehicles of the making of political ideology, venues
of hegemonic struggles, and organizational tools through which categories, actors, and ethics are injected into governing institutions. Per
Mannheim, arguably the very conceivability of something called "ideology" in Western politics is a *party effect*.[47] Mannheim identifies the
development of parties as vehicles of hegemonic struggles as a process
grounded in the history of democratization: at first political ideology
originates with the "absolute state," which "showed that politics was
able to use its conception of the world as a weapon." But then came
parties: "with increasing democratization, not only the state but also
political parties strove to provide their conflicts with philosophical foundation."[48] By the 1920s Mannheim speculated that, with the full
elaboration of democratic (that is, party) systems, a holistic "political
science"—by which he meant the integrated analysis of the whole field
of political viewpoints, as opposed to merely a "party science"—had become possible.[49] In short, liberal political orders, broadly recognized by
social scientists by the early 1940s as necessarily *party*-political orders,
both produced political ideology and opened up new possibilities for
its analysis.[50] And so, for Mannheim, to do "political science" was to
study parties as vehicles of ideology.

The link between parties and political ideology that Mannheim emphasized is no longer taken for granted in scholarship on culture and
politics.[51] This may be partly an effect of the "freezing of party sys-

tems" famously identified by Seymour Martin Lipset and Stein Rokkan (1967), which located the end of a long period of successive waves of social cleavage–driven party formation somewhere in the 1920s. But this "freezing" did not mean that parties are not, still, venues in which political ideologies are formed, struggled over, and translated into policies and programs. The one-to-one relationship between ideologies and party formation became more complex; it did not disappear. And, in any case, in the present moment it is quite clear that Western party systems are *unstuck*. Given that, it is high time to renew the Mannheimian project of linking the study of ideology with the study of parties.

Having made the case for the centrality of parties to the study of transitions from ideology to hegemony, I now turn to the need for a relational conceptualization of parties as part of a broader, *refraction* approach to the analysis of parties, representation, and hegemonic change.

Parties and Political Refraction: Beyond the Party-Society Problematic

Much current thinking about parties centers on what I call the *party-society problematic*. According to this problematic, parties change for one of two reasons: they react to the electorate, or the electorate reacts to them. So, to the question of leftism's reinventions over time, the party-society problematic offers two, and only two, sorts of answers: either parties did it or electorates did.

This way of thinking lends itself to a market-like conception of party politics: parties "supply," voters "demand." Within the framework the stereotypical "sociological" stance emphasizes "demand side" processes in which shifting demographics and changing social cleavages shape parties and programs. In a more stripped-down version of a demand-driven story, Anthony Downs's (1957) "median voter" approach posits that parties in a majoritarian, two-party system will converge on whatever appeals to the broadest swath of voters. The happy outcome, either way, is that parties respond to what (most) voters want.

The party-society problematic, however, sets aside the whole question of what goes on inside parties. By assuming that representation (responding to publics) and leadership are somehow separable, it also excludes any consideration of the possibility that one can have parties and democratic systems *without* meaningful representation. This way of thinking may work for abstract, ahistorical conceptions of economic markets, but it does not work for the analysis of historical dynamics in democratic politics.

Indeed, a long, distinguished line of thinking about politics takes representation and leadership as component parts of a whole. This conception can be found, for instance, in the early sixteenth-century writings of Niccolò Machiavelli, who famously described the dual necessity of politics in terms of consent *and* force: to do politics is to "make a nice use of the beast and the man."[52] Machiavelli was writing before the advent of mass electorates, but later thinkers—notably Max Weber and Antonio Gramsci—found his dual notion of politics equally applicable in the age of the mass party: parties have to represent, *and* they have to lead; there is no separation between the two. In this way of thinking, representation necessarily implies leadership—or, in other words, leadership *is* representation. To this we might add that, in democratic settings, parties also seek office—an imperative duly noted by Weber, who saw parties as fundamentally power-seeking organizations oriented toward mastery in and over the state.

The summary picture that emerges, of parties as entities that marry representation and leadership in service of office-seeking, breaks with the party-society problematic, situates parties with respect to states, and reopens the matter of parties' internal dynamics. The joining of the two halves of the party-society problematic thus brings parties themselves, and contestation within them, back into view.

Breaking with the party-society problematic also attunes us to concerns other than representation-through-leadership and office-seeking: political parties' deeply cultural nature. As Gramsci well understood, marrying leadership and representation requires a certain capacity to shape how people see things. In other words, just like states, parties cultivate, or seek to cultivate, a specifically cultural or symbolic capacity.[53] Accordingly, Gramsci saw parties as more or less bounded, internally differentiated entities that are compelled to always try to do three things at once: win, represent, and *shape how people think*. Accordingly, Gramsci argued that the modern party has three elements. First is "the mass element," which is "composed of ordinary, average" people "whose participation [in the party] takes the form of discipline and loyalty, rather than any creative spirit or organizational ability." This element is, in other words, made up of groups the party represents—without whom, Gramsci notes, "the party would not exist." But the first element alone is not sufficient: represented groups "are a force in so far as there is somebody to centralize, organize and discipline them," without which "they would scatter into an impotent diaspora and vanish into nothing."[54] The party must therefore also have a second leadership element—or, in his words, a "principal cohesive element, which centralizes nationally," pushing the masses' "power of innovation . . . in a certain direction, according to certain lines of force, certain perspectives, even certain premises."[55]

Gramsci then insists, however, that parties have a third, "intermediate" element that "articulates the first . . . with the second and maintains contact between them . . . morally and intellectually." The figures who do this work of intermediation are intellectuals of a certain sort: they are "organic," grounded in the "mass element," linking it to the operations and deliberations of party leadership.[56] In other words, parties have in-house experts who, depending on how those experts are positioned, generate conceptions of the world and, in so doing, imbue parties with a capacity to reconcile the tension between representation and leadership.

In light of Gramsci's thinking we might, then, restate parties' triple orientations thus: power-, or office-, seeking; representation (which implies, necessarily, leadership); and *truth-claiming*. For present purposes, however, three modifications to Gramsci's conception of the party are in order.

The first is a shift in emphasis from parties' "elements" to a concern with *actor-orientations*. Following Gramsci's tripartite conception of the party, this means taking power-seeking, representation, and truth-claiming as orientations rather than essential characteristics. Here parties become networks of relations in which actors are defined by their aims and priorities, or investments, rather than being slotted into hard-bounded categories. Parties, in other words, can be thought of as relational networks caught up in the pursuit of three aims—all essential, none perfectly reconcilable with, or reducible to, the other. This way of thinking defuses the impulse to essentialize, or strictly typologize, party actors: power-seekers can *also* be invested in representation; truth-seekers (party experts) can *also* be office-seeking politicians; and so forth. With this modification parties are not only *relational* but also constitutionally anchored to other fields of activity: power-seeking operates via linkages with the state (party-state relations); vote-seeking operates through engagements with constituencies, social movements, and civil society (party-civic relations); truth-seeking involves an orientation toward cultural and expert professions and spheres of activity (party-expert relations). By extension, a conception of parties that joins Gramscian insights with relationality gets us away from a concern with what is "external" or "internal" to parties, orienting us, instead, toward the ways in which party relations intersect with, and are shaped by, neighboring fields.

A second modification engages with the perennial problematic of the intellectual. This involves turning the intermediary role of the party expert into a question: party experts *may* do the intermediation that Gramsci describes, or they may not. In-line with arguments that the problematic of the intellectual as a social type can be usefully replaced with a concern with how experts acquire "the capacity to make a public intervention,"[57] the problematic of party experts is not whether they are "organic" but rather whether they have a *capacity to intermediate*.

Who are party experts? Gramsci pointed to journalists and newspapermen, but in the present they might include journalists, speechwriters, academics, legislative aides, public relations specialists, consultants, pollsters, think tank "wonks," and campaign managers. They could be labor representatives, businesspeople, or financiers; they might also be politicians or political aspirants. Recalling our concern with *actor-orientations,* the important thing is not party experts' title or category but how they are oriented: they specialize in the production of truth claims, building authority and esteem within party networks on that basis. Stated differently: party experts are the figures who invest themselves in the production of language, conceptions, and truth claims that parties wield in their efforts to pose as rightful representatives and bearers of the power to govern. As such, party experts shape how parties speak, produce parties' means of representation, address the question of who (or what) is to be represented, and formulate competing logics of government.

Party experts are central players in my account of leftism's twentieth-century reinventions. This focus coincides with, and potentially complements, the present-day "articulation" perspective in political sociology—admirably formulated by Cedric de Leon, Manali Desai, Clhan Tugal, Dylan Riley, Dan Slater, and others—which holds that parties are proactive forces in the construction and constitution of political identities, driving group formation in public life.[58] Gramsci is clear, however, that articulation requires articulators. One of my aims, therefore, is to resuscitate Gramsci's emphasis on parties' third element, the party expert, and an accompanying concern with parties' capacities for intermediation, as a complement to emergent sociological concerns with articulation.

This brings us to a third, and final, modification to the Gramscian conception of the party: the metaphor of articulation does not capture, exactly, the relational conception of parties that I advocate as an alternative to the party-society problematic. I suggest, instead, the metaphor of *refraction*. A refraction approach to the study of political parties hinges on (1) a relational conception of the party as a social terrain that is (2) riven by three irreducible orientations (winning office, representation, and truth-claiming) and that, as such, is (3) anchored to administrative (state and government), civic, economic, and cultural terrains. In order to resuscitate the Mannheimian and Gramscian projects of linking the study of politics and culture with the study of parties, a refraction approach suggests (4) a particular concern with parties' cultural infrastructure, including their *means of education, socialization, and knowledge production; party-expert relations;* and the formation of *party experts;* and (5) making party experts' *capacities for intermediation* an explicit explanatory object.

My call for a refraction approach to the study of political parties is akin to other culturally oriented moves in the study of states and state formation, ranging from James C. Scott's seminal *Seeing Like a State* (1999) to the works of Pierre Bourdieu, Timothy Mitchell, Julia Adams, Ann Orloff, Phil Gorski, Mara Loveman, Nicholas Wilson, and others.[59] My approach is distinguished, however, by grounding in relational and field-theoretical thinking, treatment of biographically situated first-person accounts as analytically meaningful rather than anecdotal, and its basis in the triple-relational conception of the political party described above. With this in mind, in the next section I describe the methodological implications of a refraction approach to the study of political parties in general and leftism's reinventions in particular.

METHODOLOGICAL APPROACH: ANALYZING REFRACTION

Leftism's twentieth-century reinventions are what the historical sociologist Charles Tilly termed a "large process": a broad, cross-national pattern of change over a relatively long time period. This kind of problem does not conform to what the sociologist Andrew Abbott calls "general linear reality."[60] Nor, indeed, does the relational conception of the political party laid out thus far lend itself to variable-based analysis. How, then, does one proceed?

Insisting that macro-historical questions do not imply strictly macrohistorical answers, Tilly suggested that one can gain insight into big changes by attending to the specific, the personal, or the "micro."[61] Tilly's focus on the relationship between "structures" and the "experiences of real times, places and people" recalls the contextually sensitive, meaning-oriented *verstehen* approach of Max Weber. The notion that experience is necessary rather than incidental to social explanation can also be found in the notion of *praxis* in the Marxian tradition, Pierre Bourdieu's concepts of *practice* and *habitus,* and the concerns of John Dewey with *conduct.*[62] Bourdieu, for instance, insists that the task of the sociologist is to learn from, not to override, the practical knowledge of social agents:

> [T]here is a practical knowledge that has its own logic, which cannot be reduced to that of theoretical knowledge; that, in a sense, agents know the social world better than the theoreticians.[63]

Probably the most famous statement on the importance of attending to the experiences of actors comes from C. Wright Mills, who argued that the "task and promise" of sociology was to place people in history—in his words, to grasp "history and biography and the relations between the two."[64]

There is a noteworthy distinction to be made, however, between the macro/micro language of Tilly and the practice-orientations of Marxian, pragmatist, and Bourdieusian lines of thinking. The distinction is between a *dualist* perspective that joins macro and micro—expressed in the linguistic duo of "top-down" versus "bottom-up"—and a *field* perspective in which the macro-micro distinction is simply *collapsed*. In the words of the sociologists Neil Fligstein and Doug McAdam, a field-theoretic perspective centers on local or meso-level social orders, wherein the effects of external institutional processes and historical events depend on "the way incumbents and challengers interpret and deploy . . . 'resources' in the service of the specific strategic action projects they undertake."[65] In other words, as John Levi Martin explains, in a field way of thinking causal force "impinges 'from the inside.' "[66] My conception of parties as relational terrains, emphasis on inside-out analysis, and metaphor of refraction are grounded in these field-theoretic orientations.

So far the integration of field theoretic concerns with practice and practical knowledge into comparative and historical sociological scholarship remains limited.[67] People's positions, experiences, and perspectives enrich much historical analysis but usually do not do much explanatory work. This is not for lack of resources: Philip Gorski, George Steinmetz, David Swartz, Gil Eyal, and Gisèle Sapiro, among others, have produced helpful statements on how Bourdieu's thinking bears on historical analysis.[68] Recent work in world-systems research and on race and intergenerational mobility, notably Bruce Haynes and Syma Solovitch's *Down the Up Staircase*, moves in promising biographical directions.[69] But, as yet, most comparative and historical scholarship does not mobilize Bourdieu's notions of *practice* or *habitus* or (more importantly) the intention behind them.[70] Historical and comparative sociology generally treats people's situations and self-accounts as interesting, but merely anecdotal, indicators of other, more important things.

In contrast, a refraction approach to the study of leftism's reinventions pays careful attention to historical and economic context but places heavy explanatory emphasis on party-based social actors' trajectories, self-accounts, relational positions, and proximate struggles. In a refraction perspective parties are more like prisms than pinballs; the social relations that constitute them are determinants of how parties interpret the world and formulate courses of action. Given the tripartite, relational concept of the political party described above, and the centrality of cultural production, truth-claiming, and party experts therein, an especially important element of party-political social relations are the activities, institutions, people, and resource investments through which parties produce knowledge about the world, educate and socialize publics, and contribute to the making of experts. I refer to the elements of party-political social relations through which parties seek to naturalize certain ways of seeing things as general interpretations of one's experience and political interests using the term *cultural infrastructures*.

To understand parties' cultural infrastructures I begin, for each party, with an account of its "genesis and structure."[71] Parties' origin stories identify key features of the historical moment—the economic context, the development of political institutions, the geopolitical setting— through the prism of the party, focusing especially on the "formation stories" of (left) party experts.[72] Because I am interested in left parties' economic language, and in order to facilitate comparison, I focus on similarly situated, generationally comparable economic party experts across parties and time periods (more on this below). From this starting point, I adopt a biographical approach that traces experts and party-expert relations through time in order to grasp their conditions of existence, proximate struggles, and historically specific styles, skills, and dispositions—or, using Bourdieu's term, to get a sense of *habitus*. I am especially interested in how party experts understand politics and their place in it (their *professional ethics*), how that understanding is shaped by their positions with respect to parties and other institutions, and the implications of those ethics for party experts' *capacities for intermediation*.

Unlike the micro-macro distinction favored by Tilly, my approach operates on the understanding that there is no hard line between the two. In Bourdieu's usage, *habitus* is an effect of socialization—or, in the summary of Loïc Wacquant, "the way society becomes deposited in persons in the form of lasting dispositions, or trained capacities and structured propensities to think, feel, and act."[73] If *habitus* is socialized subjectivity, then understanding the *habitus* of the party expert grants insight into the institutions through which party experts are socialized.

Stated in the terms of the sociologists Daniel Hirschman and Isaac Reed, in the biographical "formation stories" of party experts one can identify institutional developments and organizational cross-relationships that make them possible and that might orient them toward viewing the world in a certain way.[74] One can, in other words, track historical change from the inside out.

This approach preempts overly strong assumptions about the priority of any particular unit of analysis—organizations, nation-states, and so forth. An analysis that traces the institutional locations and trajectories of party experts makes no assumption, for instance, that their experiences and trajectories are nationally bounded. It thus allows us to move beyond the party-society problematic and to incorporate growing recognition in historical sociology as to the significance of inter- and transnational forces in the making of social change.[75] At the same time, by centering the analysis on similarly situated figures across parties and time periods, my approach retains the advantages of a comparative perspective. And so, while the story of leftism's reinventions that follows centers on *national* political parties and seeks to generate definite comparative insights, a refraction approach nonetheless preempts reflex tendencies to both false dualisms and methodological nationalism.

In short, a refraction approach involves the study of historical change from the inside out, centered on the formation, infrastructural conditions, and orientations of party experts. The next task, then, is to think carefully about how, exactly, one identifies party experts in the first place—that is, the analytical entry point. I focus on generationally comparable party actors who occupy *structurally similar* locations in their respective worlds and who become well-recognized experts on matters of economics and finance. Practically speaking, because of the differences between European and American political institutions, I had to approach this in two ways.

First, in the Western European context, I start with the trajectories of left parties' *first ministers of economics and finance*. From that starting point, I focus on successive finance ministers and ministers-in-waiting, incorporating new advisory networks and institutions as they develop through time.[76] In other words, I begin with finance ministers but then move with the institutions, looking beyond ministers of finance to the formation and population of new party research arms, offices and advisory positions in finance ministries, new departments and state agencies (like the Department of Economic Affairs [DEA] in Britain), and new advisory bodies (like the Sachverständigenrat, or Council of Economic Experts, in [West] Germany).

I do realize that, for the reader, my focus on a particular figure, in a particular office, may seem a narrow entry point. But I would argue that the parties involved justify the method. The SPD, SAP, and Labour Party are membership-based, hierarchical, parliamentary organizations, in which appointments to powerful offices are drawn from top-level party ranks. In those ranks the position of minister of finance, or minister-of-finance-to-be, has always held a special place. A cross-party comparison that begins with left parties' first finance ministers thus affords insight into forms of distinction inside the party and institutional arrangements that made certain kinds of party experts possible. This then becomes a historical baseline against which later experts, and their own conditions of possibility, can be compared—and, by extension, through which important changes in parties' cultural infrastructure can be identified as explanatory objects.

In my analysis of the American Democratic Party, however, I proceed differently. First, because of American parties' history of periodic realignments, the Republican and Democratic parties of the 1900s cannot be treated as though they are simply organizational continuations of the Republican and Democratic parties of the 1800s. For this reason, one cannot begin with either of the major parties at birth and go from there; instead, I begin with the Democratic Party in the early 1930s, and take special care to document when, where, and how it became "left" in a way that was comparable to center-left parties across the Atlantic.[77] A second concern has to do with the figure of the party expert in the American case. American cabinet appointments tell us little about the Democratic Party's internal hierarchies and forms of distinction if cabinet appointments do not draw from the party's executive—which they do not, because there is no such thing. Beginning with Democratic Treasury Secretaries in the 1930s would more likely lead into American business and finance than into the Democratic Party. The major American parties certainly have their hierarchies, but they are not bureaucratized membership organizations like their European counterparts. They have always been made up of fluid, relatively weakly bounded factional networks in which professional trajectories depend a great deal on electoral fortunes, committee appointments, and—especially—relationships to presidential candidates.[78] And so to identify party experts among Democrats I focus on networks with ties to candidates and political campaigns, and especially those who become presidential advisers on economic questions.[79]

As with any method, a refraction approach has its strengths and weaknesses. A chief strength is an aversion to explanation by way of conceptual oppositions that falsely impose mutually exclusive ways of accounting for the world. A biographical and historical analysis centered on similarly situated party experts across party and time periods allows the analysis to "travel" across institutions, organizations, and territorial boundaries; to retain the advantages of comparison without falling into the trap of methodological nationalism; and to make actors' experiences, ethics, and perceptions central rather than marginal to social explanation. An emphasis on experts' formation stories renders the institutions through which they move, and the techniques and resources they mobilize, analytically central.

Another strength of my approach is that, while the construction of the thing to be explained (leftism's reinventions) is built on a historical periodization, a biographical and relational view makes it impossible to treat time periods in isolation from each other. By looking at things biographically, one can see how parties and political language change in an intergenerational way, in which party leadership and expert networks in one period shape, and sometimes directly cultivate, the party's future spokespeople. And so periodization provides a structure to the explanatory puzzle, but it does not wall off one period from the next.

A final strength is an ability to incorporate, rather than simply ignore, the fact that parties, and their politics ("leftism," "conservatism," "liberalism"), may well be very different in *kind* across time and place. Analyzing parties by focusing on how, and through whom, they advertise themselves to electorates and articulate their policies, paired with a specific interest in the trajectories, institutional positions, and worldviews of party experts, makes American and European parties comparable without flattening the differences between them or treating their politics as continuous across time.

My approach also, of course, has certain difficulties and weaknesses. One is that my entry into the worlds of parties is necessarily selective, skewed toward dominant elites. To my mind this is defensible because I am interested in tracking and explaining how parties speak, and those who speak for parties are, by definition, elite. Another is that the fruits of a multicountry refraction approach will inevitably be limited by the cultural origins, resource dependencies, and linguistic constraints of the—in this case, American and English-speaking—analyst. I fully acknowledge both limitations and leave the final evaluation of their impact up to the reader.

Another difficulty is practical, having to do with the standardization of biographical information regarding both deceased and living historical figures. In the case of the deceased, the historical record is adequate to the task. Given that I deal with high-profile public figures, I am able to draw on biographies and, wherever possible, personal memoirs and autobiographies, not to mention public statements, third-party interviews, and secondary scholarship. But I cannot speak with them, and I cannot fully grasp their relationships, experiences, and worldly concerns. Neither can I tell their stories in the rich, interpersonal detail that I would like—or, at least, not in the space of a single book. So the method requires that the analyst make a great number of decisions, big and small, about what to dig into and what to gloss over. This is simply unavoidable. Again, the verdict on the gravity of this concern is up to the reader.

Different difficulties are inherent in the analysis of the living, the most obvious being that reliable historical records on living figures are limited, closed, or nonexistent. This becomes a concern in my analysis of party experts in the 1990s, especially. Given the high profile of many of the living persons involved, interviews are theoretically possible but difficult, and, in my experience, there is little that high-profile public figures say in an interview that cannot also be found in third-party interviews, newspapers, magazines, and in their own published writings. On the upside, modern political operatives are fond of writing memoirs, and, in a digital age, they now have blogs, online CVs and professional bios, well-maintained Wikipedia pages, and personal and professional websites. These can be rich sources of information, especially if one is interested (as I am) in a combination of information on professional trajectories (that is, CV-level information) and personal perspectives.

And so this is how I proceed. In order to typify expert profiles as consistently as possible over time, I prioritized the collection of basic biographical information—birth and death dates, training and credentials, professional appointments. I supplement this information with oral histories, diaries, memoirs, self-authored retrospectives, third-party interviews, professional and political publications, speeches, biographies, and autobiographies, with the singular aim of understanding how party experts emerged and became influential inside parties; what roles they played in interpretive struggles and the production of programmatic language; and whether (or not) they developed capacities for intermediation. For living figures I also draw, with care, from personal websites, professional CVs, and other online sources. I make every effort to situate all this information in time and place, using statistical data on political and economic developments, organizational datasets, news sources, and a very broad range of secondary literatures.

My purpose in the analysis of all first-person statements is not to derive from them objectively factual accounts of events. Rather, my aim is to get a sense of social actors' comparative trajectories, relational positions, and personal perspectives. In other words, I want to know about experts' personal senses of the "game"—who their allies and opponents are, the terms they use to make those distinctions, how they understand the world and their position in it, what they strive for, and why.

Finally, in order to understand the 1990s in particular, between 2010 and 2014 I had a series of informational conversations with a handful of figures who have been involved in center-left and third way circles in Europe and the United States. These conversations pointed me in very useful directions, allowed me to confirm that I had correctly identified key party experts, and gave me a better sense of the central movers in efforts to redefine mainstream leftism in the 1980s and 1990s.[80]

At this point we have summarized the general puzzle that drives the book (leftism's reinventions), the major conceptual and analytical concerns that the puzzle calls forth, and the specifics of a refraction approach to resolving the puzzle. We now turn, finally, to a preview of the explanation itself: what drove leftism's reinventions?

THE ARGUMENT (THREE WAYS),
AND ALTERNATIVES THERETO

This book develops two broad explanatory arguments. The first is that the relationship between party organizations and experts (the *party-expert relationship*) is the social basis of leftism's rhetorical forms (socialist, economistic, neoliberalized) over time. Stated differently: the language produced by left parties expresses a certain perspective on the world, and the central bearers of that perspective are socially situated *party experts.* We can boil this down to a simple proposition: there is a genetic link between the social situation of party experts and the way left parties speak. This is an empirical and causal claim, for which I provide backing in the pages to follow, but it is also grounded in the essentially Durkheimian-*cum*-Bourdieusian postulate that the way social agents classify, organize, and describe the world, or agents' "perceptual schemes," expresses a shared or similar position in "a given social formation."[81] This postulate suggests that, by explaining party experts' conditions of possibility and social locations, we can also explain the discursive parameters that leftism, as expressed by left parties, takes over time.

What, then, drove the initial formation of the left party expert between the late 1800s and the 1920s? The first and most basic condition, of course, was the formation of left parties. In Western Europe the mass party of the socialist left was born of struggles against the state that featured, from the cultural field, members of the growing occupations of "agitation" and radical journalism and, from the economic field, labor movements. Early, European-style left parties emerged at the intersection of socialist cultural terrains and workers' movements and, in the process, put in place the conditions of the first left party experts: the party theoretician. Notably, partly because American mass parties preceded the consolidation of a centralized state in the United States, the conditions of the party theoretician across the Atlantic were absent.[82]

In order to understand leftism's reinventions after about 1930, the crucial thing to understand is why party experts' profiles and social locations *changed* between the 1930s and the 1960s and again between the 1960s and the 1990s. Here two historical developments are key: first, the rise of an alliance, or interdependence, between professional economics and left parties by the early 1960s; second, the weakening, or reconfiguration, of that alliance thereafter.

Stated in the broadest conceptual terms, both the rise and fall of economics-left party interdependence had the same underlying cause: *interfield tension*. This argument also has roots in an old sociological proposition: namely, the Weberian argument that social development can be seen as a history of the proliferation of social orders (or fields), which are riddled with both intra- and interfield tensions.[83] The argument, in short, is that interfield tension drove leftism's reinventions by remaking party-expert relations, driving the formation of new kinds of party experts, and shaping the trajectory of intraparty definitional struggles.

This argument can be elaborated theoretically, historically, and heuristically. For theoretically inclined readers, I first elaborate in the language of field theory. For the nontheoretically inclined, I then tell essentially the same story in a more concrete, historical, inside-out way. Finally, for the visually inclined, I present my argument heuristically.

Causal Account: The Theoretical Version

In a field-theoretic language, the general driver of the rise and fall of interdependence between left parties and professional economics was *interfield tension*: first, between the political and economic fields; second, between the political and cultural fields.

In the first reinvention, starting in the 1920s and 1930s, growing tensions between the political and economic fields drove mainstream economics and political leftism into a historically novel alliance. The specific character of interfield tension involved what I call a *Polanyian moment,* or an intensification of Polanyi's "double movement": an opposition between protection-seeking and market-advancing forces, brought to a head by economic crisis, in which old ways of doing things break down and new political-economic arrangements become possible.[84] In field theoretical shorthand, this can be characterized as a tension between the economic and political fields. In the worlds of parties, this interfield tension, or Polanyian moment, generated deep intraparty struggles in which authoritative economic knowledge was both a means and a site of contestation. In the worlds of universities and academic

professions, it also drove intergenerational contention (that is, contention between older-generation academics and their younger-generation
progeny), redirected the concerns of young economists-in-the-making
toward questions centered on the structural causes of poverty, inequality
and unemployment, and drew young economists into both administrative agencies and party networks.

Party theoreticians initially preempted the influence of younger-
generation economists, but as they were drawn into, and became more
powerful within, party elites, a new, interdependent relationship was
born between professional economics and left parties—one that worked,
in part, via the research departments of organized labor. This relationship made possible the *economist theoretician,* who ported a professional ethic that married economic analysis to political strategy—that
is, a *Keynesian ethic.* As an intermediary between government, parties,
organized labor, and a well-regarded academic profession, the economist theoretician's capacity for intermediation was, historically speaking,
relatively high.

But the fact of interdependence—that is, a situation in which left
parties relied on Keynesian economists to formulate and scientifically
legitimate their agendas, while Keynesian economists, in turn, relied on
left parties to validate, consecrate, and make effective their particular
brand of economics—generated a new interfield tension: between economics (a cultural field) and the political field. This tension, like that
between the economic and political fields in Polanyian moments, had to
do with distinctive authority bases, or logics: inhabitants of cultural fields
are prestige-seekers whose credibility depends on their reputations as
objective, credentialed scholarly professionals, but the inhabitants of
political fields are power-seekers whose credibility depends on the ability
to wield political influence. In this sense, to be an "economist" *and* a
left party expert is not likely to be a durable state of affairs. Rather,
recognition of economists' political investments will tend to render the
economics-politics relationship a matter of professional contention, and
recognition of politicians' fealty to economists' truth claims, rather than
represented groups and political allies, will tend to undermine their political power.

These tensions fueled what the sociologist Cristina Mora calls a
"cross-field effect."[85] Economics became more politicized and internally
contentious, creating new openings for dissenting economists—some

neoliberal, some not—who challenged Keynesian notions of the roles and responsibilities of economists-in-politics and shaped the making of a younger generation. In the US, another cross-field effect was the forging of novel relationships between professional economics and parties of the right. With the onset of economic and political instabilities from the late 1960s, economics' politicization and the rise of new professional ethics fueled a turn away from domestic politics and toward international and financial concerns. As the sociologist Marion Fourcade and others have shown, late twentieth-century economics became a much less nationally grounded affair, acquiring distinctly *transnational* and *financialized* orientations.[86]

Transformations in economics reformatted—or, in a sense, retrofitted—the cultural infrastructure of left parties, giving rise to a new sort of left party expert: the transnationalized, finance-oriented economist (TFE). The TFE, as a bearer and guardian of the truth of markets, had a relatively low capacity for intermediation, tending to offer market-centered prescriptions that did not necessarily appeal to left constituencies, and thus generated strategic dilemmas for left parties. For this reason, the complement to the rise of the TFE was the proliferation of new kinds of experts—policy specialists and strategists—in left party networks who did the work of reconciling economic initiatives with electoral communication and figuring out workable, market-friendly reform strategies in nonmarket policy domains. This helps to explain why neoliberalized leftism featured not only a new market–centrism but also an intensification of politics-by-public-relations and an embrace of market- and work-friendly social welfare reforms.

Causal Account: The Historical Version

In the early 1900s the premier left party experts in Western Europe were socialist *party theoreticians*. Party theoreticians became intellectuals not because of academic recognition, university employment, or working-class experience but rather via involvements with newspapers, weeklies, journals, community institutions, and educational activities that were housed within, or were intimately connected with, left parties. Rudolf Hilferding of the German SPD, Fredrik Thorsson of the Swedish SAP, and Philip Snowden of the British Labour Party were all born between the mid-1860s and mid-1870s, came of age alongside the cross-national formation of mass socialist parties, and were recognized economic experts—but they had no formal training in economics or political economy, and were not academics. They also did not rise to intellectual prominence via labor movements. Rather, they established themselves as party experts through active participation in the formation and activities of socialist societies, clubs, associations, news outlets, and party-based theoretical journals—that is, a historically specific cultural infrastructure that emerged in reaction to industrial change and political repression. In the United States, where mass parties were not socialist and had, until recently, dominated American political institutions, Hilferding, Thorsson, and Snowden had no clear counterpart.

In the late 1920s and 1930s, however, a growing conflict between balanced budget, gold standard orthodoxies and democratic demands (in particular, for social insurance and unemployment protections) situated party theoreticians at the center of deepening political contention. Socialisms notwithstanding, party theoreticians generally had little to offer beyond fiscally conservative orthodoxies. The standoff that ensued fueled the recruitment of younger-generation, university-educated experts into the fray—in particular, socialist-friendly young men with training and credentials in what were then becoming more autonomous and statistical economics professions. Examples of these young recruits include Ernst Wigforss and Gunnar Myrdal in Sweden, Hugh Dalton and Hugh Gaitskell in Britain, and Gerhard Colm and Heinrich Deist in Germany. In the United States, figures with similar generational profiles—for example, Lauchlin Currie, Leon Keyserling, and Seymour Harris—became integral to the emergent, New Deal, liberal faction of the Democratic Party.

When one looks beneath center-left parties' "Keynesian" turns between the 1930s and the 1960s (the timing varied), one finds, invariably, that new kinds of hybrid experts—partly party men, partly academic economists, sometimes linked with the research arms of organized labor—were writing programmatic language, informing campaign speeches, participating in the making of new organizational and administrative niches for technically trained economists in politics and government, and speaking to publics on behalf of left parties. In a very real sense, this period was defined by ties between mainstream economics professions and center-left parties, borne by *economist theoreticians* who spent their professional lives moving in between academe, organized labor, states, and left parties. Reflecting that position, economist theoreticians' professional outlook centered on the necessity of marrying economic analysis to political strategizing, communication, and consensus-building; the ethic of the economist theoretician was to fit sound analysis and policy prescriptions to electoral and strategic realities, providing a living link between science and politics.

But the formation of the economist theoretician gave rise to both political and professional opposition—which, in turn, fed back into left parties. A clear example of this cross-dynamic can be found in the opposition between the American economist theoretician Walter Heller, the chairman of JFK's Council of Economic Advisers, and the Chicago-based, neoliberal economist Milton Friedman.[87] In the mid-1960s the two men opposed each other not only on technical economic questions but also on what economists-in-politics should do: for Heller, the economist's task was to reconcile economic analysis with political necessities in a discretionary way; for Friedman, the economist's task was to define rules rather than exercising discretion, reworking political institutions in a way that sets free the morally superior, impersonal, law-like forces of the market. In Friedman's conception of the economist, in other words, there was no discretion—there were only the dictates of the science of markets. This opposition was symptomatic of a broader professional opposition that reached well beyond the United States and that was rooted in the recognition of economists and publics alike that Keynesian economics had a leftward tilt. This recognition fed professional struggles that contributed to economics' internationalization, the generation of new theories that backed claims as to the futility of Keynesian demand management, and a deepening orientation to business and finance. The result was a new kind of left party–affiliated economist, the TFE—figures like Lawrence Summers in the United States, Ed Balls in the United Kingdom, and Klas Eklund in Sweden. The TFE remained left-affiliated but saw the world in a more market-centered way than his or her predecessor, played an important role in the interpretation of the meaning of economic instabilities in the 1970s, and contributed to the delegitimation of Keynesian economist theoreticians.

TFEs' new authority inside left parties strained the relationship between center-left political elites and organized labor. The TFE tended to

offer proscriptive, market-centered economic advice—for instance, pre-
scribing deregulation and strict monetary policy amid an oil-price-
induced inflationary crisis—that was removed from, and sometimes at
odds with, center-left politicians' strategic concerns and consensus-
building needs. In recognition of this irreconcilability, center-left aides
and strategic advisers (for whom the 1970s was a formative experience)
created new centers for the production of politically relevant, center-left
(or "progressive") expertise. Meanwhile, ever-closer electoral margins
prompted greater demand for a specifically strategic brand of expertise—
that is, experts specialized in winning, or "spin." From the 1990s forward,
as the role of the economist-in-left-politics became more specialized,
circumscribed, and market-centered, the prominence of policy specialists and strategic experts grew. The neoliberalization of center-left politics thus acquired two of its more notable complements: a proliferation
of political experts and policy specialists and a turn to politics-by-public-
relations via the mobilization of private political consultants.

Causal Account: The Heuristic Version

A heuristic diagram of my general explanatory account is given in
Figure 1.1.

   The figure indicates major differences across historical periods in the
left party–expert relationship, how the locus of party experts changed
over time, the interfield tensions that drove reinventions, and the characteristics of party experts in each phase. A particularly important inflection point in the arc of the story is the formation of interdependence
between left parties and economics from the 1930s to the 1960s—an
important, but arguably underestimated, feature of what is sometimes
termed the "Keynesian era." It was *because* of interdependence that
cross-field effects became possible, such that what happened in left party
politics mattered for economics and what happened in economics mattered for left party politics.

Alternative Accounts

To my knowledge, the general puzzle of Western leftism's twentieth-
century reinventions has never been formulated as an explanatory

Western leftism	Social foundations: the party-economics relationship and the party expert	Left party–economics relationship	Party experts: ideal type and social location
around 1920: socialist	left parties* party expert economics	weak or nonexistent	party theoreticians (United States: n/a)*
			social location: in-house/party-dependent; background in journalism, "agitation"
	reinvention #1: driven by tensions between political and economic fields (a Polanyian moment)		
around 1960: economistic	left parties party expert economics	interdependent and direct	economist theoreticians
			social location: professional economics and politics (hybridity)
	reinvention #2: driven by tensions between cultural and political fields (economics, party politics)		
around 1995: neoliberalized	economics party experts professionalized politics left parties	circumscribed and mediated	transnationalized, finance-oriented economists (TFEs), strategists, and policy specialists
			social location: **TFEs:** globalized economics and finance. **Strategists:** consultancies, media. **Policy specialists:** progressive think tanks, foundations, etc.

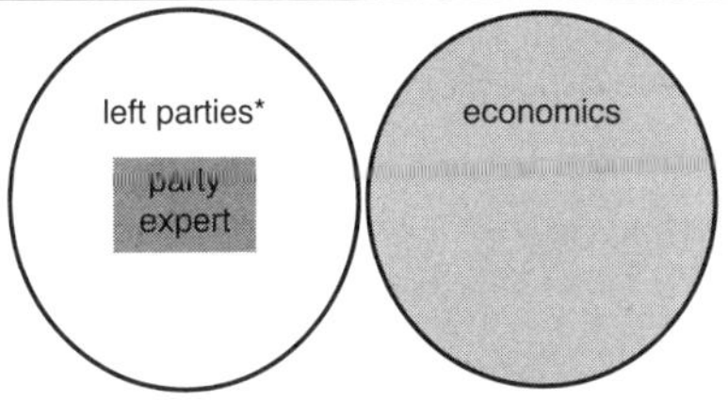

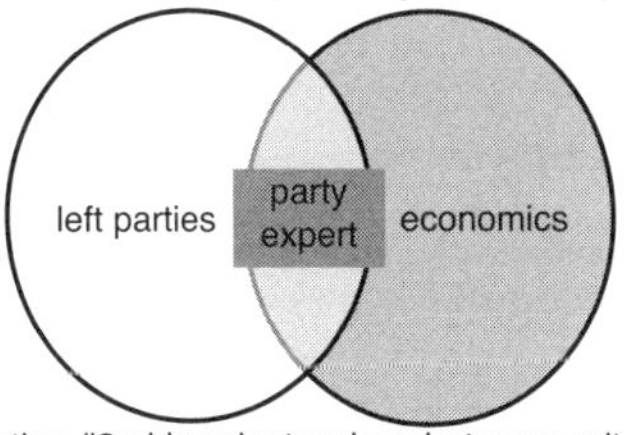

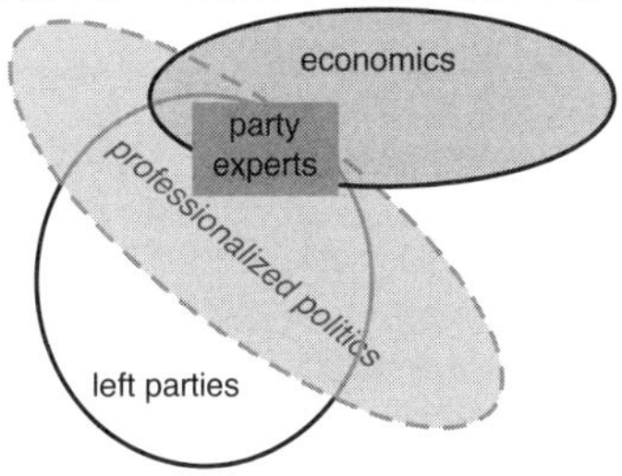

* The Democratic Party was not "left" in a Western European sense (or in the eyes of the American public) until the late New Deal period. And, of course, it was never socialist. See Chapter 5.

Figure 1.1 Leftism's reinventions: An overview.

problem. As a result, I am unable to delve into how my argument squares, or doesn't, with other accounts.

There are, however, specific accounts of leftism's midcentury, econo-mistic reinvention, most notably the "end of ideology" thesis—in which mass consumerism, the growth of the middle class, and the decline of the industrial working classes wrought a generalized decline of "ide-ology" (a term implicitly conflated with Marxist socialism) in mainstream politics.[88] The fundamental problems with this account, to my mind, are dual: a faulty conception of Keynesian-inflected economistic leftism as, by definition, nonideological and a problematic understanding of party change as a mechanistic process in which external forces (demographic and economic change) exert a unidirectional "push" on parties. I have outlined my own understanding of ideology above, and I delve further into the end of ideology claim in the following pages—especially in Chapter 4.

There is also a heterogeneous body of work on the third way phenomenon.[89] The terms of the debate on the third ways, however, often veer toward the normative, engaging implicitly or explicitly with problematics of blame, ideological capitulation, or betrayal—or, alternatively, defensive claims that the third ways remained "true" to social democratic principles and traditions. A more helpful line of analysis focuses on the discursive parameters of third wayism, and how they varied (or not) relative to leftisms past, but this line of work is not always clear on what, exactly, drives variation.[90]

There is, of course, a huge literature in the social sciences that deals with the broad question of how and why parties change.[91] None of that literature addresses the specific puzzle that drives this book. But it does suggest at least four, general sorts of accounts that can be applied to the question of leftism's reinventions: *electorate-driven, economics-driven, elite- (or party-) driven,* or *driven by intraparty, interfactional struggles.* My general response, to *all* of these accounts, is twofold. First, all are true in a way, but they rely on a faulty conception of the political party. Second, a refraction approach does not reject but rather *incorporates* these modes of explanation, on sounder conceptual footing. I elaborate on this in Chapters 7 and 8.

PREVIEW OF THE REST OF THE BOOK

The next chapter focuses on establishing the main explanatory puzzle: leftism's two reinventions. It uses a content analysis–based index of party programmatic trends to document the central puzzle of the book: leftism's two reinventions. Chapter 3 then develops an origin story of the formation of the left party expert that begins at socialism's Western European cradle. Starting from the late 1800s, I track the making of socialist leftism in Germany, Britain, and Sweden through the consolidation of mass parties of the left. I emphasize that left parties were not just power- or office-seeking organizations with a working-class, or trade union, arm; they were also entities that invested considerable time and resources in the creation of a specifically cultural infrastructure and the pursuit of knowledge-producing activities—including journalism, economic analysis, educational and community activities—with the aim of cultivating socialist and social democratic ways of seeing the world. Symptomatic of left parties' early infrastructural development was the formation of a particular kind of in-house economic expert: the party theoretician.

Chapter 4 gives an account of the transition from socialist to *economistic* leftism between the 1920s and the 1960s in Western Europe. I show how, amid interfield tensions in a Polanyian moment, party theoreticians tangled with, and were eventually displaced by, credentialed and university-affiliated economists—some, especially in Western Europe, with strong ties to the research arms of organized labor. The outcome was the formation, varying in timing and strength, of economistic leftism, which was built on a historically novel interdependence between left parties and professional economics. Indigenous to the new party-economics connection was a new kind of Western European, left party expert: the economist theoretician. I develop a similar analysis of the American Democratic Party in Chapter 5, tracing how and when it became "left" in the 1930s and thence, like European center-left parties, became a bearer of economistic leftism, and host to economist theoreticians, by the 1960s.

Chapter 6 offers an analysis of how the mid-late century, left party–affiliated economist theoretician saw politics and his role in it (the *Keynesian ethic*). It highlights the historical institutional arrangements that made economist theoreticians possible, and in which the Keynesian ethic was grounded, and how those arrangements changed from the 1960s forward. In particular, I consider how neoliberalism as a specifically intellectual project enters into the story of a move from Keynesian to neoliberal ethics, and the ways in which new alliances between economics and the political left drove a reorganization of fields of political expertise—especially of a leftist sort. I emphasize how the rise of a new economics of the right fed into the politicization of economics in general, younger-generation economists' interpretations of the economic events of the 1970s, and the professional delegitimation of the economist theoretician. Despite the ongoing leftward lean of Western economics professions, by the 1980s mainstream economics became a producer not of economist theoreticians bearing Keynesian ethics but of TFEs bearing neoliberal ethics. Last but not least, I also discuss two important sites for the making of new party experts: a new network of think tanks and other organizations keyed to the production of a "progressive" expertise and the proliferation of political consultancies.

Chapter 7 shifts back to parties, focusing on the making of the American New Democrats. I link the collapse of the Keynesian ethic to Democrats' frustrations with economists' politically insensitive and strategically counterproductive prescriptions in the 1970s, and then I show how that experience fed into efforts to remake Democratic theory and practice in the electorally dismal years of the 1980s. Until the arrival of the Clinton administration, people behind those efforts were many and diverse—strategic aides, policy specialists, politicians, financial elites—but economists, and particularly academics, were notably absent. I show, finally, how transnational- and finance-oriented economists (TFEs) and New Democratic experts jointly shaped the making of American neoliberalized leftism during the first Clinton administration. Chapter 8 extends the analysis of leftism's second reinvention to Sweden, the United Kingdom, and (West) Germany, showing how tension-driven changes in the party-economics relationship shaped neoliberal transitions in Western European leftism. I emphasize that, because of the transnationalization of economics and transatlantic exchanges between experts and political elites, changes in Western Europe were not independent from the American experience—and, perhaps most interestingly, these exchanges helped to remake Western European leftism in a distinctly "progressive" way.

Finally, in the conclusion, I summarize, clarify, and consider present-day symptoms and implications of neoliberalized leftism. A core question this whole analysis raises is whether today's center-left parties have the infrastructural capacity to meaningfully represent the poor, disadvantaged, disenfranchised, and financially anxious groups that have always been leftism's most important constituencies—and, by extension, whether they can truly cultivate not only progressive policies but also progressive political identities.

CHAPTER TWO

From Socialist, to Economistic, to Neoliberalized Leftism

> Since in the realm of politics the only knowledge that we have
> is a knowledge which is limited by the position which we
> occupy, and since the formation of parties is structurally an
> ineradicable element in politics, it follows that politics can be
> studied only from a party viewpoint.
>
> —Karl Mannheim, 1936

THIS CHAPTER establishes the book's explanatory puzzle: Western leftism's two twentieth century reinventions: first from socialist to economistic leftism (between the 1920s and the 1960s), second from economistic to neoliberalized leftism (between the 1960s and the 1990s). Following Karl Mannheim's directive to join the study of ideology with the study of parties, I map out three qualitatively distinct ways in which left parties characterized the world over time, focusing especially on economic language. The main empirics used in this chapter are mainstream political parties' election-year programs and manifestos.

The analysis proceeds in two parts. The first part takes a look at election-year programmatic excerpts of the SPD, the SAP, the Labour Party, and the Democratic Party around 1920, 1960, and 1995. Locating these parties historically, I show that, in the non-American cases, programmatic rhetoric clearly shifted from socialist to economistic, and then from economistic to neoliberalized, ways of characterizing the world. I also show that Democratic Party rhetoric was decidedly non-socialist, and in no clear way "left," around 1920, but by about 1960 it spoke in a technical, economistic language that was very similar to European center-left parties' rhetoric at that time. In other words, sometime between 1920 and 1960 Democratic and Western European center-left programmatic language converged. Then, as the century wore on, Democratic and Western European center-left rhetoric shifted more or less in tandem. By the 1990s all four parties spoke with the hallmark vocabulary that came to be known as "third way" leftism: pragmatism, work-centered welfarism, and market-friendliness.

Shifting to a different set of comparisons—over time, across the political spectrum, and across political-cultural "regimes," to use Gøsta Esping-Andersen's term—the second part of the analysis offers a more general picture of programmatic trends in mainstream party rhetoric over the course of the postwar period.[1] Here I develop a quantitative index of neoliberalism (the *neoliberalism index*) spanning *all* mainstream parties, center-left and center-right, across twenty-two Western countries from 1945 to 2005. Making use of a unique dataset that quantifies election-year manifestos according to positive and negative emphases on various topics over time, the neoliberalism index is grounded in my understanding of "neoliberalism" as a particular way of thinking about what government should do, by what means, and for whom.[2] Building on existing scholarship, I define neoliberal political thinking as the embrace of three things: economic privatization, deregulation, and liberalization as the *means* of government; work-centric welfare reforms, as opposed to security and decommodification, as the *ends* of government; and business and white-collar, as opposed to blue-collar and poor, constituencies, as answers to the question of government *for whom*. This quantitative analysis is capable of speaking to the Gramscian question of whether the late twentieth century was really an age of neoliberal hegemony in Western countries, evident on both the right *and* the left.

And, indeed, the neoliberalism index shows that between the early 1970s and the 1990s the programs of Western center-left parties moved toward emphases on economic privatization, deregulation, and liberalization; work-centric and market-friendly welfare reforms; and business and white-collar constituencies. With all due acknowledgment of the myriad problems of anachronism and cross-Atlantic distinctions in political terminology involved in the use of the term "neoliberal," programmatic data show that postwar center-right parties were always more market-friendly (or "neoliberal" in the specifically 1990s sense of the term) than parties of the mainstream left and, more importantly, that the most significant historical change in post-1970s Western political language was on the left—not on the right.

THE FIRST ANALYSIS: PROGRAMMATIC EXCERPTS

The German SPD, the Swedish SAP, and the British Labour Party consolidated into organized national parties between the late 1860s and 1900. The SPD, the precocious and powerful bearer of international Marxist socialism, was established in 1875, with roots dating to 1869. The other two soon followed: the Swedish SAP dates to 1889; the British Labour Party was formally established as the Labour Representation Committee (LRC) in 1900, with roots dating to 1881 or, depending on how one dates things, 1868.[3] But it was not until the 1910s that explicitly socialist, labor-representing political parties became institutionalized features of their respective political landscapes. By the year 1920 socialist, labor, and social democratic parties in many Western countries—with the exception of the United States—were growing in strength and size. They were also shifting into the category of "center-left," as socialist parties fractured in the wake of the Bolshevik Revolution, the formation of the Soviet-led Third International (established in 1919), and the proliferation of communist parties thereafter. As this very fracturing indicates, the 1920s marked out an increasingly unstable political and economic (or Polanyian) moment.

Around 1920 the three European center-left parties considered here offered electoral-year narratives that centered on the polarizing and wealth-concentrating effects of capitalism, the inevitability of class struggle, the ownership of the means of production, and the question of a socialist future. The 1921 program of the SPD, a particularly heavyweight player in the world of organized political leftism at that time, painted a thoroughly Marxist portrait of the world:

> The *capitalist economy* has [concentrated] . . . production under the control of a relatively small number of large owners, it has separated . . . *workers* from the *means of production* and trans-

formed them into propertyless *proletarians*. It has increased economic inequality. . . . It has thus made the *class struggle for the emancipation of the proletariat* a historical necessity and moral demand. . . . The Social Democratic Party . . . fights for the rule of the people . . . , organized by the renewal of society in the socialist public spirit.[4]

The solution, the SPD argued, was the extension of public ownership, or "[c]ontrol of the Reich over the *capitalist ownership of the means of production,* especially of interest groups, cartels and trusts," and the nonbureaucratic, democratic management of "public bodies."[5]

Accounts of the Swedish SAP note that, by 1920, it had abandoned Marx and Marxism—and yet, based on its program, one might never have guessed.[6] The SAP's 1920 program appealed to the Swedish public in a language that was not easily distinguishable from the SPD's. Just like its German counterpart, the SAP attributed the problems of the moment to concentrated ownership in a capitalist mode of production, leading to class conflict and exploitation:

> Social democracy differs from other political parties [because] it would *completely transform bourgeois society's economic organization.* . . . The main cause of defects [in] our civilization is the fact that the *capitalist mode of production* puts the *ownership of the means of production* in the minority's hands, condemning the majority to propertylessness and . . . creating *antagonism between workers and capitalists.* . . . *Capitalist private property* has . . . become a means for the propertied to deprive the working people the fruits of their labor. . . . [E]xtraction continues to favor an *ever more concentrated and ever more powerful capitalist rule.*[7]

As for the SPD, the SAP's solution was social, cooperative, nonbureaucratic control, especially in "natural wealth, industrial, credit institutions; transport and communication routes." "Social" and "community" enterprises were to be managed by experts, workers, and consumers. Companies could be privately owned, but would be subject to "social control." All of this, the SAP told its publics, was the extension of a natural process in which capitalism generates a working class organized against capitalists. In the SAP's account, capitalism makes *workers into an opposing movement.* They organize themselves against exploitation, as producers in trade unions and consumers in cooperative societies in a still ongoing, ever more immense . . . *struggle between workers and capitalists.*[8]

And then there was the British Labour Party. Founded in an explicitly "revisionist," non-Marxist, and decidedly middle-class version of socialism from the start, Labour's 1918 programmatic language was actually no less radical, ownership-focused, or critical than that of the SAP or the SPD around the same time. Labour, too, described a deeply contradictory economic system that was pushing exploitation and inequality to a breaking point, paving the way for a new politics:

> The individualist *system of capitalist production,* based on the *private ownership* and competitive administration of land and capital, with its reckless "profiteering" and *wage-slavery* . . . ; with the monstrous inequality of circumstances which it produces . . . may, we hope, indeed have received a death-blow. With it must go the political system and ideas in which it naturally found expression.[9]

Labour, too, argued for democratic economic control and social ownership:

> [T]he Labour Party insists on Democracy in industry as well as in government. It demands the *progressive elimination from the control of industry of the private capitalist, individual or joint-stock;* and the setting free of all who work . . . for the service of the community.[10]

Last but not least, Labour's programmatic language paired social ownership with an emphasis on expert knowledge:

> What the Labour Party looks to is *a genuinely scientific reorganisation of the nation's industry* . . . on the basis of the *Common Ownership of the Means of Production ["Clause IV"]; the equitable sharing of the proceeds* . . . and the adoption . . . , of those systems and methods of administration and control that may be found, in practice, best to promote, *not profiteering, but the public interest.*[11]

There are, of course, shades of difference in these three programs; these parties formed via distinctive routes that are explored in the next chapter. But the basic structure of their programmatic rhetoric was strikingly uniform, built using common socialist concepts and frames of reference.

The Distinctiveness of American Rhetoric

The American Democratic Party's 1920 platform had a different tone. Considerably older than Europe's socialist and labor parties, much less centralized, and not clearly ideological, the Democratic Party was its own kind of political animal. It was not "left" in a European sense; it had never been socialist; its chief power centers were not in Washington, D.C.; and it certainly did not understand itself as the organized political and ideological arm of the working classes. The Democratic Party moved in a political order fundamentally unlike Western Europe's, featuring a national state that was still becoming a centralized, technocratic, administrative entity, a process that was linked to professionally driven progressive movements.[12]

The Democratic Party's 1920 platform (of James M. Cox and his running mate, Franklin D. Roosevelt) expressed the distinctiveness of American party politics. The platform emphasized expert-informed policy-making—especially on budgetary matters—that echoed the antipartisan, anticorruption themes of early twentieth-century American progressivism:

> We pledge the Democratic Party to a policy of *strict economy in government expenditures,* and to the enactment and enforcement of such legislation as may be required to *bring profiteers before the bar of criminal justice.* . . . We reaffirm the traditional policy of the Democratic Party in favor of a tariff for revenue only and confirm the policy of *basing tariff revisions upon the intelligent research of a nonpartisan commission, rather than upon the demands of selfish interests,* temporarily held in abeyance. . . . In the interest of economy and good administration, we favor the *creation of an effective budget system,* that will function in accord with the principles of the Constitution.[13]

The Democratic Party of 1920 did touch on concerns with capitalism; the tensions between labor and capital could hardly have been ignored in that period. But the party spoke of these things in a register that lacked the trademark themes of Marxist socialism.

More specifically, the 1920 Democratic platform lacked the central Marxist theme of intensifying class struggle. While recognizing labor-capital relations as an important problem, the party emphasized the resolution of labor strife in a Wilsonian tone of progressive reformism, humanism, and government in the public interest:

> The Democratic Party is now, *as ever, the firm friend of honest labor and the promoter of progressive industry.* . . . Under this administration have been established employment bureaus to bring the man and the job together; have been peaceably determined many bitter disputes between *capital and labor;* were passed the Child-Labor Act, the Workingman's Compensation Act . . . , the Eight-Hour Law . . . and a code of other wholesome laws. . . . *Labor is not a commodity; it is human.* . . . At the same time, the nation depends upon the products of labor. . . . The whole people, therefore, have a right to insist that justice shall be done to those who work, and in turn that those whose labor creates the necessities upon which the life of the nation depends. . . . *Labor, as well as capital, is entitled to adequate compensation. Each has the indefeasible right of organization, of collective bargaining and of speaking through representatives of their own selection.* Neither *class,* however, should at any time nor in any circumstances take action that will put in jeopardy the *public welfare.*[14]

In short, the Democratic Party in 1920 cast itself as a bearer of progressive reformism and reasoned compromise in the general interest, but not as a representative of the working classes or a voice of socialist leftism.

In the New Deal years Democratic language shifted in ways that could be read as more left, in a European sense—but certainly not in a Marxist or socialist tone, and only by imposing a term on American party life that was not particularly meaningful at the time. The 1936 Democratic program replaced the language of "capital" with "business," retained an emphasis on labor and collective bargaining rights, and highlighted the efforts of the New Deal state to place both labor and business on the road to "freedom and prosperity"—all within an orthodox framework of sound government finance.[15] It decried the "concentration of economic power" but stopped well short of the hallmark socialist response to this concern (socialization), emphasizing instead the importance of antitrust laws. The difficulty of calling Democratic (or, indeed, any) party politics "left" at this moment is that, with reference to the major political parties, the term simply was not a particularly meaningful one. No reference appears, in either Democratic or Republican platforms between 1932 and 1940, to "left" or "right" as party-political categories.[16]

The Transatlantic Turn to Economistic Leftism

By 1960, of course, the Western political landscape was changed in myriad ways—by the Second World War, the birth of a new Western economic order with the United States at its center, and the onset of the Cold War, to name only a few. Accordingly, the language of mainstream leftism was different not only in content but also in geographical scope. All four parties, American Democrats included, converged on a shared language that was nonsocialist, strikingly optimistic, and distinctly economistic.[17]

Probably the most controversial case in this regard was the once-Marxist German SPD. In 1959 the SPD famously broke with its Marxist legacy with its Bad Godesberg Program. The program was subdued in rhetoric but optimistic in spirit, describing party goals in terms of growth, fair distribution, "full employment," stable money, and increased productivity:

> The goal of Social Democratic economic policy is the *constant growth of prosperity and a just share for all in the national product*. . . . Economic policy must secure *full employment whilst maintaining a stable currency, increase productivity and raise general prosperity*. To enable all people to take part in the country's growing prosperity there must be *planning to adjust the economy* to the constant structural changes in order to achieve a balanced economic development.[18]

No longer telling a tale of capitalist exploitation and class struggle, Bad Godesberg expressed a faith in technical economic planning, executed through the budget: in the SPD's words, "Such a policy *demands national accounting and a national budget.*"[19] Last but not least, Bad Godesberg featured a phrase that became West Germany's most famous political translation of Keynesian economics: "as much competition as possible, as much planning as necessary." The full passage reads as follows:

> The state cannot shirk its responsibility for the course the economy takes. . . . The Social Democratic Party therefore favours *a free market wherever free competition really exists.* Where a market is dominated by individuals or groups, however, all manner of steps must be taken to protect freedom in the economic sphere. *As much competition as possible—as much planning as necessary.*[20]

This rhetoric, we will see, was strikingly close to that of the SAP and the Labour Party.

By 1960 the SAP spoke as the dominant party of government that it then was, but with a familiarly economistic voice. The SAP's 1960 program proclaimed the success of the labor movement and "social democracy" (that is, itself) in the achievement of broadly shared growth, the defeat of unemployment and concentrated ownership, and the establishment of "full employment" as the central goal of economic policy in Sweden and beyond:

> Under Social Democracy's . . . leadership . . . [t]he labor movement has played a leading role in the . . . expansion of political democracy. . . . Through legislation and trade union struggle, private equity owners' autocracy has been broken, and the *majority of the people have been able to increase their share in [economic growth].* The development of state, municipal and cooperative enterprise has . . . created . . . the *democratization of ownership. . . . The threat of unemployment has decreased* thanks to a reorientation of economic policies, and *full employment* in several countries is set as a goal.[21]

Around the same time the British Labour Party spoke in a less confident tone relative to the SAP, but it used a similarly economistic language, with emphasis on full employment, stable prices, and budgetary management:

> We do not say that the task of combining an *expanding economy with full employment* and *steady prices* is an easy one. Indeed it will remain impossible until we have a Government which is *prepared to use all measures, including the Budget,* in order to expand production and simultaneously to ensure that welfare is developed and prosperity fairly shared.

Among the more striking features of Labour's 1959 program was its faith in technical economic management:

> To achieve planned economic expansion and *full employment without raising prices* requires a *buoyant demand to stimulate British industry;* a high rate of *investment* as the basis of raising productivity; an *energetic application of science in all phases of our economic life;* a *favourable balance of payments* including the development of Commonwealth trade; and a *strong pound.*[22]

The language of the SPD, the Labour Party, and the SAP around 1960 was thus very close—but, then again, their rhetoric had always been similar.

Perhaps the most interesting feature of the economistic language of center-leftism around 1960 is that, by that time, the Democratic Party spoke it, too. Indeed, the Democratic Party's 1960 platform (the year of the Kennedy-Johnson ticket) deployed a language that was very close to that of the SPD, SAP, and Labour Party:

> We Democrats believe that our *economy can and must grow* at an average rate of 5% annually. . . . We pledge ourselves to policies that will achieve this goal *without inflation.* . . . As the first step in speeding economic growth, a Democratic president will put *an end to the present high-interest, tight-money policy.* . . . We are committed to *maximum employment, at decent wages and with fair profits,* in a far more *productive, expanding economy.*[23]

No longer concerned with building administrative capacity, the Democratic Party now proclaimed the budget's usefulness as a tool of economic management, alongside interventions in private sector price-setting as needed, in the pursuit of "full employment":

Inflation has its roots in a variety of causes; its cure lies in a variety of remedies. Among those remedies are *monetary and credit policies properly applied, budget surpluses in times of full employment, and action to restrain "administered price" increases* in industries where economic power rests in the hands of a few. A fair share of the gains from increasing productivity in many industries should be passed on to the consumer through price reductions. . . . The Democratic Party reaffirms its support of *full employment as a paramount objective* of national policy.[24]

In short, by around 1960 all four parties had converged on a distinctively *economistic* leftism, projecting a confident vision of the expertly managed economy. All framed the world in technocratic, economistic terms, assuring publics that they possessed the know-how to intervene in economies precisely, scientifically, and as necessary. For economistic leftism the aim was not socialism so much as full employment—the hallmark theme of Keynesian economic management. The means was not socialization but rather expert economic know-how.

A Note on the "End of Ideology"

A few comments on my interpretation of programmatic rhetoric around 1960 are in order. Some readers might be surprised that I treat socialist and economistic leftism as essentially equivalent kinds of things, when one could argue that socialist leftism was ideological but economistic leftism was technical. Indeed, starting in the 1950s a number of scholarly observers—Raymond Aron, Edward Shils, Daniel Bell, Seymour Martin Lipset, Philip Converse—interpreted the newly technical language of mainstream left parties as qualitatively different from socialism.[25] For them it marked an "end of ideology," driven by rising affluence and electoral change: essentially, as the electorate got richer, parties dropped socialist and class appeals. End-of-ideology advocates contended that distinctions between left and right, liberal and conservative, no longer moved people because the electorate had changed. By moving away from socialism, left parties were merely responding to that fact with a nonideological, technical language, in an effort to win the most votes from a broadly centrist, affluent public.

But one can argue that the end of ideology account was built on two errors: first, it conflated ideology with Marxist socialism and, by extension, presumed that the non-Marxist, technical language of economics was not ideological; second, it assumed that parties' programmatic language was a pure response to self-evident, linear changes in the electorate, when in fact those changes were neither self-evident nor linear. I'll briefly elaborate on each point in turn.

A first problem with the end of ideology account is its presumption that Marxist socialism was ideological, but the language of Keynesian economics was technical, practical, and pragmatic—that is, nonideological. But, in fact, one can see in the party programs of the early 1960s a definite theoretical vocabulary, closely associated with a definite academic profession. This kind of specificity is precisely what sociologists of knowledge have long understood as political ideology: a worldview about the means and ends of government that expresses the positionality of the temporally and socially situated people who produced it.[26] Seen in this way, one of the great ironies of the end of ideology claim is that it was itself an ideological move, attempting to universalize a historically and socially specific way of seeing things by calling it technical.

Once Keynesian-economistic leftism is recognized as ideological in the sociology-of-knowledge sense, the difficulty with the second notion—that economistic leftism was an expression of the demands of the increasingly affluent median voter—becomes problematic. In the first place, the median voter did not articulate the language of Keynesian economics and insert it into parties' programmatic language; people in and around parties did. When we consider this, the assumption that the median voter's preferences could explain the specific language of economistic leftism starts to look too mechanical and simplistic, ignoring the question of who was speaking for parties—that is, defining programmatic vocabularies—around 1960.

One might also consider whether the increasingly affluent electorate can accurately be characterized as a *unified* electorate. This was, after all, the eve of the notorious sixties, in which it became perfectly clear that the electorate was not unified at all. The late 1960s and early 1970s, in fact, saw a resurgence in the strength and vitality of Marxist- and socialist-inflected lines of thinking—not only via European communist parties touting "Eurocommunism" but also *within* center-left parties, especially among their younger ranks. Can we assume, then, that Keynesian economics had somehow become the natural language of a unified, mainstream electorate? At best, this seems doubtful.

In short, the end of ideology thesis identified important reasons why parties changed their language, but by categorizing socialism as ideology and economism as ideology's absence, it preempted consideration of the possibility that economistic leftism had specific social bases, too. By extension, it failed to ask who was speaking for parties and how they acquired the authority to do so. It could not (and did not) offer any way of theorizing or anticipating the very different kind of politics that followed economistic leftism.

The Second Reinvention: Neoliberalized Leftism

By the mid-late 1990s Western center-left parties again spoke in a qualitatively distinctive register. Historians and social scientists alike noted left parties' acceptance of market forces, in particular financial markets, as beyond their control; a willingness to accept limitations on, and privatizations of, the welfare state; and an acceptance "that equality . . . may be tempered by the need to preserve incentives and competition."[27] The political scientist Peter Hall identified similar themes in 1990s "third way" political rhetoric: business-friendliness and market-friendliness; a shift away from public spending and toward "moral issues," including crime; and a new understanding of unemployment as "a supply-side problem to be addressed by manpower policy and changes in labour-market arrangements."[28] Gone was the tone of optimism, mastery, and distributional equality that underpinned economistic leftism around 1960; gone, also, was the language of a careful, technical calibration of a mixed economy. What we find, instead, is an emphasis on the forces of markets, and a recalibration of government and policy according to certain understandings of what market forces can and cannot do.

These changes are evident in the programmatic rhetoric of all four parties dealt with here. The SPD, whose Berlin Program of 1989 was updated in 1998, situated "the market" as an autonomous, self-correcting force, but one that could not by itself meet social, environmental, and protective needs:

Within a democratic framework, the market and competition are indispensable. The *market* effectively coordinates the vast diversity of economic decisions. . . . The *market is an instrument for compensation between supply and demand;* it is, embedded in a suitably adapted framework, an efficient instrument for controlling demand and supply. . . . But the market cannot ensure *full employment, distributional justice or environmental protection.*[29]

Meanwhile, in its 1990 program the Swedish SAP described a new world in which domestic authority had lost ground, such that no nation or party could go it alone. The SAP's confident tone of national stewardship in 1960 became an acceptance of internationalized economic, cultural, and "market conditions," requiring cross-national cooperation in order to manage social and economic life in a "sustainable" way:

Completely new problems have arisen. . . . [O]ver a hundred years after the modern labor movement began to emerge in Europe and formulated demands for a transformation of society . . . [t]oday's [situation] is in many ways more difficult. . . . *On its own, no nation can secure its safety and survival. . . . Internationalization* has already taken place—*in market conditions—in terms of capital, labor, technology, information and mass media.* . . . [S]tates . . . must work together to eliminate mass poverty and relaunch *sustainable economic and social development,* boost trade . . . , overcome economic crises . . . and promote science and technology development.[30]

In place of the directive, scientific management of national economies for the sake of full employment, the SAP would now pursue "[e]conomic policies designed to promote employment for all," partly via public employment and training opportunities that would facilitate "societal readiness to cope with changes."[31]

Perhaps the clearest instances of a new language of leftism emerged along the Anglo-American axis. In Britain, the 1997 program of "New Labour" declared itself a "party of ideas and ideals but not of outdated ideology." Combining an anti-"dogmatic" pragmatism ("[w]hat counts is what works") with emphasis on the "modern," New Labour declared that it would adapt the policies of the Thatcher and Major years rather than rejecting them wholesale:

The objectives are radical. The means will be *modern*. . . . Some things the Conservatives got right. We will not change them. It is where they got things wrong that we will make change. We have *no intention or desire to replace one set of dogmas by another.*[32]

Like the SAP and SPD, Labour also described global markets as forces beyond national control:

In economic management, *we accept the global economy as a reality* and reject the isolationism and "go-it-alone" policies of the extremes of right or left.[33]

Gone from Labour's rhetoric was scientific economic management and full employment. New Labour aimed instead for "stable economic growth with low inflation," competition, and shifting unemployed young people "off benefit and into work." Famously, the clause that had come to be known since its initial appearance in 1918 as the centerpiece of Labourite socialism, the common ownership of the means of production (Clause IV), was now nowhere to be found.

New Labour's 1997 manifesto appeared five years after the 1992 "New Democrat," Clinton-Gore platform of the American Democratic Party. That platform, too, offered a combination of pragmatism, non-inflationary growth, and jobs (but not full employment), presaging New Labourite themes. At the center of the New Democratic platform's much-noted departure from the party's New Deal, liberal past was its emphasis on a "third way" between "do-nothing" and "big" (or "tax and spend") government, business-friendliness, and the power of "market forces":

Our Party's first priority is *opportunity—broad-based, non-inflationary economic growth* . . . and *jobs* for all. . . . *We reject both the do-nothing government . . . and the big government theory* that says we can hamstring business and tax and spend our way to prosperity. *Instead we offer a third way.* . . . *[W]e honor business as a noble endeavor,* and vow to create a far better climate for firms and independent contractors. . . . We believe in *free enterprise and the power of market forces.*[34]

In summary, the hybrid language of third way leftism had at least three features: a clear market-friendliness, antidogmatic pragmatism, and a brand of welfarism that elevated work, adaptability, and personal responsibility over security and state provision. This combination was most clearly on display in the programs of the New Democrats and New Labour, but could also be found in the language of the SPD and the SAP.

This language was not "neoliberal" in any singular or straightforward way, nor was it interchangeable with the language of the center-right. Center-left parties' blend of market emphases with pragmatism and work-centric welfarism was distinctive. I take it for granted that neoliberalized leftism cannot simply be characterized as a "shift to the right"; nor can it be characterized as simple neoliberalism. This is the reason for my use of the term *neoliberalized* leftism. It is also important to keep in mind that an analysis of leftism's second reinvention needs to account for *all* of third wayism's rhetorical patterns—including its antipathies to "dogma," its commitments to pragmatism and the "modern," its skepticism of government-centered policy solutions, and its move away from protective welfarism—and not just its market-centrism. Third wayism, as I will show in the next section, had special historical significance and should be treated as such.

A SECOND LOOK: THE QUESTION
OF NEOLIBERAL POLITICS

The cross-party and cross-period sampling of programmatic excerpts given thus far shows that the language of leftism changed in ways that are consistent with my argument that there were two significant reinventions during the twentieth century: from socialist to economistic leftism and then from economistic to neoliberalized leftism. It also shows that, even though the Democratic Party was never a bearer of socialist leftism, its programmatic language tracked right alongside its Western European counterparts' in roughly the latter half of the twentieth century. But the analysis thus far does not answer the question of whether leftism's reinventions were systematic and widespread or how they compared with the politics of the right; nor does it provide unambiguous support for my claim that third wayism was an especially important departure in the trajectory of Western leftism. The analysis thus far might also give the impression that neoliberalized leftism's epicenter was chiefly along the U.S.-U.K. axis, and thus perhaps a symptom of leftism in Anglo-liberal countries specifically rather than a general reinvention, as I have claimed. This section examines these possibilities. Tracking broad trends using cross-national data on the programs of mainstream parties across twenty-two Organization for Economic Cooperation and Development (OECD) countries from 1945 to 2008, I confirm, in particular, the rise of an age of neoliberal politics, including a specifically neoliberalized leftism, in the third way period.[35]

Interlude: What's "Neoliberal"?

First, however, a brief historical note on neoliberalism's specific, late-century meaning, and how that meaning emerged, is in order. Traceable to the efforts of a transatlantic network of intellectuals, and especially economists, from the early 1930s (which I discuss in more detail in Chapter 6), by the late 1990s the term "neoliberal" meant something fairly novel in social scientific scholarship and political life. With notable variations across countries, the term "neoliberal" came to refer to a new, international common sense in which market competition was understood to be the best solution to all kinds of problems, and as both the means and ends of good government.[36]

This was new (or "neo") in at least a couple of senses. A first sense has to do with its institutional and intellectual origins. This brand of neoliberalism was first formulated within interwar and late wartime, transatlantic intellectual circles as a historically specific response to the statist, welfarist, protective, Keynesian, and national and international regulatory institutions that were then in formation. This specific context is the only way to understand why, in policy terms, neoliberalism translated into a specific package of reforms that targeted those very institutions: liberalization of trade in goods and capital, the privatization of state institutions and industries, the depoliticization of decision-making on economic and monetary policies, and the separation of regulatory authority from the executive branch—including the creation of a politically independent central bank. Late twentieth-century neoliberalism was also "neo" in a second sense: as noted by the political thinker Michel Foucault, it took markets and market competition not only as the end of government but also as its *means*.[37] Stated in the terms of the sociologist Emile Durkheim, neoliberalism is a way of thinking in which markets are sacred, and nonmarket coordinating, regulatory, deliberative and distributive institutions—including both the state and democratic politics—are profane.[38]

Neoliberalism was thus distinctive in Western liberalism's long history. It also was not intrinsically right (or left). But because of the strongly antigovernment, promarket rhetoric and policies of the center-right during the Thatcher and Reagan years, not to mention those administrations' direct ties to neoliberal economists, the term took on a definite right-leaning connotation after the 1980s. And yet, rooted in the Latin *liber* ("free man"), in the late 1700s "liberal" was associated with an egalitarian, Western politics that tilted left, being linked with opposition to aristocratic and monarchical rule.[39] In the late 1800s, as socialist and workers' movements changed the political landscape and generalized demands for protection clashed with gold standard constraints, the term "New Liberalism" emerged to denote British Liberal politicians' embrace of social reformism.[40] In the United States neither "liberal" nor its variants had particular left-right associations in the late 1800s; as we will see, liberalism became associated with "left" in the American context with the rise of the New Deal.[41] Decades later, in the early 1980s, American use of "neo-liberal" was reborn in the vernacular of the Democratic intelligentsia, referring to younger-generation critics of unreconstructed New Deal liberalism.[42] Notably, in all cases "neoliberal" modified things, programs, ideas, and people on the political left. The relationship between neoliberalism and rightness that crystallized in the 1980s was a novelty, not an inevitability.

Neoliberalism, as noted, also had specific historical, intellectual, and geographical origins.[43] I explore these more thoroughly in Chapter 6; for now I will simply note that in this book I refer to the intellectual networks of people and organizations that built neoliberalism into a definite way of seeing the world as the "neoliberal project." The existing historiography of the neoliberal project shows that it was born not in mainstream politics but rather in opposition to it.[44] Here one can simply point to the fact that the Mont Pèlerin Society (MPS), a well-documented vehicle of the neoliberal project's formation, was founded out of a sense of marginalization within the emergent Bretton Woods order—that is, without any clear political alliances.

By the early 2000s a growing body of scholarship documented the transnational formation of the neoliberal project well beyond the MPS and its linkages with free market economics (especially in the United States), parties of the mainstream center-right, national governments, and international financial institutions.[45] But conflations of neoliberalism with political rightness, as if their pairing was natural or inevitable, can obscure understandings of how and why it became a generalized "ism." Can we correctly say that mainstream politics, and not just the politics of the right, became neoliberal? It is to this question that we now turn.

The Neoliberalism Index

The figures presented in this section are based on a *neoliberalism index* that, using programmatic data from the Comparative Manifestos Project,[46] breaks down parties' programmatic emphases into three components: emphases on order and commodification rather than protective welfare (the ends of government); on *laissez-faire* rather than regulated economic exchange (the means of government); and on business, middle-class, and professional constituencies rather than blue-collar workers, the poor, and the unemployed (the answer to the question of "government for whom"). The components are standardized around the zero-line, creating an index in which positive values indicate parties' net positive emphases on policies that are commonly associated with neoliberalism in its specifically late twentieth-century sense.

The limitations of the resulting index include a risk of anachronism, since neoliberal meant something specific in the 1990s and did not mean anything in particular between the 1940s and the 1970s; the related problem of imposing continuity on discontinuous historical periods; and using a rather blunt instrument to capture complex political developments. The qualitative and historical analysis offered so far, which should be kept in mind throughout the analysis to follow, mitigates these risks. And, limitations notwithstanding, the neoliberalism index does have a singular strength: it provides a simple, quantitative, over-time measure that can help us evaluate the proposition that mainstream Western politics in general, and center-left politics in particular, shifted in a neoliberal direction in the later decades of the twentieth century.

The Trends

Figures 2.1 and 2.2 map programmatic trends, as measured by the neo-liberalism index, across *all* mainstream parties, center-left and center-right, for the whole postwar period. In Figure 2.1, the shaded sections within each bar refer to changes in the components. In order to get a sense of variation in the measure over time, the line in Figure 2.2 tracks party-level standard deviations, weighted by parties per country.

Figure 2.1 shows that neoliberal themes became increasingly evident in the electoral programs of *all* mainstream parties across twenty-two

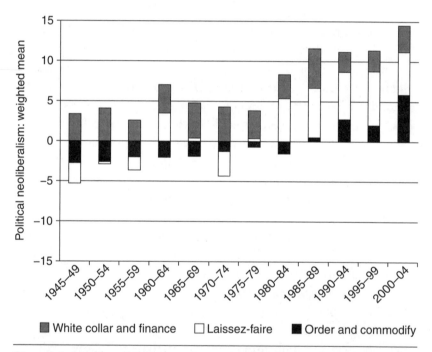

Figure 2.1. Neoliberalization in mainstream party programs in twenty-two OECD countries, 1945–2004 (weighted five-year averages). Data source: *Mapping Policy Preferences I* and *II* datasets (Budge et al. 2001; Klingemann et al. 2006). Author calculations.

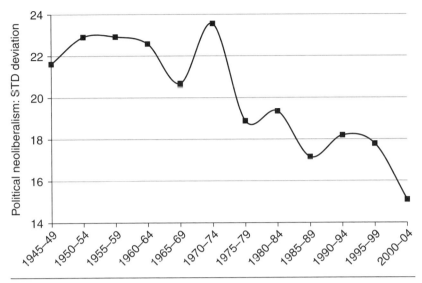

Figure 2.2. Cross-party programmatic variation among center parties in twenty-two OECD countries (weighted party-level standard deviation in five-year periods). Data source: *Mapping Policy Preferences I* and *II* datasets (Budge et al. 2001; Klingemann et al. 2006). Author calculations.

Western countries between the mid-1970s and 2004. The figure shows that post-1970s mainstream parties increasingly made election-year appeals on the basis of a new notion, historically speaking, of what government is for and how it should operate: government's responsibilities were primarily to be market-supporting; educational self-investment, work, and law and order took precedence over protective welfarism, decommodification (that is, limiting human dependence on labor market participation for basic survival), and regulation.[47] Figure 2.2 shows that, since the 1970s, this was an increasingly uniform trend.

Importantly, the parties that changed most dramatically in the late postwar period were those on the left—not the right. Figure 2.3 shows that center-right parties have always leaned toward themes that are now understood as "neoliberal" (keeping in mind that this term had no particular meaning, and certainly not its current one, prior to the 1990s). *It was thus parties of the left, and not the right, that moved most definitively over time,* crossing onto "neoliberal" (net positive) terrain in the 1980s. Notably, the American Democrats are not exceptional prior to the 1990s

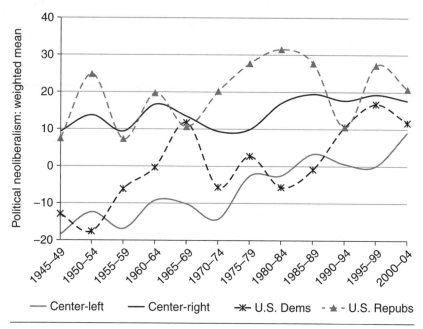

Figure 2.3. Neoliberalization in center-left and center-right programs in twenty-two OECD countries (weighted five-year averages, with U.S. parties for comparison). Data source: *Mapping Policy Preferences I* and *II* datasets (Budge et al. 2001; Klingemann et al. 2006). Author calculations. Note that, for comparative consistency, the Democratic/Republican trends are also grouped by five-year averages, which throws off the trend lines somewhat. The 1968 Democratic program featured an unusual degree of emphasis on business, prosperity, free enterprise (referencing, in particular, the Kennedy tax cuts), and educational opportunity (referencing the civil rights movements and the 1965 Elementary and Secondary Education Act), which probably accounts for the appearance of a precocious Democratic "neoliberalism" in the late 1960s (Democratic Party 1968).

relative to center-left parties elsewhere—though from the 1990s (since the Clinton years) they did emerge at the leading edge of the neoliberalizing trend.

What is the weight of the various components of neoliberalism on left and right? Figure 2.4 shows component trends across the left-right axis.

Parties of the center-left flipped to positive on all three components by the early 2000s—starting between the early and late 1970s, fluctu-

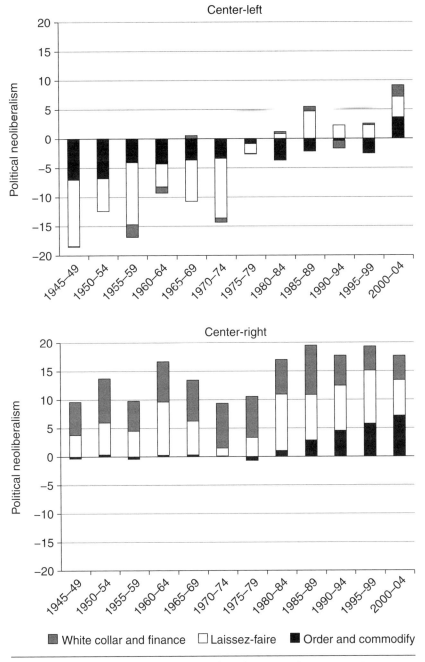

Figure 2.4. Neoliberalization in center-left and center-right programs in twenty-two OECD countries, with components, 1945–2004 (weighted five-year averages).

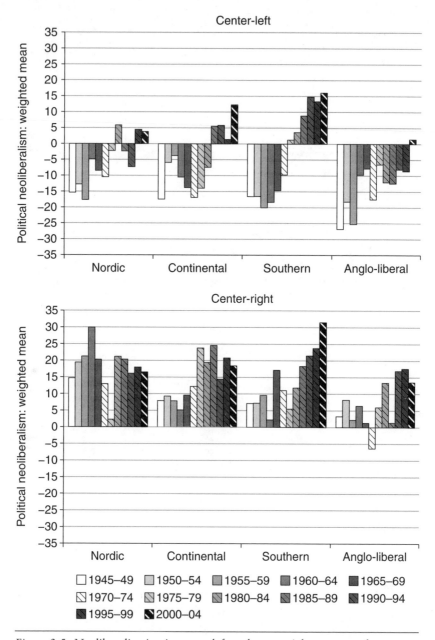

Figure 2.5. Neoliberalization in center-left and center-right programs by regime*, 1945–2004 (weighted five-year averages). * See the Methodological Appendix for a listing of countries in each regime. The trend for southern countries should be interpreted with caution, since only Italy is included for the entire time period; the figure includes Greece, Italy, Portugal, and Spain from the late 1970s forward.

ating into the 1990s, and gaining momentum in the first years of the new millennium.

An influential tradition in comparative welfare states research argues that the early postwar period featured the emergence of different "regimes" or "worlds" of welfare capitalism: Western countries with liberal cultural and political traditions (the United States, the United Kingdom, Canada, Switzerland, and the Antipodes) developed less protective, more means-tested, and less decommodifying welfare institutions relative to Nordic, continental (except Switzerland), and Southern European (Italy, Spain, Greece, and Portugal) countries.[48] Given that history, we might expect that left parties' programmatic neoliberalization was mainly characteristic of the Anglo-liberal regime. Figure 2.5, however, shows that this expectation would be wrong.

The largest programmatic changes took place in what were, according to some arguments in the welfare states literature, the least likely places: continental, Nordic, and southern countries (but note that, prior to the mid-1970s, the "southern" category includes only Italy, since the other countries in this category were not democratic systems before that time).

Across the board, then, trends in the neoliberalism index suggest that center-left parties in all four regimes did, indeed, shift in market-friendly ways after 1970. Overall, the patterns shown here are consistent with an argument that in the last decades of the twentieth century there emerged a new, market-centric political logic across the left-right spectrum as to what governments' responsibilities are and the means they should use—that is, a cross-partisan *neoliberal politics*. The most striking change was to be found on the left, not the right. And the change was, historically speaking, most marked in non-Anglo-liberal, Western European countries.

CONCLUSION

Taken together, a textual analysis of programmatic language and the political neoliberalism index paint a historical picture that is consistent with my characterization of Western leftism as having undergone two twentieth-century reinventions—first from socialist to economistic leftism and then from economistic to neoliberalized leftism. But establishing the puzzle is easier than explaining it, which is the task to which we now turn.

The analysis begins with the making of socialist leftism, which was inextricably bound up with the formation of the socialist mass party from the 1860s forward. This curious political animal was a European invention, and so the story starts there.

CHAPTER THREE

The Genesis and Infrastructure of Socialist Leftism

> How do we know that a new field has appeared or that an old
> one has disappeared? . . . In standard sociologese, we look for
> a new elite and a new ideology.
> —Philip Gorski, 2013

> [T]he original is the place where a certain number of things
> are formed . . . that, once formed, pass unnoticed.
> —Pierre Bourdieu, 1990

WHEN THE GERMAN SPD, the Swedish SAP, and the British Labour Party first entered government in the early twentieth century, they appointed people with strikingly similar profiles to the top economic posts of their respective administrations: minister of finance (or, in the United Kingdom, chancellor of the exchequer). This person was a man who was born between the mid-1860s and the mid-1870s who had come of age alongside, and to a considerable extent *within*, mass socialist parties. This figure was, in the sociologist Philip Gorski's phrasing, symptomatic of a new elite: more highly educated than most, known for his journalistic intellectual work, party-based, and broadly recognized as an economic expert of a specifically socialist sort. But he had no formal training in economics and was not an academic. Rather, he established himself as an authority on economic questions via involvements with socialist societies, clubs, and associations; newspapers and journals; and emerging party-political circles. Partly thanks to underground networks formed in an age of considerable political repression, the social world of this early left party expert was not limited by, or coterminous with, national boundaries. The party theoretician was incubated in and dependent on the capillary institutions of the emergent, transnational, mass parties of the socialist left.

This chapter analyzes the forces that gave rise to the figure of the socialist party theoretician, situating him within the broader trajectory of socialist leftism's formation. The analysis highlights that socialist leftism's composition featured three intertwined elements—mass parties, organized labor, and socialist knowledge-producing institutions—and the party theoretician's situation therein. I focus on the biographical trajectories of the first socialist finance ministers (or the equivalent) in Germany, Sweden, and the United Kingdom—respectively, Rudolf Hilferding, Fredrik Thorsson, and Philip Snowden. Tracking party theoreticians' formation in three countries, I show how the making of mass socialist parties gave rise to a "new elite and a new ideology." The party theoretician was notable for his origins in socialist journalism, his limited connections to labor movements, and his lack of formal training or credentialing in economics or political economy. I argue that this tells us something about socialist expertise more generally: it was party-dependent, distinctive from labor movements, and at most weakly connected to academe.

The present analysis, which combines a biographically sensitive field approach with historical and comparative analysis, also affords insight into Western leftism writ large, which underwent a major reconfiguration starting in the mid-late 1800s: a marriage of two different things, "socialism" and "left." Before the 1860s "left" parties were radical and liberal, not socialist. But after the 1860s, as the leaders of socialist parties-in-formation agitated for socialist way of seeing the world, often via venues that were originally liberal sites of political and educational activity, left *became* socialist. Party theoreticians, in a certain sense, embodied this transformation.

This story deviates from accounts of left party formation that see organized labor as the heart and soul of turn-of-the-century leftism. There are very good historical reasons for this view, but it is not the whole story. I will show that a strictly labor-centric story cannot explain the existence of the party theoretician or the broader cultural terrain to which he was indigenous. In other words: if we tell the story of left parties as a tale of the rise of labor movements, we have no way of explaining how the party theoretician came to exist.

Indeed, *none* of the figures I consider in this chapter became party experts thanks to their working-class origins or ascendance through the ranks of organized labor. Hilferding and Snowden had no notable background in labor movements; Snowden had a history of hostilities with union leadership. Thorsson was an organizer of sorts—in the parlance of the time, an "agitator"—but he agitated to make workers socialist (as opposed to liberal), not for worker organization *per se*. What Hilferding, Thorsson, and Snowden did have in common were affiliations with clubs, newspapers, associations, and societies that were distinctively *socialist* organizations. Understanding the formation of party theoreticians thus requires engagement with the history of socialism and socialist institutions, understood as a definite infrastructural terrain made up of specifically socialist organizations and knowledge-producing practices, which was distinctive from the institutions of organized labor. As we will see, socialism was grounded in a wide array of organizations, relations, and practical activities, especially (but not only) print journalism, through which people defined, enacted, cooperated, and built themselves as socialists.[1]

A NOTE ON ANALYTICAL AIMS

This chapter mobilizes biographical, autobiographical, and secondary materials to trace the making of socialist parties and party theoreticians. I provide what the sociologists Daniel Hirschman and Isaac Reed call a "formation story": an institutionally grounded explanatory account of the making of a certain kind of party, and the worlds that made a certain kind of historical figure possible, at the intersection of labor movements, socialism, and party-building.[2] What resulted was an (initially) extra-parliamentary, power-seeking organization with an *economic* arm in the form of organized labor and a *cultural* arm that defined and cultivated socialist ways of seeing, thinking, and acting. I will show that Hilferding, Snowden, and Thorsson were indigenous to socialist parties' cultural (socialist) arms but had varying—and sometimes very weak—relationships to socialist parties' economic arms (organized labor). In all three countries, party theoreticians' ascent into powerful positions in left party governments was made possible by the fact that, for the most part, mass socialist parties were worker-dependent, but intellectual-led.

Via a cross-national formation story of parties and party theoreticians, this chapter builds a baseline against which later leftisms (economistic, neoliberal) can be compared. Party and party theoreticians' formation tell us something important about left party–expert relations in the early 1900s: *the formulation of leftist politics, policies, and programs took shape in the party and in affiliated cultural, and specifically journalistic, institutions.* The flipside of this was that turn-of-the-century left parties formed on the basis of their own, distinctive, cross-national cultural terrain—one that, relative to socialist and labor parties' main competitors (liberal parties), was decidedly *not* university-based or tightly interconnected with the professionalizing social sciences.

THREE PARTIES, THREE PARTY THEORETICIANS

Before digging into the formation of left parties, there is an important historical question to address. How did "left" and "socialist" become overlapping categories? This is a complex question, but the answer can be stated simply: leftism and socialism converged because socialist parties married them to each other. Socialist parties fused different civil activities—specifically, socialist cultural production (journalism, theory-building, political-economic analysis, public lecturing) and workers' movements—within power-seeking political organizations. Thus formed, socialist parties were realizations of a kind of organization that, before the 1860s, could only be imagined.

Imagined Parties: Leftism, Socialism, and Labor

When Karl Marx and Friedrich Engels wrote the *Manifesto of the Communist Party* in 1848, there was no such thing as a communist party. According to the historian James H. Billington, the notion of a communist or "ideological 'social party' " built on a fusion of "the destiny of the proletariat" with the "pretensions of science" was a figment of Marx's "prophetic imagination."[3]

What did exist in 1848 was an organization of exiled German radical workers: the Communist League (established in London in 1847), which began as the League of the Just (established in Paris in 1836). The league, which was not a party in any formal sense, commissioned Marx and Engels to write its manifesto.[4] In 1848 there were also other organizations calling themselves "socialist" or "communist." Both terms had many meanings: "socialism" first cropped up in political parlance in England and France twenty or thirty years earlier, in the 1820s, and acquired general currency from about 1850.[5] Linked to its emergence was a "Socialist and Communist literature" (in Marx and Engels's phrasing), grounded first in French radical journalism and then, after the failed revolutions of 1848, in underground, cross-national networks of radical German exiles.[6] Last but not least, in 1848 there were formally organized radical, liberal, and "bourgeois" or "democratic" political parties.[7] But when Marx and Engels wrote of the communist party in 1848, they were giving form and voice to an entity not yet born.

Marx and Engels' writings are indications that, until the late 1800s, the category "left" referred more to radical liberalism than to socialism. Indeed, the term predated socialism by a considerable stretch. In the conventional account "left" was born as a political category in revolutionary France in May 1789: the French Estates General, convened under Louis XVI, was physically organized "in a continuous semicircle from the most radical and egalitarian on the left to the most moderate and aristocratic on the right."[8] Representatives of the aristocracy (the first estate) and of the clergy (the second) sat to the right of the presiding chair, and representatives of the middle classes (the third estate) sat to the left. The left-right distinction spread to other countries along with revolutionary politics, and Napoleon's empire.[9] Signaling the growing generality of the distinction in Europe, left parties established between the late 1700s and the late 1800s were variably "liberal," "whig," "democratic," "radical," "progressive," and "popular"; Denmark's and Norway's liberal parties (established in 1870 and 1884, respectively) were simply "left" (venstre).[10]

But by the turn of the twentieth century socialism and communism had taken up a place under leftism's umbrella. This had everything to do with the cross-national, but German-centered, formation of mass socialist parties. As noted by the historian Geoff Eley, socialist parties made "democracy social."[11] Central here was the rise of labor movements, mass strikes, and the "social question." But the efforts of self-understood socialists to persuade the memberships of otherwise liberal workers' organizations and associations to embrace socialism as their creed were just as central. In these efforts, socialist journalism, lecturing, and education were indispensable tools.

Journalism and the Socialist Party Spirit

The historian James H. Billington argues, in fact, that the professional enterprise of revolutionary journalism inspired the very *idea* of the socialist party. The *Communist Manifesto* was written "precisely when [Marx] was perfecting his mature profession as a journalist" in Brussels.[12] For Marx, "journalism had the responsibility of creating "party spirit"—which "preceded the firm idea of a political party."[13] The notion of party spirit—a party that joined theory and practice, philosophy and politics—was grounded in lived experience: not only was "[j]ournalism the only income-producing profession practiced by Marx, Lenin, and many other leading revolutionaries during their long years of powerlessness and exile"; journals like Marx's *Neue Rheinische Zeitung* were organizational bases on which Europe's socialist and social democratic parties later formed.[14] The Italian political theorist Antonio Gramsci tells a similar story of Marx and the making of the party: Marx "had a sense for the masses" thanks to "his journalistic and agitational activities." As a result, Gramsci argues, Marx's "concept of [political] organization" was bound up with organizational experience in "craft organization; Jacobin clubs; secret conspiracies by small groups; [and] journalistic organization."[15]

Notice that socialism, just like organized labor, featured people, organizations, activities, and the production of tangible things—including a particular conception of what a party is, or should be. And yet there remains a social scientific tendency to treat labor as an active, organizational phenomenon from which left parties emerged and treat socialism as a way of thinking.

Marx and Engels are partly to blame. They fostered the notion that parties, socialist or not, were the ideological extensions of economic classes. Ignoring the conditions of his own existence, Marx viewed socialism as a refined, scientific expression of working-class experience—that is, a way of thinking grounded in a class but articulated by intellectuals. In this understanding socialist parties were bearers of working-class ideology and thus the natural representatives of organized labor. Parties and labor were "Siamese twins," in the phrasing of a founding leader of the Austrian Social-Democratic Workers Party (Viktor Adler).[16] Probably not coincidentally, this was what socialists wanted labor leaders and workers' movements to believe, too.

But, as Marx's own life attests, socialism had an organizational and practical terrain: clubs, lecturing societies, and journalism, often seeded by liberal elites and associations, which then served as sites of representative struggle between socialists and liberals. In a certain sense, early liberal parties and associations provided the terrain on which socialists reinvented organized political leftism.[17] It was not easy: neither working-class people nor trade union leaders simply accepted that socialist intellectuals should speak for them. The naming of some late nineteenth-century left parties using the terms "workers" or "labor," but others "socialist" or "social democratic," signaled these tensions.

In short, labor, socialism, and left parties were not born conjoined; their marriage was forged. The first party to achieve this with notable success, serving as an important model for socialist parties elsewhere, was the German Social Democratic Party, or SPD.

The German SPD

By the late 1800s the German SPD was *the* model of the mass socialist party. Working partly through homegrown liberal associations and workers' education initiatives, the makers of the SPD wielded socialist journalism, referents, and ways of thinking in the pursuit of workers' loyalties. In the end they drove the national-level centralization of German organized labor and played a key role in the making and sustenance of a transnational cultural infrastructure that supported the diffusion of a specifically socialist leftism.

The SPD's ability to do all this had to do not only with electoral power but also with a deep embeddedness in local institutions, cross-national linkages, and diverse investments in knowledge production.

Reacting partly to state repression, the early SPD devoted considerable energy to the production of literature, newspapers, and journals; educational activities; and cultural and community involvements. It developed, in other words, a specifically cultural infrastructure. By the early twentieth century this infrastructure had given rise to a certain type of party elite: figures who were at once party leaders and in-house socialist theoreticians.

Thanks in part to the special place of the SPD in the formatting of socialist leftism, mass party organizations came to be understood by Marxist intellectuals and party leaders in the early 1900s as more than an extension of workers' movements and a means to office-holding: they were also central to the production of socialist knowledge and the cultivation of socialist culture. Party organization and theoretical production, in other words, were to be tightly interwoven—a sentiment expressed with particular force by Vladimir Lenin in 1905:

> Down with non-partisan writers! Down with literary supermen! Literature must become part of the common cause of the proletariat, "a cog and a screw" of one single great Social-Democratic mechanism set in motion by the entire politically-conscious vanguard of the entire working class. Literature must become a component of organised, planned and integrated Social-Democratic Party work.[18]

Making the Two-Armed Party

To see how the two-armed socialist party developed—that is, a party form linked to workers' movements and a distinctive cultural infrastructure—we begin with the early formation of the SPD, which had two organizational precursors. One was the General German Workingmen's Association (the Allgemeiner Deutscher Arbeiterverein, or ADAV), established in Leipzig in 1863.[19] Although it is sometimes understood as a labor organization, the ADAV understood itself as a political party with a definite intellectual agenda.[20] Socialist but not Marxist, it was "a working-class party, whose highly centralized structure provided the president with nearly dictatorial powers"—in-line with the convictions of its founder and first leader, Ferdinand Lassalle (1825–1864).[21] The second SPD precursor was the Social Democratic Workers' Party (Sozialdemoktratische Arbeiterpartei, or SDAP). Formally founded in

Eisenach in 1869, it was led by Wilhelm Liebknecht (1826–1920) and August Bebel (1840–1913), both of whom were associates and followers of Karl Marx.

Both the ADAV and the SDAP were built through struggles that played out on liberal terrain, by figures with connections—not always friendly—to Marx. Lassalle, a litigator who was active in the radical left in 1848 and then became a student of Marx's, reentered politics in the early 1860s upon the invitation of the Leipzig Central Committee of the Workingmen's Education Societies. Founded by liberals, the societies sought to address the "social question" in accordance with *laissez-faire* inclinations, with education and self-help. When its Leipzig committee asked Lassalle to give an address on "the working-class movement, and the tactics it should pursue," Lassalle spoke about the need to build a working-class party to challenge the dominance of liberals and to seek universal suffrage, partly on the belief that "democratic intellectuals" would otherwise remain powerless.[22] Following up with the establishment of the ADAV as a means to both political and intellectual ends, Lassalle tightly policed its intellectual ranks.[23]

The SDAP—commonly referred to as the "Eisenachers" or the "Eisenach Party"—also built itself on liberal foundations. Liebknecht and Bebel worked, in particular, through the League of German Workers' Clubs (the Verband Deutscher Arbeitervereine, established in 1863).[24] Bebel, the son of a noncommissioned officer and an orphan who grew up in poverty, had deeper roots in the labor movement than Lassalle, but he was introduced to Marx through Lassalle's pamphlets.[25] The significance of the transnationality of radical and socialist cultural networks is clear in this regard, and in the lives of early socialist leaders in general: Liebknecht, a middle-class "democratic intellectual," was exiled in London for thirteen years after the failed German revolution, where he joined the Communist League and became a friend of Karl Marx and his family. Returning to Germany in the early 1860s, Liebknecht became a representative of Marx and the International in Germany, against the Lassalleans.[26]

Thanks to Liebknecht and Bebel, the Verband adopted the program of the International in September 1868.[27] In August 1869 Liebknecht and Bebel founded the SDAP, remarkable for its more decentralized structure relative to the Lassalleans, its Marxist socialism, and its linkages to the International Working Men's Association, or First International (1864–1876).[28] Galvanized by the rise and fall of the Paris Commune; the legal persecution of Bebel, Liebknecht, and (later) the Lassalleans;[29] and Germany's 1871 unification, the ADAV and SDAP merged in 1875 in Gotha, forming the Socialist Workers' Party of Germany (Sozialistische Arbeiterpartei Deutschlands, or SAPD). Its first platform, the Gotha Program, was not explicitly Marxist—prompting Marx, who feared the Lassalleans had won, to send a stern criticism in a letter in May 1875, which Liebknecht reportedly kept under wraps.[30] The Gotha Program was nonetheless framed with Marxist terminology and, bearing a hallmark of Marx and Engels's "scientific socialism," was couched in claims to the superiority of science as a means of historical analysis and political action.

Merging the centralized ADAV with the decentralized, multisited Verband, the SAPD was a formidable political machine—and also a target of the Prussian state. Pushed underground by repressive measures that culminated in Prussian antisocialist legislation effective from 1878 to 1890, the party's reemergence in 1891 as the SPD was built on an explicitly Marxist platform. Its 1891 Erfurt Program was written by Karl Kautsky (1854–1938), founding editor of *Die Neue Zeit* and, by then, "the "pope" of socialism."[31] The Erfurt Program served as an important model for socialist parties in other countries.[32] Driven by the consolidation of the SPD, in the same year (1891) the General Commission of German Trade Unions (Generalkommission der Gewerkschaften Deutschlands, later renamed the Allgemeiner Deutscher Gewerkschaftsbund [ADGB]), or General German Trade Union Confederation, was established.

Thus was born the model two-armed party of the socialist left: a child "of democracy, of mass franchise, of the necessity to woo and organize the masses" (in Max Weber's words).[33] By 1898 the SPD was the largest party in popular votes (27.2 percent); in 1905 it established a constitutionally formalized, central office of permanent officials; by 1910 it had committees in all but 16 of Germany's 297 parliamentary districts. By 1912 it had a plurality of parliamentary seats (110 out of 397) and, by 1914, 120 labor secretariats.[34] The SPD was so organizationally effective that even conservative parties would imitate it.[35]

There can be no doubt that the SPD's effectiveness depended on its economic arm—that is, on organized labor. But a highly developed, specifically socialist cultural arm—shaped decisively by state repression and transnational networks—was also indispensable.

The Formation of the SPD's Cultural Terrain

From its beginnings, the SPD invested heavily in cultural production:

> Between 1876 and 1878 the Social Democratic publishing business flourished. . . . In 1876, the former party organs of the Lassalleans and Eisenachers were merged into the *Vorwaerts,* henceforth the official organ of the Social Democrats until it was suppressed two years later. At the same time, the party founded a literary journal, *Die neue Welt,* edited by Bruno Geiser, Liebknecht's future son-in-law. Then at the congress of 1877, the delegates endorsed the establishment of *Die Zukunft,* the first "scientific" periodical of the German Social Democrats. . . . As of 1876 the Social Democrats had twenty-three political newspapers, but within a year eighteen more were added.[36]

By 1878 there were forty-seven party newspapers, "about a fourth of which appeared as often as six times weekly."[37] *Vorwaerts* was a chief source of income for Liebknecht.[38]

Predictably, then, in 1878 the Prussian and imperial government's antisocialist legislation took particular aim not only at the SPD's economic arm but also at its cultural institutions.[39] On the one hand, trade unions were targeted indiscriminately.[40] On the other hand, government authorities aimed for the total destruction of the SPD's means of cultural production. Section 14 of the 1878 legislation stated:

> On the basis of the prohibition, the publications concerned are to be confiscated wherever found for the purpose of distribution. The confiscation may include the plates and forms used for reproduction; in the case of printed publications in the proper sense, a withdrawal of the set types from circulation is to be substituted for their seizure, upon the request of the interested parties. After the prohibition is final, the publication, plates, and forms are to be made unusable.[41]

The SPD's three major newspapers, the *Vorwärts,* the *Berliner Freie Presse,* and the *Hamburg-Altonaer Volksblatt* were all suppressed, eliminating a source of income for many (Liebknecht among them) and ceasing production for roughly 45,000 subscribers. By June 1879 the German police had suppressed 405 periodical and nonperiodical publications.[42]

It is in this period that the transnationalism of the SPD's cultural terrain became especially important for the formation of socialist leftism. Using the intellectual, political, and economic resources available to the now partly underground SPD, the antisocialist law fostered the gestation of Marxist socialism in marginality. German socialist leaders gathered in Zurich—the "foremost meeting place for exiled radicals, students and thinkers from the Tsarist Empire," the Balkans, and the United States— alongside peers from other places.[43] A new, underground German social democratic newspaper, the *Sozialdemokrat,* was first produced in Zurich on September 28, 1879, and was distributed via an impressive operation that came to be known as the Red Army Postal Service. Eduard Bernstein (former editor of *Die Zukunft*) would soon become the new paper's editor.[44] In Zurich, Bernstein befriended Karl Kautsky, a fellow exile, a former student of history, philosophy, and economics at the University of Vienna, and a member of what is now the Austrian Social Democratic Party (SPÖ).[45] By 1883 Kautsky had become the editor of the German SPD's new, "rigidly Marxian" theoretical magazine, *Die Neue Zeit.*[46]

Marxism's consolidation as a scientific basis of German socialist leftism started in Zurich during the time of the antisocialist laws and consolidated in Erfurt. In Zurich, Kautsky and Bernstein jointly drafted a new party program with the aim of reestablishing the SPD on a more definitely Marxist basis—that is, on "the historico-economic definition of Socialism which Marx had sketched in the Communist Manifesto and developed in *Das Capital.*"[47] Upon the repeal of the antisocialist laws in 1890 (on the heels of "phenomenally successful elections"), the SPD held its first party congress in Halle, where Bebel and Liebknecht called upon the party to prioritize cultural activities by developing the "circulation and influence of its press" and concentrating on "influencing public opinion . . . by argument and information."[48] This, Liebknecht emphasized, was the only route to success, as open conflict with the ever-more powerful state was "the road to disaster."[49]

Between 1890 and the early 1900s the party established its own bookshop and allocated a significant portion of membership revenues (by one report, more than 50 percent of its 1890s expenditures) to "agitation" expenses and "support of the press." It produced and disseminated journals, leaflets, brochures, pamphlets, newspapers, and books. It also established a press bureau and information service (the Sozialdemokratische Partei Korrespondenz). Its labor secretariats dispatched "692,000 items of information and legal advice" to its supporters in 1914.[50]

In 1907 the SPD also established the Party School (Parteischule) as a "purveyor of ideological training at the highest level."[51] The Party School had all the trappings of a formal educational setting: an image from around 1907 shows twenty-four adult students arranged in a modern classroom, stacked with bookshelves on one side and a chalkboard at the front, eight faculty at the head of the room, and the famous SPD theorist Franz Mehring at the podium.[52]

Meanwhile, the SPD's newspapers, journals, and weeklies, not to mention socialist-sympathetic but non-SPD-owned publications, were too numerous to count. By World War I the German "socialist press . . . reached an all-time high of 1.5 million subscribers," with the average party member receiving more than one weekly or monthly publication.[53] Pocket diaries or Volkskalender, featuring "useful information as well as snippets of socialist propaganda," were "distributed free or sold cheaply mainly among the rural population"; W. L. Guttsman estimates that "[t]heir total number may well have exceeded the million mark as the party's printing works produced in 1906 some 350,000 diaries for a few of the [rural German] areas alone."[54] In addition to Vorwärts (1876), the Socialdemokrat (the SPD-in-exile's paper), and Die Neue Zeit (1886), Die Gesellschaft was established in 1924.

In an age when formal education was not widespread, SPD leaders prioritized educational and theoretical activities. Kautsky feared that "[w]ithout knowledge of the goal and insight into the laws of historical development, the proletariat would go astray."[55] Through the party, the "best minds of the working class" could discover the truths of socialism and put them into practice.[56] In the early twentieth century the SPD was a full-fledged educational and community institution, sponsoring popular entertainment, family events, holidays, libraries, lectures, and seminars ranging from arithmetic and linguistics to Marxist theory, vocational training, and art and culture.[57] Aiming to provide a "total environment" for its members—a *Vaterhaus und Lebensinhalt* (parental home and life substance)—an SPD member could live within the party from cradle to grave:

> [An SPD member] could read the party's newspapers, borrow from its book clubs, drink in its pubs, keep fit in it gyms, sing in its choral societies, play in its orchestras, take part in the so-called people's theatre organizations, compete in its chess clubs, and join, if a woman, the SPD women's movement, and, if young, the youth organization. When members were ill, they would receive help from the Working Men's Samaritan Federation. When they died, they would be cremated by a social-democratic burial club.[58]

The SPD's cultural arm thus extended into localities and communities, cultivating a German social democratic "subculture," producing socialist intellectuals in-house whose writings reached both domestic and transnational audiences.[59]

Essential to this world was the Second International (1889–1916), now an organization of political parties (as opposed to a conglomeration of labor movements, social reformers, exiled radical and secret associations, and sympathetic journalists and intellectuals) that was anchored by the SPD. The International was one basis of theoretical Marxism's development into an internationalized intellectual enterprise in which "criticism respected no frontiers."[60] Engels relied heavily on the SPD's *Die Neue Zeit* (edited by Kautsky until 1917) as a vehicle for the translation and dissemination of Marx's work, working also to build and sustain "an extraordinary network of international socialist contacts, rapidly expanding with the new socialist parties"—each with their own cultural arms.[61] The *Neue Zeit* and its counterparts in other countries—*Le Devenir Social* in France, the *Social Democrat* in Britain (1897–1913), and the Italian Socialist Party's *Avanti!* (started in 1896).[62] It was on this terrain that Marx's works were consolidated and disseminated, along with those of Engels, Kautsky, Bebel, and Liebknecht, as well as newcomers of a younger generation that included Antonio Labriola (1843–1904), Franz Mehring (1846–1919), Georgi Plekhanov (1856–1918), and Paul Lafargue (1842–1911).[63] This generation systematized historical materialism "as a comprehensive theory of man and nature, capable of replacing rival bourgeois disciplines."[64] It was this cultural terrain, at once German and transnational, that made possible the SPD's chief theoretician by the late 1910s: Rudolf Hilferding.

Rudolf Hilferding

The SPD first entered government in 1919, as part of the Weimar coalition. It would then return in 1923 and again from 1928 to 1930. Whenever the SPD had control over the office of finance minister (in the last two SPD-coalition governments), they filled it with the same person: Rudolf Hilferding.

Born in 1877 in Austro-Hungary two years after the SPD was established, Hilferding was the son of a middle-class Jewish family of Polish origins. He trained in medicine at the University of Vienna, where he took an interest in socialism. From 1893 he participated in a student group that gathered to discuss socialist literature, which later joined with some young university teachers to create the Freie Vereinigung Sozialistischer Studenten und Akademiker. This association, headed by Max Adler, with Karl Renner, Otto Bauer, and others, would later become home to the leading "Austro-Marxists" of the Austrian SPÖ.[65]

Hilferding worked as a physician, writing about Marxist socialism on the side. In 1902 he sent a critical review of Austrian economist Eugen Böhm-Bawerk's marginalist critique of Marx's *Das Kapital* to Kautsky's *Die Neue Zeit*. We might recall that it was during this time that the SPD was ramping up its investments in journalistic and theoretical production, in the wake of the end of antisocialist legislation. Kautsky did not publish Hilferding's essay (it was too long), but was impressed.[66] Hilferding then established his own theoretical journal, *Marx-Studien,* with Adler in 1904; with Adler and Renner he also founded *Die Zukunft (Future)* and helped to initiate Vienna's first workers' school in 1903—a few years prior to the establishment of the SPD's Party School. The SPD leader August Bebel invited Hilferding (on Kautsky's suggestion) to become a regular contributor to *Die Neue Zeit*.

The SPD's cultural arm made it possible for Hilferding to leave medicine and do full-time intellectual work. Bebel recruited him to move to Berlin in 1906 as an instructor for the SPD's new Party School. On the side, he also worked for *Die Neue Zeit* and the SPD's official journal, *Vorwärts*.[67]

Finally free to dedicate himself to intellectual pursuits,[68] Hilferding published his masterwork, *Finance Capital,* in 1910. *Finance Capital* set out to understand the "processes of concentration which, on the one hand, 'eliminate free competition' through the formation of cartels and trusts, and on the other, bring bank and industrial capital into an ever more intimate relationship."[69] Hilferding argued that capitalism—with the concentration of business, growth of monopoly, the growing centrality of banks, and the underpinning of the state—was organizing itself into a less crisis-prone system over time, in a socialist direction.[70]

Hilferding's editorial work and the publication of *Finance Capital* put him on a fast track into SPD leadership. From 1912 he became a *Vorwärts* representative to the party council, which advised the executive.[71] Having established himself as a Marxist intellectual through party institutions, Hilferding thus gained direct influence over SPD policy-making.

The SPD splintered during World War I and in the aftermath of the Bolshevik Revolution; for a time Hilferding left the party.[72] But by 1922 he returned, becoming the chief editor of the SPD's new theoretical journal, *Die Gesellschaft,* at its founding in 1924. This was an important position. Between 1925 and 1928 *Die Gesellschaft* had a readership of about 4,400, circulating "mainly among social democratic political leaders and intellectuals." Its contributors included "Kautsky, the liberal historian Friedrich Meinecke, trade unionist Fritz Naphtali, socialist Ferdinand Tönnies, historian Arthur Rosenberg, philosophers Hannah Arendt and Herbert Marcuse, and Menshevik leader Alexander Schifrin"[73] From there Hilferding moved up through party ranks.

From his perch at *Die Gesellschaft,* Hilferding became the chair of the SPD's program commission. He was also placed on the SPD's "national list of *Reichstag* candidates," which "virtually assured his yearly reelection without . . . having to personally campaign."[74] Now the SPD's "chief ideologist," a member of its executive committee, and a member of the Reichstag, until 1933 he shaped party policy practically and theoretically.[75] Among other things, Hilferding was central to the formulation of the party's 1925 program.[76] According to SPD secretary Fritz Heine, Hilferding had become "the most respected Marxist theoretician in the executive."[77]

The Conditions of the SPD Party Theoretician

What made Hilferding's ascendance possible? Clearly the development of organized labor was a condition, insofar as it was central to the party as a whole—but organized labor had little to do with Hilferding's professional trajectory. Instead, Hilferding's ascent had to do with his intellectual accomplishments, themselves dependent on socialism's cultural terrain—in particular, the SPD's in-house publications and its party school. Hilferding's ascent also had to do with a disproportionate authority of intellectuals in party leadership.

As we have seen, intellectuals had dominated the SPD's leadership since the days of the Lassalleans and Eisenachers.[78] Once the ADGB was formed it provided essential organizational resources and membership bases to the party, but agenda-setting authority was a prerogative of the intellectual-dominated party executive. The SPD's oligarchical structure, duly noted by Robert Michels at the time, rendered it "a gerontocracy . . . with little consultation of the rank and file." Hilferding was part of a relatively closed cadre of older-generation officials and theoreticians who were accustomed to defining problems, priorities, and programs for the rest of the organization, including the trade unions.[79]

Hilferding's prestige also had to do with the rarity of educational credentials, in general, for people of his generation. In 1905, around the time Hilferding came to Germany to work for the SPD's Party School and journals, less than 1 percent of the German population had a university education. As of 1913, when Hilferding was advising the party executive as editor of *Vorwärts*, the German population aged fifteen to sixty-four had, on average, slightly less than seven years of formal schooling.[80]

This perhaps helps to explain why the SPD became, in effect, a credentialing institution in its own right. Graduating 203 students between 1907 and 1914, the Party School was an avenue into editorial positions on party newspapers, administrative positions in the party bureaucracy, and jobs as union officials.[81] In turn journalists and editors, the second-largest group in the party bureaucracy (after organized labor) by the 1910s, were unusually likely to track into the core of the party's leadership. In Guttsman's words:

> Even more than trade union officials [journalists] were enmeshed in the agitational and organisational work of the party. . . . An editorial post was a major milestone in the career of many SPD leaders . . . journalists remained a principal occupational group among Social Democratic leaders and parliamentarians right through the Weimar period.[82]

The SPD's cultural arm also offered a sort of career track to the limited, but nonetheless growing, numbers of university-educated offspring of the German middle classes whose professional aspirations were frustrated by limited opportunities and anti-Semitic discrimination.[83]

Hilferding's ascent was thus symptomatic of a specifically Social Democratic pathway to becoming a political intellectual by vocation. The ranks of young SPD intellectuals working for the socialist press swelled around the turn of the twentieth century.[84] They were "prominent in the debates and discussions at the party's annual conferences" and "an important part of the Social Democratic Fraktion . . . in the German parliament."[85] Max Weber noted journalists' special place in socialist parties, commenting in his 1918 lecture "Politics as a Vocation" (first published in 1919) that "the journalist has had favorable chances only in the Social Democratic party," unlike the "bourgeois parties."[86]

As the Swedish case shows, neither the centrality of journalists and party-based intellectuals nor the figure of the party theoretician was unique to the SPD.

The Swedish SAP

In a still largely agricultural context, the Swedish SAP emerged in 1889 on a Marxist platform that self-consciously emulated the SPD's Erfurt Program. Understood by some as a movement before its time, SAP formation also had its own, specific, transnational position, influenced especially by social democratic movements in Norway and Denmark. As in Germany, the party took shape amid growing worker unrest, new liberal social reformism, and antisocialist elite political sentiment.

The SAP emerged without the extraordinary state repression that shaped the making of the SPD, but it was not totally free of opposition. Swedish political and religious elites in the late 1800s regarded socialism as "almost a criminal movement." The Swedish government proposed its own antisocialist law in the same year the SAP was founded, but it was struck down in the lower house of the Riksdag.[87]

The SAP, like the SPD, was grounded in liberal workers' clubs and associations turned socialist by "agitators." Instances included the Ystad Workers' Association and the Sundsvall Workers' Club (established in 1884). Others, like the Stockholm Social Democratic Club (established in the early 1880s) and another organization by the same name at the University of Uppsala, were socialist from the start. In the account of the Swedish journalist Herbert Tingsten, "The Social Democrats sought to make the trade union movement socialist, and they succeeded."[88]

Also like the SPD, SAP formation drove the national-level centralization of Swedish labor: the Swedish Federation of Trade Unions was established well after the SAP, in 1899. At first, party membership was a prerequisite for trade union membership.[89] This didn't last very long, but by 1907 the SAP coordinated union activity, maintained a local presence via 427 labor communes, and had built a membership of 133,388—a prewar peak.[90] By the 1910s the SAP was commanding around 30 percent of the vote, winning the largest single number of votes in 1917 for the first time. In 1924, at 41 percent of the vote, it was the leading party by a wide margin.

The SAP's Cultural Arm

The SAP was built on a transnational cultural terrain that overlapped with, and was anchored by, German socialist leftism in the age of the SPD. At the same time, Swedish socialist cultural and journalistic institutions developed both against and within Swedish liberalism. Once established the SAP not only prodded workers to organize on the national level; it also extended its cultural arm, especially, into adult education.

The party's founders, all middle-class and most with unusually high levels of formal education, spent the 1880s lecturing, writing, educating, and agitating for socialism; many moved in transnational networks. August Palm (1849–1922), who brought SPD-style social democracy to Sweden from Germany, was no proletarian: a Swedish tailor and the son of a schoolteacher, he was orphaned at age ten and lived in northern Germany in the 1870s. Palm is credited with delivering the first social democratic speech in Sweden in 1881, drawing heavily from the SPD's Gotha Program. In 1882 he established a newspaper called the *People's Will* (*Folkvilan*); in the same year he published the first Swedish social democratic political program, a translation of the Danish Gimle Program of 1876 (also based on the Gotha Program).[91] In 1885 Palm established the newspaper *Social-Demokraten* in Stockholm, which became an important tool of public education in Swedish socialism.

Palm's journalistic, lecturing, and other semi-educational pursuits were typical of SAP founders, although Palm was older and less formally educated than his peers. Other SAP founding figures—Hjalmar Branting (1860–1925), Fredrik Sterky (1860–1900), and Axel Danielsson (1863–1899)—were a decade younger, all college-educated in Uppsala.[92] There they got involved with social democratic organizations and moved into journalism as an outlet for radical intellectual work.[93] In 1885 Branting became the editor of *Tiden;* in Malmö, *Arbetet* was founded by Danielsson in 1887. Sterky was involved in the founding of Palm's *Social-Demokraten.*

Socialist newspapers fed into the making of the SAP and drove a whole transformation of mass journalism in Sweden.[94] The SAP continued its journalistic activities once it was established and, like the SPD, extended its reach into adult education.[95] Driven initially by farmers, early Swedish adult education took multiple forms: folk schools, libraries, study circles, and lectures.[96] In service of liberal reformism, adult education was a tool for supporting "democratic processes and training people to exercise their newly acquired political power."[97] By 1912 the SAP effectively had a folk school of its own: the Brunnsvik People's College.[98] Like the SPD's Party School, the Brunnsvik folk school provided a site for the cultivation, employment, and education of future generations of SAP leadership.

The SAP's cultural investments also extended to the SAP-affiliated Workers' Educational Association (Arbetarnas Bildningsförbund, or ABF, established in 1912); the Trade Union Confederation (Landsorganisationen, or LO); and the Cooperative Wholesale Society (Kooperativa Förbundet). Working closely with Brunnsvik, the ABF became the largest society of its kind in Sweden.[99] The SAP's cultural terrain thus expanded as the party formalized.

Expressing this broader process, it was through party-affiliated journalism, lecturing, and socialist "agitation" that another party theoretician, Fredrik Thorsson, became the SAP's go-to economic expert.

Fredrik Thorsson

The SAP entered government for the first time in 1917, in coalition with the Liberal party. With Nils Edén (a Liberal) as prime minister, Branting served initially, and briefly, as minister of finance. Fredrik Thorsson then took the position from 1918 to 1920.[100] In 1921 Thorsson returned as finance minister, to 1923. By the time Thorsson died unexpectedly in 1925, he was the longest-serving finance minister of a SAP party-in-government.

Thorsson's formation as a SAP theoretician developed at the intersection of craft-based trade associations, emerging workers' organizations, journalistic "agitation," and socialism's transnational cultural terrain. Born in 1865, Thorsson's parents both died by the time he was nine. His guardian, a farmer, sent him to learn shoemaking (his father's trade) at the age of eleven. By 1883, aged eighteen, Thorsson had received his certification with the Ystad Crafts Association.[101] Now an independent "journeyman," Thorsson set out for the south (Malmö)—where, a few years earlier, August Palm had given public lectures on social democracy, and early socialist workers' organizations were taking shape.[102] Thorsson worked at a shoe factory but, finding the dues too expensive, did not join the union. Leaving Malmö, Thorsson traveled to Denmark, where he witnessed the 1884 victory of an alliance of social democrats and radicals.

Thorsson moved to Stockholm in 1885, one year after Sweden's franchise reform of 1884, where he became more deeply involved in socialist agitation. In Stockholm he was finally persuaded to join a workers' organization: the Shoemakers Worker Association, established in 1882.[103] After assisting the association's recruitment activities and drawing attention as a speaker, however, Thorsson found himself unemployable: socialist "agitation," as it was then known, was a risky business. By the fall of 1885 he moved again, to Uppsala, then back to Stockholm, and then north to Sundsvall. There, in 1887, he authored the union work program of Sundsvall shoemakers.[104] With the expansion of worker organization and the franchise, competition between liberals and socialists for workers' loyalties in Sundsvall, and elsewhere in Sweden, was intensifying. In this context Thorsson was known as a shoemaker-*cum*-agitator.[105]

Partly thanks to his involvements with socialist newspapers, Thorsson became an intellectual of sorts. He helped to establish the northern liberal-radical newspaper *Norrlänningen* in 1887, intervening in order to ensure that the paper would have a socialist column. The paper became a point of contention between liberals and socialists in the late 1880s. In Thorsson's account, "[T]he breaks were quite sharp between new [socialist] and old [liberal] philosophies in the trade union world."[106] The struggle hinged on workers' "true" interests: Thorsson and fellow socialists felt that workers' dire situations could not be addressed with a moderate, liberal politics. To make his case, in 1888 he published a story on the working conditions of Norrland sawmill workers in Danielsson's *Arbetet*, describing workers as "slaves" with long hours and no job security, living in decrepit company-provided housing.[107] Thorsson's impassioned contributions to *Norrlänningen* and *Arbetet* established him as a "bold" young socialist known for "energy and endurance without equal."[108]

The Sundsvall socialists finally established their own journal, *Revolt*, in the winter of 1888.[109] Symptomatic of a deepening socialist-liberal rift, only one issue ever produced. Because Thorsson helped distribute it to workers, that single issue got him fired. Already unable to work in Sundsvall, Thorsson had gone to a sawmill about a mile away, where he worked "like a slave from Monday to Friday," pursuing socialist activism and journalism on weekends. Despite efforts by his manager and coworkers to protect him, the sawmill owner threatened Thorsson's job, and he left for Ystad.[110]

At this point Thorsson's formation and that of the SAP merged. Palm, Branting, Sterky, and Danielsson (among others) established the SAP in

1889. Around that time, the editor of *Norrlänningen* finally shifted his allegiances to socialism, affiliating his paper with *Arbetet*. In 1890 the *Norrlänningen* editor made Thorsson his Ystad correspondent.[111] Thorsson also became the head of the socialist-dominated Ystad Workers' Association. At twenty-four years old, he was now a socialist agitator, journalist, and leader of a branch of a new mass party.[112]

For Thorsson, "socialist" meant workers organized for their class-specific interests under a socialist banner. The claim was not merely that workers should organize politically; it was that socialism was the theoretical language of workers' political representation. Thorsson's agitation aimed to shift the loyalties of workers, many of whom were already organized in liberal clubs and associations. In the account of a biographer and colleague, Thorsson "worked for socialism":

> Working for socialism ... [Thorsson] organized meetings, fenced premises, advertised under [socialism's] ... name, pasted posters, lectured, appeared in debates, led demonstrations, staged carnivals, wrote in newspapers, begged for money, sold tickets, sang in the choir and played the theater.[113]

In time, Thorsson's efforts helped to make Ystad a center for socialist-based worker organization in Sweden.

Thorsson became leader of his home district in southern Sweden and was elected to the Riksdag for Ystad in 1902.[114] He was about thirty-seven years old and, in the Riksdag, one of a select few: since 1896, Branting had been the only SAP member holding a parliamentary seat; when Thorsson joined him, the number of SAP seats came to a total of four.[115] But SAP parliamentary numbers rose to thirteen (1905), then to thirty-four (1908), and finally to sixty-four in 1911. From 1921, when Branting began intermittent service as prime minister until his death in 1925, Thorsson was an important presence at his side.[116]

The Conditions of the SAP Party Theoretician

Thorsson's roots were more grounded in organized labor than Hilferding's, but Thorsson was an "agitator"—a term that, at the time, referred specifically to the journalists and public lecturers who spoke for socialism.[117] Had Thorsson not been an agitator, he may never have come to the attention of Danielsson or linked with Danielsson's

Arbetet. Thorsson's professional trajectory, like Hilferding's, depended on opportunities made available to him by the cultural arm of a party-in-the-making.

There are other similarities to the German case. The SAP was worker-fueled but not worker-led. This had partly to do with the problem of merging the leading edge of a party representing newly enfranchised workers into a closed, elite, national political establishment. The SAP was the first party in Sweden to form outside of parliament; before 1889, Swedish political parties were factions of the Riksdag, not mass organizations. SAP leadership had to operate in a political world from which most Swedes, including those the SAP represented, were excluded. As in Germany, university-level education in Sweden was a rarity. In the late 1870s, when Branting and other future SAP leaders were at the University of Uppsala, tertiary enrollment for their age group was probably less than 1 percent; tertiary enrollment more than a decade later, in 1890, was still a little under 2 percent.[118]

The prominence of the agitator in early SAP leadership points to a party-centered mobility regime in which a university education helped, but could not be a prerequisite. Passage through socialist journalism was a functional substitute for formal credentials. This can be seen in the demographics of the party's rank and file versus its leadership around the turn of the twentieth century. Delegates to early party congresses were predominantly "workers and craftsmen"; before World War I about 80 percent of SAP members were trade union people.[119] But "none of the official leadership of the party came from unions."[120] Instead, journalist-agitators, like Thorsson, dominated official positions.[121]

We now come to the British Labour Party, the formation of which also had linkages to transnational (and specifically German) networks, but was also more clearly union-driven. Nonetheless, Labour, too, gave rise to its own version of a party theoretician, born chiefly of party-affiliated knowledge-producing and journalistic institutions.

The British Labour Party

The British Labour Party, as it was officially named in 1906, was an outgrowth of an organization called the Labour Representation Committee (LRC, established in 1900). As the name indicates, Labour's foundation was much more union-driven than either the SPD or the SAP. But unions were not the sole drivers. Many kinds of organizations, in fact, came together to constitute the party. By the 1920s the young Labour Party was self-consciously organizing itself in the image of the SPD and deeply invested in cultural production.[122]

The LRC's establishment, more specifically, was driven by the Trades Union Congress (TUC, established in 1868) parliamentary committee's 1899 decision, in response to legal persecution, to seek electoral power in conjunction with socialist and cooperative organizations. The latter included the (Marxist) Social Democratic Federation (SDF, formerly the DF, established in 1881), the Fabian Society (established in 1884), and the Independent Labour Party (ILP, established in 1893).[123] The novelty of the LRC was not the organized political action of trade unions but rather their alliance with socialist and cooperative organizations. From the start, there were tensions between the two. In the account of British historian Alastair Reid, "[T]he trade unions were generally pursuing improvements in their members' position within the existing social framework," but "the socialists . . . had a variety of visions of fundamental social reconstruction" and "saw Labour as the embryo of a new force in British politics which would challenge the Liberals for the leadership of progressive opinion."[124]

Labour's multiple roots, anchored by organized labor and varied socialist and cooperative organizations, show in the lives of the party's founding figures. The ILP's Keir Hardie (1856–1915), for instance, built his career through a combination of labor activism, journalism, and party organization. The largely self-educated son of working-class parents, Hardie began working life at age eleven, as a "trapper" charged with keeping mineshafts ventilated. After a combination of labor organizing activities and party-based journalism, and an encounter with Engels in 1887, Hardie abandoned involvements with the Gladstonian Liberals for socialism, calling for labor's independent political representation.[125] He started a journal called the *Miner* in 1887. But it was as founder of the Scottish Labour Party (established in 1888) and the *Labour Leader* (1894) that Hardie became a known political voice.[126]

In 1906 the LRC won twenty-nine seats in the general election and renamed itself the Labour Party, with Keir Hardie as its first chairman.[127] Labour's electoral success was made possible, in part, by a secret noncompetitive pact with the Liberal Party (1903). Labour became the main party of opposition in 1922 and entered government for the first time in 1924 in coalition with the Liberals. The event unfolded amid a haze of controversy over Labour's competence to rule, fears of the dawn of socialism in Britain, and suspicions of Labour's association with Russian communism. By this time the party's cultural terrain was singularly intertwined with the educational, research, and theoretical activities of the Fabian Society.

Labour's Cultural Terrain

Hardie's *Labour Leader* was one of various socialist newspapers and pamphlets circulating in the last two decades of the 1900s. There was also the SDF's *Justice* (established in 1884) and the Socialist League's *Commonweal* (1885). And, last but not least, there were the tracts and pamphlets of the Fabian Society. Founded by Sidney and Beatrice Webb, George Bernard Shaw, and others in London in 1884, the Fabian Society was formally integrated into the party's executive at its foundation.[128] By the 1910s Fabians were key forces in the production of Labour's programmatic rhetoric and practical policy orientations.

The Fabian Society was a site of the sometimes collaborative, sometimes oppositional, liberal-socialist relationship also found in other countries. A *de facto* credentialing institution that both produced socialist theoreticians and provided publication outlets for socialist intellectual work, from its beginnings the Fabian Society focused its energies on cultural and educational activities, targeting both political elites (especially in the Liberal Party) and the general public. Like Fredrik Thorsson, Fabians worked through existing liberal associations, cooperative societies, and trade unions to educate workers, delivering educational lectures on topics ranging from socialism, trade unionism, and cooperative organization to economics and the poor law.[129] The Webbs, Shaw, and other leading members built their intellectual reputations via Fabian Society–based publications and events, engaging with Marxism and marginalist economics and formulating their own contributions to an economic theory of rent.[130]

The Webbs and fellow Fabians are well noted for their middle-classness and civil service ties, their commitment to evolutionary (as opposed to revolutionary) socialism, and their faith in social science as a means of progressive government. Acting on this faith, they established the London School of Economics and Political Science (LSE) in 1895 as an autonomous institution dedicated to the pursuit of scientific social knowledge in service of "social reconstruction."[131] The Webbs also established the *New Statesman* magazine in 1913, an independent venue that was to remain "absolutely untrammeled by party, or sect, or creed."[132]

Meanwhile, inside the Labour Party—despite its union-led origins, and even though unions provided essential resources—Fabians came to dominate Labour's programmatic activities by the 1910s. At first, the largely nonsocialist Trades Union Congress (TUC) dominated early Labour leadership.[133] The LRC executive consisted of seven trade unionists and five socialists. Among those five, only one was Fabian; two were ILP, and two represented the (Marxist) SDF. Ramsay MacDonald, a Fabian Executive Committee (since 1894) and founding ILP member, was the LRC's secretary. The union-socialist relationship was not always easy: "trade unionists tended to be rather suspicious of the socialists," while "socialists tended to be rather dismissive of the trade unions."[134] But, soon after Labour acquired parliamentary seats in 1906, the Fabians became more dominant practically and programmatically.

Ironically, the growth of British trade unions—driven, in part, by state restrictions on union rights in 1900—contributed to the Fabians' rise within Labour leadership. Partly this was due to union-driven attrition of the competition. As union affiliates proliferated, the Liberal Party agreed to a noncompetitive deal with Labour, securing the new party's position.[135] But, in 1901, the SDF withdrew in protest of Labour's nonsocialist trade unions. The Labour executive was thus left to trade unionists and Fabian socialists.[136] Finally, in 1909 the Osborne judgment made direct union contributions to parties illegal, which had the unexpected effect of stabilizing the party's financial basis and granting it greater autonomy from union control.[137]

When MacDonald took over party leadership in 1911, Fabians were more central to the party's programmatic direction than in the days of the LRC. An MP since 1906, described as a charismatic "master of organization and strategy" with "a relatively coherent ideology," MacDonald had modest roots, but he was not a union man.[138] The illegitimate son of a housemaid and a farm laborer in Scotland, Mac-Donald left formal schooling after age fifteen and became a teacher and then a clergyman's assistant; he joined the DF (soon to be the SDF) in 1885. He then moved to London, where he became involved in the Socialist Union. An honorary secretary and executive member of the Fellowship of the New Life (the Fabian Society's predecessor), MacDonald was one of the Fabian Society's first lecturers.[139] MacDonald studied Marx's work but, rejecting it as out-of-date, embraced instead the revisionist thinking of Eduard Bernstein.

MacDonald's fellow Fabian, Sidney Webb, defined Labour's twentieth-century program. In September 1917 Webb drafted Labour's first formal policy statement, *Labour and the New Social Order,* which became the basis for Labour's 1918 constitution. Webb's constitution included the (in)famous Clause IV, calling for the "common ownership of the means of production, distribution, and exchange." The constitution would remain in effect until 1928; Clause IV would last into the 1990s.[140]

After 1918, some argue that Labour increasingly looked to the SPD as an "organizational model."[141] As the historian Stefan Berger explains, "Like the SPD, the Labour Party built up a network of local parties with a mass individual membership, created a viable Labour Party press and built up a Labour movement culture."[142] This was driven especially by Herbert Morrison, a central force in the making of the London Labour Party (LLP), whose first contact with the SPD was probably a July 1910 visit to its urban strongholds (Hamburg, Leipzig, Berlin, Frankfurt). After 1918, partly due to Morrison's emulative efforts, Labour became more SPD-like in terms of its cultural investments, especially:

> Local parties appointed paid organisers and secretaries; general management committees set up sub-committees which dealt with finance, literature, education, culture and other social/recreational activities; sometimes literature secretaries of educational officers were appointed.[143]

Morrison was not alone in his admiration, and in-person observation, of SPD organization: Ramsay MacDonald, Arthur Henderson, and Keir Hardie were also admirers. Via the Fabian Society, meanwhile, German party intellectuals also built ties between Labour and the SPD—most famously in the case of Eduard Bernstein.[144]

It was on this party-centered, transnationally connected cultural terrain that Philip Snowden emerged as a theoretician—that is, "the acknowledged authority to whom all, from Keir Hardie downwards, automatically turned" and the default choice as chancellor of the exchequer.[145]

Philip Snowden

Like Hilferding and Thorsson, Snowden was the go-to appointee for the second most powerful position in the British government: chancellor of the exchequer, the closest equivalent to a German or Swedish minister of finance.

Born in 1864, Snowden was raised a weaver's son in a small and religious (Wesleyan Methodist) community in Yorkshire. He was educated in private and boarding schools until about age sixteen, but then he had to seek employment after his parents went bankrupt. Snowden trained to be a solicitor and entered the British civil service (Inland Revenue) after passing the exam in 1886. But it didn't last: Snowden's civil service career was cut short due to a disabling illness.

Snowden turned to reading and writing, reconstructing himself after 1891 as a socialist "agitator" (to use Swedish terminology) through a combination of socialist- and Labour-affiliated electoral pursuits, public lecturing, and political journalism. After a series of invited local addresses, he acquired an uncontested spot on the Cowling parish council in 1894. He then joined the new ILP, led by Keir Hardie, and became an ILP parliamentary candidate in 1895.[146] Thenceforth committed to "earning his bread as a traveling Socialist preacher," Snowden made a living publishing his lectures as pamphlets (notably a popular 1903 lecture, "The Christ That Is to Be") and became the editor of the *Keighley Labour Journal* in 1898.[147]

Snowden thence rose through the ILP's ranks, joining the executive committee of the Keighley ILP in 1899 and becoming an LRC/Labour Party candidate in the early 1900s.[148] After moving to Leeds in 1902, where he made a living as a lecturer and journalist, he was elected as Labour's Member of Parliament (MP) for Blackburn (1906). Chairman of the ILP since 1903, in the meantime he took over Hardie's paper, the *Labour Leader,* and made it into a major party publication.[149]

Snowden was known for his writing and speaking abilities, and among his many influential contributions to Labour and Fabian thinking were books on socialism, finance, suffrage, and other topics.[150] Dependent on income from parliamentary allowances and journalistic proceeds, Snowden joined the recently established National Union of Journalists in 1908.[151] By this time Snowden occupied an undisputed role as the party's main economic expert.[152]

Snowden built himself as an expert through civil service work, self-education, journalism, and party-affiliated institutions. Like many British socialists at the time, he engaged with Marx and Marxist thinking through the works of H. M. Hyndman.[153] Being from a modest background and (unlike Hilferding, but like Thorsson) having no university education, Snowden learned about taxation and public finance via civil service experience and by reading budget speeches—including those of Sir Robert Peel, a figure closely identified with the construction of gold standard institutions.[154] Thus equipped with a formal education; a brief civil service record; extensive experience in socialist lecturing, journalism, and editorial work; and "rigid self-training in the classic principles of Gladstonian finance and *laissez-faire* economics," Snowden was the party's recognized authority on economic questions by the late 1910s.[155]

The Conditions of the Labour Party Theoretician

What made Snowden's ascendance possible? As in the cases of Hilferding and Thorsson, it was not the trade unions—that is, Labour's economic arm. Rather, Snowden's rise had to do with *de facto* credentialing in institutions and activities that were connected with the Labour party-in-formation, at a time when formal and university education was a rarity—especially among the nonaristocratic.

Snowden's more than ten years of formal education was unusual for a man of his generation, especially in Labour circles. In 1913 the average formal education in the adult population (aged fifteen to sixty-four) was about 7.3 years.[156] Formal education was particularly scarce inside Labour: between 1918 and 1935, 72 percent of Labour's members had only an elementary education (compared with 4 percent and 14 percent of Conservatives and Liberals, respectively); 11 percent had attended a university (versus 69 percent of Conservatives and 21 percent of Liberals). Meanwhile, the training grounds of Britain's political elite—Eton, Harrow, Oxbridge, the elite military academies—were hardly teeming with, or welcoming to, Labour-friendly socialists. Compared to someone like Winston Churchill (a graduate of Harrow who, in 1953, won the Nobel Prize in Literature) Snowden was hardly a natural fit with Britain's sanctified parliamentary elite.

The matter of qualification for intellectual work was an explicit concern for Labour and Fabian leadership. In G. D. H. Cole's account, around 1914 there were "114 trade-union-sponsored M.P.s, fifty were miners, by far the largest group. . . . [H]ardly any unions sponsored what Beatrice Webb was wont to call 'brainworkers.'"[157] Snowden himself, when confronted with the unprecedented prospect of a (minority) Labour government in 1924, expressed concerns regarding the ill fit between workers-turned-Labour MPs and the category "Parliamentarian":

> Half the Labour members who had been returned to this Parliament were new to the House of Commons. The new members were nearly all Trade Union nominees and had little knowledge of general politics. The Government treated the insignificant Opposition with indifference, amounting almost to contempt. During the first eighteen months of the life of this Parliament the leader of the Labour group was Mr. William Adamson, a Fifeshire miner. . . . Mr. Adamson was an honest fellow with a good deal of Scotch shrewdness. He possessed few of the qualities necessary for the leadership of a political party. He was in no sense a Parliamentarian.[158]

For Snowden, the fact that "Parliamentarian" was inherently exclusive of "worker" presented serious practical problems. Labour MPs had to be able to communicate with, and command the respect of, both fellow politicians and civil service officials. The need for intellectual respect was tied to Labour's prospects as a party of government. Surely this was an important condition of Snowden's ascent.

What *cannot* explain Snowden's ascent, however, was the support of, or his experiences with, trade unions, much less any sort of consensus among workers that Fabians deserved to speak for them. Snowden had a history of disagreement with, and by some reports disdain for, the party's union affiliates (a feeling that was likely mutual).[159] Two of Snowden's more notable works, *The Living Wage* (1912) and *Socialism and Syndicalism* (1913), were effectively responses to trade union hostility, having been published after Snowden failed to support the strikes of 1910 and 1911. During the 1926 general strike, Snowden reaffirmed this lack of support.[160] In short, the conditions of Snowden's ascent had everything to do with the special problems faced by a party representing the working classes, and the cultural institutions and activities such a party necessarily developed in that context—but very little to do with experiences in, or the support of, organized labor.

SOCIALIST LEFTISM AND ECONOMICS AROUND 1920: WEAK TIES

So far, this chapter has explored the conditions that made possible three socialist party theoreticians, showing how their formation stories tracked through left parties' specifically *cultural*—that is, educational, intellectual, journalistic, knowledge-producing—infrastructure. The cultural arms of the SPD, the SAP, and Labour made the party theoretician possible. The party theoretician's ascendance, in turn, was symptomatic of socialist intellectuals' general dominance in left party executives in the early 1900s. Socialism appears in this account not only as a set of ideas but also as an institutional, practical, and organizational terrain, no less than organized labor.

Party theoreticians' prominence was also symptomatic of something else—or, more precisely, the *absence* of something else. In all three cases considered here the academic social sciences, and especially professional economics, featured hardly at all in the making of socialist party experts. This was indicative of the state of the social sciences at the time: turn-of-the-century economists, or political economists, were relatively few in number and state-centric in orientation. They tended to be liberal leaning and were broadly hostile to Marxism and socialism. And so it is perhaps unsurprising that, for the most part, leftist economic knowledge was produced in-house. The relationship between academic economics and left parties was, by extension, weak or nonexistent.

In this section I develop a brief account of the formation of the social sciences, and especially of economics, in relation to left parties, in order to substantiate this broad claim.

German Social Sciences, Economics, and the SPD

Prussian social sciences were unusually institutionalized by the turn of the twentieth century. Chairs in economics were relatively common-place, already, by the late 1700s; full institutionalization then commenced in the late nineteenth century.[161] By 1905 there were more than one hundred economics professors in German-speaking universities—more than three times that of France.[162]

German economics was also "cameralist": a science of the state. Specialized courses of study in economics initially emerged as part of the training for civil servants, an addition to dominant training in law. Economics was thus a practical discipline meant to aid in public administration. Centered on applied and social policy questions, its orthodoxies were rooted in the work of W. Roscher, of the German Historical School.[163]

In the 1870s formal ties between the German state and economics consolidated in the form of the Verein für Sozialpolitik (Association for Social Policy, hereafter VfS). Symptomatic of what was then known as the "new liberalism," and partly a response to the looming "social question," the VfS was established in 1872 to promote social reform in the wake of the Franco-Prussian war, German unification, the intensification of labor politics, and the growing strength of social democratic political organization. Founding figures included Gustav Friedrich von Schmoller (1838–1917), Adolph Wagner (1835–1917), Ernst Engel (1821–1896; director of the Prussian Statistical Bureau), and Lujo Brentano (1844–1931).[164] The VfS was a decidedly hybrid organization with a varied membership drawn from chambers of commerce, official and voluntary associations, towns, university institutes, the civil service, and journalism.

Social reformist but not Social Democratic, the VfS's "academic" or "arm-chair" socialists focused on the cultivation and training of civil servants and the formulation of policies to address "the condition of German workers and the threat of a social revolution," without abandoning a liberal economy.[165] They rejected Manchester (or Smithian) political economy, calling for state-led efforts to bolster the middle classes.[166] Schmoller and Wagner articulated the institute's focus in terms of class inequality, labor unrest, and the unsavory prospect of revolution.

The VfS operated officially at a distance from parties and partisanship, although its members were "expected to support the state and the government in its actions, and . . . to refrain from excessively partisan politics, at least in public."[167] In practice, however, elite affiliates of the VfS did have partisan leanings of a liberal sort: Wagner was a conservative member of the Lower House of the Prussian Diet from 1882 to 1885 and then a member of the Upper House from 1910 to 1917.[168] Schmoller was "devoted to the ideals of liberalism."[169] Brentano, an economic historian and an advocate of trade unions, had similar commitments.[170] They were not friends of the SPD.

In fact, the VfS had an antagonistic relationship with the SPD from the start. For Schmoller, counterbalancing Social Democratic advances in German politics using state-led social insurance measures was one of the VfS's central purposes: "For him, a resolution of the social question would break the spearhead of German social democracy."[171] The VfS was formally open to "moderate" Social Democrats, but SPD representatives were critical of the VfS, refusing to join or speak at its meetings until the 1890s; they were never central to VfS proceedings.[172] Even after the SPD won the largest single proportion of the German vote in 1903, it was still "seen by the right and the political core of the dynastic state as 'the internal enemy,' against whom it was legitimate to consider a rollback of the limited forms of democratic participation that existed."[173] This was not necessarily true of younger generation leading figures in the VfS—for instance, Max Weber (1864–1920) and his brother Alfred (1868–1958)—but neither were SPD affiliates: Max played a founding role in the German Democratic Party, and was also involved in the construction of the Weimar constitution, despite his general aversion to direct political involvement; his brother was involved with the National Liberal Party.[174] Max Weber engaged with Marxist thinking and encouraged others to do the same, but only because he aimed to show that SPD-style Marxist orthodoxy, which he viewed as a cause of the deterioration of German politics, was misguided.[175] By one report, "there were no outright Marxists or Social Democrats among German academic economists before 1918."[176]

By 1920, in the wake of the Bolshevik Revolution, the VfS's political engagements were changing, as was the relationship between Marxism and the German academy. But Weimar-era social scientists' engagements with Marx and Marxism did not translate into an easy or cooperative relationship between German academics and the SPD elite. Here Werner Sombart (1863–1941) is an interesting case in point: a graduate of the University of Berlin (1888) and peer of Max Weber, Sombart was known as "an academic exponent of Marx," recognized by Engels himself for his engagements with *Das Kapital*.[177] Appointed at the University of Breslau in 1890 and, from 1904, as coeditor (with Max Weber) of the *Archiv für Sozialwissenschaft und Sozialpolitik*, Sombart succeeded Wagner (his mentor) in his chair of economics at the University of Berlin, after Wagner's death in 1917. But Sombart's engagements with Marx limited his academic opportunities; in time, he "swung . . . sharply from Marxism to ultra-conservatism to national socialism."[178] Notable also is Robert Michels, who was excluded from the academy due to his SPD membership.[179]

As we will see, the left party–economics relationship was also weak in Sweden in the 1910s.

Economics and the SAP

Swedish economics also professionalized early. It was established as a discipline in 1739 at Uppsala University. The establishment of a chair in economics in 1741 made Sweden the first Western country outside of the German territories to do so.[180]

The professionalization of Swedish economics began in earnest, however, from the 1870s. The establishment of the Swedish Economics Society (Nationalekonomiska Föreningen, or NF) in 1877 was an important event in the process. Like the VfS, the NF was hybrid: it began as a gathering of "a group of men at the Hotel Rydberg in Stockholm at the invitation of the President of the Board of Trade" and former minister of finance, Carl Fredrik Waern. Thus initiated by business elites and state officials, the early NF was dominated by politicians.[181] The NF, which had linkages to the German VfS, was also a conduit of information about German social insurance developments, which were imported into Swedish political debates in the 1880s.[182] Sweden's Liberal government at the time, led by the reform-oriented Adolf Hedin, followed up by establishing a government committee that produced a series of proposals for social insurance legislation. Voluntary sickness insurance funds were established in 1891.[183]

Grounded in the liberal principles of free competition, free trade, and unrestricted economic activity, the Swedish economics profession's "first generation" included Knut Wicksell (1851–1926), David Davidson (1854–1942), Gustav Cassel (1866–1944), and Eli Heckscher (1879–1952).[184] Credentials in "economics" were, however, rare: Wicksell's degree was in mathematics and physics (1869); Davidson received his PhD in law (1878); Cassel's degree was in mathematics (1895). Heckscher, alone among them (but also younger), received a PhD in economics in 1907.[185]

Like the social scientists of the VfS, this early generation was notable for public involvements and governmental advising, but kept a distance from parties. Wicksell, Heckscher, and Cassel served "as journalists-lecturers-debaters-opinion makers and as members of parliamentary committees," but "remained in academia rather than entering political careers"; none "tried to become a member of the parliament or gain a political position in the government."[186] Wicksell, a once imprisoned "radical political thinker," was a prominent participant in the NF.[187]

Insofar as first-generation Swedish economists were involved with parties, they leaned liberal: they "strongly rejected" Marxism and were critical of SAP-associated socialism.[188] Socialist and Marxist academics could be found—for instance, August Strindberg (1849–1912) and Gustav Steffen (1864–1929)—but they are not remembered as prominent founders of Swedish economics. Steffen, for instance, was a professor of economics and sociology at Gothenburg University from 1903 and, by 1911, a socialist parliamentarian with Fabian affinities, but he is not remembered as an economist. Expelled from the SAP between 1917 and 1922, Steffen exerted no clear influence on the party's programmatic development.[189] In Tingsten's account, up to 1920 "[n]o qualified economist joined the party who was able to lead or stimulate a debate" about socialism.[190]

By this time economics was, however, in transition. In 1917 Wicksell pushed along the discipline's professionalization by establishing the Political Economy Club—a much more academic institution than the NF—in Stockholm, which lasted until 1951. As we will see in the next chapter, the club provided a "professional forum for the exchange of ideas" that differed markedly from the more politician- and official-dominated NF. But, still, its senior members remained liberal and non-partisan by inclination. And so, like the SPD, around 1920 the SAP's relationship to the social sciences, economics included, was markedly weak. We now move, briefly, to the British case.

British Social Sciences, Economics, and the Labour Party

The British Social Science Association (SSA, formally the National Association for the Promotion of Social Science), founded in 1857 on the model of the British Association for the Advancement of Science (established in 1831), had liberal and statist affinities reminiscent of the German VfS and the Swedish NF. Widely noted as a politician-led organization, the SSA was "[n]ever an academic forum," but rather "an adjunct to government" or (in a *Times* 1862 description) an "outdoor Parliament." Symptomatically, the Whig Party's Lord Brougham was the SSA's first president.[191] The association focused on practical questions of administration and reform, eschewing scientific and theoretical work.

We should note here that, despite British economics' long history, it in fact *professionalized* relatively late.[192] Deeply involved with the making of gold standard institutions and advocacy of free trade during the early British Empire, British economists formed London-centered clubs and associations in the 1820s. Among them was the Political Economy Club, founded in 1821 by Thomas Tooke (1774–1858)—a *de facto* economist who had been a Russian trade merchant and was, at the time of the club's founding, governor of the Royal Exchange Insurance Company.[193] The club's members included David Ricardo (1772–1823), Thomas Malthus (1766–1834), and John Stuart Mill (1806–1873). Like Tooke, Ricardo was not an "economist" in the present-day sense of the term: he was a "[s]tockjobber and loan contractor" from 1793 to 1814, and a "[c]ountry landowner" when the Political Economy Club was founded.[194] East India Company associations were common among the club's members: Malthus, a clergyman, held the post of professor of political economy with the East India College, in

Haileybury (1805–1834); Mill was a clerk for the East India Company from 1823 to 1858 and, later, a Liberal MP (1865–1868).[195]

British economics' professionalization started in earnest around 1890 and would not be complete for two or three decades to come. Early markers include the establishment of the British Economic Association (1890, later the Royal Economic Society), the *Economic Journal* (1891) at Cambridge, Alfred Marshall's *Principles of Economics* (1890), and the Oxford-based *Economic Review* (1891). The *Economic Review* was "a product of the moral/humanistic wing of the so-called 'new' movement in British economics," comparable to the "Katheder" socialists of the VfS in Germany, traceable to Arnold Toynbee.[196] The scientific-versus-ethical distinction between the *Journal* and the *Review* expressed oppositions between historicism versus deductivism, characteristic of the "English *methodenstreit*" at that time.[197]

Notably, until the early 1900s someone like Philip Snowden would not have been able to pursue a specialized course of study in "economics" even if he tried. In the historian Colin Cross's words, "There was no real science of [British] economics for him to study."[198] In the early 1900s the profession had three main centers—Cambridge, Oxford, and the LSE. Cambridge economics, built by Alfred Marshall and Arthur Cecil Pigou, dominated. But economics was not a stand-alone subject, much less a professionally autonomous discipline. In the sociologist Marion Fourcade's summary:

> By the end of the nineteenth century, economics classes represented a small part of the general training in history (e.g., at Oxford) or moral science (e.g., at Cambridge). Political economy was still regarded as a practical subject whose place in the elite university tradition remained controversial.[199]

Cambridge did not have its prestigious economics "tripos" until 1903, thanks to Marshall's efforts to establish "the intellectual relevance of the subject at a venerable institution that saw itself as the sanctuary of the classical tradition."[200]

And so British economics, initially "small and close-knit," came to fruition as an autonomous profession built on mathematical formalization only in the 1930s.[201] The case of Britain's most famous economist,

John Maynard Keynes, speaks to the discipline's late professionalization. Keynes earned his degree in mathematics, not economics, in 1905 (under Marshall and Pigou). His formal economics training was "limited to one term's postgraduate work."[202] Keynes became a professional economist through a combination of lecturing at Cambridge (from 1908) and on-the-job civil service work.

In the 1910s and early 1920s academic economists who did not go into the civil service tended to be *ad hoc* advisers, or they worked through the Liberal Party, or both.[203] The most heavyweight players in economic policy-making, however, were Treasury officials. More specifically, a cadre that included Sir John Bradbury (1872–1950), Sir Basil Blackett (1882–1935), Sir Otto Niemeyer (1883–1971), Sir Frederick Leith-Ross (1887–1968), Sir Richard Hopkins (1880–1955), and Sir Ralph Hawtrey (1879–1975) were the premier authorities.[204] Together, this set stood for the "Treasury view": a strict adherence to gold standard orthodoxies, including small, balanced public budgets; spending cuts when revenues fall; tax increases if necessary to make ends meet; and an aversion to loan-based government financing.[205] The last practice was particularly important, as government lending "would have to offer better terms than those available elsewhere," thus "crowding out" private investment.[206] An elite consensus that was proudly grounded in the legacy of the eighteenth-century Scottish enlightenment thinkers David Hume and Adam Smith, the Treasury view encapsulated the gold standard *zeitgeist*.

But, as John Maynard Keynes would later (irritably) note, the Treasury view was not grounded in state-of-the-art economics.[207] It was also not borne by state-of-the-art *economists*. With the exception of Hawtrey (who had a BA in mathematics from Cambridge), the Treasury officials listed above were "'generalists' . . . experienced in examining arguments and evidence critically, but whose knowledge of economics was limited to the reading they had done in preparation for the Civil Service examination, or subsequently in their own time."[208]

Held at bay from power in government, some economists cultivated ties to the Liberal Party, in particular. This was especially true of Keynes, who became closely involved with the Liberal Party after it was voted out of government, after fourteen years in office, in 1922. With William Beveridge (then head of the LSE), Keynes led Liberal summer schools that, initiated by David Lloyd George, aimed to reinvigorate the party by cultivating "rising young intellectuals and influential policy makers."[209] The schools became "a platform from which the economists and other experts" presented research results and "proposals for remedying social evils" to Liberal Party leadership and rank and file.[210] Liberals also sought to install economists in the civil service: in late 1923 Beveridge called for a cabinet-level, super-ordinate organization for economic advising headed by "a person of high authority in the science of economics, and of corresponding authority in the public service."[211] The presumable aim, which went unfulfilled, was to install a Liberal-friendly permanent staff of economists in the British government.

By contrast, ties between British economics and the Labour party in the 1910s and 1920s were in their infancy, insofar as they existed at all—a fact duly noted by the Labour historian Colin Cross.[212] Instead, Labour relied heavily on its Fabian research infrastructure. Starting in 1912, the Fabian Research Department (later the Labour Research Department, or LRD) was "a bustling office for the investigation of the social problems," producing "a stream of reports" on social insurance, cooperatives, agriculture, and the international labor movement (among other topics).[213] The LRD was the party's core resource until it was displaced in the early 1920s.[214] Fabians also shaped the party's knowledge-producing activities from within the executive: Labour's National Executive Committee (NEC) innovated a new system of nine advisory committees, establishing a model that other British parties would imitate.[215] In these initiatives, however, academic social scientists tended to be junior participants. This was partly an effect of the youth of British social scientific professions and also of the programmatic dominance of a small cadre of older-generation Labour elites that included Ramsay MacDonald, Philip Snowden, and Arthur Henderson.[216] There were plenty of economists in Labour's sundry advisory circles, but the party's more senior members outranked them. And so, like the SPD and the SAP, the Labour Party around 1920 had considerable cultural and knowledge-producing investments, but they were largely in-house—extending very little into the professionalizing discipline of British economics.

CONCLUSIONS

This chapter traces socialist parties' formation in three countries with a focus on the emergent cultural and organizational terrains that made possible three party theoreticians. Rudolf Hilferding (German SPD), Fredrik Thorsson (Swedish SAP), and Philip Snowden (British Labour Party). My focus on similarly situated figures across three left parties is a means to understanding the broader party-expert relationship that underpinned European socialist leftism. I show that, in all three countries, left parties formed on definite cultural, knowledge-producing and journalistic institutions, rooted in transnationalized activities of "agitators," that were distinctive from organized labor. I also show that, until the 1920s (or so), the academic social sciences were well connected to liberal parties and associations but were marginal to the party-centered, journalistic, in-house cultural infrastructure that made possible the party theoretician.

In a certain sense all of this was symptomatic of a broader period that the historian Daniel Rodgers describes as an "age of amateurs."[217] Gilded Age politics featured diverse, nonprofessionalized forms of expertise that regularly crossed national boundaries, binding European and North American socialists, progressive reformers, and political elites (among others) in transnational and transatlantic relations of exchange. This diversified field of Western expertise was not definitively anchored in the state or the university or in any particular profession. It was also geopolitically patterned, being centered especially on the culturally influential institutions of prewar Germany. In this world party theoreticians were "amateur" in the sense that they were not technically or formally trained in social or economic analysis or credentialed in social sciences or economics. They received *de facto* credentials in the party-centered, heavily journalistic, cultural institutions of Western socialisms.

In the next chapter I consider how the cultural institutions that underpinned socialist leftism changed in fundamental ways during and after the 1930s. In particular, I consider how a Polanyian moment drove the formation of stronger ties between left parties and academic economics, producing a new leftist infrastructure and a new sort of party expert, between the 1930s and the early 1960s.

CHAPTER FOUR

European Leftism's First Reinvention

> Suppose that by the working of natural laws individuals pursuing their own interests . . . always tend to promote the general interest at the same time! . . . This is what the economists are supposed to have said. No such doctrine is really to be found. . . . It is what the popularisers and the vulgarisers said.
>
> —John Maynard Keynes, 1926

IN THE LAST CHAPTER we considered the European socialist party theoretician's formation and, more generally, the journalism- and party-dependent making of socialist leftism. This chapter analyzes how, between the 1920s and the 1960s, European socialist leftism gave way to a new, economistic leftism that, unlike its predecessor, was built on a deep interconnection between economics professions and left parties.

To grasp the novelty of this interconnection, we first have to discard any impulse to essentialize economics—including any assumption that the term "economics" refers to the same kind of profession, and the same sorts of professionals, regardless of time and place. As John Maynard Keynes argued in 1926, the notion that professional economics is mainly a carrier of purist *laissez-faire* doctrines is not now, nor has it ever been, accurate. Questions about the form and extent of government—when government can leave economic forces alone, when it cannot, and, should intervention be necessary, the form intervention should take—have always been among economics' most central concerns.[1] Economists' answers to these questions are many and varied—like economics professions, and economists themselves. Indeed, when we refer to an "economist" in the 1930s versus, say, the early 1960s, we are not talking about the same *kind* of figure in terms of training, credentials, professional comportment, partisan leaning, or institutional situation.[2] Nor can one take for granted economists' capacity to inform policy-making or shape politicians' thinking.[3]

Indeed, in the 1920s and 1930s Keynes and other young bearers of a new economics tried to persuade parties-in-government, left and otherwise, that they could and should borrow and spend in order to end unemployment and kick-start economic growth. Their arguments, however, ran against the common sense of the gold standard era and, for the most part, fell on deaf ears. From the 1930s forward, however, economists bearing policy advice that was once out-of-bounds acquired considerable political authority, transforming heterodoxy into orthodoxy in the process. By the 1960s "Keynesianism," commonly associated with the use of deficit spending in order to smooth over business cycle troughs and maintain full employment, but more broadly referring to a distinctly managerial approach to economic policymaking, was a new political common sense. Inside left parties, the Keynesian era featured a significant novelty: academic and professional economists doubled as politicians, advisers, policy-makers, strategists, and spokespersons, occupying the very positions that party theoreticians once held. I call this new economist-*cum*-left-party-expert an *economist theoretician*: a historically specific kind of economist who moved in between politics, government, and professional and academic economics. A key historical bearer of economistic leftism, the economist theoretician's displacement of the party theoretician was indicative of a broader set of transformations—in left parties, in professional economics, and in the ties between them. Like the link between socialism and leftism in the late 1800s, the left party–economics connection on which economistic leftism depended was not inevitable; it, too, was forged.

This chapter traces the fitful ascendance of the economist theoretician within European left parties and, with him,[4] the making of economistic leftism between the interwar years and the 1960s. My account begins with the emergence of a Polanyian moment: a standoff between protection-seeking and market-making in the 1920s and 1930s. This standoff fueled political and administrative struggles over economic truths that were linked, in turn, with intergenerational struggles within economics professions. Over time these interconnected struggles produced a historically novel interconnection between economics professions and left parties.

The analysis proceeds in two parts. The first shows that, as long as party theoreticians held power, they preempted or deflected young, credentialed, statistics-bearing economists who sought to influence left parties-in-government. This preemption was the backstory of a well-noted, and particularly curious, feature of interwar politics: left parties-in-government tended to be economically "conservative" (as the term is now understood), even in the face of serious unrest and economic crisis.[5] The second part of the story is that, in time, some of the very same kinds of economists who once failed to influence left parties-in-government displaced the socialist party theoretician. Borrowing the language of the sociologists Gil Eyal and Larissa Buchholz, from the 1930s forward economists built a considerable "capacity to make a public intervention," especially in and through center-left parties.[6] But, while this was very much a cross-national development, economists' new capacities to intervene did not materialize in the same way or at the same time across countries: economists' new public capacity became apparent in Sweden in the early 1930s, in the mid-1940s in the United Kingdom, and in the late 1950s in West Germany.

How can we explain the rise of left party–economics interdependence in general, as well as variations in the timing across countries? My answer to the first question centers on how the Polanyian moment that began to unfold in the 1920s—that is, deep tensions between the prevailing economic system and protection-seeking political demands—called gold standard orthodoxies into question and intensified administrative demand for, and partisan struggles over, basic economic truths (like the scale of unemployment). These struggles reached into centers of elite education, shaping intergenerational struggles inside economics professions by drawing students toward the study of economics even as economic orthodoxies were being called into question. At the same time, left parties' growing presence in elite university and educated circles was marked by a proliferation of clubs, associations, and other social outposts that served as *de facto* recruitment sites for young leaders. In sum, economistic leftism's origins are to be found in a Polanyian standoff that drove political disputation over economic truths and intergenerational disputation within economics, even as left parties were reaching ever more deeply into universities.

To explain variation in timing, I highlight distinctive dynamics across countries. In Sweden the growing problem of unemployment, generational rebellion within a relatively well-established economics profession, and sudden turnover in SAP leadership fueled a remarkably early ascendance of the economist theoretician. In Britain, where the Labour elite held young economists at bay in the 1930s, wartime engagements generated the crucial opening for the rise of new experts and forms of expertise. In Germany, and then West Germany, the Nazi interregnum; occupying forces' influence in the building of the West German state; the dominance of a specifically German school of economics (ordoliberalism) in alliance with the Christian Democratic Union (Christlich-Demokratische Union, or CDU); and the taint of Stalinism on all things Marxist held economistic leftism at bay, shaping the SPD's late economistic turn.

A final theme of this chapter is that, thanks to their positioning in between politics and economics, economist theoreticians had a notable *capacity for intermediation*. The 1960s economist theoretician played many roles: part politician and part professional economist, he was also an occasional electoral strategist, public communicator, bureaucratic operative, and intermediary between left parties-in-government and trade unions. As we will explore further in Chapter 6, the economist theoretician tended to see the economist-in-politics as a bearer of scientifically informed but politically sensitive policy strategies that could be used to facilitate negotiation and consensus-building. The economist theoretician's capacity to intervene was linked to a certain view of how to be an economist that reflected a distinctly hybrid, or—in-between, institutional location.

A THEORETICAL PRELIMINARY: RATIONALITY, BELIEF, AND POSITION

The story told here hinges on a basic sociological premise that how we think and how we are institutionally situated—that is, belief and social position—are linked. Long central to the sociology of knowledge, and fundamental to classical thinking in a lineage that stretches from Weber and Durkheim to Bourdieu, this premise lends itself to a particular way of thinking about rationality and interest as a matter of perspective—and thus as multiple, situated, and context-specific.[7]

This situated notion of rationality, what we might call situated reason, informs both stories told in this chapter—that is, the story of would-be economist theoreticians' preemption in the 1920s and 1930s, and of their ascendance thereafter. In the story of preemption, one might note that party theoreticians' refusal to countenance arguments that left parties-in-government should spend their way out of economic trouble—documented below—is puzzling. Left parties' working-class constituencies demanded action, and the ability of left parties-in-government to stay in office depended on a proactive response. In difficult economic times, however, the options were limited: either borrow in order to meet demands on the government or raise taxes and reduce spending in order to balance the budget. Party theoreticians could have mobilized young economists' nonorthodox recommendations to legitimate borrowing, allowing left parties to appease working-class constituencies and preserve their parties' positions in government. But, as I will show, they did not.

How can we explain this? Party theoreticians' "conservative" commitments become easier to grasp if we consider how a certain course of action that might appear to work against an actor's interest might appear, to the actor, as perfectly sensible. Key to this is a flexible, context-contingent conception of "interest." In the words of Pierre Bourdieu (who preferred terms like "reasonable" and "strategic" to "rational"), "There is not *an* interest, but there are *interests,* variable with time and place, almost infinitely so."[8] Stated differently, rather than asking whether an actor is rational or not, we should situate strategic, reasoned action in context, with careful attention to the investments and social positions of those involved.

Accordingly, the present analysis seeks not only to trace pathways from socialist to economistic leftism but also to understand party theoreticians' "conservative" commitments via a historical inquiry into how their worlds, and their positions in it, made the defense of orthodoxy appear the sensible thing to do.[9] By the same token, if left parties finally embraced economists' truth claims—which, sooner or later, they all did—then we should find that this was linked with a definite shift in the profile and social position of left parties' dominant experts.

THE MAKING OF A POLANYIAN MOMENT

As Karl Polanyi famously argued, the seemingly irresolvable problem of reconciling human and political institutions with a disruptive, polarizing, all-commodifying economic order came to a head in the 1920s and 1930s thanks to the classical gold standard system—or, more precisely, thanks to the "vain effort to save it."[10] The gold standard order, which stretched from about the 1820s to 1931 (when Britain was forced to abandon gold), was linked with British Empire and provided a mechanism for the equilibration of economic exchange between and within countries. National currencies were maintained at a fixed price in terms of gold, so that "any disturbance away from the natural distribution of gold . . . would lead to an equilibrating process through arbitrage on the gold market. Gold flows, by changing a nation's money supply, would then also change its price level."[11] The gold standard was, in theory, an automatic mechanism that would keep prices steady and growing. And indeed, at the gold standard's peak—between 1880 and 1913—a "free world market for goods, capital, and labor" came closer than ever to a living reality.[12] International financial transactions were relatively unrestricted and, after a deflationary period from 1873 to 1896, prices steadily rose. The gold standard system became, in Polanyi's account, the "faith of the age," uniting groups of all political stripes. In Polanyi's words: "[T]he essentiality of the gold standard to the functioning of the international economic system of the time was the one and only tenet common to men of all nations and all classes, religious denominations, and social philosophies."[13]

But in an age of expanding political rights the gold standard also generated systemic problems. Deflationary price adjustments were endemic to the gold standard system, which hit farmers' profits and workers' jobs and wages especially hard. By the late nineteenth century, those groups were also voters. Unemployment, meanwhile, was becoming a significant public issue—a combined effect of urban industry and trade union formation, the 1873–1896 downturn, new awareness of business cycles, liberal social reformism, and a proliferation of

surveys and statistics on social and economic conditions.[14] These new
statistics helped to legitimate the claim that poverty could be structural,
and not simply a cultural or behavioral problem ("pauperism," in British
terminology).

The gold standard ushered in an intensification of political contestation that ebbed and flowed with the business cycle. In the United States,
which implemented manhood suffrage in 1870, a populist movement
of farmers and workers—coinciding almost perfectly with the 1873–
1896 recession—captured the Democratic nomination in the person of
William Jennings Bryan (a "Silver Democrat").[15] True to Polanyi's
analysis, the gold standard was the backbone of a "completely mone-
tized economy" in which "currency had become the pivot of national
politics."[16] The movement behind Bryan foundered after he failed to
win the presidency and, as economic conditions improved, American
voter turnout declined until the 1920s (see Figure 4.1).

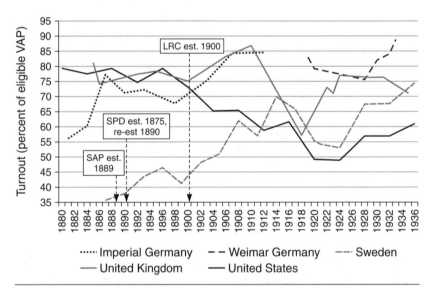

Figure 4.1. Voter turnout as a percentage of the eligible population, 1880–1936.
Notes: The LRC (Labour Representation Committee) was a precursor of the
Labour Party. Sources include Dave Leip's Atlas of U.S. Presidential Elections;
U.S. House of Representatives; Peters and Woolley, The American Presidency
Project; Falter, Lindenberger, and Schumann 1986; F. W. S. Craig 1974, 1977;
Statistika Centralbyrån/Statistics Sweden (SCB). Statistical Database:
Democracy.

Things looked different in European countries, where for much of the gold standard period many people simply could not vote. In Sweden, voting was virtually nonexistent before 1887; eligibility was highly restricted until 1911. By one estimate less than 10 percent of the Swedish population was enfranchised for the entire nineteenth century, reaching about 8 percent by 1905 and 20 percent by 1915.[17] Swedish turnout was exceptionally low around the turn of the twentieth century, but climbed to unprecedented heights by 1913.

Imperial Germany and the United Kingdom implemented manhood suffrage in 1871 and 1884, respectively. Both countries, however, imposed significant limits on voter eligibility. The United Kingdom imposed severe property restrictions; the German state dealt with workers' demands and the rising popularity of the SPD in the 1880s with aggressive suppression. In the 1880s less than 9 percent of the British population and about 20 percent of Germans had access to the vote. That figure remained relatively unchanged in Germany into the 1910s; it grew to a mere 18 percent in the United Kingdom in the same period.[18]

Turnout within the limited ranks of the eligible, however, was high and increasing in both countries in the lead-up to World War I (see Figure 4.1). By the 1920s voting was again on the rise, this time in a context of universal suffrage. A combination of broad political rights, economic instability, and deepening unrest brought many European socialist parties—now "center-left," due to a proliferation of communist (far left) parties after 1917—into government. Center-left parties built their electoral appeal, in part, on the promise that they would govern the economy according to the needs and demands of economically hard-hit constituencies. But the gold standard system, by design, allowed very little wiggle room.

An early political response to the standoff was to stray from principles of *laissez-faire* in order to protect, in a limited way, what Polanyi called "fictitious commodities": land, labor, and money.[19] Early social insurance legislation—which generally emerged in an effort to defuse popular unrest (and social democratic movements)—can be read in exactly these terms. But, as Polanyi noted, these efforts only created new problems: between the 1880s and the 1920s workmen's compensation and sickness, pension, and unemployment insurance programs committed Western governments to costs that tended to grow during

Table 4.1   Social insurance legislation passed prior to 1930

	Industrial accident	Sickness	Pension	Unemployment
Germany	1884*	1883*	1889*	1927*
Sweden	1901/1916*	1891	1913*	NA
United Kingdom	1906	1911*	1908*	1911*

Source: Flora and Heidenheimer 1982.
* = compulsory
American social insurance programs are discussed in Chapter 5.

downturns—that is, as tax revenues declined. Insofar as this added to domestic economic problems and exacerbated international instabilities (the "balance of powers" system, in Polanyi's terminology), the whole political and economic edifice of the gold standard order was at risk.

These dynamics, in which the expansion of the gold standard system developed in tandem with new protections of fictitious commodities, which then generated new economic and political difficulties, can be seen in all the cases considered here. Germany, Sweden, and the United Kingdom all had social insurance laws on the books well before the 1929 crash. In Germany and the United Kingdom, enrollment was mostly compulsory (see Table 4.1).

German and British government expenditures reached about 25 percent of GDP by 1920. The United Kingdom, exceptional among the cases considered here for its compulsory sickness, pensions, *and* unemployment insurance by 1911, had a gross public debt of more than 120 percent of GDP in 1920—far above the Western average of about 60 percent.[20] During Germany's exceptional period of hyperinflation in 1922–1923, commonly understood as an effect of the "war guilt" clause of the 1919 Treaty of Versailles, inflation climbed more than 200 percent. The Polanyian moment was thus especially profound in Germany and Britain in the 1920s and 1930s. In Sweden and the United States, where taxes and transfers were more like 10 percent of GDP, budgetary pressures were less extreme, but still present.[21] And, of course, there was the triple problem of international instability, mass unemployment, and severe labor unrest.

In this context the production of economic facts became a newly important and politically fraught enterprise. Lacking standardized government statistics, the scope and scale of unemployment was a matter of dispute with no decisive metric. As relief and unemployment claims grew, labor unrest intensified, and new surveys of the working population got under way, some argued that there was a rapidly escalating unemployment problem that was structural in nature.

In Britain, unemployment insurance statistics with industrial classifications became available from July 1923, but they were not widely used.[22] Figures provided by unions indicated that from the early 1920s there were large numbers of people who were willing but unable to work and that the ranks of failed job-seekers spiked dramatically from the late 1920s, especially in Germany and the United States (see Figure 4.2).

By these metrics, industrial unemployment rates roughly doubled in Sweden and the United Kingdom, and tripled in Germany and the United States, after 1929. In the United States, industrial unemployment remained very high into the 1930s, spiking after a 1937 recession and then receding in 1938 and 1939.

The convergence of left party power, growing voter eligibility and participation, social insurance commitments, labor unrest, skyrocketing

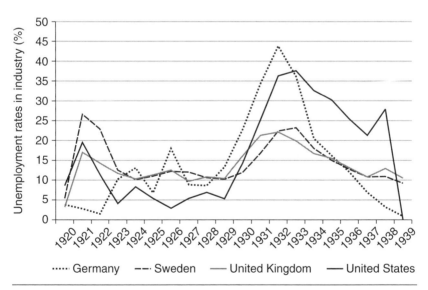

Figure 4.2. Industrial unemployment rates (union figures), 1920–1939. Data source: Eichengreen and Hatton 1988.

unemployment, and contestation over the measurement and scale of economic problems between the 1920s and 1930s fed into the making of a Polanyian moment in which market society presents itself as an alternative to, rather than a means of, human existence, and new political and economic pathways—some democratic, some not—become possible.[23] Those pathways were determined, in part, by political elites' capacity to decisively define the problem, respond to constituencies, and calm unrest in a way that reconciled political and economic demands. The question of a new political and economic settlement was when, not if; in Polanyi's words, "[I]t was only a question of time."[24]

When we look inside left parties during this time, one of the notable symptoms of this moment was the emergence of a clear opposition between the orthodoxies of party elites, including party theoreticians, and the heterodoxies of younger-generation, formally trained, statistics-bearing economists. Many economists, alongside statisticians, labor union experts, and others, relied on new statistical resources to formulate arguments that contravened gold standard orthodoxies. But, as we will see in the following section, party theoreticians-*cum*-ministers-of-finance had their own understandings, wielded considerable authority in their parties and, when in office, also wielded the authority of the state. To a certain extent, they could decide what was true.

PART ONE: INTERWAR PARTY THEORETICIANS VERSUS PROFESSIONAL ECONOMISTS

In the interwar period party theoreticians were what some political sociologists call "incumbents" in their respective parties.[25] Thanks to left parties' electoral success, party theoreticians also became powerful state officials: Thorsson, Hilferding, and Snowden became ministers of finance (specifically, in Snowden's case, chancellor of the exchequer). But political unrest and economic trouble presented interwar party theoreticians-*cum*-state-officials with a problem. Climbing unemployment, social insurance commitments, and shrinking revenues had only three solutions: bring in more revenue, cut spending, or borrow. The mainstream position was what we might now call "conservative" or "austere," or what some at the time called *laissez-faire*: governments should cut spending, balance budgets, shore up business confidence, and restore the gold standard order.

Oddly enough, socialist party theoreticians did not dissent from the *laissez-faire* position; they defended it. Some young economists did dissent, however—among whom John Maynard Keynes (1883–1946) is surely the most famous. In 1924 Keynes, bemoaning the amateurism of the "vulgarisers," announced to an audience at Oxford University that "change was in the air": *laissez-faire* was a failed mythology in economics, if not yet in the political mainstream.[26] What was later termed the "new economics" (or Keynesianism) drew heavily on mathematical, probabilistic, and statistical argumentation to posit that governments need not stand back helplessly in bad economic times; rather, they could borrow, spend, reverse the depression, and reap the rewards of increased tax revenues.

Political elites did not, however, embrace either the arguments or the statistical proof martialed by young economists. This was not for lack of trying. Keynes, a vocal member of advisory committees to the Labour government between 1929 and 1931, confronted many noneconomists— Treasury civil servants, Labour officials—who rejected his conceptual and technical argumentation.[27] These disagreements sometimes involved odd juxtapositions of party affiliation and policy position: Keynes was a longtime advocate of the Liberal Party known for his aversion to Labour, but at one point he famously declared himself "the only socialist present" in the company of the Labour prime minister Ramsay MacDonald.[28]

Keynes was hardly the first to argue that economic forces do not necessarily correct themselves without considerable help. In Sweden the mathematician-*cum*-economist Knut Wicksell (1851–1926) argued in 1897 that prices need not be self-correcting and could theoretically "rise and rise and rise" if banks maintained very low interest rates over a long period of time (and could, on the other hand, "fall and fall and fall" at high interest rates); in 1907 Wicksell presented his arguments to English-speaking audiences in the British *Economic Journal*.[29] In the late 1800s the German merchant-*cum*-economist Silvio Gesell (1862–1930) "developed the idea of constantly depreciating money," but he "failed to attract serious attention" and ended up a "rank outsider" in German economics.[30] In the United States, popular books by Waddill Catchings and William Foster, a businessman and an English professor (respectively), mobilized allegory and analysis in the 1920s to argue that the "dilemma of thrift" could be resolved by government-driven, business-informed efforts to boost consumer spending and should not be left to the whims of economic forces.[31] Their 1928 *Road to Plenty* was influential at home and was translated into five languages. Many others—politicians, trade union leaders, statisticians, social reformers—joined the chorus of dissent.

Socialist party theoreticians, however, paid little heed. Hilferding, Snowden, and Thorsson held fast to the notion that deficit spending was a limited means of short-term relief that should not be large-scale or prolonged and could not be used to short-circuit recessions.[32] New statistical argumentation and mathematical reasoning made no significant impression on them. And, as ministers of finance and powerful figures in their respective parties, they were fully capable of blocking or pre-empting the arguments of those with whom they disagreed. This they did, regardless of their brand of socialism (Marxist, Fabian, revisionist) and despite the political consequences.

The question, of course, is why—to which we now turn.

Incumbency at Work: Party Theoreticians versus the "New Economics"

In theory, the only resolution to a Polanyian moment is a rebalancing of the relationship between market imperatives and protective political demands, in which the former is subordinated to the latter; the *status quo* is not an option. In this context one might have expected party theoreticians to pick the truth that best suited them, and their parties, by embracing pro-spending arguments with a resounding "yes." One might also expect that the especially dire economic conditions confronted by the SPD and Labour parties-in-government, described above, would have led the leadership of those two parties to embrace the new economics early and enthusiastically. But on both counts one would be wrong. Not one left party-in-government broke from orthodoxy until after the gold standard collapsed in 1931; Snowden, Thorsson, and Hilferding were all keepers of the faith. And the Swedish SAP—not Labour or the SPD—was the first to make a break.

Fending off the Upstarts in Germany: The WTB Episode

Rudolf Hilferding is well noted for his resistance to loan-financed deficit spending in the interwar years.[33] Existing accounts focus on what I will call the WTB episode: an effort led by economists to persuade Hilferding to embrace a large-scale, loan-financed public employment initiative in 1932. The chief protagonist of the WTB (Woytinsky-Tarnow-Baade) episode was Wladimir Woytinsky (1885–1960), a Russian economist and statistical specialist who was, at the time, the head of the Statistical Bureau of the ADGB.[34] The other protagonists included Fritz Tarnow (1880–1951), chairman of the Woodworkers' Union; Fritz Baade (1893–1974), an SPD parliamentarian, agricultural expert, and protégé of Hilferding's; and Professor Gerhard Colm (1897–1968), a young academic from Kiel with notable statistical expertise but no particular SPD connection.[35] Two of them were at least fifteen years younger than Hilferding (who was born in 1877); others were not only younger but were also representatives of the SPD's economic arm (organized labor), as opposed to its executive or theoretical leadership. By all accounts Woytinsky, eight years Hilferding's junior, was the WTB plan's initiator and driving force.

Hilferding famously rejected the WTB plan in the dire period just before Hitler's rise. This rejection is sometimes chalked up to Hilferding's unwavering commitment to orthodox Marxism. This is the suggestion, for instance, of the political scientists Sheri Berman and Mark Blyth, the historian (and Hilferding biographer) William Smaldone, and Wladimir Woytinsky himself.[36]

And yet this decontextualized account of Hilferding, one of the premier Marxist intellectuals of his time, feels caricatured. Hilferding and the SPD had a lot to lose in 1932 (see Figure 4.3), and every reason to be intervention-friendly.

Furthermore, Woytinsky's account of Hilferding is self-contradictory: in some places Woytinsky describes Hilferding as opportunistic and open to compromise, not dogmatic or intransigent. The economic historian Harold James similarly characterizes Hilferding as possessed of a "rather undogmatic skill" in economic analysis.[37]

How can we reconcile these different Hilfderdings? One way is to abandon the effort to essentialize Hilferding's ideological inclinations,

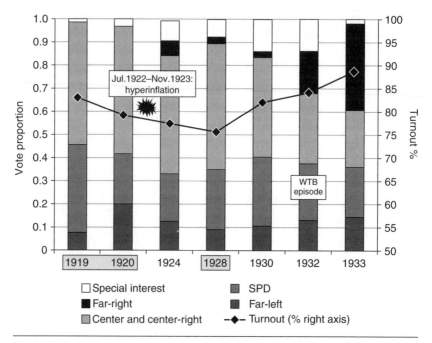

Figure 4.3. German vote proportions in election years, with voter turnout, 1919–1933 (years in shaded boxes=SPD in government). Data source: See Figure 4.1.

considering instead the history and context of the WTB episode, the relative positioning of Hilferding and Woytinsky, and the dynamic processes that preceded Hilferding's rejection of the WTB plan.

The Incumbent versus the Upstarts

Weimar Germany was exceptionally democratic and wracked by political fracture. In 1917 the SPD split with the establishment of the Independent Social Democrats (USPD); in 1918 the Communist Party (KPD) formed with a membership of over 100,000; shortly after, the German Worker's Party (later the Nazi Party) was established.[38] Meanwhile, in 1918 major strikes and the looming threat of a worker revolution prompted the German government to subsidize food, coal, and employment. The revolt subsided in 1920 with the failed Kapp Putsch (an attempted right-wing coup), followed by a bloody suppression, aided by forces of the far-right and abetted by the SPD, of the left-wing Ruhr uprising.

In the meantime the 1919 Treaty of Versailles came into effect. The government imposed taxes to balance the budget, but reparations payments precluded balance, and inflation rose dramatically. Inflation really took off in July 1922—Germany's famous episode of hyperinflation— after the right-wing assassination of the foreign minister Walter Rathenau.[39]

On the heels of all this Hilferding became finance minister, for the first time, in 1923, and called for austerity in the form of more restrictive monetary policy and higher taxes. Faced with right-wing opposition, Hilferding was forced to resign in October.[40] But austerity came nonetheless: hyperinflation ended in November 1923, when the German government pegged the mark to the U.S. dollar and curtailed "profiteering" with rent and price controls. Small property owners and farmers were especially affected. When the mark weakened in April 1924, the Reichsbank restricted credit, causing a series of business failures.[41] In Germany's 1924 elections the far-right made significant gains.

At this time Hilferding was the founding editor of the elite SPD journal, *Die Gesellschaft*. In that role he exhibited an aversion to the statistical reasoning that was then becoming a hallmark tool of young professional economists. In 1927, for instance, Hilferding had a falling out with Woytinsky—who sought to publish in Hilferding's journal— over a dispute as to the statistical testability of the labor theory of value. In Woytinsky's account, Hilferding opposed the notion that statistical analysis was a meaningful way to test the theory.[42]

Woytinsky was recruited into the executive of the trade union association, the ADGB, partly because of his opposition to the SPD's theoretical and programmatic leadership.[43] By the time Hilferding returned as finance minister in 1928, then, his opposition to Woytinsky was both epistemological and institutional. Hilferding was again forced to resign in December 1929, but he remained influential in the Reichstag and in the SPD.[44] His dispute with Woytinsky, now inseparable from tensions between the SPD executive and union leadership, continued.

In 1930 Woytinsky and his ADGB colleagues began to challenge Hilferding's estimation of the depth of Germany's economic problems, mobilizing new statistical estimates of seasonally adjusted unemployment produced by Woytinsky.[45] The ADGB board sought to persuade SPD leadership that the economic situation was going from bad to worse. SPD leadership, preoccupied with reparations, initially rejected the ADGB's assessment of a deepening crisis of unemployment. Woytinsky responded with a public campaign for reflation and large-scale public works, launched in national and international labor publications: the ADGB's journal *Die Arbeit;* a 1931 book (*Internationale Hebung der Preise als Ausweg aus der Weltkrise*); and a series in the International Labour Organization's (ILO) *International Labour Review.* In the meantime, in at least two ADGB board meetings after Britain's 1931 departure from the gold standard, Woytinsky openly challenged Hilferding's assessment of its implications.[46] The opposition between them was at once epistemological, ideational, and positional.

Heterodoxy Deflected

The controversy came to a head in 1932 when, on the heels of German chancellor Heinrich Brüning's resignation, the SPD called upon Woytinsky to present his proposals to a panel of party and union representatives. Hoping that this was a turning point, Woytinsky recruited Tarnow, Baade, and Colm to his aid. (Reportedly, he also tried but failed to recruit Keynes, via the ILO.[47]) Woytinsky and his colleagues presented the WTB plan to party leaders in May 1932. They proposed targeted, loan-financed government action to boost employment and production, including large-scale public works that would generate a million new public sector jobs, which would then stimulate consumer demand.[48]

However, in a much-cited exchange recounted by Woytinsky, Hilferding framed the WTB plan as an attack on Marxism and summarily rejected it.[49] Woytinsky later paraphrased Hilferding thus:

"Colm and Woytinsky are questioning the very foundations of our program, Marx's theory of labor value. Our program rests on the conviction that labor, and labor alone, creates value. Prices deviate from labor values under the impact of the interplay of supply and demand. Depressions result from the anarchy of the capitalist system. Either they come to an end or they must lead to the collapse of this system. If Colm and Woytinsky think they can mitigate a depression by public works, they are merely showing that they are not Marxists."[50]

Woytinsky reports that the SPD deputies "listened to [Hilferding] like an oracle." Woytinsky objected, arguing that the WTB plan had nothing to do with any particular value theory.[51] But Otto Wels, a colleague of Hilferding (who, Woytinsky says, had nodded off), awoke and furiously objected in Hilferding's defense.[52] The meeting broke down *along the very axis of opposition that separated Woytinsky and Hilferding:* union representatives favored the WTB plan, and the party representatives—except Baade—voted against.[53]

On the matter of deficit-financed, large-scale public works, Smaldone comments that Hilferding "was more conservative than many on the right."[54] And yet Hilferding's resistance to the WTB plan is difficult to chalk up to conservatism, Marxism, or indeed any particular ideological leaning. Woytinsky and Hilferding had a history of epistemological opposition; Woytinsky was junior to Hilferding, in a party known for its hierarchical tendencies; and the two occupied opposing positions in the leadership-union divide. Surely Hilferding's beliefs mattered, but his preemption of the WTB plan cannot be separated from the oppositions in which he and Woytinsky were situated.

Preempting the Interlopers in Britain

To bolster my case as to the inseparability of perspective and position, we turn to a very different case—and a very different party theoretician. Philip Snowden of the British Labour Party, who also confronted economists bearing nonorthodox, statistical argumentation in the 1920s and early 1930s, was no Marxist. And yet, like Hilferding, Snowden was unwilling to consider loan-based financing of public works unless it sat within the boundaries of "sound finance"—that is, if necessary, modest, and affordable in the short term.[55] Snowden's budgetary conservatism and immunity to the persuasive power of numbers were surely matters of belief, but, as in Hilferding's case, Snowden's beliefs were inseparable from his position within the Labour Party and, by extension, Labour's position in British politics.[56]

Unlike the SPD, the Labour Party was a relatively recent arrival on the political scene in the 1920s. Plagued by suspicion and doubt, Labour first entered a coalition government in 1924 amid considerable public alarm; Ramsay MacDonald became prime minister, and Snowden became chancellor. The City of London openly opposed Labour; some accused it of Bolshevik sympathies. Commanding only about a third of the vote before 1935 (see Figure 4.4), Labour's electoral success was heavily dependent on the Liberals' reluctant agreement to make way.[57]

In this context Labour elites, Snowden among them, worried about the party's respectability, which was viewed as inseparable from its electability and capacity to govern. In Snowden's assessment, "The Labour Party was composed in the majority of new and undisciplined members who would expect the Government to do all sorts of impossible things."[58] Concerned with everything from qualified personnel to appropriate dress, party leaders worried about perceptions of Labour's

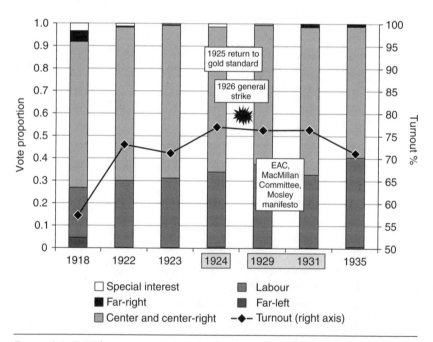

Figure 4.4. British vote proportions in election years, with voter turnout, 1918–1935 (years in shaded boxes=Labour Party in government). Data source: See Figure 4.1.

competence, its undereducated membership, and the need to rein in an unruly rank and file.[59] Snowden, lacking prestigious Oxbridge credentials, worried about establishing socialist expertise as a valid means of economic policy-making. Facing "accusations of confiscation and bolshevism," Labour elites had deep legitimacy concerns.[60]

Snowden responded with a show of budgetary competence that was at once explicitly socialist and a performance of conformity with the orthodoxies of sound finance. As chancellor he set out "to lay down a distinctively Socialist approach to financial affairs and . . . mount an effective challenge to the experts in the big parties."[61] In early 1924 MacDonald and Snowden announced to the House of Commons that the first Labour government would not abandon the Liberals' declared priority of returning Britain to the gold standard at 1914 parities.[62] Snowden presented a detailed, conservative first budget that, by all reports (including Snowden's), earned the respect of Liberals and civil servants alike.[63]

The Incumbent versus the Interlopers

Inside Labour, however, dissent festered, and young economists bearing statistical arguments (among others) tried to intervene. A proposal for a "capital levy," or wealth tax, is one example: the young Labour economist Hugh Dalton (1887–1962) made the case for the levy. More than ten years younger than Snowden, Dalton was Cambridge-educated and had close ties to party leadership (the Webbs, Arthur Henderson). He exerted enough sway to make the capital levy an important component of Labour's 1922 election campaign, but Snowden then "discreetly buried" the levy proposal, having "decided, for electoral reasons, to play it down."[64]

The prerogative of the Labour executive to ignore junior members' proposals is significant here because, in the 1920s, Labour's credentialed economists *were* junior.[65] Snowden was advised by a "team of Labour economists, who supplied views . . . which differed in several respects from the 'Treasury view'" and often had the support of organized labor, but none of those economists sat on the party's National Executive Committee (NEC).[66] And, since Snowden chaired the NEC's finance and trade committee after the 1922 elections, union leadership and professional economists—socialist or not—were no match. And so, for instance, when Ernest Bevin (Transport and General Workers Union) and Walter Citrine (TUC) borrowed from Keynes in the early 1920s to argue for more spending, it was to little effect.[67] Snowden dismissed trade union leaders' refusal to accept the insurmountable fact of budgetary limitation as evidence of their incapacity to grasp the basics of the situation.[68]

In the end Snowden and MacDonald's bid for legitimacy failed. The first Labour coalition government was tainted with suspicion of Soviet sympathies and lasted less than a year. The new Conservative chancellor of the exchequer, Winston Churchill, made good on the promise to return to the gold standard at prewar parities. By fiat British prices were set about 10 percent higher than prices in competitor countries. As in Germany, the effects were felt especially by left party constituencies: unemployment rose and wages fell, especially in coal mining; a 1926 general strike amplified trade union demands.[69]

Heterodoxy Preempted

Through all of this, and in the run-up to the 1929 election, new economics (and new economists) featured most prominently in *Liberal*, not Labour, politics. Thanks especially to Liberal summer schools run by Keynes and Beveridge,[70] the alliance between Oxbridge economics and the Liberal Party was tighter than ever. Keynes personally formulated and advertised the Liberal program, which called for large-scale infrastructure projects financed with deficit spending.[71] On March 1, 1929, Lloyd George pledged that a Liberal government would reduce unemployment to normal within a year.[72]

What this meant for Labour was that opposing the Liberals came hand in hand with rejecting Keynes, deficit financing, and the new economics.[73] Labour's program (*Labour and the Nation*), written by Snowden, Cole, and MacDonald, rejected the Liberals' "madcap finance" in favor of tax-based financing—"probably," the Keynes biographer Robert Skidelsky remarks, "a Snowden inspiration."[74] *Labour and the Nation* became the basis of Labour's 1929 election manifesto.[75] But the Liberal–new economics relationship failed to swing the vote:

Labour's vote came in at 37 percent, with the Liberals at just under 24 percent. In 1929 the new coalition government featured Labour at the helm.

Returned to the chancellor's office, Snowden established committees to inform government policy but also deflected input of a nonorthodox variety. Snowden established two advisory committees, the Economic Advisory Council (EAC) and the Macmillan Committee on finance, to make policy recommendations. The EAC included cabinet members, union leaders, industrialists, bankers, scientists, economists (including Keynes), and a historian; the Macmillan Committee featured Bevin, Keynes, and Bank of England and Treasury officials.[76] Union leadership complained that its access was, at best, erratic; Keynes's calls for spending were famously ineffectual.[77] The LSE economist Lionel Robbins accused Keynes of avoiding the real problem: labor market rigidity due to unemployment insurance and the inflexibility of wage rates.[78] The Treasury official Sir Thomas Leith-Ross criticized Keynes for inhabiting a "world of abstractions."[79] Snowden, meanwhile, managed both committees such that nonorthodox positions got little traction.

Other challenges met a similar fate. When Christopher Addison (1869–1951), a cabinet member, raised the possibility of leaving the gold standard, Snowden reportedly insulted him and ended the discussion.[80] Oswald Mosley (1896–1980)—a former Conservative, then an independent, who became a Labour MP in 1926—and John Strachey (1901–1963) also led a challenge. Drawing partly from Keynes and partly from continental economic thinking, Mosley and Strachey took up the ILP's call for "socialist planning" and the deliberate expansion of working-class purchasing power from about 1925.[81] In 1930 Mosley famously called for loan-financed public works, a national plan, import controls, and a smaller party cabinet. Both, however, were positioned on what had become Labour's ILP "left wing"—from which Snowden, at the time, was actively distancing himself.[82]

Two features of Snowden's reaction to Mosley highlight the inadmissibility of new economic thinking for the party theoretician and suggest that this inadmissibility was inextricably connected to Snowden's position. One was the marked incredulity with which Snowden rejected Mosley's Keynesian arithmetic. In Snowden's words:

[Mosley] submitted that his proposals would find employment for 730,000 persons at a cost of £10,000,000 a year! The finance of these schemes would not stand a moment's consideration. . . . As one instance of the absurdity of his finance he calculated that pensions of £1 a week for men at 60 with 10s for their wives if married, would, provided they were given to 390,000 persons, over a period of fifteen years involve a net cost to the State of £2,500,000![83]

A second notable feature of Snowden's reaction was the significance of Mosley's outsider status. Snowden, speaking not only for himself but for Labour leadership as a whole, cast Mosley's plan as the inappropriate intervention of an overly ambitious interloper:

[Mosley's] attempts immediately after he joined the Party to give the movement a new programme were strongly resented. It was felt that he was a man on the make, and was using the Labour Movement as an instrument for satisfying his ambition.[84]

In Snowden's estimation Mosley's math was not to be believed and his intentions were not grounded in a genuine commitment to Labour. The meaning of Mosley's numbers could, in other words, be dismissed on the basis of his position with respect to the party. Citing Mosley's history of partisan infidelity and doubts as to "the sincerity of [his] professions of Socialism," Snowden would not tolerate the mere suggestion that Mosley was to be taken seriously.[85]

In the end, however, Snowden's own orthodox commitments worked against the party. Faced with a budgetary standoff within party ranks, the second Labour government broke down in 1931. Snowden and MacDonald famously betrayed the party by advocating cuts to unemployment insurance and then agreeing to form a national government with the other major parties.[86] Both Snowden and MacDonald were summarily ejected; Snowden was a socialist party theoretician no more.

Abdication, Not Heterodoxy: Fredrick Thorsson and the Myth of the Swedish Exception

The case of the SAP in the 1920s is especially important for my argument that left party theoreticians' rejection of the new economics had to do with the linkage between *belief* and *position*—or, in other words, the way in which what they found thinkable expressed their situation in their parties' cultural arms. Other analyses hold up the SAP as the case that proves that ideas, separate from position, are causal. In the account of the political scientist Sheri Berman, for instance, the interwar SAP was an ideationally flexible social democratic party that, lacking the dogmatic Marxist commitments of the German SPD, weathered the economic storm of the 1920s and 1930s.[87] Berman rightly emphasizes that the SAP embraced the new economics much earlier, and fared much better than its counterparts, in the interwar years. But, when we look more closely, it is not at all clear that SAP elites were uniformly more ideationally flexible than SPD or Labour leadership; rather, it depended on who, exactly, spoke for the SAP on economic questions.

It turns out that, as long as the party theoretician Fredrik Thorsson was in charge, the SAP's budgetary stance was indistinguishable from Hilferding's SPD and Snowden's Labour Party. In other words: as long as the chief SAP expert was a party theoretician, the Swedish case was not exceptional at all. In Thorsson's opinion the SAP government had no choice but to step down in 1923 because, given budgetary constraints, the party could not govern according to its principles in bad economic times because it would be compelled to betray its priorities in service of a balanced budget. The next government, he argued, would have to solve economic problems by halting wage increases and considering increasing custom duties or prohibiting imports, not by borrowing to kick-start the economy.[88]

Why, then, did the SAP embrace the new economics? This brings us to the second part of this two-part analysis: how the forging of new ties between economics, economists, and left parties, in Sweden and elsewhere, became the social basis of leftism's first twentieth-century reinvention: the move from socialist to economistic, or Keynesian, leftism.

PART TWO: ECONOMISTIC LEFTISM'S FORMATION IN SWEDEN, BRITAIN, AND (WEST) GERMANY

We begin with Sweden because the SAP was, indeed, an exception to the rule in the early 1930s, because of its particular openness to the nonorthodox arguments of professional economists. But Swedish exceptionalism was not therefore a result of the generalized ideational flexibility of the SAP as a whole. Rather, the SAP's precocious turn to "Keynesianism," well before Keynes's *General Theory* (1936), had to do with the orientations of a newly ascendant sort of party expert: the economist theoretician.

The SAP's Precocious Turn to "Keynesianism"

In 1925 the SAP underwent a sudden change in leadership. After a period of illness Thorsson died unexpectedly; so, also, did the SAP's leader, Hjalmar Branting. A few months prior to Thorsson's death the *New York Times* announced that a younger party member named Ernst Wigforss (1881–1977) would become the SAP government's minister of finance. Perhaps figuring that a socialist is a socialist, the *Times* reporter commented that the event brought "no new political forces into the Cabinet."[89] But Wigforss, more than fifteen years Thorsson's junior, actually brought important novelties to the office.

Recall from the previous chapter that Thorsson became a SAP party expert by virtue of socialist "agitation" and journalistic work. If we place Uppsala-educated figures like Branting, Sterky, and Danielsson alongside Thorsson (who had no higher education), what they all had in common was entry into the SAP elite via public lectures, socialist organizational activities, and socialist newspapers. But Wigforss's path was different. He attended Lund University from 1899, studied linguistics, acquired a doctorate, and became a docent in Scandinavian languages and a gymnasium teacher in Lund, then Göteborg. He considered himself an "agitator," too, but agitation was never what he did for a living: Wigforss was an academic, not a journalist or newspaper editor, and was recruited into SAP circles as part of a general effort to bring a new, university-educated cadre of young leaders into the party.

At Lund Wigforss got involved in radical student politics by way of an association called Den Yngre Gubbarna ("The younger old men," or DYG, established in 1896).[90] There he befriended the rebellious liberal economist Knut Wicksell, a professor and honorary DYG member. The DYG was agnostic on socialism—possibly thanks to Wicksell, who warned students "against hasty decisions."[91] But by 1903 a split was forming in radical student ranks, marked by the establishment of a Social Democratic Youth Organisation (SSU). This split reached into the DYG as early as 1906.[92] The SSU was later the site of an organizational splinter in the SAP that gave rise to the Left-Socialist (later Communist) Party, established in 1917.

Wigforss stayed on the social democratic side of the split. His notion of what socialism meant was never grounded in Marxism. In his *Materialist Conception of History* (*Materialistisk historieuppfattning*) of 1908 (published in English in 1970) Wigforss embraced the Marxian emphasis on political power, economic and political evolution, and the critique of private property, but he rejected economic determinism and Marxian pretensions to science.[93] In his memoirs Wigforss attributed any revolutionary inclinations he might have had to the Swedish Romantic Viktor Rydberg, not Karl Marx.[94] Since socialism was not inevitable, Wigforss argued that socialists should take power and do the "work of reorganizing society" themselves, proactively moving Sweden toward a "provisional utopia."[95]

Wigforss's non-Marxist bent, or "revisionist" thinking, was squarely in-line with the SAP's turn away from Marxism, more or less at the party's establishment, in the context of a decidedly less hostile state than that faced by the SPD.[96] In this respect, he was not very different from Thorsson. What did distinguish Wigforss relative to Thorsson, however, was his academic path into party leadership and, through that pathway, his eventual transformation into a *de facto* professional economist.

From Lund Wigforss moved to Göteborg, where he worked as a teacher until 1911. By then the SAP had an extensive on-the-ground local presence, partly in the form of youth clubs. A self-described radical "youth clubbist" himself, Wigforss favored a particular coffeehouse, the Verdandikafé, where he could mix with working youth and like-minded "academics."[97] Wigforss was aware that, within the SAP, he moved in a rarefied, university-educated milieu: his affection for the Verdandikafé had to do with a dissatisfaction with "graduates who enter the labor movement and become familiar with their party colleagues" but "continue to practically live their daily lives among academic peers."[98]

Returning to Lund, Wigforss first met Branting in 1911 or 1912.[99] He then began his political career in 1919, aged thirty-eight, when he won a seat in the Upper House along with forty-seven other Social Democrats (up from nineteen).[100] Upon entering the Riksdag, Wigforss set about developing a new SAP program. The resulting draft—which included a right to employment, protections for workers, health and other services, educational opportunity, progressive taxation, worker codetermination, and economic efficiency—was rejected, but party leaders nonetheless recognized Wigforss as "one of the party's foremost young theoreticians."[101] Wigforss represented a younger, university-socialized generation of up-and-coming party elites that included Rickard Sandler (1884–1964), a former Brunnsvik teacher and founder of the ABF, and Per Albin Hansson (1885–1946).

Moving up rapidly, Wigforss became a member of the party directorate in 1920 (until 1952) and a consulting member of the Branting Cabinet in 1924, moving into Thorsson's position upon the latter's illness. Wigforss's generational peer, Rickard Sandler, became prime minister in 1925. After serving as minister of finance in 1925–1926, Wigforss joined the SAP's executive committee in 1928.

As Wigforss and Sandler were taking charge, SAP party-expert relations were shifting. Historically, Swedish economics had liberal affinities and a powerful public presence but kept a distance from party involvements. But in the 1920s the economics profession was growing and, drawn into deepening contestation over economic truths, was increasingly imbricated with partisan contestation.

The Imbrication of Swedish Economics
and Partisan Politics

In the 1920s Wicksell's Political Economy Club, in Stockholm, was a site of generational rebellion. Young, neo-Wicksellian economists began to object to their mentors' "use of economic theory in legitimizing liberal economic policy standpoints."[102] Gunnar Myrdal (1898–1987—hereafter G. Myrdal to distinguish him from his spouse, Alva Myrdal, herself an influential academic and Swedish politician) made a particularly dramatic break. After defending his dissertation (1927) and taking a post at the University of Stockholm, G. Myrdal used the club as a forum for criticism of his elders, whom he accused of failing to distinguish between fact and value. After a series of university lectures, G. Myrdal published a full statement on the argument in 1930: *The Political Element in the Development of Economic Theory*.[103] Effectively issuing a "declaration of independence of the younger generation of Swedish economists from the older generation," G. Myrdal laid the basis of what would later become known as the "Stockholm School."[104]

An oddity of the Stockholm School, however, was that even as G. Myrdal accused his elders of confusing politics and science, he and his peers blurred the line in practice by developing the very party ties that their mentors avoided. G. Myrdal, as we will see, became very close to Wigforss and the SAP. This contrasted with Gustav Cassel, G. Myrdal's adviser, who was "perhaps the best-known economist on the international scene in the 1920s" but was never party-connected and took pride in his political independence.[105] Cassel's students—including G. Myrdal, Bertil Ohlin (1899–1979) and Gösta Bagge (1882–1951)— were active, respectively, in the SAP, the liberal Folkpartiet, and the Conservative party; some became party leaders (see Table 4.2).

The deepening relationship between economics and party politics in Sweden had partly to do with the growing technical and statistical demands that the government placed on economists in turbulent times. In the late 1920s and early 1930s the Swedish government increasingly turned to academic economists for technical advice. The Unemployment Committee (UC), established in 1927 by a non-SAP government, became a "meeting place for economists and politicians interested in the causes and cures of unemployment"—described by one economic historian as a sort of "advanced workshop in macroeconomics."[106] The UC was so economist-intensive that between 1931 and 1933 its demands nearly eclipsed the Political Economy Club's activities.[107] As shown in Table 4.2, the UC became an important outlet for younger-generation Swedish economists' professional advancement, providing fodder and institutional support for a number of dissertations that would later become foundational works of the Stockholm School. And, as economists were drawn into the state, they were also drawn into parties.

The Role of the Economist Theoretician in the
SAP's Economistic Turn

In 1930 the SAP returned to government, importing Wigforss into the Ministry of Finance. From this powerful perch Wigforss linked the SAP party-in-government with the Stockholm School. As a friend and admirer

Table 4.2 The Swedish Stockholm School (listed chronologically by year of birth)

Name	Degree and institution	Academic appointments (with start year)	Party affiliation	Political offices/ government appointments (with start date)	Unemployment committee?
Lindahl* (1862–1960)	PhD (law), University of Lund, 1919	Professor, University of Gothenburg (1932)	—	Adviser to the Riksbank (1931); League of Nations (1936); Treasury (1937)	[No]
Bagge** (1882–1951)	PhD (economics), University of Stockholm, 1917	Associate professor, economics, University of Stockholm (1917); founding director of the University of Stockholm Institute for Social Sciences (1920)	Conservatives (leader)	Council and school board member, Stockholm, 1913–1918	Yes
Kock (1891–1976)	—	—	SAP (cabinet)	SAP's first female cabinet member, late 1940s	Yes
G. Myrdal* (1898–1987)	PhD (law), University of Stockholm, 1927	Professor, Institut Universitaire des Hautes Etudes Internationales, Geneva (1931); chair of Political Economy and Public Finance (1931) and professor (1961), University of Stockholm	SAP (Riksdag)	Senate (1934, 1942); Riksbank (board member); minister of commerce (1945)	Yes. Key report: "The Economic Effects of Fiscal Policy"
Ohlin** (1899–1979)	PhD (economics), University of Stockholm, 1924	Professor, Stockholm School of Economics and Business Administration (1929); University of Copenhagen (1924)	Folkpartiet (leader)	Parliament (1930); minister of trade (1944); assistant secretary, Economic Council (1920)	Yes. Key report: "Monetary Policy, Public Works, Subsidies and Tariffs as Means against Unemployment"

A. Johansson* (1901–?)	PhD (economics), University of Stockholm, 1934	Stockholm Högskola; University of Lund (1943)	Close ties to labor movement	—	Yes. Dissertation published as UC report ("Wage Movements and Unemployment")
Hammarskjöld* (1905–1961)	PhD (economics), University of Stockholm, 1934	—	SAP	Undersecretary of the Treasury (under Wigforss, starting 1936; adviser to the Riksbank (from 1935)	Yes. Dissertation published as Unemployment Committee (UC) report ("The Dispersion of the Business Cycle")
Lundberg** (1907–1987)	PhD (economics), University of Stockholm, 1937	Director, National Institute of Economic Research (1937) (Konjunkturinstitutet); professor, University of Stockholm	—	Riksbank (1934)	[No]
Svennilson (1909–1972)	—	—	—	—	Yes

Sources: Fregert 1991, pp. xvii–xxi; Metelius 1991, p. 101; Nobelprize.org, accessed August 15, 2013; Jonung 1991, pp. xvii–xx; 5–6; Hansson 1991, pp. 168–213; www.hetwebsite.org/het/schools/sweden.htm; Ohlin 1937a.

* Denotes the narrower set of members of the Stockholm School given by Hansson (1991).

** Many had trained outside of Sweden as well: Bagge studied at Johns Hopkins University, 1904–1905; Lundberg studied at American universities as a Rockefeller fellow, 1931–1933; Ohlin studied abroad at Grenoble, Oxford, and Harvard, receiving an MA from Harvard, 1923.

of Wicksell, whom Wigforss knew from his university days, Wigforss was fully engaged with developments in economics in Sweden and England.[108] An active UC participant, among Wigforss's memos on unemployment and business cycles was one that presaged the 1958 Phillips curve credited to the British economist A. W. H. Phillips (thereafter advanced by the American economists Paul Samuelson and Robert Solow).[109] As a member of the UC, Wigforss was uniquely positioned to play a dual role as both an important party elite and a *de facto* academic economist.

Three events, all in 1932, crystallized the new SAP-economics relationship. First, Wigforss became the first-ever noneconomist to be granted membership in the Political Economy Club.[110] Second, G. Myrdal joined the SAP, whereupon he wrote an essay calling on the SAP to embrace expert-led economic planning. As Wigforss became a *de facto* economist G. Myrdal was establishing "his credentials as an 'insider' " with SAP elites.[111] Third, the SAP signaled its embrace of a new theoretical basis by dropping a hallmark policy of socialist leftism—the socialization of the means of production—from its manifesto.[112]

As finance minister Wigforss, aged fifty-one, made Stockholm economics the explicit scientific foundation of the SAP's 1933 crisis program.[113] Developed under Wigforss's auspices during 1931–1932, the program called for large-scale, loan-financed public works, direct taxes, and reduced defense spending. The prime minister's speech announced the program at the commencement of the fourth SAP government; soon after, G. Myrdal followed with a memo advocating expansion-oriented deficit spending. Written on Wigforss's invitation, G. Myrdal's memo was appended to a 1933 budget message to the Riksdag in January 1933, leaving little doubt as to the new program's expert basis.[114] The SAP thus became an early progenitor of economistic leftism, grounded in a whole new relationship between the party and the economics profession.

The SAP's new budgetary approach paid off in more ways than one. Industrial unemployment dropped from 23.2 percent in 1933 to 15 percent in 1935; unemployment insurance was introduced in 1934. In 1938 Wigforss happily reported in the *Annals of the American Academy of Political and Social Science* that, true to the government's promises, by 1936–1937 income from public investments far exceeded

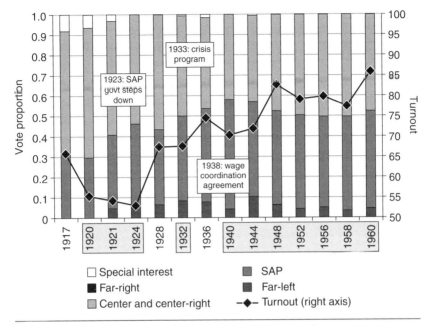

Figure 4.5. Swedish vote proportions in election years, with voter turnout, 1917–1960 (years in shaded boxes = SAP in government). Data source: See Figure 4.1.

interest payments on public debt. The successful crisis program also enabled the SAP to build crucial alliances in the form of a formal agreement with the Farmer's Party and, in 1938, an agreement on wage coordination (the Saltsjöbadsavtalet, or Saltsjöbaden Agreement) between the Trade Union Confederation (Landsorganisationen, or LO) and the Employers Association (Svenska Arbetsgivareföreningen, or SAF).[115] Here, again, Wigforss was a driving figure.[116] From that point forward, as Figure 4.5 shows, the SAP established itself as Sweden's major party of government.

The exceptionality of the SAP in the early 1930s—but not before—is hard to explain without attention to Wigforss's positional novelties. Unlike the party theoretician, Wigforss was a living bridge between the SAP and Swedish economics. He was, by his own account, an "agitator" turned financial expert, "more or less versed in the science that economists do."[117]

The Move to Trade Unions: The "LO Economist"

What then unfolded in Sweden was a new era of interdependence between the SAP and professional economics. By the mid-1940s a professional economist or economist-in-training, especially one based in
Stockholm, was likely to find him- or herself engaged in SAP circles and
governments. Because of the SAP's formalized relationship to the LO,
which had its own connections to credentialed economists, the SAP-
economics relationship extended, also, into organized labor. This ar-
rangement gave rise to a particular sort of economist theoretician on
the Swedish political scene: the SAP-affiliated LO economist. Famously,
LO economists Gösta Rehn (1913–1996) and Rudolf Meidner (1914–
2005) became the widely acknowledged architects of the Swedish model
in the early postwar period, acquiring a level of public influence that
"went well beyond the norm" for nonacademic economists in Sweden.[118]

Rehn and Meidner were both affiliates of Stockholm School economists, including G. Myrdal, Erik Lundberg, and Ingvar Svennilson.[119]
Rehn and Meidner's path was markedly different from that of the party
theoretician. Meidner was German (from Breslau) and, having witnessed the Reichstag fire in 1933, migrated to Sweden, where he acquired an academic position at Stockholm University (then Stockholm
University College).[120] Rehn, who was raised by a (liberal) municipal
clerk, was neither a Marxist nor a student of socialism. A member of
the leftist association SSU and affiliated with its journal, Clarté, Rehn
did not study socialist classics, was at odds with his peers during the
Moscow Trials in 1936, and never favored a popular front during World
War II.[121] Rehn never completed his doctorate because of his political
commitments, and he dedicated little of his writing to academic work.[122]
Yet he was well trained in the techniques and reasoning of what is sometimes called Keynesianism, but was actually a specifically Swedish economics. By the time Meidner was recruited into the LO in 1945 as
director of its new research department (established in 1943) Rehn was
already doing periodic work for it—and was, in this sense, the first LO
economist.[123]

From their LO positions Rehn and Meidner became particular sorts
of economist theoreticians, situated at the intersection of academe, the
SAP, and organized labor. In Meidner's posthumous account the LO

leadership had a highly directive role in its economists' research—and Rehn, economist or not, never ceased "to regard himself as a trade union man."[124] Thus situated Rehn and Meidner linked the SAP to the economics profession and mediated the relationship between the SAP party-in-government and the trade unions.

More formal cooperation with SAP leadership began in 1943 with a council made up of the SAP, the LO, the Social Democratic Women's Federation, and the SSU—a body associated with Wigforss, the Myrdals, the head of the LO research department (Richard Sterner), and Rehn.[125] The LO economists' hybrid position—in economics, organized labor, and the SAP elite—allowed a certain degree of flexibility in occasionally tense relations between unions and the party. For instance, after World War II Rehn mobilized technical economic argumentation in order to ease the LO away from price controls, despite trade union resistance. He was not always successful—he was not able to facilitate selective (as opposed to across-the-board) wage freezes in 1949, after a devaluation, for instance.[126] Nonetheless, in his intermediary role Rehn was able to introduce, in a certain sense, a scientific third party—economics—into the not always amiable relationship between the SAP-in-government and the trade unions. In the 1949 debate on wage freezes Meidner recounts that

> Rehn could draw upon the fund of serious thinking . . . on pay policy in a full employment economy. A wage freeze in a booming economy with high export profits was, to us economists, a textbook example of an absurd policy doomed from the outset to failure.[127]

Perhaps most importantly, the LO economists took the apparent trade-off between unemployment and inflation—the crux of the Keynesian postwar problematic—as a "political choice" to be resolved, with the government's facilitation, via analytically informed compromise.[128]

The famed Swedish model, first proposed by Rehn and Meidner in 1951, expressed the LO economists' way of seeing things: built into the economics of the Swedish model was an assumption of the necessity of mediation, negotiation, and compromise. It featured a three-pronged formula that included productivity for social ends, coordinated wage bargaining covering all unions, and a solidaristic wage policy in which wages were to be determined by work rather than employers' profits.[129] In the description of the Swedish political scientist Jonas Pontusson, the model "promoted productivity growth by accentuating profit differentials among firms and removing obstacles to factor mobility," since it was explicitly aimed at keeping firms competitive by limiting their opportunities to profit at home (especially via restrictive fiscal policies meant to transfer profits into public savings—that is, into pension funds) and forcing firms into price competition via international trade.[130]

Meidner later argued that the Rehn-Meidner model was surely an effect of the situation of those who created it: it "credibly could only be conceived within a trade union movement."[131] It was, most fundamentally, a recipe for the resolution of the inherently oppositional interests of capital and labor, constructed on recognition that neither side could grow too powerful. In Meidner's retrospective account:

> We were aware of the risk that powerful unions which are guaranteed full employment are strong enough to jeopardize the stabilization policy through aggressive wage claims. However, we rejected the idea that unions should be disciplined by unemployment. Our preference was for collective self-discipline imposed by the union's own wage policy. This was conceived within the framework of an ideology based on the notion of solidarity, promoting a wage structure which reflected the kind of work and skill rather than the profitability of the firm.[132]

First presented in a 1951 report to the LO congress, the Rehn-Meidner model was introduced as SAP government policy in 1957–1958. The occupant of the office of finance minister remained important: the appointment of Gunnar Sträng (1906–1992), the union-friendly son of a garbage collector, as minister of finance in 1955, by which time Rehn was working at the finance ministry as a research officer, facilitated its enactment.[133] By 1960 the Swedish model, a policy instantiation of the intermediary worldview of the LO economist, was in full effect.

And so the SAP's precocious embrace of the new economics, which hinged on the worldviews and activities of a specific sort of party expert, became the basis of a distinctively economistic leftism in Sweden.

Similar processes, with important variations in timing, would also unfold in Britain and West Germany.

Labour's Economistic Turn: Hugh Dalton and the Making of the "Gaitskellites"

In the 1920s Keynes's relationship with the Labour Party was principally one of mutual dislike. Keynes, an avowed Liberal, made a point of proclaiming his lack of sympathy with Labour; likewise, Labour leaders were put off by Keynes's dismissals of the party's intellectual and political competence, and found Keynes's associations with Lloyd George and Oswald Mosley suspect.[134] The birth of a Labourite *economist theoretician* was nonetheless rooted in the development of a profession in which Keynes was a formative influence.

As in the case of Ernst Wigforss in Sweden, the story of Labour's deepening interconnection with professional economics can be told through the trajectory of a particular figure: economist-*cum*-Labour politician Hugh Dalton (1887–1962). We have seen that Snowden curtailed Dalton's influence in the 1920s, but in the 1930s Dalton moved into the leadership vacuum created by Snowden and MacDonald's ejection from the party. From there Dalton recruited a number of like-minded young economists into Labour's political and advisory ranks, including James Meade (1907–1995) and Dalton's protégé, Hugh Gaitskell (1906–1963). The recruitment of Keynesian economists into the British government then accelerated during wartime, partly thanks to Dalton's efforts. By 1944 Labour economists were playing a central role in the formulation of the party's economic program. And by the early 1960s Dalton's young economist recruits were prominent party leaders, rendering the linkages between British economics and Labour unmistakable.

One of the most interesting facets of Dalton's story is how it shows that, while Labour's Keynesian turn was wrapped up with the British state's wartime demand for economists, it was also grounded in longer-term changes in the relationship between the Labour Party and the economics profession. Well before World War I the young Labour Party began to reach ever more deeply into university settings, and especially into Oxbridge, even as British economics professionalized, autonomized, and engaged itself more deeply in both government and party-political life. With this groundwork in place, and with Dalton elevated into the Labour executive, the Labour Party's marriage with Keynesian economics consolidated during World War II.

Dalton and the Labour-Fabian-Oxbridge-Economics Relationship

In the early 1900s the institutionalization of economics as a distinctive academic discipline intersected with the expanding presence of the Fabian Society in Britain's most prominent universities.

Oxbridge had long been (and remains) the central training ground of the British political class. In the early 1900s it was also hostile territory for socialists and for Labour Party sympathizers. But Labour's increasing electoral popularity from 1906 fueled more interest in Oxbridge chapters of the Fabian Society, the membership of which more than doubled between 1906 and 1908.[135] Between the early 1900s and the 1930s—as the gold standard unraveled, unemployment rose, and political unrest escalated—politically minded Oxbridge students were drawn both to the discipline of economics and to socialist, Fabian, and Labour Party circles, all of which had a growing campus presence.

Hugh Dalton, a contemporary of Ernst Wigforss, was one such student. Born to a family with strong connections to the British Royal Family, schooled at Eton, and gone "up" to King's College, Cambridge, in 1906, Dalton was hardly born to be a socialist. Nor did his path look like that of the party theoretician: Dalton was no agitator; his trajectory looked nothing like the journalism-to-party path of Philip Snowden.[136] Dalton arrived at Oxford a "Tory Democrat," taking inspiration from Joseph Chamberlain. But, even so, by the end of Dalton's first term he was both a socialist and a member of the Cambridge Fabian Society.

At the time, Fabian summer schools served as a sort of training and socialization tool for Oxbridge and other young recruits to the Labour Party. Through the summer schools Dalton developed an association with Beatrice Webb, who eyed him as a future Labour politician. By the start of his third year at Cambridge Dalton was the president of the Cambridge Fabians, and he would soon become acquainted with

Keynes. In his final year Dalton took Keynes's economics course and, breaking from family tradition, switched from mathematics to the "modern subject" of economics.[137]

Fortunately for Dalton, who failed in a series of bids for a Labour seat between 1918 and 1922, an academic career in economics was a perfect complement to the unpredictable life of an aspiring Labour politician. In 1919 Dalton took up a position as a lecturer at the LSE, which was then run by a total of seventeen full-time instructors. Dalton played an important role in the making of the still-fledgling LSE economics department, while also elevating his own stature as an academic economist.[138] In 1920 he published his first book, *Some Aspects of the Inequality of Incomes in Modern Communities*, which fused Dalton's knowledge of economics with his socialist convictions. The book dealt with the individual distribution of incomes (as opposed to its aggregate distribution across land, labor, and capital), providing "a neatly argued intellectual justification for what Dalton understood by the word socialism in its economic manifestation."[139] In 1922 Dalton then published an academic textbook, *Principles of Public Finance,* which would become "for many decades a basic text" in Britain and elsewhere.[140]

Thanks to Dalton's growing academic reputation and a close connection to Beatrice Webb—and despite the fact that Dalton was, as yet, unable to win an election—in 1921 he became more involved with Labour as an economic expert. In 1922 he became one of two Cambridge-trained economists to join a new subcommittee of the NEC, assembled to develop a programmatic stance on the question of a capital levy (a tax on the wealthy), which then became part of Labour's 1922 campaign.[141] But, as discussed above, Snowden put the initiative on a back burner.

Dalton persisted in his pursuit of elected office as a Labour MP. In a last-ditch effort in 1924, Labour listed him for a district it thought it was likely to lose. But 1924 was to become the year of the first Labour government, and Dalton became the (surprise) first Labour MP of Camberwell, Peckham, in South London.[142] Now both an economist and a Labour MP, Dalton was then among the junior economists in Labour's advisory ranks who tried, but failed, to sway Snowden on the budget. As a member of the Parliamentary Labour Party (PLP), however, he stood out as an economist in a "party of novices."[143]

An internal shake-up in Labour's leadership after 1931 in the wake of Snowden's and MacDonald's expulsion finally made room for Dalton's ascent. In 1931 Dalton used his position at the NEC to establish the Policy Committee, which he then chaired continuously from 1936 to 1944. With the advent of a wartime coalition government, in which Labour officials had sway over ministerial appointments, Dalton became minister of economic warfare (1940–1942) and then minister of the Board of Trade (1942–1945). By the early 1940s, now a Labour MP, governmental minister, and the party's Policy Committee chairman, Dalton was unrivaled in his influence on the NEC. The Policy Committee became Dalton's "personal instrument during the key period when post-war policy was being formed."[144]

Dalton was not a prominent advocate of Keynesian economics *per se*, but he was a very important point of connection between the Labour executive and an increasingly Keynesian profession. In the 1930s and 1940s Dalton actively recruited and promoted professional economists who had trained and collaborated with Keynes. Dalton thus became a node through which Keynesian economists gained greater access to, and influence over, Labour policy-making.

This would have been impossible in the absence of fertile recruitment grounds. Here it is important that connections between Labour, the Fabian Society, and academic economics deepened in the turbulent 1930s. One connection took the form of the New Fabian Research Bureau (NFRB), established at Oxford in 1931 by young Fabians under the leadership of G. D. H. Cole and Margaret Cole. Among the NFRB founders, who were motivated by disillusionment after Labour's failure in 1931 and frustrations with the Fabian "Old Gang," were economists connected to Keynes—although Keynes himself avoided it.[145] The NFRB's young economists included the future Labour leader Hugh Gaitskell, the future economics Nobel Prize winner James Meade, and the future Labour prime minister Harold Wilson (1916–1995). In time the NFRB also included Richard Kahn. A fellow at King's College and former Keynes student, and by then Keynes's close collaborator, Kahn later became famous for elaborating the concept of the "multiplier," and he was singled out by Keynes for intellectual credit in the preface to *The General Theory of Employment, Interest and Money* (1936).[146]

Centered at Oxford, the NFRB's network extended to Cambridge and London and into the Labour Party. In 1938 the NFRB merged into the London arm of the Fabian Society and took over the Fabian executive—a sensible move given that the NFRB's research output outpaced the London-based Fabian Society in the 1930s. G. D. H. Cole became the Fabian Society's new head.[147]

The Labour-Fabian-economics intersection overlapped with two other nodes of economist-heavy policy discussion in the 1930s. One was the XYZ Club (or City Group), founded in January 1932 as a means of cultivating ties between Labour and finance (the City of London). Another was an NEC subcommittee on finance and trade. Dalton was involved with both.

The founding of the XYZ Club is a subject of some disagreement, attributed by some to Nicholas Davenport (a friend of Keynes) and by others to the banker Vaughan Berry.[148] In any case, thanks to Dalton's "prompting," Gaitskell and two other Keynesian economists, Evan Durbin (1906–1948) and Douglas Jay, joined the XYZ Club, with Gaitskell as its secretary; the Hungarian-*cum*-British economist Thomas Balogh, then appointed alongside Gaitskell in the Department of Political Economy of University College London (UCL), was also a member.[149] Dalton used his connections to the XYZ Club to shape the deliberations of the NEC, referring "loftily to his 'experts' at [its] meetings."[150] As chair of the finance and trade subcommittee, Dalton pulled Gaitskell and Durbin onto that body as well.[151]

Dalton's young recruits provided him with a network that linked a younger generation of British economists to the City of London and with Labour leadership. As such, a whole new party-expert configuration informed Labour's programmatic deliberations in the 1930s. Dalton developed his next book, *Practical Socialism for Britain* (1935), partly through exchanges with Jay, Gaitskell, and Durbin. The book, which advocated economic planning informed by the new economics, became a blueprint for the next Labour government.[152]

The Party-Economics Relationship during Wartime

The culmination of the marriage of Labour and British economics took shape during the wartime coalition government, which opened up new opportunities for economists and brought Labour officials back into ministerial offices. On the one hand, Oxford became a "place of academic refuge for numerous exiles from the Nazi regime."[153] Central here was the Institute of Statistics, established in 1935 under the directorship of the Russian economist Jacob Marschak, which became home to a number of exiled economists. The institute was another site in which XYZ-connected economists—Balogh, Jay, Gaitskell, plus Harold Wilson—continued their mutual engagements.[154] On the other hand, as Dalton moved into positions of governmental power, he brought an increasingly densely interconnected cadre of young economists along with him.

Dalton moved to the powerful Board of Trade from the Ministry of Economic Warfare in February 1942. There he acquired power over "a wide empire," including rationing, wartime controls, and (toward the end of the war) postwar planning.[155] From his new position Dalton persisted in his collaboration with, and promotion of, Labour economists. Perhaps the clearest and most consequential effect was Labour's *White Paper on Employment Policy* of 1944, an early draft of which was written by the NFRB participant James Meade.[156] Famously, the white paper became the basis of the Labour government's commitment to Keynesian policies for full employment in 1944–1945.[157]

Having shaped the programmatic agenda of the party, Dalton and his economist recruits also influenced the formation of the postwar British state. When Labour became the party of government in 1945 under Clement Attlee, Dalton became one of the new government's "Big Five" leaders (with Ernest Bevin, Herbert Morrison, Stafford Cripps, and Attlee) and chancellor of the exchequer. In that position Dalton authored no fewer than four Labour budgets, through which the government's Keynesian employment program was implemented. When Dalton stepped down Stafford Cripps briefly succeeded him, but Cripps was soon replaced by Dalton's protégé, Hugh Gaitskell, who served as chancellor from 1950 to 1951.[158]

The Intermediary and Interfactional British Economist Theoretician

In the case of the SAP, the party-economics relationship hinged on economist theoreticians situated, specifically, in the LO. In the case of Labour, the party-economics connection extended especially into the party executive. Thus positioned, the Labour economist theoretician nonetheless took up an intermediary role between trade unions and the party elite, but was also caught up in the left-right factional divides that defined Labour's intraparty oppositions in the postwar period.

Dalton himself was not exactly Keynesian, but Gaitskell and many of his peers were. As such, they contended with others in Labour ranks who prioritized a more straightforwardly socialist (that is, not Keynesian) agenda, which centered on the nationalization of private industries. Labour's 1945 manifesto thus featured the language of Keynesian economics—demand management, full employment—but also called for an expansion of the public sector. The program's emphases on nationalization were thanks partly to the efforts a Labour MP, Ian Mikardo, who had been drafted into the party by the activist Wilf Canon.

During this time the economist theoretician could be found on both sides of the party's internal left-right divisions. On the left, Balogh joined with two of his economist colleagues in 1950 to restart a 1947 initiative (*Keep Left*) called *Keeping Left,* which called for economic controls, more public ownership, and a partnership between government and centralized coordination with trade unions on wage bargaining.[159] Balogh was also linked to a cadre of economist-heavy, revisionist leadership with relatively friendly union relations that formed around Gaitskell in the 1950s—later known as the moderate "New Thinkers," or simply "Gaitskellites" (see Table 4.3).[160]

Table 4.3 does not present an exhaustive list of the Gaitskellite revisionists—which, to be sure, did not consist strictly of economists. Among the most famous revisionists was, and remains, the noneconomist Anthony Crosland, whose 1956 *The Future of Socialism* remains a landmark event in revisionist Labour thinking.[161] Nonetheless, economists' new centrality in Labour's leadership, their imbrication with Labour's internal left-right divisions, and their distinctive status as intermediaries in the party-union relationship were all notable in the time of the Gaitskellites.[162]

The SPD's Delayed Economistic Leftism

In the 1920s a number of would-be party experts could be found in the SPD's junior ranks. Fritz Baade, Hilferding's protégé (and the "B" in

Table 4.3 Dalton's recruits—the making of the Gaitskell generation of revisionists (listed chronologically by year of birth)

Name	Birth–death	University	University subject	Other activities	Graduate institution
Dalton, Hugh	1887–1962	King's College, Cambridge, MA, 1906–1909	Economics [switched from mathematics]	Fabian Society, from 1906	LSE (DSc, 1913)
Durbin, Evan	1906–1948	New College, Oxford, BA, 1924–1927	Zoology (2nd); philosophy, politics, and economics (PPE) (1st), 1927	NFRB; XYZ Club	UCL
Gaitskell, Hugh	1906–1963	New College, Oxford, 1924–1927	PPE (1st), 1927	NFRB; University of Vienna (1933–1934)	None
Meade, James	1907–1995	Oriel College, Oxford, BA, MA, 1927–1930, 1933	PPE (1st), 1930 [switched from Greats]	Labour Club, NFRB, Cambridge Circus (1930–1931)	Hertford College, Oxford

Major work(s)	Academic appointment(s)	Political/party appointments	Government positions
Inequality of Incomes, 1920; *Principles of Public Finance,* 1922	LSE, lecturer/reader in economics, 1914, 1920–1936	Labour MP, 1924–1931, 1935–1962; NEC Policy Committee, 1931; life peer, 1960	Minister of Economic Warfare, 1940–1942; Board of Trade, 1942–1945; chancellor, 1945–1947
Purchasing Power and Trade Depression, 1933; *Socialist Credit Policy,* 1933, revised 1935; *The Problem of Credit Policy,* 1935; *Personal Aggressiveness and War,* 1938 [with John Bowlby]; *The Politics of Democratic Socialism,* 1940; *What Have We to Defend?,* 1942, *Problems of Economic Planning,* 1949	Lecturer, New College, Oxford; lecturer, LSE, 1930–1945	Failed runs for Labour MP, 1931 and 1935; Labour MP, 1945–1948	Economic Section of the War Cabinet (with Lionel Robbins, Harold Wilson); Attlee's assistant, 1942–1945; Dalton's parliamentary private secretary, 1945–1946; parliamentary secretary, Ministry of Works, 1947–1948
Chartism, 1929; "Four Monetary Heretics," in G. D. H. Cole, ed., *What Everyone Wants to Know about Money,* 1933; *Money and Everyday Life,* 1939; *The Challenge of Co-existence,* 1957	Lecturer in economics, Workers' Educational Association; UCL, lecturer/reader, political economy, 1928–1939; head of department, 1938	Failed run, 1935; MP, 1945; opposition leader, 1955–1963; party leader, 1955	Ministry of Economic Warfare (with Dalton), 1939–1945; minister of fuel and power, 1946; minister of economic affairs, 1950; chancellor, 1950–1951
An Introduction to Economic Analysis and Policy, 1936; *The Economic Basis of a Durable Peace,* 1940; *National Income and Expenditure* (with Richard Stone), 1944; *Planning and the Price Mechanism,* 1948; *Theory of International Economic Policy,* 1951; *A Neoclassical Theory of Economic Growth,* 1960; *Efficiency, Equality and the Ownership of Property,* 1964; [and many others]	Fellow, economics, Hertford College, Oxford, 1930–1937; LSE professorship, 1947–1957; professorial fellow, Christ's College, Cambridge, 1959–1974; professor, Cambridge, 1957–1968; Nobel Prize in Economics, 1977	None	Economic Section of the War Cabinet, 1940–1945; head of the Economic Section, January 1946–1947

(continued)

Table 4.3   (continued)

Name	Birth–death	University	University subject	Other activities	Graduate institution
Jay, Douglas	1907–1996	New College, Oxford, 1926–1929	Humanities, 1929	NFRB	All Souls College, Oxford
Wilson, Harold	1916–1995	Jesus College, Oxford, 1934–1937	PPE (1st), 1937 [switched from history]	NFRB [later, Fabian executive committee]	University College, Balliol, Oxford

Sources: Howson 2004; Haseler 1969; Durbin 1985; Blaug 1986.

the WTB episode), was one of them. So was Heinrich Deist (1902–1964), who became a member of the Young Socialist Workers organization in 1918 and studied economics, law, and political science at the universities of Leipzig, Hamburg, and Halle.[163] As a student Deist was in a group of young party intellectuals, the Hofgeismarer circle, which aimed to save the SPD from "dogmatic atrophy" in the 1920s.[164] But how any of these figures might have shaped the SPD's economic language between 1933 and 1946 cannot be known. After Hitler came to power the SPD was outlawed; the Nazis seized SPD property and banned socialist press operations.[165] The path of the SPD party expert, of any sort, was closed. By April 1933 SPD officials and politicians were forced into camps or exile; many did not survive the Hitler regime.[166]

In May 1933 the SPD sent a subset of its leadership abroad to establish an executive-in-exile (termed Sopade). It landed first in Prague, moved to Paris, and wound up finally in London under the leadership of Erich Ollenhauer (1901–1963). Ollenhauer, an SPD member from the age of seventeen, joined the party executive in the same year that Hitler came to power. In London, with the Labour Party's support, Ol-

Major work(s)	Academic appointment(s)	Political/party appointments	Government positions
The Socialist Case, 1937; *Unemployment: The Douglas Jay Report*, 1959; *Socialism in the New Society*, 1962; [and others]	Fellowship, All Souls College, Oxford, 1930–1937 and 1968–1996 [also a journalist: *Times, Economist, Daily Herald*]	MP, 1946–1983	Ministry of Supply, 1940–1943; Board of Trade, 1943–1945, personal assistant to Attlee in Labour government of 1945; economic secretary to the Treasury, 1950–1951; president of Board of Trade, 1964–1967
New Deal for Coal, 1945	Junior Research Fellow, University College, Balliol, 1938; Oxford, full fellow of university college, 1944	Labour's candidate list, 1944	Department of Mines of Board of Trade, 1941; Attlee government/president of Board of Trade, 1945; PM, 1964

lenhauer cofounded the Union of German Socialist Organizations in 1941, providing the SPD with organizational continuity during the war.

The SPD's expert ranks suffered heavy losses. Hilferding went to France, but Vichy officials turned him over to the Nazis, and he died in captivity, probably by suicide.[167] Many German-speaking intellectuals, socialist and otherwise, migrated to the United Kingdom, the United States, and elsewhere. Economics was deeply affected; by one estimate, in the 1930s "[t]he world share of leading economists living in German-speaking countries . . . declined from 15 per cent among the dead to 3 per cent among the living."[168] Some economists remained—for instance, Walter Eucken (1891–1950), at the University of Freiburg—but the Nazis brought the famed "historical school" to an end: the *Archiv für Sozialwissenschaft,* the prestigious journal of the Verein für Sozial-politik (VfS), was shut down.[169]

SPD members who stayed in Hitler's Germany either kept a low pro-file or joined the resistance and suffered the consequences. Deist became a government administrator but was dismissed for "political unreli-ability"; he joined the Nazi Party in 1938 to avoid surveillance and thence pursued a lower-profile career in accounting. Viktor Agartz (1897–1964), a lecturer for the seminar of Free Trade Unions at the University of Cologne before 1933, also went into accounting.[170] Kurt Schumacher (1895–1952), who joined the SPD in the late 1910s while pursuing his doctorate in law and political science, had been a political editor of the *Swabian Tagwacht* in Stuttgart in the 1920s and contributed to a famous speech by the SPD's Otto Wels in the Reichstag session of March 23, 1933, opposing the Enabling Act that brought Hitler to power. Schumacher joined the resistance, but he was imprisoned in concentration camps from 1933 to 1943.[171]

The New Terrain of German Economics, 1920–1940s

Nazi rule altered the whole institutional landscape of German higher education, including economics. In the process it provided a certain impetus for the production of the scientific, apolitical economist.

Here a 1920s generational rebellion within economics, comparable to events in Swedish economics, is significant. The rebellion involved a struggle of younger-generation economists—based, in particular, at the University of Kiel—against the preeminence of the historical economics of the VfS. Leading figures included Alexander Rüstow, Adolph Löwe, Gerhard Colm, Walter Eucken, and Wilhelm Röpke (that is, a mix of liberals and socialists of various stripes). The young economists' efforts first crystallized in interwar discussions of the problem of reparations payments: in 1928, facing off with political elites (including Hilferding) and older-generation, historical school economists, they argued that economic analysis indicated that Germany would have to pay its debts. After the VfS rejected their claims on epistemological grounds, members of the younger generation established a group called "the Ricardians," led by Rüstow. The Ricardians were united in opposition to the VfS and in the commitment to (in Rüstow's words) the "will to social objectivity" (via economic theory and analysis). Objectivity, the Ricardians argued, could foster an economic science that was above politics, bridging the liberal-socialist divide.[172]

The Ricardians scattered, however, in 1933. The socialist economists Eduard Heimann (1889–1967), Adolph Löwe (1893–1995), and Gerhard Colm (supporter of the WTB plan) ended up in New York, at the

New School for Social Research. The liberal economists Alexander Rüstow (1885–1963) and Wilhelm Röpke (1899–1966) went to the University of Istanbul.[173] A Nazi-era holdout remained in Freiburg, centered on Walter Eucken—who, in the 1930s, became an anchor point of a novel body of liberal economic thought, ordoliberalism, which amalgamated legal theory, free market thinking, and Christian ethics into a distinctive concept of the state as the architect of competition and free enterprise (as opposed to a "night watchman"). This distinctive school first announced itself on the eve of Hitler's rise, in two 1932 statements from Rüstow and Eucken.[174]

Meanwhile, at Kiel, a particularly scientistic, mathematical brand of economics informed the training of students and fostered openness to the mathematical logic of Keynes and the British Keynesians.[175] In the early 1930s Kiel was the training site of Karl Schiller (1911–1994), who leaned more toward (liberal) socialism than the ordoliberals but shared ordoliberals' belief in an apolitical, scientific economics.[176]

Last but not least, institutes connected to industry provided a home to statistically oriented economists and economists-in-training, providing sites of connection between economists, business, and officials of occupied Germany's fledgling governing institutions. Notable in this last category was the Institute for Economic Observation of the German Finished Goods Industry in Nuremberg (the Vershofen institute) and, later, the Institute for Industrial Research (IIR), founded in 1942 by Ludwig Erhard (with funding from the Reichsgruppe Industrie).[177] Erhard (1897–1977) had an economics doctorate but could not become a professor; his mentor prevented him from completing his habilitation, possibly due to Erhard's liberal convictions. Erhard was thus an economist by training, sympathetic to the economics of Rüstow and Eucken, but also an in-between figure who straddled "the boundary between the scholarly world and politics" as an adviser to business and public organizations.[178]

An economics profession deeply shaped by the Nazi interregnum—depleted of socialists, strong in its scientific commitments, with important centers in Kiel and Freiburg and linked to industry—provided raw materials as the Allied forces began to build the West German state. Between 1946 and 1948 the American and British occupying authorities drew on economists' familiarity with the German economic landscape—not to mention their contacts with industrialists and business owners—for guidance and assistance. Ludwig Erhard, the ordoliberal-affiliated founding director of the IIR, became the head of the American zone's Council for Economics in 1946.[179] In the same year Viktor Agartz, who shared the British embrace of planning, became the chief of the British Central Office for Economics in Minden. For a brief time Agartz headed the Economics Committee of the Bizone, established in January 1947. In 1948, however, Erhard took Agartz's place.[180] Under Erhard the committee's economist-heavy staff included Eucken, Alfred Müller-Armack, and Karl Schiller, who was by then a full professor and a local SPD administrator in Hamburg.[181]

The occupying authorities thus incorporated German economists into the first institutions of the fledgling West German government be-fore the reinitiation of electoral democracy. In the process they brought Schiller, Erhard, and other economists into working relationships. And, because West German economics had been recentered on scientific objectivity in the turbulent 1930s, when it came to the practice of eco-nomics Erhard-the-ordoliberal and Schiller-the-socialist-Keynesian saw eye to eye.

Erhard's ordoliberalism was, at first, politically orphaned. In 1945 the Christian Democrats (Christliche Demokratische Union, or CDU) in the British occupation zone declared its commitment to a "socialism of Christian responsibility"—which entailed an embrace of economic planning, industrial nationalization, and workers' codetermination rights, as laid out in the CDU's 1947 Ahlen Program.[182] These commitments did not mesh with ordoliberal thinking.[183] Ordoliberal economists' most obvious point of entry into West Germany's new democratic order was the liberal Freie Demokratische Partei (FDP), but it was the smallest of the major parties. For that reason, Erhard reportedly kept his dis-tance.[184] Meanwhile, the SPD, reestablished by Schumacher and others in 1946, made its opposition to ordoliberalism clear in the wake of Erhard's unilateral decision to eliminate price controls in 1948. It was not until 1949, when Erhard finally affiliated with the Christian Demo-crats—who agreed to embrace Erhard's economics in return (albeit uneasily)—that ordoliberal economics acquired a definite party avenue into West German government.[185]

As the 1940s drew to a close the stature of Schiller, then SPD-affiliated but not especially influential, began to rise within the party. This was not a foregone conclusion. In 1946 the SPD, under the leadership of Schumacher and with Agartz as the main SPD economic expert, affirmed its historical grounding in Marxism, calling for socialization in the accustomed vocabulary of class, economic democracy, and public ownership.[186] In 1948, however, Agartz moved to the Economic-Scientific Institute of the trade unions (now the Wirtschafts- und Sozialwissenschaftliches Institut, or WSI; but until 1971 the Wirtschafts-Wissenschaftliches Institut, or WWI), in Düsseldorf.[187] Here it becomes important that the new, national organization of West German trade unions, the Deutsche Gewerkschaftsbund (DGB), was recently established (its founding congress was in October 1949, just after Konrad Adenauer's [1876–1967] election as West Germany's first [CDU] chancellor) and, unlike its predecessor, was non-party-affiliated. In this context struggles within the union movement were linked to those in and over the SPD, but they were not coterminous.[188] And so Agartz's departure left a void. As early as 1948, SPD leadership acknowledged the party's need for a new theoretical vocabulary: in the account of the SPD party official Fritz Erler (1913–1967), the party had a serious "scientific deficit."[189]

At the time, Karl Schiller was a prominent SPD economist who had been on the Economics Committee of the Bizone, was known for his scientific commitments, and was a full professor, a city economics minister (Hamburg), and a parliamentarian.[190] We might note, also, that ordoliberalism was recognized by the DGB and SPD alike as a common foe. The SPD objected to Erhard's policies from the start, and trade unions' recognition of Erhard's ordoliberalism as antagonistic drove the DGB's programmatic revisions in the decades to come.[191] And so, formal separation between the DGB and the SPD notwithstanding, Keynesian economics was recognized by the SPD and trade unionists alike—and especially by the more "rightist" figures among them—as a potential asset in the ordoliberal-dominated years of Adenauer and Erhard.[192]

It was in this context that Schiller, together with Heinrich Deist, became a leading Keynesian within the SPD. By contrast with Agartz's Marxian-inflected thinking and emphases on the impossibility of competitive price-setting and the need for public ownership—which shaped the DGB's 1954 Action Program—Schiller advocated for "indirect" steering through monetary, income, price, and taxation policies, grounded in what was perhaps a singular familiarity with Keynesian economics.[193] Keynesianism became a *de facto* basis of SPD-DGB partnership: Schiller and Deist were, in turn, allied with the Keynesian head of the DGB's economics section, Ludwig Rosenberg (1903–1977), and DGB chief economist Dr. Rolf Wagenführ.[194]

The rise of the SPD economist theoretician also had to do with the fact that, in 1950s West Germany, the taint of Marxism was a significant liability. In the words of the political scientist Kurt Shell, in West Germany "More than anywhere else on the continent . . . Marxism was totally discredited through its identification with Stalinism and the DDR [Deutsche Demokratische Republik] dictatorship."[195] And so it mattered that, in the lead-up to the 1953 election, the SPD enlisted Schiller to aid in the formulation of its Aktionsprogramm, but its Marxist language remained.[196] Predictably, the Christian Democrats successfully used the SPD's Marxist vocabulary against it by painting Marxism as a "road to Moscow" in 1950s campaigns (see, for instance, Figure 4.6). After receiving only 29 percent of the vote in 1953, SPD leadership worried about public perceptions that placed it "far to the left of its actual policies."[197]

After Schumacher's death Erich Ollenhauer, the new SPD chairman, managed a series of programmatic revisions in which Schiller was central, culminating in the 1958 Stuttgart conference and, a year later, the 1959 Bad Godesberg program.[198] In addition to a notable absence of any reference to Marx, Marxism, or socialization, the new program married the "Freiburg imperative" (competition) with the language of Keynesianism. Its famous key phrase, "as much competition as possible, as much planning as necessary," was (and is) widely attributed to Schiller. A few years later, at DGB congresses between 1962 and 1963, the DGB followed suit with a Keynesian program of its own.[199]

A few important features of the SPD's economistic turn are notable here. First, in the account of Harold K. Schellenger Jr., Bad Godesberg was built on a self-conscious shift, orchestrated by SPD leadership, toward academics and away from party "functionaries." In other words, Bad Godesberg signaled a definite move toward a more academically

Figure 4.6. "All Marxist Paths Lead to Moscow." CDU election poster, 1953.
Reproduction source: German History in Documents and Images (GHDI).
© Bildarchiv Preußischer Kulturbesitz.

dependent SPD. This is significant partly because academics were not
dominant forces in the SPD executive at the time: in 1958 only two of
the executive's eleven paid members, and fourteen of forty-four unpaid
members, had doctoral degrees; only three "were active in academic or
research vocations." But the commission in charge of programmatic revision, appointed in 1955 by the party executive, was academic-heavy:
eleven of its twenty-nine members "were academics of some kind."[200]
This is also notable in light of the antipathies between the SPD and the

VfS before the Third Reich. The SPD's economistic turn can also be read as an expression of a *de facto* SPD-DGB alliance built, specifically, on the shared Keynesian orientations of the "right" factions of both organizations.

Last but not least, we should note that the specifically Keynesian economism of Bad Godesberg did not accord with the dominant economics of West Germany at that time, which remained ordoliberal—a state of affairs that began to change around 1962, when Keynesian demand management was becoming synonymous with modern economics cross-nationally and especially, as we will see in the next chapter, in the United States. The effect of this was to imbue the SPD's DGB-allied, Keynesian-economistic leftism, and the party experts who ported it, with a new authority.

Revisiting the "End of Ideology"

The SPD's move away from Marxism, together with developments elsewhere, has been read as symptomatic of an "end of ideology" rooted in the growth of the middle class, mass consumerism, and the decline of the industrial working classes.[201] But, setting aside the problem of defining what is and is not "ideology," this account skips over goings-on inside the socialist, laborite, and social democratic parties to which end-of-ideology thinkers often referred. More importantly, the end of ideology account fails to acknowledge that, in the 1950s, a theoretical language with its own ideological tinge (in the eyes of its critics) *replaced* Marxist terminology.

Surely changing demographics fed into the SPD's programmatic revision, but they did not determine, automatically, a turn to Keynesian economics. Nor could one argue that the Keynesianism of Bad Godesberg was a safe political bet, the only game in town, or a by-product of union influence. Preempted by the public stature of the Freiburg School, Keynesianism was never the dominant orthodoxy of German economics. The independence and strict monetary policies of the Bundesbank, built on ordoliberal thinking, constrained the economic policy options of any party-in-government.[202] Last but not least, as we have seen, the DGB's programmatic turn to Keynesianism, and against Marxian language, followed Bad Godesberg rather than preceding it.[203]

In part, the SPD's embrace of a Keynesian vocabulary was symptomatic of the growing postwar influence of economists in many Western countries, including West Germany—an influence signaled, in the first place, by the marriage of ordoliberal economics and the Christian Democrats. The SPD's Keynesian turn was also linked to the problem of having associations with Marx in the age of Stalin. This was an electoral problem, but it was also linked, in turn, with intraparty struggles: SPD party officials' office-seeking priorities and economics-friendliness ran up against the more radical tendencies of younger party members. Similar struggles are traceable within the DGB. The turn to academics, and specifically Keynesians, was thus inextricable from intraparty power struggles. Schiller himself later noted that academic involvement in the making of Bad Godesberg was a strategic tactic in pursuit of "ideological reform"—that is, a means to the abandonment of Marxism and the radical elements who favored it.[204]

In this light, one problem with understanding Bad Godesberg as an end of ideology is that it accepts a historically specific, and contested, notion of technified liberal economics as nonideological, when in fact its ideological status was contested. Indeed, some inside party ranks complained that the technical language of competition, planning, and full employment was merely ideology of a different sort. In the words of one dissenter, it was "liberal ballast"; others argued that the abandonment of socialization was capitulation to "the whimsies of bourgeois sociology and economics."[205] Some voiced the suspicion that the language of Keynesianism masked a shift in the party's electoral strategy that involved the subordination of its principles to public opinion for the sake of winning, as opposed to using campaigns to advance an ongoing project of education and socialization into a socialist way of seeing the world.[206] The SPD's Keynesianism, however, was a way of seeing, made possible by a certain configuration of political and academic institutions and borne by a certain kind of party expert—to which we now turn.

The World of, and by, the SPD Economist Theoretician

If the SAP economist theoretician was notable for his anchoring in SAP-affiliated trade unions, and the Labour economist theoretician for his prominence in the party executive and imbrication with intraparty opposition, Schiller was notable for his identification with a scientized profession in which Keynesianism was an economics of the center-left that only briefly achieved the status of orthodoxy. In the 1960s it became possible, albeit briefly, to be a *scientific* West German Keynesian economist, as opposed to a partisan, ideological, SPD- or trade union–affiliated Keynesian economist. In this context the "end of ideology" referred to the end of the SPD's Marxian-inflected socialism, but it did not mean the end of theoretically grounded mainstream leftism.

The rise of Karl Schiller and others like him was thus symptomatic of a peculiar moment in (West) German history in which Keynesian economics, for a time, achieved a semi-nonpartisan public standing. And yet, at the same time, German economists often had more or less implicit partisan leanings. Here we might consider West Germany's major economic research institutes—which were (and remain) important intermediaries between the academy, government, and politics. These include the Berlin-based Deutsches Institut für Wirtschaftsforschung, or DIW Berlin (originally the Institute for Business Cycle Research), first established in 1925; the IFO-Institut, established in 1914; the Hamburgischen Welt-Wirtschafts Archiv (HWWA), established in 1908; the RWI-Leibniz Institute for Economic Research, formerly the Rheinisch-Westfälisches Institut für Wirtschaftsforschung (RWI), established in 1926; and the Institut für Weltwirtschaft (IfW), established in 1914. Focusing on the leadership of DIW Berlin, for instance, one finds that its president from 1945 to 1968, Prof. Dr. Ferdinand Friedensburg (1886–1972), was also a cofounder of the CDU.[207] But the DIW president from 1968 to January 1974, Dr. Klaus-Dieter Arndt (1927–1974), was an SPD member since 1946, an SPD parliamentarian, and an important figure in the Federal Ministry of Economics under Schiller. Upon his early death in 1974, Arndt was remembered for both his SPD loyalties and his strong self-identification as a professional economist.[208]

The peculiarity of the moment can also be seen in the making of the Council of Economic Experts (Sachverständigenrat, or SVR), established by the Bundestag in 1962, based on a curious convergence between Erhard, the trade unions (which demanded "modern" economic management via an "independent body of experts"), and Social Democrats, including Schiller.[209] On the one hand, Erhard reportedly favored an institutionalized economics advisory board in the hope that it might have a depoliticizing effect, making "objective" information available to the public and to the government—although he worried that it could become a lever for Keynesian management that "was not compatible with the market economy."[210] Erhard himself proposed, in 1958, a committee of experts on social and economic policy, but he was not able to get the government's or his own party's endorsement.[211] By this time Schiller was also a public advocate of advancing economics' role in West German policy-making: a 1956 report from the Ministry of Economics' Advisory Council, and a follow-up article by Schiller in *Zeit*, called for the establishment of a scientific council.[212] Finally, with Erhard as chancellor, the SVR—which was made up of five economists, one nominated in consultation with the trade unions and another in consultation with employers—first met in 1963.

The SVR's formal independence from parties-in-government contrasted, for instance, with the American Council of Economic Advisers (CEA, established 1946).[213] And yet, at the same time, the SVR's origins were deeply political—a legacy that left a definite imprint on the composition of its appointees. Indeed, for Erhard a body like the SVR could serve a partisan purpose: "the hope was that economists' expert analyses would . . . undercut the critiques of the Left" in light of the SPD's Keynesian turn in Bad Godesberg.[214] And, in a sign of the times, most SVR members' "views remained close to those of the unions and the SPD until the late 1960s."[215]

It was in this context that Schiller came to new prominence as the SPD senator for economics in West Berlin, having been appointed by the city's young mayor, Willy Brandt (1913–1992). In the critical period after the 1961 construction of the Berlin Wall, Brandt and Schiller attracted international attention for their skillful management of the city's economy. After Deist, the head of the SPD Economic Policy Committee, died in 1964, Schiller took his place; by 1965 Schiller was both a member of the Bundestag and the economics spokesman for the SPD Fraktion. With the party chairmanship of Willy Brandt the SPD's full embrace of professional economics, and of the economist theoretician, was complete.

When the SPD joined the coalition government in 1966 Schiller, trailed by a "team of eggheads," became minister of economics and

then, also, of finance (1971). The "eggheads" included Johann Schöll-
horn, an economics doctorate (1922) who had worked under Müller-
Armack and Erhard; Christian Schlecht, from Freiburg (doctorate
1925); and Wilhelm Edmund (economics doctorate, 1929). Ever focused
on careful, clear, technical communication, Schiller also brought with
him two economics graduate students from Munich, Albrecht Müller
and Ulrich Pfeiffer, as "ghostwriters."[216] West Germany then famously
embarked on its first (and only) experiment with an explicitly Keynesian
economic program: the 1967 Stability and Growth Law. Characteristically for the economist theoretician, Schiller viewed the law as inseparable from "concerted action," which involved regular engagement and
close cooperation with representatives of labor and employers.[217]

CONCLUSIONS

Left parties' move away from budgetary orthodoxy and turn to professional economics was not simply an effect of revelatory new ideas or
the failures of old ones, nor is it accurately summarized as an end of
ideology. Rather, it expressed a whole reconfiguration of the relationship between economics and left parties that was initiated in a Polanyian
moment, and was characterized by a deepening intersection of left parties and professional economists. The result was a cross-national pattern
in which two different sorts of fields, one cultural (professional economics) and one political (left parties), depended on, and shaped, each
other. This interdependence was embodied by the figure of the economist theoretician.

In the next chapter we trace the American Democratic Party's turn
to economistic leftism—a story that is inextricably linked to the process by which the Democratic Party became "left."

CHAPTER FIVE

Economistic Leftism, American-Style— or, Making the Democrats "Left"

> Having no children of his own, he made Harvard, the
> Democratic Party, Stevenson and Kennedy, New England, and
> his students part of his extended family.
>
> —Paul Samuelson, 1975, describing Seymour Harris

F OR SOME READERS the American Democratic Party's appearance in a book on left parties might seem odd. The Democratic Party was born of neither socialism nor industrial labor movements; from a European perspective, it has never been "left." And yet by 1960 the Democratic Party spoke in an economistic language that was very similar to that of the SAP, the SPD, and the Labour Party. This raises two questions. One is why the Democrats spoke in an *economistic* language; the other is why a party that was not born left spoke a *leftist* language of any sort. Stated differently, the question in the American case is not just how the Democrats developed their own economistic language but also how the party became, comparatively and in public perception, "left."

A glimmer of the answer appears in the posthumous description of the economist Seymour Harris, above, by his colleague Paul Samuelson. In Samuelson's description Harris appears as a man straddling two worlds: academic and political, Harvard economics and the Democratic Party. Harris's very existence signals that the two worlds had a certain connection. The fact that Harris was influential in New Deal and Democratic circles signals that the connection was important. We have seen in the previous chapter how a very similar connection developed between the Labour Party, the SAP, the SPD, and the economics professions in their respective countries, and how that shaped the policies and programmatic language of those parties. In other words, by about 1960 one finds a pattern of institutional relationships, an interdependence, between parties and economics, embodied in national varieties of an essentially similar figure who spoke in a particular political vocabulary: the economist theoretician.

In the United States, the formation of the economist theoretician originated in processes that are by now familiar. From the 1930s forward the Democratic Party extended its reach into universities and academic professions, and professional economists became more involved with the Democratic National Committee (DNC), Democratic campaigns, and the formulation of Democratic programs and policies. The thing that stands out here is that, in the absence of a formal, bureaucratized political party, the organizational vehicles that made the Democratic-economics tie an enduring one were different: they took the form of more or less formalized institutions in between the DNC, Democratic campaigns, and economics' academic centers—especially in the Northeast. In the end, thanks to these intermediary institutions, Seymour Harris and figures like him became taken-for-granted features of a *de facto* liberal and Democratic landscape—even though, historically speaking, the Democratic economist theoretician was actually a novelty.

An important starting point in the Democrats' economistic turn was Franklin D. Roosevelt's (FDR) 1932 presidential candidacy. FDR entered the White House a bearer of balanced budget orthodoxy but, famously, left a Keynesian—or something close to it. This story is well told, but its tellers tend to focus on policy and the state, not on political parties. The economist Herbert Stein and the sociologist Margaret Weir, for instance, give careful accounts of how some New Deal advisers formed a "pro-spending network" in the 1930s and then worked to refashion FDR's budgetary thinking in the wake of the 1937 recession.[1] Existing accounts of this period and the ensuing construction of the Keynesian era in the United States, however, generally focus on the policy effects of ideas, expertise, and government agencies. Current sociological research on economics' influence, meanwhile, highlights that it is "mediated by local circumstances and meso-level social structures," focusing on economics' "broad professional authority," its "role in the cognitive

infrastructure of policymaking," and "the institutional position of economists in government."[2] The literatures on economics, politics and
policy-making attend very little to parties, the structure of party-expert
relations, and the trajectories and positions of party experts.

My focus, by contrast, is the party. More specifically, it is the evolution of Democratic party-expert relations before, during, and after the
rise of the New Deal pro-spenders. Building on the analyses of Stein,
Weir, and others, I use memoirs, oral histories, biographies, and other
materials to look at the trajectories of experts in and around Democratic presidential candidates and administrations through time. My
aim is to understand not only when and how the Democrats turned to
Keynesian economics (and econom*ists*)—that is, to explain the rise of
the Democratic economist theoretician—but also how a party that was
not left before the 1930s came to speak a recognizably left, economistic
language.

The chapter proceeds as follows. I first outline some of the oddities
of American politics and parties, which create an apples-and-oranges
problem if one seeks to compare the Democratic Party with its European counterparts. I then offer a way to deal with the problem: the loose
structure of the major American parties calls for attention to teams or
networks of players around politicians, rather than the occupants of
official party positions. Using this approach, I trace party-expert networks around Democratic presidents and presidential candidates (FDR,
Harry Truman, Adlai Stevenson, John F. Kennedy [JFK]) through four distinctive periods. Focusing on FDR, the first period is between the 1920s
and the late 1930s, when the party began to reach into economics and
vice versa. A second phase, still in FDR's time, was the emergence of
more institutionalized ties between the federal state, the national Democratic Party, and New England–centered professional economics between 1939 and 1946. These ties enabled the Democratic economist
theoretician to move seamlessly between politics and academe. The third
period, between 1946 and 1960, centers on Truman, the failed candi-
dacies of Adlai Stevenson, and finally JFK. This period featured a shift
in the economist theoretician's world from the state to new intermediary institutions between academe and the Democratic Party party,
conditioned by FDR's death, postwar demobilization, and the Democrats'
loss of the presidency. During this time Keynesian academic economists

became closely involved with the Democratic National Committee (DNC), Democratic campaigns, and the education and liberalization (in the New Deal Democratic sense) of presidential candidates. This positioning made possible a fourth period, starting around 1960, in which Democratic economist theoreticians moved seamlessly back into the executive during JFK's presidency.

Ultimately, I show that the making of American economistic leftism had certain similarities to Western European dynamics—in particular, it was driven by the coincidence of a Polanyian moment, intergenerational rebellion in professional economics, and growing political demands for authoritative economic expertise. But the specificity of American parties generated a distinctive institutional pattern: the formation of intermediary institutions through which, in the absence of a formal, centralized party organization, connections between the Democratic Party and academic economics were cultivated and sustained during Republican administrations and the early Cold War.

SPECIFICITIES OF THE AMERICAN CASE

In 1920 there was no such thing as a Democratic theoretician comparable with, say, Rudolf Hilferding. This had to do with the peculiar organization of American parties and political institutions. American political language was also highly specific: around 1920 the opposition between the major American parties had little to do with the categories "left" and "right." And so, while the development of American social sciences had transatlantic comparabilities, American political development before the 1930s was distinctive.

American Economics-Party Relationships
before the 1930s

As elsewhere, the American social sciences started to become modern academic professions in the late 1800s. The American Social Science Association (ASSA) was established in 1865, and it then split off in the mid-1880s into the American Historical Association (AHA, 1884) and the American Economic Association (AEA, 1885).[3] The rationalizing social sciences and their brethren (law, history) fueled the expansion of a new American intelligentsia that was politically engaged but not party-aligned. If anything, it was *antiparty*. New progressive professionals made a case for the primacy of expertise, professionalism, and objectivity over patronage and party government.

This distancing from parties can be seen in the drift of journalism at the time. Historically partisan newspapers, for instance, were shifting toward independence. A notable instance was the historically Republican *New York Times,* which became officially nonpartisan in 1896.[4] Meanwhile, a burgeoning field of magazines, including the *Atlantic Monthly, Century, Forum, Harper's Weekly,* and the *Nation,* marked out the nonparty terrain of progressives. When the *New Republic* was established in 1914, it became a premier outlet for the new American progressive and a platform for the advocacy of expertise and professionalism in government and policy-making.[5]

Economics, in particular, distanced itself from partisan involvements. As the sociologist Marion Fourcade has shown, economics tended to present itself as a producer of useful, apolitical, scientific knowledge for consumption by philanthropies, business, and the state.[6] In the 1910s and 1920s economics made important inroads into the federal state with the establishment of the Federal Reserve in 1913, the Treasury-based Bureau of the Budget (BOB) in 1921, and, in 1922, the Department of Agriculture's Bureau of Agricultural Economics (BAE).[7] The BAE became the first federal office with designated positions for credential-bearing economists. Other economics-friendly government outposts followed, especially in the Departments of Commerce (which Herbert Hoover did much to expand) and Labor.[8] The National Bureau of Economic Research (NBER), established in New York City in 1920, fortified emerging professional circuits between economics and government agencies.

But for the most part economists' professional reach did not extend into the major parties. A notable exception was the Progressive Party in Wisconsin, which had close ties with the institutionalist economist John Commons. Nationally, however, before the 1930s there was no such thing as a campaign economist or a specifically Democratic (or Republican) economics.

American Politics

Early twentieth-century American political life was also distinctive because it featured a party-political language that was heavy on rights but indifferent to left-right distinctions. The term "left," originating in revolutionary France and becoming a common referent in the emergent worlds of parties in mid- to late nineteenth-century Europe, had no particular relevance to Democratic-Republican distinctions before the 1930s.

The irrelevance of left-right distinctions can be seen both in historical newspapers and in politicians' rhetoric. In the *New York Times* between the 1850s and the 1920s phrases using "left" and "right" often referred to directions of movement, sides of the body, military conflict and strategy, sport (especially boxing and football), or European politics, but they did not refer to parties or party oppositions.[9] In American presidency documents from the 1800s through the 1930s—platforms, addresses, press conferences, and other documents—the term "right" appears mainly in the sense of right versus wrong or with reference to legal or human rights; "left" appears mainly in the sense of being left out, left on one's own, or left behind. The phrase "the left" usually referenced a position in physical space, not the political spectrum.[10]

These differences point toward an apples-and-oranges problem that complicates the cross-Atlantic comparison of parties. As Max Weber once observed, turn-of-the-century Democratic and Republican parties were not born as centralized, "ideological" mass organizations on the European model (or, more specifically, the model of the prototypical SPD).[11] Then, as now, American parties were organizationally distinct: more decentralized, permeable and non-membership-driven. Before the late 1900s they were grounded more in state and local level, as opposed to national level, organizations: the Democratic and Republican National Committees, or DNC and RNC, were established in 1848 and 1854, respectively, but were not capable of the kind of centralized control that might have rendered them comparable to European party executives. Another marker of American parties' distinctiveness is the nonexistence of party platforms in presidential politics until 1840, even though mass parties had been around since the 1790s (or earlier, depending on whom one asks).[12] The major U.S. parties in the nineteenth and early twentieth centuries spoke a shared language of liberalism, rights, and freedoms.

And, of course, no major American party was ever explicitly socialist. In the late 1800s the term "socialism," alongside "communism," made appearances in Republican and Democratic rhetoric mainly so candidates could establish what they were *not*.[13] As far as class affiliations, the Democratic Party had populist tendencies and made labor appeals in the 1800s and early 1900s, but organized labor was not formally party-allied—a fact that has inspired many inquiries into the question of why a European-style left party "never happened here."[14]

A party that is not built on theory does not invest in the production of theories, or indeed of theor*ists*. The Republican and Democratic parties probably were not organizationally capable of producing a party theoretician in any case. The major American parties are now, as then, fluid, factional, and weakly bounded. Officially, they do not have powerful national executives, dues-paying memberships, or annual programmatic conventions; what they have instead, intermittently, are nonparty associations and organizations that function, more or less, as parties-within-parties. The DNC and RNC are essentially agencies for campaigning, candidate sponsorship, and voter mobilization; they have never been independent bureaucracies capable of directing Democratic policy or decisively policing party ranks.[15]

A consequence is that Hilferding, Snowden, and Thorsson had no clear counterpart in the United States around 1920. In the 1910s and 1920s Carter Glass of Virginia (1858–1946)—a Democratic newspaperman-turned-state-senator in 1899, a U.S. representative in 1902, and Treasury secretary from 1918 to 1920 under President Woodrow Wilson—was perhaps the closest approximation to a Democratic Party theoretician. Historically, U.S. Treasury secretaries had backgrounds in business and finance, but Glass was a printer's apprentice at age thirteen and then a reporter for the *Lynchburg Daily News*. On social and civil rights Glass was no progressive (to say the least); in economics, he was largely self-taught. He nonetheless famously helped to develop and pass the Federal Reserve Act in 1913 and, two decades later, the Glass-Steagall Act, or the Banking Act of 1933. But, while

Glass was very influential in national economic policy, he had no bureaucratically protected claim to expert authority in the national Democratic Party. There was no office that would have made this possible.

Why Are American Parties Different?

All this might prompt a question: why are American parties so different? One argument centers on the historical development of parties and states, in which either parties drove state formation or *vice versa*.[16]

In Western Europe, states drove party formation. European parties organized in the image of the strong, centralized, pre-democratic European states that were the main objects of party struggles. When out of office they organize themselves in a state-like format, forming formal or *de facto* shadow cabinets of ministers-in-waiting. An effect is that, just as one can clearly identify who is the Swedish or German government's minister of finance, one can also identify who in a major party out-of-government is its likely finance-minister-to-be.[17]

In the United States, by contrast, parties *drove* national state formation. Up to the turn of the twentieth century the federal government was what the historian Stephen Skowronek terms a "party state": a relatively small entity dominated by two mass patronage parties.[18] By the 1920s a more professionalized, administrative, nonparty national government had taken shape, thanks partly to the efforts of progressive reformers.[19] But the Democratic and Republican parties remained dominated by patronage and factional politics, were centered more in states and localities than in Washington, D.C., and did not organize themselves as national governments-in-waiting.

And so, while the U.S. government has a national office that approximates the European-style position of finance minister (the secretary of the Treasury), the major American *parties* have no organizational position in which a Republican or Democratic Treasury-secretary-to-be awaits his or her turn in government. To be sure, party experts could be found in the 1920s and 1930s—for instance, Democratic politicians who made special claims to expertise on monetary, budgetary, or financial matters. But, lacking any executive position inside the national party through which they could institutionalize their expert claims, they had no lock on the ability to define what was, and was not, authoritative Democratic (or Republican) economic knowledge.

DEALING WITH AMERICAN SPECIFICITIES:
THE METAPHOR OF THE GAME

How should one approach the analysis of party-expert relations in the Democratic case, then? Here the metaphor of the game, and especially the distinction between *players and positions,* is helpful.[20]

Parties, like all organizations, are arenas of struggle and collaboration. In a tightly organized, hierarchical European party, the person who aims to secure influence over the party's programmatic direction has a definite target: the party executive. From the executive one acquires, by virtue of powers invested in the office, considerable authority over the party's policies and practices.[21] If the party wins its way into government and our party official becomes a minister, his or her authority is enhanced. This was the trajectory of Thorsson, Snowden, and Hilferding in the 1920s and of Wigforss, Dalton, and Schiller after them. In these cases, particular individuals can be used as analytical starting points because of the structural similarities of their formal positions in their respective parties.

In the more decentered Democratic Party, however, there is no official position to take as a starting point. Except for the DNC, which does not set policy, there is no Democratic executive, separate from politicians-in-office, with programmatic authority. No player secures uncontestable directive or veto authority over the party's goals and positions; the structure of the game remains relatively fluid. In this situation, one has to focus on *networks of players.*

Thinking this way allows for a comparison that does not proceed as if all parties are the same. The American Democratic and Republican parties are not structured such that one can grasp party-expert relations by starting with officials inside parties who are designated as Treasury-secretaries-to-be—there is no such thing. But presidential candidates and sitting presidents can be treated as the centers of gravity of party-expert networks, and these networks can be traced over time. This is the approach adopted here.

PHASE ONE: THE FORMATION OF THE PARTY-ECONOMICS RELATIONSHIP, 1920s–1930s

The analysis begins with the network around FDR during his presidential campaign of 1932, with an eye to understanding, especially, how this network fed into the making of the pro-spenders inside the New Deal state. From there I turn to party-expert relations' development after 1938, centered on the persons of Harry Truman, Adlai Stevenson, and JFK.

FDR and the Coalescence of the Pro-Spenders, 1920s–1938

Figures forming the 1930s "pro-spending network," so termed by Margaret Weir, included heads of major New Deal agencies (Harry Hopkins of the Works Progress Administration [WPA], Harold Ickes of the Public Works Administration [PWA], Rexford Tugwell of the Federal Emergency Relief Administration [FERA], economists and statisticians providing data and technical support [Leon Keyserling at the Agricultural Adjustment Administration (AAA), Leon Henderson at the National Recovery Administration (NRA)], and administrators at the Federal Reserve [Mariner Eccles, Lauchlin Currie]). In terms of professional backgrounds, they bridged many worlds: of progressive reformism and social work, law and economics, business and finance, government and administration.

How did the pro-spenders come together? Two institutional paths stand out. One ran between the New York state Democratic Party—specifically, FDR's 1932 political campaign—and the White House. Another ran between professional economics and state and federal governments.

The First Path: FDR's 1932 Campaign and the White House

The first path begins with a search for new expertise in the uncertain years of the Great Depression. More specifically, it begins with a decision by FDR's campaign manager, a Columbia-educated lawyer named Samuel I. Rosenman (1896–1973), to recruit academics in the hope that they could help the campaign address the novel problems of the Depression.[22] Rosenman's recruitment of academics, largely from Columbia, was unconventional; FDR agreed on the condition that academic recruits to the campaign were kept under wraps.[23]

The resulting "brains trust"—a term coined by the *New York Times* reporter James Kieran that evolved into the (capitalized, singular) "Brain Trust"[24]—was heavy on prominent Columbia law professors, including Raymond Moley (1886–1975) and Adolph Berle Jr. (1895–1971). Berle, an accomplished legal and economic scholar with ties to Woodrow Wilson, was then emerging as an influential critic of the structure of ownership of modern corporations—a reputation that was consolidated with the 1932 publication of *The Modern Corporation and Private Property*, coauthored with Gardiner Means.[25]

The Brain Trust also featured a singular Columbia economist, Rexford Tugwell (1891–1979). Tugwell was an institutionalist, a now-minor contingent of the economics profession with strongly progressive inclinations that was at its peak influence in the interwar years.[26] Tugwell's fellow institutionalists included John Commons (1862–1945) at the University of Wisconsin, a labor-friendly Progressive who, as a close adviser to the Progressive Wisconsin governor Robert La Follette, helped to originate the so-called "Wisconsin Idea"—that is, a conception of the state of Wisconsin as "a laboratory for wise experimental legislation aiming to secure the social and political development of the people as a whole."[27] Other contemporaries, also at Columbia, were Wesley C. Mitchell (1874–1948) and John M. Clark (1884–1963).[28] The institutionalists were advocates of planning and direct government intervention to boost consumption, but they had no particular theory of deficit spending as a tool of macroeconomic management.[29] In other words, they were not "Keynesians"—a term that, four years prior to the publication of Keynes's *General Theory*, had no definite meaning.

Tugwell was among the few Brain Trusters who transitioned into the New Deal government. After FDR's March 1933 inauguration, Tugwell became assistant secretary, then undersecretary, of agriculture.[30] (This was perhaps due to Tugwell's expertise in agricultural economics, which by that time had a long-standing professional outpost in the Department of Agriculture.) Tugwell later directed a unit of the Federal Emergency Relief Administration (FERA), an agency initially created by

Herbert Hoover in 1932 that was expanded and given more authority with the Federal Emergency Relief Act of May 1933. Thus situated, Tugwell became an important node in the making of the pro-spending network.

The Second Path: Professional Economics
and State and Federal Governments

The backdrop to Tugwell's arrival in Washington was a deepening connection between economics and government agencies. Labor unrest and factory accidents fueled mounting public concern and new government demands for reliable information. The 1911 fire at the Triangle Shirtwaist Factory in New York City, which killed 146 people, drew a great deal of public attention. The fire focused the attention of reformers, statisticians and economists, policy-makers, labor leaders, and business elites alike on the need for reliable statistics that could inform matters of policy and public concern. FDR had just become a New York state senator, in 1910.

. The 1911 fire was especially significant for economics. In its aftermath the New York legislature established the Factory Investigating Commission, which focused on the production of detailed information on factory conditions. The commission brought together state legislators (Al Smith and Robert Wagner) with social reformers (Frances Perkins), lawyers, labor arbitrators, statisticians, and experts of various sorts. As such, it was a nexus through which figures of varying political leanings, bearing different sorts of resources—expertise, political power, financial means—forged connections.

One such connection, between two expert witnesses named Malcolm Rorty and Nahum Stone, was the kernel of what later became the National Bureau of Economic Research (NBER). Rorty was a politically moderate engineer at the American Telephone and Telegraph Company and had built a professional reputation as a statistician with a 1903 memo on the application of probability theory to traffic control.[31] Stone was a labor- and socialist-friendly economist and former wage dispute arbitrator and governmental adviser, who reportedly took "the trouble, when he was young, to translate Karl Marx's *Critique of Political Economy.*"[32] They disagreed politically, but would meet again

via the New York City Mayor's Unemployment Committee. In spite of
Rorty's opinion of Stone as a "dangerous radical," he sought Stone out
after reading a fair-minded, critical review of an early work on national
income that Stone authored for the *Intercollegiate Socialist*.[33] The two
began a discussion about the possibility of a new research center that
would produce reliable, objective data on the distribution of national
income.[34]

The NBER's foundational aim was the construction of national income accounts. At the time, figures of many political persuasions agreed
that reliable, objective national accounts were a much-needed statistical
resource. Stone insisted that objectivity required an organization composed of "well-known economists representing every school of economic thought from extreme conservative to extreme radical who
should associate with them representatives of all important organized
interests in the country: financial, industrial, agricultural, labor, etc."[35]

In 1917 Rorty sought out three prestigious economists to aid the effort: Edwin Gay (of the Harvard School of Business and an associate of
the Rockefeller Foundation, established in 1914), Wesley C. Mitchell
(who would become AEA president in 1924), and John Commons (then
the AEA president). These three, with Stone and Rorty, a banker (George
Roberts, National City Bank), a statistician (Allyn Young, Cornell), a
Yale-based government adviser (Thomas Adams), and a labor journalist
(John P. Frey), formed a committee in June 1917 to define the new
organization. With the final impetus of World War I, during which inadequate information hampered the mobilization effort, the Commonwealth Fund got the project off the ground with a 1919 contribution of
$24,000.[36]

The NBER came to life in January 1920 in New York City, with Gay
as president and Mitchell as research director.[37] Its nineteen-member
board of directors was politically inclusive, but eschewed representation
from the Treasury or Federal Reserve. The board included AEA and
American Statistical Association (ASA) representatives, as well as
economists linked to Yale, Harvard, and the universities of Chicago,
Wisconsin, and Pennsylvania.

The NBER served, in part, as a *de facto* government research agency.
Among the NBER's first major projects was a study of employment
fluctuations initiated in 1921, at the request of Herbert Hoover (then

the secretary of commerce). To do the project the NBER enlisted the aid of the Russell Sage Foundation, the American Association for Labor Legislation, and the Bureau of Railway Economics.[38] Meanwhile, NBER researchers also pursued the construction of national income accounts. In 1922, with the help of a Columbia economics student named Simon Kuznets (1901–1985), a Russian immigrant, the NBER published its first complete series.[39] In the process, the NBER connected Washington to academic economic departments and research foundations.

As a cross-channel between government and economics, the NBER was part of the institutional terrain on which the New Deal administration was built. By the time Tugwell was recruited into the Brain Trust, economists, economists-in-training, and government agencies were ever more enmeshed with each other. This was true, especially, for economics departments in the Northeast. Economics' connection to the federal state strengthened in 1931, when the U.S. Senate passed a resolution calling for an official series of national income statistics. Soon after Simon Kuznets—who was by then teaching part-time at the University of Pennsylvania—was recruited to the U.S. Department of Commerce to head its new research initiative.[40]

Ties between the economics profession and the federal state provided a fertile recruiting ground from which pro-spenders, including Tugwell, were pulled in the New Deal administration. Inside professional economics, there was also a push: the discipline was becoming increasingly attractive for those concerned with the major issues of the day (unrest, unemployment, depression), but younger recruits also often found that economics professors were unwilling to countenance deviations from gold standard orthodoxies.

Coalescence of the Pro-Spenders

The pro-spenders' coalescence began in earnest when, in the fall of 1933, a short-lived recovery became a first "Roosevelt recession." In this context, budgetary struggles inside the administration intensified.[41]

At the time, presidential advisory channels ran mainly through departments. The executive office was relatively small, hovering at around one hundred full-time staff right up to World War II and consisting of a single unit.[42] Inside the Treasury, Henry Morgenthau Jr. (1891–1967) and Lewis Douglas (1894–1974), FDR's director of the Bureau of the Budget, were powerful voices of budgetary moderation. Academic economists in the Treasury, including Jacob Viner (University of Chicago) and James Harvey Rogers (Yale), were either equivocal on spending (Viner) or, in Rogers's case, a nonorthodox voice in the wilderness.[43] Morgenthau's and Lewis's conservatism was in-line with "the widely accepted view of professional economists before the Depression" and FDR's personal positions.[44] Spending advocates in other branches of the administration, especially Harry Hopkins (head of the Works Progress Administration [WPA]) and Harold Ickes (secretary of the Interior and head of the Public Works Administration [PWA]), were not effective counterweights. As heads of special New Deal agencies whose positions would clearly benefit from increased spending, they were prone to accusations of "special pleading" and "sensitive to the charge of loose spending."[45]

The federal government, however, lacked a comprehensive civil service capable of blocking new appointees. No administrative barrier preempted the pro-spenders' recruitment of like-minded people.[46] This is where Tugwell, his connection to FDR, and his grounding in a profession that was becoming a *de facto* research arm of the federal state, became most consequential.

The Utah-based businessman Mariner Eccles (1890–1977), whom Weir identifies as an especially important pro-spender, was a Tugwell recruit.[47] The two first crossed paths via a chance encounter with Stuart Chase (1888–1985), who was then "a popular writer on economics" and an originator of the term "New Deal." Chase became acquainted with Eccles after hearing him give a speech in Utah.[48] Eccles, who never went to college and had no formal training in economics, nonetheless embraced theories of underconsumption then associated with William Foster and Waddill Catchings. In Stein's account, "Tugwell and his associates were delighted to find a *banker* with these views, and decided that he must have a place in Washington."[49]

Via Tugwell, Eccles entered into the pro-spenders' network first and the federal administration second. In November 1933 Eccles attended a dinner that included Tugwell, Henry Wallace (secretary of agriculture), Mordecai Ezekiel (1899–1974; economic adviser to Wallace), Hopkins, Jerome Frank (of the Agricultural Adjustment Administration, or AAA), and others, at the then-new Shoreham Hotel in Washington,

D.C.[50] Their conversation centered on the development of "arguments on how a planned policy of adequate deficit financing could serve the humanitarian objective" while also ending the depression, ultimately balancing the budget via "increased production and employment."[51] In 1934 Eccles joined the New Deal administration as Morgenthau's assistant, having been appointed by FDR on Tugwell's reference.[52] Thus embedded inside the federal administration, Eccles became FDR's 1934 nominee as governor of the Federal Reserve, extending the pro-spending network-in-the-making into the central bank.

The trajectory of another pro-spender, Leon Keyserling (1908–1987), also entered Tugwell's orbit. Born in Charleston, South Carolina, the son of a successful agricultural producer, businessman, and local politician, Keyserling attended Columbia University and studied economics starting in 1924. Keyserling first met Tugwell as a Columbia economics undergraduate. After pursuing a law degree from Harvard (1931), Keyserling returned to Columbia to pursue a PhD in economics, working under Tugwell.[53] When Tugwell moved into the New Deal administration, Keyserling was soon to follow: he first went to D.C. to work on a short-term basis as an attorney in the AAA.[54] As a legislative aide to Senator Robert Wagner (D-NY) from 1933 to 1937 he helped to draft a $3.3 billion public works bill: the National Industrial Recovery Act's (1934) wage and collective bargaining sections; "portions of the Amendment to the National Housing Act (the Federal Housing Administration) in 1934–1935; portions of the Social Security Act and the National Labor Relations Act [NLRA] (the Wagner Act) in 1935; and the US Housing Act in 1937."[55]

Some pro-spenders came to D.C. via FDR's New York–based party network, if not necessarily via Tugwell. Mordecai Ezekiel, like Tugwell, entered the administration via FDR's 1932 campaign.[56] Hopkins, who had a background in social work, entered the New Deal state via a professional connection to FDR: under FDR's governorship Hopkins was head of New York's Temporary Emergency Relief Administration (TERA).

Others, meanwhile, came to D.C. thanks mainly to the professional circuits that linked the economics profession to government agencies. In some cases, those circuits were sufficient in themselves. Consider, for instance, the trajectory of another pro-spender, Leon Henderson (1895–1986). A graduate of Swarthmore College (1920), Henderson had only an undergraduate degree but became an "economist" as an instructor at the Wharton School of Commerce and Finance and the Carnegie Institute of Technology. From Wharton Henderson moved to a position as deputy secretary of the Commonwealth of Pennsylvania, and then he became a researcher with the Russell Sage Foundation in New York City. Moving via the same circuits in which the NBER was enmeshed, Henderson came to D.C. to work for the National Recovery Administration (NRA) in 1934, under General Hugh Johnson. Quickly promoted to director of research and planning, Henderson acquired a reputation in the New Deal administration for predicting both an upswing in 1934 and the 1937 recession via an analysis of consumption statistics.[57] After the Supreme Court invalidated the NRA in 1935 Henderson became secretary to the Senate Committee on Manufactures.[58] Henderson's path thus tracked through economics, then into one of the departments that was closely tied to the NBER, into state government, and then into a (also NBER-connected) New York City foundation, before it finally intersected with the New Deal administration.

Circuits of connection between economics and the New Deal state created professional outlets for young economists who rejected academic orthodoxies. Well into the 1930s most prestigious academic economics departments remained both antispending and antipartisan, and the Harvard economics faculty was no exception. An important case was that of Lauchlin Currie (1902–1993), a Canadian-born Harvard economist.[59] When, in early 1934, Currie persuaded five fellow Harvard instructors to write to FDR in support of "increased government expenditures" and "deliberate departure from the gold standard," the signatories were denied tenure after the letter was released to the *New York Times*.[60]

Currie nonetheless became a New Deal pro-spender, courtesy of his professional ties to economists in the federal state. Via a connection to Viner (in the Treasury), Currie found his way into a position at the Treasury starting in July 1934.[61] There he found, in Mariner Eccles, "a common enthusiasm for bold, unorthodox fiscal and monetary programs."[62] Currie provided Eccles with technical arguments and quantitative indicators that were becoming a *sine qua non* of many young economists' skill-set by the 1930s. Currie's technical contributions supported Eccles's favored program of spending-driven economic expansion.[63]

The historian of economics William Barber suggests that Currie's turn to government as a fugitive of the academic profession, and especially the Harvard economics department, was not exceptional. Paul Samuelson writes, for instance, that Seymour Harris was left "hanging on at Harvard for fifteen years without tenure" due to his "inflationist," nonorthodox positions; in the late 1930s Harris still "had little company as a Keynesian on the Harvard faculty."[64] Galbraith recalls that, in 1936, the Harvard Department of Economics dismissed as eccentric a suggestion from junior members that John Maynard Keynes be numbered among the leading economists of the day.[65] In the words of Robert Skidelsky, American economists mainly responded to Keynes's most famous work "with a mixture of hostility and incomprehension."[66] As a result, Barber contends that economics' intolerance of departures from orthodoxy chased "[a] number of the profession's more imaginative younger talents" into "officialdom."[67]

Making Economics Keynesian: How the Pro-Spenders
Changed the Profession

The development of a pro-spending, Keynesian presence in federal officialdom acted *back* on the economics profession. While many "Roosevelt economists" never attracted academic recognition (they were "righteously excluded from professional honors," Galbraith reports), others moved from D.C. back into the academic world and then shaped the direction of the profession from inside.[68]

Alvin Hansen (1887–1975) was important in this process. A graduate of the University of Wisconsin, Hansen first came to D.C. in 1933 from the University of Minnesota as director of research for the Commission of Inquiry on National Policy in International Economic Relations. Then forty-six years old, Hansen was an established academic economist. He arrived in Washington neither a Keynesian nor a pro-spender, but after moving to an economic advisory position to Secretary of State Cordell Hull in which he became part of discussions on Social Security Hansen changed his positions.

From government Hansen then moved to Harvard, starting in the fall of 1937.[69] Just three years before, Currie and others were denied tenure for the very same pro-spending inclinations that Hansen now had. Again, as recently as 1936 the Harvard economics faculty rejected the suggestion that Keynes was among the discipline's most influential figures. And yet Hansen now became one of two chairs of the university's new Graduate School of Public Administration, with a co-appointment in the economics department.[70]

The effect on economics was significant. At Harvard Hansen offered an influential fiscal policy seminar that, despite a continuing hostility to Keynes among senior faculty (including Joseph Schumpeter), became a "workshop in which the new concepts of Keynesian economics were hammered out and tested."[71] The "old economics" was still the standard curriculum, but "almost every evening from 1936 onwards almost everyone in the Harvard community discussed Keynes."[72] The historian Robert Skidelsky notes that "[m]ost of the leading American names associated with the Keynesian Revolution—[Paul] Samuelson [1915–2009], [John Kenneth] Galbraith [1908–2006], James Tobin [1918–2002], Robert Solow [1924–], Seymour Harris [1897–1974]—passed through Harvard in the 1930s."[73] After Hansen's death in 1975, the *American Economic Review* described him as "one of those heretics who eventually converted the church."[74]

Making the Democrats Economistic: How the
Pro-Spenders Changed the Democratic Party

The pro-spenders' influence in the New Deal state also affected the Democratic Party. During FDR's 1936 campaign the DNC hired its first campaign economist: Leon Henderson. By some reports the addition was not totally welcome. The economist Paul Samuelson, for instance, later recounted that

[Henderson] allegedly reported to duty to Charles Michelson, I think it was . . . Mike [who] was supposed to have said, "You see these buttons on the sleeve of my coat? They're not worth a god damn, but everybody says I've got to have them. That's the way I feel about an economist on this campaign."[75]

In the same year another economist, Leon Keyserling, became an important force in the Democratic Platform Committee, then led by Senator Robert Wagner.

Keyserling, who was central in the drafting of the large amount of New Deal legislation that originated in or passed through Senator Wagner's office, stood out especially for his role in the making of the 1935 National Labor Relations Act (NLRA) and, by extension, a *de facto* alliance between the Democratic Party and organized labor. Keyserling later described the importance of the NLRA in precisely these terms:

> I have always thought rightly or wrongly that both economically and politically, and politically I mean in the sense of shaping events to come, [the NLRA] was the most influential act of the New Deal. Its influence on the economic side doesn't need to be discussed because organized labor grew from three million to a peak of twenty million probably, under the act, and its great political influence was that this was really the basis of the historic affiliation of labor with the Democratic Party, which with slight variations is persistent till this day.[76]

Soon after, Keyserling's work turned to drafting the Democratic Party's 1936 platform. In his account:

> I made the first draft of the Democratic platform in 1936, the entire draft, in Senator Wagner's office. It later got over to the White House where Sam Rosenman and others changed the style and the format considerably, but the content was the same.[77]

None of this meant the Democratic Party was officially Keynesian, of course. Nor did it indicate that the party now had a definite academic affiliation: the economists drawn into Democratic campaign and programmatic operations were New Dealers, not academics. But they were also pro-spenders. The end result, by the late 1930s, was a certain affinity in the orientations of economists then exerting increasing influence in the state, the Democratic Party, and the academic side of the economics profession.

Expanding ranks and academic prominence bolstered the pro-spenders' growing influence in the New Deal administration. Around the same time Eccles entered into the New Deal administration, Lewis Douglas resigned from his position at the BOB, in protest of FDR's failure to balance the budget. FDR appointed an acting director (Daniel Bell, a civil servant) and began to work around, not with, the agency.[78]

Meanwhile, budgetary troubles deepened. Income taxes were not generating enough revenue to pay for New Deal programs or preexisting commitments—including, especially, veterans' benefits.[79] FDR affirmed his commitment to sound finance in the lead-up to the 1936 election, on Morgenthau's encouragement. But in the spring of 1936 social insurance promises ran up against what was then understood as a serious budgetary shortfall: Congress passed a veterans' bonus increase, overriding a veto, and the Supreme Court invalidated an agricultural processing tax, leaving the government short by $620 million. With the onset of recession in 1937, the situation became increasingly dire. In spite of it all, FDR remained opposed to the idea that deficit spending could resolve the Depression.[80]

Finally, in early 1938 FDR accepted the pro-spenders' diagnosis, espousing deficit spending to stimulate the economy amid fears of another depression. Famously, FDR's decision originated in consultation with Hopkins, Henderson, and (accidentally) Beardsley Ruml, but excluded Morgenthau, in March 1938.[81] On April 14 FDR called for almost $3 billion in emergency spending and loans, over Morgenthau's objections.[82]

FDR's fateful shift, of course, did not happen in a vacuum. It should be situated within the thickening web of relationships between the government, the party, and the economics profession by 1938. The mainstreaming of Keynesianism in professional economics should also be understood in that context. In the same year FDR changed his mind, in fact, Hansen was the AEA president. Hansen's presidential address presented his "own version of the [Keynesian] theory of secular stagnation." Also in that year, economists in and around Cambridge, Massachusetts issued "the first manifesto of the young Keynesian school, *An Economic Program for American Democracy.*"[83] The *Program* was signed by seven economists: Richard V. Gilbert, George H. Hildebrand Jr., Arthur W. Stuart, Maxine Y. Sweezy, Paul M. Sweezy, Lorie Tarshis, and John D. Wilson.[84] In short—and by no means coincidentally—FDR moved in a Keynesian direction at the very moment Keynesianism was emerging as a mainstream position of younger-generation academic economists.

American Politics, European Categories

The implications went well beyond policy. Recall that, as recently as the 1920s, the terms "left" and "right" had little connection to the major political parties. But in the late 1930s there emerged an image of American party politics in which the categories "left" and "right" aligned, albeit imperfectly, with a Democratic-Republican distinction. In this new landscape the "Roosevelt Democrats" were, unmistakably, left and the term "liberal," once a cross-party linguistic frame, now had the imprimatur of New Deal, democratic, economistic leftism.

A pair of articles, published in June and August of 1937 by the *New York Times* reporter Delbert Clark, illustrates the change.[85] Writing first on the Republican Party, Clark observed that conservative Republicans, who "shiver at the rise of organized labor as a political force," were considering the possibility of a "Conservative Party" that would "purge itself of all advanced theories and practice," espousing "states' rights and a large measure of individualism."[86] Clark explains that the "Roosevelt Party" was now, unmistakably "left"—a term that had become roughly equivalent to "liberal." Conservative Democrats, Clark reports, feared being left out as FDR remade "the party [as] a truly left ... homogeneous organism" composed of progressive Republicans, "socialists, Communists, the bulk of organized labor and various ... wing fringes." Left and liberal had become interchangeable thanks to FDR's and his advisers' efforts to "reconstruct [the party] along liberal, up-to-date lines."[87] But Clark also expressed a suspicion that academics were actually in control: the "cap-and-gown kitchen cabinet" had "more influence with [FDR] than [the "left-wingers"] have."[88]

Clark's two articles were both accompanied by political cartoons by Oscar Edward Cesare. A cartoon on the Republicans portrays the Republican elephant confronting a turning point: the elephant can turn "to the right," "to the left," or down the "middle road" (see Figure 5.1).

As shown in Figure 5.1, "left" has an academic association: the elephant atop the sign pointing "to the right" wears a businessman's top hat, but the elephant pointing "to the left" wears an academic mortar-

Lost in the political jungle—Which way out for the G. O. P. elephant?

Figure 5.1. Imagery of the Republican Party, 1937: "Lost in the political jungle—Which way for the G.O.P. elephant?" Cartoon by Oscar Edward Cesare. Source: D. Clark 1937b, *New York Times*.

board. This association between academicism and leftism appears, also, in the cartoon of the Democratic Party (Figure 5.2).

In Figure 5.2, FDR (the "New Dealer") also wears a mortarboard—while, apparently, losing control of the Democratic donkey. An "Old Dealer," presumably a southern Democrat, sits in the middle, reluctantly along for the ride, while a "left-winger"—perhaps a young socialist, or a labor representative, or both—grabs the reins from the rear.

Several things about these articles, and the cartoons accompanying them, are worth noting. First, their characterization of the American political axis in terms of a left-right distinction contrasts with the irrelevance of the very same distinction *as recently as the 1920s*. Second, the

Three men on a donkey—Can they all stay on?

Figure 5.2. Imagery of the Democratic Party, 1937: "Three men on a donkey—Can they stay on?" Cartoon by Oscar Edward Cesare. Source: D. Clark 1937a, *New York Times.*

packaging of liberal, left, organized labor, academicism, and the Democratic Party stands out. The novel association of (Democratic, liberal) leftism with intellectualism harks back to arguments raised earlier as to the infrastructure of party leftism in Europe around the turn of the twentieth century. Recall how, in Chapter 3, Europe's mass parties of the left had two arms: one grounded in organized labor, the other in knowledge production (socialism). Recall, also, how neither the Republican nor Democratic parties formed on the basis of ideology. And yet by 1937 the Roosevelt Democrats are left, labor-connected, and academically backed. This looks a lot like a two-armed party of the left, albeit with a knowledge-producing arm grounded in academe rather than socialism.

References to academics in Clark's *New York Times* articles were nonspecific, but other sources conveyed the sense that FDR's "cap-and-gown kitchen cabinet" was not made up of just any academics; it was composed, specifically, of economists. In September 1937, for instance, the Republican Senator A. H. Vandenberg called for a new coalition against the "Roosevelt party," arguing that "[t]here are practical ways for the Government to economize," but "it can't be done by 'liberals'" or "cockeyed economists."[89] Other major news outlets also took note of the shifting role of economists inside the New Deal administration.[90]

PHASE TWO: BUILDING THE DEMOCRATIC ECONOMIST THEORETICIAN'S WORLD, 1939–1946

The notion that the American government could and should proactively maintain high levels of employment found its first official expression in a report by Alvin Hansen, Currie, and others, the *Annual Report of the Secretary of Commerce for the Fiscal Year 1939*.[91] Hansen and Currie then "set out to educate Congress and the public at large on the 'new' economics" in 1939 testimony to the Temporary National Economic Committee (TNEC).[92] Last but not least, Hansen's *Fiscal Policy and Business Cycles* (1941) "gave the flesh of American statistics to the bones of [Keynes's] abstract theory," and it featured a statistical appendix by Paul Samuelson.[93] Indeed, according to Stein, in the 1940s young Keynesian economists—now *representatives*, not fugitives, of the academic world—became "the 'back-room boys' of Washington."[94] The same profession that once kept a firm distance from politics was now closely involved with the New Deal faction of the Democratic Party.

In the 1950s figures like Paul Samuelson, James Tobin, Kermit Gordon, and John Kenneth Galbraith were able to remain prestigious economists no matter how deep their partisan ties. All became Democratic speechwriters, *de facto* personal tutors of Democratic candidates, and campaign strategists in the 1950s, with especially close links to Adlai Stevenson and John F. Kennedy. Nonetheless, Samuelson and Tobin also went on to win Nobel Prizes for their contributions to economics. What this indicates is that they moved a world in which one could be "in politics" without risking their scientific prestige. How was this duality possible?

To answer this question one needs to grasp the institutional world to which the economist theoretician was indigenous. This world emerged from at least three processes: a renewed recruitment of pro-spenders, *by* pro-spenders, in the wake of their 1938 victory; new federal demands for economists in service of wartime mobilization; and academic-political relationships that both underpinned the making of the Employment Act of 1946 and reorganized the federal executive in a way that "naturally" favored the economist theoretician. In a certain sense, the economist theoretician built the very institutions that made his duality possible. I'll deal with each in turn.

With the pro-spenders' 1938 victory came appointments to powerful positions from which they were able to recruit the like-minded. After Harry Hopkins became secretary of commerce he created the Division of Industrial Economics and appointed Richard Gilbert, also a signatory of the Keynesian manifesto of 1938, as its head. Gilbert staffed the division with other Keynesians, including Walter Salant.[95] In the meantime, Hansen continued to move between Cambridge and the federal government, using his dual position to push for Keynesian policy and build advisory channels for academic economics. Hansen returned to Washington in 1940 as an adviser to the Federal Reserve and to the National Resources Planning Board (NRPB).[96]

As economic advisory channels in the executive were revamped in the late 1930s, pro-spenders were first in line for hiring. Executive reorganization began when FDR, partly in response to difficulties harnessing the support and assistance of the BOB under Douglas, appointed the Committee on Administrative Management (the Brownlow Committee) to rethink the presidential advisory apparatus. The result was, in 1939, the establishment of the Executive Office of the President (EOP).[97] As part of the reform the BOB moved to the EOP from the Treasury. Under the directorship of Harold Smith (until 1945), the BOB established a new fiscal division. The division's chief economist was none other than Gerhard Colm—who, we may recall, was one of the players in the conflict between economist pro-spenders and Hilferding in Germany in 1932 (the WTB episode).[98] The EOP also featured six new executive assistants, including Lauchlin Currie: the first professional economist to become a formal presidential adviser.[99]

A second driver in the making of the economist theoretician's world was significant federal demand for economic calculation, and thus economists, in service of wartime mobilization. The NRPB (of which Hansen was a member), the Defense Advisory Commission (1939), the Office of Price Administration (OPA, 1941; headed by Leon Henderson and chaired by Paul Porter), the National War Labor Board (NWLB, established in January 1942), and the Economic Defense Board (EDB, later the Board of Economic Warfare [BEW], 1942; headed by Vice President Henry Wallace) fortified the positions of existing economists-in-government and drew a younger generation of technically trained economists into Washington's political networks.[100]

Academic-political relationships that gave rise to the Employment Act of 1946 were a third important element of the world that made the hybrid economist theoretician possible. Key figures in the drafting of the act—especially Keyserling, with Hansen's support—essentially devised institutional arrangements in their own image.

The initial bill called for a reorganization of the executive, declared a universal right to employment, and made employment a federal responsibility.[101] It also proposed a national production and employment budget that would anticipate shortfalls in private investment, requiring the government to provide compensatory investment as necessary.[102] In the end the 1946 Employment Act eliminated the employment budget in the original bill, and made no specific commitments on future government action. It also failed to establish institutional bases for the planning of compensatory investment.[103] For these reasons, the act has been understood as a limited attempt at installing Keynesianism in federal policy-making—or, in one assessment, as a failure of "social Keynesianism" in favor of "business Keynesianism."[104]

For present purposes, the Keynesian-ness of the final Employment Act is less important than the relationships that underpinned it and the way in which those relationships left an imprint on the federal government after 1946. Reflecting on how "a group of economists, political scientists, and politicians" formulated the original bill, the Harvard-based education professor Stephen Bailey later remarked that

> this temporary confluence of professions may have been of more importance than the Employment Act itself. . . . What is new is the degree of our own self-consciousness that an interdependency exists. One of the salutary results of the Employment Act has been the forcing together of professional economists and professional politicians on a scale hitherto unknown in this country.[105]

In 1972 the *American Economic Review* (*AER*) reflected on the Employment Act in similar terms, highlighting the ties between New Deal officials, Democratic politicians, and Keynesian economists that formed the act's *social* basis. The *AER* recalled how, in the making of the act, a relatively small number of Keynesian economists "established themselves as influential advisers to" FDR, New Deal pro-spenders (like Wallace, Ickes, Hopkins, and Henderson), later New Dealers of the wartime state (like Chester Bowles), and "various Senators and Congressmen."[106]

Advisory relationships between officials, Democrats, and Keynesian economists informed the institutional imprint left by the Employment Act on the federal state. In particular, the act reorganized the government in a way that accommodated and elevated the figure of the economist theoretician within the EOP and in Congress.

From the start Keyserling viewed organizational concerns as central to the bill. In 1944 he wrote a prize-winning essay that called for a new apparatus of macroeconomic management featuring "institutional devices for approximating in some respects the parliamentary system," including a permanent "American Economic Committee which was composed *jointly* of members of the Cabinet and members of the Congress," and which would "draft the American economic goal." Keyserling argued that the goal should be integrated into State of the Union addresses and the committee should follow with "frequent reports to Congress."[107]

The proposal in that essay, Keyserling would later recount, was "to a very large extent" the seed of what would become, in 1946, the Council of Economic Advisers (CEA).[108] More specifically, the 1946 act created a three-member CEA inside the EOP and, in Congress, the Joint Economic Committee (JEC).[109] This diverged from the unified structure Keyserling originally envisioned, but nonetheless amounted to a much-expanded and more economist-centered advisory structure in the executive, with a parallel agency in the legislature. The BOB lost control over fiscal analysis, which was shifted over to the CEA.[110]

Recall that, in the 1920s, professional economics' federal outposts were strongest in the Departments of Agriculture and Commerce and that in the 1930s they expanded but remained department-based. After 1946, with the CEA, the profession reached into the heart of the executive. The CEA's creation strengthened existing linkages between the late New Deal state and Keynesian economics, specifically: as Stein comments, "Members of the school tended to know, prefer, and recruit others."[111] The CEA's birth also raised economics' profile and professional stakes. Struggles over the boundaries and definition of the term "economist," and what the relationship should be between economic science and overt politics, intensified.

This intensification was directly linked to the CEA. The 1946 Employment Act did not specify that an economics PhD was necessary for CEA appointment: candidates were qualified by virtue of "training, experience and attainment."[112] Nor was there any explicit assumption that academics were the best or most qualified CEA appointees.[113] Informally, political loyalties—known and suspected—mattered, too.

In the end the first CEA head was Edwin Nourse (1883–1974). An older-generation agricultural economist, Nourse was a past AEA and Social Science Research Council president with "good professional credentials"—meaning he was not too closely affiliated with the New Deal and unobjectionable for both business and labor. This combination of qualities required a delicate balance that a number of possible candidates, including Alvin Hansen, couldn't strike.[114] Nourse later attributed his appointment to his combination of academic standing, respectability in business circles, "a strong line of support from the agricultural area," and "a very favorable attitude from labor."[115] A fellow CEA appointee, John D. Clark, was similarly cross-positioned. Trained as a lawyer but also an economics PhD, Clark was an oil industry executive before becoming the dean of the University of Nebraska School of Business.[116]

The third CEA appointee was Leon Keyserling. More than twenty years Nourse's junior, Keyserling was an economist by reputation, but he lacked a PhD or a record of academic publication. Known as a New Dealer, Keyserling had been deeply involved in Democratic programmatic and campaign operations since 1936: he was "very actively involved" in the "translation of economic . . . ideas into the political process" as an assistant in Wagner's and, through Wagner, other senatorial campaigns. His party investments ran deep: Keyserling prepared the draft Democratic Platform in both 1940 and 1944.[117]

Contention ensued along predictable lines. Nourse later described how his "scholarly approach" was similar to Clark's and thus "very satisfactory"; however, Nourse's relationship with Keyserling was strained.[118] Nourse conceived the CEA as a scientific body that should operate at a distance from politics, but Keyserling "believed in a politically active council."[119] As Nourse later recounted:

> Keyserling . . . resented any exclusive contact of the chairman with the President. But he tried to establish, and *did* establish, his personal relations with Clark Clifford, the President's close adviser.[120]

Keyserling's influence-seeking through political channels, in a decidedly nonscientific mode, showcased his professional differences with Nourse and strained the relationship between them. Nourse's later assessment was that the problem had to do with Keyserling's lack of a PhD:

> [Keyserling] knew perfectly well that he had made himself a competent economist. . . . Although he was as competent as more than half of the profession, he didn't have that recognition and it bothered him. So it was an inferiority-superiority complex there that . . . made the relationship trying.[121]

Unwilling to fully invest in the fight—and, professionally speaking, free to disengage and return to academic pursuits—Nourse finally stepped aside; Keyserling replaced him.

It turned out, however, that a political CEA was also a vulnerable CEA. In late 1952, thanks to controversy over Keyserling's overtly political style in the context of a cross-party conservative coalition in Congress, the CEA's appropriations were slashed by 25 percent. Funds ran out as of March 1, 1953, six weeks after Dwight D. Eisenhower arrived in office. The CEA's original staff—which included many figures who were associated with the New Deal administration—was dispersed.[122]

Left with a relatively empty shell to fill as he pleased, Eisenhower concentrated more power in the position of CEA chairman and filled it with Arthur F. Burns (1904–1987). A student of Wesley C. Mitchell and a Columbia professor, Burns was, at the time, the head of the NBER (now in Cambridge). Burns reinvented the CEA in a more academic form.[123] The result was a professional outpost in the executive that helped to secure economists' new role as points of interconnection between politics and the academy, while still retaining their academic stature.

But even an academicized CEA in a Republican White House retained—or so some suspected—a certain Democratic flavor. Burns himself had been a "Democrat for Eisenhower" in the 1952 campaign.[124] He later told of his difficulties finding fellow economists who "were not too closely identified with the previous administrations" and "would agree to work for President Eisenhower."[125] In the end he found Neil H. Jacoby (1909–1979; Chicago PhD, 1938), a business school dean at the University of California, Los Angeles, and the (considerably older) Walter W. Stewart (1885–1958) from Princeton, who did not have a PhD in economics.[126] Future Eisenhower CEA appointees drew from Stanford, the University of Michigan, and Yale; three of them, Joseph S. Davis, Paul McCracken, and Henry Wallich, were Harvard PhDs (1931, 1948, and 1944, respectively).[127]

Perhaps the prominence of Harvard credentials on the CEA explains why, by some reports, its de-Democratization was never complete. According to Tobin, Eisenhower "purged Washington of Democratic Keynesians but found that many of the economists recruited in partial replacement were also contaminated."[128]

PHASE THREE: BUILDING ACADEMIC-PARTY TIES, 1946–1960

Despite the new public stature of Democratic economists by 1946, by that time the New Dealers' influence in Washington was actually at the precipice of a decline that began with Harry Truman's arrival in the presidency in 1945, accelerated with wartime demobilization, and deepened during the Eisenhower years. And yet, somehow, the economist theoretician survived—and would later return, as powerful as ever, in the JFK administration.

Truman (1884–1972), a farmer, World War I captain, haberdasher, and Jackson County Court judge from Missouri, was not of the New England establishment. The "intellectual liberals" did not connect with him as they did with FDR; in fact, they bore a grudge against Truman since he replaced Henry Wallace (a liberal "hero") as vice president in 1944. For them Truman was "a machine politician of no great stature."[129]

Many New Dealers left Truman's administration or, thanks to postwar demobilization, were forced to leave. New Dealers' governmental influence further declined in the 1950s with Eisenhower's presidency, the onset of McCarthyism, Republican and conservative opposition to Keynesianism, and deep fractures in the ranks of the American "progressive" left.

How did the economist theoretician survive? Partly his survival was thanks to the institutions described above: the CEA and other agencies provided points of connection and bases of influence, even without a Democrat in the Oval Office. But there were other reasons, too. One was Keynesian economics' security in the academy, which provided Keynesians with a professional basis from which they could weather and resist conservative attacks. The other was a loose Democratic Party terrain that included the DNC, Democratic congresspeople, state-level parties, unofficially liberal economic consultancies, policy committees, and advisory networks. This terrain helped to keep ties between academe, Washington, and the Democratic Party alive and well.

Sheltering the Storm in Academe

Keynesianism solidified its place in economics during precisely the period in which conservatives and McCarthyites ramped up the persecution of domestic communism. Individually economists were hardly insulated from McCarthyism, but Keynesianism's integration into economics as a discipline helped to keep it very much intact. And through academic channels Keynesian economists, regardless of political leanings, acquired greater status and prestige.

The first Keynesian textbook in the United States, by Lorie Tarshis (1911–1993) of Stanford University (and formerly at Tufts), emerged in 1947: *The Elements of Economics*.[130] Tarshis had attended Keynes's lectures at Cambridge between 1932 and 1934 as Keynes' *General Theory* was being written, and he was among many students who found in Keynes a symbol of hope and a source of inspiration in difficult economic times.[131] Tarshis's textbook was adopted at all the Ivy League universities, and many others, but was also an object of attack.[132]

The economist Paul Samuelson describes how Tarshis's textbook was "almost killed" by "vicious political and personal attacks on him as a 'Keynesian-Marxist' "—a term popularized by Herbert Hoover.[133] Fellow economists later recounted how "the textbook . . . was quickly attacked by some of its conservative readers . . . beginning as early as August, 1947," amounting to "an overt attempt to prevent the use of the book."[134] They also tell of letters received by Stanford's president, Donald Tresidder—including one from Hoover—condemning Tarshis and his textbook as socialist, communist, un-American, and a threat to the American economic and cultural order.[135] In the end, however, the academic world provided cover: Tarshis would go on to chair the Department of Economics at Stanford.[136]

The story of a second Keynesian textbook, by Paul Samuelson (*Economics: An Introductory Analysis,* 1948), also shows how the academic world sheltered Keynesianism—not so much out of friendliness toward its economics *per se,* but rather to defend institutional autonomy and preserve academic prestige. As Samuelson was developing the textbook, he made use of preliminary versions in his Massachusetts Institute of Technology (MIT) classes that "came under intense attack from several MIT businessmen alumni and board members." But when one of them insisted that Samuelson submit the text to "a good man like Professor Fairchild of Yale" to "cleanse out its heresies," MIT's president, Karl Compton, intervened on Samuelson's behalf. Compton wrote to the businessman that, in Samuelson's recounting, "any time one of his professors became censorable by some outsider, he would hand in his own resignation from office."[137]

Samuelson's textbook became the best-selling textbook in economics' history. Perhaps it helped that Tarshis's textbook paved the way and that Samuelson—who was familiar with Tarshis's example and thus cognizant of the need to write his textbook in a way that would defend it against critics—"wrote carefully."[138] Samuelson did not present the textbook as simply "Keynesian" but rather as a presentation of a new classical economics, or what he termed the "neo-classical synthesis," that had no overlap with Marxist economics.[139] The fifth through seventh editions, released between 1961 and 1967, sold more than 1.1 million copies, as opposed to sales of just over 600,000 of the 1950s editions (released between 1951 and 1958).[140]

The survival of the Keynesian economist theoretician in the 1950s was thus partly thanks to Keynesianism's mainstream status in the academy. Academic economics provided a prestigious, relatively politically insulated professional home for otherwise Democratic Keynesians—one that was fortified to the extent that Samuelson's textbook became the disciplinary standard. But there was also another basis of the economist theoretician's survival: academic economists' active ties to the DNC, Democratic campaigns, and Democratic candidates.

We might consider, for instance, Paul Samuelson. Samuelson became famous as an economist thanks to his textbook and, especially, after he received the Nobel Memorial Prize in Economic Sciences in 1970. But in the 1950s Samuelson was much more than an economist. He was part of a network of academics, lawyers, politicians, labor leaders, and New-Dealers-in-exile who were actively involved in the campaign and programmatic activities of the national Democratic Party. In this Samuelson had plenty of company; his Democratic Party–involved colleagues included Seymour Harris, James Tobin, Richard Gilbert, John Kenneth Galbraith, Kermit Gordon, Walter Heller, Robert Solow, and Robert Nathan.

The Move to the Democratic Party

The Democratic economist theoreticians constituted a ready resource of policy advisers and campaign speechwriters, and even a Democratic interest group in their own right, between the late 1940s and 1960. They helped to create and sustain a range of entities—including the Americans for Democratic Action (ADA), the Finletter group, and the Democratic Advisory Council (DAC)—with close ties to congressional and state-level politicians, the DNC, the CEA, platform committees, and the Democratic presidential campaigns of Adlai Stevenson and JFK. Inspired by the example of the Finletter group in particular, JFK's campaign team recruited ADA-connected economist theoreticians to educate the candidate on the campaign trail. Three of them—Heller, Gordon, and Tobin—would then become Kennedy's CEA appointees.

The ADA

Between 1941 and 1947 the Democratic-liberal inheritors of the two-armed "Roosevelt Party" established a *de facto* satellite of the Democratic Party: the ADA. The roots of the ADA are to be found in a split within the ranks of the liberal-progressive American lefts, which was partly over the question of Soviet communism, but should also be seen as a struggle over the control and definition of New Deal Democratic liberalism. The ADA became one of at least three centers of ongoing connection between the national Democratic Party, Democratic presidential campaigns, and economist theoreticians through the 1950s.

Looking to distance themselves from communist-friendly "progressives," various self-understood liberals established the ADA's predecessor, the Union for Democratic Action (UDA), in order to carve out an organizational niche for people who were democratic and anticommunist, but also supporters of New Deal–style, Keynesian-backed, proactive domestic policy. In 1941 they established the UDA in New York City. After absorbing the New York Liberal Party in 1944, the UDA moved its main offices to Washington, D.C.

In January 1947 the UDA reinvented itself as the Americans for Democratic Action, or ADA. Unable to tether an unruly Democratic Party to their agenda, ADA founders—who included Leon Henderson, Hubert Humphrey, Eleanor Roosevelt, Wilson Wyatt (a Kentucky Democrat), Eugenie Anderson, James Loeb Jr., and many others—built the new organization in order to sustain the New Deal, liberal-Democratic position in a rightward-moving political moment. The ADA's founding meeting featured enough prominent New Dealers that the event's chair, Elmer Davis, described the gathering as "the United States Government in exile."[141] Former War Production Board (WPB) and OPA employees, economists central among them, were well represented. Paul Porter, a former OPA chairman and by then head of the American economic mission to Greece, was "Truman's personal envoy" to ADA events.[142]

Partly via the ADA, New Deal liberalism, once a primarily domestic politics, was also defined in foreign policy terms: the ADA agenda featured interventionism in foreign policy in support of the Truman doctrine, activism in domestic economic and social policy, the application of Keynesian economic management in service of full employment, and the promotion of the democratic spirit of the New Deal. Porter's participation showcased a link between foreign and domestic economic policy that was then at the core of Democratic liberalism and that the ADA shared with the Truman administration despite liberal intellectuals' aversion to Truman. The ADA's declared foreign policy position aligned with the Truman doctrine: spending on foreign aid, specifically for Greece, with the purpose of communist containment.[143] On domestic policy the ADA advocated full employment, low prices by means of price controls, a higher minimum wage, tax relief for low earners, housing, and farm supports. As ADA founder James Loeb Jr. would later recall, "[W]e called it a 'two-front fight for democracy both at home and abroad.'"[144]

For some, the ADA is a case study in the history of postwar American liberalism.[145] But ADA's existence points to the fact that American liberalism was, like socialism, an institutional and organizational terrain brought to life by certain practices and socially situated people. It was also (and remains) a *stake* that structured and organized Democratic competitions and collaboration. Those dynamics played out amid the very tripartite relations that Gramsci once described: between party politicians, represented groups that included organized labor, and cadres of academics and other sorts of experts. In the last category, Keynesian economists featured prominently.

In the 1950s the liberal-Democratic nexus of relations sustained the world of the economist theoretician through the era of Eisenhower and McCarthyism. The ADA built and maintained linkages between politicians and politicians-to-be (Hubert Humphrey, Chester Bowles), economists-*cum*-New-Dealers (Leon Keyserling, Leon Henderson), and later-generation "back-room boys" (Robert Nathan, John Kenneth Galbraith)—not to mention lawyers (James Loeb Jr. [1908–1992]), non-economist academics (Arthur Schlesinger Jr), labor leaders (Walter Reuther, Philip Murray, Sidney Hillman), and others.[146]

The ADA helped to sustain the economist theoretician by keeping Keynesian academics connected to the Truman administration and actively involved in Democratic economic policy-making. Immediately after its March 1947 convention, for instance, the ADA commissioned an economic report, led by Chester Bowles, on economic stabilization and the avoidance of depression after the war. Bowles's committee members included Seymour Harris (the Harvard economist, formerly at the BEW [1942]), John Kenneth Galbraith (an editor of *Fortune*, formerly of the Department of Agriculture and then the OPA soon to join the Harvard economics faculty [1949]), Alvin Hansen (then at Harvard), Richard Gilbert (at that time a consulting economist to Schenley Industries, Inc.; formerly on the Harvard economics faculty and then director of the OPA [1941–1946]), and Robert Nathan.[147]

Of those listed above, Nathan stands out as an interesting exception: he was the only one who did not have an economics PhD, but he earned *de facto* credentials as an economist. Nathan had been a trainee of Simon Kuznets, helping to build national income statistics at the Commerce Department; he then joined the WPB and TNEC during the war. He also held a JD from Georgetown University and had the distinction of having founded the first economics consulting firm in Washington, D.C.: Nathan Associates, in late 1945.[148] But, other than Nathan, all of the Bowles Committee members had both economics PhDs and Harvard affiliations. And all the members, including Nathan, had deep roots in New Deal and wartime federal agencies.

By most reports their professional relationships ran deep: in the 1940s, for instance, Nathan, Gilbert, Leon Henderson, and Lauchlin Currie participated in an informal group that called itself "the goon squad." Meeting every Monday, the goon squad policed and promoted the operations of the WPB. At the same time, they also extended their reach into the operations of the national party: in 1944 Nathan and Henderson were both on an independent fund-raising committee for the FDR-Truman campaign.

In the late 1940s and early 1950s, then, the ADA was keeping professional relationships among New Dealer economist theoreticians active. It also sustained the liberal-labor connection, having an especially strong relationship with the Congress of Industrial Organizations (CIO). When Taft-Hartley passed by a Republican-dominated Congress in June 1947, the ADA-CIO relationship strengthened: between 1947 and 1948 union support to the ADA more than doubled, from $22,000 to $55,000. By the time of the ADA's February 1948 convention, its executive committee had a close working relationship with both CIO and American Federation of Labor (AFL) leadership.[149]

The ADA also functioned as an organizational center through which ties to the Truman administration could be maintained. The economists of Truman's CEA, Nourse and Keyserling, embraced the ADA economic program as closely aligned with the administration's. And although ADAers remained ambivalent about Truman, in 1948 the president took the advice of Special Counsel Clark Clifford and courted the ADAers to support his campaign. (The idea was to fend off Wallace's third-party threat [the Progressive Party] by keeping liberals close.) In exchange for support of his campaign, Truman offered ADAers top positions and emphasized their highest-priority issues: "high prices, housing, the Marshall Plan, tax revision, conservation of natural resources in the West, and civil rights."[150] The ADA and the DNC then joined forces during the 1948 election, placing ADAers in an important position of influence in the making of the Democratic platform.

In the early 1950s the ADA maintained its ties to the Truman administration and its involvements in presidential campaigns. It was, in a sense, part of the circuit that ran from the ADA, to the White House, to the DNC, and into Democratic campaigns, with academic (especially northeastern, and economic) and union-centered nodal connections to boot. As a case in point, in 1951 one of the ADA founders, James Loeb Jr., left for a temporary White House assignment. From there Loeb nearly moved to the DNC, but instead he became an organizer of the "Draft Stevenson" campaign; from there he then became the executive director of Averell Harriman's campaign.[151]

The ADA circuit was especially central to the 1950s campaigns of Adlai Stevenson, who was the darling candidate of the liberals and the Cambridge economists. In 1952 three ADAers, Wilson Wyatt, Arthur Schlesinger Jr., and John Kenneth Galbraith, served as Stevenson's campaign chairman (Wyatt) and speechwriters (Schlesinger and Galbraith). At that point Stevenson was no friend of unions, nor was he a believer in Keynesian economics; his ADA advisers tried to temper his leanings. But pressure from Republicans and the RNC, intent on associating the ADA with communism, prompted Stevenson to distance himself. Ultimately, thanks to Republican pressure, ADAers were frozen out of the Stevenson campaign.[152]

In the 1950s times became harder for the ADAers, who were forcibly distanced from the administration during the Eisenhower years. Galbraith later recounted how "[f]or two decades, Washington had seemed an accessible and friendly place," but

> it would now be a closed, forbidden city. . . . I had come, without ever realizing it, to think of myself as part of a permanent government. I too was now out of office.[153]

The ADA soon became a target of McCarthy's prosecutions. Meanwhile, its labor ties substantially weakened when, in 1955, the AFL merged with the CIO and the new entity (AFL-CIO) engaged in direct, independent lobbying and legal pursuits. In 1954 labor contributions made up 26 percent of the ADA's income, but they were only 10 percent by 1959.[154]

The Finletter Group and the DAC

Undeterred, the ADA worked through alternative channels. Among them was the Finletter group, organized in 1952 by Thomas Finletter to educate Adlai Stevenson—who, as mentioned, was no Keynesian and was not particularly interested in economic issues.[155] The aim was thus, in a sense, to liberalize Stevenson by training him in economics and other subjects close to the liberals' hearts. Meeting in Finletter's New York apartment, the group remained active in the lead-up to Stevenson's second candidacy in 1956. Arthur Schlesinger Jr. was an important presence, as were many of the Cambridge-centered and party-connected economists—including Alvin Hansen, now near retirement from Harvard (in 1956).[156] As Paul Samuelson, who was also involved, later recalled:

> Tom Finletter had organized a brain trust for Adlai Stevenson. I'm sure that I was recruited to that group through [John] Kenneth Galbraith and Arthur Schlesinger Jr. and Seymour Harris. Alvin Hansen had some connections.[157]

In 1955–1956 Walter Heller and James Tobin were also connected with the group.[158]

The 1956 election, a failure for the Democratic liberals, brought the establishment of yet another ADA-connected entity: the Democratic Advisory Council (DAC), chaired by the DNC's Paul Butler.[159] Based in D.C., the DAC was a "rather smallish group" that included Eleanor Roosevelt, Herbert Lehman, Averell Harriman, and Harry Truman (who was, according to Finletter, not a major participant), among others. Both Roosevelt and Harriman were ADAers. Links to the ADA also featured prominently among the experts who prepared papers and headed DAC committees: for instance, Dean Acheson chaired the DAC's Committee on Foreign Policy, and John Kenneth Galbraith chaired the DAC Committee on Domestic Policy.[160]

The (now) DAC-ADAers placed their hopes in another presidential run by Adlai Stevenson, but the 1958 elections were a disappointment: both Bowles and Finletter were defeated in the Democratic primaries.[161] Schlesinger's analysis was that the Democrats' 1958 defeat had to do with the party's failure to listen to its intellectuals. He wrote in the *New Republic* that "[a] party which seeks to qualify itself for responsibility in an age of national and international crisis is not well advised to begin to do so by blowing out its own brains."[162]

The DAC kept connections between economist theoreticians and the heights of the Democratic Party intact, but it was its predecessor—the Finletter group—that became an important model for the Kennedy campaign. Like Stevenson, JFK did not begin his political career known for his interest or acuity in modern economics; for their part, ADAers were not immediately convinced of JFK's liberal credentials. But, thanks to Democratic economist theoreticians, JFK was educated to become a liberal—which meant, naturally, to be educated in the language and logic of Keynesian economics.

Kennedy's connection to ADAers, which probably originated in regional, New England ties between the Massachusetts senator and Cambridge academics, was initially thin. As Samuelson explains:

John F. Kennedy became my congressman in Cambridge in 1946, after he returned from war service as a naval officer. I believe that his connections with the academic community were very sparse at that time.[163]

Consistent with Samuelson's account, in 1952 JFK was not the Cambridge economists' favored Senate candidate, in part because of their aversion to Joseph Kennedy. Against the senior Kennedy, the economist theoreticians supported Henry Cabot Lodge. They found JFK to be an unlikely bearer of Keynesianism in Democratic politics: as a senator JFK was on the Joint Economic Committee (JEC), but the economists who frequently testified before that body had the impression that JFK had no particular interest in "the academic abstract issues of fiscal policy."[164] But this began to change when Samuelson finally met JFK in 1958, at a "well-received" speech at the MIT faculty club.[165]

By 1959 the Kennedy campaign, inspired by lore of the Finletter group, turned to the same economists who educated Stevenson. As Samuelson recalled:

> [W]hen John F. Kennedy decided that he was going to go for the presidency and had his staff and they were aiming for the presidency, there was a mystique of the Finletter group. They wanted the best of everything and since there had been a marvelous Finletter group, of which they had heard so much, they wanted to have one too.[166]

Kennedy's campaign team, Ted Sorensen and Archibald Cox, met with Samuelson in late 1959 to persuade him to participate on the Kennedy campaign, even though he and others like him still favored Stevenson. In Samuelson's recounting:

> The argument was the following: here was a man who would play a great role in American history whether he made the presidency or not. If he made the presidency, he would be important. He wanted the best advice. He did not want personal loyalty. He did not need our votes, he wanted our ideas. It was under those circumstances that I agreed to cooperate.[167]

Samuelson, knowing it would be difficult to find academics who supported Kennedy, referred Sorensen to Tobin, who joined the campaign.[168]

Two of the economists who would later appear on Kennedy's CEA (Heller, Tobin) were thus directly involved in Kennedy's education in economics on the campaign trail. The linkages involved were grounded in Cambridge, on the one hand, and the ADA, on the other. Heller and Kennedy first met during a presidential campaign visit to Minneapolis, having been "strongly recommended" by the Democratic senator (and ADAer) Hubert Humphrey.[169] Kermit Gordon was also referred to Kennedy via the "Cambridge group." Kennedy originally wanted to appoint Paul Samuelson as CEA chairman, but Samuelson was then at MIT and reluctant to go, and Kennedy was concerned about appearing too dependent on Cambridge.[170]

PHASE FOUR: THE DEMOCRATIC ECONOMIST THEORETICIAN'S RETURN TO THE STATE

The Democratic-Keynesian alliance reached its peak in the Kennedy-Johnson years. JFK's administration featured not only a singularly influential CEA but also a large contingent of current and former ADA members.

On the eve of Kennedy's inauguration, the president-elect informed his economic team of his intent to make the White House "a pulpit for public education in economics."[171] Via JFK's CEA—chaired by Walter Heller (1915–1987) and filled out by James Tobin and Kermit Gordon—the administration's monetary policies were oriented toward national economic stability and growth, questions of interest rates and the supply of money were weighed against "economic circumstances," and the principle of balanced budgets as a goal in itself was set aside.[172] Communicated by Heller and the general public in 1961, the media dubbed it "the New Economics."[173]

Given the shared intellectual and political trajectories of members of the CEA under Heller, not to mention JFK's Keynesian coaching since his days on the JEC, it is perhaps not surprising that Heller's CEA exhibited an unusual degree of professional camaraderie. As Tobin later commented:

> I think there is wide agreement that the 1960s were the best years of [the] CEA's life, that under Heller's leadership the CEA achieved greater standing with the president, the rest of the federal govern-

ment, the Congress, the press, the economics profession, and the general public than at any other time. During the 1960s the small CEA staff . . . certainly reached unrivaled heights of quality, dedication, and *esprit de corps.*[174]

This period of extraordinarily friendly state-Democratic-economics relations extended beyond the CEA. Through the ADA other economists, academics, and New Deal liberals entered into the Kennedy administration alongside Heller, Gordon, and Tobin. By one estimate around forty past or current ADA members could be found inside the Kennedy administration.[175]

But, in a sign of problems to come, the academic, economic, and ADA presence in the White House was not lost on outside observers, nor was it always viewed positively. Political cartoons in the *Cincinnati Enquirer,* the *Holyoke (Mass.) Transcript-Telegram,* and the *Columbia State* in South Carolina caricatured Kennedy playing a "New Frontier Policy" piano score by "ADA advisers" to a rapt audience of ADAers including Bowles and Galbraith; being held at gunpoint by a scruffy ADA bandit demanding "political payment" in the form of "more liberalism"; and trapped in a cage made up of the letters "ADA," deaf to entreaties of a frantic taxpayer.[176] Some conservatives saw the ADA's presence as ominous proof of the arrival of an ideological party of the left in the White House: an article in the *National Review* directly compared the JFK government and the British Labour government of 1924.[177]

CONCLUSION: TOWARD A GENERAL ACCOUNT
OF ECONOMISTIC LEFTISM

The story of the making of American economistic leftism can be recapped as follows. At the onset of the Great Depression American economists, for the most part, operated at a distance from partisan politics. In 1930 there was no such thing as a campaign or White House economist, and no clear notion that such a thing was necessary. Economists, especially of an agricultural sort, had connections with government agencies. Economics was neither Republican nor Democratic. The nonpartisanship of American economics differed from professional counterparts in Western Europe, which had historical ties to liberal (as opposed to religious, monarchical, and conservative)—and *not* socialist, social democratic, or Labour—parties.

But, as the Polanyian dynamics of the 1920s and 1930s set in, protective countermovements—manifested in unrest over factory conditions, workers' rights, and controversies over unemployment—set off new political and intellectual dynamics. On the one hand, political struggles over economic facts, including the causes and extent of unemployment, intensified; on the other hand, economists-in-training, whose ranks (and professional opportunities) were growing partly *because* of intensified public contestation over economic facts, challenged gold standard economic orthodoxies. Here we find that American and Western European contexts had an important similarity: mainstream academics and political elites alike rejected economic thinking that ran against gold standard, balanced budget orthodoxies. When Keynesian analysis finally broke into mainstream American economics between 1937 and 1948, Hoover and others likened it to Marxism.[178] Republican anti-Keynesianism at this time extended across the aisle, well into Democratic ranks.

Between the 1932 presidential campaign and the early New Deal period, however, the entry of new, younger-generation, Keynesian economists into the professional and political mainstream took shape via a party-centered network: the White House–based pro-spenders. Elements of this network extended into academe, and especially to Cambridge, Massachusetts, and played an important role in making Keynesianism into academic orthodoxy. Keynesianism also became an implicitly *Democratic* economics; Keynesian economists became Democratic educators, strategists, speechwriters, and formulators of programs and policies. This economist-heavy Democratic network shaped the formation of the Executive Office of the President, which in turn fortified Keynesian economics' academic stature—a process marked, especially, by the 1946 establishment of the Council of Economic Advisers (CEA) in the White House. Keynesian economists thus rose to the peak of the academic profession, became the unofficial economists of the Democratic New Dealers, and inscribed the Democratic-Keynesian relationship into the executive branch.

The 1950s marked a period of Keynesian economists' relative exclusion from the heights of the federal state. But, thanks especially to the ADA, they stayed closely involved in national politics and in the selection and economic education of Democratic presidential aspirants. Indeed, by the time of JFK's presidential run Keynesian economists' involvement in Democratic presidential campaigns was taken for granted. In Samuelson's words, "[T]he people around [John F.] Kennedy, and Kennedy himself probably, had a feeling that they needed some economists," even if "they weren't sure just why."[179]

Taking a transatlantic view, we can now say something about the reasons for newfound affinities in the outlook, vocabularies, and orientations of European social democrats, Labour's revisionists (or Gaitskellites), and American Democratic liberals around midcentury: an *interdependent* party-economics relationship, embodied in the figure of the economist theoretician. We can also identify distinctive features of the American move to economistic leftism that were by-products of the United States' peculiarly noncentralized political parties: the formation of more or less formal intermediary institutions, like the ADA and the Finletter group, that sustained linkages between professional economists and the Democratic Party during Republican administrations and the early Cold War.

Based on the analysis thus far, Figure 5.3 offers a graphic summary of the causal dynamics behind Western leftism's economistic reinvention, and the making of center-left economist theoreticians, in Western Europe and the United States. A key outcome, in all cases, was the making of a new party-expert relation that undergirded what is sometimes called the "Keynesian era": interdependence between mainstream, professional economics and left parties.

In the next chapter I consider the figure of the midcentury, center-left economist theoretician more closely, with an eye to how his situation between academe and politics aligned with a certain view of the economist's role in politics and public life. I focus, in other words, on the *Keynesian ethic* of the economist theoretician: an understanding of the economist-in-politics as a politically savvy mediator and communicator whose task was to fit scientific knowledge to the imperatives of politics and the strategic priorities of parties-in-government and for whom

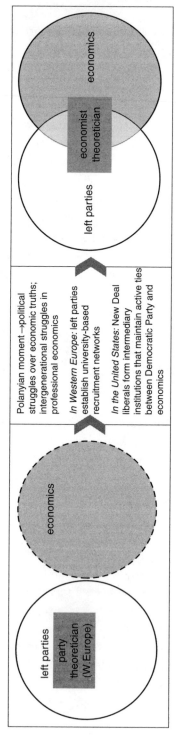

Figure 5.3. The drivers of interdependence in leftism's first reinvention. This figure maps out the causal processes driving "reinvention #1" in Figure 1.1.

economic management necessarily entailed negotiation and consensus-building. I then show that the implicit partisanship of the economist theoretician gave rise to criticism and opposition, both professional and political. From the 1960s an increasingly politicized economics profession became host to a new sort of economist, who saw the world in a very different way.

CHAPTER SIX

Interdependence in the Making of Leftism's Second Reinvention

The detached, Olympian, take-it-or-leave-it approach to Presidential economic advice—the dream of the logical positivist . . . simply does not accord with the demands of relevance and realism.

—Walter Heller, 1966

[T]he role of the market . . . is that it permits unanimity without conformity; that it is a system of effectively proportional representation. . . . The wider the range of activities covered by the market, the fewer are the issues on which explicitly political decisions are required.

—Milton Friedman, 1962

WALTER HELLER is a prime example of the kind of left party expert that I have characterized as an economist theoretician. Heller and his ilk, we have seen, did much more than analyze the economy and advise policy-makers. Economist theoreticians played intermediary roles between left parties, constituencies (in particular, organized labor), employers, and government agencies; they formulated and implemented economic policies on the basis of an assumed need for negotiation and consensus-building; and they participated in the construction of advisory institutions that consolidated professional economists' roles in government, politics, and public debate.

Heller's remarks, above, suggest that economist theoreticians also had a certain conception of the economist-in-politics: to be a voice of scientific reason, and yet remain attuned to real-time political necessities and strategic concerns. This *Keynesian ethic* surely expressed his experiences of moving in between professional economics, left parties, and parties-in-government. In other words, in the same way that the orthodox economic commitments of Europe's socialist party theoreticians' expressed their dependence on, and centrality to, socialist parties (and, by extension, their *luck* of ties to academe), the Keynesian ethics of economist theoreticians expressed their situation at the (new) intersection of politics and professional economics.

Not all economists, of course, were economist theoreticians, nor did all economists share the Keynesian ethic. The second quotation given above, from the famous Chicago economist Milton Friedman (Heller's contemporary), attests to this. For Friedman the economist's task was not to manage the economy in a politically attuned way, but rather to speak on behalf of the market and, by supporting the market's extension, to limit the scope of political decision-making. In other words the economist should be attuned to markets, not politics.

Long associated with the efforts of marginalized postwar neoliberals to legitimate a new brand of free market thinking, Friedman had his own political ties—of a right-leaning, conservative, and Republican sort. He is now among the best-known figures associated with the neoliberal project.[1] In both of these respects (among others), he was hardly a typical economist. Nonetheless, just as Max Weber could cite Benjamin Franklin's thinking as a distillation of the Protestant ethic, Friedman's comments suggest a distinctively *neoliberal ethic*—one that is striking in contrast with its Keynesian counterpart.[2] And Friedman was, in his way, extraordinarily influential in American economics. Because the Keynesian era was defined not only by economics, but also by the extension of American hegemony, the reach of a Chicago economist of Friedman's generation could extend well beyond national boundaries.

Yet we should not overestimate the strategic influence of any particular economist, or of economics in general. Nor can an account of neoliberal economists, who had no discernible reach into center-left parties, suffice as an explanation of leftism's second reinvention. But a concern with neoliberal ethics, as opposed to neoliber*als*, shifts the explanatory focus to the economics profession as a whole. And that profession, as we have seen, was interdependent with left parties by the early 1960s.

A concern with professional ethics also draws one's attention to the fact that Heller's and Friedman's differences cannot be reduced to

Keynesianism versus monetarism, or the relative importance of fiscal versus monetary policy, or the relative virtues of states versus markets. These characterizations overlook the fact that the neoliberal challenge to Keynesianism entailed a definite set of claims as to what economists can and cannot do and still call themselves economists. They also take no particular account of the fact that the bearers of neoliberal ethics, like economist theoreticians, were historically, professionally, and politically situated. In short, the neoliberal challenge to Keynesianism was not just a battle of ideas; it was a contest over economists' credibility, waged by people with political leanings and, perhaps more importantly, professional investments. Much was at stake: without scientific credibility, economist theoreticians were merely partisans.

Taking the contrast between Keynesian and neoliberal ethics as a starting point, this chapter considers how mid-twentieth-century interdependence between mainstream economics and center-left parties, and tensions therein, set the stage for leftism's second reinvention. This requires rethinking the Keynesian era in a party-centered way. Specifically, I argue that new linkages between professional economics and center-left parties—or *interdependence*—created the novel possibility of cross-field effects, in which changes in economics had direct implications for left parties in particular, and changes in left parties had direct implications for economics. This dynamic, I argue, lies at the heart of leftism's second reinvention.

The chapter proceeds as follows. After some conceptual and historical preliminaries, I make the case for understanding interdependence as a basis of economics' unusual capacity for political intervention in the twentieth century. I then turn to an analysis of Keynesian ethics. In particular, I offer a "most different systems" comparison of the perspectives of an American and a West German economist theoretician—Walter Heller and Karl Schiller—on the public roles and responsibilities of economists. Documenting striking similarities in Heller's and Schiller's professional ethics, this analysis suggests that economist theoreticians shared a notion of the economist-in-politics as an agent of economic management whose success depended on a certain sensitivity to the strategic necessities of parties-in-government.

I then consider the conditions and implications of Keynesian ethics. Economist theoreticians' ability to maintain professional esteem, despite their party investments, was conditional on their power and prestige within the economics profession. And in the 1960s, even as economics was growing in size and public influence, economist theoreticians confronted new professional threats. Turning to the oft-referenced "collapse of Keynesianism," I emphasize the challenge to the likes of Heller that the neoliberal ethic represented, especially insofar as Friedman and others like him acquired a new capacity for public intervention. And acquire this capacity they did, via at least three routes: the international proliferation of free market think tanks, new alliances with parties of the center-right, and professional channels made possible by the considerable public stature of the (Keynesian) economics profession.

How, specifically, did all this affect left parties? I identify at least two dynamics. First, free market think tanks' new prominence in center-right politics prompted a mimetic organizational response on the center-left: the construction of a new international network of "progressive" think tanks, foundations, magazines, and research institutes. Like socialist leftism's newspapers, journals, and weeklies, this terrain was linked with the formation of a new sort of left party expert: the progressive policy specialist. Second, the neoliberal challenge both fueled the politicization of economics and shaped professional interpretations of emergent economic troubles (in particular, "stagflation") as a definitive case against the Keynesian ethic. In other words, the neoliberal challenge rendered the making of domestically grounded, politics and government-oriented economists like Walter Heller improbable. As economics turned to markets it also became an increasingly transnationalized profession, increasingly centered on business and finance. In other words Western economists remained, by and large, left-leaning, but came to be grounded more in finance than in politics and attuned more to problems of international markets—especially financial markets—than to problems of domestic government. I refer to this new sort of economist as the transnationalized, finance-oriented economist (TFE).

The formation of the progressive policy specialist and the TFE had a curious complement: the strategist, or "spin doctor." Anchored to the burgeoning profession of political consulting, the strategist had little to do with professional economics. But in the concluding sections I suggest that there was a connection, or complementarity, between the TFE and the strategist: the displacement of intermediary economist theoreticians by market-representing TFEs prompted party elites to seek out strategic experts who were responsive, borrowing Heller's phrasing, to "the demands of relevance and realism." This sets the stage for a more grounded, refraction analysis of leftism's second, neoliberalized reinvention in the chapters to follow.

CONCEPTUAL PRELIMINARIES: PARTIES, ECONOMIC EXPERTISE, AND CROSS-FIELD EFFECTS

This chapter builds on existing literature on the late postwar relationship between economic expertise and Western politics. At the same time, however, it also calls into question a dominant conception of the political as primarily consisting of states and governing institutions, without any particular attention to political parties.

The sociologist Marion Fourcade, for instance, characterizes the period from the 1930s to the 1960s—that is, the period in which left parties and professional economics became interdependent—as one marked by economics' "emergence as a technique of government . . . and, more generally, as a tool for the exercise of public expertise." "Economic knowledge, like any form of knowledge," Fourcade adds, "is always deeply intertwined with politics."[3] But there is little indication in Fourcade's analysis of the postwar leftishness of Western economics and economists, or of Keynesian economics' deep interconnection with parties of the left. Fourcade's masterful *Economists and Societies* (2009) makes frequent reference to political parties, but it does not systematically historicize or situate the party-economics relationship.

The treatment of parties as incidental, rather than analytically central, is generally symptomatic of contemporary literature on politics, experts, and professional economics. Parties are often referenced but not explicitly theorized, for instance, in John Campbell and Ove Pedersen's otherwise laudable formulation of "knowledge regimes" as a pillar of political economy[4] and in an important article on the "political effects of economists" by the sociologists Daniel Hirschman and Elizabeth Popp Berman (2014). Hirschman and Berman rightly note that "meso-level social orders affect the political influence of economists" and that one needs to consider the specifics of economists' 'institutional position.'"[5] But "institutional position" seems to refer to positions with respect to states and governing institutions, not parties: Hirschman and Berman point out that the processes by which economists gain position are "messy and political" and that little research attends to "how economists attained their positions inside the state and its networks," but they stop short of referencing parties directly.[6]

The omission of parties has analytical consequences. For instance, by contrast with my party-centric account of the making of the 1946 Employment Act and the CEA in the United States (Chapter 5), a story without parties overlooks the role, and historical novelty, of the Democratic Party-economics relationship in the making of Keynesian institutions.[7] The same can be said of economics-left party ties in Western European countries. A partyless story also misses an important source of historical change: alliances between knowledge-bearing experts and political power-seeking entails an inevitable tension, or opposition, that has long been recognized as historically consequential.[8] In other words, a tendency to conceptually submerge political parties obscures the dynamic, tension-ridden relationship between politics and expertise that shapes historical transformations.

Attention to party-economics relationship is as central for understanding the rise of the Keynesian era as it is for grasping the neoliberal transition that followed. The period from the 1930s to the 1960s was special not only because economics became central to modern government, but also because left parties and mainstream economics became *interdependent*. But, like the pairing of socialism and left parties-in-formation in Western Europe in the mid- to late nineteenth century, the twentieth-century alliance of economics and center-left parties was forged. That forging then generated new historical possibilities.

Interdependence was important because it generated the possibility of what the sociologist Cristina Mora calls "cross-field effects:" a historical dynamic in which "change in field A sparks concurrent, co-constitutive changes in field B," even as "changes in field B lead to changes in A."[9] Stated in Mora's terms, the newly interdependent relationship between economics (a cultural field) and party politics (the political field) generated cross-field effects between the 1960s and the 1990s that shaped leftism's second reinvention.

Given the submergence of parties in existing scholarship on economics and politics, however, an analysis of cross-field effects in the making of neoliberalized leftism requires not only conceptual, but also historical, groundwork. To this we now turn.

HISTORICAL PRELIMINARIES: INTERDEPENDENCE IN THE MAKING OF THE KEYNESIAN ERA

Keynesianism, like socialism and neoliberalism, involves a certain set of ideas about how economic life worked, how it should be managed, and the place of the state therein. In his most famous academic work, *The General Theory of Employment, Interest and Money* (1936), Keynes formalized the notion that market forces are fundamentally unstable in the short to medium term, and may stagnate for long periods of time at unnecessarily high levels of unemployment, as a fundamental problematic of macroeconomics.[10] Taking aim at "classical economics" and especially Say's law—which states (in Keynes's words) that "the aggregate demand price of output . . . is equal to its aggregate supply price," and so "there is no obstacle to full employment"—Keynes built his case by focusing on oversaving and underinvestment.[11]

Insisting that classical economics was out of touch with reality, Keynes argued that investment responds to many factors other than the supply of money and that governments can and should deal with depressions by boosting spending and raising aggregate demand, thus producing a "multiplier" effect that would more than compensate for the costs of borrowing.[12] In Peter Hall's concise summary, Keynes thence developed three prescriptions: policy-makers could use demand management to shape growth and employment; fiscal policy is at least as important as monetary policy as an economic management tool; and rather than continually striving for balanced budgets, governments should borrow during recession and save in periods of growth.[13]

Keynes, who thought (in Robert Skidelsky's account) that "economics was over-addicted to 'specious precision,'" wrote *General Theory* in a primarily verbal format, with a smattering of equation-heavy interludes (for instance, on the "employment function").[14] But in time *General Theory*'s arguments were "whittled down to four equations and two curves," formalized in the IS-LM (investment-saving, liquidity preference–money supply) model initiated by John Hicks (1937) and developed by Franco Modigliani, Lawrence Klein, Alvin Hansen, James

Tobin, Paul Samuelson, and others.[15] Another important elaboration of Keynesian thinking came in the form of the Phillips curve, originated by A. W. Phillips in 1958, which identified an inverse historical relationship between rates of unemployment and wage inflation in Britain between 1861 and 1957.[16] By the 1960s the Phillips curve was broadly accepted in macroeconomics and, because it offered a way of managing economic systems by manipulating unemployment via budgetary policy (taxation and public spending), was an important tool of policy-oriented economic analysis.[17]

The mathematical elaboration of Keynesianism-after-Keynes, of which the Phillips curve was symptomatic, was central to economics' formation as a tool of modern government—including, of course, left parties-in-government.[18] Mathematicization helped Keynesian economics come to fruition as a new policy science able to enact a decidedly mechanical vision of the economic world.[19] "[E]conomists, especially those seeking a scientific economics, have always been inordinately fascinated by *machines*," explains the economist and philosopher of science Philip Mirowski.[20] The development of macroeconomic statistics, innovations in computing, and calculative techniques for specifying, say, productivity or inflation at a given level of unemployment rendered "the economy" subject to deliberate governmental management and brought the metaphor of the engine-like economy to life.[21]

One should note here that quantitative Keynesian macroeconomics emerged in a very particular geopolitical moment in which empire was giving way to a world of nation-states that was soon defined fundamentally by the Cold War, East-West divide. This emerging world was situated within a postwar Bretton Woods international architecture that was famously characterized by John Ruggie (following Karl Polanyi) as "embedded liberalism."[22] Meanwhile colonial empires gave way to sovereign nations that took sides, or were caught in between, the communist East and a capitalist West. And with the emergence of a world of nation-states came a specifically national way of thinking about economic life. As explored in the work of Timothy Mitchell, Daniel Breslau, Philip Mirowski, and Daniel Hirschman, the foundational object of Keynesian macroeconomics, "the economy," was a construction born no earlier than the 1930s, grounded in a mechanical imagination in which economies were like engines that could be run at "full throttle" but were prone to "overheating."[23] Keynesian macroeconomics' development was linked to these postwar geopolitical transformations, especially insofar as it was capable of rendering (national) economies calculable.

Notable, also, is the United States' newly powerful postwar geopolitical position, which was enshrined in the Bretton Woods Accord of 1944. The accord, premised on an understanding that the Great Depression and World Wars I and II as having originated in capitalism run amok, gave rise to the International Monetary Fund (IMF), the World Bank, and a new international monetary architecture that hinged on the U.S. dollar. Bretton Woods thus established a politically managed international system in which the United States was a lynchpin, postcolonial nation-states were on the rise, and the reach of Western capitalism was more of a question than an established fact. This was the context of about a thirty-year period of industry-driven, postwar economic growth in Western countries, in which the institutions of "welfare capitalism" (managed economies, strong unions, relatively generous safety nets) helped to ensure that profits were broadly shared across most income-earning groups.

INTERDEPENDENCE AS A MEANS TO PUBLIC INTERVENTION

In the era of embedded liberalism the economics profession became central to politics and government in a whole new way. The Keynesian era was significant in part because an academic profession generated guiding metaphors, technical devices, and terminological shortcuts that helped to organize a whole era of modern Western history.[24] Without the technical vocabulary of Keynesian economics, the mere task of describing the institutions of midcentury Western politics is nearly impossible. In this sense postwar economics was not merely a technology of government or a tool of policy-makers; it was *constitutive* of political life and conceptions of what it meant to govern.

Economics' constitutive role is well recognized, if easily exaggerated or oversimplified, in current scholarship. In Hirschman and Berman's analysis economics' influence goes well beyond the technical tools used to inform and structure decision-making: "economics discourse" in general "reshapes how non-economist policymakers understand a given issue."[25] For scholars of "performativity," economics' influence in public life extends from the practical activities and technical products of economists. Here postwar economics not only organizes politics and policy decision making, it also (in the terms of Michel Callon) "performs, shapes, and formats the economy."[26]

But the means and conditions of economics' performativity are not always perfectly clear in existing research. We have seen that, in the 1920s and 1930s, economists' advisory access and knack for mathematical and statistical argumentation was not a sufficient means to political power. Nor do sheer numbers of economists in government agencies or political institutions automatically translate into influence. As the historian of economics A. W. B. Coats reminds us, "A tiny handful of strategically placed individuals with direct access to powerful decisionmakers may . . . be far more influential than a mighty host of trained economists."[27] What, then, imbued economics with considerable capacities for public intervention?

In a sense, the analysis thus far has already addressed this question: economists' incorporation into left parties, born of a Polanyian moment, created important channels of intervention. In other words, party-economics interdependence was a key means to public intervention. But there is more to it than this. The science and technology studies scholars Donald MacKenzie and Yuval Millo have shown that both network locations and membership in a morally grounded, professional community have been key conditions of economics' performative influence.[28] In a study of the making of the Chicago Board Options Exchange, MacKenzie and Millo argue that performativity operates via actor-networks engaged in practical action on the basis of shared concerns with "reputation and respect."[29] The broader implication is that the performative force of economics, and indeed any body of knowledge, is conditional on both *network ties* and the *moral meanings* that inhere within them.

Interdependence and Network Ties

True to MacKenzie and Millo's arguments, my analysis thus far shows that networks in and around left parties were central channels through which Keynesian economists acquired performative capacity. It was only after economists became deeply enmeshed with elite left party networks, displacing party theoreticians, that Keynesian economists shaped left parties-in-government and programmatic language. Interdependence was also a driver of economists' growing presence in postwar government: in the 1960s and early 1970s—when left parties-in-government were relatively commonplace in Western countries—the ranks of professional economists grew to new highs in the United States, the United Kingdom, and elsewhere.[30]

The rise of a specifically Keynesian economics in the 1960s is especially notable in West Germany, given the historical influence of ordoliberalism there. West Germany saw "a remarkable growth in the number, scale, and importance of economists and economic research institutions" in the 1960s, according to the historian of economics Harald Hagemann.[31] It was in this period that the dominance of Freiburg ordoliberalism waned, along with Erhard's authority, and questions considered Keynesian—the management of a full employment economy, "restraining inflationary pressures, avoiding external disequilibria," and "fine-tuning"—became the order of the day.[32]

Credentialed economists' public prestige also reached an arguable peak in the 1960s.[33] Here we might note that both Walter Heller and Karl Schiller, against background images of jagged graph lines that clearly suggest a certain technical mastery, graced the covers of *Time* and *Der Spiegel* in the 1960s.[34] We might also note *Time* magazine's famous 1965 declaration of economics' mastery in public affairs:

> Economists have descended in force from their ivory towers and now sit confidently at the elbow of almost every important leader in Government and business. . . . They have proved that they can prod, goad and inspire a rich and free nation to climb to nearly full employment and unprecedented prosperity.[35]

This message of economics' mastery was a common theme, echoed in other popular literature of the time.[36]

In short, there is good reason to think that interdependence was a key basis of the kinds of network ties that imbued mid-century Keynesian economics with performative potential. What, then, of the "moral meanings" to which MacKenzie and Millo refer? Did Keynesian economists' share political leanings and conceptions of "reputation and respect" that bore the imprint of interdependence with left parties?

INTERDEPENDENCE AND MORAL MEANINGS

Keynesian economics is well noted for its affinities with the broadly social democratic principles of welfare capitalism.[37] Many prominent Keynesians had well-documented leftward leanings—noted, for instance, by Paul Samuelson in 1971:

> [I]n this country most economists have been associated with the critics of the ruling elite, the business elite—favoring the Democratic programs of the New Deal, Fair Deal, New Frontier, and Great Society, rather than the rugged individualism of Herbert Hoover and/or Barry Goldwater or the moderated versions of Eisenhower and Nixon.[38]

In 1976 Everett Carll Ladd Jr. and Seymour Martin Lipset confirmed Samuelson's assessment of American economics' Democratic inclinations.[39] This then becomes cross-nationally significant if we consider that Samuelson's widely used economics textbook, with its narrative of a unified "neo-classical synthesis," anchored the discipline in the United States and elsewhere.[40]

Recent surveys document a persistent leftishness in Western economics professions. In a 2005 survey in the United States, Democrat-leaning economists outnumbered Republican-leaning economists by a ratio of about three to one.[41] A 2012 survey suggests that the ratio may have declined, but a Democratic lean remains in evidence: 56 percent of economists surveyed were Democratic, and less than 21 percent were Republican.[42] Research on the political leanings of European economists identifies a similarly leftward professional bent.[43] The historians Avner Offer and Gabriel Söderberg, in an exhaustive survey of research on the politics of economists, highlight the leftward leanings of economists across the transatlantic divide.[44]

Political leanings are but one kind of moral sentiment, however. Important, also, is how economists see their professional roles and responsibilities. Marion Fourcade draws our attention, for instance, to Keynes's 1924 characterization of the "master economist":

> The master economist must possess a rare combination of gifts. He must . . . combine talents not often found together. He must be mathematician, statesman, historian, philosopher—in some degree. He must understand symbols and speak in terms of the general, and touch abstract and concrete in the same flight of thought. He must study the present in light of the past for the purpose of the future.[45]

Keynes' commentary here becomes unsurprising when we take into account that Keynes himself played many roles—as a civil servant, an academic, an economic journalist, and a Liberal party expert—and that British economics in Keynes' time was historically the province of "leisured gentlemen, enlightened businessmen, intellectuals, journalists, statesmen, and civil servants."[46] More generally, the notion that economists' worldview is linked to their institutional situation finds strong support in Marion Fourcade's cross-national account of how the shape and structure of the state has shaped the making of very different sorts of economists in the United States, the United Kingdom, and France.[47]

By extension, if the present emphasis on economics-left party interdependence is well placed, then we should find that economist theoreticians' self-conceptions, or professional ethics, comport with their positioning at the intersection of left parties and economics. In short, we should find that economist theoreticians were bearers of a distinctly *Keynesian ethic* that expressed the experiential and situational fact of interdependence. The following analysis evaluates this claim.

THE KEYNESIAN ETHIC: SCHILLER AND HELLER COMPARED

To explore the proposition that interdependence was linked with a distinctively Keynesian ethic, this section compares the professional worldviews of Karl Schiller (1911–1994) and Walter Heller (1915–1987). Schiller and Heller are usefully compared because, at first glance, one might expect them to have little, if anything, in common. In the language of social scientific comparativists, Heller and Schiller moved in "most different systems."[48]

The development of the American Democratic Party and the (West) German SPD could hardly be more different: the Democratic Party is older, historically continuous, weakly bounded, and relatively decentralized; it was never formally allied with organized labor and never socialist or Marxist. The SPD is younger, historically discontinuous, and labor-connected and has been a case study in bureaucratic centralization since Robert Michels's *Political Parties*.[49] Until Bad Godesberg the SPD was self-consciously Marxian, a line of thinking that has always been anathema to both of the great American parties. American and West German economics also differ in important ways: postwar American economics in the United States had internal divisions—especially between Harvard and MIT and the University of Chicago—but no major disruptions in the twentieth century, and the profession was increasingly Keynesian after the 1930s. By contrast, Nazism and the East-West division fractured German economics, which then reemerged in West Germany with Freiburg school ordoliberalism at its center.

How, then, did Heller and Schiller understand the relationship between science and politics, and their place in it? For an answer from Karl Schiller, I use essays written between 1953 and the early 1960s, published in 1964, titled *The Economist and Society* (*Der Ökonom und die Gesellschaft*).[50] From Walter Heller I draw from lectures delivered at Harvard University in March 1966, published later that year as *New Dimensions of Political Economy*.

DIFFERENT WORLDS, SHARED ETHICS

In the foreword to *The Economist and Society*, published in 1964, Schiller describes the moment as one defined by Keynesian problems ("optimal economic growth and full employment") and the increasing application of science to policy. "[T]he organization of economic life is to a considerable extent determined," Schiller states, "by what is researched and taught at universities." Schiller titled his book, he notes, in recognition of "the tension between rationality and spontaneity, theory and action, program and reality" that the new public role of scientific economics brought to the fore.[51] Heller's *New Dimensions* articulates similar themes, remarking that he deliberately uses the terms "political economy" and "political economist" because the "new economics" refers to new political *"uses* of economics rather than the *substance."*[52] What had changed was not economics itself but rather its relationship to public life.

For both men economics' growing public role meant, necessarily, a retreat of emotion, ideology, "spontaneity," and partisanship. Heller notes that, thanks to "conceptual advances and quantitative research," "emotion" was giving way to "reason."[53] Likewise, Schiller explains that, as economics' political reach expands, politics becomes driven more by reason rather than "ideologies" or "dogmas"; economics' advance was pushing back the frontier of "spontaneity" by making politics "pragmatic."[54] In modern economics' synthesis of "two great masses of ideas," namely, "socialism and liberalism," Schiller asserts that "something new is really coming to the surface": politics was unified on the basis of a "modern economic policy."[55]

"Modern" meant scientifically grounded—that is, backed by a politically autonomous, consensual economics profession—and yet more politically central. The former was necessary to the latter. Schiller emphasizes how economics' formation as a specialized, cumulative, consensual scientific endeavor, giving rise to the pure economist, underpinned the unification of modern economics. "For more than 25 years, the simple expression 'economics' or 'economist' has been increasingly used," as opposed to the "state scientist" or "national economist," he notes.[56] Heller tells a similar story of increasing scientific autonomy and its importance for the "political economist." The economist now has a "new, more responsible—and more exposed—role as a presidential adviser and consensus-seeker," Heller explains, but that exposure is not too great thanks to steady scientific advancement and "growing professional consensus."[57]

The message, from both, is that the political economist can maintain his place at the boundary of science and politics so long as economics remains a noncontentious, politically autonomous, cumulative endeavor. Thankfully, Heller explains, economists of both the academic and the applied sort "take for granted that the government must step in to provide the essential stability at high levels of employment and growth that the market mechanism, alone, cannot deliver."[58] Modern economists agreed that economic management was government's rightful concern.

Neither comments on party affiliations or political leanings, however obvious. Schiller was, by 1964, a longtime member of the SPD, central to economic policy-making in the parties-in-government of Hamburg and Berlin, and noted for his role in Bad Godesberg; in 1964 Schiller joined the executive committee of the SPD, and in 1965 the party delegated him from Berlin to the Bundestag.[59] Heller's Democratic connection was also clear: it was through the Keynesian-Democratic connection, after all, that Heller was "thrust into the limelight from academic obscurity."[60] And yet Heller keeps his political affiliations implicit, characterizing the Kennedy-Johnson administrations for bringing together the language and understandings of "men of affairs" and "modern" economists, but never noting that these were specifically Democratic administrations.[61]

The economist theoretician was thus grounded primarily in cumulative science, not politics—and yet he was also, undeniably, politically aligned. Both acknowledge this indirectly, pointing to the differences between economics and politics and highlighting the delicate task of negotiating between them. Heller, for instance, explains that the economist theoretician cannot be too political or too academic if he is to reconcile "good economics" with "good politics." Fortunately, he explains, the 1946 Employment Act requires the economist to stay grounded: a "detached, Olympian, take-it-or-leave-it approach to Presidential economic advice—the dream of the logical positivist . . . simply does not accord with the demands of relevance and realism and the requirements of the Employment Act," and so the economist theoretician has no choice but to stay "within the technical limits of his analysis" while operating "deep in the heart of realism."[62]

Schiller makes a similar point when he describes how economists who, like him, "leave the universities" and take on the role of the "economic practitioner" encounter an essentially foreign setting. "Two quite different . . . attitudes meet" in this situation, Schiller explains: the economic practitioner encounters "the man of the situation, who is experienced, intuitive and instinctive"—the "entrepreneur," the "trade union leader," the "administrator." But the economic practitioner has a different orientation: "by virtue of his scientific training" he relies on analysis rather than strategic instinct.[63]

The key was a certain professional malleability, including a willingness to adapt to political necessities. Schiller describes how the economist-in-politics brings science and politics together by playing multiple roles that sometimes involve the use of technical skills for political ends: economist advisers worked "not only as consultants but as entrepreneurs, managers and officials" and, sometimes, as an "economic astronomer" that ties economic forecasts to political calendars—for instance, offering growth forecasts to inform the determination of an election date.[64] The economic practitioner uses models to calculate the effects of different courses of action for use by the "politician, entrepreneur or trade union leader."[65]

Schiller also points to the ways in which economists use language to organize political debates. In Schiller's account the economist provides "mental images"—terms like "public interest," "maximum social product," and "general equilibrium"—that can serve as "models of practical thought."[66] But the task was not to eliminate politicians' strategic maneuverability: "We must always point out that not everything is quantifiable and calculable and that much is unpredictable, and thus space must be left for the free and spontaneous decision."[67]

Similarly, Heller elaborates on the economist's insertion of "semantics" into political language.[68] The economist may set parameters on politics, and may even define the terms of politics itself—but he does not snuff it out. Heller emphasizes that the economist needs to offer strategically helpful advice that is linked in the minds of politicians to definite economic effects, especially growth, if he is to maintain his influence. Economists' ability to take credit for growth, and the fact that growth offered leverage to President Johnson (LBJ) and enhanced the United States' geopolitical position, allowed them to sustain their political influence. Thanks to growth, Heller explains, LBJ was able to finance wartime operations and make the United States "a showcase of modern capitalism"; sustain a positive balance of payments that strengthened its international bargaining position; and tame the forces of domestic partisanship, since the president did not have to finance federal programs by "robbing Peter to pay Paul."[69]

Apparently, Heller and Schiller shared a certain ethic concerning who the economist was, or should be. Part of that ethic was a recognition that scientific standing depended on the backing of a broadly consensual scientific profession. But, at the same time, the economist-in-politics had to stay grounded in political realities, playing multiple roles and offering prescriptions, choice sets, and forecasts that meshed with political exigencies. In short, economic advising had to be scientifically grounded but politically sensitive and strategically adaptable.

NEW ECONOMISTS, NEW LEFTISM?

Hints of a Keynesian ethic can be found in accounts of other economist theoreticians with whom we are now familiar. The historian Michael Bernstein recounts that James Tobin "firmly believed" that economic advice had to jibe, specifically, with partisan concerns:

> Yale's James Tobin . . . firmly believed that "[a] neutral nonpartisan Council [CEA], if one could be imagined, would simply not provide advice of interest to the President." The chief executive, in his view, surely needed "professional" as well as "disinterested advice," but it necessarily had to come from those who "share[d] his objectives and his concern for the record of the Administration."[70]

Hugh Gaitskell's biographer, Brian Brivati, notes Gaitskell's characteristic tendency to see "modern economics" and distributional ends of the Labour Party as separate but wholly reconcilable; Brivati emphasizes Gaitskell's decidedly domestically centered, planning-oriented conception of the economics profession, noting that he "did not believe in the efficacy of markets."[71] June Morris offers a similar portrait: in the 1930s Gaitskell was "less concerned with the theory of economics than with its practical application to the miserable conditions of poverty, inequality and high unemployment."[72] Last but not least, there is surely no more famous expression of a managerial, politically attuned, Keynesian professional ethic than the Rehn-Meidner model in Sweden.

Positioned in between economics and national politics, the economist theoretician had a characteristically national, managerial, party-friendly way of thinking about economic processes and the public role of the economist: for the economist theoretician economics was a science of economies and their political management, not a science of apolitical markets. This would be hard to understand without an understanding of the peculiarly hybrid social location of economist theoreticians: the Keynesian era may have been (paraphrasing Walter Heller) the Age of the Economist Theoretician, but the Keynesian economist theoretician was deeply enmeshed in social democratic, laborite, and New Deal–liberal party networks. True to MacKenzie and Millo's arguments, Keynesian economists shared practical and moral self-conceptions.[73] What this meant, however, was that by changing the ethics, understandings, and orthodoxies of mainstream economics it had become possible, also, to change leftism. To this we now turn.

CHANGING LEFTISM BY CHANGING ECONOMICS

Long ago Karl Mannheim pointed out that when politics becomes scientific, science becomes political.[74] In theory, then, the scientifically disinterested yet politically invested Keynesian economist theoretician was an unlikely figure. As economist theoreticians understood, a situation in which a knowledge-producing profession is wrapped up with partisan politics is a fragile state of affairs.

In this light, one of the more remarkable aspects of the 1930s-1960s period was that economist theoreticians' partisan affiliations were essentially hidden in plain sight. This was the case, for instance, for Karl Schiller, who remained an "economist" despite the fact that (in the words of international affairs scholars Stephen Silvia and Michel Vale) "[a]ll of the leading Keynesian economists . . . were in the Social Democratic Party."[75] The same can be said of Gunnar Myrdal, Gösta Rehn, and Rudolf Meidner, whose roles in the programmatic development of the SAP were significant facets of what has been noted by historians of economics, rather generically, as postwar Sweden's "economist-intensive" politics.[76] In the United Kingdom the hybridity of figures ranging from Hugh Dalton and James Meade in the 1940s to Hugh Gaitskell, Harold Wilson, Thomas Balogh, and Nicholas Kaldor points to the same state of affairs.[77] All these figures embodied Granovetterian networks that linked left parties to professional economics, making possible economics' performative capacity in political life. But, at the same time, that capacity depended on economist theoreticians' standing as bearers of technical expertise—partisan affiliations notwithstanding.

New challenges to the professional standing of economist theoreticians emerged, however, in the mid-to-late 1960s. Here we come, inevitably, to the notorious "collapse of Keynesianism" and the birth of "stagflation"—that is, the Phillips curve–defying, cross-national, concomitant rise of inflation and unemployment that was first noted around 1965. We turn to this story here, with a particular focus on the American context (I deal with European countries more fully in Chapter 8).

Stagflation and the Collapse of Keynesianism, Revisited

The story of the collapse of Keynesianism is often linked up with the resurgent problem of inflation. Indeed, the economist and economic historian Michael A. Bernstein locates the extinguishing of "the prestige and the confidence" of Keynesian economists in the mid-1960s, amid inflation rates that reached 4.5 percent by mid-1968—which were broadly attributed to the income demands of overly powerful workers (the "wage-push" inflation thesis).[78] This then gave way to a concern with "stagflation"—a term that probably originated with Britain's Conservative shadow chancellor of the exchequer, Iain Macleod, in 1965.[79] By 1977 stagflation had become a well-defined, international concern— marked by 1977 report by a group of economists who, under the auspices of the OECD, backed the argument that, in the face of the Vietnam War, a "European wage explosion," the breakdown of the Bretton Woods exchange rate system, and the oil price shocks of 1973–1974 (with a second on the way, unbeknownst to the report's authors, in 1979), Keynesian management had become more a problem than a cure.[80] Bernstein recounts how, with the onset of inflation in the mid-1960s professional economics and "its leading disciples would never be the same."[81]

And yet the collapse of Keynesianism did not simply present itself as the self-evident consequence of inflation troubles; it emerged from a series of interpretive struggles in the context of left party-economics interdependence. Here the social and political locations of some of Keynesianism's more prominent critics are worth considering. Ian Macleod, for instance, was a prominent Conservative MP in the 1960s who used the term "stagflation" as part of a broader critique of the Labour government's use of Keynesian economists and economic calculation as a means of challenging the authority of the Treasury.[82] Restated in the terms of the present analysis, the problem of stagflation was born in Britain as a partisan critique of interdependence between Labour and Keynesian economics. We might also note the social and political locations of the authors of the aforementioned OECD report, "Towards Full Employment and Price Stability." The authors included eight economists: Paul McCracken (professor at the University of Michigan and Nixon's former CEA chairman—of which more below), Guido Carli (governor of the Bank of Italy), Herbert Giersch (director of the Institute for World Economics at Kiel University and a former member of the German SVR), Attila Karaosmanoglu (the International Bank of Reconstruction and Development's [IBRD—later the World Bank] director of development policy and a former Turkish deputy prime minister for economic affairs), Ryutaro Komiya (professor at the University of Tokyo), Assar Lindbeck (director of the Institute for International Economic Studies, Stockholm University), Robert Marjolin (former Organization for European Economic Cooperation [OEEC, later the OECD] secretary-general and vice president of the Commission of the European Economic Community—of which, also, more below), and Robin Matthews (a master of Clare College, Cambridge, and former Drummond Professor of Political Economy, Oxford).[83] The Republican affiliation of the group's chairman, and the international and nonacademic professional locations of three of the authors, are noteworthy—particularly since, as argued by the sociologist Aaron Major, the OECD had long been a postwar transnational outpost of classical liberal orthodoxies in an otherwise Keynesian period.[84]

In short, the stagflation debates and the collapse of Keynesianism involved interpretive struggles that cannot be cleanly divorced from partisan and professional investments. As such, they should be situated historically, with respect to the left party–economics connection that, by the 1960s, was hidden in plain sight. Inflation was a statistical and experiential fact to be sure, but its full weight was not felt until the 1970s, and its causes and implications were matters of debate. That debate played out partly within an economics profession in which, despite Heller's and Schiller's depiction of economics as a consensual scientific community, was in fact internally differentiated, increasingly politicized, and changing in form and scope.

The Politicization of Economics

If Keynesianism started to collapse in the mid-1960s, Walter Heller didn't seem to notice. In 1966 Heller reported that American economics' status as a consensual, Keynesian scientific community was very much intact. "The basic structure of the Keynesian theory of income and employment—and even the basic strategies of Hansenian policy for stable employment" he asserted, "are now the village common of the economics community."[85] Bearers of dissent, in particular the Chicago economist Milton Friedman (1912–2006) were, for Democratic-friendly economist theoreticians like Heller, fringe elements. Samuelson's popular textbook framed Friedman's economics as more political than scientific: as late as 1973 "Chicago School libertarianism" appeared as an add-on to the main text under the heading "Conservative Counterattacks against Mainstream Economics."[86] When Friedman famously told *Time* magazine that "we are all Keynesians now" in 1965, Heller summarized the profession's response thus: "'Amen.'"[87]

And yet, in that same moment, economics' image as a "village common" was on the verge of decline. References to economics and economists in news media between the 1960s and the 1980s suggest growing perceptions of an openly politicized discipline. Figure 6.1 charts the tallies of a simple count of U.S. news articles using partisan modifiers—"Democratic" versus "Republican," or "liberal" versus "conservative"—of the terms "economics" or "economist(s)." As the figure shows, partisan and political modifiers were very rare in news references to economics and economists in the 1950s. But such modifiers started to become more common in the 1960s, and took off in the 1970s and 1980s.

Figure 6.2 tracks articles with partisan modifiers as a percentage of all articles referencing economics and economists, restricted to the use of party-specific terms: "Democratic" and "Republican." It shows we find a similar pattern: party-specific references to economics and economists start to become more common in the 1960s, and become particularly frequent in the 1970s and 1980s. References to specifically

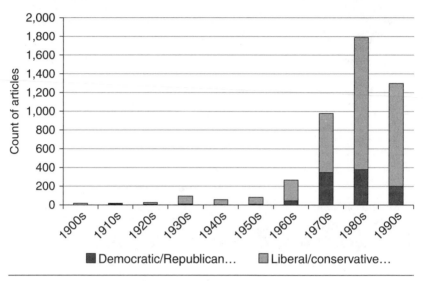

Figure 6.1. U.S. news articles using partisan modifiers of "economics/
economist(s)," 1900s–1990s. Source: ProQuest Historical Newspapers,
December 29, 2015. Newspapers searched include the *New York Times, Wall
Street Journal,* and *Los Angeles Times* and various state and local newspapers.

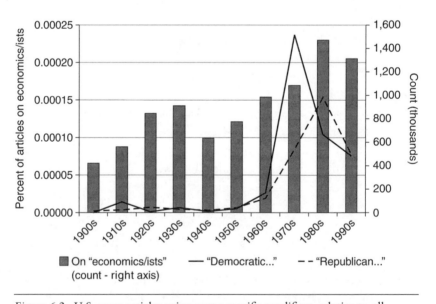

Figure 6.2. U.S. news articles using party-specific modifiers, relative to all
articles on economics topics, 1900s–1990s. Data source: see note for Figure 6.1.

"Democratic" economics and economists became much more common in the 1970s; an upward trend in references to "Republican" economics and economists, most pronounced in the 1980s, follows closely behind.

These trends suggest that a striking transition in the public stature of American professional economics began in the 1960s: a fading nonpartisan veneer. We will see in the following chapters that this was not a uniquely American phenomenon: Western European economics professions also exhibited a marked politicization in the 1960s and 1970s. On reconsideration, then, one can reasonably interpret Samuelson's assessment of Milton Friedman and his ilk as elements of a professional fringe as a political claim, launched in a time of deepening opposition between the (majority) Democratic and (minority) Republican economists of whom Friedman was leading figure.

What, then, was the nature of the neoliberal, or Friedmanite, dissent? To this we now turn.

The Neoliberal Dissent

A year after Heller's Harvard lectures, Friedman became the president of the AEA and delivered a well-known address declaring the return of monetary policy to the macroeconomic imagination. The address articulated a novel distinction between "natural" and "market" unemployment (borrowing from Wicksell's theory of interest), emphasizing the importance of expectations of inflation and arguing that the Phillips curve trade-off between inflation and unemployment was, in fact, temporary.[88] Sooner or later, Friedman famously argued, the trade-off would vanish.

Friedman's analysis was not broadly accepted in 1967, but as AEA president he could hardly be described as professionally marginal. By that time Friedman was also a well-published popular writer on free market economics (having published, for example, *Capitalism and Freedom* [1962] and essays in *Business Week*) and a prominent figure in emerging media of the new conservative right (appearing, for example, on William F. Buckley's *Firing Line* television series, which began in 1966[89]). Friedman was also an adviser to Barry Goldwater's 1964 Republican campaign and, in 1968, an adviser to Richard Nixon. From a media viewpoint—judging, for instance, by Friedman's appearance on

the cover of *Time* magazine—by 1969 Friedman was Heller's functional equivalent.

What distinguished Friedman from Heller was not his status as an
economist and public intellectual, but rather his position within the economics profession, his free market views, and his rightward stance in
a partisan divide that, by the 1960s, crossed through the economics
profession. Friedman was linked to a novel formation of American conservatism that linked Chicago-style, neoliberal economists with anticommunist, "neoconservative" New York intellectuals and a "fusionist"
contingent that served as a unifying force (of which Buckley was foremost).[90] By the late 1960s, in other words, American economics' ability
to maintain the pretense of being a nonpolitical discipline was breaking
down. And new sorts of economists, bearing new ethics, were in the
making. As these processes unfolded it would become increasingly difficult, if not impossible, for a figure like Heller to persuasively claim to
speak on behalf of a consensual, Keynesian profession.

The Anti-Managerial, Anti-Discretionary, Neoliberal Ethic

The fracturing of economics was on full display in November 1968,
when Heller and Friedman engaged in a debate at a strikingly well-
attended event hosted at the New York University Graduate School of
Business Administration.[91] In that exchange Heller explained his differences with Friedman in terms that went well beyond the question of
fiscal versus monetary policy. Rather, at issue were distinctive understandings of the world: whether it was made up of domestic economies
to be managed according to national priorities (the economist theoretician's view) or whether its central truth was the territorially untethered
market—that is, generalized market forces out there (the Friedmanite,
or neoliberal, view).

These essentially ontological viewpoints had implications for conceptions of the proper role of economists and economic managers. To
characterize the difference between himself and Friedman on this point,
Heller posed a rhetorical question:

[S]hould we rely on the Federal Reserve authorities to adapt monetary policy flexibly to changing economic events and to shifts in fiscal

policy, or should we instead not only enthrone money supply but encase it in a rigid formula ... ? In other words, should we adopt the Friedman rule and replace Bill [William McChesney] Martin [the Federal Reserve chairman] at the Fed with an exponential curve . . . ?[92]

Heller, of course, favored human discretion over exponential curves. But Friedman saw things differently. For him the economist was a bearer of scientific knowledge *about* markets, not a technician capable of telling markets what to do. The economy was not a national engine but rather a set of forces beyond the reach of politics, political institutions, and the powers of the state and should be treated as such.

As early as 1953 Friedman argued that, just as physicists reported on the workings of the natural world, economists should be the scientific truth-tellers of the price system. This, for Friedman, had clear implications for how economics should be done and the activities economists should undertake. In a controversial argument for "positive economics," Friedman contended that the profession's

task is to provide a system of generalizations that can be used to make correct predictions about the consequences of any change in circumstances. Its performance is to be judged by the precision, scope, and conformity with experience of the predictions it yields. In short, positive economics is, or can be, an "objective" science, in precisely the same sense as any of the physical sciences.[93]

The market, like gravity or the sun, was beyond the reach of politics, policy-makers, and economists alike.

Friedman's response to Heller in 1966 restated this view quite clearly. He did not propose a "rigid rule," he explained, but merely that policy should be adjusted to "[t]he automatic pilot" of "the price system"—that is, "the market system." The market, he argued, has its own laws: "It isn't perfectly flexible, it isn't perfectly free, but it has a good deal of capacity to adjust." And if it's "going to work," then economists should advocate for a "basic, stable framework" in the form of a "constant rate of increase in the price of money."[94] Friedman went on to refute the claim that discretion in economic policy was then, or had ever been, the source of postwar American economic growth. American economic success was thanks not to Keynesian "fine tuning" but rather to scientifically informed central bank policy.[95] An implication was that the pragmatic, politically attuned, intermediary ethic of the Keynesian economist theoretician was simply misguided.

Friedman's way of seeing things can be characterized as a specifically *neoliberal ethic*. Like its Keynesian counterpart, it was grounded in a particular position, or institutional viewpoint. This is where the neoliberal project becomes important to the story of leftism's second reinvention.

Enter the Neoliberal Project

Friedman, like Heller, occupied a particular position with respect to his profession, and with respect to politics. He sat at the intersection of at least three social worlds: Chicago economics, the American conservative movement, and the neoliberal project. The three were, in a way, so deeply intertwined with each other in the 1970s and 1980s that they cannot really be separated. Institutionally speaking, however, each had distinctive histories and institutional bases.

Here at least three characteristics of the neoliberal project's formation and organizational terrain are worth noting: its consolidation in (marginalized) opposition to the Bretton Woods order; its Anglo-American and economics-centeredness, yet cross-national geographic scope; and its alliance with center-right parties, on both sides of the Atlantic, by the 1980s.

Consolidation in Marginalization

With roots dating to the 1930s, the neoliberal project was an attempt of intellectuals, journalists, and businessmen to resuscitate and reformulate the "liberal creed" in response to the birth of the Keynesian order. The neoliberal project first took shape in a forum in Paris between 1939 and 1940 called the Colloque Walter Lippman, organized by the French philosopher Louis Rougier. The colloquium included a range of academics, businessmen, civil servants and continental economists—including, notably, Raymond Aron and Robert Marjolin from France, the Austrians Friedrich Hayek and Ludwig von Mises, and the German ordoliberals Wilhelm Röpke and Alexander Rüstow.[96] The group did not exactly hang together—the Germans, for instance, derided their Austrian colleagues—but they did produce a draft manifesto in which they identified "the price mechanism as the best way to obtain the maximal satisfaction of human expectations" and the state's responsibility to construct a legal order that was "adjusted to the order defined by the market," among other things.[97]

After World War II, with considerable backing from financial and business interests (for instance, what is now Credit Suisse and the Volker Fund), the neoliberal project's organizational footing took shape in 1947, with the first meeting of the Mont Pèlerin Society (MPS) in Switzerland.[98] Figures associated with the University of Chicago (Friedman, Fritz Machlup, Frank Knight) and the LSE (Friedrich Hayek, Lionel Robbins, Karl Popper) featured among various European and American academics, journalists, and others in attendance.[99] The MPS thence elaborated on the colloquium's initiative with a draft statement of aims in which it identified the "competitive market" as the singular locus of "individual freedom," private ownership as the only antidote to a concentration of power, and the growth of state power as the erosion of "free society."[100]

The historian Angus Burgin emphasizes how marginality—that is, "perceptions of public irrelevance, impediments to academic advancement," and "countless political defeats"—defined the making of the MPS and the neoliberal project writ large.[101] The 1930s, Burgin notes, was "a period of extraordinary isolation for academic opponents of government intervention," whose views were received as "the prattle of outmoded cranks."[102] Neoliberals' marginality deepened between the 1936 publication of Keynes' *General Theory* and the 1960s. This was important, especially insofar as it fostered a sense of community, and because it rendered the MPS' leading figures "reluctant to endanger their scientific authority by wading into venues of popular debate," focusing instead on exerting influence within the economics profession.[103]

Anglo-American and Economics-Centered Transnationality

Around the same time the MPS was getting off the ground, the neoliberal project acquired an important base at the University of Chicago.

By 1947 both Friedman and Hayek were on Chicago's faculty, situated within a cross-departmental network that spanned the Committee on Political Thought, the economics department, and the law and business schools. The Chicago economics department long had a reputation for conservatism, but this new configuration became the breeding ground of a distinctively free market, economics-driven, cross-disciplinary "Chicago School."[104]

By the 1950s MPS-connected networks extended well beyond Chicago, and beyond academe. Important here was a new breed of research organization: the part scholarly, part political, business-affiliated free market think tank.[105] Free market think tanks can be traced back to a few origin points. Among them is the Foundation for Economic Education (FEE), established in 1946 by a Los Angeles–based businessman named Leonard Read, who was connected to the Chicago School and the Volker Fund. As a continuation of business opposition to the New Deal, the FEE was very much a political organization.[106] More importantly, it was a model, a training ground, and a resource for efforts to build similar organizations in the United States and abroad.

One extension was the Institute of Economic Affairs (IEA), established in London in 1955. The IEA's founder, Antony Fisher, became a central force behind the establishment of free market organizations in the United Kingdom and abroad. These included the Social Affairs Unit, established in the United Kingdom in 1980 with IEA support; the British Centre for Policy Studies (1974); and the Adam Smith Institute (1977).[107] Fisher also supported the establishment of the free market Fraser Institute in Vancouver in 1974 and, in 1981, the Atlas Economic Research Foundation in Arlington, Virginia.

Meanwhile the neoliberal project extended further into American economics, through which it played an important role in shaping a politically influential, increasingly transnationalized profession.[108] In 1974 and 1976, respectively, Friedrich Hayek and Milton Friedman—both past MPS presidents—won the Nobel Prize in economics; other MPS presidents, including George Stigler (1982 Nobel, MPS president 1976–1978), James Buchanan (1986 Nobel, MPS president 1984–1986), and Gary Becker (1992 Nobel, MPS president 1990–1992), followed.[109] New free market foundations, meanwhile, deepened the intersection between academe and the neoliberal project: the John M. Ohlin Foundation, the Scaife Foundations, and the Lynde and Harry Bradley Foundation extended support to the law and economics program at the University of Chicago and to new centers on public choice at the Virginia Polytechnic Institute and George Mason University.[110]

In time Fraser and Atlas became nodes in a network of free market organizations that was near global in scope, centered especially in North America and the United Kingdom, and that featured more than 500 members.[111] To give a sense of this network's temporal development and geographical scope, Figure 6.3 tracks the regional diffusion of Atlas member organizations by the end of 2004 using data on the founding dates of 403 affiliated organizations. (This is a subset of a total of 513 affiliates by 2008, of which 464 have known founding dates.)

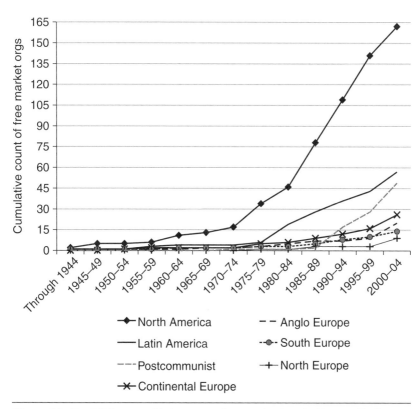

Figure 6.3. Establishment of Atlas network organizations in Europe, Latin America, and North America, ≤2004 (n=403). Author calculations. See Methodological Appendix for further details.

Figure 6.3 shows that, while some Atlas-affiliated organizations in North America (Canada and the United States) existed well before the 1970s, the vast majority emerged afterward. Outside of North America, nearly all were founded in the 1980s or later. In Germany, home to six Atlas-affiliated think tanks by 2008, important exceptions include the ordoliberal Walter Eucken Institute and the FDP-associated Friedrich Naumann Stiftung (FNS), founded in 1954 and 1958, respectively. By 2008 a full 176 (34 percent) of a global network of 513 Atlas-affiliated free market institutes were in the United States, of which only 10 (of 163 with known founding dates) existed before 1970. The United Kingdom was home to 22 Atlas organizations by the end of 2008 (4 percent of the total)—of which only 2 predated the 1970s, and more than half (12) were founded between 2000 and 2006. In Sweden, home to 4 Atlas organizations as of 2008, only 1 predated the year 2000: Timbro, established in 1978.[112]

In its guise as an expanding, business-connected global network of think tanks, the neoliberal project looks a lot like a social movement. Among its sustaining narratives was an interpretation of twentieth-century history as a global "war of ideas" between "government planning" and "market ideas," in which certain figures (Friedrich Hayek, Antony Fisher) are "top generals."[113] Sociologically speaking, this sort of imagery lends coherence and meaning to a social movement, signaling that the neoliberal project was at once an intellectual and a *moral* initiative. By the 1980s this initiative was clearly allied with politics and parties of the center-right.

Alliance with the Center-Right

By the 1980s the neoliberal project extended directly into center-right politics in the United States, the United Kingdom, and elsewhere. One indicator of this is the 1983 establishment of a free market international organization of center-right political parties: the International Democrat Union (IDU), established by Margaret Thatcher (United Kingdom), George H. W. Bush (United States), Jacques Chirac (France) and Helmut Kohl (West Germany), among others—and informally dubbed the "Freedom International."[114] Compared with its closest sibling, the Liberal International (LI, founded in 1947), the IDU's principles placed noteworthy emphases on free enterprise, free trade, private property, democracy, an independent judiciary, and limited government, but they did not echo the LI's concerns with community, poverty, multilateralism, or the concentration of power.[115]

The IDU signals that, by the 1980s, a new center-right politics had emerged that laid its own claims to grounding in mainstream economics. To grasp the implications, one might consider that before the1980s the pool of party-friendly, professionally reputable economists was decidedly shallow. Nixon's CEA chairman, Paul McCracken (PhD, Harvard, 1948—associated with the 1977 OECD report), commented on this very fact when he noted that, when he accepted his CEA assignment, he

> had not reckoned with the problem that if all three of the nation's Republican economists wouldn't do their duty, Mr. Nixon might not have a Council of Economic Advisers at all.[116]

Another Nixon CEA member, Herbert Stein (PhD, Chicago, 1958), later echoed McCracken's commentary on the rarity of Nixon-era, mainstream, Republican economists:

> We [Nixon's CEA members] were part of the small Republican branch of mainstream economists from which it was inevitable that Nixon would choose his advisers. McCracken used to say that we were the only Republican economists that Nixon could find. That wasn't exactly true. But the number who would not be considered hopelessly antediluvian, or wildly eccentric and dogmatic, or rigidly committed to business interests, was not large.[117]

But, as we have seen, by the 1980s right-leaning economists were not necessarily professionally dominant, but neither were they rare or easily dismissed as "fringe."[118] This ensured, for instance, that Republicans in the 1980s would not confront the Nixon-era conundrum of a dearth of Republican-friendly economists.[119] This development was clearly a byproduct of the transformational effects of the neoliberal project on the economics profession.

Effects on the Left

What, then, of the consequences for the left? The analysis thus far shows that characterizations of the neoliberal project as one aligned with the politics and parties of the right may be broadly correct, but they are also partial. The sociologist Johanna Bockman makes a similar argument.[120] Among other things, a conflation of neoliberalism with right-leaning politics glosses over the historical *novelty* of neoliberals' overt political alliances in the 1980s, which stand out in contrast with neoliberals' Keynesian era political marginality. More importantly, such character- izations are of little use for grasping goings-on within the left.

What were the implications of the neoliberal project, and its emer- gent alliance with the center-right, for parties of the center-left? Here two phenomena are noteworthy: first, the rise of free market think tanks prompted a countermovement on the left, in the form of a new network of "progressive" knowledge-producing organizations; second, ascen- dance of Friedmanite economics entailed, necessarily, the decline of the professional stature of the economist theoretician.

Countermovement: New Progressive Expertise

Political parties in a number of continental European countries have long had their own, officially affiliated, research foundations.[121] In West Germany, for instance, the Friedrich-Ebert-Stiftung (FES) was first established in 1925; the FDP's foundation, the Friedrich Naumann Foundation (FNS), was established in 1958; and the CDU founda- tion, Konrad Adenauer Stiftung (KAS), arrived on the scene in 1964.[122] In Sweden, we have seen that the LO's research department was *de facto* a SAP research foundation; the same is true of the Fabian Society in the United Kingdom. In the United States, Americans for Democratic Action (ADA) was a liberal Democratic research organization of sorts.

But, starting in the 1980s, leftism's party-expert terrain began to change. In 1988 the Institute for Public Policy Research (IPPR) appeared in London; a year later, in 1989, the Progressive Policy Institute (PPI), a think tank arm of the Democratic Leadership Council (DLC, established in 1985), appeared in Washington, D.C. As the century drew to a close these organizations formed a new network of foundations, institutes, magazines, and think tanks that were not necessarily formally party-affiliated, but identified themselves with a new, "progressive," expert terrain of the center-left. The *Berliner Republik* and Netzwerk Berlin appeared in Germany in 1999, as did the Arena Group in Stockholm in 2000. In the year 2000 this network acquired a new nodal center in the form of the Policy Network (London). Back in the United States, this emergent progressive network gained another node in the form of the Center for American Progress (CAP) in 2003. Finally, 2008 saw the establishment of the Foundation for European Progressive Studies (FEPS) in Brussels, the think tank of the Party of European Socialists (PES). Table 6.1 lists the names and founding dates of the forty-one organizations affiliated with the Policy Network as of 2008.

As the table shows, this new, progressive network was (and remains) much smaller than the Atlas network. But the timing of its development with respect to free market think tanks, shown in Figure 6.4, reflects an important fact: the formation of this new progressive network was a direct response to the formation, public prominence, and political effectiveness of new conservative and free market think tanks and the rise of a new market-friendly center-right in the 1980s.

Indeed, the IPPR's website credits its initiation to the thinking of a Labour-affiliated finance- and media-affiliated businessman named (Lord) Clive Hollick during the Thatcher years, starting in 1986.[123] The original prospectus for CAP directly cited conservatives' "ideas infrastructure outside of government" among its foundational motives.[124] And, while smaller in scope than its conservative and free market counterpart, the progressive network developed in striking historical parallel.

In the following chapters I delve in more detail into the emergence of third wayism inside the Democratic, Labour, and Swedish and German Social Democratic parties and the place of new progressive organizations therein, showing that organizations like PPI and the IPPR were home to a new sort of left party expert: the policy specialist, or progressive "wonk." Among the more striking aspects of this new breed of expert, historically speaking, was that he or she was *not* an academic economist—or, indeed, an academic of any sort. Nor was the policy specialist merely a reincarnation of the in-house, socialist party theoretician.

Table 6.1   Progressive center-left organizations affiliated with the Policy Network as of 2008

Name	City	Country	Founded
The Centre	Brussels	Belgium	.
Demos	Budapest	Hungary	.
Unions 21 (union-financed)	London	UK	.
Fabian Society	London	UK	1884
Joseph Rowntree Foundation	York	UK	1904
Friedrich-Ebert-Stiftung (German SPD)	Bonn	Germany	1925
Brookings Institution	Washington, D.C.	USA	1927
Wiardi Beckman Stichting (Dutch Labour Party/formally independent)	Amsterdam	Netherlands	1945
Renner Institut (Austrian Social Democratic Party)	Vienna	Austria	1972
Institute for Futures Studies	Stockholm	Sweden	1973
Work Foundation (Lancaster University)	London	UK	1984
Hellenic Foundation for European and Foreign Policy (ELIAMEP)	Athens	Greece	1988
Institute for Public Policy Research	London	UK	1988
Progressive Policy Institute	Washington, D.C.	USA	1989
European Institute (LSE)	London	UK	1991
Alfred Herrhausen Society (International Forum of Deutsche Bank)	Berlin	Germany	1992
Centre for the Study of Global Governance (LSE)	London	UK	1992
Fondation Jean-Jaurès (French Socialist Party/formally independent)	Paris	France	1992
Demos	London	UK	1994
Economic Policy Research Institute	Cape Town	South Africa	1994
European Policy Centre	Brussels	Belgium	1997

Table 6.1   (continued)

Name	City	Country	Founded
Fundación Alternativas	Madrid	Spain	1997
Per Capita	Surry Hills	Australia	1997
Centre for European Reform	London	UK	1998
Fondazione Italianieuropei	Rome	Italy	1998
Berliner Republik / Netzwerk Berlin (linked to DPZ)	Berlin	Germany	1999*
Arena Group	Stockholm	Sweden	2000*
Policy Network	London	UK	2000
Telos	Paris	France	2000*
Center for American Progress	Washington, D.C.	USA	2003
Glocus	Rome, Milan	Italy	2003
Community: The Union for Life (trade unions)	London	UK	2004
Slovak Governance Institute	Bratislava	Slovakia	2004
Social Europe journal	London	UK	2005*
Gauche Réformiste Européenne	Brussels	Belgium	2006
Global Policy Institute (London Metropolitan University)	London	UK	2006
Das Progressive Zentrum (DPZ)	Berlin	Germany	2007
Les Gracques	Paris	France	2007
Foundation for European Progressive Studies	Brussels	Belgium	2008
Instituto Igualdad (Socialist Party of Chile)	Santiago	Chile	2008
Terra Nova	Paris	France	2008

Source / notes: See the Methodological Appendix. Where founding years could not be identified, the year of first publication is listed (marked with "*"). Research assistance provided by Brian Veazey.

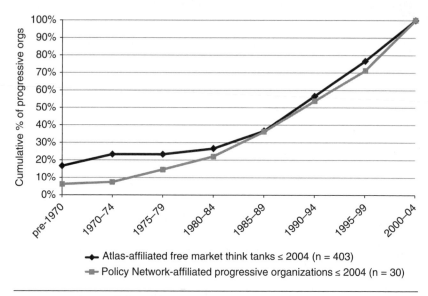

Figure 6.4. The parallel proliferation of free market and progressive organizations: cumulative percent founded, ≤2004. Author calculations. See Methodological Appendix for further details.

Rather, the organizational home of the policy specialist was a relatively new world of "think tanks."[125]

The Delegitimation of Keynesian Professional Ethics

What, then, became of the economist theoretician? This brings us to another way in which the neoliberal project mattered for leftism. In addition to supporting the formation of prominent economists of the right, neoliberal project–affiliated economists also shaped the ethics and orientations of the profession more broadly. Insofar as the influences of Milton Friedman and others, especially at Chicago, informed a professional interpretation of inflationary trouble as proof of Keynesianism's scientific deficiencies, the neoliberal project became an important force in the decline of the economist theoretician.

Recent research on citation patterns in economics suggests that the writings of free market economists exerted outsized influence in the profession cross-nationally, well into the twenty-first century.[126] Friedman's arguments for "positive economics," "monetarist" macroeconomic management (treating monetary policy, managed according to strictly scientific criteria, as the most important element of economic policy), and a "natural rate" of unemployment, as they were taken up and worked out by figures after him, were particularly important.[127]

Central here are the "rational expectations" arguments of two economists with Chicago affiliations: Robert E. Lucas Jr. (1937–; PhD, Chicago, 1964) and Thomas J. Sargent (1943–; PhD, Harvard, 1968; visiting professor, Chicago, 1976–1977).[128] The rational expectations claim was that the market, not policy-makers, defined the limits of "full" employment, and more broadly that the whole notion of purposive economic management was misguided. Rational expectations arguments were important not only because of their implications for the Phillips curve (which were laid out by Friedman in his 1967 AEA address) but also because of their implications for Keynesian economists' professional and scientific standing. As Sargent later explained, "Rational expectations undermines the idea that policymakers can manipulate the economy by systematically making the public have false expectations."[129] In the late 1970s Lucas, Sargent, and others extended this into a general argument in favor of rule-based (as opposed to discretion-based) monetary policy.[130] In their words:

[T]he central fact is that Keynesian policy recommendations have no sounder basis, in a scientific sense, than recommendations of non-Keynesian economists or, for that matter, noneconomists.[131]

The argument went well beyond theories of inflation and unemployment *per se*: echoing the same themes of the Heller-Friedman exchange in 1966, the rational expectations case was against Keynesian-style, managerial discretion and for Friedmanite rule-based decision-making. From a rational expectations viewpoint, mainstream scientific economics was, by 1979, on the side of rules, not discretion.

Recall that the term "stagflation" was introduced in 1960s Britain, naming what was then a specifically British concern, in the context of a Conservative MP's criticism of Labour's uses of Keynesian economics, and economists, as a means of government. The rational expectations arguments, by contrast, centered on the 1970s, were keyed to the

American experience, and were formulated by economists, for economists. A particularly notable aspect of this formulation was the way in which the inflationary 1970s, which had unambiguous origins in sudden hikes in oil prices by the Organization of Petroleum Exporting Countries (OPEC), was interpreted ahistorically as a matter of scientific proof. In Lucas and Sargent's words:

> [M]acroeconometric models were subjected to a decisive test in the 1970s. . . . [T]he models of the late 1960s predicted a sustained U.S. unemployment rate of 4 percent as consistent with a 4 percent annual rate of inflation. Based on this prediction, many economists at that time urged a deliberate policy of inflation. . . . The inflationary bias on average of monetary and fiscal policy in this period should, according to all of these [Keynesian] models, have produced the lowest average unemployment rates for any decade since the 1940s. In fact, as we know, they produced the highest unemployment rates since the 1930s. This was econometric failure on a grand scale.[132]

Lucas and Sargent emphasized that this did not suggest a wholesale abandonment of Keynesianism for "other faiths." But, since Keynesian discretionary management was no longer scientific, they announced that scientific economists were turning their attention to new concerns. "Fewer and fewer economists are involved in monitoring and refining the major econometric models; more and more are developing alternative theories of the business cycle," Lucas and Sargent observed. Economists turned to "the theoretical casualties of the Keynesian Revolution, to the ideas of Keynes' contemporaries and of earlier economists whose thinking has been regarded for years as outmoded."[133]

Absent from Lucas and Sargent's account is reference to oil prices or geopolitical instability. Keynesian demand management failed not because of geopolitically rooted disruptions, but because the science behind Keynesian demand management was, and had always been, wrong. Notably, this was not intended as a political argument, nor is there any reason to think that it had definite political motivations. Lucas and Sargent later described their work as nonideological; Sargent recently described himself as pro-Keynes and "a fiscally conservative, socially liberal Democrat."[134] Nonetheless, the rational expectations account fed into politically inflected transnational and national debates as to the meaning and implications of inflation—featuring prominently, for instance, in the 1977 OECD report of McCracken and his colleagues, which helped to extend the rational expectations indictment of the Keynesian ethic across Western settings.

As we will see in the following chapters, the rise of rational expectations was inseparable from a turn to neoliberal ethics in professional economics. The implications of the profession's embrace of markets, and move away from concerns with domestic political economy, were not lost on economists themselves. In 1984 Philip A. Klein, an economics professor at Pennsylvania State University, wrote in the *Journal of Economic Issues* that many of his "fellow economists," in their "return to the market," had abandoned their ethical responsibilities. Supply-side economics, monetarism, and rational expectations (what Klein termed "new classicism") amounted to "a rationalization for avoiding his [the economist's] basic responsibility to participate in the continuing national debate about the emergent value premises reflected by any ongoing economy," Klein argued.[135] By extension, the new classicists

> do not appear to dwell on the condition of the economy (or the people in it) after their policy prescriptions have been enacted. Thus the condition of our economy after the supply-sider has had his tax cuts, after the monetarist has achieved his constantly growing money supply, and after the rational expectations people have rid us of reasonably forecastable efforts to intervene never seems to get discussed in any detail.[136]

Klein concluded that "the new classicists are all ignoring a fundamental obligation of the economist."[137] In 1998, Mark Blaug echoed Klein's concern in the form of a question: "Is there any way back to the policy-relevant, problem-solving kind of economics that was the norm in the 1940s, 1950s, and perhaps the 1960s?"[138]

The Formation of the TFE

As Lucas and Sargent noted, after the discrediting of Keynesianism the profession developed in new directions. Here two features of the post-1970 development of economics, well documented by the economist Franck Jovanovic and the sociologist Marion Fourcade (among others), are important: its internationalization and finance-oriented turn. The end result was the making of a very different set of Western economic professions, which were home to a very different sort of economist: the transnationalized, finance-oriented economist, or TFE.

We might note, first, that Lucas, Sargent, and Wallace published some of their most important statements not in generalist economics venues but in financial economics journals: the *Journal of Money, Credit and Banking,* the *Journal of Monetary Economics,* the Federal Reserve Bank of Minneapolis *Quarterly Review,* and other publications of central banks. In 1977 Lucas became an associate editor of the *Journal of Monetary Economics.* Neither Lucas's nor Sargent's professional CVs list government work or political appointments, with the exception of the military or a Federal Reserve bank, between the 1960s and the 1980s.[139] This is notable, in part, because financial economics was practitioner-centered and largely historical in orientation before the 1960s; it was not a scientific subfield of the mainstream discipline.[140] But after 1965, partly thanks to the contributions of Eugene Fama, a graduate student at the Chicago School of Business, and, at MIT, Franco Modigliani (plus considerable advances in computing), financial economics became an important scientific subfield. Indeed, Marion Fourcade and her colleagues identify a turn to finance, and the accompanying ascendance of business school-based economists, as one of the most striking developments in the profession in the late twentieth century.[141]

The flipside of the birth of financial economics was the financialization of economic and corporate life—the symptoms of which include a disproportionate growth of financial profits as a proportion of GDP and corporate profits after the 1970s, the expansion of "securitization and tradable financial instruments, a corporate turn to "profiteering and cost-saving," and "the use of credit to shore up consumption under real wage stagnation."[142] Economics and noneconomists alike note a connection between financialization and financial economics. In Fourcade's account, "The rise of finance and microeconomics, on the one hand, and the market liberalization of economies, on the other, have opened up new jurisdictions in the private world, turning economic knowledge into a successful corporate activity."[143] In the account of the two-time CEA member Alan Blinder, economics took on a new role not just in the analysis of markets but in the making of them. "One might have assumed that economists would have to adjust their models to fit reality, rather than the other way around," he notes, "[b]ut economists appear to have bent reality (at least somewhat) to fit their models."[144] Blinder cites the making of financial markets—alongside the collapse of Eastern socialism, privatization, and the rise of shareholder value in corporate life—as a case in point.

The rise of finance and financial economics coincided with major transformations in transnational monetary and financial government, especially in Europe. One was the reinvention of European integration as a market-making project starting in 1985, culminating with the establishment of the European Central Bank (ECB) in 1998 and the introduction of a new currency, the euro, in 1999. Another was the growing independence, and power, of central banks relative to national authorities, even as they became more interconnected cross-nationally. During the 1990s no fewer than fifty-four countries in Eastern and Central Europe, Western Europe, Latin America, Africa, and Asia made statutory changes to autonomize central banks or granted autonomy by nonstatutory means.[145] The ECB is well noted for its extraordinary autonomy, which was written directly into provisions in the 1992 Treaty on European Union (TEU) that prohibited it and eurozone national banks from either seeking or taking "instructions from Community institutions or bodies, from any government of a Member State or from any other body."[146] Likewise, the treaty prohibited EU institutions and national governments from seeking to influence the decisions of either the ECB or the eurozone national central banks. Partly due to the power and influence of the German Bundesbank in the process of building the eurozone, the ECB stood out among its peers for its particularly high degree of independence when it was established.[147]

As central banks became more autonomous, they also became more powerful relative to their counterparts in other branches of government (for instance, finance ministers), more tightly linked with international financial institutions, and generally more "scientized."[148] This, too, had consequences for the development of economics professions. The scientization and internationalization of central banking involved the formation of cross-bank networks of credentialed economists with their own "epistemic clan structures," sizable bank-based research departments, in-house academic journals, and a distinctively transnational, bank-centered apparatus for the production of economic and professional knowledge.[149] Notable, also, was an intensification of network ties across ministries of finance, central bank governing boards, European Commission economic directorates, and Bretton Woods financial institutions from the 1970s forward—a process traceable to the 1950s, linked to expanding international capital flows, monetary instability, and European integration.[150]

This went hand-in-hand with the construction of a "European" economics with notable links to finance and financial institutions. Two anchor points, established in the mid-1980s, were explicitly intended as counterparts to the U.S. National Bureau of Economic Research and the American Economic Association: the Centre for Economic Policy Research (CEPR), established in London in 1983, and the European Economic Association (EEA), established in 1984 in Brussels but now in Milan. Notably, the CEPR is closely connected to national and transnational financial institutions, but keeps a formal distance from partisan involvements.[151] Its funding base is spread across private, public, and nonprofit organizations, but, as of 2013, its corporate members included no less than thirty-one central banks plus the Bank for International Settlements (BIS), more than a dozen corporate banks (including Citigroup, Credit Suisse, J. P. Morgan, and Lloyds), and two finance ministries (the Cypriot Ministry of Finance and the British Treasury).[152]

In the end, then, what we find is the construction of a whole new internationalized, financialized professional ecosystem. Alongside the emergence of the progressive policy specialist, the politicization of economics, the delegitimation of the economist theoretician, and the rise of a more market-centered, finance-oriented mainstream economics profession, then, the post-1960s period featured a transformation of economics into a globalized profession that was increasingly removed from domestic political investments and more tightly interwoven with public and private finance. This new professional ecosystem fostered and sustained the making of a new kind of economist: the transnationalized, finance-oriented economist, or TFE.

Thus far, I have laid out key ways in which Western expertise, especially the economic expertise on which center-leftism depended, changed fundamentally after the 1960s. I have also tracked the neoliberal project's role in the formation of new progressive experts, the decline of the Keynesian ethic, and the formation of the TFE. The cumulative effect was that the cultural infrastructure of leftism was radically transformed between the 1960s and the 1990s.

What were the implications of the demise of the economist theoretician? Klein's critical analysis of the new classicists suggest that neoliberal ethics emptied professional economics of its capacity for producing domestically grounded economists capable of addressing practical political concerns. To whom, then, could left parties turn? Here we come to yet another kind of expert: the strategist.

NEOLIBERAL ETHICS AND THE RISE
OF THE STRATEGIST: A CONNECTION?

At first glance, the figure of the professional political strategist, or "spin doctor" appears unconnected to the story of left parties, economics, and neoliberalism told thus far. Indeed, historically, the rise of political consulting had little to do with any of these things. One of my key arguments in the chapters to follow, however, is that the post-1970s decline of the economist theoretician, the rise of the TFE, and the growing prominence of the figure of the professional strategist were interconnected.

Born in California in 1933, political consulting originated as a form of business mobilization. The first political consulting firm, Campaigns, Inc., formed in service of business efforts to block the gubernatorial candidacy of the socialist historian Upton Sinclair.[153] But as the sociologist Daniel Laurison explains, "Through the first half of the twentieth century, political parties were the primary mobilizing force during campaigns" in the United States, as in other countries.[154] In the 1960s, this changed: American candidates increasingly assembled "their own campaign teams of staff and consultants" in the later twentieth century.

Markers of political consulting's professional consolidation include the 1968 establishment of the American Association of Political Consultants (AAPC) and of new training centers and credentials in political strategy and campaign management—for instance, American University's Campaign Management Institute or advanced degrees in political campaigning from George Washington University's Graduate School of

Political Management.[155] By the mid-1990s the AAPC had counterparts in the United Kingdom (the Association of Professional Political Consultants, established in London in 1994) and Austria (the European Association of Political Consultants, established in Vienna in 1996); in 2002 the Deutsche Gesellschaft für Politikberatung, or German Association of Political Consultants (de'ge'pol), was established in Berlin. The summary result, in Laurison's words, was "the rise of a new type of political actor—the professional political consultant"—sometimes termed (with more or less derogatory intent) the "spin doctor" in media and public debates and notable for his or her specialization in a specifically *strategic* form of political expertise.[156]

The political consultant is not a uniquely American figure, but the profession as a whole seems to have a distinctly American flavor. Existing comparative and cross-national research emphasizes the relatively under-professionalized state of "European consultants and political managers," Europe's relative lack of "specialized university courses" in campaigning and political marketing, and the United States–centrism of European campaign professionals.[157] Fritz Plasser and Gunda Plasser find in a large survey that, as of 2002, familiarity and experience with American campaigns was, from the perspective of "most European consultants and party managers," high among the "requirements" of campaign professionals.[158]

In the 1990s political consulting extended into European settings alongside the advancement of European integration. The construction of European cross-national alliances of parties alongside the European Parliament (EP) and the push to further empower the EP in the 1992 Treaty on European Union (TEU) extended domestic party politics' professionalization into Brussels. On the European level, Plasser and Plasser note, "advertising and communications managers of the social democratic or socialist parties provide forums for transnational contacts" in which "leading party campaign experts exchange and analyze their professional experiences and discuss current strategies."[159] These events, they observe, feature a distinctive American presence: "US consultancy businesses are regularly invited to report on the newest trends and innovations in American campaign practices."[160]

Political consulting, in the United States and abroad—like any profession—is internally differentiated. Dennis W. Johnson, for instance, makes a distinction between "amateur" consultants who have a special interest in a particular candidate versus more detached professionals.[161] But, in light of the analysis thus far, the figure of the strategist is notable in at least one respect: unlike the party dependence of socialist party theoreticians in the 1920s, or the academic affiliations of economist theoreticians in the 1960s, strategists are indigenous to a private, for-profit profession. And, as I will argue in the next chapters, they were also part and parcel of leftism's second reinvention.

CONCLUSIONS

The figures of the progressive policy specialist, the TFE, and the strategist, and their specific roles in the making of third way leftism across national contexts, are the stuff of the next two chapters. One of the things I aim to show is that, while the emergence of political consulting and the rise of the strategist had little to do with economics, center-left parties' reliance on TFEs and their turn to strategists in the 1980s and 1990s were connected: the more TFEs' emphases focused on the market, the more center-left parties turned to specialists in "spin" to attract voters. With this, we now turn to the inside-out story, or refraction account, of leftism's second reinvention in the United States, with the making of the New Democrats.

CHAPTER SEVEN

New Economists, New Experts, New Democrats

> The political ideas and passions of the 1930s and 1960s
> cannot guide us in the 1990s. . . . We believe the Democratic
> Party's fundamental mission is to expand opportunity, not
> government. . . . The free market, regulated in the public
> interest, is the best engine of general prosperity. . . . We believe
> a progressive tax system is the only fair way to pay for
> government. We believe in preventing crime and punishing
> criminals, not explaining away their behavior. We believe the
> purpose of social welfare is to bring the poor into the nation's
> economic mainstream, not maintain them in dependence.
>
> —DLC New Orleans Declaration, March 1990

THE AMERICAN DEMOCRATIC PARTY changed fundamentally between the upheavals of 1968, the rise of "New Politics" liberalism in the 1970s, and the 1985 foundation of the Democratic Leadership Council (DLC)—home of the "New Democrats" (quoted above). Changes in the party were at once organizational and programmatic: organizationally, procedural power shifted toward Washington, D.C.; programmatically, the party became "progressive"—or, in my terminology, *neoliberalized*. Just like its economistic predecessor, neoliberalized Democratic leftism expressed a distinctive relationship between expertise and the party's leading faction. In this chapter I trace the rise of DLC-style progressive leftism and the party-expert relations underlying it, with particular emphasis on the role of a reformatted economics profession, the neoliberal ethic, progressive policy specialists, and new strategic professionals.

New Democratic party-expert relations were distinctive, in part, for what they *lacked:* a strong core of prestigious academic economists. This lack was symptomatic of changes in the party-economics relationship that are not quite captured by the familiar phrase "the collapse of Keynesianism." What collapsed was not so much Keynesian thinking in Democratic circles, but rather the population of prestigious, party-affiliated economists porting *the Keynesian ethic.* In the 1970s a new opposition emerged in the ranks of Democratic Party experts between economists bearing neoliberal ethics and noneconomist advisers who, motivated partly by exasperation with the political insensitivity of market-centric economists, focused their efforts on political strategy.

This opposition within the ranks of Democratic Party experts fed directly into the formation of the DLC and its knowledge-producing arm, the Progressive Policy Institute (PPI). Notable for its D.C.-centeredness, a dependence on corporate and financial (as opposed to union) support, and minimal academic connections (economists included), the DLC-PPI's new marriage of analysis and political strategy took the form of New Democratic "progressivism," featuring the triple theme of opportunity, responsibility, and community. New Democratic progressivism deliberately omitted liberal themes of redistribution, equal outcomes and welfarism; also absent were Keynesian themes of maximal employment and cooperative economic management. The New Democrats called for an efficient, work- and opportunity-promoting, tough-on-crime government that would shape American economic life by promoting markets, investment, and personal responsibility, achieving redistributive and progressive ends mainly via taxation.

A central argument of this chapter is that the eclectic language of the New Democrats was a social effect of the disparate forms of expertise behind it. New Democratic eclecticism expressed the fact that strategic and scientific economic expertise, once channeled through the singular figure of the economic theoretician, now came from different corners. It also expressed a party-expert configuration in which the professional economist remained important, but played a more *circumscribed* role. Economists now took a backseat on matters of political strategy; they informed, but were not necessarily lead figures in, the development of noneconomic policy positions. When it came to economic policy,

however, transnationalized and finance-oriented Democratic economists (TFEs) played important roles as truth-tellers and guardians of
the market. I demonstrate this by focusing on the first Clinton administration's prioritization of balanced budgets over public investment, the
North American Free Trade Agreement (NAFTA), and the handling of
the 1994–1995 Mexican peso crisis, showing that TFEs played a specific role as drivers of international market-making and as spokespeople for, and sometimes saviors of, the market. I also show that
Democratic losses in the 1994 midterm elections tipped the scales in
favor of neoliberalized leftism by empowering strategic experts and
DLCers over liberals in Congress and in the White House.

Overall, this chapter offers a *refraction* account of American leftism's
second reinvention. My account takes parties as internally contested,
relational terrains that refract the meaning and interpretation of events
(economic events or electoral change, for instance) in ways that are
patterned by the actor-orientations that characterize party networks:
power-seeking, truth-claiming, and representation. In a refraction account the trajectories and social conditions of the truth-claimers, or
party experts, are central to the explanation of how, and for whom,
parties speak. In order to clarify the distinctive features of this approach
we begin, first, by considering the strengths and weaknesses of alternative modes of explanation.

THE TROUBLE WITH EXISTING ACCOUNTS

There are at least four existing explanations of the New Democrats in
existing research. A first account centers on electoral necessity: the New
Democrats had to adapt to the programs, strategies, and appeal of the
neoconservative right in order to win. In this understanding New Democratic politics emerged because the party adopted the policies of its
competitors in order to meet the demands of "clients" (that is, voters).
In the language of organizational sociology, the New Democrats were
an effect of "mimetic isomorphism."[1] This is a specific case of a more
general kind of account that attributes the New Democratic turn to
electorate-driven demands.

There is truth in this account, but there are also problems with it.
One is that neither the DLCers nor their predecessors understood them-

selves as adapting to or co-opting Republican programmatic orientations (even when, in the case of 1996 welfare reform, this is precisely what happened). The organizational precursor of the New Democrats, the Committee on Party Effectiveness (CPE), built itself on a critique of Reagan Republicanism, advancing an agenda centered on "fairness" that had little in common with neoconservative thought or free market economics; figures who drove the making of the DLC formulated their efforts with reference not to Republicanism but rather to the history of their own party, grounded in their take on the legacies of Democratic presidents ranging from Andrew Jackson to JFK.[2] The DLCers' most immediate rivals were liberal Democrats, not Republicans; for that reason, initiatives like NAFTA and welfare reform were understood as New Democratic *intraparty* victories. A mimicry story at best ignores, and at worst distorts, the actual process that generated New Democratic politics.

There are also problems with electorate-driven accounts in general. First and foremost, the claim that New Democratic politics enjoyed widespread electoral support is at best overstated and at worst simply incorrect. In the first place, Clinton's electoral appeal was precisely that he brought together two kinds of voters—liberals (including the union vote) *and* socially and economically conservative (white, male) middleclass voters—and so his popularity cannot be read only in terms of his New Democratic appeal.

More importantly perhaps, electoral history does not bear out a definitive story of widespread or enduring voter support for New Democratic politics. First, voting trends from the 1960s to the 1990s were marked by a broad decline in voter turnout, reaching a new low in 1996—that is, the year of Clinton's reelection (see Figure 7.1). Second, third party and independent candidates, especially Ross Perot, took an unusually high percentage of the popular vote (Perot won almost 19 percent), and the third party vote remained relatively strong in 1996 (see, again, Figure 7.1). Clinton did not win the majority of the popular vote in either election. Third, during the Clinton years congressional Democrats underwent an electoral slide that, except for a brief respite during the financial crisis of 2007–2008, is with us still (see Figure 7.2). This is not strong evidence of voters' embrace of New Democratic politics—or, indeed, of the politics of *either* of the major parties—in the 1990s.

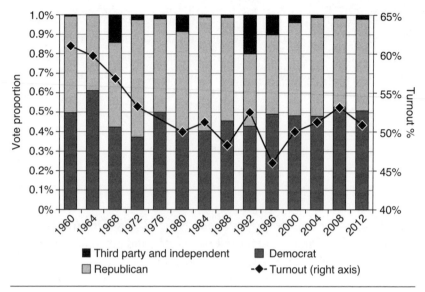

Figure 7.1. U.S. vote proportions in presidential election years, with voter turnout, 1960–2012. Data source: U.S. House of Representatives; Armingeon et al., 2016.

A final problem with an electorate-driven account is that the policies considered by New Democrats to be among their biggest victories hinged not on the Democratic Party's electoral strength but rather on its Congressional weakness. *As a result, there is no easy way to tell if the Democrats' electoral decline in the Clinton years was in spite of the party's New Democratic turn or because of it.* The 1996 welfare reform is sometimes understood as a combined result of popular opinion (expressed in the 1994 midterm vote against the Democrats) and Clinton's capitulation to Republican neoconservatives in Congress. But the 1992 vote trended against the Democrats, too, shifting in favor of third party and independent candidates—in continuation of a steep, continuous decline that began in the 1980s (or mid-late 1970s, arguably) (see Figure 7.2).

DLCers interpreted the Republican midterm victory as a repudiation of Clinton's stubbornly liberal proclivities and, later, viewed the 1996 work-centric welfare reform as *their* policy victory (even though it originated as a Republican bill). Liberal Democrats, meanwhile, argued that 1994 Democratic losses had to do with union and working-class alienation after NAFTA and that the 1996 welfare reform was a betrayal of

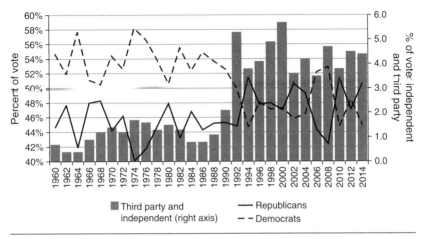

Figure 7.2. Congressional popular voting, U.S. House of Representatives, 1960–2014. Data source: Armingeon et al. 2016, Comparative Political Dataset.

Democratic constituencies that would only further alienate voters. The New Democratic interpretation won, but it is hard to separate their interpretive victory from the fact that they also won the struggle for dominance of the party. This suggests a dynamic that is more complicated than a simple voters-demanded-and-New-Democrats-responded story: electoral trends were interpreted in competing ways *within* the Democratic Party, and the winning interpretation was closely linked to the intraparty rise to power of the DLCers relative to congressional and liberal Democrats.

In short, an account in which neoliberalized Democratic leftism was simply "what voters wanted" is, at best, partial. This brings us to a second kind of account: a *party- or elite-driven* story, in which the New Democratic turn was an elite-led project, rather than a response to electoral demand. This, too, has truth to it—the CPE and the DLC were, to be sure, elite-led; a party-driven account is also a better fit with the curious fact that New Democrats' strength appeared to be a function of the Democratic Party's losses. But a problem here is that a party-driven account requires selectively rejecting the stories New Democrats themselves tell. New Democrats made a strong case that their whole initiative was a response to the demands of "mainstream" voters. It may be that this was, factually speaking, false, but this does not mean that New

Democrats did not *believe* themselves to be responding to mainstream voters. Another problem is that, like an electorate-driven account, a party-led story simply overlooks the intraparty factional competitions that, in fact, gave rise to the New Democratic project. In other words, the party-driven story cannot explain why some elites (the New Democrats) won and other elites (liberals, old and new) lost.

We now come to a third kind of explanation: the New Democrats emerged out of a compulsion to adapt to new economic circumstances in a globalized age. Stated differently, Democratic politics changed because economic realities changed. I'll call this the *economics-driven* account.

The difficulty with an economics-driven account is the assumption that economic circumstances—"stagflation," "globalization"—and the meanings thereof simply presented themselves as is, rather than being interpreted and defined by people with competing perspectives and interests. It is not clear that one can draw a straight line from stagflation and globalization to "opportunity, responsibility, and community." And, more fundamentally, an economics-driven account assumes that economic forces come first and politics second—that is, that the New Democrats were not themselves implicated in the *definition and promulgation* of new economic realities. And yet it is not at all obvious that this is true.

This can be illustrated by considering post-1970 U.S. macroeconomic trends in the context of neoliberalized Democratic leftism's formation— originating during the Carter presidency (1977–1981), acquiring a definite organizational basis and programmatic language with the establishment of the DLC-PPI, and consolidating during the first Clinton administration, 1993–1997.

First, a look inside the Carter administration in the late 1970s shows that recession and inflation did not generate settled or consensual diagnoses of economic problems' causes and implications.[3] We have seen that, within American professional economics, some took the experience of the 1970s as a reason to conclude that the scientific validity of Keynesian demand management, grounded in the Phillips curve theorem of an inflation-unemployment trade-off, was dead. And indeed, from the 1970s to 2005 the relationship between inflation and unem-

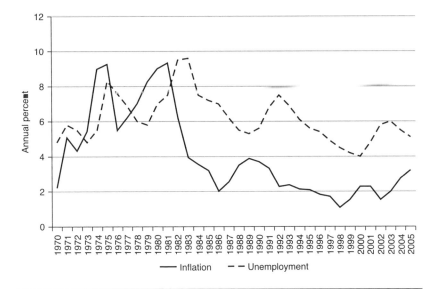

Figure 7.3. Inflation and unemployment in the United States, 1970–2005.
Data source: World Bank, World Development Indicators (WDI); International
Labour Organization (ILO).

ployment was modestly positive (see Figure 7.3). But in politics, and especially in Democratic circles, the lessons to be learned from the 1970s were matters of dispute. Many viewed the inflationary 1970s as effects of temporary oil price shocks and concluded that more, not less, economic management and coordination was needed. Indeed, the following pages will show that this interpretation was alive and well in the 1980s and 1990s. Keynesianism may have collapsed in economics, but it did not collapse in the Democratic Party.

What an economics-driven account tends to miss is that, inside parties, economic difficulties prompt fractures over interpretations and possible courses of action—not consensual perceptions of agreed-upon facts. Democratic economists, politicians, and strategic aides interpreted the events of the 1970s in variable ways. In this sense, the early 1980s drop in inflation shown in Figure 7.2—widely attributed to the decision of Paul Volcker, the Fed chairman, to raise interest rates—was symptomatic of an intraparty fracture in which (certain) Democratic economists'

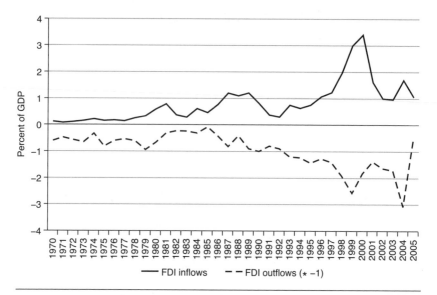

Figure 7.4. Foreign direct investment (FDI) inflows and outflows, United States, 1970–2005. Data source: World Bank, World Development Indicators (WDI). Note: for ease of visual interpretation, the percent of GDP in FDI outflows is multiplied by −1.

interpretations won.[4] The question, then, has to be extended beyond any particular economic event to the problem of *why* one set of actors' interpretations won over others.

Another consideration, also bearing on an economics-driven account, is the timing of "globalization," and in particular the globalization of finance, relative to the formation of New Democratic politics. Here one can simply note that the United States' embrace of global finance emerged *after* Clinton's election, unfolding most dramatically in the late 1990s (see Figure 7.4). Figure 7.5 shows, also, that the American financial balance of payments situation fundamentally changed during the second Clinton administration, continuing into the administration of George W. Bush.

Considered in conjunction with the central role of the New Democrats in the making of NAFTA, the timing of these trends calls into question the presumption that New Democratic politics was simply a compulsory adaptation to new, global economic forces. Instead, one

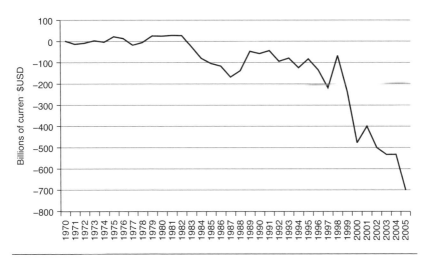

Figure 7.5. U.S. financial balance of payments, 1970–2005. Data source: World Bank, World Development Indicators (WDI).

could make the case that New Democratic forces were *drivers* of American economic and financial globalization.

There is a final, fourth account of the New Democrats. This kind of explanation, which I'll call an *interfactional* account, traces the origins of the New Democrats' market-friendly turn to intraparty contestation. An interfactional account is not exclusive of the accounts described thus far, but it stands apart for its treatment of intraparty relations, factional struggles, and interpretive processes as causal forces. This is the approach in Kenneth Baer's *Reinventing Democrats,* which describes the New Democrats' emergence as "a profound change in the Democratic Party." Rejecting the notion that New Democratic politics marked "a craven attempt to mimic the GOP" or a simple adaptation to "radical change in the condition of the country or in the electorate," Baer argues that, despite a lack of grassroots support, the New Democrats' "new public philosophy, and the electoral success apparently tied to it, was the product of a conscious and sustained effort" by New Democratic players "and their most important organizational form, the Democratic Leadership Council (DLC)."[5] In short, changing electoral, party-organizational, and economic circumstances may have conditioned party change, but the proximate sources of neoliberalized leftism were intraparty struggles—which involved deliberate factional efforts to steer programmatic development based on their own interpretations of events.

The interfactional account finds a lot of support here. But the concept of "faction" does not, in itself, differentiate in any systematic way among types of party actors (politicians, experts, activists), nor does it address qualitative differences between dominant party spokespeople across time periods. But New Democratic experts—which included journalists-turned-aides, think tank "wonks," private sector and financial economists, and wealthy trustees—were distinctive, especially in comparison with the economist theoretician of the 1960s. Grasping this necessitates, in turn, consideration of the historical development of the institutions in which party networks are grounded and party actors are formed. Stated simply, the people who make up party factions are both *differentiated* from each other and different *in kind* over time. Party actors see the world in distinctive ways; to the extent that they shape party program-building and communicative strategies, their distinctive ways of seeing shape how parties see, too. But an interfactional account tends to treat factions as undifferentiated, historically equivalent units, making it difficult to explain why any particular party, faction, or actor forms and projects distinctive interpretations of the world.

In a refraction account, by contrast, economic, demographic, and institutional changes are channeled through intraparty, interfactional, interpretive struggles; parties and party factions are internally differentiated and historically specific; and party experts are a key component of party infrastructure because of their variable capacities for intermediation. To this we now turn.

ORIGINS: NEW POLITICS, INTERFACTIONALISM, AND THE RISE OF STRATEGIC EXPERTS

The undoing of the Keynesian-era liberal elite began in the 1960s, with the rise of civil rights, feminist, and antiwar movements. This kicked off a long period of *disarticulation* and *intraparty contestation* in which formerly loyal Democratic voters divorced themselves from the party that, since the New Deal, dominated American partisan identification

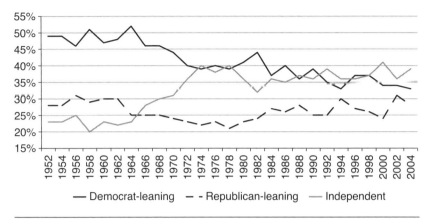

Figure 7.6. Trends in party identification ("strong" or "weak" versus independent), 1952–2004. Data source: American National Election Studies, via Stanley and Niemi 2015, Table 4.1. Author calculations.

(see Figure 7.6). As Democrats' ability to command voter loyalties declined from the 1960s forward, factional struggles for control of nominations, agendas, and policies intensified.

After violent upheavals at the Chicago Democratic Convention in 1968, the balance of power inside the Democratic Party shifted away from the New Deal liberal elite. In 1968 liberals closed ranks around their candidate (and a longtime ADAer), Vice President Hubert Humphrey, shutting out his competitor for the nomination, the favorite of the antiwar movement, Eugene McCarthy. Facing a tough contest with Richard Nixon and lacking appeal for newly mobilized protest groups, the Humphrey campaign turned to a new kind of expert: Joseph Napolitan (1929–2013). Napolitan specialized in tailoring campaigns according to weekly polls. His role was novel enough that, lacking a formal title, he created the term "political consultant" for himself.[6] There thus emerged, in the crucible of 1968, a novel role in national-level Democratic political campaigns for bearers of specifically strategic expertise.

As discussed in the previous chapter, political consulting was not new, but it was increasingly prominent. Napolitan's appearance on the Humphrey campaign marked an important inflection point in this broad shift. In the same year Napolitan was also a driver in the establishment of the American Association of Political Consultants (AAPC). The decline of a strongly Democratic-identified electorate and ensuing intensification of electoral competition, it would seem, promoted the rise of the political consultant by focusing candidates' concerns on problems of electoral strategy.

Meanwhile, in the wake of 1968, the Democratic bearers of New Deal liberalism lost control. A twenty-eight-member commission, selected by DNC Chairman Fred Harris and led by Senator George McGovern (and, later, Representative Donald Fraser), transformed the events of 1968 into a mandate to revise the party's convention rules. The resulting McGovern-Fraser reforms of 1972 afforded greater representation, albeit in a quota-like way, to groups associated with New Politics movements—especially racial/ethnic minority groups and women. The powers of New Deal liberals and trade unions declined; Baer reports that the dominance of New Politics reformers on the commission was such that "the AFL-CIO pulled its lone commissioner from the body in protest."[7] McGovern won the Democratic nomination in 1972.

After 1972 the representational composition of Democratic delegations changed, but procedural control also shifted upward, toward the national level. Symptoms included the imposition of national-level rules on what had been highly variable state and local delegation systems; adoption of a national charter in 1974; and initiation of a regular system of midterm conferences (among other things). In short, the party became more "porous" in ways that offset the power of the New Deal elite and trade unions, but also became a more national organization.[8]

The two shifts, toward New Politics liberals (representationally) and the national level (procedurally), were to some extent at odds. The failed McGovern campaign—the staff of which included Bill Clinton—served, for some, as proof that the party's new structure was not a recipe for electoral success. Amid a party in which power was now newly exercised from the top down, the party's New Politics turn begat new forms of opposition. The year 1972 thus saw the birth of the Congress-based Coalition for a Democratic Majority (CDM), which took inspiration from a 1970 book by Walter Scammon and Ben Wattenberg called *The Real Majority*.[9] The CDM, which included the famous Democratic "neoconservatives" Daniel Bell, Daniel Patrick Moynihan, and Irving Kristol, interpreted McGovern's failure as proof of Scammon and Wattenberg's poll-based analysis of a white working-class aversion to the abandonment of social issues.[10] It asserted that the "real majority" in the United States was, in fact, economically liberal and socially conservative. This conclusion did not sit easily with the new makeup of Democratic delegations or with the party's quota-oriented procedures, which the CDM explicitly opposed.[11]

White southern Democrats (like Sam Nunn [D-GA]) tended to align with the CDM's socially conservative, pro-military stances.[12] But the year 1974 brought a major congressional victory for Democratic politicians, many of them non-southerners; Democrats gained four seats in the Senate and forty-nine seats in the House. The new Democratic freshman class shifted the power-position of southern Democrats like Nunn, unseating three long-standing, powerful, southern Democratic committee chairmen (another had been ousted a year earlier).[13] The post-1960s decline of the Democratic Party in the South thus, in a sense, finally took root in 1974, as younger-generation Democrats from places like Wisconsin, Illinois, and Washington displaced congressional Democratic "southerners who were there forever."[14]

This new Democratic class reshaped the governmental economic advisory institutions built by its New Deal predecessors. The float of the dollar in 1971 and mistrust of the presidency engendered during the Watergate scandals prompted the new Democratic Congress to create the Congressional Budget Office (CBO), fueling the politicization of economics that is tracked in the previous chapter. The CBO, established via the Budget and Impoundment Act, was intended as a counterweight to the Office of Management and Budget (OMB)—the objectivity of which Democratic congresspeople "had come to question" in the Nixon years.[15] The OMB and CBO thence produced estimates that tended to diverge when the White House and Congress were controlled by opposing parties.[16]

THE CARTER YEARS: FRACTURING AND OPPOSITION IN DEMOCRATIC EXPERTISE

On the eve of Jimmy Carter's election, then, the Democratic Party was congressionally powerful but internally divided, and economic advisory institutions forged in the New Deal era were fractured and politicized.

Monetary stability and inflation, closely linked with volatility in oil prices (which was, in turn, inextricable from Western involvements in the Middle East), shaped the American experience from the start of the 1970s. For some economists the significance of the inflation problem was its implication for Keynesian theory; for Carter's late-stage inflation adviser, the economist Alfred (Fred) Kahn, and his appointee to the Federal Reserve, Paul Volcker, the solutions involved a combination of energy deregulation and monetary policy (raising interest rates). What this meant, in practice, was that energy prices would go up even as the economy slipped more deeply into recession. But for Carter's noneconomist advisers, and indeed for Carter himself, the significance of inflation and oil prices was political, inseparable from the United States' foreign oil dependencies, and linked to the fate of the administration and the Democratic Party. Their solutions included Keynesian-style management of wages and prices, plus energy policies that could diminish the country's oil dependencies.

The two interpretations, and their solutions, were at odds. Not surprisingly, in the late stages of the Carter administration Democratic economists and noneconomists did not always get along. The experience left those in the latter category convinced of the need for a new, specifically Democratic economic analysis, with or without economists' input. The fracture was fueled, in part, by the new prominence of poll-based, strategically specialized experts in party-expert networks. Significant here was the young pollster Patrick Caddell, who innovated polling techniques aimed at figuring out how to shape, as opposed to read, public opinion.[17] Unlike George Gallup or Elmo Roper, Caddell tried to identify issues that voters did not like or were unfamiliar with, and then he looked for ways of framing them in order to garner approval.[18] The approach was tailor-made to the pressing question of which voters needed to be reached and why, but it came up short on the question of how. Early in Carter's presidency Caddell advised the president to focus on young, educated, suburban professionals and called for a "fundamentally new ideology" that was "neither traditionally liberal nor traditionally conservative"—but, he added, he was not sure what such an ideology would be.[19] Like Joe Napolitan, Caddell ported a form of expertise that was closely tailored to electoral and strategic concerns.

Some of Carter's advisers and cabinet members, meanwhile, remained decidedly "Keynesian" in their thinking. Notions of a trade-off between unemployment and inflation and the usefulness of managerial "fine-tuning" persisted. Carter's labor secretary, F. Ray Marshall (1928–; PhD, economics, University of California, Berkeley), for instance, later framed his advocacy of a government-driven jobs program in terms of a conventionally Keynesian trade-off between unemployment and infla-tion.[20] Carter's Council on Wage and Price Stability, which mimicked the Nixon administration's response to inflation, also spoke to the on-going legitimacy of union-friendly, Keynesian-style managerialism in the administration.

Carter's CEA's economists—against a background of broader con-cern that unions were driving "wage-push" inflation—did not, however, support a key component of wage and price coordination: *mandatory* guidelines. The Council on Wage and Price Stability was a Keynesian institution, but its content was not. In the account of Bert Carp, Car-ter's chief domestic policy adviser and staff director:

> Nixon faced almost exactly the same problem [of inflation], and he slapped on wage and price controls and got himself reelected. Right? . . . Carter looked at this and decided to do the right thing, sort of. . . . [W]e had everything about wage and price controls, except the wage and price controls. . . . We completely re-established the Nixon price control program, except we said compliance was voluntary; and of course, there was no compliance. . . . We had the weekly reports, meetings, we brought people, jawboned 'em. We did everything ex-cept control either wages or prices, and nobody paid any attention to us at all.[21]

There are indications that the curiously Keynesian-but-not nature of Carter's wage and price policies had to do with an emergent opposition between political and academic orientations. Carp, for instance, later recounted that Carter's decision to make controls mandatory had to do with his respect for economists' advice: "Carter, being a very respon-sible person, was unable to not listen to the economists.[22]

In the later years of Carter's one-term presidency the schism became clearer. At least two appointments are especially notable here. One is that of Alfred (Fred) Kahn (1917–2010; Yale PhD), whom Carter appointed in 1978 in a dual role as adviser on inflation and chair of the Council on Wage and Price Stability. The other appointment made on the heels of a major cabinet shake-up and a notable shift in the tone of Carter's public communication was that of Democratic economist Paul Volcker (1927–) as head of the Federal Reserve, effective August 1979.

Kahn, a specialist in the economics of deregulation, came into his new position in October 1978. He arrived from a position at the head of the Civil Aeronautics Board (CAB), where he had been since 1977, having earned a reputation as both "an old-fashioned Democrat" and a deregulator of American airlines. Kahn found Carter's selection of an economist of deregulation as a Keynesian-style regulator surprising, although he later explained that he was not opposed to wage and price controls ("I think it's pragmatically something that may do some good," but "it doesn't interest me professionally").[23] From Kahn's perspective, the way to manage prices was by deregulating markets and letting competition do the work. Assured by Carter that his responsibilities would include "the entire range of government policies that might have a bearing on inflation," Kahn took up his new position on October 25, 1978.[24]

At once a spokesperson for the administration and an advocate of deregulation (especially in trucking, health care, and energy), Kahn's appointment was meant to convey that the government had inflation in hand—and yet, at the same time, Kahn offered prescriptions that tended to make the administration appear self-contradictory.[25] Kahn later recounted that he considered himself no expert on the political implications of his advice: "How many times is an issue so clear that you can simply tell a President, 'Deregulate crude oil,' or 'Don't deregulate crude oil'? That was a terribly difficult and complicated decision involving political aspects."[26] His public communications, instead of building momentum behind presidential initiatives, sometimes fueled congressional efforts to block legislation that the administration supported (for instance, price controls on sugar).[27]

By the summer of 1979, as oil prices climbed in the wake of the Iranian Revolution, the administration's situation was deteriorating. In July Carter shifted his communications strategy away from a nuts-and-bolts focus on energy and inflation, criticism of OPEC, and calls for reduced foreign oil dependence, shifting instead to themes of American consumerism and public morality. The result was Carter's "malaise" speech, given on July 15, 1979, amid fuel shortages, gas lines, and a restive American public. Caddell supported Carter's rhetorical move, but his economist advisers, among others, did not.[28] Shortly thereafter Carter surprised everyone by summarily firing and reconstituting much of his cabinet and senior advisory staff.[29]

Carter's shake-up involved a new appointment to the chairmanship of the Federal Reserve: Paul Volcker, who took up the post in August 1979. Volcker was (and remains) a Democratic economist, albeit of a particular sort: holding a BA from Princeton University (1949) and an MA from the Harvard Graduate School of Public Administration in political economy and government (1951), Volcker attended the LSE in 1951–1952 but did not pursue a doctorate. He became a *de facto* economist by virtue of a professional trajectory that centered in finance, not academe: after early work in central bank research (in particular on securities), he moved between Chase Manhattan Bank, government (the Treasury), and an academic appointment at the Woodrow Wilson School at Princeton University. Volcker earned professional esteem partly as a player in negotiations over the valuation of the dollar and the closing of the gold window under Nixon in 1971—and was, by extension, integrated into the internationalizing world of economics and finance that is described in the previous chapter.[30] As the head of the New York Federal Reserve since 1975, Volcker was also acquainted with the theories of Milton Friedman and the rational expectations arguments of Robert E. Lucas Jr. and Thomas J. Sargent.[31]

Carter knew that Volcker supported bank independence and restrictive monetary policies and that high interest rates would not bode well for his electoral fortunes. Volcker, for his part, knew that his inclinations did not square with Carter's political concerns.[32] Carter nonetheless appointed him, effective August 6, 1979—just a few months after Lucas and Sargent declared the impossibility of scientifically grounded Keynesian "fine tuning."[33] F. Ray Marshall objected:

> I think it was a bad idea to appoint Paul Volcker. . . . I still think it was a mistake to do it. I think that if our analysis of the cause of inflation was correct, it was mainly because of external oil price shocks. . . . [T]herefore what they wanted to do was to let the workers

pay for it with high unemployment. But it wouldn't just be the workers paying for it. The Democratic Party was going to pay for it. The President was going to pay for it.[34]

True to Marshall's assessment, Volcker commenced with the implementation of austere monetary policies that were hard on inflation, and on Democratic interests.

Carter later complained that Volcker's anti-inflation campaign undermined his presidency by appearing to render it impotent.[35] More generally, he recounted his frustration with the ambiguity of economic advice, policy disagreement among economists, and economists' seeming insensitivity to the necessities of politics. In Carter's words:

> The problem was, and this is so patently well-known that its almost stupid to say it, you could talk to five economists about macroeconomic policy and they'd all give you a different version. Then you got down and said, well, OK, what are we going to do about it? . . . I wasn't a theoretician sitting in an ivory tower just being absorbed with the excitement of discussing economics.[36]

In Marshall's assessment, the administration's failed price and wage controls and Volcker's appointment were both symptomatic of a larger problem: the abandonment of consensus-building, fueled by "economics colleagues" who believed not "in consensus" but rather in "letting market forces take over."[37]

In the end some Carter administration veterans came to view economists as either incapable of doing or unwilling to do the work of reconciling economic advising with consensus-building and strategizing. This had little to do with regard for economists and economics, *per se*.[38] It had to do, instead, with a sense that economists could not solve economic problems and, more importantly perhaps, that they lacked a feel for the political game. Stuart Eizenstat later commented that the Carter administration was replete with "Ph.D. economists," and yet it "presided over an economy with double-digit inflation and interest rates and a recession."[39] Economists' advice "was sometimes grating to me, and to others," he added, "because it lacked political sensitivity."[40] In short, economists no longer seemed able to straddle the worlds of politics and science.

All this was, for some, a formative experience. Among those for whom it was formative was the future founder of the DLC: Al From (1943–). Through From's trajectory, in particular, one can see how the divorce of economic advising and political strategizing shaped the rise of the New Democrats.

NEW EXPERTS, NEW DEMOCRATS:
FROM CARTER TO CLINTON

Trained in journalism (BA and MA) at Northwestern, From initially came to D.C. as part of a journalistic start-up called the Medill News Service. Turning down a job at the *Chicago Daily News*, From went to work for Sargent Shriver as a journalistic evaluator of War on Poverty programs, joining a number of "young lawyers and journalists" recruited to report on how the programs were faring.[41] Originally from South Bend, Indiana, From acquired through this work firsthand knowledge of civil rights struggles in the South.[42] From there he worked in various capacities in the Senate including, for a time, a position in Edmund Muskie's (D-ME) office. Having taken on the Shriverian principle that government programs should have self-corrective mechanisms, in the Senate From worked partly on budgetary issues, producing (for instance) a bill on "countercyclical revenue sharing," for "antirecession aid to states and cities" that was tied to unemployment rates since, in From's words, during a recession "tax revenues go down and demands for services go up." In other words, he helped to formulate a Keynesian-style, automatic mechanism for resolving (whether or not From thought of it in this way) a core dilemma of welfare capitalism.[43]

In 1979 From entered the Carter administration as deputy advisor to the president on inflation, giving him an up-close view of the emergent divorce of Democratic economics and Democratic strategy. Noting how hard inflation was on middle-class families (including his own), From later emphasized how the experience of rising inflation and dropping public approval "helped shape my philosophy."[44] Out of this experience, From developed a certain understanding of what constituted a successful policy: the key is not the interest coalition behind it, but rather the aftereffects once a policy is in place. With the example of Carter's wage-price guidelines in mind, From concluded that strategic thinking about the timing of policy effects relative to the rhythms of electoral politics, in particular, was essential.[45] He thus arrived at a conclusion that is reminiscent of the Keynesian ethic: successful policy-making had to be keyed to the rhythms and necessities of politics.

In the 1980s, From was also among a variety of politicians, journalists, aides, and experts who worried that New Politics liberalism was eating away at the Democratic Party's "mainstream" support. For From, this concern was linked to a belief that the inflationary 1970s, and perceptions of the Carter administration as economically incompetent, drove middle-class disaffections. All this suggested a need for a new Democratic program that married strategy, policy, and rhetoric.[46]

Meanwhile economics' public profile as a consensual, nonpolitical profession continued its steep decline. Ronald Reagan's campaign famously mobilized the arguments of "supply-siders," prompting mockery of Reagan's "voodoo economics"—that is, an economic program that, grounded in the logic of the Laffer curve, included increased defense spending, cutting taxes, and balancing the budget.[47] Reagan defended himself by laying claim to the backing of "fine economists,"[48] whose identity became clear enough in his administration: Reagan appointed Milton Friedman, by then a recipient of the Nobel Prize (1976), to the new Economic Policy Advisory Board, which was separate from the CEA. Five (out of eight) of the board's economists were Chicago-trained. Over the course of Reagan's two terms a considerable number (five) came to the board from posts in financial institutions (the Federal Reserve, the Treasury) and business or management schools.[49]

Flanked by economists of a particular sort, Reagan passed his famous tax-cutting Omnibus Budget Reconciliation Act in 1981, leaving monitoring and evaluation in the hands of a politicized OMB—whose director later went on record with a remarkable confession of efforts to manipulate the interpretation of the policy's success.[50] Economics was just as central to politics as ever—perhaps more so—but the Age of the Economist, grounded in a consensual (and implicitly Democratic) profession, had passed.

First Steps: The Committee on Party Effectiveness

The first steps in the making of New Democrats emerged jointly from intraparty struggles, the Carter experience, the fall of the economics–

Democratic Party alliance, and the electoral success of Reaganite Republicanism. Out of this conjuncture emerged the New Democrats' institutional predecessor: the Committee on Party Effectiveness (CPE).

The early years of the Reagan administration sparked new efforts among House Democrats—specifically House Democratic Caucus leader Representative Gillis Long (1923–1985; D-LA) and Al From (who became Long's aide), alongside fiscally conservative Democrats unhappy with the growing deficit—to tighten and redirect the Democratic message.[51] The result was the CPE, established after the 1980 election by Long and From.[52]

Through the CPE Long, newly powerful after successfully maneuvering into the leadership of the House Democratic Caucus (in a surprise victory over Tip O'Neill), brought together a group of younger-generation Democrats. In From's account, "Gillis turned out to be the guru of all these young leaders like Tim [Timothy] Wirth and Dick [Richard] Gephardt and Al Gore [Jr.] and Gerry [Geraldine] Ferraro and others"—all of whom were new arrivals to Congress in the mid-1970s.[53] The CPE—and, later, the DLC—has been characterized as a project driven by southern Democratic politicians in response to the success of the Republican "southern strategy," but the makeup of the CPE suggests a more complicated geographical basis: in total thirty-seven congressional representatives joined the CPE, roughly one-third southern (38 percent), western or midwestern (32 percent), and northeastern or mid-Atlantic (30 percent).[54]

It is clear, however, that for From the CPE was a logical extension of views formed in the Carter years. In the early 1980s From continued to view inflation as a driver of middle-class disaffection with the Democratic Party: "All the analysis that I had done—and I did a lot more in those four years I was in the caucus—basically showed that we were losing middle-class voters." If they got "on the right side of the inflation issue," From reasoned, the Democrats also had a shot at getting "back to middle-class voters" and thus restoring middle-class Democratic loyalties.[55] By extension, the party's capacity for analysis had to be resuscitated.

The first step involved a noteworthy repurposing of the House Democratic Caucus. In the 1970s, in From's perspective, the caucus was a casualty of intraparty struggles:

> [W]hat we did with the caucus was that we made it the incubator of ideas and message. . . . The Democratic Caucus in the House is the oldest political institution in America other than the Speakership. . . . It had an illustrious history. . . . When I took over, it was at the end of a dormant period, because . . . the liberals grabbed hold of the caucus, they opened all the meetings to the public, and they used it basically as a stage. So the leadership tried to shut it down.

Out of the (literal) rubble of intraparty struggles, From assembled the raw materials of a new in-house, party-based, programmatic infrastructure:

> I went up to the caucus office, and it was a room with no windows on the seventh floor of the Longworth Building—piled with rubble, telephones, telephone wires. . . . So I cleaned it out. Some Republican Congressman—poor soul—who was next door had a conference room, and he stuck his conference table outside the door—big mistake. I moved it into our office, re-covered it, and around that table we began the New Democrat movement. . . . Gillis formed this little group called the Committee on Party Effectiveness [CPE], which met every Tuesday—and sometimes even more than that up there—and they talked about politics and policy.[56]

In 1981, because Long delegated leadership over the CPE due to health problems, From acquired singular authority in the effort.[57]

The CPE Economic Agenda: The Collapse of Keynesianism?

In the lead-up to midterm elections the CPE centered 1982 Democratic campaigns on the theme of "fairness," defined in opposition to Reagan administration policies. To this end it produced a series of reports, ranging across agriculture, labor, nutrition, education, senior citizens, housing, women and minorities, and foreign aid, titled the "Fairness Packet."[58] In September 1982, in an effort led largely by From and Wirth, the CPE also published a more concise, seven-point Democratic policy statement that came to be known as the "Yellow Book" or "Yellow Brick Road" (officially titled *Rebuilding the Road to Oppor-*

tunity: A Democratic Direction for the 1980s).[59] The Yellow Book covered "long-term economic policy, housing, small business, women's economic issues, the environment, crime, and national security"—but, as noted by the political scientist Karl Gerard Brandt, it "reflected the diversity of House Democrats' political ideologies."[60] It was, in other words, still a liberal document.

But, according to From, there was an important novelty in the Yellow Book's economic vocabulary: growth. The use of "growth" may seem "like a pretty silly thing," From later noted, but "through the '70s, growth wasn't part of the Democratic litany."[61] The turn to growth, however, was hardly framed in a free market, rational expectations, or Reaganesque way. Indeed, the CPE's separate report on long-term economic policy, *Rebuilding the Road to Opportunity: Turning Point for America's Economy* (led by Long, Wirth, and Richard Gephardt, with From on the staff), called for a series of government-centric initiatives: national investment in manufacturing and high tech, preservation of family farms, job retraining to help workers transition between industries, and reducing foreign oil dependence.[62] The reference to oil dependence no doubt expressed Democrats' ongoing interpretation of the inflationary 1970s as an energy problem, as opposed to a failure of economic science.

A particularly interesting indication of CPE Democrats' ongoing Keynesian inclinations is the committee's call for a new advisory institution to support and reinforce the links between economic analysis, consensus-building, and policy-making, providing a new forum for negotiation among business, labor, academe, and government. Early on, under the heading "The Democratic Way," the report states this quite explicitly: "Achieving economic growth will require a partnership among labor, small business, big corporations, universities, and government."[63] To this end, the CPE called for the creation of a new forum: the Economic Cooperation Council.[64]

The fact that the report calls for *any* new center of economic advising is itself noteworthy. Governmental advisory institutions by this time were hardly in short supply: in Congress and the White House alone at least four separate agencies, the CEA, OMB, CBO, and JEC, provided economic analyses, budgetary projections, and research-based forecasts, not to mention the many various economist-heavy departmental agencies.

What, then, explains the call for yet another governmental basis of economic advising?

On this question the report cites a disconnect between domestic and international economic analysis, on the one hand, and between economic analysis and political cooperation, on the other, with clear reference to the experience of the 1970s. First, it describes the need for "a center of American expertise" capable of providing an "early warning system to detect flaws or weaknesses in our domestic enterprises before those weaknesses become debilitating or even fatal." Had such a body existed in 1970, the report argues, it could have anticipated changes in international oil production and "the whole course of economic history might well have been different." Second, it could evaluate "global economic trends" in order to "assess the strengths of our competitors in the international arena" in a way that links forecasting with public communication: the new council would have the "capability to forecast where we should be in three or six or ten years," within "a national arena for clarifying complex economic choices and building broad support for public initiatives." Finally, the council would "combine the ability to assess future economic trends with a membership that would help build a partnership around solutions to major economic problems."[65]

The Economic Cooperation Council, in short, would be a site for joining national and international economic analysis with communication, negotiation, and politically acute advising. The new body's members and staff would be "representative, distinguished, respected and influential," featuring "top quality staff with . . . specialized talents that combine analytic skills with an understanding of the American political process."[66] In other words the new council would be a bearer of Keynesian ethics, with or without economists.

The CPE task force's economic recommendations were symptomatic of the so-called "collapse of Keynesianism," but not in the usual sense of the phrase. In fact, on budgetary matters early 1980s Democratic positions remained broadly liberal in the Keynesian, pro-deficit sense. One analysis, by the Conservative Democratic Forum (CDF), identified 45 House Democrats as budgetary conservatives, 41 as moderates, and 156 as liberals.[67] Pro-deficit liberalism remained intact despite intensifying efforts to police party ranks and voting habits.[68] After the passage of new rules in 1983, in fact, preferences given to loyal party-line voters in committee appointments often meant that budgetary conservatives were passed over.[69] In the early 1980s, in short, it was far from clear that Democratic inclinations had become any less Keynesian in a broad (Phillips curve) or strict (pro deficit) sense.

What we do find in the wake of the Carter years, however, are indications that CPE Democrats did not view professional economics, Keynesian or otherwise, as natural bearers of Democratic economic policy-making. Instead they saw the power-seekers—that is, elected party elites—as the rightful holders of definitional authority.

Reasserting Party Control

After the 1982 midterm elections CPE Democrats could make some claim to electoral success: Democrats made significant midterm gains in the House, bringing in fifty-seven (mainly fiscally conservative) freshmen Democrats, but gained no advantage in the Senate. More important than electoral gains, however, were CPE-driven efforts to shift party procedures and reassert elite control.

The nomination process was an important target. In Baer's account, "CPE Democrats knew that to make changes they desired in the public philosophy of the party, they had to steal a page from the playbook of the New Politics faction."[70] The result was the Hunt Commission of 1980–1982, chaired by North Carolina governor James B. Hunt Jr., which aimed to bring "elected officials back into party affairs" in order to "make the nominating process more representative of the party's rank and file."[71]

The Hunt Commission included AFL-CIO representatives, "the Senate Democratic Conference, state party chairs, and the House Democratic Caucus."[72] But some understood the Hunt Commission as having the singular purpose of marginalizing New Politics liberals. "The whole theory," in one New Democrat's words, was "for the elected wing of the party to exercise a kind of countervailing force to the ideologues and the interest groups."[73] In From's account: "Basically the party had divorced itself from its elected officials. . . . I cut the deal on the super delegates because we wanted to bring electeds back."[74] Despite AFL-CIO involvement, Baer notes that From "wanted Democratic congressmen to flex their new institutional muscle, challenge the early endorsement strategy of powerful interest groups (e.g., AFL-CIO, NEA [National Education Association]), and become prominent players in the nominating process."[75]

The result was a significant increase of conventional delegation slots reserved for "governors, large-city mayors, members of Congress and state party chairs as unpledged delegates to its national convention."[76] A plan drafted by Geraldine Ferraro and Mark Siegel created "add-on slots" for state party chairpersons and "allocated four hundred additional unpledged delegate positions to the states."[77] Superdelegates made up 8 percent of the delegates at the party's 1980 convention, but 15.5 percent in 1984.

In sum, by 1984 the decline of loyal Democratic voters (especially in the South), the experience of the inflationary 1970s, conflicts between economic advising and political interests inside the Carter administration, and the ascendance of Reagan fueled not one but *two* fractures inside the Democratic Party: first, the formation of a new party faction, marked by its opposition to New Politics Democratic liberalism (understood as a politics of "blacks, Hispanics, unions, gays, feminists, and the elderly," or simply the "fringe") and concerns with returning to the "mainstream"; second, the end of a once taken-for-granted alliance between professional economics and Democratic Party politics.[78] The latter hinged not on criticism of economics *per se,* or any clear recognition of goings-on within the economics profession, but rather on an apparent irreconcilability between what economists-in-politics advised and what Democratic strategy required.

The superdelegate system did not, at first, work in the way its creators envisioned.[79] Reflecting the fact that many party elites were still of the old liberal, New Deal or New Politics, sort ("paleoliberal," in the terminology of opponents), Walter Mondale secured the 1984 nomination, defeating a favored candidate of CPE Democrats: Gary Hart.[80] From encouraged the Mondale campaign to avoid liberal pandering, drawing (in Baer's words) "men and whites to the Democratic ticket by adopting a message with broad national appeal, one that would pledge to hold the line on spending." But the campaign did not take From's advice. From feared that a younger generation of potential Democrats—especially white men—would "never join the party."[81] For the CPE

Democrats, the 1984 Democratic program proved that "the inmates had taken over the asylum."[82]

The Distinctiveness of New Democratic Party-Expert Relations

After Long's death in 1985, From and a fellow aide, Will Marshall (1952–), set their sights on moving beyond the Democratic Caucus. Reportedly starting with "a budget of just $400,000" that was "cobbled together at fundraisers starring [Chuck] Robb, former President Jimmy Carter, and K Street Democratic eminence Bob [Robert] Strauss" (treasurer, then chair, of the DNC from 1970 to 1977), the Democratic Leadership Council (DLC) was established in 1985 with From at its head and Marshall as policy director.[83] The aim was to rival the DNC—in From's words: "After a few abortive efforts to try to elect a DNC chairman, we figured we couldn't do that so we'd do our own deal."[84] The DLC was initially chaired by Gephardt, with From as executive director; its congressional affiliates drew from CPE circles and From's broader networks of contacts in the Senate (Lawton Chiles, Sam Nunn) and the House (Chuck Robb, Bruce Babbitt). Spurred by Democratic electoral losses in 1988, in 1989 the DLCers established a small in-house think tank, the Progressive Policy Institute (PPI). Soon after Bruce Reed (a would-be journalist-turned-congressional-aide, formerly Senator Al Gore's first speechwriter and self-described "idea guy") took over as the DLC's policy director.[85]

The composition of the PPI's early leadership is worth noting. At the helm was Will Marshall, a 1975 graduate of the University of Virginia (English, history) who had worked, like From, as a journalist (in Virginia). From there Marshall became "press secretary, spokesman and speechwriter" in the Senate campaign of North Carolina governor Jim Hunt and then worked with Long and served as a House Democratic Caucus chairman in the days of the CPE. The PPI also had a cofounder and vice president: a Harvard-trained economist, Robert J. Shapiro (1953–), who had been working since 1986 as the associate editor of *U.S. News and World Report* and before that (1981–1986) as legislative director and economic counsel to Senator Daniel Patrick Moynihan, advising especially on taxation and budgets.[86]

The structure of the DLC-PPI had the makings of a two-armed party: politicians at the helm, dedicated to knowledge production and oriented toward middle-class and mainstream constituencies. For From, the necessity of investment in knowledge production was taken for granted: "[I]f we were going to be an idea place, we needed an idea center," and so "that's why we created the PPI" and its magazine, the *Mainstream Democrat*.[87] The New Democratic electoral base (the "mainstream") was, to a certain extent, theoretical—an amalgamation constructed on the basis of polls, public opinion surveys, and interpretations of their meaning in light of election results. Via relationships between DLC-affiliated representatives and their voting constituencies, however, the DLC's connections to voters were also quite real.

What, then, was distinctive about the DLC-PPI configuration? Recalling the account of the ADA given in Chapter 5, a comparison is perhaps helpful. From, in fact, considered the ADA a precursor of the DLC-PPI, especially because they shared the aim of saving liberalism by reforming it (in the ADA's case, by situating Democratic liberalism as anticommunist).[88] And the DLC and ADA had similar origins: White House and congressional exiles initiated the formation of both, recruiting the like-minded along the way. Structurally and historically, however, the DLC-PPI and ADA were different in important respects.

First, unlike the ADA, the DLC was not deeply grounded in networks of academics and government-connected, PhD-bearing experts. By comparison the DLC-PPI stands out for the absence of academics, and especially economists, among its most prominent figures. Also, the DLC sought to supplant the DNC instead of cooperating with it. A final distinction is detectable in the two entities' representative bases. Unlike the ADA, which had particularly strong ties to the CIO before the mid-1950s, neither the PPI nor the DLC incorporated labor representatives into its leadership; instead, the DLC-PPI is noted—sometimes critically—for its corporate and financial sponsorship.[89]

The absence of union ties deserves explanation. Partly it had to do with the geographical bases of DLC politicians: recall that CPE membership was about two-thirds southern, western, and midwestern. One could also point to labor's numerical decline—which began in the 1960s but was accelerating in the 1980s (see Figure 7.7).

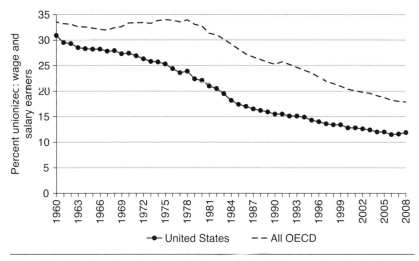

Figure 7.7. Trade union density, 1960–2008, United States and all OECD. Data source: OECD.

But numbers were not necessarily the main basis of union influence with Democrats; financial ties were also crucial. Recall that until 1955 unions provided the core of the ADA's financial support; after 1955, with the AFL-CIO merger, that basis declined, but the union-Democrat financial relationship continued via candidates and campaigns. But, DLCers saw unions as wielders of too much power over Democratic politicians, pushing the party away from the mainstream—and were not alone in that assessment.

Corporate and financial sponsorship, it seems, allowed the DLCers to challenge Democrats' union dependencies. In 2001 a *Prospect* journalist, Robert Dreyfuss, noted:

By 1990 the combined DLC-PPI operation boasted revenues of $2.2 million, a big chunk of which came from a single source, New York hedge fund operator Michael Steinhardt, who pledged $500,000 a year for three years. (Steinhardt, whose actual donations came to half that in the end, was named chairman of the newly formed PPI's board of trustees, before falling out with the DLC in the mid-1990s.) . . . By 1990 major firms like AT&T and Philip Morris were important donors.[90]

Steinhardt—a 1960s-era Goldwater supporter who later described how, in the 1970s and 1980s, he "moved left as the world moved to the right"—confirms that he was, "by far, the DLC's largest financial contributor, donating a minimum of $250,000 per year for nearly 10 years." Steinhardt's financial support was complemented by participatory access: "Early on, I became [the DLC's] legal chairman. . . . I also became chairman of . . . the Progressive Policy Institute."[91] In short, the DLC's notable lack of union affiliation was probably made possible by its corporate and financial ties. These ties provided Democratic politicians—as we will see, in Clinton's case—with alternative sources of support if they broke with union priorities.

Last but not least, one can also compare the ADA's and DLC-PPI's structure and organizational contexts. Like the ADA, the DLC tried to ground itself beyond D.C., initiating an effort to seed state-level chapters in the late 1980s. In From's account, "We needed money but we also needed troops."[92] But the effort failed:

> We've never been any good at it. We had a one-person field department. . . . We had people from all over who were interested, particularly in the parts of the country where the Democratic Party was in deep trouble. . . . So people wanted to organize. . . . We put together, really, shells of chapters. We had a leadership of chapters.[93]

Aside from the logistical difficulties of nationwide organizing, the DLCers seem to have been unwilling to engage in the complicated management and *quid pro quo* horse-trading that would have been essential to the effort.[94] And so the DLC remained an "office-holder organization."[95]

What allowed the DLC to persist in this decidedly D.C.-centered, elite format? Here it is important that the DLC-PPI was part of the new organizational ecology of "think tanks"—which simply didn't exist in the ADA's early years. As the sociologist Thomas Medvetz shows, the proliferation of political think tanks in the 1970s–1980s drove the formation of a whole new organizational terrain dedicated to the production of policy knowledge.[96] Indigenous to the think tank ecosystem was the policy specialist, or "wonk," distinctive for his (or, finally, her) orientation to the production of policy knowledge that tailored scholarly insight, journalistic appeal, and sensitivity to the fast-ticking rhythms of politics. By the 1980s, academics (and anyone else) were increasingly compelled to navigate the world of think tanks in order to gain entry into national politics. This may help to explain the DLC's D.C.-centeredness and its lack of deep academic ties.

New Democratic leftism, like its economistic predecessor, thus had its own organizational terrain, representational orientations, institutional dependencies, and characteristic experts. The New Democratic expert was most likely a journalist-turned-aide, a think tank "wonk," a private sector economist, a "relatively affluent" (in Steinhardt's term) trustee, or some combination.[97] This was the basis on which a new brand of Democratic politics—"not liberal, not conservative, but progressive," in Steinhardt's words—was built.[98]

None of this is to say that the New Democratic project was not, as its protagonists assert, about "ideas." The point is merely that all ideological initiatives play out in context, carried forth by socially situated actors. In democratic settings, political ideologies become effective in government and policy-making via networks of actors in and around political parties. In this sense the DLC-PPI project was no different, and no less distinctive, than the forces behind the making of socialist or economistic leftism. But in a specific sense the New Democrats' were special indeed: their efforts were backed by connections to finance and corporations rather than organized labor and grounded, not in academic economics, but in an increasingly self-contained world of professionalized politics.

The Demarcation of New Democratic "Progressivism"

In the late 1980s a central aim of the DLC-PPI was crafting a cultural infrastructure and, through it, a coherent programmatic message. "What we spent all our time on was figuring out what we were going to say and checking the message, the philosophy of opportunity, responsibility, and community," in From's recounting.[99] The low profile of economists in the effort has been noted, but of course some academics were involved. In a 2004 interview, Bruce Reed named exactly two: William (Bill) Galston (1946–) and Elaine Kamarck (1950–), both political scientists.[100]

Galston and Kamarck played a special role in the effort to demarcate New Democratic "progressivism" as a distinctive factional politics, defined by its opposition to Democratic "liberalism." At the time Galston (PhD, political science, University of Chicago) was on the faculty of the University of Maryland's School of Public Affairs; Galston first entered politics while on the faculty of the University of Texas at Austin in 1982, when he became the issues director for the presidential campaign of Walter Mondale (1982–1984) and then, in 1988, joined Al Gore's campaign for the presidential nomination.[101] Galston and Kamarck became prominent in the DLC crowd after Galston delivered a successful 1989 speech on Democratic policy and, shortly after, published a "political manifesto" with Kamarck as coauthor in September 1989, via the PPI, called *The Politics of Evasion*.[102] The political scientists provided an important strategic rationale for a self-consciously factional initiative, defining DLC "progressivism" by contrast with its "liberal" alternative.

By this time From and other DLCers recognized their project as a factional struggle, which was comparable to the Reagan neoconservatives' in the Republican Party. After losses in 1988, From's argument for a factional break took on new weight:

> I did a memo . . . in November 1989 . . . where I said, "What we need is a revolution in our party like Reagan had in his." We had to understand that if we drew lines that some of our friends would fall on the other side of those lines. Could we have done that in 1988? The answer is no. But a third election where you get your ass kicked makes people say, "Maybe these guys aren't so goddamn stupid as we thought."[103]

The DLCers recognized, however, that a successful bid for the presidency required liberal support. Partly for this reason, in the late 1980s From and the DLCers began to court the governor of Arkansas, Bill Clinton, to become the next DLC chair.

Clinton's record as a former McGovernite (that is, a New Politics liberal) and a successful governor seemed to have the potential to bring together liberals and DLCers in a joint effort to "modernize" liberalism. Despite the doubts of some DLCers—in particular Steinhardt, who understood Clinton as a bearer of "left-wing liberalism"—From saw in

Clinton a man of exceptional political and oratorical skills, endowed with a singular strategic capacity.[104]

Enticed by a chance at the presidency, Clinton became chair of the DLC in March 1990, where he remained until August 1991. A 1990 New Orleans conference was Clinton's first event as DLC chair. There the DLC presented the closest thing it had to a party manifesto: the New Orleans Declaration, emphasizing opportunity, free markets, progressive taxation, crime and punishment, and work-friendly welfare. The declaration was written via an exchange between two politicians and three DLC experts: Clinton, Nunn, From, Marshall, and Reed.[105]

The language of the New Orleans Declaration reflected the DLCers' sharpening opposition, in particular, with Democratic civil rights leaders, especially Jesse Jackson (1941–). In this charged context, small rhetorical gestures took on outsize meaning. From explains, for instance, that "fairness meant to people, 'We're going to take from you to give to somebody else,'" but "[o]pportunity meant that everybody had a chance to get ahead."[106] Jackson received the declaration's emphasis on "equal opportunity, not equal outcomes" as a challenge to civil rights concerns; it "got us into trouble," From later noted.[107]

In light of this opposition, it becomes difficult to read the DLC's definition of "mainstream" in a nonracialized way. From and the DLCers had a tendency to conflate mainstream with white and male. (This demographic category, one should note, was once cleaved to the Democrats on the basis of the party's support of organized labor—but, for the DLCers, mainstream did not mean unionized.) The confrontation with civil rights leadership reportedly made DLC Democrats, and especially Clinton, uncomfortable, but From saw Jackson, and not the whole civil rights community, as the DLC's real opposition.[108]

By May 1991 the New Democrats' factional break was clear. As Clinton's bid for the presidency warmed up, the DLC held a first convention in Cleveland, Ohio, featuring about 800 delegates from Congress, state and local governments, and various corporate and interest groups. Jackson was refused a slot in the event's lineup of speakers.[109] The choice of location was symbolic; the event was to mark the Democratic Party's return to the American heartland and mainstream American beliefs: free enterprise and hard work; country and community; freedom, equality and fairness. In Cleveland DLC delegates formalized their principles in the *New Choice Resolution*.[110] Afterward, thanks to Bruce Reed, the New Democratic program was boiled down to the New Democrats' hallmark trilogy: opportunity, responsibility, and community.[111]

In October and November 1991 Clinton gave a series of three "New Covenant" campaign speeches at Georgetown University, viewed by DLCers as key statements of New Democratic progressivism. Reed and Clinton jointly wrote the speeches, which dealt with three topics (community, economy, and security), with help from others (Galston, Shapiro, and George Stephanopoulos).[112] Although heavily DLC-informed, the speeches were striking in part for their eclectic inputs; the second New Covenant speech, on the economy, involved not only Reed and Shapiro but also (in Reed's account) "about 50 memos from various people around the country [Clinton] had met, that he'd known for years, and whose ideas he'd asked for."[113] Criticizing politicians as a whole, the speeches pronounced the death of old politics and "stale theories" and positioned New Democratic progressivism as a politics of the forgotten, economically downtrodden, overtaxed and underserved American middle class.[114] In the first New Covenant speech Clinton introduced his famous promise, at Reed's suggestion (because the speech needed "a policy proposal that would make news") to "put an end to welfare as we have come to know it."[115]

Economics without Economists: The Clinton Campaign

The Clinton campaign's economic plan featured a mix of middle-class tax cuts, infrastructure spending (with emphasis on construction jobs), and the expansion of lending and credit—for mortgages and businesses, in particular—with some controls on credit card interest rates. The fundamental aim, as Clinton emphasized in his second New Covenant speech, was a "high-wage, high-growth, high-opportunity economy." This "won't come from government spending," but rather it will come "from individuals working smarter and learning more, from entrepreneurs taking more risks and going after new markets, and from corporations designing better products and taking a longer view." "We're going to reward work, expand opportunity, empower people," he added—"we are going to win again."[116] As the campaign wore on, it would become famous for its singularly economy-centered slogan, coined by the strategist James Carville: "It's the economy, stupid!"

Where did the "Clintonomics" of the 1992 campaign come from? Here, not only eclecticism, but also economists' low profile, stands out. As a Yale graduate and former Rhodes Scholar, Clinton's personal networks included plenty of academics.[117] A long list of economists, including Paul Samuelson, James Tobin, Kenneth Arrow, Lawrence Klein, Robert Solow, Franco Modigliani, and (of course) Walter Heller, endorsed Clinton during the campaign.[118] But many of Clinton's most prominent economic advisers, often identified (still) in news media as "economists" (for example, Robert Reich, Eugene Sperling, Ira Magaziner, Roger Altman), are not credentialed in economics.[119]

In Reich's account, in fact, the Clinton campaign did not have a formal economic team. Reich, who advised the campaign from afar, was in Cambridge, on the faculty of Harvard's Kennedy School of Government, at the time (Reich, a supporter of Robert Kennedy and Eugene McCarthy in the 1960s, was associated with Clinton as a fellow Yale Law School student and 1968 Rhodes Scholarship recipient).[120] Eugene (Gene) Sperling (1958–), who was on the campaign staff, is a graduate of Yale Law School and former student of the Wharton School of Business and had worked on Michael Dukakis's 1988 campaign.[121] Also among Clinton's advisers was the PPI's Robert Shapiro. Shapiro's professional CV lists him as the campaign's principal economic adviser, but Reich later recalled ("to the best of my memory") that the Clinton campaign had no "official economic team with an official head." Instead, he said, "[t]here were about five or six of us who advised."[122]

Other accounts support the conclusion that the Clinton campaign was neither clearly connected to, nor deeply informed by, professional or academic economists. On the subject of NAFTA, for instance, the sociologist Malcolm Fairbrother identifies a curious disconnect between the Clinton campaign's economic rhetoric and mainstream neoclassical economic thinking. Fairbrother reports that "the advisors who won over both Clinton and [Mickey] Kantor [Clinton's campaign manager] were not economists, but a team of advisors without training in economics," who formulated the argument that NAFTA would generate

American jobs. Clinton, over the protests of the independent candidate Ross Perot, famously made job-promotion claims central to his pro-NAFTA argumentation, in spite of criticism from the prominent economist Paul Krugman "for their ignorance of mainstream trade economics."[123]

THE STRUGGLE OVER THE SOUL OF THE PRESIDENT, *REDUX:* THE FIRST CLINTON ADMINISTRATION

With Clinton's arrival in the White House in 1992 the New Democrats had achieved an important victory. But, in contrast with the ADA's pervasive presence in JFK's administration, the DLCers did not flood the White House upon Clinton's arrival in it. Clinton, who some DLCers continued to suspect was a liberal in New Democratic clothing, became the target of in-house advisory struggles. And herein lies an interesting fact, belying a story in which the neoliberalization of Democratic leftism was merely capitulation to the neoconservative right: DLCers would later cite the years from 1995 to 1997—that is, *after* the advent of a Republican-dominated, Newt Gingrich–led House of Representatives—as the key period in which New Democrats prevailed over their liberal rivals. In other words, the DLC understood their success as a function of the weakness of congressional Democrats. A more accurate assessment, then, would have to be that neoliberalized leftism was an *intraparty* factional victory, not a helpless capitulation to the Republican opposition.

Despite Al From's prominent role in Clinton's transition to the White House, many advisers in the first Clinton administration—including Reich—were neither DLCers nor "progressives," but rather self-understood "liberals." And there are good indications that, in the early years of the first Clinton administration, the liberals had considerable sway.

Reich, Sperling, From, and others played parts in the making of the Clinton administration. Reich, author of the investment-oriented *Work of Nations,* was responsible for building Clinton's economic team.[124] Among Clinton's economic advisers, in whose appointments Reich and Sperling played a significant role, were Ira Magaziner (1947–; a Rhodes

Scholar alongside Clinton), the economist Lawrence (Larry) Summers (Harvard PhD, 1982; nephew of Paul Samuelson; on the Harvard faculty and then the World Bank from 1991), and the economist Laura D'Andrea Tyson (1947–; MIT PhD, 1974; University of California, Berkeley). The *New York Times* reported that Robert Shapiro, Robert Rubin (1938–; Goldman Sachs cochairman), and Roger Altman (of the Blackstone Group, in New York, and a friend of Clinton's from Georgetown) would advise Summers.[125] The administration also featured Leon Panetta, former chairman of the House Budget Committee, as head of the OMB. Lloyd Bentsen (1921–2006; of the Senate Finance Committee; Dukakis's 1988 running mate) was Treasury secretary, with Summers as undersecretary. The CEA, chaired by Tyson, included Joseph Stiglitz (MIT PhD, 1967; a Princeton professor) and Alan Blinder (1945–; MIT PhD, 1971; also from Princeton). Clinton appointed Reich secretary of labor.

DLCers mainly appeared in domestic policy appointments: Reed and Galston became co-deputies of Clinton's Domestic Policy Council (DPC), assisting Carol Rasco.[126] Steinhardt later noted, disappointedly, that "[f]ew professionals at the DLC were appointed to the government positions they had sought."[127] The result was an internally diverse administration that included liberals, academics, DLCers, strategists and speechwriters, well-established Democratic politicians, and financial elites. DLCers were hardly a clear or coherent majority.

Two post-NAFTA dynamics seem to have shifted the administration's tendencies, nonetheless, in a neoliberalized direction. On economics, an advisory structure that privileged transnationalized, finance-oriented economists (TFEs) and advisers tended to corral Clinton toward balanced budgets and free trade. This became especially clear after NAFTA, as the administration's economic concerns shifted to maintaining international markets during the Mexican peso crisis, consolidating the primacy of TFEs. A second dynamic centered in domestic policy-making: DLCers' and political strategists' influences grew to the extent that liberal- and union-backed congressional Democrats weakened, clearing the way for a final abandonment of New Deal liberalism's most hallowed vehicle—the federal state—and fulfillment of the promise to "end welfare as we know it."

The Victory of TFEs and Neoliberal Ethics

Early on, the key issue within Clinton's economic team was the matter of the deficit. The deficit became a more central concern, especially, as new estimates came to light during the transition. The economic team split on the deficit before its arrival in the White House. Reich remained unconcerned with the "deficit *per se*"—for him, the concern was the deficit-to-GDP ratio, and so the chief problem was growth. Reich lists Rubin, Summers, and Altman among the "concerned," but not Tyson, Sperling, or Stephanopoulos.[128] Clinton kept Reagan's appointed head of the Federal Reserve, Alan Greenspan, in place, adding a particularly heavyweight player to the ranks of the "concerned."[129]

Clinton's advisory structure placed Robert Rubin at the head of a new body, the National Economic Council (NEC), making Rubin "a senior presidential adviser with *de facto* Cabinet rank."[130] The reported rationale for the NEC's creation was to fulfill Clinton's campaign pledge of making economic policy just as important as foreign policy in the White House.[131] Al From, for his part, viewed the NEC as a fulfillment of the CPE's 1982 proposed Economic Cooperation Council.[132] Signaling ongoing cognizance of the role of fractured economic advising in the downfall of Jimmy Carter, the NEC was also meant to keep relations between warring advisers settled.[133] But, with Rubin—who was closely connected to, and met regularly with, both Greenspan and Summers—at its head (where he remained until January 1995, then becoming Treasury secretary), the NEC effectively reversed FDR-era efforts to center budgetary and economic advising in the executive by shifting it back toward the Treasury.[134] The NEC included Panetta, Bentsen, Summers, Reich, and the CEA economists, but some insiders later described the NEC as dominated by "the Rubin side" of the administration.[135] In Galston's analysis, "[I]t was pretty clear that Rubin had won the big game, and Reich and company had lost it."[136]

The result was the Omnibus Budget Reconciliation Act, signed into law by Clinton in August 1993, which balanced the budget partially via modest increases in top marginal personal and corporate tax rates. Notably, with the input of the economist David Ellwood, the budget increased the progressivity of the tax system by expanding the earned income tax credit (EITC). But an investment and stimulus package, strongly advocated by Reich, did not materialize. In its absence, the years of growth that followed brought, also, increasing wage inequality.

The DLCers also viewed the signing of NAFTA, in November 1993—which responded to some environmental concerns, but lacked protections sought by unions—as a policy win.[137] But in NAFTA's wake the attentions of the "Rubin side" were soon drawn to the Mexican peso crisis, which began in December 1994. During this episode, the distinctive orientations of Clinton's TFEs are clear.

A default by Mexico, which became the United States' third-largest trading partner thanks to NAFTA, prompted an impressive effort at consensus-building, political strategizing, and aggressive intervention led by Rubin, Greenspan, and Summers. The aim was both remedial and preventative, meant to head off "a chain reaction" that "could lead investors to pull back from emerging markets around the world," slowing down American economic growth by (in the Fed's estimate) "1/2 to 1 percent a year."[138] Rubin (who was by then Treasury secretary), Greenspan, and Summers went to a remarkable effort to build support for a U.S. intervention of at least $25 billion, despite awareness that "[p]utting public funds on the line was likely to be massively unpopular and politically risky."[139] Mexico, they realized, "couldn't be rescued without the side effect of helping some investors," but Summers, in particular, worried that a Mexican default would potentially hinder "the global movement toward trade and capital market liberalization and market-based reforms." Repurposing a military dictum—that intervention is warranted "only when American interests are at stake," and then only "with an overwhelming level of force" (the Powell Doctrine)—the trio recommended a financial outlay large enough to "make a considerable psychological difference to the markets."[140] With Clinton's blessing they took their case to Capitol Hill, garnering the support of Republican (Newt Gingrich) and Democratic leadership. In the end congressional opposition proved overwhelming; the administration instead provided $20 billion from the Treasury's Exchange Stabilization Fund. The effort turned out to be a revenue-boosting investment of sorts, albeit not along the lines Reich and the liberals envisioned: after recovering, Mexico repaid its debt to the United States plus $1.4 billion in interest, coming to a profit of $580 million.[141]

There is much to note in this story, including the laborious effort required of Clinton's economic advisers to keep international markets up and running. Rubin's, Summers's, and Greenspan's deep investments in a creative repurposing of political capital, economic analysis, public funds, and symbolic tools (in this case, military doctrine) in service of propping up the advance of markets suggests that economic life needed as much management as ever, but the understanding of what was to be managed was wholly different. International markets, not the domestic economy or the interest conflicts therein, were the objects of management. Here we might hark back to the previous chapter, in which I described the distinction between the Keynesian and the neoliberal ethic thus: if, in the Keynesian view, the economist's role is to ground economic analysis in the realities of domestic politics, in the neoliberal view the economist is to fit political institutions to the truth of the market. Neither Rubin nor Summers are "neoliberals" in a historically meaningful sense (Greenspan surely is), but both are bearers of neoliberal ethics thus defined.

The "Death of Liberalism at Its Own Hands" and the 1996 Welfare Reform

If TFEs were central to the early Clinton-era focus on international markets, strategists and specialists were key players in the push for market-friendly domestic policies. This became clear after the midterm elections of 1994, after which unrest festered among some DLCers in the wake of Republican gains. The problem, in their diagnosis, was that Democrats were losing because Clinton was not staying true to New Democratic promises. Steinhardt, among others, was upset with the primacy of a health care initiative, not least because of the role of Hillary Clinton, who was viewed by Steinhardt and others as a liberal force. The lack of progress on welfare and entitlement reform, displaced by the health care initiative, was another source of frustration.[142]

But DLCers were strengthened after the Republican takeover of Congress in the 1994 elections, because Clinton's attention was now recentered on strategic concerns. What ensued was a kind of competitive mimicry—that is, co-optation of Republican initiatives—in which strategic expertise was central. By many reports the later-notorious backroom strategist, Dick Morris (famous for "triangulation"), gained increasing advisory influence.[143] Several administration insiders later noted that Clinton began to consult secretly with Morris.[144] Galston emphatically asserted that the internal dynamic of the administration changed completely.[145] From speculated that Morris, who "sometimes didn't know which party he was running a campaign for," was likely a liaison between the White House and congressional Republicans.[146]

But the Republican takeover also tipped things in favor of DLCers. Within the administration, DLCers like Bruce Reed gained in influence, at the expense of liberals. At least two events consolidated, in the perspective of DLCers and liberals alike, the victory of progressivism before the end of Clinton's first term. The first was Clinton's January 1996 State of the Union address, in which dismayed liberals witnessed a Democratic president pronouncing the "era of balanced budgets and smaller government." In Clinton's famous words:

> We know big Government does not have all the answers. We know there's not a program for every problem. We know, and we have worked to give the American people a smaller, less bureaucratic Government in Washington. And we have to give the American people one that lives within its means. The era of big Government is over.[147]

For George Stephanopoulos the speech signaled the end of a Democratic Party that was "unified by the belief that government could promote the common good."[148] It was, in his words, "dishonest and vaguely dishonorable, as if we were condemning Democrats from Franklin Roosevelt to Lyndon Johnson to the trash heap of history for the sake of a sound bite. . . . It showed, as speechwriter Michael Waldman said when we left the Oval, 'the death of liberalism at its own hands.'"[149]

The second event was work-friendly, time-restricted, limited-eligibility welfare reform. In August, when Clinton signed the Personal Responsibility and Work Opportunity Reconciliation Act of 1996 (H.R. 3734), Democratic outcry intensified.[150] A series of high-profile figures in the administration resigned in protest.[151] Reich declined to return for Clinton's second term.[152]

CONCLUSIONS

This chapter traces the long transition from 1968 to the rise of neoliberalized leftism in the 1990s inside the Democratic Party. Like its economistic predecessor, neoliberalized leftism was grounded in distinctive party-expert relations, featuring three sorts of figures: the TFE, the strategic expert, and the policy specialist. The role of the neoliberal project in the production of these experts was indirect, but important: it made such a thing as a mainstream Republican economist possible, contributing to the politicization of the economics profession and the discrediting of the economist theoretician; it also played a central role in the formation of the TFE—who, political leanings notwithstanding, saw the world in terms of the primacy of markets. By providing a model in the form of free market think tanks, the neoliberal project also provided direct inspiration for the making of the DLC-PPI.

The role of the neoliberal project, insofar as it was centered on the reformatting of professional economics, was largely a force emanating from what some sociologists term the *cultural field*. An especially central source of Democratic third wayism was the relationship between this cultural field and the Democratic Party—or what I have termed *interdependence*. Field interdependence created the possibility of "cross-field effect," in which (in the present case) changes in economics reached directly into Democratic Party networks and the experiences of party actors.[153] With the rise of the neoliberal ethic among Democratic and Republican economists alike, the unification of scientific economic analysis and political strategizing—a dual role once played by the singular figure of the economist theoretician—came to an end. Economists' prescriptions appeared to Democratic insiders as a problem to work around, not a means of government, consensus-building, or political communication. The break between analysis and strategy created a niche for experts specialized in communication and programmatic strategy—with or without economists. Out of this break was born the New Democrats, an initiative driven by elected politicians and strategic aides who came of age in the Carter and Reagan years.

The final consolidation of neoliberalized leftism unfolded inside the Clinton administration, thanks to the combined power of TFEs to secure and defend the steady advance of globalizing markets and DLC-connected specialists and strategists who, as the ranks of liberal Democrats in Congress declined, became more influential in presidential policy-making. I have argued that two processes that are sometimes cited as causes of Democratic neoliberalization—the declining electoral appeal of the Democrats and economic globalization—were partly *effects* of the party's neoliberal turn.

We now turn to Western Europe in order to investigate how, and to what extent, center-leftism on the other side of the Atlantic followed a similar trajectory.

CHAPTER EIGHT

Making Western European Leftism "Progressive"

> Fairness and social justice, liberty and equality of opportunity, solidarity and responsibility to others—these values are timeless. . . . To make these values relevant to today's world requires realistic and forward-looking policies . . . Modernisation is about adapting to conditions that have objectively changed, and not reacting to polls . . . [W]e need to apply our politics within a new economic framework, modernised for today, where government does all it can to support enterprise but never believes it is a substitute for enterprise. The essential function of markets must be complemented and improved by political action, not hampered by it. We support a market economy, not a market society.
>
> —Tony Blair and Gerhard Schröder, *Europe: the Third Way/ Die Neue Mitte*, 1998

T HIS CHAPTER EXTENDS the analysis of leftism's second reinvention to Sweden, Britain, and (West) Germany. My aim is twofold: to track the distinctive paths followed in those countries and to build a more general account of the dynamics of leftism's neoliberalization between the 1980s and the early 2000s. Engaging first with alternative accounts, and then moving chronologically through the neoliberalization of the SAP, the Labour Party, and the (West) German SPD, I elaborate on how interfield dynamics—in particular, tensions between happenings in professional economics on the one hand and inside left party networks on the other—shaped Western leftism's neoliberalization.

The story of Western European leftism's second reinvention is cross-national and comparative, but it is also transnational and European.

Viewed as cross-national cases, each of the parties considered here is important in its own way. The Swedish Social Democrats' neoliberalization stands out for (at least) four reasons: early timing, the special place of the Swedish social model in Western leftism's history, the continuous numerical strength of Swedish organized labor, and an especially tight and long-standing relationship with professional economics. In the United Kingdom, the making of New Labour has outsized significance because Labour's program still officially favored the nationalization of industry into the early 1990s, rendering its transformation especially stark. Last but not least, the (West) German case is important because of the SPD's special history as the once dominant model of a mass party of the socialist left; because West Germany, which remained a major industrial exporter in the later twentieth century, did not have the same degree of inflationary trouble seen in other countries in the 1970s; and because of the brevity and historical significance of its Keynesian interlude—in which an otherwise recognized Social Democratic, trade union–friendly economics was, if only briefly, also mainstream economics. The (West) German trajectory is also notable for its punctuation by East-West unification, German centrality in Europe's market-making and monetary unification in the 1980s and 1990s, and the relatively late arrival of German-style third wayism—which materialized after 1998, by which time third way politics had already taken root elsewhere.

The transnational and European aspects of Labour's and the SPD's neoliberalization indicate that leftism's second reinvention, like the making of socialism and economistic leftism before it, was not nationally bound. New Labour, for instance, is also important for its similarities to, and direct interconnections with, the American New Democrats and as an important conduit of third wayism's internationalization. And, as the 1998 *Third Way* statement by Blair and Schröder (quoted above) attests, Western European center-left elites at the end of the century moved in transnationalized and Europeanized circuits. Indeed, it was through those circuits that third wayism became an international "progressive" project. The term "progressive" signals, also, the centrality of Bill Clinton and the New Democrats (who had an aversion, for domestic political reasons, to "socialism") to this effort.[1] In this sense, Western leftism's second reinvention involved a historical novelty:

the American Democratic Party, which has never been socialist or social democratic, played a crucial role in making Western European
leftism "progressive."

ACCOUNTING FOR WESTERN EUROPEAN
LEFTISM'S SECOND REINVENTION

In the previous chapter I outlined four ways of explaining neoliberalized
leftism—electorate-driven, elite- or party-driven, economics-driven,
interfactional—and the difficulties therein. I then developed a refraction
account of the New Democrats, attending closely to the ways in which,
from a starting point of interdependence between economics and American Democratic leftism, changes in politics and in economics drove a
series of cross-field effects—creating new kinds of economists, politicizing the economics profession, and creating an opposition between
economic and strategic expertise in Democratic ranks. In this section I
extend this analysis to Western Europe, first, by considering how non-
refraction accounts fare as explanations of neoliberalized leftism. I focus
especially on the electorate-driven account and a partly electorate-
driven, partly economics-driven explanation that has special significance in European contexts: that left parties neoliberalized because of
the postindustrial decline of organized labor. While both accounts have
value, I argue that historical data on voting and union strength offer
only limited support. Rather, the trends suggest that leftism's neoliberalization demobilized voters and weakened the party-union relationship. This sets the stage for a fuller analysis that begins with the SAP's
early neoliberalization in the 1980s, and then moves to the subsequent
formation of New Labour (1997) and the German New Middle
(1998–1999).[2]

The Electoral Account

In the previous chapter I argued that electorate-driven explanations of
the New Democrats rest on debatable claims regarding voter appeal.
Similar patterns are evident in the Western European context.

Consider, for instance, the Swedish case. The SAP's neoliberal turn
became clear in 1982 and, in the short term, appeared to be elector-

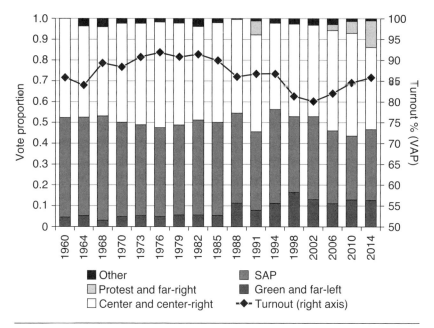

Figure 8.1. Swedish vote proportions in election years, with voter turnout, 1960–2014. Data source: Armingeon et al., 2016.

ally successful: in 1985 and 1988 the SAP sustained a level of voter support that was broadly consistent with its strong postwar electoral history. But in 1988 the SAP's grip on voter loyalties slipped, as the green and far-left vote rose to an unprecedented 11.3 percent (see Figure 8.1).

Finally, in the 1991 election, amid controversy over Sweden's entry into the soon-to-be European Union, the far-right (New Democracy) vote rose to an unprecedented 6.7 percent and the SAP suffered its worst result (37.7 percent) in postwar history. The SAP recovered in 1994, but its governmental dominance masked an underlying electoral weakness: from 1994 forward its share of the vote settled at a new low, while far-left and far-right parties' vote margins grew. Given these trends, we cannot take for granted that the SAP's market-friendly turn responded in any clear way to what the electorate wanted.

British and (West) German vote patterns tell a similar story. In Britain, the Labour Party fractured in 1981, when a centrist contingent broke off to form the Social Democratic Party (SDP), cutting significantly into

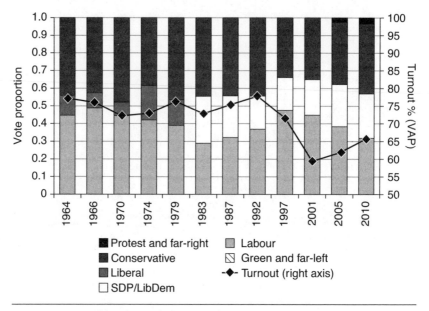

Figure 8.2. British vote proportions, in election years, with voter turnout, 1964–2010. Note: Votes for the Social Democratic (SDP) and Liberal Democratic parties are shaded differently because of the SDP's significance for Labour's electoral fate after 1981. Data source: Armingeon et al., 2016.

the Labour vote. After a long, ensuing period out of government, the party rebranded itself as New Labour in the run-up to the 1997 election, reclaiming the centrist vote—some of which had been lost to the SDP—and taking a decidedly market-friendly tack in its economic policies. British voter turnout dropped to a historic low in 2001, and in 2010 Labour's share of the vote declined to a level not seen since the early Thatcher era—even as new far-right forces appeared on the political horizon (see Figure 8.2).

In the (West) German case, where the SPD's neoliberalization became evident after 1998, a similar decline in voter turnout and rise of non-mainstream voting followed—first to the SPD's left and then to its right (see Figure 8.3).

In sum, left parties' neoliberal turns were followed, initially, by declining turnout and narrowing electoral margins. Increasing turnout thereafter benefited far-left and far-right parties. These patterns render as dubious, at best, the argument that Western European leftism's neo-

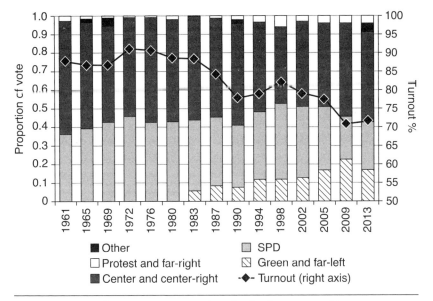

Figure 8.3. West German vote proportions in election years, with voter turnout, 1961–2013. Data source: Armingeon et al., 2016.

liberalization was electorally driven. They can also be read in a different way: as indications that the third way era demobilized voters and undermined loyalty to center-left parties, making way for new, nonmainstream competitors.

The Thesis of Working-Class and Union Decline

The question of the party-union relationship is central to the analysis of Western European leftism because of the particular histories of socialist, social democratic, and laborite parties.[3] Here the famous contributions of the political scientists Adam Przeworski and John Sprague are relevant: in 1988, Przeworski and Sprague argued that "electoral socialism" was doomed for demographic and economic reasons.[4] Because the working classes made up a declining proportion of the electorate, mainstream left parties would have to resort to class compromise, ceasing to exist as working-class organizations in the process. In terms of the explanatory alternatives laid out thus far, the decline-of-the-unionized-working-class thesis is a hybrid argument in which party change is partly electorate- and partly economics-driven.

There are several difficulties with the thesis of working-class decline, however. First, it treats working-class identity as an economically
determined given, ignoring cultural aspects of class identity and, more
importantly, the possibility that parties can, and have, played an important role in the *formation* of class-based understandings of political
interests. But in turn-of-the-century Sweden and Germany, left party
formation was a *driver* of organized labor's coalescence as a national
political force, not *vice versa*.[5] In other words, it is not the case that class
identity exists first and parties come second.[6]

Another difficulty with the decline-of-electoral-socialism thesis is that
it fits uncomfortably with the case of the American Democratic Party.
The story of "electoral socialism" excludes Democrats, and yet their
central place in the trajectory of Western center-leftism from the late
1930s forward—tracked in earlier chapters of this book—is a historical fact. There can be no account of center-leftism's neoliberalization
that excludes the Democratic Party.

And then there is a final problem: Western leftism's neoliberalization
has no stable correlation with the numerical strength of organized labor.
In the countries considered in this book, only American unions underwent a steady, long-term decline after the 1960s (see Figure 8.4). British
and (West) German union density remained high until the early 1990s,
beginning a steady (but very gradual, in the British case) decline from
that point forward.

Last but not least, Sweden's unionization rates remained unusually,
and consistently, high. And yet the SAP was an early mover in leftism's
second reinvention: the party tacked in a market-friendly direction *in
the early 1980s*, even as Swedish union density was on the rise. The
quantitative decline of unions simply does not work as a general explanation of neoliberalized leftism.

Of course, sheer numbers and political strength are not the same. The
qualitative strength of the party-union relationship may be the more
crucial consideration. Here the argument of *mutual divorce*, advanced
by the professor of politics Chris Howell, is important: the central story
of the post-1970s left party–labor relationship, he argues, was a "mutual distancing of party and union movement" that "occurred everywhere."[7] A question, then, is whether the mutual divorce of unions and
left parties drove neoliberalized leftism or whether leftism's neoliberal-

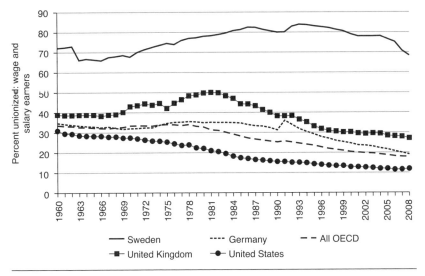

Figure 8.4. Cross-national trends in union density, 1960–2008. Data source: OECD.

ization caused the mutual divorce that Howell describes. The assessment of the Democratic case in the previous chapter suggests that neoliberalization drove mutual divorce, not *vice versa*. I will argue that the same is true for Western European leftisms—to which we now turn.

THE ECONOMIST-INTENSIVE NEOLIBERALIZATION OF SWEDISH LEFTISM

The SAP's neoliberal turn began with the Palme government of 1982. It is striking for at least two reasons: the growing strength of Swedish trade unions at the time and the fact that the SAP was as precocious in its neoliberalization as it was in its turn to economics.

The Politics of Economists in the Age of the Swedish Model

Observers of Swedish politics often characterize the period from the 1940s to about 1973, featuring the LO economist and the Rehn-Meidner model, as an era of consensual politics.[8] But Sweden's fabled postwar golden age had its critics.

In 1948 the non-party-affiliated Stockholm economist Erik Lundberg (1907–1987), a former mentor of Gösta Rehn, complained that economists' "arguments based on more refined theory are inexorably rejected by [Swedish] officials."[9] In the 1950s Lundberg engaged with Rehn in public debate, expressing concerns about regulation and the welfare state as a problem of the concentration of power in the hands of "bad politicians, bad administrators, bad economists and bad business men."[10] Working at the Konjunkturinstitutet (KI) from 1937 (the year of its founding) until 1955, Lundberg "did not disparage politicians en masse" but was skeptical of forecasting and overly simple answers to complex economic problems.[11] Pressure to endorse the government's positions was ultimately enough to prompt Lundberg's resignation from the KI in 1955.[12] Two years later he took up Bertil Ohlin's chair at the Stockholm School of Economics, where he remained a critic.[13]

Lundberg's dissent points to tensions within Swedish economics over the practice of economic science and the public role of economists in the fabled age of the Swedish model. These tensions could be found, also, *inside* the SAP. They were evident, in particular, in the relationship between the SAP-in-government and its appointees to the Bank of Sweden (the Sveriges Riksbank, or SEB).

The SEB's long-standing subordination to SAP government priorities was a source of intraparty tension. In the early postwar years, for instance, the SAP government imposed low interest rates on the SEB in order to promote housing construction. The bank was "made to purchase government and mortgage bonds," over the objections of its governor, Ivar Rooth.[14] SEB efforts to raise interest rates in the late 1940s and early 1950s were denied, and the SAP government kept a firm hold on credit in order to "maximize investment and keep inflation in check."[15] The effort to link bank practices to party interests extended into bank appointments: in 1955 the SAP Prime Minister Tage Erlander appointed Rooth's successor, Per Åsbrink (1912–1994), a university-educated SAP "party man" with a newspaper background.[16]

But Åsbrink's professional and personal connections were neither nationally contained nor party bound. They reached into both international financial institutions and into professional economics. Encouraged by Rooth to deepen his international contacts, Åsbrink joined the governing board of the Bank for International Settlements (BIS), attending its monthly meetings in Basel.[17] The historians Avner Offer and Gabriel Söderberg argue that Åsbrink "absorbed anti-Keynesian sentiments" via cross-connections with other central bankers and that, at home, he looked to academic economists for allies.[18] Åsbrink would remain at the head of the SEB until 1973, becoming a *de facto* economist—marked by the award of an honorary Stockholm School doctorate (1973)—along the way. In the background was the deepening process of European economic integration, which fueled the joint transnationalization of both economics and financial authorities. The year 1960 saw the founding of the European Free Trade Association (EFTA), made up of seven countries, including Sweden; in the 1970s, EFTA countries either joined the European Economic Community (EEC) or signed bilateral free trade agreements with the EEC.[19]

Under Åsbrink the SEB was an important basis of cross-field connection with transnationalizing finance and professional economics. It was also a site of intraparty opposition. Åsbrink demanded tighter credit and "attacked the national wage bargain as being conducive to inflation," garnering accolades from his peers in West Germany and the United Kingdom.[20] In 1957 he then raised the discount rate without consultation.[21] After a stern reminder that the "government had complete responsibility and authority over taxation and interest rates," Åsbrink reluctantly conceded.[22]

SAP intraparty tensions fed back into the formation of the economics profession, in Sweden and beyond. With a windfall in-hand from the surprise rate increase, in the early 1960s Åsbrink began to make the case that the SEB should create a new scientific foundation—which would become, in 1969, the Nobel Prize in economics.[23] This story is well-told by Offer and Söderberg, who track how the prize's establishment unfolded as a kind of "coup" within the party, in which SEB social democrats intervened in economics' prestige structure as a means of intraparty struggle. Åsbrink took the lead in the making of an economics Nobel with the aid of a younger Stockholm-trained SEB adviser named Assar Lindbeck (1930–; PhD 1963). Lindbeck, a fellow Social Democrat who was also "inclined toward heresy," was at the time a professor at Stockholm and a research professor at Columbia University.[24] Lundberg joined in the effort, as did Gunnar Myrdal.[25] The Nobel

Foundation, the Swedish Royal Academy of Science, and the SEB approved the new prize in May 1968.[26]

This brief account raises at least two interesting possibilities: it suggests that Swedish economists played a very special role in economics' professional internationalization, and that professional internationalization was, in turn, inseparable from the SAP's interdependence with professional economics.[27] Indeed, it would seem that the impetus behind the making of the prize, not to mention the financial resources that made it possible, *originated in an SAP intraparty struggle*. In other words, the making of the Nobel Prize in economics was part of a larger dynamic of cross-field effects: SAP intraparty struggles shaped economics' cross-national development and events within the economics profession, including its internationalization, acted back on SAP intraparty struggles.[28]

Neoliberalism and the Reformatting of Swedish Economics

Swedish economics' postwar internationalization, especially from the 1970s, is well documented. The Swedish economists Bo Sandelin, Nikias Sarafoglou, and Ann Veiderpass, for instance, highlight the profession's postwar expansion, specialization, internationalization, and more American orientations.[29] Noting North American influences, Sandelin and his colleagues describe "a denationalization of Swedish economics" and "a shift from German and Austrian to American influences" in the late twentieth century.[30] In the 1970s about half of Swedish economics dissertations were in English, but after 1991 *all* of them were. By the year 2000 observers described a profession that no longer oriented itself toward domestic audiences and concerns.[31]

Others note new contestation among Swedish economists in the 1970s, the subsequent demise of managerial Keynesianism's legitimacy, and, in the 1980s, the rise of a rule-bound, anti-discretionary, Swedish-style new classicism—that is, in other words, the rise of neoliberal professional ethics. The transition played out in the pages of the periodical *Ekonomisk Debatt* (*ED*): established in 1973 as a journal of the Swedish Economics Association (NF) by the young economists Assar Lindbeck and Nils Lundgren, with support from foundations and

Swedbank, *ED*'s very existence was itself a marker of contestation with the discipline, and financial involvements therein.[32] By about 1980 *ED* articles treated "the problems of Keynesianism" as "so serious that it should be regarded as inferior to other macroeconomic approaches."[33] By the early 1980s a decidedly neoliberal ethic emerged in Swedish economics, informed by American new classicism and associated with the economist Hans Tson Söderström (a student of Lindbeck's).

Intraparty Struggles

Changes in Swedish economics were never entirely separate from go-ings-on inside the SAP, where economic troubles and labor unrest between the late 1960s and the mid-1970s strained the party-union relationship. Additional sources of tension centered within organized labor. Between 1950 and 1970 the main white collar union, the Con-federation of Professional Employees (Tjänstemännens Centralorgan-isation, or TCO) grew disproportionately, creating rifts with the LO. Among the rifts was "resistance to the egalitarian thrust" of LO wage policy by a TCO affiliate, the Central Organization of Professional Employees (Sveriges Akademikers Central Organisation, or SACO), whose membership was distinguished by "possession of a university degree."[34]

In the late 1960s, however, labor-based economist theoreticians con-tinued to play their accustomed intermediary role—for instance, in a cooperative effort by the TCO, SAF, and LO research directors, Gösta Edgren, Karl-Olof Faxén, and Clas-Erik Odhner (respectively), to de-velop a joint agreement on wage negotiation procedures that came to be known as the EFO model (so titled based on the names of the lead figures involved).[35] Reflecting the LO's continuing influence, the effort culminated in the LO's successful imposition of a "solidaristic wage policy . . . over much of the rest of the labor market."[36]

This did not, however, settle unrest in trade union ranks. In the wake of wildcat strikes in 1969–1970, in the 1970s the SAP government initially responded in a typically Keynesian, labor-friendly way: it ex-panded public control over investment through the extension of collec-tive bargaining, culminating in the industrial democracy reforms of 1972 and the Codetermination Act of 1976, which required negotiation over corporate decisions affecting the workforce.[37] But, in 1976, as

Keynesianism was embattled in the pages of *ED*, the SAP's historical privileging of the LO economist faltered.

A key inflection point was a 1976 plan drawn up by Rudolf Meidner proposing wage-earner funds that would require large companies to turn around 20 percent of their profits into new shares for wage earners, which would then remain as working capital under the control of the firms that made the profits. This, Meidner argued, would enforce wage solidarity, reconcile profit-seeking with labor-friendly redistribution, and promote employee participation in corporate decision-making.[38] The LO approved the Meidner plan at its 1976 congress, but SAP leadership—which lost control of government in 1976 and would return in 1982—deflected the initiative by means of an expert commission.[39] According to the British sociologist Robin Blackburn, SAP leadership "did not share Meidner's vision."[40]

The question, then, is why SAP leadership ended its long-standing willingness to rely on the LO economist as its chief economic policymaker. Why were the wage earner's funds a step too far? Some, including the political economist Mark Blyth, answer this question by focusing on business mobilization channeled through economics, linked to the neoliberal project, and realized in the policies of the center-right. Blyth documents how the main employers' association (the Svenska Arbetsgivareföreningen, or SAF), viewing the funds as an assault on private property, mobilized financial resources that dwarfed the LO's in a fight against the funds. By the early 1980s SAF spending competed with expenditure levels of *all* of Sweden's major parties combined.[41]

The SAF's mobilization was channeled partly through long-established centers of employer-funded research—in particular, the Center for Business and Policy Studies (SNS). The SNS, an early postwar institution founded in 1948 on the model of the New Deal–friendly U.S. Committee for Economic Development (CED), is a historically moderate organization but, amid controversies and a growing membership in the 1970s, it situated itself as a bridge into government and a site of public debate for dissenting economists. To this end the SNS established the four-member Economic Policy Council, on which Erik Lundberg was a "driving force."[42] The council was an advocate of alternatives ("different models of profit-sharing") in the debate over wage earners' funds, and "a sounding board and conversation partner to the Ministry of Finance."[43] SAF mobilization also operated, however, on the neoliberal project's terrain, via a newer publishing house, Timbro (established in 1978), which is part of the SAF-funded Free Enterprise Foundation and the Atlas Foundation's free market think tank network. Looking to the United States, the SAF also solicited a report from the American public choice economist Gordon Tullock (1922–2014) in 1978.[44]

Understandably, Blyth places particular emphasis on the alliance between business and the political right—with the aid of neoliberal economists and organizations—as drivers of the Swedish model's decline.[45] The conservative ("bourgeois") government that came into power in 1976 abandoned demand-supporting fiscal policies and enacted two devaluations in 1977, followed by another in September 1981.[46] This right-centered story, however, is of little help when it comes to events within the SAP and its break with the LO economist.

On this count another point raised by Blyth is more helpful: the shifting orientations of Swedish economists. Two economists, Hans Tson Söderström (1945–; PhD 1974, Stockholm) and Johan Myhrman (1937–1997), are central here. Both were affiliates of the Stockholm Institute for International Economic Studies (IIES) and of the SNS. Myhrman was also a Timbro affiliate, a student of Friedrich Hayek and the German-*cum*-American monetarist economist Karl Brunner (1916–1989), and an adherent of public choice.[47] But neoliberal connections were not a constant: Söderström, an early 1970s PhD student of Lindbeck's, was a prominent and influential Social Democratic economist.[48]

Söderström's political location points to the weaknesses of a story that centers too much on the right and that fails to consider cross-field dynamics in which changes in economics shaped the SAP, and *vice versa*. SAF mobilization may explain the policies of the 1976 center-right government, and it is true that the SAP was weakened in the 1970s—but, returning to government in 1982, the SAP would remain dominant (with an interruption in the early 1990s) until the end of the century. To get to the question of neoliberalization on the left, the analysis needs to consider left party–economics interdependence.

Indeed, a key background fact to the SAP's break with Meidner from 1976 was the LO economists' loss of the backing of the mainstream profession, manifested in the open opposition of well-known Social Democratic economists. The wage-earner funds proposal, for instance, prompted Lindbeck (Söderström's mentor) to resign from the SAP in 1976 in protest. In the 1980s, while incorporating monetarist and rational expectations theories into his work, Lindbeck became an influential promulgator of the (disputed) diagnosis of Swedish "Eurosclerosis": that is, the argument that the country risked long-term economic stagnation due to "welfare state, taxation, and . . . other forms of political interventions into market forces."[49] Lindbeck was joined by fellow Social Democratic economist Ingemar Ståhl, coiner of the term "Suedosclerosis," who had been Lindbeck's early 1960s collaborator in the advocacy of market alternatives to rent control. In time Ståhl would become one of the few Swedish economists to join the MPS.[50]

Offer and Söderberg portray Lindbeck as a professional pivot point among Social Democratic economists, leading them toward a perspective that had a certain neoliberal hue. In Offer and Söderberg's account, Lindbeck specialized in the development of formal (that is, not evidence-based) analysis of welfare state and social democratic institutions from a perspective that, by treating the abstract ideal of a perfect market as the comparative reference point, tended to find those institutions wanting.[51]

Meanwhile, Söderström served in the SNS Economic Policy Group in 1980–1981 and was also on the SAP government's 1981 Expert Commission on Wage Earner Funds—that is, the commission through which SAP leadership deflected Meidner's 1976 proposal.[52] From the late 1970s through the 1980s, the period in which the *Ekonomisk Debatt* settled on "the crisis of Keynesianism" as "a historical fact" and set about formulating alternatives, Söderström was the journal's managing editor (1977–1978) and was then on its editorial board (1979–1999).[53]

In short, while Myrdal's generation of Stockholm School economists shifted the profession toward an alliance with the SAP, the post-Lindbeck generation appears to have shifted the SAP toward a new way of seeing things in which the chief imperative was to refit SAP economic policies to the truth of the market. To this story we now turn.

The War of the Roses

In the spring and summer of 1982 Erik Åsbrink (Per Åsbrink's son) and Michael Sohlman (1944–), by then "the two main social democratic economic advisers," were formulating a revolution in SAP economic thinking at the behest of Gunnar Sträng's protégé, the finance-minister-in-waiting Kjell-Olof Feldt (1931–).[54] Joined by Klas Eklund (1952–) and others, Feldt's "crisis group" was charged with drafting the new government's economic program.[55] After 1982 the group came to be known as the "*kanslihushögern*": the right flank of the SAP government in the finance ministry ("MoF rightists," in Eklund's translation[56]).

The *kanslihushögern* originated in 1979 amid controversies over the wage earners' funds and the rise of "norms-based" thinking in Swedish economics. In Eklund's account it began as a movement of young Social Democratic economists that included Eklund, Erik Åsbrink, and Lars Heikensten (1950–), who were united in their opposition to "[v]ulgar Keynesianism and overbidding politics." The movement consolidated in a "union of Social Democratic economists" who could "gradually become a modern think tank for the party"; Eklund chaired the group, which he later estimated at more than one hundred members.[57]

Eklund tells how he and his colleagues aimed to reeducate SAP leadership in "modern economic theory" via seminars, debates, public memos, and direct contact with party leadership. In January 1981 Eklund published an article in the *Dagens Nyheter* calling for a "Swedish historic compromise": labor would have to accept "the stagnation of real wages and public services" in exchange for business acceptance of some variant of the wage-earner funds.[58] Eklund also sought to build a stronger public profile by soliciting "support and co-operation from better-known colleagues," including Villy Bergström (1938–), an Uppsala-trained economist and editor of the SAP's *Tiden,* who would become both head of the Trade Union Institute for Economic Research (FIEF) and an SNS affiliate; Harry Flam (1948–), a Berkeley- and Stockholm-trained IIES colleague of Söderström, editor of *Ekonomisk Debatt* and future SNS board member (1987–1993); Carl Hamilton (1946–), an LSE-trained, Stockholm economist and future Liberal parliamentarian; Nils Lundgren (1936–), a Stockholm-trained economist and soon-to-be chief economist for PK-banken; and Karl-Göran Mäler (1939–), an environmental economist.[59]

The six economists published a strident article in *Arbetet* that earned the group the title of the "sextuplets."[60] Appealing to the public, in Eklund's telling, "as economists and active social democrats," they criticized the conservative government's economic reforms for being too timid: neither devaluation nor marginal tax cuts were deep enough, consumption was too high, and productivity was too low. "The Swedish economy's problems are so large and well defined," they argued, "that most economists—regardless of party affiliation—are agreed on the main features of the necessary economic policies."[61] They emphasized that the SAP, as the party of labor, had a special responsibility to put a check on the demands of its core constituency: if it failed to break with the prioritization of "full employment and equitable distribution of wealth," the alternative was "forced Thatcherite policy in Sweden." It was now the "responsibility of the workers' movement" to get the country to swallow this "bitter medicine."[62]

Eklund describes the article as a trigger of "far-reaching debate, inside and outside the party."[63] Union-connected economists, led by the trade union economist Carl Johan Åberg," were a basis of opposition.[64] The historian Jenny Andersson quotes one participant at the 1981 SAP conference arguing that "[w]e should send these cuts back to where they came from . . . the theoretical world of liberal economists!"[65] But Eklund persisted, producing a 1982 book on "the need for firm-handed politics" (*The Grim Truth*) and a SAP party pamphlet, while also delivering lectures for the Young Social Democrats and other SAP organizations.[66]

The Formation of the SAP-Affiliated TFE

What sorts of experts were the leading protagonists of the *kanslihush-ögern*, as described by Eklund? With the exception of Feldt, all were in their thirties or late twenties around 1980. They were not LO economists, elected politicians, or academics; all are recognized as economists, whether or not they have economics PhDs. Their easy access to SAP intraparty debates can only be explained with reference to the well-established historical interconnections between Swedish economists and the SAP elite. Allied—as shown in the sextuplets' profiles, elaborated further below—with colleagues who had diverse professional affiliations, the MoF rightists' network extended into business circles (the SAF, SNS), transnationalized finance and Swedish economics, and both the liberal and social democratic parties. Insofar as they came together via shared experiences that were grounded in transnationalized and financial institutions, they fit the profile of the TFE; insofar as they understood their task in terms of refitting SAP economic policies to the truths of markets, they were also bearers of neoliberal ethics.

Feldt, the most senior figure, became an SAP economic expert under Sträng at the Ministry of Finance in the 1970s. Feldt's outlook, like Per Åsbrink's at the SEB, seems to have been shaped by incorporation into transnational finance: his engagements with the OECD, the BIS, and the IMF, in Offer and Söderberg's account, instilled in him a conviction that the SAP had "to stop attempting to control the economy, and to expose Social Democracy to international competition."[67] In a way, however, the more interesting figure is Feldt's most junior counterpart, Klas Eklund, for whom long-standing ties between the SAP and Swedish universities, and espccially between academic economics and the Ministry of Finance, was a key point of entry into the party's expert ranks.

In his intellectual biography Eklund tells of his journey from 1968-inspired radicalism after a year attending American high school, to the Stockholm School in 1972 (where he earned a licentiate degree, but "fell short of the doctor's thesis"), and finally into the SAP, which he joined in 1978. Eklund describes the move as a self-conscious abandonment of "the Left," in the radical Marxist sense, via training in economics: "I found Marx and Lenin being intellectually defeated by Popper, Keynes, Samuelson, and Schumpeter." At Stockholm Eklund worked with Professor Erik Dahmén (who was "also an advisor to the Wallenbergs at Enskilda Banken") before being recruited into the Ministry of Finance.[68] In Eklund's account, he and his student colleagues at the Stockholm School found an easy path into the SAP because intraparty economists, including Erik Åsbrink, were looking for anti-Keynesian allies.[69] That Eklund, by his own account, was recruited *because* of his anti-Keynesian bent is significant because it speaks to the centrality of party-economics ties in the making of cross-field effects.

Michael Sohlman followed a different, more transnational, trajectory. Sohlman, who has a BA from the University of Uppsala (1968), did "[f]urther postgraduate studies in economics and political sciences at the Universities of Uppsala and Stockholm," but his online professional biography does not list a doctorate or academic appointments.[70] From SAP government positions he moved to the Ministry of Finance in 1974, also joining the Permanent Swedish Delegation to the OECD of Paris as a financial counselor. Moving to the SAP Department of Parliamentary Research in 1981, in 1982 he was head of planning and budget director in the Ministry of Finance, leaving in 1987. In 1992 Sohlman became the executive director of the Nobel Foundation.[71]

In the next section I will show that, characteristically for TFEs, younger-generation economists behind the SAP's market-friendly turn shared the sense that their task was to fit the policies of the SAP government to the emergent necessities of international markets—which they were, at the same time, also helping to construct.

The Neoliberalization of the SAP

In the wake of another oil price shock the SAP won the 1982 election and returned to government in 1983. At this point there could be little doubt as to who won the war of the roses. The crisis program of the MoF rightists became part of the SAP's 1982 election campaign, "presented as the Social Democrats' alternative to social dismantling."[72]

The new SAP government's "third way," or "third path" policy (*tredje vägens politik*) launched with an unprecedented 16 percent devaluation, a tighter budget "to break inflation and to signal the end of devaluation," and a host of "supply-side" reforms that included liberalizing finance and tax reform.[73] On the heels of the devaluation Feldt made it clear that "compensatory nominal wage increases would not be corrected by expansionary fiscal measures *or* by new devaluations."[74] The introduction of market devices into public services was also important: the Ministry of Finance aggressively advocated "the introduction of various types of . . . 'quasi-markets' in the social services sector," in which "the provision of services is separated from direct political control, and the role of government is reduced to that of 'purchasing" services' from competitive bidders." Competition was also encouraged via Swedes' exercise of choice in service provision.[75]

Notably, the third way SAP government embraced a diluted version of the wage-earner funds and continued to situate full employment as its main objective. Party leadership was also aggressively anti-neoliberal in tone. Erlander's successor, Olof Palme, declared unemployment a threat to human well-being and democratic stability, aggressively defending the trade union movement and the welfare state. Around 1985 Palme pursued "an enthusiastic campaign against 'neo-liberalism' "—a term that referenced the neoconservative, pro–free market right, particularly in Britain and the United States.[76] As the SAP government rolled out third road policies, it still maintained full employment as a central objective.[77] Yet the new government clearly rejected Keynesian means to Swedish social democracy's ends.[78] Rather, it appeared to move in lockstep with the formation of Swedish-style new classicism in economics.

By the mid-1980s Söderström sat at the head of both the SNS (CEO, 1985–2002) and the SNS Economic Policy Group (chair, 1984–1994). Thus situated, he made the case for rule-based economic policies—a Swedish version of the kind of anti-discretionary thinking expressed by Milton Friedman—mainstream. In the SNS's official history, the rationale for the move was the experience of "stagflation": since "the theory of rational expectations and supply side economics put the focus on the need to create long-term favorable conditions for economic growth through deregulation, comprehensive tax reform, and a monetary policy focused on price stability," in the 1980s "the [SNS] Economic Council put forward the idea of a norm-based stabilization policy and price stability as the overriding norm for economic policy," with a target inflation rate of between 2 and 4 percent.[79] Sure enough, in 1985 the SAP government announced that it was ending political discretion in monetary policy and that it would not borrow to finance its debt but would rely instead on foreign holders of Swedish currency. In the account of the Swedish scholar Magnus Ryner, the financial and monetary arm of the SAP-in-government saw the end of monetary political discretion in favor of the discipline of international financial markets as the best means of managing inflation: "The Ministry of Finance and the Central Bank reasoned that when unions, social service agencies and individuals took increased interest rate sensitivity into account, their propensity to consume would decline."[80]

On March 1, 1986, Palme was assassinated while walking home from the cinema, and was succeeded by Ingvar Carlsson (1934–). Neither SAP rhetoric nor economic policy changed considerably after Palme's death, but Swedish economic management changed in a decidedly anti-Keynesian way. Inflation returned in the late 1980s, and in

1989 the SAP government abandoned exchange controls. Shortly thereafter Feldt announced, at a conference in Stockholm, that Sweden was
opening its doors to foreign banks.[81]

The effects of Sweden's financial liberalization are shown in
Figures 8.5 and 8.6. As the figures show, the effects of the SAP government's new financial and monetary policies quickly set in: flows of foreign investment grew markedly in the 1990s and, under Göran Persson
(1949–, Swedish PM 1996–2006) in particular, Sweden's financial balance of payments went sharply positive.

Later, in 1999, Eklund—by this time a Chief Economist at the SEB—
wrote in an "intellectual biography and manifesto" that Swedish "[p]arty
politicians and interest organizations" had yet to fully grasp "just how
radically Sweden is going to change due to globalization and the open
economy." In a mode that is reminiscent of the anti-discretionary,
market-centered arguments of Milton Friedman in his 1960s exchanges
with Walter Heller, Eklund called on Swedish political elites to attune
themselves to the necessities of markets: the "forces of globalization,"
Eklund argued, would have to be embraced if SAP politicians wanted

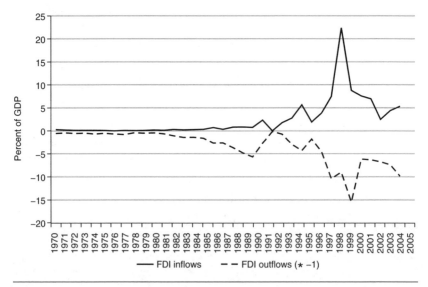

Figure 8.5. Foreign direct investment (FDI) inflows and outflows, Sweden,
1970–2005. Data source: World Bank, World Development Indicators (WDI).

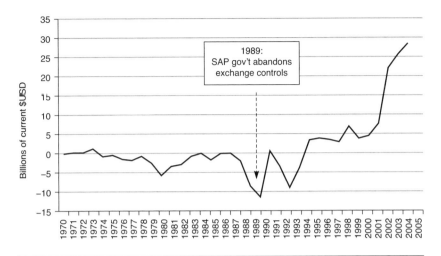

Figure 8.6. Sweden's financial balance of payments, 1970–2005. Data source: World Bank, World Development Indicators (WDI).

to "advance prosperity."[82] By this time, Eklund's words were undoubtedly true—but third road economic policy had played no small part in creating that new reality.

Neoliberal Ethics, the Divorce of Theory and Strategy, and Party-Labor Disarticulation

The question of whether or not the SAP of the mid- to late 1980s was, despite its rhetoric, "neoliberal" is not a very helpful one. Feldt was later adamant that the party's aim was to avoid neoliberalism, not to embrace it.[83] These self-accounts should be taken at face value. The question, then, is how it was possible for SAP leadership to understand third road policies, no matter how market-friendly, as anti-neoliberal. The analysis thus far suggests that this disconnect was a cross-field effect in which intraparty struggles drove changes in economics, and changes in economics shaped interpretive and programmatic struggles within the SAP.

Among the consequences, one stands out: the SAP could no longer hold the party-labor relationship together. Initially the SAP's third road policies had the desired effect in terms of Sweden's balance of payments, industrial competitiveness and profits, and a balanced budget. Unemployment declined to very low levels by 1989. But in the 1990s, even after the SAP returned to government in 1994, unemployment never returned to the sustained lows of the Keynesian era. Meanwhile, the Swedish economy remained Keynesian, in the Phillips curve sense: from 1970 to 2005 the correlation between inflation and unemployment rates in Sweden remained almost perfectly negative (–0.80). But, as shown in Figure 8.7, the historical prioritization of full employment was abandoned between 1991 and 1992 for the sake of keeping inflation low—ushering in a new era of inverted Keynesianism in Sweden.

With the return of unemployment came the end of wage solidarity and a considerable weakening of the party-union relationship.[84] Containing wage demands was key to the party's ability to manage the Swedish economy; to this end, the SAP government depended on the strength of corporatist institutions and the willingness of union leadership to agree to wage constraint.[85] In the 1980s, union leadership was thus in the contradictory position of both representing workers and being a lever for the containment of wage demands, even as third road policies suggested that SAP leadership was no longer committed to facilitating compensatory trade-offs.[86] By increasing private sector profitability at

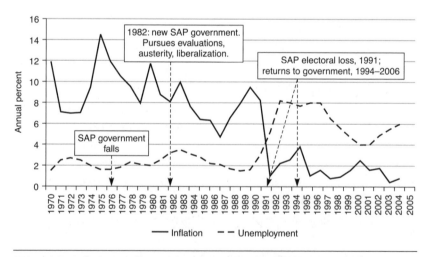

Figure 8.7. Inflation and unemployment in Sweden, 1970–2005. Data source: World Bank, World Development Indicators (WDI); International Labour Organization (ILO).

the expense of the public sector and making the labor market a zero-sum game from the perspective of workers, third way policies undermined the basic foundations of Swedish wage coordination. By extension, they destabilized the SAP-union relationship writ large. "The (correct) perception that profits were not channeled into productive investments, but into speculation and expansion abroad," Ryner comments, "further undermined the legitimacy of government policy in trade unions circles."[87]

The effects of the breakdown in the SAP-union relationship, also a basis of the party's ability to build cross-party coalitions, were manifest by the end of the 1980s. Carlsson offered his resignation after the Riksdag rejected an austerity package: the Swedish Communist Party would not agree to wage and price freezes.[88] An attempted government-imposed freeze on wages, prices, and dividends plus prohibition on strikes produced across-the-board discontent, and the government was forced to step down. As the SAP led an initiative for EU membership, its public opinion ratings dropped below 30 percent—the SAP's lowest level since the 1920s. The SAP lost the September 1991 elections and, despite a comeback in 1994, would never fully regain its electoral strength.[89] In the end, Ryner argues, third road policies amounted to the self-sabotage of the SAP.[90]

The Decline of Economists-in-Politics and the Move to New Experts

Toward the end of the century some Swedish economists noted that, after the 1980s, the profession's public role changed.[91] Economic advisory commissions, once led by full professors of economics and LO economists, became less academic and more dominated by economists linked to the finance ministry. Sandelin and his colleagues attribute this to the decline of Keynesian calculation as a tool of long-term planning and to a changing "stock of economists," thanks in part to increasing numbers of "competent economists in the Ministry of Finance" and elsewhere.[92] They argue that economists' direct participation in Swedish government, politics, and public discussions diminished, highlighting that economics professors were no longer prominent in parliament or government.[93] In 2000 they forecasted that, as authority over economic policy-making shifted to Brussels, Swedish economists' role in domestic public affairs would continue to decline.[94]

Among the more interesting complements of economics' declining public role was a new volatility in the office of finance minister. In striking contrast with the long tenures of his predecessors, Feldt was minister of finance only until 1990, when he resigned.[95] The incoming SAP government of 1994, led by Carlsson and then Persson (from 1996), received critical attention for high turnover and autocratic decision-making and appointment practices.[96] Eklund, whose professional trajectory might have made him a likely candidate for finance minister, instead became chief economist of the SEB in 1994, where he immersed himself (by his account) in learning about "the international economy."[97] Erik Åsbrink served briefly as finance minister (1996–1999) but was succeeded not once but twice by figures with little grounding in economics: Bosse Ringholm (1942–) and then, in 2005, Pär Nuder (1963–; master of laws degree, Stockholm; Persson's former minister of policy coordination).[98]

Also notable are new career pathways between the finance ministry, private finance, and financial consulting. Erik Åsbrink went into private industry and, as of 2011, was an international advisor to Goldman Sachs. Nuder became a strategic counselor to the Albright Stoneridge Group, "where he advises clients on global financial trends and provides strategic advice to clients seeking to enter the European market"; he is also adviser to "the Nordic private equity fund EQT and the venture capital fund Northzone."[99] Domestically grounded, non-financial, SAP-connected economists did not disappear, of course—but neither could one say that the economist theoretician was still at the intermediary, interpretive, managerial, strategic, and coordinating heart of SAP economic policymaking.[100]

And yet parties still need to build policy agendas and communicate them with voting publics. And so, unsurprisingly, in the economist theoretician's wake came new experts. Strategic experts became especially noticeable: the SAP's 1994 campaign became (in)famous for featuring three American political consultants: Bill Hamilton, Phil Noble, and Rick Ridder.[101] According to the Swedish political scientist Lars Nord, this had to do with the SAP's weakened ability to mobilize voters in a context of declining party identification, rising split-ticket voting, and the media's growing independence from partisan affiliations. The SAP's turn to American-style professional campaigning was a marker of a new style of politics in Sweden, featuring a focus "on political personality and character, frequent use of opinion polls, a central role for PR consultants and political marketing, a television-driven media agenda, and professionalization" in political communication.[102]

In the years between 1996 and 2006 the Persson government made an especially clear move to politics-by-public-relations. Existing research tracks a remarkable increase in public relations staff in the Government Office and, within it, the Office of the Prime Minister. "[O]fficials working inside the Government Office claim that there will soon be no room left for proposals and measures that cannot be presented in attractive press releases," noted Göran Sundström in 2008. Under Persson, Sundström notes, the number of press secretaries in the prime minister's office increased from one to six, there was a "major intake of 'spin-doctors' into the Government Office," and "political messages in the form of story-telling made a real breakthrough."[103]

It was also during the Persson years that an initiative to transnationalize third wayism, anchored in the relationship between Blair, Clinton, and their respective advisory networks, coalesced. The effort originated in London- and U.S.-based exchanges between Blair and Clinton in early 1998, in the run-up to the G8 Summit in Birmingham in May of that year—during which Blair and Clinton also held a seminar at Chequers. By September 1998 the initiative broadened to include Persson, Romano Prodi (Olive Tree Coalition, Italy), and Wim Kok (Labor Party, Netherlands), among others (the SPD leader Gerhard Schröder was invited, but could not attend).[104] The chief advisory movers had familiar profiles: "policy people" (or, in my terms, policy specialists) and "campaigners" (strategic experts—especially pollsters).[105]

In time, as the 1998 third way events transitioned into a "progressive governance" conference series—a moniker chosen with the explicit intention of avoiding the American politics-unfriendly taint of socialism—many varied academics, consultants, pollsters, and industry-connected figures would be drawn into the effort.[106] These included, from Sweden, Christer Sturmark, an "internet entrepreneur, founder of Cell/Cell Ventures, writer, and member of the boards of Fame Studios, NordNet, Roaming Factory and Municel." It also included Joakim Palme, then a

"Reader at the Institute for Social Research (SOFI) at the University of Stockholm.[107] But Sidney Blumenthal, a particularly prominent mover on the American side, made clear from the start that the initiative was not grounded in the "arcane ideology" of "intellectuals": third wayism was grounded in the "practical experience" of election-winning politicians who "operate in the real world."[108]

Specificities of Swedish Leftism's Second Reinvention

My account of neoliberalization in the Swedish case can be summarized thus. The politicization of economics was both an *effect* of the profession's interdependence with leftism and a *driver* of cross-field effects that, starting in the turbulent 1970s, informed SAP intraparty contestation and, within that contestation, efforts to redefine the party's programmatic language and agenda. Economics' politicization took the form of professional struggles which, because of interdependence, played out partly *within* the SAP. The discrediting of economist theoreticians, and the formation of new kinds of economists, including left party–affiliated TFEs bearing neoliberal ethics, followed. Inside left parties, the decline of the economist theoretician and the disintegration of center-left interest alliances drove a search for new kinds of experts—some of a specifically strategic sort, linked especially with American political consulting, but also experts drawn from non-economics disciplines and the private sector. The turn to new expertise was interconnected with the Anglo-American-driven transnationalization of third wayism—a major reason that the leadership of the most successful Western social democratic party of the twentieth century became not socialist, but progressive.

How does the story of Swedish leftism's economist-intensive neoliberalization compare with the making of New Labour? To this we now turn.

NEOLIBERALIZING BRITISH LEFTISM

In Britain, too, political fracturing was intertwined with the politicization of economics—which, because of interdependence, reached directly into the Labour Party. As in Sweden, the left party-economics connection also had international ramifications—prompting, among other things, the emergence of the problem of "stagflation." As in the United States, a turn to public relations and strategic expertise followed on the decline of the Labour economist theoretician, which complicated the party's relationship with unions and working class constituencies. As the party fractured, "modernizing" forces, drawing on new experts and expertise, became the victorious bearers of the British third way.

Politics Economized, Economists Politicized

Marion Fourcade has traced how, fueled by political and administrative demand, British economics became a growth industry between the 1940s and the 1960s. By 1950 "economics majors represented nearly a quarter of all full-time students" at Oxford, Cambridge, and Manchester "and almost 60 percent of those at the London School of Economics." In 1957 the Civil Service Commission reported that economics (including philosophy, politics, and economics, or PPE) was "the third most successful subject for recruitment into the administrative class." The 1960s and 1970s were growth years for economics in particular and the social sciences in general: economics teaching posts almost tripled, rising from 679 to 1,802, between 1960 and 1969.[109]

Is there evidence of a politicization of British economics during this period and, if so, that it had to do with left party–economics interdependence? The answer, to both questions, is yes. The 1955 establishment of the Institute of Economic Affairs (IEA), a Conservative-affiliated beachhead of the neoliberal project supported by an alliance between "the Conservative Party and captains of industry," was itself symptomatic of economics' politicization.[110]

The IEA's founders, who took the Fabian Society as a reference point, moved in a political context in which the Labour-economics relationship was both prominent and an object of Conservative criticism. Here we might hark back to Chapter 4, which described how, in the 1950s and early 1960s, British economists were imbricated with intraparty Labour factions on both the party's right (or revisionist, or Gaitskellite) flank and the "Labour Left."[111] June Morris, Thomas Balogh's biographer, makes note of critical and conspiratorial media commentary regarding Nicholas Kaldor (1908–1986; an adviser of Gaitskell until his death in 1963) and Balogh (1905–1985), who was close to Harold Wilson (understood by then as Gaitskell's rival). The two Oxbridge-based Hungarian-*cum*-British economists' proximity to the Labour elite prompted characterizations of the pair as dangerous foreigners and a proliferation of more or less derogatory nicknames—the most famous being a play on the name of Hungary's capital city: Kaldor was "Buddha" (referring to Kaldor's figure) and Balogh was "Pest" (which speaks for itself).[112] Morris speculates that "malicious and hostile gossip of the press may have limited the usefulness and value of both Balogh and Kaldor to the PM."[113]

Keeping in mind that Gaitskell and Wilson were Labour elites *and* economists, the economistic saturation of the Labour elite in the early 1960s was remarkable. But it was also an object of Conservative ire.[114] The influence of economists in the Labour Party was on full display during its 1963 campaign, famous for Wilson's "white heat" technological theme, in which Anthony (Tony) Benn (1925–2014; at that time a Wilson supporter), Thomas Balogh, Richard (Dick) Crossman (1907–1974), and Peter Shore (1924–2001) were keynote speechwriters.[115] But controversy over the economics-Labour relationship came to a head in the first Wilson government.[116]

Upon Wilson's arrival at Downing Street in late 1964 Balogh became adviser on economic affairs to the cabinet and Wilson's personal adviser; Kaldor was special adviser to the chancellor of the exchequer, James Callaghan (1912–2005). Balogh was also a member of a small advisory group known as Wilson's "Kitchen Cabinet," which also included Marcia Williams, Crossman, Shore, Benn, and others.[117] The new Department of Economic Affairs (DEA—based on a plan of Balogh's, developed at Wilson's request), alongside three other new ministries (Ministry of Technology, Ministry of Overseas Development, and Ministry of Land and Natural Resources), not to mention the Government Economic Service (GES), which created a specific basis in the civil service for economists, were all markers of interdependence.[118] The DEA, in particular, was heavily shaped by Balogh, who ushered his own "friends and past pupils" into DEA positions.[119] The GES expanded especially rapidly under Labour administrations (it shrank under Thatcher); GES economists, initially centered in the DEA and the Treasury, could be found in "large concentrations" elsewhere by the late 1960s.[120] In

1964 economists also acquired a new prominence within the Cabinet Office in the form of a small team charged with assisting Wilson on economic policy.[121]

Quantitative markers give a sense of the economistic shift in the British state under Labour governments in the 1960s and 1970s: the first Wilson government featured a nearly twentyfold increase of economists in the British civil service; only 21 economists were on the civil service payroll in 1964, but there were 408 by 1978.[122] The Labour-driven "economization" of Whitehall was contentious among civil service administrators—not necessarily because it involved economists, but because of the creation of a new civil service category of politically appointed "irregulars" who, in Peter Hennessy's words, appeared to civil servants as "the thin edge of a wedge of politicization which has advanced ever since."[123] In other words, what appeared from the perspective of economics as a successful professional colonization of the civil service was, from the perspective of Whitehall—given economics' Labour ties—the politicization of the state.

The making of the DEA was also indicative of Labour's long-standing battle with the Treasury, which now played out as a sort of economistic proxy war.[124] The DEA's predecessor, the National Economic Development ment Council (NEDC), had been around since 1962 (established by Harold Macmillan's Conservative government), but Balogh found it inadequate. The DEA, Balogh argued, would both bring modern economic managerial techniques to Britain and counterbalance Treasury power. Balogh, a critic of "the amateurish culture of the mandarins," saw the DEA as a way of revolutionizing the civil service from within, shifting its economic involvements toward income policy and government industrial intervention.[125] In a dynamic that is reminiscent of intraparty tensions between SEB appointees and LO economists inside the SAP, Balogh had a long record of criticizing the Bank of England—which, for its part, is said to have tried to prevent Balogh's appointment to an Oxford (Balliol) fellowship.[126] In recognition of the DEA's malicious intent, Treasury officials referred to the DEA as the "Department of Extraordinary Aggression."[127]

It was an important moment. If successful, the DEA would not only address the emergent problematic of Britain's economic decline—a theme popularized since Andrew Shonfield's 1958 *British Economic Policy since the War*—but also challenge the question of economic competence that hung over Labour from its beginnings.[128] But the DEA, hemmed in from the start by Wilson's commitment to avoiding devaluation (with Balogh's backing—although he changed his mind in 1965), produced an economic plan that was never realized.[129] As the decade progressed, the Labour government's dependence on technical economic calculation attracted growing political derision and academic criticism.

The Making of "Stagflation"

In this context, in which the Labour elite had essentially hitched its quest for proof of economic competence to the technical prowess of economics, "stagflation" was born as a renewal of old Conservative criticisms. It was coined in November 1965 in the House of Commons by the Conservative MP Iain Macleod as part of a broad critique of Labour's economic policy "and, in particular, of the policy on Productivity, Prices and Incomes"—which, Macleod claimed, "imperils the standard of living and savings of Your people."[130] Macleod singled out the "Socialist" government, and the DEA in particular, as the culprit:

> We came to the General Election in 1964 without a crisis of confidence. . . . [S]terling held throughout the election and held throughout the immediate post-election period and on into November. Then the mistakes began. In our view, the first of those mistakes . . . was the formation of the Department of Economic Affairs.

The problem was the DEA's circumscription of the powers of the chancellor and, by extension, the Treasury:

> [T]he result of this [the DEA] was that the Chancellor of the Exchequer was, for a time at least, reduced to counting candle-ends. . . . He was the first Chancellor . . . who had no true responsibility for the economy.[131]

Regarding the Labour government's "inflationary" budget, Macleod praised the Bank of England for averting a devaluation, but he argued that the domestic economy's situation was dire—and that the DEA's head, Secretary for Economic Affairs George Brown, was making things worse by failing to control wages. Macleod concluded:

> We now have the worst of both worlds—not just inflation on the one side or stagnation on the other, but both of them together. We have a sort of "stagflation" situation and history in modern terms is indeed being made.[132]

Macleod argued that, even as the DEA was "building a dam that is bound to burst in an economy where incomes are swiftly rising while production is completely stagnant," the chancellor (Callaghan) was elevating inflationary expectations with bad figures. Referring to a speech in Scotland in November, Macleod cited Callaghan's misstatement—that wages had increased by 8 percent in as many months—and interpreted the error as an indicator of Callaghan's intelligence:

> [W]e assumed the Chancellor must have some figures of his own and must have known what he was talking about. It turns out that he did not. . . . [W]hat, in fact, was "discreetly admitted in Whitehall last night" was that "we gave him the right figures—but, of course, the fellow cannot read."[133]

Academic critiques, from within economics, complemented conservative criticisms. In 1968, for instance, the Cambridge economist Terence W. Hutchison's (1912–2007) *Economics and Economic Policy in Britain, 1946–1966* questioned whether technical economics was a reliable basis of policy-making via an analysis of errors in forecasting.

Lasting only until 1969, the DEA—then headed by Peter Shore—would go down in history as a short-lived failure with outsize significance. Its demise paralleled a decline in Balogh's influence, as Wilson turned increasingly to ministers for strategic advice. Balogh's advice was "less regarded," partly due to a low point in the Balogh-Wilson relationship amid a "gold crisis weekend" in 1968, in which Roy Jenkins (1920–2003), the chancellor (and a former student of Balogh's), confronted the humiliating prospect of turning to "Washington" for credit. The situation, in Jenkins's account, was "desperate"; Wilson and Jenkins were convinced that a second devaluation would be "total political disaster." Finding his advice singularly unhelpful, Jenkins and Wilson grew "very impatient with Balogh."[134]

After 1968 Balogh's fate was similar to Meidner's: he became an economist theoretician whose moment was past. Balogh became a life peer in 1968; Kaldor followed in 1974. Around the same time, some commentators identified an expert vacuum in Labour's expert ranks. In Roger Backhouse's account, the DEA's failure left party leaders "suspicious of all systematic economic theories."[135] In retrospect, some viewed the DEA episode with exasperation at the blind faith in economic expertise that it symbolized.[136]

In 1970 the Wilson government gave way to the Conservative government of Edward Heath, which faced a serious (but moderate, in retrospect, by current standards) unemployment problem: rates increased from around 2.5 percent to 3.7 percent by 1972.[137] Conservative policy of more spending, reduced taxation, and wage controls nonetheless remained "Keynesian." Amid escalating inflation after the 1973 oil price shock the government, unwilling to comply with trade union demands for price controls in housing and utilities, "called an election on the platform of who rules Britain" in February 1974. The Conservatives lost to Labour, which campaigned on the claim that its "historic and special relationship with the trade unions" would allow it to "generate a better climate for industrial relations."[138]

In 1974 Labour returned as part of a minority government, having won seats but not the popular vote. Harold Wilson was again prime minister. But, in the meantime, new oppositions had opened up between Gaitskellite-descended revisionists, union leaders, and young party activists. Revisionists mobilized public relations specialists, who "argued that Labour's image was 'increasingly obsolete' " and called for "modern public relations techniques to rethink the party's image," especially for younger voters—bolstering the revisionist case that the party needed to abandon its class image and, perhaps, also its relationship to trade unions.[139] In response, union leaders and young Labour activists formed the Campaign for Labour Party Democracy (CLPD). The Labour Party of the 1970s thus became home to a new constellation in which the remnants of the Gaitskellites, shorn of their ability to build their politics on the advice and scientific reputation of Keynesian economists, turned to new kinds of strategic experts—and, in the process, became merely a faction on the party's right flank.[140]

"Keynesian" Policy without Keynesian Economics: The Wilson-Callaghan Government

The second Wilson government arrived near the peak of Britain's first spike in inflation (see Figure 8.8).

On the understanding that union-driven wage increases were driving inflation, the government set its sights on voluntary restraint in the form of a "'Social Contract' with the trade union movement."[141] In the account of the economic historian Jim Tomlinson, Labour claimed that it "could 'do a deal' with the trade unions" that would improve the economy and reduce inflation "while not increasing unemployment," while also "avoiding the confrontations between government and organized labour that had characterized the years of the Heath government."[142] But, in a marked shift from the economistic strategy embodied by the DEA, the pursuit of wage restraint now worked largely through a public communications campaign that aimed to persuade union members and working-class housewives to embrace it.

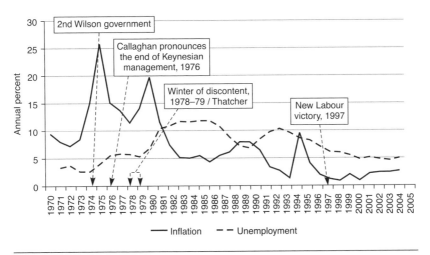

Figure 8.8. Inflation and unemployment in the United Kingdom, 1970–2005. Data source: World Bank, World Development Indicators (WDI); International Labour Organization (ILO).

In the wake of Labour's embrace of politics-by-public-relations, how-ever, the party-labor relationship began to collapse. The new government's central communications vehicle, the Counter-Inflation Publicity Unit (CIPU), substituted opinion research and public communication for the DEA's economist-intensive, technical managerialism. Geoffrey Goodman, formerly an industrial editor for the *Daily Mirror* ("by far the leading working-class newspaper in Britain"), was the new unit's director.[143] The restraint-by-communication strategy, however, failed. The CIPU was dissolved in November 1976; in the same year, Callaghan (the new prime minister) declared the futility of Keynesian management and the Labour government agreed to a conditional IMF loan that re-quired spending reductions. In Tomlinson's analysis, what the CIPU mainly achieved was a widespread public understanding (even among miners' housewives and trade unionists) that inflation was union-driven.[144] The move to government-by-public-relations shifted the burden of resolving economic crisis away from the government and onto orga-nized labor but, in the process, complicated the party's relationship with working class constituencies.

British academic commentary on Keynesianism's inability to diag-nose, much less cure, stagflation continued apace in the mid-1970s.[145] If the problem with Keynesian calculation in the late 1920s was an aver-sion to new "smoke and mirrors" statistical aggregates, the problem now was too much computer-driven mathematical analysis. British eco-nomic journalism, by bringing "monetarism" into the fray, reemerged as a driving force in the shaping of public economic debates—marked, in particular, by "a virulent controversy on the 'economic consequences of Lord Keynes' . . . in the *Times*."[146] In 1975 the *Economist* magazine criticized economics' failings, linking it to "the theoretical world that many economists have been patiently constructing . . . through a gen-eration of computerized economystics." "In many major British univer-sities it is being argued that the day of the econometrician is over," the magazine proclaimed; "the day of the English-speaking basic economic theorist has returned."[147]

The years 1975–1976, in Tomlinson's account, marked British Keynesianism's final collapse—not because there was an objective balance-of-payments crisis, but because of the perception of one. Cuts in public spending were made in order to make British debt more at-tractive to financial institutions, but, in the end, the government was forced to pursue an IMF loan that was conditional on further cuts.[148] Upon Wilson's resignation in 1976, James Callaghan stepped in and, famously, announced at the Labour conference that the notion that one could "spend your way out of a recession and increase employment by cutting taxes and boosting spending" was out-of-date and inflationary:

> I tell you in all candour that this option no longer exists, and in so far as it ever did exist it only worked by injecting a bigger dose of inflation and a higher level of unemployment. Unemployment is caused by pricing ourselves out of jobs quite clearly and unequivocally.[149]

Other markers of the "collapse of Keynesianism" in Britain include Robert Skidelsky's 1977 volume, *The End of the Keynesian Era*, and Hutchison's *Keynes versus the "Keynesians"... ?*, in which he argued that the practices and beliefs of Labour's prominent Keynesians—Kahn, Kaldor, Balogh, and others—had gone too far beyond Keynes's teachings.[150]

What followed was a rapid disintegration of Labour's electoral position. Labour seats were whittled away in by-elections, prompting a Labour-Liberal agreement in 1977. Inflation dropped, but unemployment climbed to a postwar peak of 5.7 percent. IMF loan conditions weakened an already fraught relationship to organized labor: alongside expenditure reductions, a requirement for the removal of industrial subsidies rendered income-related negotiations with trade unions "difficult to sustain."[151] Callaghan put off calling a general election, but new oil price shocks kicked off a new bout of inflation.[152] Despite relatively low unemployment, labor unrest grew, culminating in the "winter of discontent" in 1978–1979. Deeply fractured, Labour lost the 1979 election, making way for the rise of Margaret Thatcher.

Economics, Interfactional Struggle, and the Reconstruction of Labour's Expert Terrain

Amid the looming failure of the Labour government, figures on the British intellectual left moved to alter the contours of Labourite debate. One marker was the foundation of the journal *Marxism Today* (*MT*) in 1977, which continued publication until 1991. Edited by Martin Jacques, *MT* featured a range of both senior intellectuals and younger-generation contributors including Eric Hobsbawm (1917–2012), Stuart Hall (1932–2014), and Geoff Mulgan (1961–).

Presciently, Hall argued in *MT* in 1979 that Thatcher's "shift to the right" coincided, also, with a new "authoritarian populism"—citing, for instance, the rise of the French National Front.[153] He argued, however, that glimmers of populism were symptomatic of the intellectual disarray of the left and the political fragmentation of working-class movements. Hall pinned this fragmentation on Labour's efforts at Keynesian managerialism, suggesting that they tended to morph into a means of controlling and constraining organized labor rather than advancing its cause—although, as we have seen, it would be more correct to say that it was, in fact, a turn to politics-by-public-relations, in the wake of Keynesianism's professional and political discrediting, that broke the union-party tie.[154]

In any case, after 1979 *MT*'s founders, motived by a shared concern that Labour had no adequate response to Thatcherism, focused on developing an analysis for "New Times." The effort was premised on the assumption, now shared on the British left and right, that the age of an electorally workable party-union relationship was dead. A guiding thesis hinged on the argument that Labour would have to develop an alternative to both Thatcherism and "labourism."[155]

The Neoliberal Project: Building an Alliance between Economics and Conservatism

The advent of the Thatcher (and then Major) years had direct implications for the development of British economics. The Conservative years effectively closed off what had, since 1964, been a well-worn route in between economics, the Labour Party, and the British government. In Robert Nelson's account, the Thatcher period saw a "sharp decline in the participation and effectiveness of university economists in government policymaking" and in the "degree of interaction between university economists and government economists."[156] Fourcade similarly describes the Thatcher period as one of increasing political isolation for economists.[157]

The new Conservative chancellor, Geoffrey Howe, presented the Medium Term Financial Strategy (MTFS) with the government's 1980 budget, which expressed its "explicit commitment . . . to the ideas of rational expectations and a monetarist doctrine."[158] Thatcher's 1981 budget then broke with Keynesian logic in the most dramatic way: amid declining inflation and rising unemployment, it increased taxes by £4 billion (about 2 percent of GDP). The linkages to the neoliberal project here were clear; Thatcher's affiliation with free market think tanks and bearers of monetarist economics is well known.[159] But, for the British left, the significance of Thatcher's economic policies centered on its consequences for Labour's cultural terrain—which, as we have seen, extended into mainstream and academic economics.

In this regard, among the notable effects of "Thatcherism" was the marginalization of Keynesian economists-in-government. Kaldor, for instance, was a member of the Select Committee on Monetary Policy, and in that capacity he argued that the MTFS was essentially "an indirect way . . . to break with wage inflation by creating unemployment"—but to little effect.[160] Meanwhile, Thatcher's government offices "sought to choose their own economic advisors among economists who were regarded as politically trustworthy."[161]

The fact that Thatcherism was the most significant challenge yet to the political authority of academic economists became especially clear in 1981. In that year Thatcher's budget was met with resounding condemnation from the heights of the British academy: a letter of opposition appeared in the *Times,* authored by two Cambridge economics professors (Frank Hahn and Robert Neild) and signed by 364 academics from forty British universities. Among the signatories were Kaldor and Richard Kahn—the so-called "Two Ks" at King's College [Cambridge] who were, by then, known as "left-wing Keynesians" to economics students.[162] Cambridge faculty accounted for the statement's single largest number of signatories (fifty-four). Despite a challenge leveled at Thatcher in parliament "to name even two economists who supported her," in the rye summary of a *Guardian* journalist, "[t]he lady was not for turning,"[163]

The episode, like the failure of the DEA, acquired outsize significance—becoming an integral part, for instance, of a turn-of-the-twenty-first-century narrative of a "war of ideas" between free market thinking and "planning."[164] This narrative is partly hyperbolic, of course, but if we replace "free market thinking" with "rational expectations," and "planning" with managerial Keynesianism, it was also correct. Thatcher's "anti-Keynesianism" was grounded in argumentation that was "produced by economists who," in the words of the IEA's Patrick Minford, "would have called themselves 'Keynesian.'" On this basis, Minford responded to the *Times* protest letter with the statement that "the 364 were playing a dangerous and dishonest game."[165]

In the background were deep changes in British economics, linked with left party–economics interdependence, Conservative criticism thereof, and the rise of Thatcher. The 1970s had been a period of diversification in British higher education, offering new disciplinary avenues— sociology, urban planning—for the training of social scientists. The "shift of influence from one group of economists to another" under Thatcher, from academic Keynesians to IEA and monetarist economists, prompted a reorientation in the economics profession away from government posts. British growth, which rose in 1983 and climbed to nearly 6 percent by 1988, allowed Thatcher to back the claim that the advice of academics need not be heeded on matters of economic policy. In Nelson's account, government work started to look "outdated" to would-be economists.[166] As the British social sciences expanded and economics declined, the popularity of business education grew.[167] Fourcade thus describes an "exodus of would be academics toward the corporate sector," even as privatization and regulatory changes "opened a niche for the consultancy market and prompted the emergence of 'new' jurisdictions in the corporate world."[168] As the century drew to a close, economics degrees were "increasingly seen as points of entry into the financial professions."[169] These professional transformations had multiple sources, but their acceleration in the Thatcher years is hard to explain without first considering how economics' *de facto* Labour affiliations sparked Conservative ire.

Labour, Disarticulated

In the interim, 1982 steel workers' strikes and the yearlong 1984–1985 miners' strike manifestly failed to undermine the legitimacy of the new regime. Unemployment peaked at more than 3.2 million, while the liberalization of financial markets (in the "Big Bang of 1986") shifted the British economy in a decidedly financialized direction.[170] In a striking coincidence, the embrace of monetarism in Thatcher's 1981 budget was accompanied by the final departure of the remnants of the Gaitskellite generation: the revisionists (including Roy Jenkins) took the Downsian advice of political scientists that the "median voter" was up for grabs and formed a new Social Democratic Party (SDP).

Inside Labour, meanwhile, internecine power struggles pitted "modernizers" concerned with electability against socialist "Bennites" (referring to Tony Benn), unions, and party activists. This new world—in which Keynesian managerialism (and Keynesian managers), socialism, and unionism stood in opposition to the "center"—was the terrain in which, in the 1970s and 1980s, the party's younger generation, inheritors-in-the-making came of age.

Here the case of Peter Mandelson (1953–)—who is the grandson of Herbert Morrison and would become one of Tony Blair's highest-profile strategic advisers—is particularly interesting. Contrasting his perspective with his grandfather's, Mandelson describes his experience of Labour as a terrain defined by a zero-sum struggle between electoral viability and the socialist "hard left."[171] Mandelson, a student of PPE at St. Catherine's College, Oxford, starting in 1973, reports that he avoided the typical party institutions, the student union and the Labour Club: the union "seemed full of self-serving careerists and preening would-be Cabinet ministers" and the Labour Club "was going through one of its . . . periods of tension between right and left, social democrats and traditionalists." In time he became involved in the British Youth Council (BYC), bringing him into contact with figures in the Callaghan government.[172] After Oxford, Mandelson worked "in a distinctly Old Labour environment"—the TUC—where he

> had a crash course in how power was then wielded inside Labour. . . .
> The process was a product of a "corporatist" approach in which government, business and trade unions carved up the decisionmaking and attempted to run the economy—investment, prices and incomes—among themselves. It was an idea whose time had come and gone, if it ever arrived.[173]

Linking the failures of corporatism to Britain's IMF bailout, the winter of discontent, and Thatcher's electoral victory, and noting the TUC's hierarchical tendencies, Mandelson came to see a job with the unions, or "Old Labour," as a professional dead end.[174] In 1980–1981 Mandelson, then working for Labour's shadow transport secretary, reacted to the far-left "Bennites" by helping to organize a Labour solidarity campaign as a "counterweight . . . to give heart to the moderates and keep them in the party." Mandelson did not join the SDP in 1981, but he reports that he "did share much of their vision of what a modern left-of-centre party should be": "it should fight for fairness and opportunity" and "appeal to the centre ground"; it should not represent "sectional interests." In 1982 Mandelson left his party job, taking up a position at London Weekend Television.[175]

Soon thereafter Labour's new leader, Neil Kinnock (1942–), initiated an effort to reconfigure the party's authority structures, alliances, and cultural infrastructure. Elected in 1983, Kinnock pursued reforms aimed at empowering leadership at the expense of unions and left activists alike.[176] Proposing an internal one-member-one-vote (OMOV) policy in place of trade union block voting, Kinnock responded to the formation of the far-left Militant Tendency in 1983 by expelling its members in 1987 and created Joint Policy Committees in an effort to dilute the programmatic authority of the "Bennite" NEC.[177] In a sign of ongoing concern over resuscitating Labour's capacity to join analysis and strategy—and, it seems, of business support of incipient effort to "modernize" Labour—the year 1988 saw the establishment of a new think tank, the Institute for Public Policy Research (IPPR), "with the aim of feeding policies into his modernization of the Labour Party."[178] The making of a new Labourite party-expert configuration—office-seeking "modernizers," flanked by strategic aides and progressive policy specialists, informed by the new ethics of a changed economics profession—was under way.

New Experts, New Labour

New Labour's famous call, closely associated with the sociologist Anthony Giddens, to go "beyond left and right" was received, in some circles, as more of a political than an analytical move.[179] But when Giddens published *Beyond Left and Right* in 1994 the spatial metaphors of British politics had, in fact, shifted. Inside the Labour Party, the category "left" had become a referent for the party's backward-looking re-arguard, the "traditionalists" and the "backbenchers," in contrast with the forward-looking "frontbenchers," or "modernizers." (The term "backbencher" could be found in British political lexicon from the 1930s, but its use rapidly escalated in the 1970s and 1980s in British English-language books.[180]) This shift had a social basis: for someone like Peter Mandelson, to embrace socialism, Keynesianism, corporatism, or trade unionism was to drag Labour onto the electorally treacherous territory of the "old." In this sense, Giddens was correct.

And yet, arguably, Anthony Giddens' prominence masked British center-leftism's notable move away from academic expertise and toward a new terrain: the developing world of think tanks. Here the think tank Demos, established in 1993 by Geoff Mulgan and Martin Jacques (of *MT*), is of particular interest. The founders' aim was to establish a "cross-party think tank of the centre-left" that, in a context of declining faith in politics, could "change the terms of political debate."[181] As Mulgan would later recount: "There was little sign of imagination in any of the parties. . . . Above all we wanted to articulate an alternative to the hoarding habits of closed elites and share power."[182] Mulgan describes Demos as a reaction to *MT* and other sources of cultural and political criticism, which were prone to encouraging "contempt" at the expense of "practical problem-solving."[183] Instead, Demos would neither produce intellectual criticism for-its-own-sake nor operate in a blindly partisan way:

> We hoped to combine freedom from party affiliation with an ethos that was radical, troublesome, and appealing to insurgents rather than incumbents. . . . [T]he name [Demos] is an anagram of "sod 'em."[184]

Although Demos was Labour-inclined in the 1990s (as we will see), it innovated a site of intellectual production that was *neither* academic *nor* partisan, and thus utterly different from Labour's dominant sources of expertise in the ages of socialist and economistic leftism.

Meanwhile, inside Labour, the modernizers gained ground. John Smith (1938–1994) became Labour's leader, having served as the opposition's shadow chancellor since 1987. Smith pushed through a first step toward OMOV but otherwise struggled to rebuild party unity. In 1994, however, Smith died suddenly of a heart attack, and into his place stepped a young modernizer, Anthony (Tony) Blair (1953–)—who extended OMOV in 1996 via a reduction in the weight of the unions' block at conferences to 50 percent. In combination with changes in party composition after a new membership drive, Labour now had a changed constituency that allowed Blair to remove Sidney Webb's Clause IV—the symbol of Labour's socialist past, calling for the nationalization of industry—from the party's program.[185]

Blair brought with him a particular party-expert constellation, the making of which can only be understood in light of the decline of the economist theoretician, the fracturing of the party's relationship to organized labor, and the reformatting of Labour's cultural terrain. Labour's new party-expert constellation included, alongside Tony Blair and Gordon Brown, a distinctive trilogy of strategists, policy specialists, and TFEs—including (but not limited to) Peter Mandelson, Matthew Taylor (1960–), Charlie Whelan (1954–), and Philip Gould (1950–2011) on the strategic side; Ed Balls, a TFE; and a host of specialists and aides drawn from Demos and IPPR.

Taylor—for whom Labour's changing 1970s cultural terrain was, as for Mandelson, formative—was appointed to run Labour's "rebuttal operation" in 1994. The party's policy unit at that time was, for the modernizers, enemy territory: "a Bennite hotbed" and "thus sidestepped by Labour frontbenchers."[186] The son of a sociologist (Laurie Taylor) and a historian (Jennie Howells), Taylor was in the late Wilson/Callaghan years a sociology student at Southampton University, where he was involved in the "Bennite" wing of Labour student politics.[187] He left the student Labour organization (the University Labour Group) to start the Socialist Society and joined the Labour Party in 1978, canvassing for Douglas Jay in Battersea North. Among various jobs after university, Taylor worked at the NEDC and "flirted briefly with an academic career at Warwick Business School."[188]

A contributor to Labour's 1997 electoral manifesto and the "five pledges," Taylor helped to develop a mode of policy-making by way of policy forums that some would later cite as more demobilizing than empowering.[189] In a process that parallels the Democratic Party's combination of incorporation-by-quota and elite-driven centralization, some would later characterize the reforms Taylor helped to bring about as a move to controlled policy-making and a consensus-based (as opposed to conflict-driven) deliberative process, combined with "a reassertion of authority."[190]

Another important arrival in Labour's expert ranks was Ed Balls (1967–). At the time of the miners' strike Balls was seventeen years old and had just joined the Labour Party (at sixteen). Balls's father, Michael, was chairman of a local Labour ward.[191] Balls went to Oxford (Keble, PPE), where he reportedly joined the Labour, Tory, *and* Liberal clubs.[192] Working at Midland Bank in the summers, he completed his degree in 1988; from there he went to the Treasury and then to Harvard's Kennedy School, where he pursued an MA in public administration on a Kennedy Memorial Scholarship. At Harvard, Balls's instructors included Lawrence (Larry) Summers and Lawrence (Larry) Katz.[193] After completing his degree Balls pursued the very path that Fourcade highlights as having acquired new importance as an efficient, nonacademic pathway into British politics in the 1970s: economic journalism. At the Treasury, Balls caught the attention of the shadow chancellor, Gordon Brown, with a Fabian Society pamphlet advocating independence for the Bank of England and "a new approach to investment and to tackling unemployment."[194] Brown invited Balls to come to the Treasury on a full-time basis.

By 1994 Brown, flanked by a TFE (Balls) and a strategist (often referred to in the press as a "spin doctor") named Charlie Whelan (1954–), became the leader of a new team that would handle Labour's perennial economic competence problem. Their approach looked nothing like the Wilson-Balogh strategy of reshaping the machinery of government and challenging the power of the Treasury and the Bank of England, however. The Brown-Balls-Whelan approach, instead, was more akin to Snowden's: to reassure the media and the markets that Labour was "prudent" in the sense that, in-line with conventional economic thinking, it was committed to free markets, globalization, and central bank independence. In the *Independent*'s telling, "Brown and Balls rewrote Labour's economic strategy, ditching the old 'tax and spend' image," even as "Whelan overcame the initial scepticism of the media." The "trio created

the idea that Labour could be trusted to manage the economy pru-
dently, and that it was dedicated to getting people back into jobs
through the welfare-to-work programme."[195] The *Economist* later emphasized that Balls operated on the conviction that "a left-of-centre
government must establish credibility with the international financial
markets before embarking on redistribution" and that "supporting
free trade and globalisation was compatible with pursuing social justice at home."[196] The tactic, in other words, was to refit Labour's economic strategy to the imperatives of markets.

Labour's 1997 campaign, drawing inspiration from New Democratic
successes and strategies, featured a specific manifesto for business and
called for an end to unconditional benefits.[197] New Labour won with
more than 40 percent of the vote, versus the Conservatives' nearly
31 percent. But the political scientist Peter Mair noted that in 1997
"Labour actually won a smaller share of support than at any election
in the 1950s or 1960s, and this in an election characterized by a record
low turnout."[198] The modernizers declared the 1997 election a "land-
slide" victory, but, in the full arc of British postwar electoral history, it
was not a show of overwhelming popular support.

Famously, one of the New Labour government's first moves—to the
surprise of many, because it was not advertised during the election campaign—was to grant the Bank of England independence. Brown insisted that the New Labour government would reconcile prudent fiscal
management—borrowing in the current cycle to finance public investment, not current expenditure, with a low debt-to-GDP ratio—with
Labour's social objectives. The way in which Brown hoped to achieve
this was by giving the Bank of England independence and controlling
wage inflation by subordinating "all other economic concerns" to an
inflation target of no more than 2.5 percent.[199] As in the Swedish case,
economic policies of New Labour made a considerable contribution to
the dawn of a new age of financial internationalization in Britain (see
Figures 8.9 and 8.10).

The rise of the policy specialist in the New Labour years was also
unmistakable. Fifteen IPPR staff reportedly moved into government
jobs after the 1997 election.[200] With Mandelson's support, and despite
objections to "an apparatchik from Millbank" to his appointment,
Taylor became IPPR's director in 1999 and would remain there until

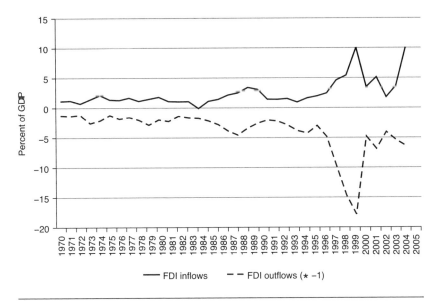

Figure 8.9. Foreign direct investment (FDI) inflows and outflows, United Kingdom, 1970–2005.

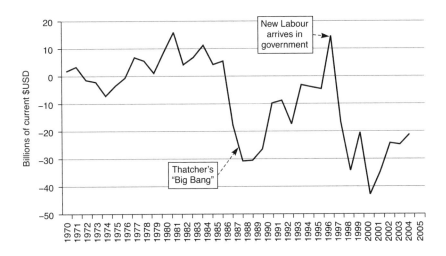

Figure 8.10. U.K. financial balance of payments, 1970–2005. Data source: World Bank, World Development Indicators (WDI).

2003.[201] During that time IPPR gained some notoriety as an advocate of public-private partnerships for public service provision based on the work of a commission backed by KPMG, Serco, and Norwich Union and chaired by Martin Taylor, a WHSmith chairman and former Barclays chief executive.[202] In 2003, at age forty-two, Taylor became the head of the Number 10 Policy Unit.[203] Demos, widely noted as an important source of experts and argumentation in the New Labour years, also became (in its own retrospective assessment) "New Labour's favourite think-tank."[204]

NEOLIBERALIZATION, TRANSNATIONAL PROGRESSIVISM, AND THE GERMAN "NEW MIDDLE"

The analyses of leftism's second reinvention thus far place cross-field effects, rooted in the relationship between economics and left parties, center-stage. To what extent were cross-field effects at work in the (West) German case?

German leftism's second reinvention unfolded within West, and then unified, Germany's unique postwar trajectory. West Germany leftism's late economistic turn was followed by the *absence* of the kind of dramatic inflationary spikes seen in the United Kingdom in the 1970s and (less so) in Sweden (see Figure 8.11). But (West) German inflation and unemployment rates did follow the X-shaped pattern, in which low unemployment took a backseat to low inflation, seen in all cases thus far. The (West) German case, in short, exhibits the same inverted Keynesianism seen elsewhere—but a much more moderate version.

As we will see, the SPD's neoliberalized "new middle" had particularly striking transnational aspects. It took root in tandem with the consolidation of Europe as a single market, the making of the euro, and the formation of the European Central Bank (ECB). It also unfolded in engagement with the transnationalizing initiative by which third wayism became progressivism. The German experience thus provides a useful window into the roles of (at least) two kinds of transnational forces in leftism's second reinvention: the Europeanization of financial governance and the international formation of new, progressive political-expert networks.

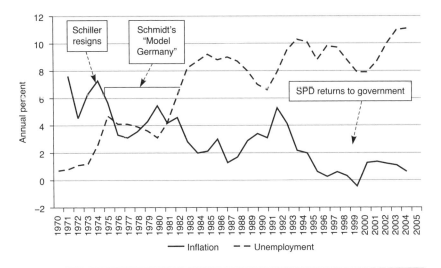

Figure 8.11. Inflation and unemployment in (West) Germany, 1970–2005. Data source: World Bank, World Development Indicators (WDI); International Labour Organization (ILO).

The 1970s "Collapse of Keynesianism," but Not the Economist Theoretician

We have seen that left parties-in-government in the United States and Britain in the 1970s, amid the politicization of economics, pursued "Keynesian" policy without Keynesian economist theoreticians, which took the form of voluntary rather than mandatory wage and price guidelines that were implemented, without success, by means of moral suasion and public relations campaigns. In Sweden, too, a TFE-led challenge, hosted in the pages of *Ekonomisk Debatt* in the 1970s, undermined the claim of LO economists as representatives of a professional consensus. In all cases, by this time, the Keynesian economist theoreticians' capacity for public intervention had considerably declined. A different dynamic unfolded in West Germany in the 1970s: SPD economist theoreticians negotiated, relatively successfully, new economic difficulties—but in the longer run they lost the backing of the profession, and saw their scientific standing decline.

In 1972 Karl Schiller, then "superminister" of both economics and finance, stepped down amid disputes over reducing spending. For a time Schiller shifted his allegiance to the CDU; his former student in economics, Helmut Schmidt (1918–2015), took his place.[205] Serving as West Germany's "hardheaded" economist chancellor from 1974 to 1982, Schmidt is broadly credited for guiding the West German economy through the oil shocks of the 1970s, lending "economic respectability" to the SPD in the process.[206] Schmidt's "Model Germany" centered on "high capital stock per employee; . . . a capacity to retain competitiveness by restraining unit labour costs; social peace . . . ; budget consolidation; and . . . a 'hard' D-Mark"—and was distinctive among center-left government strategies at the time.[207]

As in Britain, the 1970s saw the official abandonment of full employment by the SPD finance minister, Hans Matthöfer—an autodidact trade union economist who "declared that the state could not guarantee full employment, and that economic growth depended on the vitality of the private sector."[208] But Schmidt and Matthöfer remained Keynesian economist theoreticians with managerial commitments. Despite increasing rancor and discontent in the ranks of German trade unions, and notwithstanding the decline of Keynesian calculation, Schmidt is remembered as a "conciliator" who embraced austerity as a means to recovery (in particular, in the form of the Budget Structure Law of 1975) but was also able to encourage union toleration of cutbacks. In Andrei Markovits's account, Schmidt managed this "by brilliantly employing a mixture of coercion, persuasion and a genuinely close relationship with some of the unions' most important leaders," with whom he had a "unique rapport." Union leaders saw Schmidt as "a superb economic expert whose pragmatism, coupled with a genuine concern for the average worker, would provide the best combination" in the defense of labor interests.[209] Schmidt, drawing on economic advice from the chancellery's SPD-aligned Division of Planning (headed by Albrecht Müller), held regular meetings with union leadership and supported codetermination; in return, unions limited their wage demands.[210] The years 1977–1978 saw a return to stimulus in the form of the Future Investment Program (ZIP).[211] In 1979 DIW Berlin, then at the end of the presidency of the SPD-affiliated economist Dr. Karl König, backed the stimulus initiative with a report on strategies for returning to full employment.[212]

Cross-Field Effects: Fracture on the Left and the Politicization of Economics

There were, however, changes afoot in professional economics in the 1970s. Between 1971 and 1974 the SVR (Sachverständigenrat) saw its first dissenting votes—six of them—cast by a trade union-nominated member, Claus Köhler.[213] Signaling a monetarist shift in the profession from which SVR members are drawn, after 1976 the SVR "explicitly favoured supply-side policies" and thus "came to be entangled in major controversies with the trade unions."[214]

Economics' emergent politicization, as elsewhere, unfolded alongside deepening fractures in Social Democratic ranks on the one hand and important changes in West German political expertise on the other. Trade union and youth protests within the SPD in the late 1960s culminated, most dramatically, in the formation of the Red Army Faction (RAF) in 1968. The following year, in 1969, a cross-party group of Bundestag members and the Berlin House of Deputies drove the founding of a new institute, the Social Science Center (WZB).[215] Modeled on the Brookings Institution in the United States, some German analysts note that the WZB, with the Friedrich Ebert Stiftung (FES), was home to policy specialists who aimed to support a rethinking of mainstream party policies that would quell the influence of "organized interests," focusing their attentions on the SPD in the 1970s.[216] Meanwhile the DGB-affiliated WWI (the Economic-Scientific Institute [Wirtschafts-Wissenschaftliches Institut]), once home to the programmatically influential Viktor Agartz, moved away from what was regarded as academic and scientific economics—a shift signaled by a 1971 change of name: the Institute of Economics and Social Sciences (Wirtschafts- und Sozialwissenschaftliches Institut, or WSI).[217]

Unrest within the ranks of the West German left deepened in the 1970s. Schmidt's strong response to radical student groups kept the SPD in power but alienated its younger membership.[218] The party's overall membership reached an all-time peak in 1976, but declined thereafter.[219] Among the SPD's alienated youth was Oskar Lafontaine (1943–), a Young Socialist (Jusos), whom Schmidt excluded from "inner Party leadership."[220]

As in the past, West Germany's political fracturing prompted a move to scientization in the world of academe. Symptomatic here was the Blue List, an accreditation process of the German Council of Science and Humanities (later the Leibniz Association) established in 1977, creating new motivations for West Germany's prestigious research institutes to pursue high-profile university affiliations.[221] And yet, as before, the academic leadership of the institutes remained more or less explicitly politically aligned. A case in point here is the president of DIW Berlin from 1979, Prof. Dr. Hans-Jürgen Krupp—formerly the president of the University of Frankfurt. Krupp, who worked in the Ministry of Economics under Schiller and also with Helmut Schmidt, was the likely economic minister if the SPD had won under Hans Jochen-Vogel, according to Der Spiegel.[222] As a participant in the party leadership's programmatic debates, Krupp would be remembered as an economist theoretician—that is, "an economist" who "also knew when to consider political processes."[223] But, with the SPD out of government, Krupp would remain a minister-to-be.

In the early 1980s, as Helmut Kohl's chancellorship (1982—1998) targeted the power of economists within the West German state, the politicizing effects of left party-economics interdependence came into stark relief. Kohl, like Thatcher, sought to rid the federal bureaucracy of its "Socialist" elements, targeting economist-heavy divisions. The new government downgraded and moved the Division of Planning, now renamed the Division for Social and Political Analysis; SPD-allied economists, including Albrecht Müller, moved on.[224] The SVR, meanwhile, became a showcase of fracture rather than professional consensus. Between 1982 and 1984 the DIW's Hans-Jürgen Krupp, who joined the SVR in 1982 with trade union endorsement, submitted a historic seventeen dissenting votes—almost three times the historical maximum, cast by Claus Köhler between 1969 and 1974.[225] Niklas Potrafke identifies fiscal and labor market policy as main areas of dissent, concluding that trade union economists favor "comprehensive minimum wages and . . . a larger government."[226]

In this context, the institutional arrangements that made the economist theoretician possible ceased to exist. The economist theoretician was reduced, once again, to a mere Social Democratic or trade union economist. Meanwhile, West German economies, as elsewhere, internationalized, Anglicized, and turned to new professional endeavors: starting in the 1980s younger-generation economists increasingly sought international rather than domestic publication venues; German-language journals shifted to English.[227] The notion that one could be an SPD economist *and* a scientific economist was no longer taken for granted. The transition can be seen in the new leadership of DIW: Krupp's successor, Prof. Dr. Lutz Hoffman, had a career that included domestic academic appointments as well as experience as a World Bank and European Commission consultant. A *Tagesspiegel* article, noting Krupp's SPD affiliations, commented approvingly that "[p]olitical ambitions are rarely compatible with scientific research."[228]

Cut Adrift: the Noneconomistic Origins of the New Middle

During the Kohl years Willy Brandt cultivated a younger group of party leadership that would come to be known as *Brandts Enkel* (Brandt's "grandchildren") or, alternatively, the "modernizers." Lafontaine was among them; so, also, were Herta Däubler-Gmelin, Hans Eichel, Björn Engholm, Karl-Heinz Hiersemann, Klaus Matthiesen, Uli Mauter, Rudolf Scharping, Gerhard Schröder, and Heidemarie Wieczorek-Zeul. In the 1987 campaign the SPD tried, and failed, to marry working-class appeal with a green-friendly, new left platform. But the SPD's vote hit a new low, and the Greens—especially in large cities—gained strength.[229] After the 1987 elections the party's "right wing" forced Brandt out of SPD leadership, replacing him with Vogel; Lafontaine became deputy leader.

In 1989 the SPD drafted its first new program since Bad Godesberg—a process, initiated by Brandt in 1984, that unfolded in the striking absence of a Schilleresque figure. The final program's commitment included ending the arms race; a commitment to a "fair world economy," defined as access for all to "decent employment and equal treatment"; social equality; "qualitative economic growth" with "democratic" basis for decisions on production; and encouraging civil society.[230] Observers noted that the new program seemed to lack coherence on economic questions.[231]

In 1990, amid the unification of East and West Germany, the SPD suffered its worst electoral defeat since 1957. Party leaders worried that it "had become virtually unelectable."[232] What ensued was internal jockeying for control and, in the end, a shake-up of SPD leadership. Brandt died in 1992; Engholm resigned as chairman in 1993; Scharping stepped in. By 1994 the new leadership troika featured Scharping, Lafontaine, and Schröder.[233] Lafontaine was voted in as chairman over Scharping (the incumbent) in 1995 at the party's Mannheim conference.[234]

The absence of a Schilleresque figure in the SPD's leadership and programmatic deliberations by this time was symptomatic of a double process: the politicization of economics in the 1970s and 1980s and a growing European-centeredness of German economics. Indeed, in the background to the rise of Scharping, Lafontaine, and Schröder was an important shift in European monetary governance marked by the January 1994 establishment of the European Central Bank's (ECB) precursor, the European Monetary Institute (EMI). The EMI was a key element of Stage 2 in monetary unification, laid out in the Treaty on European Union (TEU). Officially an organizational basis of cross-cooperation among the eleven national central banks of the future eurozone, the EMI was partly intended to advance toward the goal of achieving national-level central bank independence by 1998. In this context, as power over monetary policy became more European than national, German economists' attention centered increasingly on Europe and European integration.[235]

In the wake of the figure of the domestically-grounded economist theoretician, the SPD's economic deliberations were cut adrift. An initial draft of SPD economic policy, some thought, placed undue emphasis on Germany's slipping economic competitiveness—a theme favored at the time by modernizers, journalists, and employers' organizations.[236] As elsewhere, the narrative of German economic decline dovetailed with calls for deregulatory initiatives. Lafontaine, who is trained as a physicist, worked with the economist Heiner Flassbeck (later Lafontaine's deputy finance minister) to challenge the narrative of decline. Flassbeck, head of the Department of Business Cycles at DIW from 1990 to 1998, "appeared in several German newspapers exposing the flaws and costly consequences of the Berlin government's economic and social policies" and criticizing the positions of "business-linked economists."[237] Lafontaine and Flassbeck challenged the rhetoric of economic crisis within the party, calling for a balanced "double strategy" of both "supply and demand."[238]

On this theme, Lafontaine made a speech that "proposed a change in direction in the SPD's economic and fiscal policy" to counter the "[n]eoliberalism and monetarism [that] had come to characterize the economic thinking of Social Democrats and trade unionists alike."[239] But the effort was unsuccessful; in Lafontaine's later account, the media accused him and Flassbeck "of trotting out the tattered old slogans of the 1970s."[240] Lafontaine later speculated that the SPD's engagement with academic and theoretical work was not what it once was, arguing that Keynes had gone the way of Marx: "[M]any who talk about Keynes have never read a word of what he wrote."[241]

Schröder, who made innovation, welfare state reform, personal responsibility and flexibility central themes in his public speeches in the late 1990s ("he even referred to Ludwig Erhard," notes one observer), emerged as the "modernizer," in contrast with Lafontaine. By one report, "prejudices, antipathies, and petty jealousies" marked their relationship, and their respective advisory networks likewise "regarded each other with mistrust."[242] Especially notable, on the Schröder side, was Bodo Hombach (1952–), a "trade union stalwart" turned campaign organizer in the late 1980s, and soon after an MP in North Rhine-Westphalia (1990).[243] In one retrospective account Hombach was central to the effort to lay claim to the legacy of Erhard; Lafontaine, who was among "Hombach's sworn enemies," reportedly caricatured Hombach as a "Teutonic Peter Mandelson."[244] During this time the SPD leadership also made a clear move to American campaign styles, making a careful study of the Clinton campaigns in particular. Key here was the SPD Secretary-General, Franz Müntefering, who "planned to initiate a campaign similar to that of the Democrats and . . . the Labour Party."[245]

In the late 1990s SPD leadership thus divided along familiar lines, with familiar experts in tow. The party's 1998 program expressed its internal division, invoking an awkward combination of markets and competition on the one hand, and full employment and distributional justice on the other. The SPD campaign slogan, "Innovation and Justice," echoed the same division.[246]

New Experts, Transnational Forces and the
Resignation of Oskar Lafontaine

By the spring of 1998 the effort to internationalize third wayism, which now included Schröder, was getting off the ground. The following month saw the publication of a now infamous 1998 Blair-Schröder statement, *The Third Way—Die Neue Mitte.* The joint statement announced, among other things, "A New Supply-Side Agenda for the Left" that, on the heels of "two decades of neo-liberal laissez-faire," would nonetheless repudiate Western leftism's Keynesian, economistic past.[247] Unlike "past social democrats" who "gave the impression that the objectives of growth and high unemployment would be achieved by successful demand management alone," the "[m]odern social democrats recognise that supply side policies have a central and complementary role to play." Alongside "welfare-to-work" reforms, lower income taxes, "[s]ound public finance," and flexible product, capital, and labor markets, the Third Way/Neue Mitte "active state" would promote "investment in human and social capital."[248] Last but not least, third wayers would build their own expert infrastructure, establishing "a network of experts, farsighted thinkers, political fora and discussion meetings" that could "deepen and continually further develop the concept of the New Centre and the Third Way."[249]

The SPD won the September 1998 election with 41 percent of the vote; Schröder was chancellor, and Lafontaine became minister of finance. But, as in the early Clinton years, the victory of *Neue Mitte* politics was no foregone conclusion. The formation of a coalition government with the Green Party (with almost 7 percent) only complicated matters.

Meanwhile, however, Europe's economic consolidation was entering a new phase. The European Central Bank (ECB) was formally founded on June 1, 1998, alongside the European System of Central Banks (ESCB; consisting of eleven Eurozone national central banks and four others), with seven months to prepare for the establishment of a single currency and to define eurozone monetary policies.[250] Shortly after Schröder's arrival in the chancellery conversion rates were fixed and the euro was introduced on January 1, 1999. In short, financial and monetary power shifted, in a very real institutional sense, beyond national control.

And yet, in a time of predominantly center-left government across EU member states, many of Lafontaine's ministerial peers were also social democrats. Here we might recall, as noted in Chapter 6, arguments that monetarism and monetary union elevated the power of central bank governors over ministers of finance.[251] We might recall also the Europeanization and internationalization of European economics professions by this time, and that the economist theoretician had given way to very different sorts of economists-in-government—as we have seen in the Swedish case.

In this context, one of the most remarkable things about Lafontaine's (short) tenure as finance minister is his relative isolation on the European political scene. In late November 1998, because Lafontaine was calling for tax harmonization across the EU, the *Sun* famously dubbed him "the most dangerous man in Europe."[252] Lafontaine was backed by Dominique Strauss-Kahn (IMF), among others, but Lafontaine later characterized New Labour's response as "chicken-hearted," and noted the obstacles imposed by the EU's Growth and Stability Pact—"the brain-child," in Lafontaine's characterization, of Hans Tietmeyer of the Bundesbank.[253] Thus embattled, on March 18, 1999 Lafontaine surprised everyone by quitting his ministerial position and, later, defecting from the SPD. Hans Eichel (1941–), a vocational teacher with little economics training but considerable financial expertise as a former premier of Hesse—which includes Germany's major financial center, Frankfurt—succeeded Lafontaine.[254] After Lafontaine resigned Flassbeck went international, becoming the United Nations Conference on Trade and Development's (UNCTAD) chief economist.[255] Describing his resignation as "a struggle to uphold a particular ideal," Lafontaine later linked the rhetoric of "modernization" to the "false ideology of central bankers," citing the strict monetary policies of the Bundesbank and the ECB, backed by the EU's Growth and Stability Pact, as the central obstacles to Keynesianism's resuscitation in Europe.[256] "Forgotten," Lafontaine notes, "were the days when Ludwig Erhard and Karl Schiller vetoed the Bundesbank's plan to raise the bank rate."[257]

Making the SPD Modern—or, Progressive

In the months after the resignation, Schröder disowned Lafontaine's economic positions and embraced Hans Eichel's year 2000 program.[258]

Eichel exempted "divestiture of shareholdings by German companies from capital gains tax" and proposed in 2001 a "single federal financial services authority" that "emulated supervisory arrangements in the City of London."[259] His *Annual Economic Report of 2000* centered on "lessons to be learnt from abroad, notably from Denmark, the Netherlands and the United States, about how to improve growth and employment; and the 'Europeanisation' of German economic policy."[260] Mobilizing a notion of Hombach's, Eichel called for learning from other countries by "benchmarking best practices," while staying focused on the "European dimension."[261] As Figures 8.12 and 8.13 show, a new opening of the German economy to financial flows and foreign investment was among its more striking features after Lafontaine's departure.

The most controversial move of the post-Lafontaine SPD-Green government, however, involved labor market reform. Responding to a report from the Federal Audit Court that accused the employment service of falsifying placement rates, Schröder appointed the fifteen-member Hartz Commission, led by Volkswagen's human resources director, Peter Hartz.[262] Two management consultancies—McKinsey and Company and

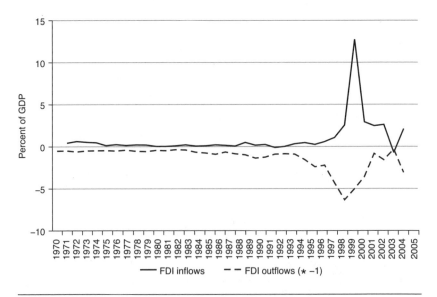

Figure 8.12. Foreign direct investment (FDI) inflows and outflows, (West) Germany, 1970–2005. Data source: World Bank, World Development Indicators (WDI).

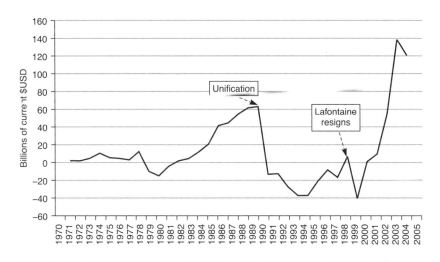

Figure 8.13. (West) German financial balance of payments, 1970–2005. Data source: World Bank, World Development Indicators (WDI).

Roland Berger Strategy Consultants—were leading partners in the Hartz deliberations, marking what one German observer describes as "the apex of [consultancies'] involvement in governmental policy-making."[263]

The commission presented its report in 2002. On the guiding principle of "support and demand," it identified a targeted 50 percent reduction of unemployment in three years. Schröder declared the Hartz reforms top priorities, promising to pass them

> without major compromises pressed for by the social partners, in particular the unions; his own party, the Social Democrats; or his smaller coalition party, the Greens.[264]

In early 2003 the thirty-five-member "pro-reform" Netzwerk group of young parliamentary SPD members—affiliated with the new, internationalized field of progressive expertise tracked in Chapter 6, and led by Hubertus Heil (a founder)—argued that elections should be read as a referendum on whether Schröder was modernizing quickly enough.[265]

After the 2002 Bundestag elections the Hartz I–IV laws passed. The most controversial element was Hartz IV, which took effect in January 2005. Hartz IV restricted social insurance benefits to the short-term unemployed and offered the long-term unemployed only basic assistance. "[A] number of smaller policy measures were introduced to increase labour market participation by 'making work pay' and activating jobseekers through job search and a take-up requirement with respect to jobs offered."[266] At least "100,000 people protested on the streets for several consecutive weeks" after Hartz IV, especially in eastern German cities.[267]

Agenda 2010 gave rise to what one observer of the German scene dubbed the "battle of the economists." Those against the initiative included Albrecht Müller, who "published a bestseller calling much of the reasoning and justifications for the Berlin government reform moves 'falsities,' 'lies,' 'myths,' and 'legends' that will ruin Germany."[268] Bofinger, a high-profile dissenting voice in the SVR, joined Müller's protest. The SVR, meanwhile, had become a very public economistic battleground, noted for "entertaining the country recently with some very public mudslinging."[269]

This "battle of economists" had its parallel in a pattern of disintegration on the left that is by now familiar. Controversies in the wake of Agenda 2010 prompted union-sympathetic SPD members to defect and form the Electoral Alternative for Labor and Social Justice (Arbeit und soziale Gerechtigkeit—Die Wahlalternative, or WASG). In 2007 WASG merged with the Party of Democratic Socialism (Partei des Demokratischen Sozialismus, or PDS), a leftover from East Germany, to create Die Linke—headed by Oskar Lafontaine. By 2008 Die Linke was the third-largest political party in unified Germany, popular with working-class voters who were once regarded as the SPD's natural constituency. Meanwhile, SPD programmatic debates—culminating in the adoption of the Hamburg Programme—drew on a variety of expert sources (the FES, the WZB, the Bertelsmann Foundation, and two management consultancies).[270]

CONCLUSIONS

The paths to leftism's second reinvention analyzed in this chapter have clear parallels, and yet each tells us something important about its unfolding. Common threads include the importance of cross-field effects, in which economics' politicization shaped intraparty dynamics, and *vice*

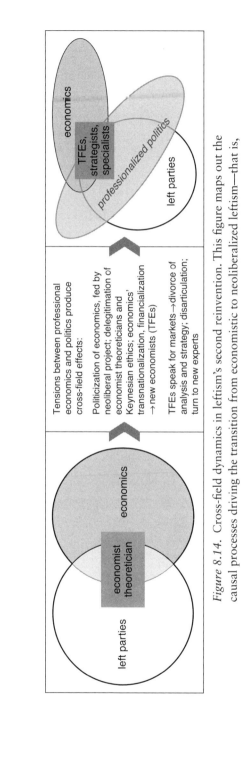

Figure 8.14. Cross-field dynamics in leftism's second reinvention. This figure maps out the causal processes driving the transition from economistic to neoliberalized leftism—that is, "reinvention #2" in Chapter 1, Figure 1.1.

versa; the relationship between politicization and the demise of the economist theoretician; the rise of more market-centric economics and economists and, in its wake, a turn to strategic expertise; and the centrality of academically untethered policy specialists, progressive think tanks, strategists, and private consultants in leftism's late-century programmatic formulations. These broad dynamics, found also in the case of the U.S. Democratic Party, are depicted in Figure 8.14.

Leftism's cross-national neoliberalization also, of course, had temporal, historical, and causal specificities. The SAP's reinvention showcases the importance of economics–left party interdependence, and of resultant cross-field effects, as drivers of leftism's neoliberalization, and a striking connection between SAP intraparty struggles and the globalization of the economics profession in the later twentieth century. Labour's reinvention draws one's attention to the centrality of intraparty factionalism, through which economist theoreticians' influence was heavily mediated, and stands out as a key point through which American New Democrats arrived on the European scene. The SPD's neoliberalization, meanwhile, showcases the significance of the Europeanization of monetary policy authority and, along with it, professional economic knowledge. The end result, in all cases, was a striking reinvention of Western European leftism that was remarkable not only for its market-centrism, but also center-left elites' embrace of a "progressive" moniker that bore the imprint of American Democratic politics—that is, a politics with no grounding in the distinctive histories of ideological mass parties of the left, and that has always avoided the taint of socialism.

CHAPTER NINE

Conclusions and Implications

> [O]ver the last few years the conviction that . . . the role of politics is merely to implement economic imperatives has become widespread. There has really been a loss of political vision in general. It is clear that the Left has suffered more as a result.
>
> —Massimo D'Alema, 2002

> [O]ne of the most striking features of modern politics is the almost complete absence of organisations representing the relatively poor. . . . Less social mobility, a more closed political elite, and a more detached and anti-political "demos," wasn't quite what we had in mind.
>
> —Geoff Mulgan, 2013

T HIS BOOK OFFERS A PARTY-CENTERED, refraction analysis of Western leftism's twentieth-century reinventions. Because language is the currency of politics—and the language of parties is, in itself, an act of representation—my analysis centers on cross-national shifts in left parties' programmatic rhetoric. Along the way, I inevitably delve into the relation between what parties say and what they do—that is, the extent to which programmatic language can be traced, also, in the policy-making activities of parties-in-government. But the *ways parties speak* remain the central object of explanation. From a sociology of knowledge perspective, this concern necessarily raises another: *who speaks for parties.*

I identify at least two significant shifts in the language and spokespersons of leftism over the course of the twentieth century. In the first shift, left parties that once spoke in a decidedly Marxist-socialist idiom began to ground their message, instead, in the technical language of modern economics. Conflicts between capital and labor transitioned into a rhetoric of technical economic management, balances between wages and prices, and trade-offs between inflation and unemployment. In the era of economistic leftism the primary aim of economic government was on the "demand side": full employment. The American Democratic Party's shift here was, in a sense, especially profound: not only did it embrace the language of economistic leftism, but it also *became left* in the process.

My formulation of economistic leftism as a phenomenon that is not different in kind from its socialist counterpart breaks with one of the major accounts of left party rhetoric at midcentury: the "end of ideology" thesis. This thesis only works if one first defines Marxist socialism, but *not* neoclassical Keynesian economics, as "ideology"—a move for which there is no consistent historical rationale. The end of ideology story overlooks the fact that economistic leftism, just like its socialist predecessor, had definite organizational, professional, and theoretical bases; it, too, was produced by socially situated, historical persons, and as such it expressed the way certain people viewed the world. Many of those people, as I have shown, were not only technical economists; they were also left party experts. By extension, the end of ideology thesis misses a deep set of institutional changes that made economistic leftism possible: novel organizational and professional intersections between mainstream economics and mainstream left parties.

The making of this new professional intersection had various historical drivers across countries—for instance, wartime demands were especially important in the American and British cases, but not in Sweden or Germany (where the SPD was temporarily ruled out of existence). Cross-nationally, however, new interconnections between left parties and professional economics had a shared, international driver: interfield tensions between political and economic forces that were built into the gold standard order.

Here it is perhaps worth a pause to consider the Polanyian, historical political economy–grounded element of my argument. In his famous work *The Great Transformation* Polanyi describes a situation in which, thanks to the construction of the gold standard and political efforts to prop it up at all costs, market society presented itself as an alternative to, rather than a means of, human existence.[1] The background to this, suggested but not made explicit in Polanyi's analysis, is the forward march of democratization. By the 1920s the "fount and matrix" of both domestic and international political-economic life was "the self-regulating market"—but the self-regulating market, grounded in the peaceable profit-seeking of *haute finance,* was "a stark utopia" that threatened human existence. As humans will do, especially if they have democratic rights, they took "measures to protect" themselves—but these efforts "impaired the self-regulation of the market, disorganized industrial life, and thus endangered society in yet another way."[2]

This situation, in which democratically untethered, transnational, finance-dominated markets or human societies, but not both, can be saved, is a *Polanyian moment.* In my analysis, between the 1920s and the 1940s left parties became crucibles in which the tension between democratic demands and the advancement of a market order came to a head. The reason for this had to do with left parties' particular position: unlike other sorts of parties, they were at once representatives of poor and working-class groups, newly legitimated political organizations, and viable as parties of government. Left parties, in other words, had gained access to the authority of the state—which centers partly, as Weber tells us, on force and extraction, but is also an authority to define, to decide what is true, and to put that understanding into legislative, classificatory, and regulatory action. And so left parties were at the center of a sort of maelstrom, a perfect storm, in which the truth of the moment was at once highly contested, some of the most restive democratic demands centered inside parties of the left, and those same parties had access to the levers of state power, including its powers over the adjudication of economic truths.

Left parties, and not only states, thus became important sites of struggle and sources of political demand for economic knowledge. There were other sources of demand, too—especially that which came directly from state agencies and administrative arms, given a major push by the advent of wartime. However, while state-driven demand for economists and the means of economic calculation helps to explain why economics and administrative states became deeply intermingled in the postwar period, it does not explain why left parties and professional economics, which were at best weakly connected (if not openly hostile) prior to the 1930s, developed a deep interdependence after the 1930s.

Indeed, my analysis shows that left parties and professional economics were, across the board, deeply interdependent by the 1950s and
1960s. To account for this I trace the processes by which, in Western
Europe, left parties in the 1920s and 1930s generated new demands for
economic expertise in order to resolve their Polanyian troubles, but incumbent party experts—socialist theoreticians—preempted the efforts
of young economists to achieve a break with orthodox economic understandings. At the same time, the rise of a Polanyian moment also
drove intergenerational struggles in professional economics, partly
because it focused the attention of young economists-in-training on
problems of unemployment and labor unrest. Some of these young
economists achieved a foothold in the junior ranks of left parties'
university-educated elites and, from that position, proceeded to facilitate
the recruitment and promotion of other academically trained economists
into left party networks. In the United States the story is different—
there were no socialist theoreticians, and so there is no story of preemption—but the recruitment and promotion dynamic was similar. What
stands out in the American case is how, in the absence of strong, centralized parties, those very recruitment networks engaged in a kind of
organizational bootstrapping by forging new intermediary institutions
in between the Democratic Party and the economics profession.

What one finds, then, by the 1960s is a new set of left party–expert
relations, grounded in close ties between professional economics and
left parties, to which a distinctive kind of professional is indigenous: the
hybrid figure of the economist theoretician. I delve into the position and
perspective of the economist theoretician in Chapter 6 and highlight the
(stark) contrast between his managerial, discretionary, Keynesian professional ethics and the rule-centered, anti-discretionary ethic of the
neoliberal. I highlight the views of Milton Friedman as an ideal-typical
bearer of neoliberal ethics, but note that a similar ethic underpinned
other formulations of new classical economic thinking in the 1970s. According to the neoliberal ethic, the economist-in-politics' job is not to
manage the economy or facilitate political discretion therein, but rather
to speak on behalf of the market, insulate it from political interference,
and push back the frontier of politics by expanding the market's reach.

It is here, in the move from economistic to neoliberalized leftism, that
the neoliberal project enters into the story of leftism's second reinven-

tion. By "neoliberal project" I mean something much more specific than neoliberal*ism* writ large: I do not mean policies or broad processes of deregulation and liberalization; rather, I mean a historically specific project of intellectuals that, with a healthy dose of business support, developed into an expansive network of economists and economics departments, law schools and legal organizations, business-funded informational and financial clearinghouses, and free market think tanks. Key activities within the neoliberal project centered on the formulation of new economic, scientific, and moral argumentation and a highly specific policy repertoire: central bank independence, privatization of public and national industries, eliminating government regulations, insulating regulatory institutions from political intervention, introducing competitive mechanisms and profit-seeking incentives into public institutions, and liberalizing international trade in goods and capital. They also centered on creating new institutional bridges into public and political life—in particular, they created new professional pathways in between the cultural terrain of the neoliberal project, governing institutions, and parties of the center-right. The neoliberal project essentially extended, over time, into a whole new, transnational cultural terrain that was home to bearers of neoliberal ethics, and that extended deeply into the economics profession.

The neoliberal project was not particularly important for the development of left party–expert relations in a direct sense, but it was *indirectly* very important indeed. Here one should take special note that interdependence between left parties and professional economics at midcentury was, in the larger scheme of things, a historical novelty. Goings-on in professional economics only matter for left parties, or indeed for any parties, if there are preexisting networks of relations that link party politics with economics professions. The making of such linkages between left parties and professional economics was a specific historical achievement, not an inevitable state of affairs.

The key argument here is that the neoliberal project was a "push" in a broader professional transformation in economics that fed into the formation of new kinds of economists bearing neoliberal ethics during a time in which economists *had become deeply imbricated with left party elite networks*. But the prestige-seeking activities of economists on the basis of truth claims are not, in the end, reconcilable with the

partisan and power-seeking dynamics of party competition. Here my
claim is that left party-economics interdependence made possible, in
turn, a new sort of interfield tension: if leftism's first reinvention was
driven by tensions between the political (democratic) and economic
fields, its second reinvention was grounded in tensions between the
political (parties) and cultural fields (professional economics). These
tensions were important precisely because they made possible *cross-
field effects.*

One cross-field effect extended from politics into economics: the politicization of economics. Founding initiatives of the neoliberal project—the MPS, the remaking of Chicago economics into the "Chicago
school,", the transnational effort to build free market think tanks—were
grounded in the initiators' recognition that mainstream economics was
implicitly an economics of the left. As we have seen, this recognition had
a certain practical truth: mainstream, midcentury Keynesian economics
was, indeed, a center-left-oriented, and connected, discipline. The politicization of economics—which involved the politicization of economic
advisory institutions-in-government and the building of new alliances
between neoliberal economists and parties of the center-right—can be
read, in part, as an *effect* of this recognition. The neoliberal project
fed into a new era of intergenerational change in the profession, laying
the scientific groundwork for the discrediting of the economist theoretician, offering new symbolic resources to center-left economist theoretician, professional opponents, and orienting younger-generation
economists toward new concerns (in particular, business and finance).
A key result was an intergenerational, professional shift toward neoliberal ethics.

These processes were shaped by political and economic instability,
inflation, and the decline of Bretton Woods arrangements in the 1960s
and 1970s—but they were not determined by them. Economic uncer-
tainties fed into both intraparty struggles and the development of
professional economics in the sense that they kicked off, yet again, new
interpretive struggles, partly because economic trouble called into question the authority of dominant party elites—including economist theoreticians who were, by then, among left parties' most important
experts, and who were losing the unquestioned backing of their colleagues in the academic side of the economics profession.

In another cross-field dynamic, extending from economics into politics, economics' intraprofessional struggles generated new scientific argumentation, and new sorts of economists, that could be mobilized in political struggles. Economic argumentation, and economists porting it, played particularly central roles in intraparty contestation in Sweden, between the SAP's autonomy-seeking central bank economists and office-seeking elected party elites—a fact that is unsurprising given the oft-noted "economist-intensive" history of Swedish politics. One also finds competitions between different sorts of economists featuring prominently in interparty contestation between left and right parties—a particularly notable dynamic in the United States and the United Kingdom. In the United Kingdom, for instance, we saw how Thatcher's exclusion and public rejection of British Keynesian academics fed back into economics' formation, reinforcing a disciplinary turn toward business and finance.

These processes were also shaped, of course, by demographic and electoral change—including, in particular, the rise of civil rights and new left youth movements, which deepened intraparty struggles over programmatic control and prompted new efforts by party elites to manage or exclude newly rebellious factions. But one of the more remarkable facets of intraparty contestation of the left, by the time we get to the 1980s and 1990s, is the extent to which professional economists' roles were *circumscribed*: economist theoreticians had once been left parties' highest-profile party experts, blending their skills as economists with political and strategic sensibilities, but the TFE's domain was the market. For TFEs, problems of political strategy and nonmarket policy domains were in the jurisdiction of new strategic experts and policy specialists. This pattern is perhaps most striking in Sweden, where the rise of the TFE was followed with a marked decline of economists in Swedish political life and the rise, in their place, of strategic experts—consultants, public relations specialists, and "spin doctors," some borrowed from the United States.

Last but not least, leftism's neoliberalization, especially in Western Europe, was tied to a fracture of the party-union relationship—but, arguably, this fracture was as much an *effect* as it was a cause of the rise of neoliberalized leftism. The reprioritization of low inflation over low unemployment happened either during neoliberalized left parties-in-government or, if it happened under neoconservative parties-in-government, it was then kept in place by left party administrations. The same can be argued regarding economic globalization, particularly of a financial sort: the return of *haute finance* (to use Polanyi's term) took off most dramatically after, and not before, parties bearing neoliberalized leftism took office.

TWO PROPOSITIONS AND THE PROBLEMATIC
OF THE SOCIOLOGY OF PARTIES

This book is, to my knowledge, the only existing work in historical sociology that treats the transformations of Western leftism as its central puzzle. There are vast literatures on socialism, Keynesianism, neoliberalism, political parties, and left parties, especially in history and historical political science. I draw heavily on these literatures, but the problematic that drives this book is a specifically sociological one, grounded in two theoretical propositions.

A first proposition is that language is an indicator of the social position, or perspective, of its producers—and the language of parties is no exception to this rule. This has definite methodological implications: a sociological approach to the study of party politics should treat changes in language as important phenomena in themselves, but attending to language alone is never enough. Language is a window into the social situation, proximate concerns, and perspectives of its producers—and so, if we are to understand language, we need to consider those situations and perspectives.

A second proposition is that historical change is grounded in the formation, development, and tension-ridden interrelations between meso-level social orders, or social fields. This can be read as something like a general, working hypothesis: the making and interrelations of fields, including cross-field effects that interfield connections make possible, are among the most important drivers of social transformations.

By grounding this whole inquiry in these two sociological propositions, I hope to contribute to an ongoing reestablishment, reworking, and resuscitation of a once lively sociological scholarship on political parties and the dynamics of party representation. Central to this effort is a third proposition, of sorts: that the key problematic, or concern, of the historical social science of parties, party politics, and party-political institutional orders should be representation—as opposed to policies, votes and elections, demographics, or ideas—and, within that general concern, parties' *capacity to intermediate.*

IMPLICATIONS: THE CAPACITY TO INTERMEDIATE

In the introductory chapter I suggested that the sociology of parties should resuscitate Mannheimian concerns with the connection between party-political life and knowledge production. Drawing from current arguments that the sociology of knowledge should concern itself with how experts acquire "the capacity to make a public intervention," I argued that the sociology of parties should concern itself with party experts' capacity to intermediate.[3]

Here I am working both with and against Antonio Gramsci. Gramsci termed the articulating, intermediary, integrative party expert the "organic intellectual." By "organic," Gramsci meant professional truth-claimers who are grounded *both* in parties *and* in the social groups that parties represent. But the question of whether an intellectual is "organic" or not, inevitably, slips into moral judgments as to which kind of intellectual is the most authentic. To avoid this slippage, I replace the problematic of organicism with a different one: the capacity to intermediate.

In Gramsci's words, the "functions" of the organic intellectual "are precisely organizational and connective."[4] But, while party experts can be conceptualized in terms of their situation in between power-seeking politicians and represented publics, this does not mean that they necessarily perform a "connective" role—that is, that party exertions are necessarily vehicles of the installation of a group-based way of thinking into the operations of government, and thus agents the making or sustenance of hegemonic projects. Anchoring Gramsci's concerns in field-theoretic sensibilities, I have emphasized that this intermediary capacity is not merely a matter of ideas or intentions; it is a matter of the professional and social location of party experts, and the way in which party experts' locations with respect to party networks as well as neighboring institutions—academe and academic professions, constituencies and represented groups, private consultancies, think tanks and foundations, and journalism, among possible others—conditions their worldviews and shapes their professional ethics. By extension, I mean to suggest that party experts, too, are representatives of sorts—and it matters a great deal for whom, or for what, they speak.

We might consider, on the question of capacities to intermediate, the contrast between the economist theoretician and the TFE. In the 1960s the Keynesian economist was part technical engineer, part pragmatic political strategist. He produced knowledge about how to manage something called "the economy," understood as an object to be managed, and then had to work to *translate* that knowledge into something politically workable. He performed the managerial economy by negotiating politics. To do this, the economist theoretician worked through political institutions—that is to say, through parties and partisan networks, not just states. His ability to "fix" the economy, to borrow Timothy Mitchell's phrasing, was contingent on his ability to navigate the political field.[5] But the TFE spoke on behalf of an object that operated beyond economists, parties, and domestic politics: the market. The market has no territoriality and no constituencies; for the TFE, it was beyond the reach of government or political power. Insofar as the TFE sees things in this way, he or she "performs" a very different economic phenomenon—one that politics serves, but cannot manage in the interests of publics. The TFE does not see the workings of the market as somehow contingent on his or her own ability to navigate politics, to be "politically sensitive." For spokespeople of markets, there is only the question of whether politics works such that markets can be free.

And so, on the question of capacities to intermediate, my claim is quite simple: economist theoreticians, not only because of the specific knowledge and skills they possessed but also because of their managerial and discretionary Keynesian ethic, had a relatively high capacity for intermediation. The key to intermediation, in this way of thinking, is an ability to marry knowledge production and scientific analysis to matters of political and electoral strategy. Manifestly, the TFE did not do this—a neoliberal ethic, in fact, opposes this kind of marriage on principle. Nor does a strategic specialist, specialized in knowledge production for the sake of winning, fit the bill.

But the capacity for intermediation is not a matter of decision; it is made possible by circumstances that are beyond the control of any particular party expert. Gramsci understood this: for him, saying that parties, via intellectuals, are vehicles of hegemony is not to say that either has perfect control over the political game, governments, or indeed the conditions of their own existence. This is in the nature of a "war of position": "The truth is that one cannot choose the form of war one wants. . . . A war of position is not, in reality, constituted simply by actual trenches, but by the whole organizational and industrial system of the territory which lies to the back of the army in the field."[6] Gramsci's contention was simply that there is a relationship between the organicism of experts and their ability to function as intermediaries and articulators. But not all experts can be intermediaries; the conditions of their own existence are not up to them.

How can we generalize this into a new way of thinking about how parties work and the conditions under which they are able to bring together the distinctive tasks of power-seeking, representation, and truth-seeking? I would suggest that, in place of Gramsci's concept of organicism, we rethink party experts in terms of their centrifugal versus centripetal tendencies—that is, whether they see the world, and especially the economic world, in a way that can bridge the divide between represented groups and party elites, or not. The new experts who drove the making of third way leftism—strategists speaking for "what wins," policy specialists for "what works," and TFEs for markets—seem to have been the latter, not the former. The question, in the current Polanyian moment, is whether today's profound conflicts will give rise to new party experts with the intermediary capacity to return voice to the voiceless.

Methodological Appendix

I. GENERAL NOTES

The central primary data mobilized in this book are biographical and autobiographical, drawn from professional CVs and biographies, online databases, obituaries, published remembrances, handbooks, historical biographies, memoirs, autobiographies, reference handbooks, third-party interviews and oral histories. A great deal of archival work was conducted online, using digital repositories. All primary sources are documented in notes to tables and figures, in endnotes, and in a separate section of the bibliography. The analysis of the 1980s to 1990s is also informed by informal conversations with academics and professionals who are, or have been, linked with third way circles, some of whom are personal and professional contacts. I offer further detail on digital repositories and on personal and professional contacts in Section II, below.

I also make use of various organizational, political, and macroeconomic datasets—some produced by others, some I constructed myself. The dataset on party programs that is used for the analysis in Chapter 2, and my uses thereof, are described in this Appendix (Section III, below). This book also mobilizes multiple self-built organizational datasets, some of which I detail here. These include, but are not limited to, a Historical Parties Dataset (HPD); a dataset of Atlas network, or free market, organizations; a dataset of progressive or center-left organizations; and a dataset of all historical members of the American Council of Economic Advisers (CEA) between 1946 and 2001. Information on the last three datasets, used in Chapters 6 and 7, are provided in this Appendix (Section IV).

II. ARCHIVAL AND OTHER SOURCES

In the course of research for this book I visited several archives in person, including the archives of the European University Institute (EUI), the London School of Economics (LSE), and the Progressive Policy Institute (PPI). But most archival sources were accessed on-line. These include the archives of the Jimmy Carter, Harry S. Truman, John F. Kennedy, and William J. Clinton presidential libraries; the Hoover Institution Library and Archives at Stanford University's the Stanford Historical Society; the Presidential Oral History Program of the Miller Center at the University of Virginia; the Bancroft Library at the University of California, Berkeley; the Friedrich Ebert Stiftung (FES) archives; German History in Documents and Images (GHDI); the German Social Democratic Party (SPD); the House of Commons Hansard Archive; the Swedish National Data Service (Svensk Nationell Datatjänst); the American Presidency Project at the University of California, Santa Barbara; the Marxists Internet Archive; and others (see the Bibliography for a full listing). The recent development of an extraordinary range of online archival resources thus made this book possible.

This book does not use formal interviews, but it is informed by a series of conversations between 2010 and 2017 with figures connected to national and transnational center-left politics. Uniquely helpful here were conversations with various figures at the Progressive Policy Institute (PPI), the (former) Democratic Leadership Council (DLC), and the Center for American Progress (CAP) in Washington, D.C. I have also spoken with various figures, especially journalists, involved in efforts to revamp American Democratic liberalism in the 1980s (who called themselves "neoliberals," and were first brought together by the charismatic *Washington Monthly* founding editor, Charles Peters), as well as contacts at the Policy Network in London, the Foundation for European Progressive Studies (FEPS) in Brussels, and Das Progressive Zentrum in Berlin. Between 2012 and 2014 I also attended several small and mainly public events, primarily in London, and usually sponsored by the Policy Network; between 2014 and 2017 I sporadically engaged in further conversations with knowledgeable contacts in Western Europe. I reference some of these conversations in Chapters 7 and 8, using the following shorthand:

- Democratic neoliberals 2013 (figures linked to the Washington Monthly)
- New Democrats 2010–2013 (figures linked to the DLC and the PPI)
- Third Wayers 2013–2017 (figures linked to British, European, and German center-left parties, especially progressive and third way organizations)

Last but not least, I make use of conference and event documentation related to a series of progressive governance meetings in the third way years, kindly provided to me by a Third Wayer. These conversations, experiences, and resources have informed my analysis of leftism's second reinvention, and I am very thankful for them.

III. PARTY PROGRAMS: THE NEOLIBERALISM INDEX (CHAPTER 2)

This analysis was first developed in an article published in 2011 in *Social Science History*.[1] The explanation to follow draws from that article.

I developed the neoliberalism index using the *Mapping Policy Preferences I* and *II* datasets, which is to my knowledge the most complete set of indicators on parties' policy positions available.[2] Spanning fifty-one countries (twenty-six OECD countries, twenty-four Central and Eastern Europe countries, and Israel—which joined the OECD in 2007), the dataset includes indicators of parties' positions in 113 policy categories based on a content analysis of election programs (manifestos) and declarations in parliamentary or congressional debate before a vote of confidence or investiture. The coding unit is the quasi-sentence, defined as "the verbal expression of one political idea or issue."[3] Each *Policy Preferences* variable represents the percent of quasi-sentences falling into a particular category relative to all quasi-sentences in the program or declaration.[4] Data on OECD countries span the entire postwar period, or for as long as countries have been democratic systems.

Since my focus is on Western democracies, I exclude Central and Eastern European (CEE) countries, Turkey, Japan, and Israel. I also exclude Cyprus and Malta because neither is included in the dataset until the late 1990s, leaving twenty-two countries in total. Focusing on parties of the center[5]—that is, excluding Green, communist, and Marxist parties on the left;[6] nationalist and anti-immigration parties on the right; and special interest or single-issue parties—I consider general trends across these twenty-two countries across the left-right divide and across political-cultural regimes.[7] Southern and Mediterranean European countries are included (Greece, Spain, Portugal, and Italy), but only Italy is accounted for before the 1970s since it is the only one of the four that has been a democratic system for the entire postwar period.[8] This means that, prior to the mid-1970s, trends for Southern European countries are only for Italy and then pick up the other three countries from 1975 forward.[9]

A listing of the twenty-two OECD countries and regime categorizations is provided in Table A.1.

Table A.1 Twenty-two OECD countries by regime

Nordic	Denmark	Southern	Greece
	Finland		Italy
	Iceland		Portugal
	Norway		Spain
	Sweden	Anglo and Liberal	Australia
Continental	Austria		Canada
	Belgium		Ireland
	France		New Zealand
	Germany		Switzerland
	Luxembourg		United Kingdom
	Netherlands		United States

I track neoliberal politics using a composite index that accounts for three sorts of shifts in emphasis in party programs: toward opportunity (education and training), law and order, and militarism rather than welfare state protections and pacifism (which appears in tables and graphs under the label "order and commodify"); toward efficiency, decentralization, free market orthodoxy, productivity, and trade openness rather than Keynesianism, regulation, national ownership, and protectionism (labeled "*laissez-faire*"); and toward financial, professional, and white-collar constituencies rather than "old" constituencies such as the working classes, labor, and trade unions (labeled "white collar and finance"). I understand these as indicators of parties' positions as to (A) the responsibilities of the state; (B) by what means the state should fulfill those responsibilities; and (C) in whose interests the state should govern (see Table A.2).

More specifically, the three components of the neoliberalism index (A, B, and C) track party positions on the following issues:

A: What are the responsibilities of the state toward its citizens?
A neoliberal notion of the responsibilities of the state toward its citizens prioritizes human capital investments, meritocracy, and labor market participation over protective welfarism: valuing opportunity in the form of education and training over social protection, favoring means-targeted rather than universal forms of assistance, and treating the unemployed punitively should they prove difficult or impossible to push into the labor market. Seven variables make up component A: I subtract emphases on welfare state expansion and peace from emphases on education expansion, welfare state limitation, law and order, and militarism.

B: By what means should the state fulfill its responsibilities?
A neoliberal conception of how the state should govern centers on the construction and preservation of market-like environments, in which private individuals make decisions according to an economically rational self-interest. To this end, property must have strong legal protections; economic exchange must be freed from political control via privatization; trade is liberalized; domestic markets are deregulated; and economic

Table A.2 The political neoliberalism index

Major category		Variable #	Variable description
A. State responsibility	Plus	505	Positive—welfare state limitation
(in graphs: "order and commodify")		506	Positive—education expansion
		104	Positive—military
		605	Law and order
	Minus	504	Welfare state expansion
		105	Negative—military
		106	Peace
B. Locus of authority	Plus	301	Positive—decentralization
(in graphs: "*laissez-faire*")		303	Government and administrative efficiency
		407	Negative—protectionism
		410	Positive—productivity
		414	Positive—economic orthodoxy
	Minus	302	Positive—centralization
		403	Positive—market regulation
		404	Positive—economic planning
		406	Positive—protectionism
		412	Positive—controlled economy
		413	Positive—nationalization
C. Focal constituencies	Plus	401	Positive—free enterprise
(in graphs: "white collar and finance")		702	Negative—labor
		502	Culture and leisure
		704	Middle class and professionals
	Minus	405	Corporatism
		701	Positive—labor

and monetary policy-making is depoliticized. Monetary policy is a priority domain and is centered on controlling inflation—a substitute for Keynesian-style demand management. Accordingly, this component draws on eleven variables dealing with parties' positions on economic issues. Emphases on efficiency and decentralization, economic orthodoxy, and productivity are counted positively; emphases on centralization, protectionism, planning, and Keynesian demand management are counted negatively.

C: Whose interests should the state serve?

Finally, political neoliberalism prioritizes business, finance, and white-collar professionals rather than trade unions, blue-collar working classes, or the poor and unemployed as part of a broader recasting of proper citizens as workers, consumers, and investors. This component uses six variables that deal with constituencies: enterprise, labor and trade unions, and middle-class professionals. I subtract emphases on labor, corporatism, and unions from those on free enterprise, leisure, and professionals.

The final index is a simple sum of categories A, B, and C. Each variable is counted equally. When a party's score is positive its emphases are more consistent with neoliberal priorities; when it is negative, the party's emphases are less consistent with neoliberal priorities. The result is a straightforward measure defined according to the theoretically anchored conception of political neoliberalism: a politics consisting of *laissez-faire*, antiwelfarist, consumer- and business-oriented, and (ironically) antipolitical, antibureaucratic emphases.[10] Though the index provides only an approximation of neoliberalism as a political thing, each component marks out emphases that are antithetical to the left themes of the "golden age" politics of the early postwar period: full employment via demand management and corporatist institutions, limitations on economic inequalities via redistribution and progressive taxation, pro-union and pro-labor appeals, and protective, decommodifying public benefits and social services provided on a citizenship basis. Descriptive statistics for all variables used are given in Table A.3.

Table A.3   Descriptive statistics (obs = party / year)—center parties only

Variable	Obs	Mean	Standard Deviation	Minimum	Maximum
Country	1,305	32.6	17.4	11.0	64.0
Party	1,305	33,050.3	17,439.9	11,320.0	64,620.0
Year	1,305	1,975.7	16.6	1,945.0	2,005.0
Fiveyear (1 = 1945–1949, . . . , 12 = 2000–2004)	1305	6.7	3.3	1.0	12.0
Regime	1,305	2.5	1.2	1.0	4.0
Center-left / right (1 = center-left)	1,305	1.6	0.5	1.0	2.0
Neoliberalism index	1,305	4.6	20.9	−75.3	75.0
Category A: commodify	1,305	−0.6	8.5	−58.3	32.0
Category B: *laissez-faire*	1,305	1.7	13.3	−72.2	52.0
Category C: white collar and finance	1,305	3.4	7.3	−24.0	70.3

IV. ORGANIZATIONAL AND OTHER DATASETS: ATLAS, FRASER, POLICY NETWORK, CEA

Three self-built datasets are the basis of the analysis of free market and progressive network organizations found in Chapter 6, and they inform the analysis of the economics-politics relationship in Chapter 7.

First, a dataset of free market think tanks affiliated with the Atlas Foundation and with the Fraser Institute was built using data from:

(1) an online Atlas Foundation directory: http://www.atlasusa.org /V2/main/acc.php, accessed between April and November 2008. The same database, it would appear, can now be found here: http://www .atlasnetwork.org/partners. At the time of data collection, a search of Atlas's global directory returned 513 organizations, for which I was able to find information on city and founding year for 464 (and 403 by the end of 2004). A full listing of all Atlas organizations in the four countries included in the present analysis is provided in Table A.4.

Table A.4   Atlas organizations in (West) Germany, Sweden, the United
Kingdom, and the United States, 2008 (listed by country and founding date)

(West) Germany	Walter Eucken Institute	Freiburg	1954
	Friedrich-Naumann-Stiftung (FDP)	Potsdam	1958
	Friedrich-August-von-Hayek-Gesellschaft E.V.	Berlin	1998
	Institute for Free Enterprise/Institut für Unternehmerische Freiheit	Berlin	1998
	Council on Public Policy, University of Bayreuth	Bayreuth	2001
	Center for European Policy	Freiburg i. Br.	2006
Sweden	Timbro	Stockholm	1978
	Eudoxa AB	Stockholm	2000
	Ratio Institute	Stockholm	2002
	Captus	Malmö	2005
United Kingdom	Institute of Economic Affairs	London	1955
	Libertarian Alliance	London	1967
	Adam Smith Institute	London	1977
	Social Affairs Unit	London	1980
	Centre for Research into Post-Communist Economies	London	1983
	David Hume Institute	Edinburgh	1985
	Social Market Foundation	Westminster	1989
	Bruges Group	London	1989
	Stockholm Network	London	1997
	Policy Institute	Edinburgh	1999
	Civitas: Institute for the Study of Civil Society	Westminster	2000
	International Policy Network	London	2001
	E. G. West Centre	Newcastle upon Tyne	2002
	Policy Exchange	London	2002
	Reform	London	2002
	Young Britons Foundation	London	2003

(continued)

Table A.4   (continued)

	Liberal Bangla	Cirencester	2004
	Project Empowerment	London	2004
	TaxPayers' Alliance	London	2004
	Venezie Institute	South Kensington	2005
	Freedom Alliance	London	2006
	Malaysia Think Tank London	London	2006
United States	American Enterprise Institute	Washington, DC	1943
	Association of American Physicians and Surgeons	Tucson, AZ	1943
	Foundation for Economic Education	Irvington-on-Hudson, NY	1946
	Mont Pèlerin Society	Alexandria, VA	1947
	Liberty Fund	Indianapolis, IN	1960
	Hudson Institute	Washington, DC	1961
	Institute for Humane Studies	Arlington, VA	1961
	American Conservative Union	Alexandria, VA	1964
	Philadelphia Society	Jerome, MI	1964
	Fund for American Studies	Washington, DC	1967
	Heritage Foundation	Washington, DC	1973
	Pacific Legal Foundation	Sacramento, CA	1973
	Rose Institute for State and Local Government	Claremont, CA	1973
	Center for the Defense of Free Enterprise	Bellevue, WA	1976
	Ethics and Public Policy Center	Washington, DC	1976
	Foundation for Teaching Economics	Davis, CA	1976
	Landmark Legal Foundation	Kansas City, MO	1976
	Southeastern Legal Foundation	Atlanta, GA	1976
	Cato Institute	Washington, DC	1977
	Free Congress Foundation	Washington, DC	1977
	Manhattan Institute for Policy Research	New York, NY	1977
	National Journalism Center	Washington, DC	1977

Table A.4 (continued)

Reason Foundation	Los Angeles, CA	1978
Beverly LaHaye Institute	Washington, DC	1979
Claremont Institute	Claremont, CA	1979
Florida TaxWatch	Tallahassee, FL	1979
Golden State Center for Policy Studies	Sacramento, CA	1979
Iran Analytical Report	Washington, DC	1979
Leadership Institute	Arlington, VA	1979
Pacific Research Institute for Public Policy	San Francisco, CA	1979
Property and Environment Research Center	Bozeman, MT	1980
Atlas Economic Research Foundation	Arlington, VA	1981
Ludwig von Mises Institute	Auburn, AL	1981
Federalist Society for Law and Public Policy Studies	Washington, DC	1982
Center for International Private Enterprise	Washington, DC	1983
Maryland Business for Responsive Government	Baltimore, MD	1983
National Center for Policy Analysis	Dallas, TX	1983
Capital Research Center	Washington, DC	1984
Center for Economic and Social Justice	Washington, DC	1984
Competitive Enterprise Institute	Washington, DC	1984
Freedom Works	Washington, DC	1984
Heartland Institute	Chicago, IL	1984
Advocates for Self-Government	Cartersville, GA	1985
Ayn Rand Institute	Irvine, CA	1985
Committee for a Constructive Tomorrow	Washington, DC	1985
Foundation for Research on Economics and the Environment	Bozeman, MT	1985

(continued)

Table A.4   (continued)

Independence Institute	Golden, CO	1985
Americans for Tax Reform Foundation	Washington, DC	1986
California Public Policy Foundation	Camarillo, CA	1986
Independent Institute	Oakland, CA	1986
Institute of Political Economy	Logan, UT	1986
South Carolina Policy Council	Columbia, SC	1986
Congressional Institute	Alexandria, VA	1987
Institute for Policy Innovation	Lewisville, TX	1987
James Madison Institute	Tallahassee, FL	1987
Mackinac Center for Public Policy	Midland, MI	1987
Media Research Center	Alexandria, VA	1987
Yankee Institute for Public Policy Studies	Hartford, CT	1987
Alexis de Tocqueville Institution	Arlington, VA	1988
Center for Security Policy	Washington, DC	1988
Commonwealth Foundation	Harrisburg, PA	1988
Goldwater Institute	Phoenix, AZ	1988
Pioneer Institute for Public Policy Research	Boston, MA	1988
Alabama Policy Institute	Birmingham, AL	1989
Buckeye Institute	Columbus, OH	1989
Center for the New West	Boise, ID	1989
Fully Informed Jury Association	Helena, MT	1989
Future of Freedom Foundation	Fairfax, VA	1989
Institute for Energy Research	Houston, TX	1989
International Society for Individual Liberty	Benicia, CA	1989
John Locke Foundation	Raleigh, NC	1989
Locke Institute	Fairfax, VA	1989
Public Interest Institute	Mt. Pleasant, IA	1989
Texas Public Policy Foundation	Austin, TX	1989

Table A.4   (continued)

Acton Institute for the Study of Religion and Liberty	Grand Rapids, MI	1990
Center of the American Experiment	Minneapolis, MN	1990
Institute of World Politics	Washington, DC	1990
Agencia Interamericana de Prensa Económica	Boca Raton, FL	1991
Beacon Hill Institute for Public Policy Research	Boston, MA	1991
Cascade Policy Institute	Portland, OR	1991
Defenders of Property Rights	Washington, DC	1991
Evergreen Freedom Foundation	Olympia, WA	1991
Georgia Public Policy Foundation	Atlanta, GA	1991
Institute for Justice	Arlington, VA	1991
Philanthropy Roundtable	Washington, DC	1991
Toward Tradition	Mercer Island, WA	1991
Independent Women's Forum	Washington, DC	1992
Science and Environmental Policy Project	Arlington, VA	1992
State Policy Network	Richmond, CA	1992
Becket Fund for Religious Liberty	Washington, DC	1993
Center for Education Reform	Washington, DC	1993
Clare Boothe Luce Policy Institute	Herndon, VA	1993
Ethan Allen Institute	Concord, VT	1993
Josiah Bartlett Center for Public Policy	Concord, NH	1993
Minaret of Freedom Institute	Bethesda, MD	1993
Nevada Policy Research Institute	Las Vegas, NV	1993
Oklahoma Council of Public Affairs Inc.	Oklahoma City, OK	1993
Progress and Freedom Foundation	Washington, DC	1993
American Institute for Full Employment	Klamath Falls, OR	1994
Constitution Society	Austin, TX	1994

(continued)

Table A.4   (continued)

Foundation for Democracy in Africa	Arlington, VA	1994
Sutherland Institute	Salt Lake City, UT	1994
Allegheny Institute for Public Policy	Pittsburgh, PA	1995
American Council of Trustees and Alumni	Washington, DC	1995
Arkansas Policy Foundation	Little Rock, AR	1995
Calvert Institute for Policy Research Inc.	Baltimore, MD	1995
Frontiers of Freedom	Oakton, VA	1995
Galen Institute	Alexandria, VA	1995
Institute for Health Freedom	Washington, DC	1996
Lone Star Foundation and Report	Austin, TX	1996
Milton and Rose D. Friedman Foundation	Indianapolis, IN	1996
Thomas Jefferson Institute for Public Policy	Springfield, VA	1996
Virginia Institute for Public Policy	Gainesville, VA	1996
Washington Policy Center	Seattle, WA	1996
Culture of Life Research and Communication Institute	Washington, DC	1997
Flint Hills Center for Public Policy (formerly Kansas Public Policy Institute)	Wichita, KS	1997
Howard Center	Rockford, Il	1997
New Citizenship Project	Washington, DC	1997
Shamie Center for Better Government	Boston, MA	1997
Citizens' Council on Health Care	St. Paul, MN	1998
Hispanic American Center for Economic Research	Washington, DC	1998
Initiative and Referendum Institute	Washington, DC	1998
Islamic Free Market Institute Foundation	Washington, DC	1998
Mercatus Center	Arlington, VA	1998
America's Future Foundation	Washington, DC	1999

Table A.4   (continued)

Center for the Study of Islam and Democracy	Washington, DC	1999
Committee for Monetary Research and Education	Charlotte, NC	1999
DonorsTrust	Alexandria, VA	1999
Faith and Reason Institute	Washington, DC	1999
Foundation for Individual Rights in Education	Philadelphia, PA	1999
Great Plains Public Policy Institute	Sioux Falls, SD	1999
Center for Cognitive Liberty and Ethics	Davis, CA	2000
Rio Grande Foundation	Albuquerque, NM	2000
Bureaucrash	Washington, DC	2001
Grassroot Institute of Hawaii Inc.	Honolulu, HI	2001
LibForAll Foundation	Winston-Salem, NC	2001
Maine Public Policy Institute	Bangor, ME	2001
Maryland Public Policy Institute	Germantown, MD	2001
Center for Policy Research of New Jersey	Bloomsbury, NJ	2002
Education Advancement Fund International	Honolulu, HI	2002
Illinois Policy Institute	Springfield, IL	2002
Maine Heritage Policy Center	Portland, ME	2002
Bluegrass Institute for Public Policy Solutions	Bowling Green, KY	2003
Prometheus Institute	New York. NY	2003
Wynnewood Institute	Wynnewood, PA	2003
Language of Liberty Institute	Prescott Valley, AZ	2004
Sagamore Institute for Policy Research	Indianapolis, IN	2004
Tennessee Center for Policy Research	Nashville, TN	2004
Center for Competitive Politics	Arlington, VA	2005
Center for Vision and Values	Grove City, PA	2005
Consumers for Health Care Choices	Hagerstown, MD	2005

(continued)

Table A.4   (continued)

Human Rights Foundation	New York, NY	2005
Institute for Trade Standards and Sustainable Development	Princeton, NJ	2005
Show-Me Institute for Public Policy	St. Louis, MO	2005
Center for Political Economy and Study of American Constitutionalism	Memphis, TN	2006
Openworld Institute	Washington DC	2006
San Diego Institute for Policy Research	San Diego, CA	2006
South Florida Freedom Initiative	Miami, FL	2006
Public Policy Foundation of West Virginia	Morgantown, WV	2006
Sam Adams Alliance and Foundation	Chicago, IL	2006
Just Facts	Florham Park, NJ	2007
Oregon Better Government Project	Tualatin, OR	2007
Platte Institute for Economic Research	Omaha, NE	2007
Alliance for School Choice	Washington, DC	.
Center for the Study of Carbon and Energy Markets	Burke, VA	.
Cuba Archive Project	Summit, NJ	.
Discovery Institute	Seattle, WA	.
Free to Choose Media	Erie, PA	.
Innovations for Poverty Action	New Haven, CT	.
Leaders for Liberty Institute	Williamsburg, VA	.
Mississippi Center for Public Policy	Jackson, MS	.
National Institute for Labor Relations Research	Springfield, VA	.
Free State Foundation	Potomac, MD	.
Matthew Ryan Project for the Study of Free Institutions and the Public Good	Villanova, PA	.
Wisconsin Policy Research Institute	Thiensville, WI	.
Young America's Foundation	Herndon, VA	.

Table A.5   Data sources on the CEA and its membership, 1946–2001

General Resources:

Naveh, David. "The Political Role of Academic Advisers: The Case of the U.S. President's Council of Economic Advisers, 1946–1976." *Presidential Studies Quarterly* 11, 4 (Fall 1981): 492–510, table 1 (p. 494) and table 2 (p. 495).

Benze, James G., Jr. "Presidential Management: The Importance of Presidential Skills." *Presidential Studies Quarterly* 11, 4 (Fall 1981): 470–478.

Carter Presidential Library CEA finding aid: http://www.jimmycarterlibrary.gov /library/findingaids/Council%20of%20Economic%20Advisers.pdf

http://www.whitehouse.gov/administration/eop/cea/about/Former-Members

Specific biographical resources:

Baily: http://www.brookings.edu/~/media/experts/b/bailym/20150717-baily-cv .pdf, accessed August 19, 2015

Baily: http://www.brookings.edu/experts/bailym, accessed August 19, 2015

Blank: http://chancellor.wisc.edu/content/uploads/2015/01/CV_Blank.pdf, accessed August 19, 2015

Blinder: http://www.princeton.edu/~blinder/vitae.pdf, accessed August 19, 2015

Bradford: LA Times obituary, 2005, http://articles.latimes.com/2005/feb/24/local /me-passings24.3, accessed August 19, 2015

Eads: undated CV, http://www.airlineinfo.com/ostpdf8/875.pdf, accessed August 19, 2015

Feldstein: http://www.nber.org/feldstein/cv.html, accessed August 19, 2015

Frankel: http://www.hks.harvard.edu/fs/jfrankel/CVJeffFrankel.pdf, August 19, 2015

Goldfeld: http://www.nytimes.com/1995/08/29/obituaries/stephen-goldfeld-55 -professor-was-chief-economic-forecaster.html, accessed August 19, 2015

Jordan: http://www.cato.org/people/jerry-jordan, accessed August 19, 2015

Lawrence: http://www.hks.harvard.edu/fs/rlawrence/LAWRENCEcvJuly2013 .pdf, accessed August 19, 2015

Malkiel: http://www.nndb.com/people/559/000133160, accessed March 27, 2014

McAvoy: http://paulmacavoy2.com/, accessed March 27, 2014

Moore: http://web.stanford.edu/~moore/Bio.html

Moore: "A History of the Moore Family" (2000), at http://web.stanford.edu /~moore/Introduction.pdf

Munnell: http://www2.bc.edu/~munnell/, accessed August 19, 2015

(continued)

Table A.5   (continued)

Niskanen: obituary, *New York Times*, by Segal, 2011—http://www.nytimes.com /2011/10/29/business/william-a-niskanen-a-blunt-libertarian-economist-dies -at-78.html?_r=0

Nordhaus: http://www.econ.yale.edu/~nordhaus/homepage/current.htm, accessed August 19, 2015

Poole: http://www.cato.org/people/william-poole, accessed September 19, 2015

Schmalensee: http://rschmal.scripts.mit.edu/docs/vitae.pdf, accessed September 19, 2015

Seevers: http://www.futuresindustry.org/gary-seevers.asp, accessed March 27, 2014

Sprinkel: http://www.reagan.utexas.edu/archives/textual/personal%20papers /SPRINKEL.htm, accessed August 19, 2015

Stewart: http://www.nndb.com/people/982/000161499

Stiglitz: http://www0.gsb.columbia.edu/cfusion/faculty/jstiglitz/download/Stiglitz _CV.pdf, accessed August 19, 2015

Taylor: http://web.stanford.edu/~johntayl/cv/TaylorCV-August-2015.pdf

Tyson: CV, http://www.haas.berkeley.edu/groups/online_marketing/facultyCV /tyson_laura.pdf, accessed August 19, 2015

Tyson: http://facultybio.haas.berkeley.edu/faculty-list/tyson-laura, accessed August 19, 2015

Weidenbaum: obituary, *New York Times*, Hershey 2014

Wonnacott: CV, http://www.econ.umd.edu/faculty/profiles/wonnacott, accessed August 19, 2015

Yellen: http://facultybio.haas.berkeley.edu/faculty-list/yellen-janet, accessed August 19, 2015

---

(2) To the Atlas data I also include organizations affiliated with the Fraser Institute, called the "Freedom Network," using data from James Gwartney and Robert Lawson (2005) and various organizational websites. This brings the total count of organizations to 464.

A second dataset, used mainly in Chapter 6, includes the affiliates of the center-left, New Labour–connected Policy Network (in London) as of 2011. This dataset was built starting with the Policy Network website (http://www.policy-network.net/links/index.aspx?id=46), numerous individual organizational websites, and organizational contacts (with assistance from Brian Veazey) between February 2009 and

October 2011. By the end of 2008 the Policy Network's website listed 41 affiliated organizations (growing to 45 during the time of our research), of which 38 have known founding dates. The analysis in Chapter 6 presents data up to the end of 2004, for 30 affiliates with known founding dates.

A third dataset, on the membership of the CEA between 1946 and 2001, draws on the resources detailed in Table A.5.

Please note: this Appendix is not an exhaustive summary of all data sources used in this book. Further explanatory details, on all sources, can be found in endnotes and the bibliography.

Notes

Preface

1. I use the term "leftism" to denote the broad array of positions, terminologies, social groupings, meanings, and organizations (especially political parties) that have been understood as "left" in Western countries between the eighteenth century and the present. I trace the history of "left" as a political category in Western Europe and the United States in Chapters 3 and 5.

2. See, e.g., Cuperus and Kandel 1998; cf. Crouch 1997; Hall 1998.

3. Crouch 1997, p. 352.

4. Giddens 1994.

5. Hall 1998, p. 9, quoting Blair.

6. I trace Western leftism's origins in Chapter 3; see also Bobbio 1996.

7. Bourdieu 1979 [1984], p. 476; see also Bourdieu and Wacquant 1992.

8. Bourdieu 1977 [2008].

9. Anderson 1976.

1. Analyzing Leftism's Reinventions

Epigraph: Mills 1959 [2000], p. 6.

1. Weber 1920 [1978], pp. 1397–1398.

2. Key 1955, 1959; see Campbell 2006 for a recent assessment. Cf. Mayhew 2002.

3. Weber 1920 [1978], pp. 1397–1398.

4. Clemens 1997.

5. Lafontaine 2009.

6. DiSalvo 2012.

7. Michels 1915 [1982]; Gramsci 1929–1935 [1971]; Eley 2002.

8. Weber 1919 [1958].

9. Mair 1990, p. 2.

10. I draw here from a long line of thinking that reaches back to Karl Marx (at least) and to the more recent "articulation" perspective of Cedric de Leon and others—discussed further below.

11. For a similar move in the sociology of state formation and colonial rule, see Wilson 2011.

12. See, e.g., Rodgers 1998; Go and Krause 2016; Mudge and Vauchez 2012, 2016. For a discussion of the move beyond methodological nationalism in "third wave" historical sociology, see Adams, Clemens and Orloff 2005, pp. 56–63.

13. The broad overview I provide in this section is substantiated empirically in Chapter 2.

14. Mannheim 1936 [1985], p. 40.

15. Foucault 1978–1979 [2008].

16. Mannheim 1936 [1985], pp. 118–138.

17. Marx 1846 [1978], p. 175.

18. Weber 1920 [1978], p. 304.

19. Foucault 1978–1979 [2008], pp. 34–39.

20. I am doing some violence here to Foucault's project: on the theme of neoliberalism Foucault took up the study of practices, not political ideology (Power 2011).

21. Marx 1846 [1978], p. 175.

22. Marx 1846 [1978], p. 175.

23. On the uses and abuses of first-person accounts in sociology, see Martin 2011.

24. Martin 2015; Gross, Medvetz, and Russell 2011.

25. Gross, Medvetz, and Russell 2011, pp. 330–331.

26. Mirowski and Plehwe 2009.

27. The following discussion draws from, and builds on, other work on the analysis of neoliberalism: see Mudge 2017.

28. Weber 1903–1917 [1949]; Durkheim 1895–1897 [1982].

29. Emirbayer and Desmond 2015, on race; Bourdieu 1989–1992 [2015], on the state; Mudge and Vauchez 2012, 2016, on the EU; V. Zelizer 2010 and also Polillo 2011, on money; Stampnitzky 2014, on terrorism; Medvetz 2012, on think tanks; Martin 2015, on political ideology.

30. Berman 2006; Weir 1992; Mudge 2008.

31. Mitchell 1998. I revisit the origins of neoliberalism as an intellectual project in Chapters 2 and 6.

32. Hirschman and Reed 2014.

33. Eyal and Buchholz 2010.

34. For a historical and analytical assessment of the field concept, see Martin 2003; see also Fligstein and McAdam 2012b.

35. Bourdieu 1985; Weber 1902 [2001].

36. Eyal 2013.

37. Mudge 2016.

38. Harvey 2005 [2009], p. 3.

39. E.g., Sassoon 1997 and Crouch 1997, on left disorientation; Peck 2010, on "soft" neoliberalism.

40. See, e.g., Derluguian 2005.

41. Bourdieu 1979 [1984] ; Bourdieu and Wacquant 1999.

42. Bourdieu and Wacquant 1992, p. 199.

43. E.g., Sassoon 1996, 1997; Andersson 2007, 2009.

44. E.g., P. Hall 1989; Weir 1992; Rueschemeyer and Skocpol 1996.

45. Prasad 2006; Babb 2001; Chorev 2007, 2013; Bockman 2011; Wacquant 2012.

46. E.g., McQuarrie 2013; Lee 2015; Lee, McQuarrie, and Walker 2015; Pacewicz 2015, 2016.

47. Mannheim 1936 [1985], pp. 36, 147–153.

48. Mannheim 1936 [1985], p. 36.

49. Mannheim 1936 [1985], pp. 148–149.

50. Schattschneider 1942.

51. For an elaboration, see Mudge 2017.

52. Machiavelli 1516 [1999], p. 56.

53. Bourdieu, Pierre. 1989–1992 [2014]; Loveman 2005.

54. Gramsci 1929–1935 [1971], p. 152.

55. Gramsci 1929–1935 [1971], p. 152.

56. Gramsci 1929–1935 [1971], p. 153.

57. Eyal and Buchholz 2010, p. 120.

58. For the most recent statement of the articulation perspective, see De Leon, Desai, and Tuğal 2015.

59. Scott 1999; Adams 2005; Bourdieu 1989-1992 [2014]; Gorski 2003; Mitchell 1999; Loveman 2005; Wilson 2011.

60. Abbott 1988.

61. Tilly 1984, p. 14.

62. Marx 1844 [1978]; Gramsci 1929–1935 [1971]; Bourdieu 1993; Wacquant 2004; Dewey 1922 [2011]. One might also include here the notion of "social skill," in an American version of field-theoretic thinking (Fligstein 2001; Fligstein and McAdam 2012b).

63. Bourdieu 1968 [1991], p. 252.

64. Mills 1959 [2000].

65. Fligstein and McAdam 2012a, 49; see also Fligstein and McAdam 2012b.

66. Martin 2003, p. 1.

67. Emirbayer and Desmond 2015, on race; Desmond 2014, on ethnography; Steinmetz 2007, 2008, on German colonialism.

68. See, e.g., Gorski 2013.

69. Derlugian 2005; Harris and McQuade 2015; Haynes and Solovitch 2017.

70. Steinmetz's work (2007, 2008) is an important exception; Emirbayer and Johnson (2008) make a similar complaint about organizational sociology.

71. Bourdieu et al. 1994.

72. Hirschman and Reed 2014.

73. Wacquant 2004, p. 315.

74. Hirschman and Reed 2014.

75. See, e.g., Go and Krause 2016; Mudge and Vauchez 2012, 2016.

76. I use the term "ministers-in-waiting" to highlight my focus on people who are *party* officials first and state officials second. The distinction is important. In Weber's take, even when party officials become state officials, they are still agents of parties. Depending on their situation, they acquire veto authority in a double sense—in the party and in the state (Weber 1920 [1978]).

77. See Chapter 5.

78. For other works that highlight the importance of parties' weak boundaries, see Weir 1992; Halfmann 2011.

79. I describe the specificities of American parties in greater detail in Chapter 5.

80. For further details, see the Methodological Appendix.

81. Bourdieu 1979 [1984], p. 468. See Durkheim and Mauss 1903 [1963]; Durkheim 1912 [1995], 1914 [1973]; Bourdieu 1986 [1996]. For an extended discussion of Bourdieu's reassertion of this Durkheimian postulate, see Brubaker 1985. For another, current application of this line of argument, see Fourcade, Ollion, and Algan 2015.

82. This analysis is laid out in much greater detail in Chapters 3 and 5.

83. Weber 1915 [1958].

84. Polanyi 1944 [2001].

85. Mora (2014, p. 184) defines a cross-field effect as follows: "change in field A sparks concurrent, co-constitutive changes in field B," even as "changes in field B lead to changes in A."

86. Fourcade 2006.

87. I explore the opposing ethics Heller, an economist theoretician, and Friedman, a neoliberal economist, in Chapter 6.

88. Shils 1955 [1968]; Aron 1957 [1968]; Bell 1960; Lipset 1960; Converse 1964; Waxman 1968; cf. Jost 2006.

89. A sampling might include Andersson 2006; Baer 2000; Bonoli and Powell 2004; Favretto 2003; Glyn 2001; Hall 2002; Johnson and Tonkiss

2002; Merkel et al. 2008; Scanlon 2001; Schmidtke 2002. The meaning of the terms "left" and "social democracy" are often fuzzy in party scholarship, a difficulty that is sometimes resolved by treating center-left parties and social democracy as coterminous (e.g., Cuperus and Kandel 1998; Merkel et al. 2008; Schmidtke 2002). Herbert Kitschelt (1994) offers a noteworthy analysis of left parties without treating them as coterminous with leftism. There is also a rich historical literature on left parties, socialism, and social democracy, some of which centers on its late twentieth-century transformations. Here the work of Donald Sassoon (1996, 1997) is indispensable.

90. See Andersson 2009.

91. For a general review, see Mudge and Chen 2014.

2. From Socialist, to Economistic, to Neoliberalized Leftism

Epigraph: Mannheim 1929–1931 [1936], p. 147.

1. Esping-Andersen 1990.

2. For further explanation of my conceptualization of neoliberalism, see Mudge 2008, 2011.

3. The British Labour Party was formed out of a cooperative effort of the Trades Union Congress (TUC), established in 1868, and various other socialist and cooperative organizations that included the Democratic Federation (later the Social Democratic Federation), established in 1881.

4. SPD 1921. Emphasis added.

5. SPD 1921. Emphasis added.

6. Tingsten 1941 [1973]; Berman 2006.

7. SAP 1920. Emphasis added; brackets indicate paraphrasing.

8. SAP 1920. Emphasis added.

9. Webb 1918.

10. Webb 1918.

11. Webb 1918.

12. Skowronek 1982; for a retrospective, see V. Zelizer 2003.

13. Democratic Party 1920. Emphasis added.

14. Democratic Party 1920. Emphasis added.

15. Democratic Party 1936. Emphasis added.

16. We will return to the categories "left" and "right" in Chapters 3 and 5.

17. I trace how the American Democrats became "left" in Chapter 5.

18. SPD 1959. Emphasis added.

19. SPD 1959. Emphasis added.

20. SPD 1959. Emphasis added.

21. SAP 1960. Emphasis added. See also D. Bailey 2009.

22. Labour Party 1959. Emphasis added. See also N. Thompson 1996. A broadcast version of Labour's 1959 program can be viewed at http://www.youtube.com/watch?v=ZN4kLQFdL5Q.

23. Democratic Party 1960. Emphasis added.

24. Democratic Party 1960. Emphasis added.

25. Bell 1960; Aron 1957 [1968]; Converse 1964; Lipset 1960; Shils 1955 [1968].

26. Mannheim 1936 [1985], p. 40.

27. Sassoon 1997, p. 4.

28. P. Hall 2002, pp. 32–34. See also Andersson 2009, p. 15.

29. SPD 1998. Emphasis added.

30. SAP 1990. Emphasis added.

31. SAP 1990.

32. Labour Party 1997. Emphasis added. This manifesto was based on a draft published in 1996 titled "New Labour, New Life for Britain," which was approved at the party convention.

33. Labour Party 1997. Emphasis added.

34. Democratic Party 1992. Emphasis added.

35. For details on the analysis of programmatic trends presented here, see the Methodological Appendix.

36. For fuller development of neoliberalism as a category, a worldview, and a set of historical developments, see Mudge 2008, 2016, 2017.

37. Foucault 1978–1979 [2008]; see also Mudge 2016.

38. Mudge 2008.

39. I elaborate on the formation of the left-right axis in the next chapter.

40. Powell 1986.

41. I elaborate on this association in Chapter 5.

42. Peters 1983; Farrell 1983; Kaus 1984; see also Chapter 7.

43. Hartwell 1995; Mirowski and Plehwe 2009; Phillips-Fein 2009; D. Jones 2012; Burgin 2012; Bourne 2013. See also Chapter 6.

44. Burgin 2012, pp. 12–15.

45. Cockett 1994; Valdés 1995; Blyth 2001; Speth 2004; Mudge 2008; Teles 2008; Gross, Medvetz, and Russell 2011. Pre-1990s social scientific scholarship on neoliberalism, in its current sense, was thin—but see Friedrich 1955; Megay 1970; Foucault, 1978–1979 [2008]. The topic then became relatively commonplace in the early 2000s. A search in the Web of Science returns 126 articles on neoliberalism between 1990 and 1999, but 1,021 between 2000 and 2009. The single largest percentage (40 percent) was in geography. Useful disciplinary overviews of neoliberalism scholarship include Harvey 2005 [2009]; Peck 2011; Hilgers 2011 (cf. Wacquant 2012); Centeno and Cohen 2012.

46. A fuller explanation of the neoliberalism index and the data sources are given in the Methodological Appendix. See also Mudge 2011.

47. The term "decommodification" is a Marxian referent, but the specific use here is attributable to Gøsta Esping-Andersen (1990).

48. Esping-Andersen 1990, 1999.

3. The Genesis and Infrastructure of Socialist Leftism

Epigraphs: Gorski 2013, Kindle loc. 6972–6974; Bourdieu 1989–1992 [2014], p. 89.

1. For a related take on the conceptualization of political ideology in field-theoretical terms, see Martin 2015.

2. Hirschman and Reed 2014.

3. Billington 1980 [2007], pp. 261–275.

4. Tucker 1978, p. 469.

5. Eley 2002, pp. 19, 21; see also Vincent 2009. Eley dates socialism's entry into political lexicon to the 1850s; Mark Bevir (2011, p. 14) argues that the term gained currency in Britain in the 1880s. Vincent (2009) locates socialism's appearance in 1827 in the British Owenite *Cooperative Magazine* and then, in February 1832, the French Saint-Simonian journal *La Globe*.

6. Marx and Engels 1848 [1978], p. 493.

7. Marx and Engels 1848 [1978], pp. 491–500.

8. Lipset 1960, p. 132; see also Zaretsky 2012; Sassoon 1996; Eley 2002.

9. Zaretsky 2012, p. 3.

10. This listing of party titles draws from the Historical Parties Database (see the Methodological Appendix). See also Eley 2002, pp. 13–22; Roth 1963. On radicalism and the difficulties of using "left" and "right," see Calhoun 2012. See Sperber 1992 for an account of radicalism in mid-eighteenth-century Germany. On French revolutionary politics between 1789 and 1848, see Sewell 1980 [1989].

11. Eley 2002.

12. Billington 1980 [2007], p. 308.

13. Billington 1980 [2007], p. 318.

14. Billington 1980 [2007], pp. 33, 318; see also Hamman 1970.

15. Gramsci 1929–1935 [1971], p. 259.

16. Cited in Ebbinghaus 1995, p. 51, n. 2.

17. Eley 2002, p. 81.

18. Lenin 1905 [1965].

19. The name has also been translated as the General German Workers' Union (R. Morgan 1965).

20. R. Morgan 1965, p. 2.

21. Lidtke 1966, p. 21.

22. Lidtke 1966, pp. 20–21. The former quotation is from E. Bernstein 1893, p. 120, cited in Lidtke 1966, p. 21. The latter quotation is from Roth 1963, pp. 42–45. See also Lidtke 1966, pp. 21–25.

23. Roth 1963, pp. 43, 47.

24. R. Morgan 1965, pp. 12–14. The Verband was intended "to safeguard Liberal political interests against the Lassallean threat"; it was "amicably divided" among liberals, socialists, and progressives. Liebknecht and Bebel's success in establishing the SDAP as a socialist organization thus "involved significant concessions on all sides" (R. Morgan 1965, pp. 12–14).

25. Lidtke 1966, pp. 40–41.

26. Roth 1963, p. 50.

27. R. Morgan 1965, p. 20.

28. On the significance of this achievement, see R. Morgan 1965, pp. 98–180.

29. The Prussian government dissolved the party organization in June 1874. See Lidtke 1966, p. 42.

30. Marx's *Critique of the Gotha Program* complained that Gotha implied that a democratic republic was a final aim rather than a transitional stage. Liebknecht kept Marx's critique out of circulation. Bebel did, however, receive a similar complaint in a letter from Engels (Lidtke 1966, pp. 44–45; for an exploration of Liebknecht's motivations, see Lidtke 1966, pp. 45–47). Marx's critique was not published until 1890–1891, in *Die Neue Zeit* (of which more below).

31. Eley 2002, p. 89.

32. Eley 2002, p. 89; Sassoon 1996, pp. 12–18; Tingsten 1941 [1973], p. 695; see also Cole 1953, p. 31.

33. Weber 1919 [1958], p. 102.

34. Eley 2002, p. 80.

35. Weber 1919 [1958], p. 102; Michels 1915 [1982]. Duverger (1954) famously emphasized the left origins of the mass party as a source of organizational "contagion" from left to right; but see Epstein (1980). See also Eley 2002, pp. 113–114.

36. Lidtke 1966, pp. 54–55. *Die Zukunft* was made possible by a considerable financial subsidy from Karl Höchberg, the wealthy son of a Jewish banking family from Frankfurt am Main.

37. Lidtke 1966, p. 55.

38. Lidtke 1966, p. 85; see also R. Morgan 1965.

39. Roth 1963, p. 24; Lidtke 1966. The legislation did not, to Bismarck's chagrin, prevent Social Democrats from running for office.

40. Lidtke 1966, p. 80.

41. Law against the Publicly Dangerous Endeavors of Social Democracy, October 19, 1878, in Lidtke 1966, pp. 339–345.

42. Lidtke 1966, pp. 79–80.

43. Sassoon 1996, p. 11.

44. Lidtke 1966, pp. 89–97.

45. Gorman 1986, p. 158.

46. Hayes 1917, p. 78.

47. Hayes 1917, p. 79.

48. Guttsman 1981, pp. 169–170.

49. Liebknecht proclaimed the futility of open conflict: "They would put us in jail or in the lunatic asylum, because this is where we would belong" (Guttsman 1981, p. 170).

50. Eley 2002, p. 80.

51. Guttsman 1981, pp. 171, 185.

52. The image can be found in Smaldone 1998, p. 38: "SPD Party School, ca. 1907."

53. Guttsman 1981, p. 172.

54. Guttsman 1981, pp. 172–173.

55. Pierson 1993, p. 64.

56. Pierson 1993, p. 65, quoting Kautsky 1891 [1971], pp. 183–189.

57. Guttsman 1981, pp. 174–188.

58. Sassoon 1996, pp. 120–121.

59. Roth 1963; see also Eley 2002, pp. 79–82.

60. Anderson 1976, pp. 13–14.

61. Eley 2002, pp. 42–45.

62. See Anderson 1976, on *Le Devenir Social*. The *Social-Democrat* became the *British Socialist* in 1912, on the heels of the formation of the British Socialist Party. Published by Twentieth Century Press, it was linked to the Social Democratic Federation and its founder, H. M. Hyndman; see H. W. Lee 1913.

63. Anderson 1976, p. 5.

64. Anderson 1976, pp. 5–6.

65. Smaldone 1998, pp. 10–11. Max Adler (no relation to Viktor Adler, founder of the Austrian SPÖ) became a professor of sociology and social philosophy at the University of Vienna in 1920. The Austro-Marxists stood out for their unusually strong ties to the Austrian academy, where Marxism was taught by "professorial Marxists" like Carl Grünberg (Smaldone 1998, p. 14; see also Anderson 1976).

66. Smaldone 1988, p. 273.

67. Smaldone 1998, p. 31.

68. Smaldone 1988, pp. 273–274.

69. Hilferding 1910 [1981], p. 21.

70. Berman 1998; Hilferding 1910 [1981]; James 1981. See Smaldone 1998, pp. 40–55, for a summary of *Finance Capital* and the book's reception.

71. Smaldone 1998, p. 56.

72. Initially divided over the question of support for the war (which motivated the establishment of the Independent Social Democrats, or USPD), party divisions materialized with the establishment of the Kommunistische Partei Deutschlands, or Communist Party of Germany, (KPD) and the Spartacus League. See Smaldone 1998, pp. 1–22.

73. Smaldone 1998, p. 142.

74. Smaldone 1998, p. 139.

75. Smaldone 1993, pp. 101, 139.

76. Smaldone 1988, p. 295; James 1981, p. 850.

77. Smaldone 1998, p. 139.

78. Roth 1963, pp. 55–56.

79. Michels 1911 [1962]; see also James 1981.

80. Ehrlich 2007, p. 20, table 1.

81. Smaldone 1998, p. 38.

82. Guttsman 1981, p. 246.

83. Pierson 1993, p. 8.

84. Pierson 1993, p. 9.

85. Pierson 1993, p. 9.

86. Weber 1919 [1958], p. 97.

87. Tingsten 1941 [1973], pp. 51, 53–56.

88. Tingsten 1941 [1973], p. 157.

89. Tingsten 1941 [1973], p. 157.

90. Eley 2002, p. 79.

91. Tingsten 1941 [1973], p. 115.

92. Tingsten 1941 [1973], pp. 118–120; see also Berman 1998.

93. Tingsten (1941 [1973] p., 123) emphasizes the particular influences of these three figures, but also a number of others.

94. Hallin and Mancini 2004; Wadbring 2003, p. 1.

95. Lund 1938.

96. Lund 1938, pp. 232–233.

97. Erickson 1966, p. 130.

98. Lund 1938, pp. 235–36.

99. Lund 1938; Erickson 1966.

100. Rickard Sandler (1884–1964) also filled the office in a short-lived SAP government of 1920.

101. Vennerström 1926, pp. 7–9. Author's translation.

102. Palm 1881.

103. Vennerström 1926, pp. 11–12, 14, 16–17. Author's translation.

104. Vennerström 1926, pp. 20–25. Author's translation.

105. Vennerström 1926, p. 25. Author's translation.

106. Vennerström 1926, p. 29. Author's translation.

107. Vennerström 1926, pp. 26–27. Author's translation.

108. Vennerström 1926, p. 32, quoting Saxon's *New Day*. Author's translation.

109. Vennerström 1926, pp. 45–46. Author's translation.

110. Vennerström 1926, pp. 51–55. Author's translation.

111. Vennerström 1926, p. 56. Author's translation.

112. Vennerström 1926, p. 66. Author's translation.

113. Vennerström 1926, p. 69. Author's translation.

114. *New York Times* 1925.

115. Mackie and Rose 1991.

116. Tingsten 1941 [1973], pp. 137–138. See also Nobel Prize 1921.

117. Palm 1881.

118. Malmberg 2007.

119. Tomasson 1941 [1973], pp. xiv–xv. The LO had journals of its own and provided campaign and financial support to SAP candidates.

120. Tomasson 1941 [1973], p. xiv.

121. Hedström, Sandell, and Stern 2000, p. 148.

122. Berger 1996.

123. The ILP was established by Philip Snowden (1864–1937), Ramsay MacDonald (1866–1937), Keir Hardie (1856–1915), and J. Bruce Glasier (1859–1920). For a succinct history of the formation of the Labour Party, see Thorpe 1997 [2008], pp. 1–35.

124. Reid 2000, p. 224.

125. K. Morgan 2004.

126. K. Morgan 2004.

127. K. Morgan 2004, p. 13.

128. Sidney Webb stood out among them for his formal academic training, in law.

129. Pease 1918 [1963], p. 125.

130. Elizabeth Durbin (1985) emphasizes that the founding Fabians appreciated Marx's critical insights but turned to Jevonian marginalism in order to build a case for the transfer of rents from the bourgeoisie to society as a whole, via the state. Bevir (2011) highlights that there was no singular theory of rent to which all Fabians subscribed.

131. Pease 1918 [1963], p. 124.

132. Fabian Society [undated].

133. Durbin 1985, p. 20.

134. Reid 2000, pp. 224–225.

135. For a concise narrative of this period of "new liberal" politics, see Durbin 1985, pp. 19–20.

136. On Labour's many socialisms and consolidation on ethical and Fabian bases, see Bevir 2011.

137. A 1911 action established MP salaries of £400 per year, so that wages would not be paid directly by unions or other organizations. The Trade Union Act of 1913 prevented unions from donating from their general funds, but allowed them to set up a separate political fund by membership ballot. This clarified the legal relationship between parties and unions and led to the establishment of dedicated political funds for Labour, giving it "a firmer base of income and budgeting than ever before" (Thorpe 1997 [2008], p. 29).

138. Thorpe 1997 [2008], p. 28.

139. Thanks to funds left by a deceased Fabian, Henry Hutchison (Pease 1918 [1963], pp. 35–36). The Fabian Society was a successor to the Fellow-ship of the New Life, formed in response to the American thinker Thomas Davidson (Pease 1918 [1963], pp. 123–124).

140. Bevir 2011, p. 308; the quotation is from Labour's 1914 constitution. See also Thorpe 1996.

141. Berger 1996, p. 172.

142. Berger 1996, p. 172.

143. Berger 1996, pp. 173–174.

144. Berger 1996, p. 174; see also D. Morgan 1979.

145. Cross 1966, pp. 40, 84, 178.

146. Tanner 2004.

147. The quotation is from Cross 1966, p. 34.

148. For a useful account of Snowden's turn to socialism, his self-support via lecturing and publication activities, and his rise within the ILP, see Cross 1966, pp. 18–48.

149. Cross 1966, pp. 59–60.

150. E.g., *Labour and National Finance* (1920) and *Labour and the New World* (1921 [1925]).

151. For an account of Snowden's dependence on journalism as a source of income, see Cross 1966, pp. 80–81.

152. Tanner 2004.

153. Snowden reportedly learned about Marx primarily via Hyndman's work; he possessed a copy of *Das Kapital* but, by his own account, never read it (Cross 1966).

154. Among other things, Peel had been one of the figures behind the Bank Act of 1844, a core institution of the gold standard era.

155. Cross 1966, p. 178.

156. Ehrlich 2007.

157. Skidelsky 1967, pp. 73–75, citing Cole 1948, p. 223.

158. Snowden 1934b, pp. 525–526, 531.

159. Cross 1966, pp. 117–123; see also Riddell 2002; Reid 2000. Snowden conflicted with union leadership over the strikes of miners, railwaymen, and dockworkers in 1910 and 1911 and openly disagreed with both the syndicalist arguments of radical union leadership and G. D. H. Cole's nonrevolutionary "guild socialism."

160. In *Socialism and Syndicalism* Snowden argued that state intervention, not strikes, was the best means of improvement in workers' lives and that workers' numbers would never be enough to counter the "middle and upper classes" (Cross 1966, pp. 118–122). On 1926, see Snowden 1934b, pp. 725–733.

161. Fourcade-Gourinchas 2001, p. 404.

162. Fourcade-Gourinchas 2001, p. 410.

163. Fourcade-Gourinchas 2001, pp. 406–407; Rueschemeyer and Von Rossem 1996, p. 123; Wittrock and Wagner 1996, p. 100. German economics' historicism was challenged in a series of disputes (the *Methodenstreit*) between the 1880s and 1910s. Ultimately, the appointment powers of the professoriate and the German state tipped the scales in favor of inductivism, facilitating the decline of classical economics in the German academy.

164. Rueschemeyer and Von Rossem 1996, p. 119; Blaug 1986. Schmoller and Wagner were both leading figures of the "younger Historical School" in German economics.

165. The latter quote is from Fourcade-Gourinchas 2001, p. 408; see also Rueschemeyer and Von Rossem 1996, pp. 120–121 and Small 1924, p. 713. Policy questions considered in the VfS's founding conferences included factory legislation, housing, and unemployment (Small 1924, p. 716).

166. Small 1924, p. 715.

167. Fourcade-Gourinchas 2001, p. 409.

168. Blaug 1986, p. 862.

169. Watrin 1979, p. 408.

170. Blaug 1986, p. 118.

171. Nau 2000, p. 509.

172. Rueschemeyer and Von Rossem 1996, pp. 121–122, 144. Franz Mehring and Rosa Luxemburg were particularly critical (Rueschemeyer and Von Rossem 1996, p. 144).

173. Rueschemeyer and Von Rossem 1996, p. 146.

174. Mommsen 1959 [1984].

175. Mommsen 1959 [1984], pp. 111–113.

176. Ringer 1969, p. 150. On the "modernist" German professoriate's tendencies toward the National Liberal and Progressive parties, see Ringer 1969, pp. 130–134. On its antipathies to socialism, Marxism, and the SPD, see Ringer 1969, pp. 146–150.

177. A. Harris 1942, pp. 807–808.

178. Blaug 1986, p. 796.

179. A. Harris 1942, p. 806. Robert Michels's difficulties in acquiring academic employment as an SPD member (until 1907) are documented by Hands (1971) and Mommsen (1959 [1984]).

180. Kuhnle 1996, p. 242. Anders Berch occupied the chair.

181. *Nationalekonomiska Föreningen* [undated]; Henriksson 1991, p. 42.

182. Kuhnle 1996, pp. 241–242.

183. Kuhnle 1996, pp. 240–253.

184. Tingsten 1941 [1973], p. 17, on liberal principles.

185. Jonung 1991, pp. xvii–xxxi.

186. Jonung 1991, pp. 3–4.

187. Lindahl 1951.

188. Jonung 1991, pp. 3–4; see also Tingsten 1941 [1973], pp. 170–173, on a 1908 debate on socialism between Heckscher, Branting, and others in Stockholm, prompted by Heckscher's criticisms.

189. Ericksson 1994. Steffen does not appear in Mark Blaug's (1986) *Who's Who in Economics.*

190. Tingsten 1941 [1973], p. 168; see also Tomasson 1941 [1973]; Eriksson 1994.

191. Goldman 1987, pp. 136–137.

192. For an in-depth analysis, see Fourcade 2009.

193. Blaug 1986, p. 837.

194. Blaug 1986, p. 715.

195. Blaug 1986, pp. 561, 598.

196. Coats 1993, pp. 178–179, citing Kadish 1986; Royal Economic Society 2012; Fourcade 2009, p. 148.

197. Coats 1993, pp. 179–180.

198. Cross 1966, pp. 40, 84.

199. Fourcade 2009, p. 131.

200. Fourcade 2009, p. 134.

201. Durbin 1985, pp. 98–99. Notable here are Robinson's *The Economics of Imperfect Competition* (1933) and Hicks's *Value and Capital* (1939 [1978]).

202. Peden 2004, p. 11.

203. Howson and Winch 1977, p. 5. Nassau Senior ascribed Britain's economic successes in 1853 to "philosophers and political economists" (Senior [1878], cited in Hutchison 1979, p. 426).

204. Howson and Winch 1977, pp. 5–6.

205. Durbin 1985, p. 48.

206. Blyth 2013, pp. 122–123; see also Skidelsky 1967, p. 57.

207. Keynes 1924.

208. On Hawtrey, see Blaug 1986, p. 379. Of the Treasury officials named above, only Hawtrey appears in Blaug's (1986) *Who's Who in Economics.* The quotation is from Peden 2004, p. 3.

209. Hoover 2003, pp. 50–51.

210. Starr 1937, p. 104.

211. Howson and Winch 1977, p. 10. The latter quotation is from Beveridge in *Nation and Athenaeum,* December 29, 1923, and January 5, 1924—a Liberal party journal controlled by a company chaired by Keynes that provided a central venue for Beveridge's arguments.

212. Cross 1966, p. 178.

213. Initially a "more or less academic institution," during World War I the Fabian Research Department participated in strikes and otherwise became more connected to the labor movement; in the process, it severed its Fabian ties, took on the name Labour Research Department (LRD), and became "an agency of the Labor Party" but remained independent of the party's executive committee, charged with compiling research and statistics (Starr 1937, p. 101).

214. Starr 1937, pp. 102–106. The LRD was displaced after 1921 by a joint Labour Party–union research venture that could be more directly controlled by both. The LRD's membership and financial situation soon declined (Starr 1937, p. 102).

215. Starr 1937, p. 106.

216. Thorpe 1997 [2008], p. 65.

217. Rodgers 1998, pp. 25–26.

4. European Leftism's First Reinvention

Epigraph: Keynes 1926 (2004), pp. 18, 22.

1. I draw here from Michel Foucault, who describes liberalism as logic of government in which the limits of the state become subject to the truth-telling, or "veridiction," of the market (Foucault 1978–1979 [2008]).

2. The multiplicity of economists and forms of economic knowledge is amply clear in Marion Fourcade's (2009) comparative analysis of economics professions in the United States, France and Britain.

3. Consider, for instance, that as of August 24, 2017, about seven months into the presidency of Donald J. Trump, no appointments had been made to the prestigious Council of Economic Advisers.

4. Generally speaking, the economist theoretician was a "he." On the predominance of men in American economics, see Fourcade, Ollion, and Algan 2015.

5. The pervasiveness of interwar budgetary orthodoxy, even on the left, remains a significant puzzle of twentieth-century Western history. See, e.g., Gourevitch 1984; Berman 1998.

6. Eyal and Buchholz 2010, p. 120.

7. Durkheim and Mauss 1903 [1963]; Durkheim 1912 [1995], 1914 [1973]; Bourdieu 1979 [1984], 1986 [1996], 1990; Weber 1915 [1958]. I discuss the link between perspective and position in more detail in Chapter 1.

8. Bourdieu 1990, p. 87.

9. For a similar approach, see Shapin and Schaffer 1985 [2011].

10. Polanyi 1944 [2001], p. 3.

11. Bordo and Schwartz 1984, pp. 3–4.

12. Frieden 2006, pp. 16–17; Quinn 2003, pp. 189–191. See also Hawtrey 1947; Eichengreen 1998; Cohen 1998.

13. Polanyi 1944 [2001], p. 26.

14. Eichengreen and Hatton 1988, pp. 3–4.

15. Sundquist 1983, pp. 106–169.

16. Polanyi 1944 [2001], pp. 25–29.

17. Goldstein 1983, pp. 4–5, table 1.1.

18. Goldstein 1983, pp. 4–5, table 1.1.

19. Polanyi 1944 [2001], pp. 79, 226.

20. Tanzi and Schuknecht 2000.

21. Tanzi and Schuknecht 2000; Skocpol 1992. The American federal government had substantial commitments in the form of veterans' benefits—a remnant of the late 1800s, in which the Republican Party substantially expanded the Civil War pension system to cover nearly one-third of elderly men in the North and elsewhere (Skocpol 1992, Kindle loc. 159).

22. Hancock 1960, p. 320.

23. Polanyi 1944 [2001], pp. 3, 245–251.

24. Polanyi 1944 [2001], pp. 19–20.

25. Gamson 1975; Fligstein 2001.

26. Keynes 1927, p. 5, cited in Burgin 2012, pp. 1–2.

27. Cockett 1994, pp. 39–45.

28. Durbin 1985 pp. 64–68; see also Skidelsky 1992, p. 363.

29. Wicksell 1897, 1907.

30. F. Meyer 1967 [1982], p. 194. See also Keynes 1936 [1964], chapter 23.

31. Foster and Catchings 1928.

32. Blyth 2001, 2002.

33. Berman 1998; Blyth 2001, 2002.

34. Woytinsky 1961, pp. 8–10.

35. On Baade, see Smaldone 1998, p. 120; Hochstätter 2006, p. 76. Discussions of the WTB plan can also be found in Berman 2009, p. 569; Janoski 1990, pp. 66–67; Garraty 1976, pp. 138–139; Garvy 1975. On Colm, see Blaug 1986, p. 177.

36. Berman 1998, 2006; Blyth 2001, 2002; Smaldone 1998, p. 167; Woytinsky 1961.

37. Woytinsky 1961, pp. 457–458. James (1981, p. 850) highlights that in the 1925 program Hilferding "displayed a considerable and rather undogmatic skill in analysing the economic situation, within an explanatory structure provided by the Marxist inheritance" that did not exhibit any "over-mechanistic Kautskyite political ideology."

38. Eley 2002, p. 178, table 11.1.

39. Hetzel 2002.

40. Smaldone 1998, pp. 127–129, 132–134. The strongest resistance came from the German National People's Party (DNVP).

41. Hetzel 2002.

42. Woytinsky 1961.

43. Woytinsky 1961, pp. 457–458.

44. Berman 1998.

45. Garvy 1975.

46. Woytinsky 1961, pp. 466, 468.

47. Garvy 1975.

48. Smaldone 1998, p. 120.

49. See, e.g., Smaldone 1998, pp. 120–121; Berman 1998, pp. 392–393.

50. Woytinsky 1961, pp. 471–472.

51. In Woytinsky's account, he responded that "[a]ny party can execute it. And it will be executed. The only question is whether we take the initiative or leave it to our enemies" (1961, p. 471).

52. Wels's response attests not only to loyalties to Hilferding within the SPD leadership but also to the problems that arise when intellectual positions are wrapped up with political stakes: for Wels, Woytinsky's truth claims *contra* Hilferding's were tantamount to calling Hilferding a liar—which could not be tolerated. Wels reportedly "pounded the desk with both fists and shouted 'Shut up! I will not permit . . . ,'" to which Woytinsky replied, "You will not permit what?" Wels responded, "You said 'it is not true,' . . . If what Hilferding says is not true he must be a liar!" (Smaldone 1998, p. 121, quoting Woytinsky 1961, pp. 471–472).

53. Woytinsky 1961, p. 472.

54. Smaldone 1998, p. 167.

55. Tanner 2004; Snowden 1934a, 1934b.

56. Cross 1966, pp. 82–83.
57. Snowden 1934b, pp. 593–599.
58. Snowden 1934b, p. 595.
59. Snowden 1934b.
60. Pimlott 1985, pp. 142–143.
61. Cross 1966, p. 82.
62. Cross 1966, p. 202.
63. Snowden 1934b.
64. Pimlott 1985, p. 143.
65. Tanner 2004.
66. Tanner 2004.
67. See, e.g., Riddell 2002, p. 296.
68. Snowden 1934b.
69. Galbraith 1977 [2001], pp. 229–230.
70. I discuss the Liberal summer schools in Chapter 3.
71. Liberal Party 1929.
72. Thomas-Symonds 2010, p. 55.
73. For a very similar account, see Thomas-Symonds 2010, p. 56.
74. Skidelsky 1967, p. 60. The phrase "madcap finance" is from *How to Conquer Unemployment: Labour's Reply to Lloyd George* (Labour Party 1929a, pp. 9–10).
75. Thorpe 1996, p. 97.
76. Howson and Winch 1977, pp. 24–27. The EAC was chaired by MacDonald and included Snowden.
77. Riddell 2002, p. 295; see also Tomlinson 1981; Fourcade 2009, p. 165.
78. Cockett 1994, p. 37; see also Howson and Winch 1977. A socialist-turned-liberal who held a chair in economics at the LSE, Robbins attributed his own liberal conversion partly to Ludwig von Mises (Cockett 1994, p. 26).
79. Leith-Ross 1930, in Peden 2004, p. 103; see also Cockett 1994. Leith-Ross graduated Balliol College, Oxford, with a prestigious degree in "Greats": "ancient history, philosophy, . . . modern philosophy, including logic, but not economics" (Peden 2004, p. 13).
80. For Sidney Webb, it was only after Britain left the gold standard that it became conceivable. Webb reportedly remarked, "We were not told we could do that" (Marquand 1977; Durbin 1985).
81. Both Mosley and Strachey—especially the latter—were responding to Soviet experiments in central planning, which borrowed on economic models developed by three (otherwise unknown) European economists: Friedrich von Wieser, one of the three founders of the Austrian School; Vilfredo Pareto, who took Léon Walras's chair of economics at Lausanne in 1892; and Enrico Barone. These models, essential to the development of mathematical neoclas-

sical economics, were first put into action by World War I Germany (Toye 2003, pp. 17–19, 25–27, 33–39; see also Bockman 2011).

82. Durbin 1985, p. 68; Thorpe 1996, p. 107; Toye 2003 pp. 33–39.

83. Snowden 1934b, pp. 875–876.

84. Snowden 1934b, p. 876.

85. Snowden 1934b, pp. 875–876. The ILP disaffiliated from Labour in 1932.

86. See Durbin 1985, pp. 12, 64–66; Skidelsky 1967, pp. 68–69; Williamson 1984.

87. Berman 1998, 2006.

88. Tingsten 1941 [1973], pp. 203–248. Vennerström 1926.

89. *New York Times* 1925a.

90. Wigforss 1950, vol. 1, pp. 98–99. Author's translation.

91. Wigforss 1950, vol. 1, pp. 189–90. Author's translation. On Wicksell's "civil courage" but nonparty investments, see Swedberg 1999.

92. Wigforss 1950, vol. 1, pp. 259–260. Author's translation.

93. Tilton 1979, p. 506.

94. Wigforss 1950, vol. 1, p. 125. Author's translation.

95. The "work of reorganizing" quotation is from Wigforss 1908 [1970]; the "provisional utopia" is from Wigforss 1926, both cited in Tilton 1979, p. 507.

96. Rothstein 1991.

97. Wigforss 1950, vol. 1, pp. 341–342; on the relationship between academics and politics, see Wigforss 1950, vol 3, pp. 413-421. Author's translation.

98. Wigforss 1950, vol. 1, pp. 341–342. Author's translation.

99. Wigforss 1950, vol. 1, p. 344. Author's translation.

100. Arneson 1920.

101. Tingsten 1941 [1973], pp. 167, 169. Among his peers were Värner Rydén, Erik Palmstierna, Anders Örne, Ivar Vennerström (Thorsson's biographer), Sigfrid Hansson, Gustav Möller, and others.

102. Henriksson 1991, p. 49.

103. Barber 2008, pp. 11–12.

104. Henriksson 1991, pp. 48–50; see also B. Ohlin 1937b; Barber 2008.

105. Jonung 1991, p. 2, 4. See also Jonung 1979.

106. Jonung 1991, pp. 11–12.

107. Henriksson 1991, p. 58.

108. Wigforss 1950, vol. 1, p. 346; Henriksson 1991, p. 58.

109. Henriksson 1991, p. 58; Phillips 1958; Samuelson and Solow 1960.

110. Henriksson 1991, p. 58.

111. Barber 2008, pp. 38–39.

112. Tilton 1979, p. 506.

113. Tilton 1979, pp. 506–508; Wigforss 1938, p. 39.

114. Tingsten 1941 [1973], pp. 286–309; Jonung 1991, pp. 5–6; see also Tilton 1979.

115. Jonung 1991, p. 11; Wigforss 1938. Social democratic parties achieved a similar alliance in Denmark in 1933, Norway in 1935, and Finland in 1937 (Sassoon 1996, p. 44).

116. On Wigforss's influence, see Steinmo 1988, p. 419.

117. Wigforss 1950, vol. 3, p. 402.

118. Meidner 1988, p. 455.

119. Jonung 1991, pp. 31–32.

120. Magnusson, Ottosson, and Hellmark 2006; Erixon and Wadensjö 2012.

121. Erixon and Wadensjö 2012, pp. 71–72.

122. Erixon and Wadensjö 2012.

123. Erixon and Wadensjö 2012.

124. Meidner 1988, pp. 455–456. Meidner notes that LO leadership exerted considerable influence over the research of its economists: its president, August Lindberg, reacted "sharply to ideas and formulations which he did not think to be an accurate reflection of LO's views" (Meidner 1988, p. 456).

125. Erixon and Wadensjö 2012, pp. 72–74.

126. Erixon and Wadensjö 2012, pp. 73–74; Meidner 1993.

127. Meidner 1988, p. 467.

128. Meidner 1993, p. 213.

129. Erixon and Wadensjö 2012, pp. 72–75, quoting Meidner 2003; see also Pontusson 1994, pp. 25–26.

130. Pontusson 1994, p. 27.

131. Erixon and Wadensjö 2012, pp. 72–75, quoting Meidner 2003; see also Pontusson 1994, pp. 25–26.

132. Meidner 1993, p. 214.

133. *New York Times* 1992.

134. Skidelsky 1992, p. 438.

135. Pimlott 1985, pp. 38–39, 41.

136. Pimlott 1985.

137. Pimlott 1985, pp. 49–62.

138. Pimlott 1985, pp. 135–137.

139. Pimlott 1985, p. 138.

140. Pimlott 1985, p. 138.

141. Pimlott 1985, pp. 142–143.

142. Pimlott 1985, pp. 148–149.

143. Pimlott 1985, p. 150.

144. Pimlott 1985, pp. 392–393.

145. Pugh 1984, pp. 162–166; Durbin 1985, pp. 79–80. The NFRB was established alongside another group that focused on political propaganda, the Society for Socialist Information and Propaganda (SSIP, pronounced "zip"). The SSIP was a platform for expressions of discontent with the gradualism of the "Old Gang" in the wake of 1931, its "Friday Club" meetings brought together Clement Attlee, G. D. H. Cole, Stafford Cripps, Hugh Dalton, Harold Laski, Arthur Pugh, and Richard H. Tawney, who produced *A Labour Programme of Action*. Although the SSIP briefly looked as if it might become a party in its own right, ultimately it dissolved and merged with the NFRB (Pugh 1984, pp. 166–171).

146. Keynes 1936 [1964], p. viii. See also Marcuzzo 2002.

147. Pugh 1984, pp. 180–182, 204–205.

148. Skidelsky names Davenport as the founder, noting that Keynes "steered well clear of such Labour Party think tanks as the New Fabian Research Bureau or the XYZ Club" (Skidelsky 1992, p. 438). Cf. Brivati 1996, p. 32.

149. Morris 2007, p. 20.

150. Brivati 1996, p. 32.

151. Brivati 1996, p. 31; Pimlott 1985, p. 393.

152. Pimlott 1985.

153. Morris 2007, p. 30.

154. Morris 2007, pp. 20, 30–35.

155. Pimlott 2004.

156. Meade was appointed to the Economic Section of the War Cabinet in 1941 and became its head in 1946, where he developed estimates of national income and expenditure.

157. Durbin 1985, pp. 13–14.

158. On Cripps, who was not an economist, see Clarke and Toye 2004.

159. Keep Left, p. 39, quoted in D. Howell 2005 [2013].

160. Brivati 1996, pp. 62–63.

161. Crosland 1956. See also Maravall 2010.

162. Haseler 1969.

163. Friedrich-Ebert-Stiftung 2016.

164. Friedrich-Ebert-Stiftung 2016.

165. Schellenger 1968, p. 32.

166. Schellenger 1968.

167. Smaldone 1998.

168. Hagemann 2000, p. 115, citing Frey and Pommerehne 1988.

169. Hagemann 2000, p. 115.

170. Friedrich-Ebert-Stiftung 2016; see also Krämer 1995.

171. Friedrich-Ebert-Stiftung 2016.

172. Janssen 2009, pp. 2–7.

173. Janssen 2009.

174. Eucken 1932; Rüstow 1932. See also Janssen 2009.

175. Lütjen 2007; Hochstätter 2006.

176. Hochstätter 2006, Lütjen 2007.

177. Mierzejewski 2004.

178. Mierzejewski 2004, Kindle loc. 241.

179. Erhard had a doctorate in economics from the University of Frankfurt am Main, where he worked under the socialist economist Franz Oppenheimer. He completed his habilitation in 1931, but it was never accepted. At the Vershofen institute and the IIR Erhard became connected with the ordoliberals, among others. After his American appointment he became an honorary professor at the University of Munich in November 1947. See Mierzejewski 2004.

180. Friedrich-Ebert-Stiftung 2016; Krämer 1995; Mierzejewski 2004.

181. Mierzejewski 2004, Kindle loc. 918; Haunhorst and Zündorf 2016; Childs 1994; Federal Ministry for Economic Affairs and Energy 2017.

182. Markovits and Allen 1984, p. 95. For the full Ahlen Program, in English, see CDU 1947.

183. Mierzejewski 2004, Kindle loc. 681–702.

184. Mierzejewski 2004, Kindle loc. 788.

185. Mierzejewski 2004, Kindle loc. 1206–1213.

186. Schellenger 1968, p. 93; Hogwood 1995; Hodge 1993, pp. 21–22.

187. Here I rely partly on a verbal account kindly relayed by Wolfgang Streeck of the Max Planck Institute for the Study of Societies (MPIfG), Cologne.

188. The DGB's internal ranks included CDU-friendly unionists, while other elements—in particular, IG Metall and its leader, Otto Brenner—were SPD-sympathetic. The DGB's first chairman, Hans Böckler, who is credited for formulating an early focus on codetermination and economic democracy, was influential with Adenauer. See Markovits and Allen 1984, pp. 95–101.

189. Schellenger 1968.

190. Haunhorst and Zündorf 2016; Hochstätter 2006, p. 51.

191. Markovits and Allen 1984, pp. 94–111.

192. Markovits and Allen 1984.

193. On the Action Plan, see Markovits and Allen 1984, p. 113. On Schiller, see Hochstätter 2006, pp. 51–54; see also Held 1982; Hagemann 2000.

194. Haunhorst and Zündorf 2016; Hochstätter 2006, p. 51; Markovits and Allen 1984, p. 115.

195. Shell 1970, p 659.

196. Hodge 1993, p. 22.

197. Hodge 1993, p. 22.

198. Markovits and Allen 1984, p. 115.

199. Markovits and Allen 1984, p. 116.

200. Schellenger 1968, pp. 94–96.

201. Shils 1955 [1968]; Aron 1957 [1968]; Bell 1960; Lipset 1960; Converse 1964; Waxman 1968; cf. Jost 2006.

202. Allen 1989, pp. 268–269.

203. Allen 1989, p. 274; see also Markovits and Allen 1984.

204. Schellenger 1968, pp. 94–96, citing an interview with Schiller; see also Schiller 1964.

205. Schellenger 1968, pp. 78, 85–86.

206. Schellenger 1968, p. 86.

207. DIW Berlin 2008 [2017]a..

208. DIW Berlin 2008 [2017]b.; see also *Der Spiegel* 1974.

209. Quotations are from Markovits 1986, pp. 106–108. The acronym SVR follows Markovits and Allen (1984) and Markovits (1986). In English-language works the acronym CEE, for Council of Economic Experts, is sometimes used to refer to the same body.

210. Tietmeyer 2003, p. 24. Author's translation.

211. Tietmeyer 2003.

212. Tietmeyer 2003.

213. Giersch 1973.

214. Allen 1989, pp. 275–276.

215. Markovits 1986, p. 108.

216. Hochstätter 2006.

217. Markovits 1986, pp. 108–109.

5. Economistic Leftism, American-Style—or, Making the Democrats "Left"

Epigraph: Samuelson 1975, p. iv.

1. Stein 1996; Weir 1992.

2. Hirschman and Berman 2014, p. 779.

3. By the end of this period, twelve American institutions offered political economy PhDs (Fourcade-Gourinchas 2001, p. 425).

4. Schudson 1998.

5. Skowronek 1982, pp. 43–44; Schudson 1998.

6. Fourcade-Gourinchas 2001.

7. Markoff and Montecinos 1993.

8. Markoff and Montecinos 1993; Barber 1981, pp. 176–177.

9. See, e.g., *New York Times* 1917. The general observation is made based on a historical news search of the *New York Times* from 1851 forward,

April 2, 2014, for "left and right," "left or right," "right and left," or "right or left."

10. Based on a term search of all documents available in the University of California, Santa Barbara, American Presidency Project, http://www.presidency.ucsb.edu/, accessed June 6, 2014.

11. Following, in particular, the work of Moisei Ostrogorski, Weber (1920 [1978]) made a strong ideological versus patronage distinction when he compared European and North American parties. See also Reichley 1992; Schudson 1998.

12. Howe 2007, pp. 573–574; Chambers and Burnham 1967 [1969].

13. Stokes 1983, p. 17. For an early reference to communism, see Cleveland 1888. Defending the tariff law of 1890 (the McKinley Tariff), in 1892 President Benjamin Harrison (R) later accused Democratic critics of making "free trader" appeals to the "workingman" that "not infrequently [were] pronouncedly communistic," defending protectionism as a means of boosting American wages and thus acting as "the only barrier against a reduction to the European scale" (Harrison 1892).

14. Sombart 1906 [1976]; Lipset and Marks 2000 [2013]; for a recent contribution to this debate, see Eidlin 2016.

15. Reichley 1992, p. 236; Ostrogorski 1902 [1982]; cf. Mayhew 2002.

16. Weber 1918–1920 [1978].

17. This structurally similar, or homologous, situation of Thorsson, Hilferding, and Snowden is what makes them especially useful, analytically speaking, as means of comparing the development of parties and the configuration of party-expert relations.

18. Skowronek 1982, p. 39.

19. Skowronek 1982; Barber 1981, p. 175.

20. For other analyses mobilizing the game metaphor and placing it in the sociological tradition, see Pacewicz 2015, 2016.

21. On the power of the executive in the SPD and the Labour Party, see Koelble 1987a Executive membership, in both parties, is elected in the convention and operates at some remove from local branches. Parliamentary membership (the Fraktion in [West] Germany or the Parliamentary Labour Party [PLP] in the United Kingdom), because of its power over policy implementation, is the primary counterpower to the executive. See Koelble 1987a, pp. 43–67; see also Braunthal 1977.

22. Rosenman 1968–1969. FDR appointed Rosenman to the New York State Supreme Court in April 1932.

23. Tugwell 1968, pp. 8–10; see also Rosenman's *Working with Roosevelt* (1952).

24. Tugwell 1968, pp. xx, 3–6.

25. Berle and Means 1932.

26. Barber 1981, p. 178; Yonay 1998; Tugwell 1968.

27. T. Roosevelt 1912 [2007], p. vii.

28. Clark was professor of economics at Columbia University, 1922–1953; during that time he also served in a series of public capacities: NRA, 1934–1935; National Resources Planning Board (NRPB), 1939–1940; Office of Price Administration (OPA), 1940–1943; Commission on Freedom of the Press, 1944–1947; Attorney General's National Committee to Study Anti-Trust Laws, 1953–1954. Columbia University Libraries, undated.

29. In theory, there is a distinction between planning and Keynesian deficit spending: one involves economic action driven or instigated by government; the other involves the use of the budget, and in particular substantial deficit spending in hard times, as a means of macroeconomic management. Planning can happen within the constraints of balanced budgets; Keynesian deficit spending, obviously, cannot. But, when it comes to historical actors, this does not mean that "planners" could not *also* be "spenders," or *vice versa.*

30. Tugwell 1968, p. xxx.

31. Rorty 1903. See also Juran 1997.

32. Fabricant 1984, p. 4.

33. Stone, quoted in Fabricant 1984, p. 4.

34. Fabricant 1984.

35. Fabricant 1984, p. 5, quoting Stone.

36. Fabricant 1984.

37. Fabricant 1984.

38. Fabricant 1984, p. 23.

39. Fabricant 1984; Kuznets 1971 [2014].

40. Fabricant 1984, p. 14.

41. Stein 1996, p. 56.

42. See Peters and Woolley 2015.

43. Sweezy 1972, p. 119.

44. Salant 1989, p. 30. The orthodox view was "that in a free market economy unemployment would be limited to the frictional and casual kind" (Salant 1989, pp. 30–31). See also J. Zelizer 2000, p. 335.

45. Sweezy 1972, p. 119.

46. Weir (1992) elaborates on the importance of the permeable federal state and the pattern of recruitment into it—see, especially, p. 34.

47. Weir 1992.

48. Stein 1996, pp. 148–149.

49. Stein 1996, pp. 148–149.

50. Mordecai Ezekiel, while working as a noncredentialed economist at the Agriculture Department's Division of Farm Management, attended classes at

the Department of Agriculture's Graduate School and the University of Minnesota, acquiring an MS in 1923. He then completed a PhD in economics at the Robert Brookings Graduate School of Economics and Government in 1926. After publishing a book on correlation analysis, working for the Federal Farm Board, and traveling to Europe and Russia on a Guggenheim Fellowship, Ezekiel returned to the Department of Agriculture to help build the AAA and, later, draft the Agricultural Adjustment Act. He became economic adviser to the secretary of agriculture in 1933. See Ezekiel, "Biographical Sketch," [undated].

51. Stein 1996, p. 56, quoting Eccles 1951, p. 131.

52. Sandilands 1990, pp. 60–61.

53. Keyserling claimed that he was an uncredited author of Tugwell's *American Economic Life and the Means of Its Improvement,* published in 1930 (Tugwell used a 1925 privately printed first edition to teach a course in economics) (Keyserling 1971). But it is not clear how the timing works out, since Keyserling did not return to Columbia until 1931.

54. Keyserling 1971, pp. 1–5.

55. Brazelton 1997a, pp. 189–190; see also Keyserling 1971.

56. Ezekiel came to know Tugwell in November 1932, when he met with him, FDR, and Morgenthau (and others) to talk about farm policy. Ezekiel [undated].

57. Ennis 1986; Barnes 1986.

58. Ennis 1986.

59. Weir 1992; Sandilands 1990, pp. 61–62.

60. Sweezy 1972, p. 117, quoting from the Harvard instructors' letter; see also Sandilands 1990, p. 54; Barber 1981, p. 178, n. 1; Galbraith 1965.

61. Stein 1996, p. 165.

62. Durr 2014, pp. 26–27; Sandilands 1990, p. 61; see also Schwarz 1993.

63. Sandilands 1990, p. 62.

64. Samuelson 1975, p. iv.

65. Galbraith 2001, p. 107, n. 7.

66. Skidelsky 1992, p. 576.

67. Barber 1981, p. 178; Carson 1975.

68. Galbraith 2001, p. 107, n. 7.

69. Stein 1996, p. 164.

70. Musgrave 1976, pp. 3–4; the other chair was filled by Heinrich Brüning, the last chancellor of the Weimar Republic.

71. Musgrave 1976, p. 5.

72. Skidelsky 1992, p. 580.

73. Skidelsky 1992, p. 580.

74. American Economic Association 1976, p. 986.

75. Samuelson, in Council of Economic Advisers 1964, p. 34.

76. Keyserling 1971, p. 12.

77. Keyserling 1971, p. 35. See also Brazelton 1997a.

78. Tomkin 1998, pp. 34–35.

79. "Throughout the 1930s, not more than 3 percent of the population ever paid income taxes. During the New Deal, the administration relied on regressive excise and payroll taxes and income taxes on the wealthiest Americans" (J. Zelizer 2000, p. 337).

80. Stein 1996, p. 57.

81. Stein 1996, p. 107.

82. J. Zelizer 2000 p. 353.

83. Stein 1996, p. 164; see also Skidelsky 1992.

84. Stein 1996, p. 165. In yet another indicator of the linkages between economists and government by that time, Stein reports that "several others who participated in drafting it did not feel free to sign it because of government connections or for other reasons.

85. Clark 1937a, 1937b.

86. Clark 1937a.

87. Clark 1937a.

88. Clark 1937b.

89. Associated Press 1937, quoting Vandenberg.

90. D. Thompson 1939.

91. Salant 1989, p. 29.

92. Barber 1987, pp. 203–204.

93. Lekachman 1966, p. 128.

94. Stein 1996, p. 165.

95. Stein 1996, p. 165.

96. Stein 1996, p. 168.

97. Tomkin 1998, pp. 34–35.

98. Stein 1996, p. 168. I discuss the WTB episode in Chapter 4.

99. Stein 1996, pp. 128–129.

100. Klausen 1999, pp. 220–221.

101. Weir 1992, pp. 42–44. See also S. Bailey 1950; Keyserling 1971.

102. Weir 1992, p. 45.

103. Weir 1992, pp. 45–47.

104. B. Jones 1972; Weir 1992.

105. Bailey 1955, p. 341.

106. B. Jones 1972, p. 131.

107. Keyserling 1971, pp. 30–31.

108. Keyserling 1971, pp. 30–31.

109. The CEA also had a support staff of about thirty or forty researchers.

110. Schick 1970, p. 531.

111. Stein 1996, p. 168.

112. Employment Act of 1946, cited in Naveh 1981, p. 492.

113. Naveh 1981, p. 493.

114. Nourse 1972, pp. 17–19.

115. Nourse 1972, pp. 17–19. In the same oral history interview Nourse described his "long association with the Chambers of Commerce, the National Association of Manufacturers and the National Industrial Conference Board and the American Management Association and so forth."

116. Naveh 1981, p. 496.

117. Wagner was, in Keyserling's description, a "very, very active campaigner." Keyserling 1971, pp. 33–36.

118. Nourse 1972, p. 21.

119. Naveh 1981, p. 496.

120. Nourse 1972, p. 22.

121. Nourse 1972, pp. 23–24.

122. Naveh 1981, p. 496.

123. Naveh 1981.

124. McClenahan and Becker 2011, p. 26.

125. Naveh 1981, p. 497.

126. McClenahan and Becker 2011, p. 26.

127. Naveh 1981; Council of Economic Advisers 2016.

128. Tobin 1976, p. 35.

129. Loeb 1970, pp. 16–18.

130. Tarshis received his PhD from Trinity College, Cambridge, in economics in 1939. He was a Carnegie Fellow at the NBER from 1939 to 1940 and then an assistant professor at Tufts University (and a U.S. citizen) starting in 1942. After serving on the U.S. War Production Board (WPB) and then in the air force, he was offered the position at Stanford, which he took up in 1945. See Gurley et al., undated.

131. Skidelsky 1992, p. 574.

132. Gurley et al., undated.

133. Samuelson 1997, pp. 157–158.

134. Gurley et al., undated, p. 4.

135. Gurley et al., undated.

136. Gurley et al., undated.

137. Samuelson 1997, pp. 158–159. Referencing other condemnations of his textbook in Bill Buckley's *God and Man at Yale* (1951), Samuelson noted that "Buckley's Yale was notorious in those days for its conservative old guard economists (Fred Fairchild, Hudson Hastings, Ray Westerfield, O. Glenn Saxon)" (Samuelson 1997, p. 158).

138. Samuelson 1997, pp. 159.

139. Samuelson 1955 [1973].

140. Samuelson later dropped the phrase "neo-classical synthesis" because "it smacked too much of complacency: perfection is at hand, economics is an exact science, blah, blah," and out of concern over "a *stagflation* problem in a mixed-economy welfare state that strove hard for full employment while at the same time helping the unemployed in a humane way" (Samuelson 1997, pp. 155–156).

141. Loeb 1970, 16.

142. Gillon 1987, p. 26.

143. Gillon 1987, pp. 26–27.

144. Loeb 1970, p. 11.

145. Gillon 1987; Brock 1962; Brinkley 1998.

146. Ericson 1979, p. 13.

147. Harris 1964; Gilbert 1939–1948.

148. Nathan 1989, pp. 30–58. Nathan, who had been among the candidates for the first chairman of the CEA, was in frequent contact with Keyserling. See also Gillon 1987, pp. 29–30.

149. Gillon 1987, pp. 41–43.

150. Gillon 1987, pp. 37–43; see also Loeb 1970, p. 19.

151. Loeb 1970, pp. 9–10, 80–87.

152. Gillon 1987, pp. 89–91.

153. Gillon 1987, p. 106, quoting Galbraith.

154. Gillon 1987, pp. 89–95, 106–107, 123.

155. Heller, in Council of Economic Advisers 1964.

156. Musgrave 1976.

157. Samuelson, in Council of Economic Advisers 1964, pp. 2–3.

158. Finletter 1972, p. 69; Samuelson, in Council of Economic Advisers 1964, pp. 2–4. See also Tobin, in Council of Economic Advisers 1964, pp. 5–6. An overlapping group was the DNC Economic Advisory Committee, chaired by Galbraith.

159. DiSalvo 2012; see also Cotter and Hennessy 2009.

160. Finletter 1972, p. 74.

161. Finletter 1972, p. 72; Gillon 1987, p. 124.

162. Schlesinger 1958, pp. 7–8; Gillon 1987.

163. Samuelson, in Council of Economic Advisers 1964, p. 1.

164. Samuelson, in Council of Economic Advisers 1964, p. 12.

165. Council of Economic Advisers 1964, p. 2.

166. Samuelson, in Council of Economic Advisers 1964, pp. 6–7.

167. Samuelson, in Council of Economic Advisers 1964, p. 13.

168. Samuelson, in Council of Economic Advisers 1964, p. 14; Solow 2004, p. 403.

169. Tobin 1991, p. 101.
170. Naveh 1981, p. 497.
171. Heller 1966.
172. Tobin 1991, pp. 101–102.
173. Tobin 1991, pp. 101–102.
174. Tobin 1991, p. 101.
175. Brock 1962, p. 12.
176. Brock 1962, pp. 13, 14, 174.
177. Brock 1962, p. 15.
178. Samuelson 1997, pp. 157–158.
179. Samuelson, in Council of Economic Advisers 1964, p. 33.

6. Interdependence in the Making of Leftism's Second Reinvention

Epigraphs: Heller 1966, p. 15; Friedman 1962, pp. 9, 24.

1. On the differentiated groups and thinkers of the neoliberal project, see Burgin 2012.

2. Weber 1902 [2001].

3. Fourcade 2009, p. xiv, 2. On this point one can simply note that, in the index of Fourcade's magisterial work on economics in the United Kingdom, France, and Britain, the entry "political parties" directs the reader to three pages within a nearly 400-page monograph (Fourcade 2009, p. 379).

4. Campbell and Pedersen 2014.

5. Hirschman and Berman 2014, pp. 2–3.

6. Hirschman and Berman 2014, p. 15

7. Hirschman and Berman (2014, pp. 13–14) attribute the 1946 Employment Act and the making of the CEA to a general increase in economists' newfound professional authority after World War II, rendering invisible the party networks in which many Keynesian economists were grounded.

8. E.g., Machiavelli 1516 [1999]; Weber 1919 [1958]; Mannheim 1936 [1985]; Bourdieu 1991.

9. Mora 2014.

10. Keynes 1936 [1964]. See P. Hall 1989, pp. 6–7, for a useful overview; Skidelsky 1992, pp. 548–571, gives a more detailed summary.

11. By "classical" Keynes meant Ricardian economics, ranging from David Ricardo and James Mill to J. S. Mill, Alfred Marshall, Francis Y. Edgeworth, and Arthur Cecil Pigou. Keynes 1936 [1964], pp. 3, 36.

12. On the multiplier—a concept developed by Richard Kahn and later elaborated by Paul Samuelson and Alvin Hansen—see Keynes 1936 [1964], pp. 245–247.

13. P. Hall 1989, pp. 6–7.

14. Skidelsky 1992, p. 540; Keynes 1936 [1964], pp. 280–291.

15. Hicks 1937. For analyses of the history of IS-LM, see Colander 2004; Boianovsky 2004.

16. Phillips 1958.

17. On the origins, history, and uses of the Phillips curve, see Sargent 1987; Leeson 1998; Kirshner 2009; Hirschman 2016.

18. Using citation patterns, Fourcade, Ollion, and Algan (2015, pp. 102–103) trace economics' growing engagements with mathematics and statistics in the postwar period, peaking in the 1960s and 1970s.

19. On the importance of quantification for Keynesian economics, see Mirowski 1988; Leeson 1998.

20. Mirowski 2002, p. 9.

21. Mitchell 1998; Mirowski 1988, 1989, 2002; see also Phillips 1958. Hirschman gives a helpful account of the Phillips curve, its hydraulic metaphor, and the Monetary National Income Analogue Computer (MONIAC) on which it was based (Hirschman 2016, pp. 109–111).

22. Ruggie 1982; Mitchell 1998, 2002.

23. This metaphor had origins dating to the 1870s, taking on a new specificity around the turn of the twentieth century through the work of economists including Ragnar Frisch in Norway, Jan Tinbergen in the Netherlands, and Irving Fisher in the United States. See Mitchell 1998; Mirowski 1989, 2002; Breslau 2003; Hirschman 2016.

24. In an analysis of priority struggles in science, Robert K. Merton highlights instances in which historical periods are identified with reference to "men who have put their stamp on science": "the Newtonian epoch, the Darwinian era, or the Freudian age" (Merton 1957 [1973], p. 298). So one could make this point a little differently, emphasizing the Keynesian era as an age defined with reference to a particular economist.

25. Hirschman and Berman 2014, p. 2.

26. Callon 1998a, p. 2.

27. Coats 1981, p. 6.

28. In a study of "economics' persuasive power" in the making of modern financial derivatives exchanges, MacKenzie and Millo show how economists' power "flowed through a Granovetterian network" (referencing the economic sociologist Mark Granovetter) that included individual economists, a consulting firm (Nathan Associates), a securities lawyer and Securities and Exchange Commission (SEC) official (Milton Cohen), and a party-in-government (the Nixon administration) (MacKenzie and Millo 2003, pp. 139-141).

29. MacKenzie and Millo 2003, pp. 139–141.

30. Siegfried 1998; Coats (ed.) 1981; Coats (ed) 2000.

31. Hagemann 2000, p. 113.

32. Hagemann 2000, pp. 117–118.

33. I document the growing public prominence of professional economists in the 1960s–1970s cross-nationally in greater detail in Chapters 7 and 8.

34. Heller appeared on *Time* magazine covers in 1961 and 1962; Schiller appeared on the cover of *Der Spiegel* in 1967 and 1971.

35. *Time* 1965.

36. See, e.g., Lekachman 1966; Roll 1968.

37. Ruggie 1982; also Centeno and Cohen 2012; Esping-Andersen 1990; Korpi 2003; Hicks and Zorn 2005.

38. Samuelson 1971 [1977], p. xiii.

39. Ladd and Lipset 1976.

40. Samuelson 1955 [1973]. Kuhn (1962) argues that the textbook is a cornerstone of "normal science," providing a basis of common professional socialization and a technical foundation for professional problem-solving in a cumulative mode.

41. Klein and Stern 2005; cf. Hamilton and Hargens 1993; Gross 2013.

42. Klein et al. 2012. See also Fourcade, Ollion and Algan 2015, p. 107.

43. A 2005–2006 survey of graduate students in European economics programs by David Colander found that most were center or center-left; only 7 percent identified as conservative. "My sense is that, in the United States, there is a slightly larger group of students falling in the conservative range than in Europe," Colander remarks, but "overall in both the United States and Europe the majority of students fall to the center left of the political spectrum" (Colander 2008, p. 218). The sociologist Johanna Bockman notes the indignation she encountered during an interview with an (unspecified) economist at the mere suggestion that his profession was conservative or right-leaning, since all the economists he knew were politically left (Bockman 2011, pp. 12–13).

44. Offer and Söderberg 2016, pp. 113–119.

45. Fourcade 2009, p. 7, citing Keynes 1924, p. 322.

46. Fourcade-Gourinchas 2001, p. 412.

47. Fourcade 2009.

48. Przeworski and Teune 1970.

49. Michels 1911 [1962].

50. Schiller 1964. Translation is by the author, with the help of Babylon software, Google Translate, and cross-checking with a German native speaker, unless otherwise noted.

51. Schiller 1964, p. vi..

52. Heller 1966, p. vii. Emphasis in original.

53. Heller 1966, p. 9. A common way of thinking among the end-of-ideologists, this way of seeing things can be found in a number of academic and scholarly settings in the 1950s and 1960s.

54. Schiller 1964, p. vi.

55. Schiller 1964, p. vi.

56. Schiller 1964, p. 3.

57. Heller 1966, pp. vii, 7.

58. Heller 1966, p. 9.

59. Hagemann 2000, p. 118; Haunhorst and Zündorf 2016; Childs 1994.

60. Leeson 1998, p. 603.

61. Heller 1966, p. 1. The Democratic affiliation of the "Phillips curve Keynesians" (Robert Solow, Franco Modigliani, James Tobin, Lawrence Klein, Heller, and [later] Arthur Okun) is duly noted by Leeson (1998).

62. Heller 1966, pp. 14–26.

63. Schiller 1955 [1964], p. 3.

64. Schiller 1955 [1964], pp. 3–4.

65. Schiller 1955 [1964], p. 7.

66. Schiller 1955 [1964], p. 8.

67. Schiller 1955 [1964], p. 12.

68. Heller 1966, pp. 16–22.

69. Heller 1966, pp. 10–12.

70. M. Bernstein 2004, p. 131.

71. Brivati 1996, p. 442.

72. Morris 2007, p. 20.

73. Heller characterizes the mid-1960s as "the Age of the Economist" (1966, p. 2; capitalization in original).

74. Mannheim 1929–1931 [1936].

75. Silvia and Vale 1992, p. 38. See also Held 1982.

76. See, e.g., Sandelin, Sarafoglou and Veiderpass 2002.

77. On the Gaitskellites and other Labourite economists in the 1960s, see Chapter 4.

78. M. Bernstein 2004, p. 149.

79. McCracken et al. 1977; see also Leeson 1998.

80. McCracken et al. 1977, pp. 37–100.

81. M. Bernstein 2004, p. 149.

82. I explore the British origins of stagflation in greater depth in Chapter 8.

83. McCracken et al. 1977, p. 6.

84. Major 2014, chapter 3.

85. Heller 1966, p. 9.

86. Samuelson 1955 [1973], p. 847.

87. Heller 1966, p. 9.

88. Friedman 1967 [1968], pp. 8–9.

89. Friedman 1968b. Buckley established the *National Review* magazine in 1955 and the *Firing Line* television series in 1966.

90. Gross, Medvetz, and Russell 2011.

91. Joseph H. Taggart, in Friedman and Heller 1968 [1969], pp. 7–8. Attesting to the public stature of the economist theoretician by that time, "[t]he response," the host later reported, "exceeded our expectations. Not only was the lecture hall filled to capacity, but an overflow audience had to be served by closed-circuit television."

92. Heller 1968 [1969], p. 17.

93. Friedman 1953, in Hausman 1984 [2008], p. 146.

94. Friedman and Heller 1968 [1969], p. 78.

95. Friedman and 1968 [1969], pp. 79–80, citing a 1953 talk given in Stockholm and a reprint in his 1968 *Dollars and Deficits,* "Why the American Economy Is Depression Proof."

96. Denord 2009, p. 48.

97. Denord 2009, p. 49, quoting from the proceedings of the colloquium.

98. Denord 2009, pp. 46–47. Rüstow "privately . . . confessed to Wilhelm Röpke what he thought of Friedrich Hayek and Ludwig von Mises: their place was in the museum. . . . It was people of their ilk who were responsible for the great crisis of market legitimacy of the twentieth century" (Denord 2009, p. 49).

99. Cockett 1994, appendix 1, pp. 336–338.

100. MPS *Draft Statement of Aims,* quoted in Mirowski and Plehwe 2009, pp. 22–24, citing Hartwell 1995, pp. 49–50.

101. Burgin 2012, p. 5.

102. Burgin 2012, p. 13.

103. Burgin 2012, p. 15.

104. Founding figures included Aaron Director, Rose Director, Frank Knight, Henry Simons, George Stigler, and Allen Wallis. Starting in 1957, George Schultz (1920–) was recruited to Chicago (Stein 1994, p. 145). For an excellent account of the conservative legal movement and its Chicago connections, see Teles 2008.

105. On the essential hybrid of think tanks, see Medvetz 2012.

106. Phillips-Fein 2009, pp. 10–11.

107. Backhouse 2009, p. 19.

108. Fourcade 2006.

109. The Fraser Institute 2004; http://nobelprize.org/nobel_prizes/economics /laureates/and http://www.hoover.org/bios/, accessed February 26, 2009.

110. Backhouse 2009, p. 20.

111. This includes both Atlas network members and the Fraser-based Freedom Network.

112. Author dataset of Atlas organizations; author calculations—see the Methodological Appendix for more information, including a full listing of

Atlas organizations in Germany, Sweden, the United Kingdom, and the United States.

113. Blundell 2001 [2007], pp. 11, 20; see also Dyble 2008.

114. Mudge 2008; Szajkowski 2005.

115. Szajkowski 2005; International Democrat Union 2005; Liberal International 2005; see also Mudge 2008.

116. McCracken 1996, p. 165.

117. Stein 1994, p. 139. Stein was a CEA member, and then chairman, under Richard Nixon and Gerald Ford.

118. On the lasting impact of free market economists on the profession, see Clark, Miller-Wilford, and Stringham 2012.

119. One might note here how the Reagan Republicans, especially Congressman Jack Kemp, made use of the work of the Stanford-trained economist Arthur Laffer, then at the University of Southern California. Laffer argued that, to a certain point, government revenues will increase as tax rates decline. He famously jotted down his notion of an inverted U-shaped taxation-revenue curve in conversation with Donald Rumsfeld in September 1974 (see http://www.polyconomics.com/gallery/Napkin003.jpg). Laffer was influenced by the economist Robert Mundell—who was MIT-trained, Chicago- and IMF-connected, and a future recipient of the economics Nobel (1999) and who was later associated with the free market Fraser Institute (Stein 1994, pp. 244–248; Fraser Institute 2004).

120. Bockman 2011.

121. For more on these foundations and national "knowledge regimes" more generally, see Campbell and Pedersen 2014.

122. Thunert 2004.

123. Institute for Public Policy Research 2012.

124. Tanden 2013, p. 1.

125. Medvetz 2012. I elaborate on this argument in Chapter 7.

126. Clark, Miller-Wilford, and Stringham 2012.

127. For a concise assessment, see Sargent 1987.

128. Blaug 1986. See also Sargent and Wallace 1976; Lucas and Sargent 1979; Lucas and Sargent 1981.

129. Sargent 2008.

130. Sargent and Wallace 1976; Lucas and Sargent 1979. Sargent published a series of works concerned with expectations and interest rates starting in 1969; his first article with "rational expectations" in the title appeared in the *Journal of Money, Credit and Banking* in February 1972. See Sargent 2016.

131. Lucas and Sargent 1979, p. 6.

132. Lucas and Sargent 1979, p. 6.

133. Lucas and Sargent 1979, pp. 6–7.

134. Jenkins 2011; Sommer 2011. In the latter Sargent is quoted describing himself as a fiscally conservative Democrat who understands "himself as a scientist, a 'numbers guy' who is 'just seeking the truth' as any good researcher does" (Sommer 2011).

135. P. Klein 1984, p. 537.

136. P. Klein 1984, p. 539.

137. P. Klein 1984, p. 544.

138. Blaug 1998, p. 25.

139. Sargent 2016; Lucas 1995.

140. Jovanovic 2008.

141. Fourcade, Ollion and Algan 2015, pp. 103–105.

142. Flaherty 2015, p. 418; see also Krippner 2005, 2011.

143. Fourcade 2009, p. 2; see also Fourcade, Ollion and Algan 2015.

144. Blinder 1999, p. 255.

145. Polillo and Guillén 2005, pp. 1771–1772.

146. European Central Bank 2000, p. 130.

147. De Haan and Eijffinger 2000, p. 396.

148. Marcussen 2009; Polillo and Guillén 2005, p. 1767.

149. Marcussen 2009, pp. 375–379.

150. Mudge and Vauchez 2012; Major 2014.

151. Centre for Economic Policy Research 2013a.

152. Centre for Economic Policy Research 2013b.

153. For a full history of the field of American political consulting, see E. Walker 2014.

154. Laurison 2014; see also Sabato 1981.

155. Berenson and Tarr 2012.

156. Sabato 1988; Katz and Mair 1995; Farrell and Webb 2000.

157. Plasser and Plasser 2002, pp. 252–253.

158. Plasser and Plasser 2002, p. 254.

159. Plasser and Plasser 2002, p. 252.

160. Plasser and Plasser 2002, p. 253, citing Plasser, Scheucher, and Senft 1999, pp. 101–104.

161. Johnson 2016, p. 3.

7. New Economists, New Experts, New Democrats

Epigraph: Democratic Leadership Council (DLC) 1990, p. 3.

1. DiMaggio and Powell 1983.

2. From 2013, pp. 114, 237238.

3. I explore interpretations of inflation inside the Carter administration at length below.

4. I investigate the victory of DLC "progressives" over "liberals" further below.

5. Baer 2000, pp. 2, 7.

6. Benenson and Tarr 2012.

7. Baer 2000, p. 22.

8. Jackson and Hitlin 1981; cf. Sorauf 1972.

9. Scammon and Wattenberg 1970.

10. Baer 2000, pp. 30–31.

11. On the politics of quotas see Miller Center 2014a, p. 20; see also Baer 2000, pp. 30–31.

12. Baer 2000, p. 32.

13. The unseated chairmen were John William Wright Patman (1893–1976; D-TX) from the chairmanship of the House Banking and Currency Committee; William Robert Poage (1899–1987; D-TX) from the Agriculture Committee; and F. Edward Herbert (D-LA) from the House Armed Services Committee. Wilbur Mills (1909–1992; D-AR) was ousted as the long-standing head of the House Ways and Means Committee.

14. From 2006, p. 12. See also Hunter 1975.

15. Engstrom and Kernell 1999, p. 822.

16. Engstrom and Kernell 1999; see also the analysis in Chapter 6.

17. Caddell entered the ranks of high-level political advising when Gary Hart, McGovern's campaign manager, hired him to work on the McGovern campaign. Joe Klein comments that "Caddell had no precise sense of what pollsters did—what sort of questions they asked or, more important, didn't bother to ask (in fact, very few people did at that point)—and so he invented his own rules as he went along, asking open-ended questions, having real conversations, digging deeper, probing the nuance and intensity of the responses" (J. Klein 2007, p. 25).

18. Judis and Texeira 2002; see also J. Klein 2007.

19. Judis and Texeira 2002, p. 120, quoting Caddell.

20. See, e.g., Miller Center 2006b, p. 2.

21. Carp 2011, pp. 22–23.

22. Carp 2011, p. 23.

23. Miller Center 2006a, p. 3.

24. Miller Center 2006a, pp. 5–6.

25. Miller Center 2006a, pp. 18–19.

26. Miller Center 2006a, p. 25.

27. Miller Center 2006a, p. 30. Kahn's abstention from defense of the administration's regulatory policies (reportedly testifying, when asked, "Let the record show embarrassed silence"), in the case of a White House–initiated bill on sugar prices, for instance, was mobilized in Congress to defeat the bill (Miller Center 2006a, p. 30).

28. Miller Center 2003; see also Wilentz 2008, pp. 96–98.

29. Hoxie 1980.

30. Silber 2012; CNN 2016.

31. Silber 2012.

32. Silber 2012.

33. Lucas and Sargent 1979.

34. Miller Center 2006b, p. 19.

35. Silber 2012.

36. Miller Center 2003, p. 64.

37. Miller Center 2006b, p. 10.

38. See, e.g., Eizenstat 1981, p. 3.

39. Eizenstat 1992, pp. 65–66. The Carter administration had economists serving, Eizenstat notes, as "Secretary of Labor, Secretary of Commerce, Secretary of Treasury, Director of the Council on Wage and Price Stability, the President's anti-inflation adviser, Chairman and Council Members of the Council of Economic Advisers, and many other senior positions" (Eizenstat 1992, p. 65).

40. Eizenstat 1992, p. 66. Eizenstat may have had in mind Alfred Kahn, whom Eizenstat famously rebuked for publicly suggesting that rising inflation could result in a "very serious depression." Kahn responded by continuing to issue warnings of inflation-induced depression, but with the word "depression" replaced with "banana." See also Hershey 2010.

41. Miller Center 2014a, p. 3.

42. Miller Center 2014a, p. 3.

43. Miller Center 2014a, p. 7.

44. Miller Center 2014a, p. 8.

45. Miller Center 2014a, p. 8.

46. Notable here is another important basis of Democratic discontent: the political-insider Democratic magazine, the *Washington Monthly,* and its charismatic editor, Charles (Charlie) Peters. Peters had also worked for Shriver; like From, he also believed that liberalism, and liberal programs, required built-in mechanisms of criticism and self-correction. In the early 1980s Peters would become the charismatic center of a group of journalists and politicians that, for a time, took on the moniker "neo-liberal"—referring, of course, not to MPS-style neoliberalism, but to a new brand of Democratic liberalism, built on the inheritance of the New Deal. Peters' "neo-liberals" overlapped and intersected with DLC networks in the 1980s, but they understood themselves—and continue to do so—as distinctive.

47. On this see Berman and Milanes-Reyes 2013.

48. Carter and Reagan 1980.

49. For information on sources on profiles of CEA members, see the Methodological Appendix.

50. Here I refer to the remarkable story of David Stockman, Reagan's OMB director, infamous for the publication of a lengthy exposé of his manipulation of budgetary information in the *Atlantic* magazine in December 1981, a few months after passage of Reagan's budget. See Greider 1981; Stockman 1986 [2013].

51. Long recruited From to aid in his efforts after Reagan's victory. From later commented that he was both out of a job and among the ranks of middle-class people who were hard-hit by inflation, and so while he "wasn't interested in the future of the Democratic Party," he "was interested in paying [his] mortgage" (From 2006, p. 9). See also K. Brandt 2009, p. 92.

52. New Democrat sources, 2010, 2013. See Methodological Appendix for details.

53. Miller Center 2014a, p. 9.

54. Author calculations; Long and Wirth 1982.

55. Miller Center 2014a, p. 9.

56. Miller Center 2014a, p. 10.

57. Miller Center 2014a, p. 11.

58. K. Brandt 2009, pp. 92–93.

59. On From and Wirth's effort, see From 2006, p. 10.

60. K. Brandt 2009, p. 93.

61. Miller Center 2014a, p. 10.

62. Long and Wirth 1982; K. Brandt, 2009, p. 94.

63. Long and Wirth 1982, p. 9.

64. Long and Wirth 1982, p. 22.

65. Long and Wirth 1982, p. 23.

66. Long and Wirth 1982, pp. 21–22.

67. K. Brandt 2009, p. 98.

68. K. Brandt 2009, pp. 99–100.

69. K. Brandt 2009, pp. 99–100.

70. Baer 2000, p. 48–49.

71. Baer 2000, p. 48–49.

72. Baer 2000, p. 48–49.

73. New Democrats, 2010–2013. See Methodological Appendix for details.

74. Miller Center 2014a, p. 10.

75. Baer 2000, p. 50.

76. Southwell 2012, p. 268.

77. Baer 2000, p. 49.

78. On "the fringe," I quote the venture capitalist Michael Steinhardt (2001, Kindle loc. 1951), who was an important funder of the DLC and PPI and a leading figure in both institutions—I return to Steinhardt below.

79. Kamarck 1986, p. 336.

80. The term "paleoliberal" comes from Democratic neoliberals, 2013. See Methodological Appendix for details.

81. Baer 2000, p. 51.

82. New Democrats 2010–2013.

83. Dreyfuss 2001. See also Miller Center 2014a, p. 11.

84. Miller Center 2014a, p. 11.

85. Reed 2004, p. 4; Hohenstein 2004.

86. Shapiro 2017.

87. Miller Center 2014a, pp. 34–35.

88. Miller Center 2014a, pp. 28–29.

89. See, e.g., Dreyfuss 2001.

90. Dreyfuss 2001.

91. Steinhardt 2001, Kindle loc. 1960–1961. Dreyfuss reported that, as of 2001, "[t]he DLC board of trustees is an elite body whose membership is reserved for major donors, and many of the trustees are financial wheeler-dealers who run investment companies and capital management firms—though senior executives from a handful of corporations, such as Koch, Aetna, and Coca-Cola, are included. Some donate enormous amounts of money, such as Bernard Schwartz, the chairman and CEO of Loral Space and Communications, who single-handedly finances the entire publication of *Blueprint,* the DLC's retooled monthly that replaced *The New Democrat*" (Dreyfuss 2001).

92. Miller Center 2014a, pp. 34–35.

93. Miller Center 2014a, pp. 34–35.

94. Miller Center 2014a, p. 35.

95. Miller Center 2014a, pp. 34–35.

96. Medvetz 2012.

97. The Board of Trustees "were diverse in almost all respects except one; we were all relatively affluent" (Steinhardt 2001, Kindle loc. 1966).

98. Steinhardt 2001, Kindle loc. 1955.

99. Miller Center 2014a, p. 24.

100. Reed 2004, p. 12.

101. Galston and Kamarck 1989; see also Galston 1999–2001.

102. Miller Center 2014c, p. 10; New Democrats 2010–2013 (see Methodological Appendix); From 2013, pp. 108–109.

103. Miller Center 2014a, p. 34.

104. Steinhardt 2001, Kindle loc. 1955; From 2006, p. 22.

105. Miller Center 2014a, p. 34.

106. Miller Center 2014a, p. 10.

107. Miller Center 2014a, p. 5.

108. Steinhardt 2001; Miller Center 2014a.

109. Steinhardt 2001, Kindle loc. 1990.

110. Its presentation is viewable on C-SPAN (http://www.c-span.org/video/ ?17890-1/new-choice-resolution).

111. Miller Center 2014a, p. 24.

112. Reed 2004, pp. 6–19; see also Baer 2000, p. 199.

113. Reed 2004, p. 19.

114. Clinton 1991a, 1991b.

115. Reed 2004, p. 18; Clinton 1991a.

116. Clinton 1991b.

117. Reich 1998.

118. See, e.g., Economists for Clinton 1992.

119. Magaziner, Reich, and Altman are all associates of Clinton and bearers of considerable expertise, but none hold PhDs in economics. See Reich 2013; Magaziner 2017; Altman 2017; Leonhardt 2011.

120. Reich 2011, 2013; see also Reich 1998.

121. Ullmann 1997.

122. Shapiro 2017. In 1991 Shapiro had become a private consultant, performing "analyses for national corporate and public sector clients on antitrust, telecommunications regulation, corporate taxation, and information technology issues." See also Reich 2010 [2011], p. 3.

123. Fairbrother 2014, pp. 1345–1346.

124. Reich 2010 [2011], p. 3.

125. Greenhouse 1992.

126. Miller Center 2014c, p. 23.

127. Steinhardt 2001, Kindle loc. 2007–2009; see also Miller Center 2014c.

128. Reich 2011, p. 7.

129. Reich 2011, p. 8. Reich later compared Greenspan's role to a "black hole": "I could only tell of his existence by the movement of other celestial bodies in his direction. . . . [H]e was the biggest deficit hawk of all and he was telling Lloyd Bentsen in no uncertain terms that the deficit had to be reduced or else the Fed would not reduce short term interest rates" (Reich 2011, p. 8).

130. Ullmann 1997, p. 26.

131. Ullmann 1997, p. 25.

132. Miller Center 2014a, p. 12.

133. Ullmann 1997, p. 25.

134. Rubin's successor was Gene Sperling. Neither are credentialed economists, although, thanks to their roles in economic policy-making, they are commonly described using the title.

135. Miller Center 2014c, p. 8; Reich 1998.

136. Miller Center 2014c, p. 27.

137. Evans and Kay 2008.

138. Rubin and Weisberg 2003, Kindle loc. 95.

139. Rubin and Weisberg 2003, Kindle loc. 119.

140. Rubin and Weisberg 2003, Kindle loc. 242.

141. Rubin and Weisberg 2003, Kindle loc. 645–648.

142. From 2007, p. 29.

143. Reich 1998.

144. On Clinton's consultations with Morris, see Reich 1998; Miller Center 2014c.

145. Miller Center 2014c.

146. Miller Center 2014b, p. 30.

147. Clinton 1996a.

148. Stephanopoulos 1999 [2000], p. 412. But, Stephanopoulos noted, the politics of it were "solid gold," with 80 percent approval at the polls.

149. Stephanopoulos 1999 [2000], p. 412. Stephanopoulos attributes the comment on "the death of liberalism at its own hands" to the speechwriter Michael Waldman.

150. Clinton 1996b.

151. Vobejda and Havemann 1996.

152. Reich 1998.

153. Mora 2014.

8. Making Western European Leftism "Progressive"

Epigraph: Blair and Schröder 1998, p. 2.

1. New Democrats 2010–2013; Third Wayers 2013–2017.

2. I deal with a strictly economics-driven explanation, that Western center-left parties neoliberalized because they had no choice in the face of globalization, in the chronological phase of the analysis to follow. I attend to the transnational and European aspects of leftism's neoliberalization especially, but not solely, in the analysis of the SPD.

3. On the birth of the two-armed (one socialist, the other trade union-based) mass party of the left, see Chapter 3.

4. Przeworski and Sprague 1988; Judt 1989. Frances Fox Piven (1989) argued that the thesis of electoral socialism's inevitable decline mistakenly defined the working class in strictly industrial terms, failing to attend to the question of party organization. Some dismissed Przeworski and Sprague's argument on epistemological grounds (e.g., Lindemann 1988).

5. See Chapter 3.

6. For a full statement on party-driven articulation, see De Leon, Desai, and Tuğal 2015.

7. Howell 2001, pp. 7–8.

8. E.g., Erickson 1966; Blomqvist 2004.

9. Lundberg 1948, quoted in G. Ohlin 1996, p. 140.

10. G. Ohlin 1996, pp. 140–141, quoting Lundberg.

11. G. Ohlin 1996, p. 140; see also Erixon and Wadensjö 2012.

12. G. Ohlin 1996, pp. 140–141.

13. G. Ohlin 1996, pp. 140–141; Erixon 2010, pp. 684–685.

14. Offer and Söderberg 2016, p. 89.

15. Offer and Söderberg 2016, pp. 89–90.

16. Offer and Söderberg 2016, pp. 90–91.

17. Offer and Söderberg 2016, p. 91.

18. Offer and Söderberg 2016, p. 92.

19. European Free Trade Association 2017. Sweden would finally join the EU, leaving EFTA, in 1995.

20. Offer and Söderberg 2016, pp. 91–92.

21. Offer and Söderberg 2016, p. 94.

22. Offer and Söderberg 2016, p. 95.

23. Offer and Söderberg 2016, pp. 95–96.

24. Offer and Söderberg 2016, p. 98; Lindbeck 2014. See also Lindbeck 1971 [1977].

25. Lindbeck 1985, p. 37; Lindbeck 2014.

26. Lebaron 2006, p. 89; Offer and Söderberg 2016, p. 106. Offer and Söderberg found that, until the 1990s, the prize committee exhibited a preference against left-leaning economists.

27. Fourcade 2006; see also Chapter 6.

28. Mora 2014; see also Chapters 1 and 6.

29. Sandelin, Sarafoglou, and Veiderpass 2000, pp. 43–44.

30. Sandelin, Sarafoglou, and Veiderpass 2000, pp. 46–47.

31. Sandelin, Sarafoglou, and Veiderpass 2000, p. 49.

32. Schück 2002.

33. Lindvall 2009, p. 717.

34. A. Martin 1984, in Gourevitch et al., p. 238.

35. A. Martin 1984, in Gourevitch et al., p. 241.

36. A. Martin 1984, in Gourevitch et al., p. 248.

37. Pontusson 1994, p. 28.

38. Pontusson 1994.

39. Pontusson 1994. On deflection and "government by Commission," see Dyson 2005.

40. Blackburn 2005.

41. Blyth 2001; 2013, pp. 10–11. See also Pestoff 1991.

42. SNS 2017.

43. SNS 2017.

44. Offer and Söderberg 2016, pp. 204–205; Blyth 2001; Atlas network dataset (see Methodological Appendix).

45. Blyth 2001, p. 20.

46. Lindvall 2009, p. 718.

47. Hakelius 1997.

48. Söderström 2017.

49. Blyth 2001, p. 16; Korpi 1996, p. 1728. Korpi (1996) offers an extended refutation of the "sclerosis" diagnosis.

50. Offer and Söderberg 2016, pp. 211–212.

51. Offer and Söderberg 2016, pp. 204–205.

52. Söderström 2017.

53. Lindvall 2009, p. 717; Söderström 2017.

54. Lindvall 2009, pp. 718–719.

55. Lindvall 2009. Walter Korpi notes that, compared with the prior SAP government, Feldt "trebled the number of academically trained economists among the top advisors within the Ministry of Finance" (Korpi 1996, p. 1729).

56. Eklund 1999 [2009].

57. Eklund 1999 [2009].

58. Eklund et al. 1981.

59. *Dala-Demokraten* 2016, on Bergström; Flam 2014; C. Hamilton 2017.

60. Eklund 1999; Eklund et al. 1981; see also Andersson 2006, p. 116.

61. Eklund et al. 1981. Author's translation.

62. Eklund et al. 1981. Author's translation.

63. Eklund 1999.

64. Andersson 2006, p. 117.

65. Andersson 2006, p. 116.

66. Eklund 1982, 1999.

67. Offer and Söderberg 2016, p. 204.

68. Eklund 1999 [2009].

69. Eklund 1999 [2009].

70. Sohlman 2016.

71. Sohlman 2016.

72. Andersson 2006, p. 116.

73. Eklund 1999. See also Andersson 2006; Steinmo 1988; Ryner 1994; Brenner and Vad 2000; Blomqvist 2004.

74. Erixon 2010, p. 691.

75. Blomqvist 2004, p. 145.

76. Fredriksson 1996, p. 15.

77. Feldt interview, Sjoberg 1999.

78. Lindvall 2009, p. 718; Fredriksson 1996, p. 19.

79. SNS 2017; see also Lindvall 2009.

80. Ryner 1994, pp. 392–393. See also Gill and Law 1988.

81. Taylor 1989.

82. Eklund 1999 [2009].

83. Ryner 1994, p. 393.

84. As noted, the problem was exacerbated by the growth of public sector employment and, with it, white-collar union confederations (TCO and SAC) and the LO's Municipal Workers' Union (Kommunal). See Ryner 1994.

85. Ryner 1994, pp. 399–400.

86. Ryner 1994. See also Panitch 1981, 1986.

87. Ryner 1994, p. 404.

88. Prokesch 1990.

89. Ryner 1994, pp. 404–405; see also Wörlund 1992.

90. Ryner 1994, pp. 402–403.

91. Sandelin, Sarafoglou, and Veiderpass 2000, pp. 55.

92. Sandelin, Sarafoglou, and Veiderpass 2000, pp. 55–56.

93. Sandelin, Sarafoglou, and Veiderpass 2000, pp. 59–61.

94. Sandelin, Sarafoglou, and Veiderpass 2000, p. 42.

95. Blomqvist 2004; see also Sjoberg 1999.

96. Sundström 2008, p. 155.

97. Eklund 1999 [2009].

98. Sundström 2008, p. 157.

99. Juntunen 2011; Albright Stonebridge Group 2017.

100. One should note here, however, the arrival of the Stockholm- and Harvard-trained economist Magdalena Andersson (1967–) as SAP Finance Minister, starting in 2014.

101. Hamilton, of Hamilton Campaigns (2007), formerly Hamilton Beattie and Staff (see B. Hamilton 2017); Noble, of Phil Noble and Associates (see Noble 2017); Ridder, of RBI Strategies and Research (see Ridder 2017).

102. Nord 2001, pp. 114–116.

103. Sundström 2008, pp. 148–155.

104. M. Walker 1998.

105. Third Wayers 2013–2017.

106. Third Wayers 2013–2017.

107. Schröder 2002b.

108. M. Walker 1998; Third Wayers 2013–2017.

109. Fourcade 2009, p. 135.

110. Fourcade 2009, p. 177.

111. Miliband 1961. See also Panitch 1979 [2003]; Coates 2003.

112. Morris 2007.

113. Morris 2007, pp. ix–x.

114. Middleton 2012, p. 13.

115. Morris 2007, p. 100. On Benn, see Brivati 2014. Shore had a degree in history from King's College, Oxford; he would draft Labour's 1966 manifesto (see Pearce 2001).

116. Owen 1965, pp. 381–382.

117. Morris 2007, pp. 121–122.

118. On the making of the new DEA, see Morris 2007, p. 101.

119. Morris 2007, p. 101.

120. Fourcade 2009, pp. 170–171.

121. Middleton 2012, p. 13.

122. On the increase of economists in the civil service, see Clifford 1997, p. 94. The statistics are from Nelson 1989, p. 8.

123. Morris 2007, p. 109, quoting Hennessy in 1964.

124. Fourcade 2009, p. 169.

125. Fourcade 2009, p. 172; Clifford 1997. See also Streeten 1992; Pimlott 1993; Morris 2007.

126. Morris 2007, p. 11. In his twenties Balogh worked for the German, French, and U.S. central banks. At the Secretariat of the League of Nations in Geneva during the 1931 collapse of the gold standard, Balogh was "cured" of his "childhood bogey of inflation" (Morris 2007, p. 13, quoting Balogh). Working in the City of London before going to Oxford, Balogh's move from finance to academe paralleled a shift "towards a more heterodox view of economics" and "from right to left" politically (Morris 2007, p. 13).

127. Clifford 1997, p. 94.

128. Shonfield 1958; see also Tomlinson 2005.

129. On Balogh, see Morris 2007, pp. 107–108. There is some puzzlement in existing research as to why Wilson was so determined to avoid devaluation. Morris suggests that it had to do with a concern with establishing Labour's competence (2007, p. 107). On the long history of the Labour elite's concern with the party's reputational competence, see Chapter 3.

130. Hansard 1965.

131. The DEA head's response indicates that this criticism was a familiar Conservative refrain: "The old fill-in about the relationships between the D.E.A. and the Treasury and the other economic production departments we have heard so often, but it gets no better and no nearer to the truth" (Hansard 1965).

132. Hansard 1965.

133. Hansard 1965; Macleod is citing the *Financial Times*.

134. Morris 2007, p. 150.

135. Backhouse 2000, p. 31; see also Panitch, Leys, and Coats 2001.

136. Bogdanor 2012.

137. Mullard 2005.

138. Mullard 2005, pp. 183–184.

139. Haseler 1969, pp. 143–146, 164–166. Stephen Haseler notes that "this image was obviously an exaggeration . . . especially as far as membership was concerned, but surveys and polls carried out at that time verified this image as a representative one" (1969, p. 144). A major survey was carried out on the party's behalf by Research Services Ltd., directed by Mark Abrams. But even before it was done, Haseler notes, "many Gaitskellites had formulated their ideas on the danger to Labour of its exclusively working-class, 'cloth-cap' association in the public mind" (1969, p. 144).

140. On factional struggles inside Labour in the 1970s, see Koelble 1987a, b.

141. Tomlinson 2014, p. 756.

142. Tomlinson 2014, p. 756.

143. Tomlinson 2014, p. 756.

144. Tomlinson 2014, pp. 756–763.

145. Rothschild 1972.

146. Fourcade 2009 p. 180.

147. *Economist* 1975.

148. Tomlinson 1981, pp. 83–84.

149. Callaghan, 1976 [2017].

150. Hutchison 1977; A. Booth 1983, p. 105.

151. Mullard 2005, p. 184.

152. The inflation-unemployment correlation for the United Kingdom for the period 1970–2005 is -0.25, but after 1980 it flips to modestly positive: 0.29.

153. S. Hall 1979.

154. S. Hall 1979, p. 16.

155. Bentham 2006, p. 169.

156. Nelson 1989, p. 14.

157. Fourcade 2009, p. 184.

158. Mullard 2005, p. 185.

159. Cockett 1994 [1995].

160. Mullard 2005, p. 186.

161. Nelson 1989, p. 13.

162. Laws 2006, pp. 106–107.

163. See, e.g., P. Booth 2006.

164. Blundell 2001 [2007]; P. Booth 2006.

165. Minford, in P. Booth 2006, p. 83.

166. Nelson 1989, pp. 13, 19.

167. Fourcade 2009, pp. 135–136.

168. Fourcade 2009, p. 183.

169. Fourcade 2009, p. 182.

170. Mullard 2005, pp. 187–188.

171. Mandelson 2010 [2011], p. 46.

172. Mandelson 2010 [2011], pp. 54–59.

173. Mandelson 2010 [2011], pp. 59–60.

174. Mandelson 2010 [2011], p. 61.

175. Mandelson 2010 [2011], pp. 62–69.

176. Wickham-Jones 2000.

177. Panitch and Leys 2001, p. 220.

178. Bentham 2006; Gibbon 2001.

179. Giddens 1994; see also Giddens 1998, 2000.

180. This tracking of the use of "backbencher" is based on a Google Ngram search for the term in British English-language books for the period 1800–2010. See http://books.google.com/ngrams/.

181. Goodhart 2013, p. 11.

182. Mulgan 2013, pp. 17–18.

183. Mulgan 2013, p. 18.

184. Mulgan 2013, p. 21.

185. Panitch and Leys 2001, pp. 228–229.

186. Gibbon 2001.

187. Laurie Taylor is "said to have inspired Malcolm Bradbury's *The History Man*" (Rowan 2003).

188. Gibbon 2001; Rowan 2003.

189. Faucher-King 2005, pp. 181–184.

190. Faucher-King 2005, pp. 184–190.

191. Routledge 1998.

192. Routledge 1998.

193. Routledge 1998.

194. Routledge 1998.

195. Routledge 1998.

196. *Economist* 2007.

197. The significance of the New Democrats, and the influence of New Democrats via transatlantic networks, is well noted in research on New Labour. See, e.g., King and Wickham-Jones 1999. On the manifesto, see Lipset and Marks 2000 [2013], pp. 274–276.

198. Mair 2000, p. 31.

199. Peston 1995.

200. Rowan 2003.

201. Gibbon 2001.

202. Gibbon 2001.

203. Rowan 2003.

204. Goodhart 2013, p. 13.

205. Childs 1994; Augstein 1995; Whitney 1984.

206. Dyson 2001, p. 135.

207. Dyson 2001, pp. 135–136.

208. Maravall 2010, p. 11; see also Padgett and Paterson 1994, p. 105.

209. Markovits 1986, pp. 131–132.

210. Markovits 1986, pp. 132–133; Berry 2005.

211. Markovits and Allen 1984, p. 149.

212. DIW Berlin 1979.

213. Potrafke 2013, p. 182.

214. Hagemann 2000, p. 120.

215. Thunert 2004; Pautz 2010b.

216. Pautz 2010b, p. 288.

217. It is also notable here that Agartz was removed from his position at the head of the WWI by trade union leadership, for being too left, in 1955. The WSI's scientific reputation deteriorated in the 1970s (Third Wayers 2013–2017).

218. Hochstätter 2006; Koelble 1987a, p. 110.

219. Koelble 1987a, p. 59.

220. Hülsberg 1987, p. 95.

221. Campbell and Pedersen 2014, pp. 158–160.

222. Krupp 1986.

223. Willy Brandt Kreis 2009.

224. Berry 2005, pp. 348–349. Müller also advised Helmut Schmidt and, in the true form of the economist theoretician, ran a number of SPD election campaigns (Engelen 2005).

225. Between 2004 and 2011 Peter Bofinger, also appointed with trade union endorsement, would also cast 17 dissenting votes. See Potrafke 2013, pp. 182–183.

226. Potrafke 2013, p. 182.

227. Hagemann 2000, p. 124.

228. Ohm 1999.

229. Padgett and Paterson 1994, p. 57; Hülsberg 1987, p. 88.

230. T. Meyer 1997, p. 130.

231. T. Meyer 1997, p. 135.

232. Lafontaine 1999 [2000], p. 19.

233. Lafontaine 1999 [2000], p. 18.

234. Lafontaine 1999 [2000], pp. 23–25.

235. Hagemann, 2000.

236. Lafontaine 1999 [2000], pp. 26–27.

237. Engelen 2005, p. 62.

238. Lafontaine 1999 [2000], p. 26.

239. Lafontaine 1999 [2000], p. 25.

240. Lafontaine 1999 [2000], pp. 26–27.

241. Lafontaine 1999 [2000], p. 29. He continues: "His doctrine was reduced to a thesis that the state had to borrow in order to stimulate the economy."

242. Sturm 2009, pp. 11–14. Translation by Kate Miller.

243. *Economist* 1999.

244. Leonard 2000, p. xii.

245. Sturm 2009, p. 11. Translation by Kate Miller. See also Gibson and Römmelle 2009.

246. See Chapter 2.

247. Blair and Schröder 1998, p. 5.

248. Blair and Schröder 1998, pp. 7–10.

249. Blair and Schröder 1998, p. 12.

250. Initial members of the eurozone were Belgium, Germany, Spain, France, Ireland, Italy, Luxembourg, the Netherlands, Austria, Portugal, and Finland. The other four members, of non-euro countries (at that time), were the banks of Greece, Sweden, England, and Denmark.

251. See also Polillo and Guillén 2005.

252. Lafontaine 1999 [2000], p. 143.

253. Lafontaine 1999 [2000], pp. 143–144.

254. I am thankful to Wolfgang Streeck for his insight on the significance of Eichel's premiership.

255. Engelen 2005.

256. Lafontaine 1999 [2000], pp. x, 30–33.

257. Lafontaine 1999 [2000], p. 32.

258. Lafontaine 1999 [2000], pp. viii, xiii.

259. Dyson 2001, p. 137.

260. Dyson 2001, p. 137.

261. Dyson 2001, p. 137.

262. Kemmerling and Bruttel 2006, p. 91.

263. Pautz 2010b; see also Pautz 2008.

264. Kemmerling and Bruttel 2006, p. 91.

265. Simonian 2003.

266. Kemmerling and Bruttel 2006, p. 92.

267. Kemmerling and Bruttel 2006, pp. 104–105.

268. Müller 2004, quoted in Engelen 2005, p. 26.

269. Engelen 2005, p. 26.

270. Pautz 2010b, p. 285.

9. Conclusions and Implications

Epigraphs: D'Alema 2002; (formerly a member of the Italian Communist Party, Massimo D'Alema was the prime minister of Italy from 1998 to 2000); Mulgan 2013, p. 21.

    1. Polanyi 1944 [2001], p. 3.

    2. Polanyi 1944 [2001], pp. 3–4.

    3. Eyal and Buchholz 2010, p. 120.

    4. Gramsci 1929–1935 [1971], p. 12.

    5. Mitchell 1998.

    6. Gramsci 1929–1925 [1971], p. 234.

Methodological Appendix

    1. Mudge 2011.

    2. See Budge et al. 2001; Klingemann et al. 2006. These data are the product of the Comparative Manifestos Project (CMP) of the Manifesto Research Group (MRG).

    3. Volkens 2001, p. 96.

    4. For further explanation, see Budge et al. 2001; for the procedures used to create the dataset, see Volkens 2001.

    5. Generally speaking, center-left parties include noncommunist socialist and social democratic parties, Labour/New Labour; and the American, Canadian, and Australian Democrats/New Democrats. Center-right parties include liberal and liberal democrat parties (European), Conservative parties, continental Democrats, the American Republicans, and Christian Democrats. Party categorizations are, as much as possible, based on the historical self-positioning of political parties within their national contexts; they are based on those given in the original dataset, checked against other sources (McHale 1983; Day and Degenhart 1984; Muller, Overstreet, Isacoff, and Lansford 2011). I deal in-depth with the emergence of the "center-left" as a political category and party type in Chapter 3.

    6. One exception is the former Italian Communist Party (PCI), which is counted as a mainstream party because it was for a considerable period Italy's main party of the left (Anderson 1976; Sassoon 1996).

    7. That is, across families of countries that share political and religious histories and have tended to develop in similar, path-dependent ways. See Esping-Andersen 1990, 1999.

    8. Portugal became a democracy in 1976; Spain in 1978; Greece in 1975.

    9. For a fuller discussion of my conceptualization of neoliberalism, see Mudge 2008, 2016, 2017; see also Chapters 2 and 6. Since data only exist for

election years, I group all policy indexes into five-year averages. Because some countries appear more than others and have more parties than others, all measures are weighted using STATA's *aweight* function.

10. I do not use factor analysis because I neither expect nor claim that all the components of the index hang together across countries in a systematic way; it is precisely the aim of this analysis both to track a general trend and to identify its many variants.

Bibliography

Historical/Archival, Biographical/Autobiographical, and News Sources

Albright Stonebridge Group. 2017. About Us: Pär Nuder. Albright Stone-bridge Group. http://www.albrightstonebridge.com/team/p%C3%A4r-nuder, accessed April 11, 2017.

Altman, Roger. 2017. Roger C. Altman, Founder and Senior Chairman. Evercore. http://www.evercore.com/team/2/all/all/bio/34, accessed March 23, 2017.

American Economic Association. 1976. In Memoriam: Alvin H. Hansen. *The American Economic Review* 66, 5: 986–987.

Associated Press. 1937. Vandenberg Urges Coalition to Fight "Roosevelt Party"; Republicans and Democrats Must Forget Old Party Lines, He Tells Michigan Rally. *New York Times,* September 19.

Augstein, Rudolf. 1995. Karl Schiller: 1911 bis 1994. *Der Spiegel,* January 2.

Barber, William. 1987. The Career of Alvin H. Hansen in the 1920s and 1930s: A Study in Intellectual Transformation. *History of Political Economy* 19, 2: 191–205.

Barber, William J. 2008. *Gunnar Myrdal: An Intellectual Biography*. London: Palgrave Macmillan.

Barr, Ann, 1997. The Swot Who Knows Best. *Independent*, March 9.

Berle, Adolph, Jr., and Gardiner Means. 1932. *The Modern Corporation and Private Property*. New York: Harcourt, Brace and World.

Blackburn, Robin. 2005. Rudolf Meidner, 1914–2005: A Visionary Pragma-tist. *Counterpunch,* December 22. http://www.counterpunch.org/2005/12/22/a-visonary-pragmatist, accessed April 30, 2014.

Blair, Tony, and Gerhard Schröder. 1998. *Europe: The Third Way/Die Neue Mitte*. Working Document #2. Johannesburg: Friedrich Ebert Foundation South Africa Office.

Blundell, John. 2001 [2007]. *Waging the War of Ideas.* London: Institute of Economic Affairs.

Booth, Philip, ed. 2006. *Were 364 Economists All Wrong?* London: Institute of Economic Affairs.

Brandt, Willy. 1960. *My Road to Berlin.* New York: Doubleday.

Brazelton, Robert. 1997a. The Economics of Leon Hirsch Keyserling. *Journal of Economic Perspectives* 11, 4: 189–197.

Brazelton, Robert. 1997b. Alvin Harvey Hansen: A Note on His Analysis of Keynes, Hayek, and Commons. *Journal of Economic Issues* 27, 3 (September): 940–948.

Brivati, Brian. 1996. *Hugh Gaitskell.* London: Richard Cohen Books.

Brivati, Brian. 2014. Tony Benn Obituary. *Guardian,* February 14. http://www.theguardian.com/politics/2014/mar/14/tony-benn-obituary.

Buckley, William F., Jr. 1951. *God and Man at Yale.* Chicago: Regnery.

Callaghan, James. 1976 [2017]. Leader's Speech, Blackpool, 1976. Labour Party. http://www.britishpoliticalspeech.org/speech-archive.htm?speech =174, accessed December 14, 2017.

Carp, Bert. 2011. Slaying the Dragon of Debt: Fiscal Politics and Policy from the 1970s to the Present. A project of the Walter Shorenstein Program in Politics, Policy and Values, conducted by Patrick Sharma in 2011. Regional Oral History Office, Bancroft Library, University of California, Berkeley.

Carter, Jimmy and Ronald Reagan. 1980. Presidential Debate in Cleveland, October 28, 1980. Online by Gerhard Peters and John T. Woolley, The American Presidency Project. http://www.presidency.ucsb.edu/ws/?pid =29408. Accessed December 3, 2017.

Center for American Progress (CAP). 2013. *Making Progress: Ten Years of Ideas, Action and Change.* Tenth Anniversary Report. Washington, DC: Center for American Progress and Center for American Progress Action Fund.

Centre for Economic Policy Research (CEPR). 2013a. About CEPR. http://cepr.org/about-cepr, accessed October 12, 2013.

Centre for Economic Policy Research (CEPR). 2013b. Supporters of CEPR. http://cepr.org/content/supporters-cepr, accessed October 12, 2013.

Childs, David. 1994. Obituaries: Karl Schiller. *Independent,* December 28.

Clark, Delbert. 1937a. The Democrats at a Turn in the Road. *New York Times,* August 29.

Clark, Delbert. 1937b. The Republicans Face a Great Decision. *New York Times,* June 20.

Clarke, Peter, and Richard Toye. 2004. Cripps, Sir (Richard) Stafford (1889–1952). In H. C. G. Matthew and Brian Harrison, eds., *Oxford Dictionary*

of National Biography. Oxford: Oxford University Press. http://www
.oxforddnb.com/view/article/32630, accessed August 7, 2013.

Clinton, William J. 1991a. The New Covenant: Responsibility and Rebuilding
the American Community. Remarks to Students at Georgetown University,
October 23. http://www.dlc.org/, accessed November 2013.

Clinton, William J. 1991b. A New Covenant for Economic Change. Remarks
to Students at Georgetown University, November 20. http://www.dlc.org/,
accessed November 2013.

Clinton, William J. 1996a. Address before a Joint Session of the Congress on
the State of the Union, January 23, 1996. American Presidency Project, by
Gerhard Peters and John T. Woolley. http://www.presidency.ucsb.edu/ws
/?pid=53091.

Clinton, William J. 1996b. Statement on Signing the Personal Responsibility
and Work Opportunity Reconciliation Act of 1996, August 22, 1996.
American Presidency Project, by Gerhard Peters and John T. Woolley.
http://www.presidency.ucsb.edu/ws/?pid=53219.

CNN. 2016. Paul Volcker Fast Facts. http://www.cnn.com/2013/01/30/us/paul
-volcker-fast-facts.

Cole, G. D. H. 1953. What is Socialism?, I. *Political Studies* 1: 21–33.

Columbia University Libraries. [Undated.] John Maurice Clark papers,
[ca. 1920] –1963. http://www.columbia.edu/cu/lweb/archival/collections
/ldpd_4078614/, accessed December 3, 2017. .

Council of Economic Advisers (CEA). 1964. Council of Economic Advisers
Oral History Interview. With Walter Heller, Kermit Gordon, James Tobin,
Gardner Ackley, and Paul Samuelson, by Joseph Pechman, August 1. Oral
History Program, John F. Kennedy Presidential Library. http://www
.jfklibrary.org/Asset-Viewer/Archives/JFKOH-CEA-01.aspx.

Council of Economic Advisers (CEA). 2016. Members of the Council of
Advisers. http://www.whitehouse.gov/administration/eop/cea/about/Former
-Members, accessed April 27, 2016. [Now http://obamawhitehouse
.archives.gov/administration/eop/cea/about/members.]

Cross, Colin. 1966. *Philip Snowden.* London: Barrie and Rockliff.

Currie, Lauchlin. 1978. Comments and Observations. *History of Political
Economy* 10: 541–548.

Dala-Demokraten. 2016. Nostalgitripp med Villy. February 7. http://www
.dalademokraten.se/opinion/ledare/nostalgitripp-med-villy.

D'Alema, Massimo. 2002. Interview with Massimo D'Alema (of the Italian
Democratic Party of the Left), by Harry Kreisler, June 11. Institute of
International Studies, University of California, Berkeley. http://globetrotter
.berkeley.edu/people2/DAlema/dalema-con.e0.html, accessed November 25, 2008.

Democratic Leadership Council (DLC). 1990. *The New Orleans Manifesto: A Democratic Agenda for the 1990s.* Endorsed by the Fourth Annual Conference of the Democratic Leadership Council in New Orleans, Louisiana, March 22–25, 1990.

Democratic Leadership Council (DLC). 1996. The New Progressive Declaration: A Political Philosophy for the Information Age. http://www.ndol.org /ndolci.cfm?kaid=128&subid=185&contentid=880, accessed December 5, 2006.

Der Spiegel. 1974. Claus Dieter Arndt. February 4. http://www.spiegel.de /spiegel/print/d-41784425.html.

DIW Berlin 1979. Eine mittelfristige Strategie zur Wiedergewinnung der Vollbeschaeftigung (Financing the Structure and Distribution Effects of a Demand-Oriented Strategy for the Recovery of Full Employment). *DIW Weekly Report,* no. 13/1979, *Working-Class Labor Market Perspectives,* pp. 139–147.

DIW Berlin. 2008 [2017]a. Ferdinand Friedensburg (1886–1972). http://www .diw.de/de/diw02.c.102419.de/ueberuns/dasdiwberlin/institutsleiter /ferdinandfriedensburg/ferdinandfriedensburg.html.

DIW Berlin. 2008 [2017]b. Klaus-Dieter Arndt. http://www.diw.de/de/diw02.c .102424.de/ueberuns/dasdiwberlin/institutsleiter/klausdieterarndt /klausdieterarndt.html.

Dreyfuss, Robert. 2001. How the DLC Does It. *Prospect,* December 19. http://prospect.org/article/how-dlc-does-it, accessed March 22, 2017.

Dyble, Colleen, ed. 2008. Taming Leviathan. London: Institute of Economic Affairs.

Eccles, Mariner S. 1951. *Beckoning Frontiers.* New York: Alfred A. Knopf.

Economist. 1975. Economics: New Oxford. Business Brief, November 29, p. 76.

Economist. 1997. New Labour's Gurus: The American Connection. November 6. http://www.economist.com/node/105528, accessed July 6, 2015.

Economist. 1999. Bodo Hombach, Germany's trouble-shooter. February 18. http://www.economist.com/node/186932, accessed December 6, 2017.

Economist. 2007. April 28. The Think-Tanks that Miss the Target. June 7.

Economists for Clinton. 1992. On Clinton's National Economic Strategy. *Challenge,* September–October.

Eichengreen, Barry, and Tim Hatton, eds. 2012. Interwar Unemployment in International Perspective. Dordrecht: Springer.

Eizenstat, Stuart. 1981. Stuart Eizenstat Exit Interview, by Emily Soapes. Presidential Papers Staff, Jimmy Carter Presidential Library. https://www .jimmycarterlibrary.gov/research/oral_histories.

Eizenstat, Stuart. 1992. Economists and White House Decisions. *Journal of Economic Perspectives* 6, 3: 65–71.

Eklund, Klas. 1982. Den bistra sanningen: Om Sveriges ekonomi och de kommande magra åren [The Grim Truth: On Sweden's Economy and the Coming Years]. *Tidens debatt*. Stockholm: Tidens Förlag.

Eklund, Klas. 1999. An Intellectual Biography and Manifesto. http://www .klaseklund.se/, accessed May 31, 2014.

Eklund, Klas, et al. 1981. Nu krävs en svensk historisk kompromiss. *i Dags Nyheter*, January 21.

Engelen, Klaus C. 2005. Battle of Economists. *International Economy*, Winter, 22–62.

Ennis, Thomas W. 1986. Leon Henderson, a Leading New Deal Economist. *New York Times*, October 21. http://www.nytimes.com/1986/10/21 /obituaries/.

Erixon, Lennart, and Eskil Wadensjö. 2012. Gösta Rehn (1913–96)—en otålig samhällsreformator. *Ekonomisk Debatt* 40, 8: 71–82.

Eucken, Walter. 1932. Staatliche Strukturwandlungen und die Krise des Kapitalismus. *Weltwirtschaftliches Archiv* 36: 297–323.

European Central Bank. 2000. *Annual Report*. Frankfurt am Main: European Central Bank.

European Free Trade Association (EFTA). 2017. About EFTA. http://www.efta .int/about-efta/history, accessed February 19, 2017. Geneva.

Ezekiel, Mordecai. [Undated.] Biographical Sketch. Pp. 2–4 in *Papers of Mordecai J. B. Ezekiel, 1918–1975*. FDR Library. http://www.fdrlibrary .marist.edu/archives/pdfs/findingaids/findingaid_ezekiel.pdf, accessed December 7, 2017.

Federal Ministry for Economic Affairs and Energy / Bundesministerium für Wirtschaft und Energie. 2017. In Focus: Advisory Boards. http://www .bmwi.de/Navigation/EN/Ministry/Advisory-Boards/advisory-boards.html, accessed November 26, 2017.

Finletter, Thomas. 1972. Oral History Interview with Thomas K. Finletter, by Jerry N. Hess. Harry S. Truman Presidential Library. http://www .trumanlibrary.org/oralhist/finlettr.htm, accessed December 27, 2015.

Flam, Harry. 2014. Curriculum Vitae. http://perseus.iies.su.se/~flam /CVHarryFlam.pdf.

Fraser Institute. 2004. The Fraser Institute at 30: A Retrospective. Vancouver: Fraser Institute.

Fredriksson, Gunnar. 1996. *Olof Palme*. Stockholm: Svenska Institutet.

Fregert, Klaus. 1991. Dramatis Personae at the End of 1937. Pp. xvii–xxi in Lars Jonung, ed., *The Stockholm School Revisited*. New York: Cambridge University Press.

Friedman, Milton. 1953. The Methodology of Positive Economics. Pp. 3–43 in *Essays in Positive Economics*. Chicago: University of Chicago Press.

Friedman, Milton. 1962. *Capitalism and Freedom*. Chicago: University of Chicago Press.

Friedman, Milton. 1967 [1968]. The Role of Monetary Policy. *The American Economic Review* 58, 1: 1–17.

Friedman, Milton. 1968a. *Dollars and Deficits: Inflation, Monetary Politics, and the Balance of Payments*. New York: Prentice-Hall.

Friedman, Milton. 1968b. The Economic Crisis. *Firing Line*, no. 83 (January), New York. Hoover Institution Library and Archives, Stanford University. http://www.youtube.com/watch?v=N8lhLhXasVQ.

Friedman, Milton, and Walter Heller. 1968 [1969]. *Monetary vs. Fiscal Policy*. The Seventh Annual Arthur K. Salomon Lecture, Graduate School of Business Administration, New York University. New York: W. W. Norton.

From, Al. 2013. *The New Democrats and the Return to Power*. London and New York: Palgrave Macmillan.

Galbraith, John Kenneth. 2001. *The Essential Galbraith*. Boston and New York: Houghton Mifflin Company.

Galston, William. 1999–2001. William Galston. Institute of Race and Social Division, Boston University. http://www.bu.edu/irsd/lectures/galstonbio.htm, accessed March 16, 2017.

Galston, William, and Elaine Kamarck. 1989. *The Politics of Evasion: Democrats and the Presidency*. Washington, DC: Progressive Policy Institute.

Gibbon, Gary. 2001. The New Statesman Profile—Matthew Taylor. *New Statesman,* May 28. www.newstatesman.com/.

Giddens, Anthony. 1994. *Beyond Left and Right: The Future of Radical Politics*. Stanford, CA: Stanford University Press.

Giddens, Anthony. 1998. *The Third Way*. Cambridge, UK: Polity Press.

Giddens, Anthony. 2000. *The Third Way and Its Critics*. Cambridge, UK: Polity Press.

Gilbert, Richard. 1939–1948. Richard V. Gilbert Papers. FDR Library. http://www.fdrlibrary.marist.edu/archives/collections/franklin/index.php?p=collections/findingaid&id=576&q=&rootcontentid=238789#id238789.

Greenhouse, Steven. 1992. The Transition: Recruiting; Clinton Economic Advisers Get Assignments, and Heads May Turn. *New York Times,* November 19.

Goodhart, David. 2013. Preface. Pp. 11–14 in Ralph Scott and David Goodhart, eds., *Twenty Years of Ideas*. London: Demos.

Gurley, John G., Moses Abramovitz and Tibor Scitovsky. [Undated.] Memorial Resolution: Lorie Tarshis (1911–1993). Stanford University Office of the President. http://historicalsociety.stanford.edu/pdfmem/TarshisL.pdf, accessed June 6, 2014.

Hakelius, Johan. 1997. Johan Myhrman in Memoriam. *Svenska Dagbladet*. September 10.

Hamilton, Bill. 2017. Bill Hamilton. Hamilton Campaigns. http://www .hamiltoncampaigns.com/about-us/our-history/38.html, accessed December 7, 2017.

Hamilton, Carl. 2017. Carl B. Hamilton (L): Tillgänglig ersättere. Sveriges Riksdag. https://www.riksdagen.se/sv/ledamoter-partier/ledamot/carl-b -hamilton_0477013214601, accessed December 7, 2017.

Hansard. 1965. Economic Debate, House of Commons, November 17, 1965, vol. 720, cols. 1155–284. House of Commons Hansard Archives. http:// hansard.millbanksystems.com/commons/1965/nov/17/economic-affairs#S5 CV0720P019651117HOC286.

Harris, Seymour. 1964. Oral History Interview. John F. Kennedy Presidential Library. http://www.jfklibrary.org/Asset-Viewer/Archives/JFKOH-SEH-01 .aspx.

Harrison, Benjamin. 1892. Letter Accepting the Presidential Nomination, September 3, 1892. American Presidency Project, by Gerhard Peters and John T. Woolley. http://www.presidency.ucsb.edu/ws/index.php?pid=76067, accessed October 7, 2013.

Haunhorst, Regina, and Irmgard Zündorf. 2016. Biografie Karl Schiller. LeMO-Biografien, Lebendiges Museum Online, Stiftung Haus der Geschichte der Bundesrepublik Deutschland. http://www.hdg.de/lemo /biografie/karl-schiller.html, accessed December 3, 2016.

Heller, Walter. 1966. *New Dimensions of Political Economy*. The Godkin Lectures at Harvard University. Cambridge, MA: Harvard University Press.

Heller, Walter. 1968 [1969]. Is Monetary Policy Being Oversold? Pp. 13–42 in Milton Friedman and Walter Heller, *Monetary vs. Fiscal Policy*. The Seventh Annual Arthur K. Salomon Lecture, Graduate School of Business Administration, New York University. New York: W. W. Norton.

Hershey, Robert D., Jr. 2010. Alfred E. Kahn Dies at 93; Prime Mover of Airline Deregulation. *New York Times*, December 28. http://www.nytimes .com/2010/12/29/business/29kahn.html.

Hicks, John R. 1937. Mr. Keynes and the "Classics": A Suggested Interpretation. *Econometrica* 5, 2: 147–159.

Hicks, John R. 1939 [1978]. *Value and Capital: An Inquiry into Some Fundamental Principles of Economic Theory*. Oxford: Oxford University Press.

Hilferding, Rudolf. 1910 [1981]. *Finance Capital: A Study of the Latest Phase of Capitalist Development*. Ed. Tom Bottomore. London: Routledge and Kegan Paul.

Hochstätter, Matthias. 2006. Karl Schiller—eine wirtschaftpolitische Biografie. PhD dissertation, Universität Hannover.

Hogwood, Patricia. 1995. Ollenhauer, Erich (1901–1963). P. 712 in A. Thomas Lane, ed., *Biographical Dictionary of European Labor Leaders*. Vol. 2. Westport, CT: Greenwood Publishing.

Hohenstein, Kurt A. 2004. Briefing Materials: Bruce Reed. William J. Clinton Presidential History Project. February 19 and 20. Charlottesville, VA: The Miller Center.

Howson, Susan. 2004. Meade, James Edward (1907–1995). Pp. 643–648 in C. G. Matthew and B. Harrison, eds., *Oxford Dictionary of National Biography*, London: Oxford University Press.

Hunter, Marjorie. 1975. 4 Ousted House Chairmen Just Watch Parade. *New York Times*, October 22. http://www.nytimes.com/1975/10/22/archives/4-ousted-house-chairmen-just-watch-parade-4-ousted-house-chairmen.html.

Institute for Public Policy Research (IPPR). 2012. http://www.ippr.org/, accessed January 21, 2012.

International Democrat Union (IDU). 2005. Washington Declaration. Party Leaders' Meeting, July 18, Washington, DC.

Janssen, Hauke. 2009. Zwischen Historismus und Neoklassik: Alexander Rüstow und die Krise in der deutschen Volkswirtschaftslehre. Hamburgisches WeltWirtschaftsInstitut (HWWI) Research Paper 5-7. Hamburg: HWWI.

Jenkins, Holman W., Jr. 2011. Chicago Economics on Trial. *Wall Street Journal,* September 24. http://www.wsj.com/articles/SB10001424053111190 41946045765833825508849232.

Juntunen, Pirkko. 2011. Nordic Roundup: Erik Åsbrink, Goldman Sachs, AMF. Investments and Pensions Europe, July 29. http://www.ipe.com/nordic-roundup-erik-sbrink-goldman-sachs-amf/41540.fullarticle, accessed February 20, 2017.

Kautsky, Karl. 1891 [1971]. *The Class Struggle (Erfurt Program)*. Trans. William E. Bohn. New York: W. W. Norton.

Keynes, John Maynard. 1924. Alfred Marshall, 1842–1924. *Economic Journal* 34, 135: 311–372.

Keynes, John Maynard. 1926 [2004]. *The End of Laissez-Faire; The Economic Consequences of the Peace*. Amherst, NY: Prometheus Books.

Keynes, John Maynard. 1936 [1964]. *The General Theory of Employment, Interest and Money*. New York: Harcourt, Brace and World.

Keyserling, Leon. 1971. Oral History Interview with Leon Keyserling, by Jerry N. Hess, May 3. Harry S. Truman Presidential Library.

Krämer, Susanne. 1995. Viktor Agartz: Vom Cheftheoretiker zur "Persona non grata." *Gewerkschaftliche Monatshefte*, pp. 310–316. http://library.fes.de

/gmh/main/pdf-files/gmh/1995/1995-05-a-310.pdf, accessed September 28, 2016.

Krupp, Hans-Jürgen. 1986. Farthmann hat nicht zu Ende gedacht. *Der Spiegel*, March 31. http://www.spiegel.de/spiegel/print/d-13519517.html.

Kuznets, Simon. 1971 [2014]. Simon Kuznets—Biographical, Nobelprize.org. http://www.nobelprize.org/nobelprizes/economic-sciences/laureates/1971/kuznets-bio.html.

Lafontaine, Oskar. 1999 [2000]. *The Heart Beats on the Left*. London: Polity Press.

Leonard, Mark. 2000. Introduction. Pp. xi–xxix in Bodo Hombach, ed. *The Politics of the New Centre*. London: Polity Press.

Leonhardt, David. 2011. Gene Sperling 101. *New York Times*, January 5. http://economix.blogs.nytimes.com/2011/01/05/gene-sperling-101, accessed March 23, 2017.

Liberal International. 2005. http://www.liberal-international.org/, accessed December 1, 2005.

Lindahl, Erik. 1951. Till hundraårsminnet av Knut Wicksells födelse. *Ekonomisk Tidskrift* 53, 4: 197–243.

Lindbeck, Assar. 1971 [1977]. *The Political Economy of the New Left: An Outsider's View*. New York: Harper and Row.

Lindbeck, Assar. 1985. The Prize in Economic Science in Memory of Alfred Nobel. *Journal of Economic Literature* 23, 1: 37–56.

Lindbeck, Assar. 2014. Professional CV. http://perseus.iies.su.se/~alind/CV_AL_NY.pdf, accessed January 7, 2015.

Loeb, James, Jr.. 1970. Oral History Interview with James I. Loeb, by Jerry N. Hess. Harry S. Truman Presidential Library.

Lucas, Robert E., Jr. 1995. Robert E. Lucas, Jr.—Curriculum Vitae. http://www.nobelprize.org/nobelprizes/economic-sciences/laureates/1995/lucas-cv.html.

Lucas, Robert E., Jr., and Thomas J. Sargent. 1979. 1979. After Keynesian Macroeconomics. *Federal Reserve Bank of Minneapolis Quarterly Review* 3, 2: 1–16.

Lundberg, Erik. 1948. Connections between Economic Theory and Economic Policy. *Nationalökonomisk Tidskrift* 50: 53–57.

Lütjen, Torben. 2007. *Karl Schiller (1911–1994): "Superminister" Willy Brandts*. Bonn: Dietz.

Magaziner, Ira. 2017. Ira Magaziner. Clinton Foundation. http://www.clintonfoundation.org/blog/authors/ira-magaziner, accessed March 23, 2017.

Magnusson, Lars, Jan Ottosson, and Ann-Britt Hellmark. 2006. In Memory of Rudolf Meidner (1914–2005). *Economic and Industrial Democracy* 27: 7.

Mandelson, Peter. 2010 [2011]. *The Third Man.* New York: HarperPress.

McCracken, Paul. 1996. Economic Policy in the Nixon Years. In The Nixon Presidency, *Presidential Studies Quarterly* 26, 1 (Winter): 165–177.

McCracken, Paul, Guido Carli, Herbert Giersch, Attila Karaosmanoglu, Ryutaro Komiya, Assar Lindbeck, Robert Marjolin, and Robin Matthews. 1977. *Towards Full Employment and Stability.* A report to the Organization for Economic Cooperation and Development (OECD) by a group of independent experts. Paris: OECD.

Meidner, Rudolf. 1980. Our Concept of the Third Way: Some Remarks on the Socio-Political Tenets of the Swedish Labour Movement. *Economic and Industrial Democracy* 1: 343–369.

Meidner, Rudolf. 1988. Gosta Rehn as an LO Economist. *Economic and Industrial Democracy* 9, 4: 455–474.

Meidner, Rudolf. 1993. Why Did the Swedish Social Model Fail? *Socialist Register* 29: 211–228.

Meidner, Rudolf. 2003. Några tankar vid ett seminarium, *Den svenska modellens ekonomiska politik.* Stockholm: Atlas Akademi.

Middleton, Roger, ed. 2012. *Inside the Department of Economic Affairs. Samuel Brittan: The Diary of an "Irregular," 1964–6.* Oxford: Oxford University Press for the British Academy.

Mierzejewski, Alfred C. 2004. *Ludwig Erhard: A Biography.* Chapel Hill: University of North Carolina Press.

Miller Center. 2003. Interview with Jimmy Carter (1982). Charlottesville, VA: University of Virginia. November 29, 1982. Retrieved from https://millercenter.org/the-presidency/presidential-oral-histories/jimmy-carter-oral-history-president-united-states.

Miller Center. 2006a. Interview with Alfred Kahn (1981). Charlottesville, VA: University of Virginia. December 10-11, 1981. Retrieved from https://millercenter.org/the-presidency/presidential-oral-histories/alfred-e-kahn-oral-history-chairman-council-wage-and.

Miller Center. 2006b. Interview with F. Ray Marshall (1988). Charlottesville, VA: University of Virginia. May 4, 1988. Retrieved from https://millercenter.org/the-presidency/presidential-oral-histories/ray-marshall-oral-history-secretary-labor.

Miller Center. 2014a. Interview with Al From (2006). Charlottesville, VA: University of Virginia. April 27, 2006. Retrieved from http://millercenter.org/oralhistory/interview/al-from-2006.

Miller Center. 2014b. Interview with Al From (2007). Charlottesville, VA: University of Virginia. Retrieved from http://millercenter.org/oralhistory/interview/al-from-2007.

Miller Center. 2014c. Interview with William Galston (2004). Charlottesville, VA: University of Virginia. April 22-23, 2004. Retrieved from https:// millercenter.org/the-presidency/presidential-oral-histories/william-galston -oral-history-deputy-assistant-president.

Miller Center. 2014d. Interview 1 with Bruce Reed (2004). Charlottesville, VA: University of Virginia. February 19-20, 2004. Retrieved from https:// millercenter.org/the-presidency/presidential-oral-histories/bruce-reed-oral -history-february-2004-domestic-policy.

Mont Pèlerin Society. http://www.montpelerin.org, accessed March 15, 2007

Morgan, Kenneth O. 2004. Hardie, (James) Keir (1856–1915). In H. C. G. Matthew and Brian Harrison, eds., *Oxford Dictionary of National Biography*. Oxford: Oxford University Press. http://www.oxforddnb.com /view/article/33696, accessed June 7, 2014.

Morris, June. 2007. *The Life and Times of Thomas Balogh*. Brighton, UK: Sussex University Press.

Mulgan, Geoff. 2005. My Time in the Engine Room. Politics, *Guardian,* April 22. http://www.theguardian.com/politics/2005/apr/23/election2005 .labour, accessed June 7, 2015.

Mulgan, Geoff. 2013. Demos—Many Successes but One Big Failure. Pp. 17–24 in Ralph Scott and David Goodhart, eds., *Twenty Years of Ideas*. London: Demos.

Müller, Albrecht. 2004. *Die Reformlüge: 40 Denkfehler Mythen und Legenden mit denen Politik und Wirtschaft Deutschland ruinieren*. Munich: Droemer.

Nathan, Robert. 1989. Oral History Interview with Robert R. Nathan, by Niel M. Johnson, June 22. Harry S. Truman Presidential Library. http://www.trumanlibrary.org/oralhist/nathanrr.htm.

Nationalekonomiska Föreningen. [Undated]. Historik. http://nationalekonomi .se/node/42, accessed April 29, 2014.

Neidhardt, Friedhelm. 2002. Issues of Reform-Oriented Politics. Pp. 3–12 in Gerhard Schröder, ed., *Progressive Governance for the XXI Century: Contributions to the Berlin Conference*. The Hague: Kluwer Law International.

New York Times. 1917. Press Is Inclined to Applaud Bethmann. May 18.

New York Times. 1925a. Sandler Swedish Premier, Succeeds Branting, Who Is Ill, but Cabinet Remains. January 25.

New York Times. 1925b. Swedish Financier, F. W. Thorsson, Dies. May 6.

New York Times. 1992. Gunnar Strang, 85, Architect of Swedish Welfare Plan. March 8. http://www.nytimes.com/1992/03/08/world/gunnar-strang -85-architect-of-swedish-social-welfare-plan.html.

Nobel Prize. 1921. The Nobel Peace Prize 1921: Hjalmar Branting, Christian Lange. http://www.nobelprize.org/nobelprizes/peace/laureates/1921/index .html/branting.html, accessed January 15, 2014.

Noble, Phil. 2017. http://www.philnoble.com/work, accessed May 2, 2017.

Nourse, Edwin G. 1972. Oral History Interview with Dr. Edwin G. Nourse, by Jerry N. Hess, March 7. Harry S. Truman Presidential Library. http://www.trumanlibrary.org/oralhist/nourseg.htm, accessed December 27, 2015.

Ohlin, Bertil. 1937a. Gösta Adolfsson Bagge. *Swedish Biographical Dictionary*, http://sok.riksarkivet.se/sbl/artikel/18992, accessed January 14, 2014.

Ohlin, Bertil. 1937b. Some Notes on the Stockholm Theory of Savings and Investment I. *Economic Journal* 47, 185: 53–69.

Ohlin, Göran. 1996. Erik Lundberg, Studies in Economic Instability and Change: Selected Writings through Five Decades by Rolf G. H. Henriksson. *Scandinavian Journal of Economics* 98, 1: 137–143.

Ohm, Martina. 1999. The New President Is to Sharpen the Profile of the DIW. *Der Tagesspiegel,* February 15. http://www.tagesspiegel.de/wirtschaft/der -neue-praesident-soll-das-profil-des-diw-schaerfen/71468.html.

Palm, August. 1881. Speech at Hotel Stockholm, Malmö, 6 November 1881. Marxists Internet Archive. http://www.marxists.org/archive/palm-august /1881/speech.htm.

Pearce, Edward. 2001. Lord Shore of Stepney. *Guardian,* September 26. http://www.theguardian.com/news/2001/sep/26/guardianobituaries .obituaries/.

Peters, Charles, and Phillip Kiesling. 1985. *The New Road for America: The Neoliberal Movement.* Lanham, MD: Madison Books.

Phillips, A. W. H. 1958. The Relation between Unemployment and the Rate of Change of Money Wage Rates in the United Kingdom, 1861–1957. *Economica* 25, 2: 283–299.

Pimlott, Ben. 1985. *Hugh Dalton: A Life.* London: Jonathan Cape.

Pimlott, Ben. 1993. *Harold Wilson.* New York: HarperCollins.

Pimlott, Ben. 2004. Dalton, (Edward) Hugh Neale, Baron Dalton (1887–1962). In H. C. G. Matthew and Brian Harrison, eds., *Oxford Dictionary of National Biography.* Oxford: Oxford University. http://www.oxforddnb .com/view/article/32697, accessed 5 Aug 2013.

Prokesch, Steven. 1990. Sweden's Social Model Shows Signs of Cracks. *New York Times,* February 20. http://www.nytimes.com/1990/02/20/world /sweden-s-social-model-shows-signs-of-cracks.html.

Reich, Robert. 1998. *Locked in the Cabinet.* New York: Vintage Books.

Reich, Robert. 2011. *Slaying the Dragon of Debt: Fiscal Politics and Policy from the 1970s to the Present, A Project of the Walter Shorenstein*

Program in Politics, Policy and Values, conducted by Patrick Sharma and Martin Meeker in 2010, Regional Oral History Office, The Bancroft Library, University of California, Berkeley.

Reich, Robert. 2013. CV. https://gspp.berkeley.edu/directories/faculty/robert -reich, accessed March 23, 2017.

Ridder, Rick. 2017. Our People: Rick Ridder. RBI Strategies and Research. http://www.rbistrategies.com/our-vision/our-people, accessed May 5, 2017.

Robinson, Joan. 1933. *The Economics of Imperfect Competition.* London: Palgrave Macmillan.

Rorty, M. C. 1903. The Application of Probability Theory to Traffic Control Problems. October 22. AT&T.

Rosenman, Samuel I. 1952. *Working with Roosevelt.* New York: Harper and Brothers.

Rosenman, Samuel I. 1968–1969. Oral History Interview with Judge Samuel I. Rosenman, by Jerry N. Hess. Harry S. Truman Presidential Library. http://www.trumanlibrary.org/oralhist/rosenmn.htm, accessed March 26, 2014.

Routledge, Paul. 1998. Profile: Ed Balls—Brown's Young Egghead. *The Independent,* March 8.

Rowan, David. 2003. Ideas Man. Politics, *Guardian,* September 7. http://www .theguardian.com/politics/, accessed May 19, 2014.

Royal Economic Society. 2012. Aims and Objectives. http://www.res.org.uk /view/aimsActivities.html, accessed December 5, 2015.

Rubin, Robert, and Jacob Weisberg, 2003. *In an Uncertain World: Tough Choices from Wall Street to Washington.* New York: Random House.

Rüstow, Alexander. 1932. Freie Wirtschaft-Starker Staat-Die Staatspolitischen Voraussetzungen des wirtschaftlichen Liberalismus. *Schriften des Vereins fur Sozialpolitik,* 187: 62–69.

Samuelson, Paul. 1955 [1973]. *Economics.* Ninth Edition. Columbus, OH: McGraw-Hill, Inc.

Samuelson, Paul. 1971 [1977]. Foreword to Assar Lindbeck, *The Political Economy of the New Left: An Outsider's View.* New York: Harper and Row.

Samuelson, Paul. 1975. Seymour Harris as a Political Economist. *Review of Economics and Statistics* 57, 1: ii–v.

Samuelson, Paul. 1997. Credo of a Lucky Textbook Author. *Journal of Economic Perspectives* 11, 2: 153–160.

Samuelson, Paul, and Robert Solow. 1960. Analytical Aspects of Anti-Inflation Policy. *American Economic Review* 50, 2: 177–194.

Sandilands, Roger J. 1990. *The Life and Political Economy of Lauchlin Currie.* Durham, NC: Duke University Press.

Sargent, Thomas J. 1987. *Some of Milton Friedman's Scientific Contributions to Macroeconomics.* Stanford: Hoover Institution.

Sargent, Thomas J. 2008. Rational Expectations. In *The Concise Encyclopedia of Economics.* Library of Economics and Liberty. http://www.econlib.org/library/Enc/RationalExpectations.html, accessed October 30, 2016.

Sargent, Thomas J. 2016. Curriculum Vitae. http://www.tomsargent.com/personal/resume.pdf, accessed December 7, 2017.

Sargent, Thomas J., and Neil Wallace 1976. Rational Expectations and the Theory of Economic Policy. *Journal of Monetary Economics* 2: 169–183.

Schiller, Karl. 1955 [1964]. Der Ökonom und die Gesellschaft. Pp. 3-14 in Schiller, Karl 1964. *Der Ökonom und die Gesellschaft: Das freiheitliche und das soziale Element in der modernen Wirtschaftspolik.* Stuttgart: Gustav Fischer Verlag.

Schiller, Karl 1964. *Der Ökonom und die Gesellschaft: Das freiheitliche und das soziale Element in der modernen Wirtschaftspolik.* Stuttgart: Gustav Fischer Verlag.

Schlesinger, Arthur, Jr. 1958. Death Wish of the Democrats. *New Republic,* September 15.

Schlesinger, Arthur Jr. 1980. The End of an Era? *Wall Street Journal,* Nov 20, p. 26.

Schröder, Gerhard. 2002a. Civil Society, the New Economy and the State: What Progressive Governance Is About. Pp. xv–xxi in Gerhard Schröder, ed., *Progressive Governance for the XXI Century: Contributions to the Berlin Conference.* Munich: Verlag C. H. Beck.

Schröder, Gerhard, ed. 2002b. *Progressive Governance for the XXI Century: Contributions to the Berlin Conference.* Munich: Verlag C. H. Beck.

Schück, Johan. 2002. 30 år av Ekonomisk Debatt. *Ekonomisk Debatt* 36: 543–548. http://www.nationalekonomi.se/filer/pdf/30-6-js.pdf, http://nationalekonomi.se/Edom, accessed April 13, 2017.

Shapiro, Robert J. 2017. Robert J. Shapiro, PhD. Precision Economics, LLC. http://www.precisionecon.com/affiliates-2/robert-j-shapiro-ph-d, accessed March 17, 2017.

Silber, William L. 2012. *Volcker: The Triumph of Persistence.* London: Bloomsbury.

Simonian, Haig. 2003. Internal Pressures on Schröder Mount. *Financial Times,* January 28, London edition.

Sjoberg, Thomas. 1999. Playboyintervjun: Kjell-Olof Feldt. *Playboy Scandinavia,* no. 5.

Skidelsky, Robert. 1967. *Politicians and the Slump.* London: Macmillan.

Skidelsky, Robert. 1983. *John Maynard Keynes: Hopes Betrayed, 1883–1920*. London: Macmillan.

Skidelsky, Robert. 1992. *John Maynard Keynes: The Economist as Savior, 1920–1937*. London: Macmillan.

Smaldone, William. 1988. Rudolf Hilferding and the Theoretical Foundations of German Social Democracy, 1902–33. *Central European History* 21, 3: 267–299.

Smaldone, William. 1998. *Rudolf Hilferding: The Tragedy of a German Social Democrat*. DeKalb: Northern Illinois University Press.

Snowden, Philip. 1920. *Labour and National Finance*. London: L. Parsons.

Snowden, Philip. 1921 [1925]. *Labour and the New World*. London: Cassell.

Snowden, Philip. 1934a. *An Autobiography*. Vol. 1. London: Nicholson and Watson, Ltd.

Snowden, Philip. 1934b. *An Autobiography*. Vol. 2. London: Nicholson and Watson, Ltd.

SNS. 2017. The History of SNS: 70 Years of Knowledge-Based Debate. http://www.sns.se/en/about-sns/history, accessed April 12, 2017.

Söderström, Hans Tson. 2017. Curriculum Vitae. http://hanstson.wordpress.com/curriculum-vitae, accessed April 12, 2017.

Sohlman, Michael. 2016. Curriculum vitae von Michael Sohlman. Eduard-Rhein-Stiftung. http://www.eduard-rhein-stiftung.de/en/awardee/michael-sohlman, accessed February 19, 2016.

Solow, Robert. 2004. James Tobin, 5 March 1918–11 March 2002. *Proceedings of the American Philosophical Society* 148, 3: 399–404.

Sommer, Jeff. 2011. The Slogans Stop Here. Your Money, *New York Times*, October 9. http://www.nytimes.com/2011/10/30/your-money/.

Sperber, Jonathan. 1991. *Rhineland Radicals: The Democratic Movement and the Revolution of 1848–1849*. Princeton: Princeton University Press.

Steinhardt, Michael. 2001. *No Bull: My Life in and out of Markets*. New York: John Wiley and Sons.

Stephanopoulos, George. 1999 [2000]. *All Too Human: A Political Education*. Back Bay Books.

Streeten, Paul. 1992. Thomas Balogh (1905–1985). In Philip Arestis and Malcolm C. Sawyer, eds., *A Biographical Dictionary of Dissenting Economists*. Cheltenham, UK: Edward Elgar.

Szajkowski, Bogdan, ed. 2005. *Political Parties of the World*. London: John Harper Publishing.

Tanden, Neera. 2013. Untitled. P. 1 in *Making Progress: Ten Years of Ideas, Action, and Change*. Center for American Progress. http://www.americanprogress.org/issues/democracy/news/2013/10/24/78000/making-progress-10-years-of-ideas-action-and-change.

Tanner, Duncan. 2004. Snowden, Philip, Viscount Snowden (1864–1937). In H. C. G. Matthew and B. Harrison, eds., *Oxford Dictionary of National Biography.* Oxford: Oxford University Press.

Tietmeyer, Hans. 2003. Die Gründung des Sachverständigenrates aus Sicht der Wirtschaftspolitik. Pp. 22–33 in *Vierzig Jahre Sachverständigenrat, 1963–2003.* Wiesbaden: Statistisches Bundesamt.

Time. 1965. We Are All Keynesians Now. December 31.

Tobin, James. 1976. Hansen and Public Policy. *Quarterly Journal of Economics* 90, 1: 32–37.

Tobin, James. 1991. Walter W. Heller (August 27, 1915–June 15, 1987). *Proceedings of the American Philosophical Society.* 135, 1: 100–107.

Tugwell, Rexford. 1968. *The Brains Trust.* New York: Viking.

Ullmann, Owen. 1997. Sperling Credentials. *International Economy.* May/June: 24–29.

Vennerström, Ivar. 1926. *F. V. Thorsson: En Minnesskrift.* Stockholm: Tidens Förlag.

Vobejda, Barbara and Judith Havemann. 1996. 2 HHS Officials Quit Over Welfare Changes. *The Washington Post,* September 12.

Walker, Martin. 1998. Clinton and Blair Set Date for Third Way Conference. Foreign Page, *Guardian,* August 14.

Wattenberg, Ben and Richard Scammon. 1970. *The Real Majority: An Extraordinary Examination of the American Electorate.* New York: Coward-McCann.

Webb, Sidney. 1918. *Labour and the New Social Order: A Report on Reconstruction.* London: Labour Party.

Whitney, Craig. 1984. A Talk with Helmut Schmidt. *New York Times Magazine,* September 16. http://www.nytimes.com/.

Wicksell, Knut. 1897. Der Bankzins als Regulator der Warenpreise, *Jahrbücher für Nationalökonomie und Statistik* 68: 228–243

Wicksell, Knut. 1907. The Influence of the Rate of Interest on Prices. *Economic Journal* 17, 66: 213–220.

Wigforss, Ernst. 1908 [1970]. *Materialistisk historieuppfattning: Industriell demokrati.* Stockholm: Tidens Förlag.

Wigforss, Ernst. 1926. Sammanträdet den 4 februari. *Ekonomisk Tidskrift* 28, 10–12: 1–31.

Wigforss, Ernst. 1938. The Financial Policy during Depression and Boom. *Annals of the American Academy of Political and Social Science* 197: 25–39.

Wigforss, Ernst. 1950. *Minnen.* Vols. 1–3. Stockholm: Tidens Förlag.

Willy Brandt Kreis. 2009. Prof. Dr. Hans-Jürgen Krupp. http://www.willy -brandt-kreis.de/pdf/ansprache_noe_krupp.pdf, accessed December 7, 2017.

Woytinsky, Wladimir. 1961. *Stormy Passage.* New York: Vanguard Press.

Biographical Dictionaries and Repositories

Arestis, Philip and Malcolm C. Sawyer. 1992. *A Biographical Dictionary of Dissenting Economists*. Cheltenham, UK: Edward Elgar.

Blaug, Mark. 1986. *Who's Who in Economics*. Cambridge, MA: MIT Press.

Friedrich-Ebert-Stiftung (FES). 2016. *Archiv der sozialen Demokratie*. http://archiv2.fes.de/, accessed September 28, 2016.

Gorman, Robert A. 1986. *Biographical Dictionary of Marxism*. Westport, CT: Greenwood Publishing.

Katz, Bernard S., and C. Daniel Vencill. 1996. *Biographical Dictionary of the United States Secretaries of the Treasury, 1789–1995*. Westport, CT: Greenwood Publishing.

Lane, A. Thomas, ed. 1995. *Biographical Dictionary of European Labor Leaders* Vol. 2. Westport, CT: Greenwood Publishing.

Nobel Prize. http://www.nobelprize.org/.

Oxford Dictionary of National Biography. 2004. Oxford: Oxford University Press. http://www.oxforddnb.com/.

Swedish Dictionary of National Biography. National Archives of Sweden. Stockholm. http://www.nad.riksarkivet.se/.

Party Publications

CDU. 1947. The Ahlen Program of the CDU (February 1947). German History in Documents and Images (GHDI), German Historical Institute, Washington, DC. http://germanhistorydocs.ghi-dc.org/subdocument.cfm?documentid=3093, accessed August 22, 2017.

Cleveland, Grover. 1888. Fourth Annual Message (First Term), December 3, 1888. American Presidency Project, by Gerhard Peters and John T. Woolley. http://www.presidency.ucsb.edu/ws/index.php?pid=29529&st=communist&st1=communism#axzz2h2ioX1Pt, accessed October 7, 2013.

Democratic Party. 1920. 1920 Democratic Party Platform, June 28, 1920. American Presidency Project, by Gerhard Peters and John T. Woolley. http://www.presidency.ucsb.edu/ws/?pid=29592, accessed September 9, 2015.

Democratic Party. 1936. 1936 Democratic Party Platform, June 23, 1936. American Presidency Project, by Gerhard Peters and John T. Woolley. http://www.presidency.ucsb.edu/ws/?pid=29596.

Democratic Party. 1960. 1960 Democratic Party Platform, July 11, 1960. American Presidency Project, by Gerhard Peters and John T. Woolley. http://www.presidency.ucsb.edu/ws/?pid=29602.

Democratic Party. 1968. 1968 Democratic Party Platform, August 26, 1968. American Presidency Project, by Gerhard Peters and John T. Woolley. http://www.presidency.ucsb.edu/ws/?pid=29604.

Democratic Party. 1992. 1992 Democratic Party Platform, July 13, 1992. American Presidency Project, by Gerhard Peters and John T. Woolley. http://www.presidency.ucsb.edu/ws/?pid=29610.

Labour Party. 1929a. *How to Conquer Unemployment: Labour's Reply to Lloyd George*. London: Labour Party.

Labour Party. 1959. *Britain Belongs to You: The Labour Party's Policy for Consideration by the British People*. London: Labour Party. http://www .politicsresources.net/area/uk/man/lab59.htm.

Labour Party. 1997. *New Labour—Because Britain Deserves Better*. London: Labour Party. http://www.fes.de/fulltext/ialhi/90057/90057toc.htm or http://www.politicsresources.net/area/uk/man/lab97.htm.

Liberal Party. 1929. *We Can Conquer Unemployment*.London: St. Clements Press.

Long, Gillis W. and Timothy E. Wirth. 1982. *Rebuilding the Road to Opportunity: Turning Point for America's Economy*. Special Task Force on Long-Term Economic Policy. Washington, D.C.: Democratic Caucus/U.S. House of Representatives.

SAP. 1920. Program för Sveriges Socialdemokratiska Arbetareparti. http://snd .gu.se/en/vivill/party/s/program/1920, accessed June 25, 2015.

SAP. 1960. Program för Sveriges Socialdemokratiska Arbetareparti. http://snd .gu.se/en/vivill/party/s/program/1960, accessed June 25, 2015.

SAP. 1990. Program för Sveriges Socialdemokratiska Arbetareparti. http://snd .gu.se/en/vivill/party/s/program/1990, accessed June 25, 2015.

SPD. 1921. Görlitz Program (Görlitzer Programm). Marxists Internet Archive. http://www.marxists.org/deutsch/geschichte/deutsch/spd/1921/goerlitz.htm, accessed September 9, 2015.

SPD. 1959. Godesberg Program of the SPD (November 1959). German History in Documents and Images (GHDI), German Historical Institute, Washington, DC. http://germanhistorydocs.ghi-dc.org/.

SPD. 1998. *Arbeit, Innovation und Gerechtigkeit*. SPD-Programm für die Bundestagwahl 1998. April 17. Leipzig: SPD. https://www.spd.de/fileadmin /Dokumente/Beschluesse/Bundesparteitag/wahlprogrammbundesparteitagle ipzig1998.pdf, accessed December 2, 2017.

Political/Electoral, Macroeconomic, and Organizational Data Sources

Armingeon, Klaus, Christian Isler, Laura Knöpfel, David Weisstanner, and Sarah Engler. 2016. *Comparative Political Data Set 1960–2014*. Bern: Institute of Political Science, University of Berne.

Arneson, B. A. 1920. Swedish Parliamentary Elections, 1919. *American Political Science Review* 14, 1: 123–125.

Atlas Foundation. Atlas Foundation Directory. http://www.atlasusa.org/V2 /main/acc.php, accessed April–November 2008.

Budge, Ian, Hans-Dieter Klingemann, Andrea Volkens, Judith Bara and Eric Tanenbaum. 2001. *Mapping Policy Preferences: Estimates for Parties, Electors, and Governments 1945–1998*, Oxford: Oxford University Press.

Craig, Frederick W. S. ed. 1974. *British Parliamentary Election Results 1885–1918*. London: Palgrave Macmillan.

Craig, Fred W. S. ed. 1977. *British Parliamentary Election Results: 1918– 1949*. London: Palgrave Macmillan.

Day, Alan J., and Henry W. Degenhardt, eds. 1984. *Political Parties of the World*. 2nd ed.. Burnt Mill, Harlow, Essex, UK: Longman.

Deutscher Bundestag, 2005. Historical Exhibition Presented by the German Bundestag: Elections in the Empire, 1871–1918. Administration of the German Bundestag, Research Section WD 1, November. http://www .bundestag.de/blob/189790/1907ef7ab16a75a7048c04b3d2558f00 /electionsempire-data.pdf, accessed 3 January 3, 2016.

Falter, Jürgen, Thomas Lindenberger, and Siegfried Schumann. 1986. *Wahlen und Abstimmungen in der Weimarer Republik 1919–1933*. Munich: C. H. Beck.

Gwartney, James. 2007. Economic Freedom of the World: 2007 Annual Report. Vancouver, BC: Fraser Institute. http://www.freetheworld.com /datasetsefw.html, accessed July 8, 2008.

Gwartney, James, and Robert Lawson. 2005. Economic Freedom of the World: 2005 Annual Report. Vancouver, BC: Fraser Institute. http://www .freetheworld.com/datasetsefw.html, accessed July 8, 2008.

Hansard Online. http://hansard.parliament.uk/.

International Institute for Democracy and Electoral Assistance (International IDEA). Voter Turnout Database. http://www.idea.int/data-tools/data/voter -turnout, accessed September 15, 2015.

International Labour Organization (ILO). 1998–2008. Labour Statistics Database. Geneva. http://www.ilo.org/global/statistics-and-databases /lang—en/index.htm, accessed November 1, 2008.

Klingemann, Hans-Dieter, Andrea Volkens, Judith Bara, Ian Budge and Michael McDonald, eds. 2006. *Mapping Policy Preferences II: Estimates for Parties, Electors, and Governments in Eastern Europe, European Union, and OECD 1990-2003*, Oxford: Oxford University Press.

Leip, Dave. [Undated.] Dave Leip's Atlas of U.S. Presidential Elections. http://uselectionatlas.org/.

Mackie, Thomas T., and Richard Rose. 1991. *The International Almanac of Electoral History.* London: Macmillan.

McHale, Vincent E., ed. 1983. Political Parties of Europe. In *The Greenwood Historical Encyclopedia of the World's Political Parties.* Vols. 1–2. Westport, CT: Greenwood Publishing.

Muller, Thomas C., William R. Overstreet, Judith F. Isacoff, and Tom Lansford. 2011. *Political Handbook of the World 2011.* Washington, D.C.: CQ Press

Organisation for Economic Cooperation and Development (OECD). Labour Force Statistics. www.oecd.stat, retrieved July 31, 2010.

Peters, Gerhard, and John T. Woolley. 2015. Size of the Executive Office of the President (E.O.P.): Coolidge–Clinton. American Presidency Project. http://www.presidency.ucsb.edu/data/eop.php, accessed December 26, 2015.

Peters, Gerhard, and John T. Woolley. 1999–2017. American Presidency Project. http://www.presidency.ucsb.edu/index.php.

Policy Network. [Undated.] Links. http://www.policy-network.net/content /244/Links, accessed April 30, 2013.

Stanley, Harold W. and Richard G. Niemi, eds. *Public Opinion and Voting: Vital Statistics on American Politics 2015–2016.* Washington, DC: CQ Press.

Statistika Centralbyrån / Statistics Sweden (SCB). Statistical Database: Democracy. http://www.scb.se/en/Finding-statistics/Statistics-by-subject -area/Democracy/General-elections/General-elections-results/Aktuell-Pong /12275/Historical-statistics-of-election-results/32065.

U.S. House of Representatives. Election Statistics, 1920 to Present. http:// history.house.gov/Institution/Election-Statistics/Election-Statistics.

World Bank. 2017. World Data Indicators (WDI). http://databank.worldbank .org/data, accessed February 14, 2017.

Secondary Sources

Abbott, Andrew. 1988. Transcending General Linear Reality. *Sociological Theory* 6, 2: 169–185.

Adams, Julia. 2005. *The Familial State: Ruling Families and Merchant Capitalism in Early Modern Europe.* Ithaca, N.Y.: Cornell University Press.

Adams, Julia, Elisabeth Clemens, and Ann Shola Orloff. 2005. Introduction: Social Theory, Modernity, and the Three Waves of Historical Sociology. Pp. 1–72 in Julia Adams, Elisabeth Clemens, and Ann Shola Orloff, eds.,

Remaking Modernity: Politics, History, and Sociology. Durham, NC: Duke University Press.

Allen, Christopher S. 1989. The Underdevelopment of Keynesianism in the Federal Republic of Germany. Pp. 263–290 in Peter Hall, ed., *The Political Power of Economic Ideas: Keynesianism across Nations.* Princeton, NJ: Princeton University Press.

Anderson, Perry. 1976. *Considerations on Western Marxism.* London: Verso.

Andersson, Jenny. 2006. The People's Library and the Electronic Workshop: Comparing Swedish and British Social Democracy. *Politics and Society* 34: 432–456.

Andersson, Jenny. 2007. Socializing Capital, Capitalizing the Social: Contemporary Social Democracy and the Knowledge Economy. Center for European Studies Working Paper 145. Institute for Contemporary History, Södertörn University College, Flemingsberg, Sweden.

Andersson, Jenny. 2009. *The Library and the Workshop: Social Democracy and Capitalism in the Knowledge Age.* Stanford, CA: Stanford University Press.

Aron, Raymond. 1957 [1968]. The End of the Ideological Age? Pp. 27–48 in Chaim I. Waxman, ed., *The End of Ideology Debate.* New York: Funk and Wagnalls.

Arter, David. 1998. An Agenda 2000 for the Nordic Region. *Economic and Political Weekly* 33, 35: PE79–PE86.

Babb, Sarah. 2001. *Managing Mexico: Economists from Nationalism to Neoliberalism.* Princeton, NJ: Princeton University Press.

Backhouse, Roger. 2000. Economics in the Mid-Atlantic: British Economics, 1945–95. Pp. 20–41 in A. W. B. Coats, ed., *The Development of Economics in Western Europe since 1945.* Routledge Studies in the History of Economics. London: Routledge.

Baer, Kenneth. 2000. *Reinventing Democrats: The Politics of Liberalism from Reagan to Clinton.* Lawrence, KS: University Press of Kansas.

Bailey, David J. 2009. *The Political Economy of European Social Democracy: A Critical Realist Approach.* London: Routledge.

Bailey, Stephen Kemp. 1950. *The Story behind the Unemployment Act of 1946.* New York: Columbia University Press.

Bailey, Stephen K. 1955. Political Elements in Full Employment Policy. *The American Economic Review* 45, 2: 341–350.

1981. The United States: Economists in a Pluralistic Polity. Pp. 175–209 in A.W. Coates, ed., *Economists in Government: An International Comparative Study.* Durham, N.C.: Duke University Press.

Barnes, Bart. 1986. Leon Henderson Dies at 91; Was First Chief of Old OPA. *Washington Post,* October 21.

Bell, Daniel. 1960. *The End of Ideology.* Glencoe, IL: Free Press.

Benenson, B., and D. Tarr. 2012. Political Consultants: History. In *Elections A to Z.* 4th ed. Washington, DC: CQ Press. http://library.cqpress.com /elections/elaz4d399.1.

Bentham, Justin. 2006. The IPPR and Demos: Think Tanks of the New Social Democracy. *The Political Quarterly* 77, 2: 166–174.

Berger, Stefan. 1996. "Organising Talent and Disciplined Steadiness": The German SPD as a Model for the British Labour Party in the 1920s? *Contemporary European History* 5, 2 (July): 171–190.

Berman, E. P., and L. M. Milanes-Reyes. 2013. The Politicization of Knowledge Claims: The "Laffer Curve" in the U.S. Congress. *Qualitative Sociology* 36, 53–79.

Berman, Sheri. 1998. *The Social Democratic Moment: Ideas and Politics in the Making of Interwar Europe.* Cambridge, MA: Harvard University Press.

Berman, Sheri. 2006. *The Primacy of Politics: Social Democracy and the Making of Europe's Twentieth Century.* Cambridge: Cambridge University Press.

Berman, Sheri. 2009. The Primacy of Economics versus the Primacy of Politics: Understanding the Ideological Dynamics of the Twentieth Century. *Perspectives on Politics* 7, 3: 561–578.

Bernstein, Eduard. 1893. *Ferdinand Lassalle as a Social Reformer.* London: Swan Sonnenschein.

Bernstein, Michael A. 2004. *A Perilous Progress: Economists and Public Purpose in Twentieth-Century America.* Princeton: Princeton University Press.

Berry, Phyllis. 2005. The Organization and Influence of the Chancellery during the Schmidt and Kohl Chancellorships. *Governance: An International Journal of Policy and Administration* 2, 3 (July): 339–355.

Bevir, Mark. 2011. *The Making of British Socialism.* Princeton, NJ: Princeton University Press.

Billington, James H. 1980 [2007]. *Fire in the Minds of Men: Origins of the Revolutionary Faith.* Piscataway, NJ: Transaction Publishers.

Blaug, Mark. 1998. Disturbing Currents in Modern Economics. *Challenge* 41, 3: 11–34.

Blick, Andrew. 2006. Harold Wilson, Labour, and the Machinery of Government. *Contemporary British History* 20, 3: 343–362.

Blinder, Alan. 2016. How the Economy Came to Resemble the Model. Pp. 255–270 in Robert Crow, ed, *The Best of Business Economics: Highlights from the First Fifty Years.* London and New York: Palgrave Macmillan.

Blomqvist, Paula. 2004. The Choice Revolution: Privatization of Swedish Welfare Services in the 1990s. *Social Policy and Administration* 38, 2: 139–155.

Blyth, Mark. 2001. The Transformation of the Swedish Model. *World Politics* 54, 1: 1–26,

Blyth, Mark. 2002. *Great Transformations: Economic Ideas and Institutional Change in the Twentieth Century.* Cambridge: Cambridge University Press.

Blyth, Mark. 2013. *Austerity: The History of a Dangerous Idea.* Oxford: Oxford University Press.

Bobbio, Norberto. 1996. *Left and Right: The Significance of a Political Distinction.* Trans. Allan Cameron. Chicago: University of Chicago Press.

Bockman, Johanna. 2011. *Markets in the Name of Socialism: The Left-Wing Origins of Neoliberalism.* Stanford, CA: Stanford University Press.

Bogdanor, Vernon. 2012. Inside the Department of Economic Affairs: Samuel Brittan, the Diary of an "Irregular" (1964–66)—Review. *New Statesman*, August 15. http://www.newstatesman.com/.

Boianovsky, Mauro 2004. The IS-LM Model and the Liquidity Trap Concept: From Hicks to Krugman. *History of Political Economy* 36 (Annual Supplement): 92–126.

Bonoli, Giuliano, and Martin Powell, eds. 2004. *Social Democratic Party Policies in Contemporary Europe.* London and New York: Routledge.

Booth, Alan. 1983. The "Keynesian Revolution" in Economic Policy-Making. *Economic History Review,* New Series, 36, 1 (February): 103–123.

Bordo, Michael D., and Anna J. Schwartz. 1984. *A Retrospective on the Classical Gold Standard, 1821–1931.* Chicago: University of Chicago Press.

Bourdieu, Pierre. 1968 [1991]. *The Craft of Sociology: Epistemological Preliminaries.* Berlin: Walter de Gruyter.

Bourdieu, Pierre. 1977 [2008]. Giving Voice to the Voiceless. Pp. 70–77 in *Political Interventions : Social Science and Political Action.* London, New York: Verso.

Bourdieu, Pierre. 1979 [1984]. *Distinction: A Social Critique of the Judgement of Taste.* Cambridge, MA: Harvard University Press.

Bourdieu, Pierre. 1986 [1996]. *The State Nobility: Elite Schools in the Field of Power.* Oxford: Oxford University Press.

Bourdieu, Pierre. 1989–1992 [2014]. *On the State: Lectures at the Collège du France, 1989–1992.* Cambridge, UK: Polity Press.

Bourdieu, Pierre. 1990. *In Other Words: Essays Towards a Reflexive Sociology.* Trans. Matthew Adamson. Stanford, CA: Stanford University Press.

Bourdieu, Pierre 1991. *Language and Symbolic Power.* Edited and with an introduction by John Thompson. Cambridge: Harvard University Press.

Bourdieu, Pierre. 1993. *The Logic of Practice.* Cambridge, UK: Polity.

Bourdieu, Pierre, and Loïc Wacquant. 1992. *An Invitation to Reflexive Sociology.* Chicago: University of Chicago Press.

Bourdieu, Pierre, et al. 1994. *Weight of the World.* Stanford, CA: Stanford University Press.

Bourdieu, Pierre, and Loïc Wacquant. 1999. On the Cunning of Imperialist Reason. *Theory, Culture and Society* 16, 1: 41–58.

Bourne, Ryan. 2013. Lady Thatcher's Relationship with Friedrich Hayek and Milton Friedman. *Pieria,* April 10. www.pieria.co.uk/, accessed August 31, 2015.

Brandt, Karl Gerard. 2009. *Ronald Reagan and the House Democrats: Gridlock, Partisanship, and the Fiscal Crisis,* Columbia: University of Missouri Press.

Braunthal, Gerard. 1977. The Policy Function of the German Social Democratic Party. *Comparative Politics* 9, 2: 127–145.

Brenner, Mats, and Torben Bundgaard Vad. 2000. Sweden and Denmark: Defending the Welfare State. In Fritz Scharpf and Vivien Schmidt, eds., *Welfare and Work in the Open Economy,* vol. 2, *Diverse Responses to Common Challenges.* Oxford: Oxford University Press.

Breslau, Daniel. 2003. Economics Invents the Economy: Mathematics, Statistics, and Models in the Work of Irving Fisher and Wesley Mitchell. *Theory and Society* 32: 379–411.

Brinkley, Alan. 1998. *Liberalism and Its Discontents.* Cambridge, MA: Harvard University Press.

Brock, Clifton. 1962. *Americans for Democratic Action: Its Role in National Politics.* Washington, DC: Public Affairs Press.

Brubaker, Rogers. 1985, Rethinking Classical Theory: The Sociological Vision of Pierre Bourdieu. *Theory and Society* 14, 6: 745–775.

Burgin, Angus. 2012. *The Great Persuasion: Reinventing Free Markets since the Great Depression.* Cambridge, MA: Harvard University Press.

Calhoun, Craig. 2012. *The Roots of Radicalism: Tradition, the Public Sphere, and Early Nineteenth-Century Social Movements.* Chicago: University of Chicago Press.

Callon, Michel 1998a. Introduction: The Embeddedness of Economic Markets in Economics. *Sociological Review,* 46, 1: 1–57.

Callon, Michel. 1998b. *Laws of the Markets.* New York: Wiley.

Campbell, James E. 2006. Party Systems and Realignments in the United States, 1868–2004. *Social Science History* 30, 3: 359–386.

Campbell, John, and Ove Pedersen. 2014. *The National Origins of Policy Ideas: Knowledge Regimes in the United States, France, Germany, and Denmark.* Princeton, NJ: Princeton University Press.

Carson, Carol S. 1975. The History of the United States National Income and Product Accounts. *Review of Income and Wealth* 21, 2: 153–181.

Centeno, Miguel A., and Joseph N. Cohen. 2012. The Arc of Neoliberalism. *Annual Review of Sociology* 38: 317–40.

Chambers, William Nisbet and Walter Dean Burnham. 1967 [1969]. *The American Party Systems: Stages of Political Development.*

Chorev, Nitsan. 2007. *Remaking U.S. Trade Policy: From Protectionism to Globalization.* Ithaca, NY: Cornell University Press.

Chorev, Nitsan. 2013. Restructuring Neoliberalism at the World Health Organization. *Review of International Political Economy* 20, 4: 627–666.

Clark, J. R., Jennifer Miller-Wilford, and Edward Peter Stringham. 2012. Beyond Kelly Green Golf Shoes: Evaluating the Demand for Scholarship of Free-Market and Mainstream Economists. *American Journal of Economics and Sociology* 71, 5: 1169–1184.

Clemens, Elisabeth. 1997. *The People's Lobby.* Chicago: University of Chicago Press.

Clifford, Christopher. 1997. The Rise and Fall of the Department of Economic Affairs 1964–69: British Government and Indicative Planning. *Contemporary British History* 11, 2: 94–116.

Coats, A. W. B., ed. 1981. *Economists in Government: An International Comparative Study.* Durham, NC: Duke University Press.

Coats, A. W. B. 1993. *The Sociology and Professionalization of Economics.* Vol. 2 of *British and American Economic Essays.* London: Routledge.

Coats, A. W. B., ed. 2000. *The Development of Economics in Western Europe since 1945.* Routledge Studies in the History of Economics. London: Routledge.

Coates, David, ed. 2003. *Paving the Third Way: The Critique of Parliamentary Socialism.* A Socialist Register *Anthology.* London: Merlin Press.

Cockett, Richard. 1994. *Thinking the Unthinkable: Think-Tanks and the Economic Counter-Revolution, 1931–1983.* London: HarperCollins.

Cohen, Benjamin J. 1998. *The Geography of Money.* Ithaca, NY: Cornell University Press.

Colander, David. 2004. The Strange Persistence of the IS-LM Model. *History of Political Economy* 36: 305–322.

Colander, David. 2008. The Making of a Global European Economist. *Kyklos* 61, 2: 215–236.

Cole, G. D. H. 1948. *History of the Labour Party from 1914.* London: Routledge and Kegan Paul.

Converse, Philip. 1964. The Nature of Belief Systems in Mass Publics. Pp. 206–261 in D. E. Apter, ed., *Ideology and Discontent.* New York: Free Press.

Cotter, Cornelius P., and Bernard C. Hennessy. 2009. *Politics without Power: The National Party Committees.* London: Routledge.

Crewe, I. 1982. The Labour Party and the Electorate. In Dennis Kavanagh, ed., *The Politics of the Labour Party,* London: Allen and Unwin.

Crosland, Anthony. 1956. *The Future of Socialism.* London: Jonathan Cape.

Crouch, Colin. 1997. The Terms of the Neo-Liberal Consensus. *Political Quarterly* 68, 4: 352–360.

Cuperus, René, and Johannes Kandel. 1998. The Magical Return of Social Democracy. In René Cuperus and Johannes Kandel, eds., *European Social Democracy: Transformation in Progress.* Amsterdam: Friedrich-Ebert-Stiftung.

de Haan, Jakob, and Sylvester C. W. Eijffinger. 2000. The Democratic Accountability of the European Central Bank: A Comment on Two Fairy-Tales. *Journal of Common Market Studies* 38, 3: 393–407.

De Leon, Cedric, Manali Desai, and Cihan Tuğal. 2015. *Building Blocs: How Parties Organize Society.* Stanford, CA: Stanford University Press.

Denord, François. 2009. French Neoliberalism and Its Divisions: From the Colloque Walter Lippman to the Third Republic. Pp. 45–67, in Philip Mirowski and Dieter Plehwe, eds., *The Road from Mont Pèlerin: The Making of the Neoliberal Thought Collective.* Cambridge, MA: Harvard University Press.

Derluguian, Georgi M. 2005. *Bourdieu's Secret Admirer in the Caucasus: A World-System Biography.* Chicago: University of Chicago Press.

Desai, Radhika. 1994. Second-Hand Dealers in Ideas: Think-Tanks and Thatcherite Hegemony. *New Left Review* 203: 27–64.

Desmond, Matthew. 2014. Relational Ethnography. *Theory and Society* 43: 547–579.

Dewey, John. 1922 [2011]. *Human Nature and Conduct.* Mineola, NY: Dover.

DiMaggio, Paul J., and Walter W. Powell. 1983. The Iron Cage Revisited: Institutional Isomorphism and Collective Rationality in Organizational Fields. *American Sociological Review* 48, 2: 147–160.

DiSalvo, Daniel. 2012. *Engines of Change: Party Factions in American Politics, 1868–2010.* New York: Oxford University Press.

Downs, Anthony. 1957. *An Economic Theory of Democracy.* New York: Harper and Row.

Dreyfuss, Robert. 2004. An Idea Factory for Democrats. *Nation,* March 1, 18–23.

Durbin, Elizabeth. 1985. *New Jerusalems: The Labour Party and the Economics of Democratic Socialism.* London: Routledge and Kegan Paul.

Durkheim, Emile. 1895–1897 [1982]. *The Rules of Sociological Method and Selected Texts on Sociology and Its Method.* Ed. with an introduction by Steven Lukes. Trans. W. D. Halls. New York: Free Press.

Durkheim, Emile. 1912 [1995]. *The Elementary Forms of Religious Life.* New York: Free Press.

Durkheim, Emile. 1914 [1973]. The Dualism of Human Nature and Its Social Conditions. Pp. 149–166 in Robert N. Bellah, ed., *Emile Durkheim on Morality and Society.* Chicago and London: University of Chicago Press.

Durkheim, Emile, and Marcel Mauss. 1903 [1963]. *Primitive Classification.* Chicago: Chicago University Press.

Dürr, Tobias. 2014. These Are the Days of Miracle and Wonder. *Dagens Arena,* February 13. http://www.dagensarena.se/innehall/.

Duverger, Maurice. 1954. *Political Parties.* London: Methuen.

Dyson, Kenneth. 2001. The German Model Revisited: From Schmidt to Schröder. *German Politics* 10, 2: 135–154.

Dyson, Kenneth. 2005. Binding Hands as a Strategy for Economic Reform: Government by Commission. *German Politics* 14, 2: 224–247.

Ebbinghaus, Bernhard. 1995. The Siamese Twins: Citizenship Rights, Cleavage Formation, and Party-Union Relations in Western Europe. *International Review of Social History* 40, 3: 51–89.

Ehrlich, Isaac. 2007. The Mystery of Human Capital as Engine of Growth, or Why the US Became the Economic Superpower in the 20th Century. NBER Working Paper 12868. http://www.nber.org/papers/w12868.

Eichengreen, Barry. 1998. *Globalizing Capital: A History of the International Monetary System.* Princeton, NJ: Princeton University Press.

Eichengreen, Barry, and Tim Hatton. 1988. Interwar Unemployment in International Perspective. Working Paper No. 12-88. Institute for Research on Labor and Employment, University of California, Berkeley.

Eidlin, Barry. 2016. Why Is There No Labor Party in the United States? Political Articulation and the Canadian Comparison, 1932 to 1948. *American Sociological Review* 81, 3: 488–516.

Eley, Geoff. 2002. *Forging Democracy: The History of the Left in Europe, 1850–2000.* Oxford: Oxford University Press.

Emirbayer, Mustafa, and Matthew Desmond. 2015. *The Racial Order.* Chicago: University of Chicago Press.

Emirbayer, Mustafa, and Victoria Johnson. 2008. Bourdieu and Organizational Analysis. *Theory and Society* 37, 1: 1–44.

Engstrom, Erik J., and Samuel Kernell. 1999. Serving Competing Principals: The Budget Estimates of OMB and CBO in an Era of Divided Government. *Presidential Studies Quarterly* 29, 4: 820–829.

Epstein, Leon. 1980. *Political Parties in Western Democracies*. London: Transaction Publishers.

Erickson, Herman. 1966. Adult Education and Swedish Political Leadership. *International Review of Education* 12, 2: 129–143.

Ericson, Jack T., ed. 1979. Americans for Democratic Action Papers, 1932–1965. A Guide to the Microfilm Edition. Sanford, NC: Microfilming Corporation of America.

Ericksson, Ingalill. 1994. Den Svenska Sociologins dolda Historia—fallet Gustaf Steffen/The Hidden History of Swedish Sociology—The Case of Gustaf Steffen. *Sociologisk Forskning* 31, 3: 44–56.

Erixon, Lennart. 2010. The Rehn-Meidner Model in Sweden: Its Rise, Challenges and Survival. *Journal of Economic Issues* XLIV, 3: 677–715.

Esping-Andersen, Gøsta. 1990. *The Three Worlds of Welfare Capitalism*. Cambridge, UK: Polity Press.

Esping-Andersen, Gøsta. 1999. *The Social Foundations of Postindustrial Economies*. Oxford: Oxford University Press.

Esping-Andersen, Gøsta, and Kees van Kersbergen. 1992. Contemporary Research on Social Democracy. *Annual Review of Sociology* 18: 187–208.

Evans, Peter, and Tamara Kay 2008. How Environmentalists "Greened" Trade Policy: Strategic Action and the Architecture of Field Overlap. *American Sociological Review* 73: 970–991.

Eyal, Gil. 2013. For a Sociology of Expertise: The Social Origins of the Autism Epidemic. *American Journal of Sociology* 118, 4: 863–907.

Eyal, Gil, and Larissa Buchholz. 2010. From the Sociology of Intellectuals to the Sociology of Interventions. *Annual Review of Sociology* 36: 117–137.

Fabian Society. [Undated]. The Fabian Story. http://www.fabians.org.uk/about/the-fabian-story, accessed June 7, 2014.

Fabricant, Solomon. 1984. Toward a Firmer Basis of Economic Policy: The Founding of the National Bureau of Economic Research. Cambridge, MA: NBER.

Fairbrother, Malcolm. 2014. Economists, Capitalists, and the Making of Globalization: North American Free Trade in Comparative-Historical Perspective. *American Journal of Sociology* 119, 5 (March): 1324–1379.

Farrell, David M., and P. Webb. 2000. Political Parties as Campaign Organizations. Pp. 102–28 in Dalton, Russel W. and Martin P. Wattenberg, eds., *Parties without Partisans: Political Change in Advanced Industrial Democracies*. New York: Oxford University Press.

Farrell, William. 1983. "Neoliberals" in Need of Constituents. *New York Times*, October 23.

Faucher-King, Florence. 2005. *Changing Parties: An Anthropology of British Political Conferences*. London: Palgrave Macmillan.

Favretto, Ilaria. 2003. *The Long Search for a Third Way: The British Labour Party and the Italian Left since 1945*. Basingstoke: Palgrave Macmillan.

Flaherty, Eoin. 2015. Top Incomes under Finance-Driven Capitalism, 1990–2010: Power Resources and Regulatory Orders. *Socio-Economic Review* 13, 3: 417–447.

Fligstein, Neil. 2001. *The Architecture of Markets: An Economic Sociology of Twenty-First-Century Capitalist Societies*. Princeton, NJ: Princeton University Press.

Fligstein, Neil, and Doug McAdam. 2012a. Response to Goldstone and Useem. *Sociological Theory* 30, 1: 48–50.

Fligstein, Neil, and Doug McAdam. 2012b. *A Theory of Fields*. New York: Oxford University Press.

Flora, Peter, and Arnold Heidenheimer, eds. 1982. *The Development of Welfare States in Europe and America*. Piscataway, NJ: Transaction Publishers.

Foster, William, and Waddill Catchings. 1928. *The Road to Plenty*. Boston: Houghton Mifflin.

Foucault, Michel. 1978–1979 [2008]. *The Birth of Biopolitics: Lectures at the Collège de France, 1978–1979*. New York: Picador.

Fourcade, Marion. 2006. The Construction of a Global Profession: The Transnationalization of Economics. *American Journal of Sociology* 112, 1: 145–194.

Fourcade, Marion. 2009. *Economists and Societies*. Princeton, NJ: Princeton University Press.

Fourcade, Marion, and Rakesh Khurana. 2013. From Social Control to Financial Economics: The Linked Ecologies of Economics and Business in Twentieth-Century America. *Theory and Society* 42: 121–159.

Fourcade, Marion, Etienne Ollion, and Yann Algan. 2015. The Superiority of Economists. *Journal of Economic Perspectives* 29, 1: 89–114.

Fourcade-Gourinchas, Marion. 2001. Politics, Institutional Structures, and the Rise of Economics: A Comparative Study. *Theory and Society* 30: 397–447.

Frey, Bruno, and Werner W. Pommerehne. 1988. The American Domination among Eminent Economists. *Scientometrics* 14, 1–2: 97–110.

Frieden, Jeffrey A. 2006. *Global Capitalism: Its Fall and Rise in the Twentieth Century*. New York: W. W. Norton.

Friedrich, Carl J. 1955. The Political Thought of Neo-Liberalism. *American Political Science Review* 49, 2: 509–525.

Galbraith, John Kenneth. 1965. *How Keynes Came to America*. Stamford, CT: Overbrook Press.

Gamson, William A. 1975. *The Strategy of Social Protest*. Homewood, IL: Irwin Press.

Garraty, John A. 1976. Unemployment during the Great Depression. *Labor History* 17, 2: 133–159.

Garvy, George. 1975. Keynes and the Economic Activists of Pre-Hitler Germany. *Journal of Political Economy* 83, 2: 391–405.

Gay, Oonagh. 2000. *Advisers to Ministers*. Research Paper 00/42. London: House of Commons.

Gibson, Rachel K., and Andrea Römmele. Measuring the Professionalization of Political Campaigning. *Party Politics* 15, 3: 265–293.

Giersch, Herbert. 1973. 10 Years of the German Council of Economic Experts. *Intereconomics* 11: 352–354.

Georgakakis, Didier, and Marine de Lasselle 2008. Where Have All the Lawyers Gone? Structure and Transformations of the Top European Commission Officials' Legal Training. EUI Working Paper RSCAS 2008/38 (December). European University Institute, Robert Schuman Centre for Advanced Studies, San Domenico di Fiesole.

Gill, Stephen, and David Law. 1988. *The Global Political Economy*. Baltimore: Johns Hopkins University Press.

Gillon, Steven M. 1987. *Politics and Vision: The ADA and American Liberalism, 1947–1985*. London and New York: Oxford University Press.

Glyn, Andrew. 2001. *Social Democracy in Neoliberal Times: The Left and Economic Policy since 1980*. Oxford: Oxford University Press.

Go, Julian, and Monika Krause. 2016. Fielding Transnationalism: An Introduction. *Sociological Review Monographs* 64, 2: 6–30.

Goldman, Lawrence. 1987. A Peculiarity of the English? The Social Science Association and the Absence of Sociology in Nineteenth-Century Britain. *Past and Present* 114: 133–171.

Goldstein, Robert J. 1983. *Political Repression in 19th Century Europe*. London: Croom Helm.

Gorski, Philip S. 2003. *The Disciplinary Revolution: Calvinism and the Rise of the State in Early Modern Europe*. Chicago: Chicago University Press.

Gorski, Philip S., ed. 2013. *Bourdieu and Historical Analysis*. Durham, NC: Duke University Press.

Gourevitch, Peter. 1984. Breaking with Orthodoxy: The Politics of Economic Policy Responses to the Depression of the 1930s. *International Organization* 38, 1: 95–129.

Gramsci, Antonio. 1929–1935 [1971]. *Selections from the Prison Notebooks*. London: Lawrence and Wishart.

Greider, William. 1981. The Education of David Stockman. *Atlantic*, December.

Gross, Neil. 2013. *Why Are Professors Liberal and Why Do Conservatives Care?* Cambridge, MA: Harvard University Press.

Gross, Neil, Thomas Medvetz, and Rupert Russell. 2011. The Contemporary American Conservative Movement. *Annual Review of Sociology* 37: 325–354.

Guttsman, W. L. 1981. *The German Social Democratic Party, 1875–1933.* New York: HarperCollins.

Hagemann, Harald. 2000. The Post-1945 Development of Economics in Germany. Pp. 113–128 in A. W. B. Coats, ed., *The Development of Economics in Western Europe since 1945.* Routledge Studies in the History of Economics. London: Routledge.

Halfmann, Drew. 2011. *Doctors and Demonstrators.* Chicago: University of Chicago Press.

Hall, Peter A. 2002. The Comparative Political Economy of the 'Third Way'. Pp. 31–58 in Oliver Schmidtke, ed., *The Third Way Transformation of Social Democracy: Normative Claims and Policy Initiatives in the 21st Century.* Hampshire, UK: Ashgate.

Hall, Peter, ed. 1989. *The Political Power of Economic Ideas: Keynesianism across Nations.* Princeton, NJ: Princeton University Press.

Hall, Stuart. 1979. The Great Moving Right Show. *Marxism Today,* January, 14–20.

Hall, Stuart. 1998. The Great Moving Nowhere Show. *Marxism Today,* November/December.

Hallin, Daniel C., and Paolo Mancini. 2004. *Comparing Media Systems: Three Models of Media and Politics.* Cambridge and New York: Cambridge University Press.

Hamilton, Richard F., and Lowell L. Hargens 1993. The Politics of the Professors: Self-Identifications, 1969–1984. *Social Forces* 71, 3: 603–627.

Hamman, Oscar J. 1970. The Young Marx, Reconsidered. *Journal of the History of Ideas* 31,1: 109–120.

Hancock, Keith. 1960. Unemployment and the Economists in the 1920s. *Economica* 27, 108: 305–321.

Hands, Gordon. 1971. Roberto Michels and the Study of Political Parties. *British Journal of Political Science* 1, 2: 155–172.

Hansson, Björn. 1991. The Stockholm School and the Development of Dynamic Method. Pp. 168–213 in Bo Sandelin, ed, *The History of Swedish Economic Thought.* London: Routledge.

Harris, Abram L. 1942. Sombart and German (National) Socialism. *Journal of Political Economy* 50, 6: 805–835.

Harris, Kevan, and Brendan McQuade. 2015. Notes on the Method of World System Biography. *Journal of World-Systems Research* 21, 2: 276–286.

Hartwell, Max. 1995. *A History of the Mont Pèlerin Society.* Indianapolis: Liberty Fund.

Harvey, David. 2005 [2009]. *A Brief History of Neoliberalism.* Oxford: Oxford University Press.

Haseler, Stephen. 1969. *The Gaitskellites: Revisionism in the British Labour Party, 1951–1964.* London: Macmillan.

Hausman, Daniel M., ed. 1984 [2008]. *The Philosophy of Economics: An Anthology.* Cambridge: Cambridge University Press.

Hawtrey, R. G. 1947. *The Gold Standard in Theory and Practice.* New York: Longmans.

Hayes, Carlton J. H. 1917. The History of German Socialism Reconsidered. *The American Historical Review* 23, 1: 62–101.

Haynes, Bruce, and Syma Solovitch. 2017. *Down the Up Staircase: Three Generations of a Harlem Family.* New York: Columbia University Press.

Hedström, Peter, Rickard Sandell, and Charlotta Stern. 2000. Mesolevel Networks and the Diffusion of Social Movements: The Case of the Swedish Social Democratic Party. *American Journal of Sociology* 106, 1: 145–172.

Held, Michael. 1982. *Sozialdemokratie und Keynesianismus: Von der Weltwirtschaftskrise bis zum Godesberger Programm.* Frankfurt / Main ; New York : Campus Verlag.

Henriksson, Rolf G. H. 1991. The Political Economy Club and the Stockholm School, 1917–1951. Pp. 41–73 in Lars Jonung, ed., *The Stockholm School Revisited.* New York: Cambridge University Press.

Hetzel, Robert L. 2002. German Monetary History in the First Half of the Twentieth Century. Federal Reserve Bank of Richmond, *Economic Quarterly* 88, 1: 1–35.

Hicks, Alexander, and Christopher Zorn. 2005. Economic Globalization, the Macro Economy, and Reversals of Welfare: Expansion in Affluent Democracies, 1978–94. *International Organization* 59, 3 (Summer): 631–662.

Hilgers, Mathieu. 2011. The Three Anthropological Approaches to Neoliberalism. *International Social Science Journal* 61, 202: 351–364.

Hirschman, Daniel. 2016. Inventing the Economy; or, How We Learned to Stop Worrying and Love the GDP. PhD dissertation, University of Michigan.

Hirschman, Daniel, and Elizabeth Popp Berman. 2014. Do Economists Make Policies? On the Political Effects of Economics. *Socio-Economic Review* 12, 4: 779–811.

Hirschman, Daniel, and Isaac Reed. 2014. Formation Stories and Causality in Sociology. *Sociological Theory* 32, 4: 259–282.

Hodge, Carl Cavanagh. 1993. The Long Fifties: The Politics of Socialist Programmatic Revision in Britain, France and Germany. *Contemporary European History* 2, 1: 17–34.

Hoover, Kenneth R. 2003. *Economics as Ideology: Keynes, Laski, Hayek, and the Creation of Contemporary Politics.* Lanham, MD: Rowman and Littlefield.

Howe, Daniel Walker. 2007. *What Hath God Wrought: The Transformation of America, 1815–1848.* New York· Oxford University Press.

Howell, Chris. 2001. The End of the Relationship between Social Democratic Parties and Trade Unions? *Studies in Political Economy* 65: 7–37.

Howell, David. 2005 [2013]. Keep Left (act. 1947–1951). *Oxford Dictionary of National Biography.* London and New York: Oxford University Press. http://www.oxforddnb.com/view/theme/92511, accessed 19 May 2014.

Howson, Susan, and Donald Winch. 1977. *The Economic Advisory Council, 1930–1939: A Study in Economic Advice during Depression and Recovery.* Cambridge: Cambridge University Press.

Hoxie, R. Gordon. 1980. Staffing the Ford and Carter Presidencies. *Presidential Studies Quarterly* 10, 3, Why Great Men are, or Are Not, Elected President (Summer): 378–401.

Hülsberg, Werner. 1987. After the West German Elections. *New Left Review* 162: 85–99.

Hutchison, Terrence W. 1968. *Economics and Economic Policy in Britain, 1946–1966.* London: Allen and Unwin.

Hutchison, Terence W. 1977. Keynes versus the "Keynesians" . . . ? London: Transatlantic Arts.

Hutchison, Terence W. 1979. Notes on the Effects of Economic Ideas on Policy: The Example of the German Social Market. Currency and Economic Reform: West Germany after World War II: A Symposium, *Zeitschrift für die gesamte Staatswissenschaft / Journal of Institutional and Theoretical Economics* 135, 3 (September): 426–441.

Jackson, John S., and Robert A. Hitlin. 1981. The Nationalization of the Democratic Party. *Western Political Quarterly* 34, 2 (June): 270–286.

James, Harold. 1981. Rudolf Hilferding and the Application of the Political Economy of the Second International. *Historical Journal* 24, 4: 847–869.

Janoski, Thomas. 1990. *The Political Economy of Unemployment: Active Labor Market Policy in West Germany and the United States.* Berkeley: University of California Press.

Johnson, Carol, and Fran Tonkiss. 2002. The Third Influence: the Blair Government and Australian Labor. *Policy and Politics* 30: 5–18.

Johnson, Dennis W. 2016. *Democracy for Hire: A History of American Political Consulting.* New York: Oxford University Press.

Jones, Byrd L. 1972. The Role of Keynesians in Wartime Policy and Postwar Planning, 1940–1946. *American Economic Review* 62, 1–2: 125–133.

Jones, Daniel Stedman. 2012. *Masters of the Universe: Hayek, Friedman, and the Birth of Neoliberal Politics*. Princeton, NJ: Princeton University Press.

Jonung, Lars. 1979. Cassel, Davidson and Heckscher on Swedish Monetary Policy: A Confidential Report to the Riksbank in 1931. *Economy and History*, 22: 85–101.

Jonung, Lars, ed. 1991. *The Stockholm School of Economics Revisited*. New York: Cambridge University Press.

Jost, John T. 2006. The End of the End of Ideology. *American Psychologist* 67, 7: 651–670.

Jovanovic, Franck. 2008. The Construction of the Canonical History of Financial Economics. *History of Political Economy* 40, 2: 213–242.

Judis, John and Ruy Teixeira. 2002. *The Emerging Democratic Majority*. New York: Scribner.

Judt, Tony. 1989. Reviews of *Aspects of International Socialism, 1871–1914: Essays by George Haupt*, by George Haupt and Peter Fawcett; *A Lost Left: Three Studies in Socialism and Nationalism*, by David Howell; *Paper Stones: A History of Electoral Socialism*, by Adam Przeworski and John Sprague. *Journal of Modern History* 61, 4 (December): 745–748.

Juran, J.M. 1997. Early SQC: A Historical Supplement. *Quality Progress* 30, 9: 73–81.

Kadish, Alon. 1986. *Apostle Arnold: The Life and Death of Arnold Toynbee, 1852–1883*. Durham, NC: Duke University Press.

Kamarck, Elaine. 1986. Structure as Strategy: Presidential Nominating Politics since Reform. PhD dissertation. University of California, Berkeley.

Katz, Richard, and Peter Mair. 1995. Changing Models of Party Organization and Party Democracy: The Emergence of the Cartel Party. *Party Politics* 1, 1: 5–28.

Katz, Richard S., and Peter Mair. 2009. The Cartel Party Thesis: A Restatement. *Perspectives on Politics* 7, 4: 753–766.

Kaus, Mickey. 1984. Too Much Technology, Not Enough Soul: The Gospel according to Randall Rothenberg. *Washington Monthly*, September, 48–54.

Kemmerling, Achim, and Oliver Bruttel. 2006. "New Politics" in German Labour Market Policy? The Implications of the Recent Hartz Reforms for the German Welfare State. *West European Politics* 29, 1: 90–112.

Key, Valdimer Orlando. 1955. A Theory of Critical Elections. *Journal of Politics* 17: 3–18.

Key, Valdimer Orlando. 1959. Secular Realignment and the Party System. *Journal of Politics* 21: 198–210.

King, Desmond, and Mark Wickham-Jones. 1999. From Clinton to Blair: The Democratic (Party) Origins of Welfare to Work. *Political Quarterly*. 70,1: 62–72.

Kirshner, Jonathan. 2009. Keynes, Legacies, and Inquiry. *Theory and Society* 38: 527–541.

Kitschelt, Herbert. 1994. *The Transformation of European Social Democracy.* New York: Cambridge University Press.

Klausen, J. 1999. *War and Welfare: Europe and the United States.* Houndmills, UK: Palgrave.

Klein, Daniel B., William L. Davis, Bob G. Figgins, and David Hedengren. 2012. Characteristics of the Members of Twelve Economic Associations: Voting, Policy Views, and Favorite Economists. *Economic Journal Watch* 9, 2: 149–162.

Klein, Daniel B., and Charlotta Stern. 2005. Professors and Their Politics: The Policy Views of Social Scientists. *Critical Review* 17, 3: 257–303.

Klein, Joe. 2007. *Politics Lost. From RFK to W: How Politicians Have Become Less Courageous and More Interested in Keeping Power than in Doing What's Right for America.* New York: Broadway Books.

Klein, Philip A. 1984. Economic Policy and the Obligations of the Economist. *Journal of Economic Issues* 18, 2: 537–546.

Koelble, Thomas. 1987a. Politics, Party Activists and Trade Unions. PhD dissertation. University of Calfornia, San Diego.

Koelble, Thomas. 1987b. Trade Unionists, Party Activists, and Politicians: The Struggle for Power over Party Rules in the British Labour Party and the West German Social Democratic Party. *Comparative Politics* 19, 3: 253–266.

Korpi, Walter. 1996. Eurosclerosis and the Sclerosis of Objectivity: On the Role of Values among Economic Policy Experts. *Economic Journal* 106, 439: 1727–1746.

Korpi, Walter. 2003. Welfare-State Regress in Western Europe: Politics, Institutions, Globalization, and Europeanization. *Annual Review of Sociology* 29: 589–609.

Krippner, Greta. 2005. The Financialization of the American Economy. *Socio-Economic Review* 3: 173–208.

Krippner, Greta. 2011. *Capitalizing on Crisis: The Political Origins of the Rise of Finance.* Cambridge, MA: Harvard University Press.

Kuhn, Thomas. 1962. *The Structure of Scientific Revolutions.* 50th anniversary edition. Chicago and London: University of Chicago Press.

Kuhnle, Stein. 1996. International Modeling, States, and Statistics: Scandinavian Social Security Solutions in the 1890s. Pp. 233–263 in Dietrich Rueschemeyer and Theda Skocpol, eds., *States, Social Knowledge and the Origins of Modern Social Policies.* Princeton, NJ: Princeton University Press; New York: Russell Sage Foundation.

Kundnani, Hans. 2005. Goodbye to the '68ers. *Prospect*, July 28.

Ladd, Everett Carll, Jr., and Seymour Martin Lipset. 1976. *The Divided Academy: Professors and Politics.* New York: W. W. Norton.

Lafontaine, Oskar. 2009. *Left Parties Everywhere?* Nottingham, UK: Spokesman Books for Socialist Renewal.

Lane, Robert E. 1966. The Decline of Politics and Ideology in a Knowledgeable Society. *American Sociological Review* 31, 5: 649–662.

Laurison, Daniel. 2014. The Field of American Political Consultants. In Michael Grenfell and Frédéric Lebaron, eds., *Bourdieu and Data Analysis: Methodological Principles and Practice.* Berlin: Peter Lang.

Laws, David. 2006. Economic Policy in the Early 1980s: Were the 364 All Wrong? Pp. 104–111 in Booth, Philip, ed. 2006. *Were 364 Economists All Wrong?* London: Institute of Economic Affairs.

Lebaron, Frédéric. 2006. "Nobel" Economists as Public Intellectuals: the Circulation of Symbolic Capital. *International Journal of Contemporary Sociology* 43, 1: 87–101.

Lee, Caroline W. 2015. *Do-It-Yourself Democracy.* New York: Oxford University Press.

Lee, Caroline W., Michael McQuarrie, and Edward Walker, eds. 2015. *Democratizing Inequalities: Dilemmas of the New Public Participation.* New York: New York University Press.

Lee, H. W. December 15, 1913. Overview of the "Social Democrat" and "British Socialist," 1897–1913. *British Socialist.* https://www.marxists.org /history/international/social-democracy/social-democrat/1913/12/overview .htm, accessed 24 November 2017.

Leeson, Robert. 1998. The Origins of Keynesian Discomfiture. *Journal of Post Keynesian Economics* 20, 4: 597–619.

Lekachman, Robert. 1966. *The Age of Keynes.* New York: McGraw-Hill.

Lenin, Vladimir. 1905 [1965]. Party Organisation and Party Literature. In *Lenin: Collected Works*, vol. 10. Moscow: Progress Publishers. http://www .marxists.org/archive/lenin/works/1905/nov/13.htm.

Leys, Colin. 2003. The British Labour Party's Transition from Socialism to Capitalism. Pp. 235–260 in David Coates, ed., *Paving the Third Way: The Critique of Parliamentary Socialism.* London: Merlin Press.

Lidtke, Vernon L. 1966. *The Outlawed Party: Social Democracy in Germany, 1878–1890.* Princeton, NJ: Princeton University Press.

Lindemann, Albert S. 1988. Review of *Paper Stones: A History of Electoral Socialism,* by Adam Przeworski and John Sprague. *American Historical Review* 93, 3 (June): 682.

Lindvall, Johannes. 2009. The Real but Limited Influence of Expert Ideas. *World Politics* 61, 4: 703–730.

Lipset, Seymour Martin. 1960. *Political Man.* Garden City, NY: Doubleday.

Lipset, Seymour Martin, and Stein Rokkan. 1967. *Party Systems and Voter Alignments: Cross-National Perspectives.* New York: The Free Press.

Lipset, Seymour Martin, and Gary Marks. 2000 [2013]. *It Didn't Happen Here: Why Socialism Failed in the United States.* New York: W. W. Norton.

Loveman, Mara. 2005. The Modern State and the Primitive Accumulation of Symbolic Power. *American Journal of Sociology* 110, 6: 1651–1683.

Lund, Ragnar. 1938. Adult Education in Sweden. *Annals of the American Academy of Political and Social Science* 197: 232–242.

Machiavelli, Niccolò. 1516 [1999]. *The Prince.* New York: Penguin Classics.

MacKenzie, Donald, and Yuval Millo. 2003. Constructing a Market, Performing a Theory: The Historical Sociology of a Financial Derivatives Exchange. *American Journal of Sociology* 109, 1: 107–145.

MacKenzie, Donald, Fabian Muniesa, and Lucia Siu. 2008. *Do Economists Make Markets? On the Performativity of Economics.* Princeton, NJ: Princeton University Press.

Mair, Peter (ed). 1990. *The West European Party System.* Oxford: Oxford University Press.

Mair, Peter. 2000. Partyless Democracy. *New Left Review* 2: 21–35.

Major, Aaron. 2014. *Architects of Austerity: International Finance and the Politics of Growth.* Stanford, CA: Stanford University Press.

Malmberg, Bo. 2007. Number of Students and Enrollment Rates in Extended Primary, Integrated-Upper Secondary, and Tertiary Education, Sweden, 1768–2002. Stockholm: Institute for Futures Studies.

Mannheim, Karl. 1936 [1985]. *Ideology and Utopia: An Introduction to the Sociology of Knowledge.* New York: Harcourt Brace.

Maravall, José Mariá. 2010. Shifting Promises: The Politics of Social Democratic Programs. Paper prepared for the conference Democracy, Democratization and Social Democracy, CEACS, Juan March Institute, Madrid, 14–15 June 2010.

Marcussen, Martin. 2009. The Scientization of Central Banking, the Politics of Apoliticization. Pp. 373–390 in Kenneth Dyson and Martin Marcussen, eds., *Central Banks in the Age of the Euro: Europeanization, Convergence, and Power.* Oxford: Oxford University Press.

Marcuzzo, Maria Cristina. 2002. The Collaboration between J. M. Keynes and R. F. Kahn from the *Treatise* to the *General Theory. History of Political Economy* 34, 2: 421–447.

Markoff, John, and Véronica Montecinos 1993. The Ubiquitous Rise of Economists. *Journal of Public Policy* 13, 1: 37–68.

Markovits, Andrei. 1986. *Politics of West German Trade Unions.* Cambridge: Cambridge University Press.

Markovits, Andrei, and Christopher Allen. 1984. Trade Unions and the Economic Crisis: The West German Case. Pp. 91–188 in Peter Gourevitch, Andrew Martin, George Ross, Christopher Allen, Stephen Bornstein, and Andrei Markovits, *Unions and Economic Crisis: Britain, West Germany and Sweden*. London: Allen and Unwin.

Marquand, David. 1977. *Ramsay MacDonald*. Berkeley: University of California Press.

Martin, Andrew. Trade Unions in Sweden: Strategic Responses to Change and Crisis. Pp. 189–359 in Peter Gourevitch, Andrew Martin, George Ross, Christopher Allen, Stephen Bornstein, and Andrei Markovits, *Unions and Economic Crisis: Britain, West Germany and Sweden*. London: George Allen & Unwin.

Martin, John Levi. 2003. What Is Field Theory? *American Journal of Sociology* 109, 1: 1–49.

Martin, John Levi. 2011. *The Explanation of Social Action*. Chicago: University of Chicago Press.

Martin, John Levi. 2015. What Is Ideology? *Sociologia, Problemas e Práticas* 77: 9–31.

Marx, Karl. 1844 [1978]. Economic and Philosophic Manuscripts of 1844. Pp. 66–125 in *The Marx-Engels Reader*, ed. Robert C. Tucker. New York: W. W. Norton.

Marx, Karl. 1846 [1978]. The German Ideology: Part I. Pp. 146–200 in *The Marx-Engels Reader*, ed. Robert C. Tucker. New York: W. W. Norton.

Marx, Karl, and Friedrich Engels. 1848 [1978]. Manifesto of the Communist Party. Pp. 469-500 in *The Marx-Engels Reader*, ed. Robert C. Tucker. New York: W. W. Norton.

Mayhew, David R. 2002. *Electoral Realignments: A Critique of an American Genre*. New Haven, CT: Yale University Press.

McClenahan, William, Jr., and William H Becker. 2011. *Eisenhower and the Cold War Economy*. Baltimore: Johns Hopkins University Press.

McQuarrie, Michael. 2013. Community Organizations in the Foreclosure Crisis: The Failure of Neoliberal Civil Society. *Politics and Society* 41: 73–99.

Medvetz, Thomas. 2012. *Think Tanks in America*. Chicago: University of Chicago Press.

Megay, Edward N. 1970. Anti-Pluralist Liberalism: The German Neoliberals. *Political Science Quarterly* 85, 3: 422–442.

Merkel, Wolfgang, Alexander Petring, Christian Henkes, and Christoph Egle, eds. 2008. *Social Democracy in Power: The Capacity to Reform*. London: Routledge.

Merkl, Peter H. 1962. Comparative Study and Campaign Management: The Brandt Campaign in Western Germany. *Western Political Quarterly* 15, 4: 681–704.

Merton, Robert K. 1957 [1973]. The Role-Set: Problems in Sociological Theory. *British Journal of Sociology* 8, 2. 106–120.

Metelius, Bengt. 1991. Comment on Earlene Craver, "Gösta Bagge, the Rockefeller Foundation, and Empirical Social Science Research in Sweden, 1924–1940." Pp. 100–102, in Lars Jonung, ed., *The Stockholm School Revisited*. New York: Cambridge University Press.

Meyer, Fritz W. 1967 [1982]. The Splendor and Misery of the Full Employment Policy. Pp. 193–204 in Wolfgang Stützel, Christian Watrin, Hans Willgerodt, and Karl Hohmann, eds., *Standard Texts on the Social Market Economy: Two Centuries of Discussion*. Stuttgart: Gustav Fischer.

Meyer, Thomas. 1997. The Transformation of German Social Democracy. Pp. 124–142 in Donald Sassoon, ed., *Looking Left: Socialism in Europe after the Cold War*. New York: New Press.

Michels, Robert. 1911 [1962]. *Political Parties: A Sociological Study of the Oligarchical Tendencies of Modern Democracy*. New York: Free Press.

Miliband, Ralph. 1961. *Parliamentary Socialism: A Study in the Politics of Labor*. London: Allen and Unwin.

Mills, C. Wright. 1959 [2000]. *The Sociological Imagination*. Oxford: Oxford University Press.

Mirowski, Philip. 1988. *Against Mechanism: Protecting Economics from Science*. Rowman and Littlefield.

Mirowski, Philip. 1989. *More Heat than Light: Economics as Social Physics, Physics as Nature's Economics*. Cambridge: Cambridge University Press.

Mirowski, Philip. 2002. *Machine Dreams: Economics Becomes a Cyborg Science*. Cambridge: Cambridge University Press.

Mirowski, Philip, and Dieter Plehwe, eds. 2009. *The Road from Mont Pèlerin: The Making of the Neoliberal Thought Collective*. Cambridge, MA: Harvard University Press.

Mitchell, Timothy. 1998. Fixing the Economy. *Cultural Studies* 12, 1: 82–101.

Mitchell, Timothy. 1999. Society, Economy, and the State Effect. Pp. 76–97 in George Steinmetz, ed., *State/Culture: State Formation after the Cultural Turn*. Ithaca: Cornell University Press.

Mitchell, Timothy. 2002. *The Rule of Experts: Egypt, Techno-Politics, Modernity*. Berkeley: University of California Press.

Moggridge, Donald, and Elizabeth Johnson, eds. *The Collected Writings of John Maynard Keynes*. Vol. 25. London: Macmillan.

Mommsen, Wolfgang J. 1959 [1984]. *Max Weber and German Politics, 1890–1920*. Chicago: University of Chicago Press.

Mora, Cristina. 2014. Cross-Field Effects and Ethnic Classification: The Institutionalization of Hispanic Panethnicity, 1965 to 1990. *American Sociological Review* 79, 2: 183–210.

Morgan, David W. 1979. The Father of Revisionism Revisited: Eduard Bernstein. *Journal of Modern History* 51, 3 (September): 525–532.

Morgan, Roger. 1965. *The German Social Democrats and the First International, 1864–1872*. Cambridge: Cambridge University Press.

Mudge, Stephanie L. 2008. What Is Neoliberalism? *Socio-Economic Review* 6, 4: 703–731.

Mudge, Stephanie L. 2011. What's Left of Leftism? Neoliberal Politics in Western Party Systems, 1945–2004. *Social Science History* 35, 3: 337–380.

Mudge, Stephanie L., and Anthony S. Chen. 2014. Political Parties in the Sociological Imagination: Past, Present, and Future Directions. *Annual Review of Sociology* 40: 305–330.

Mudge, Stephanie L. 2015. Explaining Political Tunnel Vision: Politics and Economics in Crisis-Ridden Europe, Then and Now. *European Journal of Sociology* 56, 1: 63–91.

Mudge, Stephanie L. 2016. Neoliberalism, Accomplished and Ongoing. In Simon Springer, Kean Birch, and Julie MacLeavy, eds., *The Handbook of Neoliberalism*. New York: Routledge.

Mudge, Stephanie L. 2017. Neoliberalism and the Study of "Isms." In William Outhwaite and Stephen Turner, eds., *The SAGE Handbook of Political Sociology*. Thousand Oaks, CA: Sage.

Mudge, Stephanie L. Forthcoming. States, Parties, and Expertise. In Thomas Janoski, Cedric de Leon and Isaac Martin, eds. *The Handbook of Political Sociology*. Cambridge: Cambridge University Press.

Mudge, Stephanie L., and Antoine Vauchez. 2012. Building Europe on a Weak Field: Law, Economics, and Scholarly Avatars in Transnational Politics. *American Journal of Sociology* 118, 2: 449–92.

Mudge, Stephanie L., and Antoine Vauchez. 2016. Fielding Supranationalism: The European Central Bank as a Field Effect. *Sociological Review Monographs* 64, 2: 146–169.

Mullard, Maurice. 2005. *Policy-Making in Britain*. London: Taylor and Francis.

Musgrave, Richard A. 1976. Alvin H. Hansen: Caring for the Real Problems. *Quarterly Journal of Economics* 90, 1: 1–7.

Nau, Heino Heinrich. 2000. Gustav Schmoller's Historico-Ethical Political Economy: Ethics, Politics and Economics in the Younger German Historical School, 1860–1917. *European Journal of the History of Economic Thought* 7, 4: 507–531.

Naveh, David. 1981. The Political Role of Academic Advisers: The Case of the U.S. President's Council of Economic Advisers, 1946–1976. *Presidential Studies Quarterly* 11, 4: 492–510.

Nelson, Robert. 1989. Introduction and Summary. Pp. 2–14 in Joseph Pechman, ed., *The Role of the Economist in Government: An International Perspective*. New York: New York University Press.

Nord, Lars. 2001. Americanization v. the Middle Way: New Trends in Swedish Communication. *Press/Politics* 6, 2: 113–119.

Offer, Avner, and Gabriel Söderberg. 2016. *The Nobel Factor: The Prize in Economics, Social Democracy and the Market Turn*. Princeton, NJ: Princeton University Press.

Ostrogorski, Moisei. 1902 [1982]. *Democracy and the Organization of Political Parties*. New York: Doubleday.

Owen, Geoffrey. 1965. The Department of Economic Affairs. *Political Quarterly* 36: 380–389.

Pacewicz, Josh. 2015. Playing the Neoliberal Game: Why Community Leaders Left Party Politics to Partisan Activists. *American Journal of Sociology* 121, 3: 826–881.

Pacewicz, Josh. 2016. *Partisans and Partners: The Politics of the Post-Keynesian Society*. Chicago: University of Chicago Press.

Padgett, Stephen, and William Paterson. 1994. Germany: Stagnation of the Left. Pp. 102–129 in Perry Anderson and Patrick Camiller, eds., *Mapping the West European Left*. London: Verso.

Panitch, Leo. 1979 [2003]. Socialists and the Labour Party: A Reappraisal. Pp. 159–179 in David Coates, ed., *Paving the Third Way: The Critique of Parliamentary Socialism*. London: Merlin Press.

Panitch, Leo. 1981. Trade Unions and the Capitalist State. *New Left Review* 125: 21–43.

Panitch, Leo. 1986. The Tripartite Experience. Pp. 37–119 in K. Banting, ed., *The State and Economic Interests*. Toronto: Toronto University Press.

Panitch, Leo and Colin Leys. 2001. *The End of Parliamentary Socialism: From New Left to New Labour*. London: Verso.

Pautz, Hartwig. 2008. Think Tanks in Germany: The Bertelsmann Foundation's Role in Labour Market Reform. *Zeitschrift für Politikberatung* 1, 3: 437–456.

Pautz, Hartwig. 2010a. The Role of Think Tanks in the Modernisation of the SPD. *German Politics* 19, 2: 183–199.

Pautz, Hartwig. 2010b. Think Tanks in the United Kingdom and Germany: Actors in the Modernisation of Social Democracy. *British Journal of Politics and International Relations* 12: 274–94.

Pease, Edward R. 1918 [1963]. *The History of the Fabian Society*. London: Frank Cass.

Peck, Jamie. 2010. *Constructions of Neoliberal Reason.* Oxford: Oxford University Press.

Peden, G. C., ed. 2004. *Keynes and His Critics: Treasury Responses to the Keynesian Revolution, 1925–1946.* Oxford: Oxford University Press.

Pestoff, V. A. 1991. Towards a New Swedish Model of Collective Bargaining and Politics. In Colin Crouch and Franz Traxler, eds., *Organized Industrial Relations in Europe: What Future?* Aldershot, UK: Avebury Press.

Peston, Robert. 1995. *Brown's Britain.* London: Short Books.

Peters, Charles. 1983. A Neoliberal's Manifesto. *Washington Monthly,* May, 8–18.

Phillips-Fein, Kim. 2009. *Invisible Hands.* New York: W. W. Norton.

Pierson, Stanley. 1993. *Marxist Intellectuals and the Working-Class Mentality in Germany, 1887–1912.* Cambridge, MA: Harvard University Press.

Piven, Frances Fox. 1989. Is There an Electoral Path for Socialists? Review of *Paper Stones: A History of Electoral Socialism,* by Adam Przeworski and John Sprague. *Contemporary Sociology* 18, 1 (January): 65–67.

Plasser, Fritz , Christian Scheucher, and Christian Senft. 1999. Is There a European Style of Political Marketing? A Survey of Political Managers and Consultants. Pp. 89–112 in *The Handbook of Political Marketing,* ed. Bruce I. Newman. Thousand Oaks, CA: Sage.

Plasser, Fritz, and Gunda Plasser 2002. *Global Political Campaigning: A Worldwide Analysis of Campaign Professionals.* Westport, CT: Greenwood Publishing.

Polanyi, Karl. 1944 [2001]. *The Great Transformation: The Political and Economic Origins of Our Time.* Boston: Beacon Press.

Polillo, Simone. 2011. Money, Moral Authority, and the Politics of Credit-worthiness. *American Sociological Review* 76, 3: 437–464.

Polillo, Simone, and Mauro F. Guillén. 2005. Globalization Pressures and the State: The Global Spread of Central Bank Independence. *American Journal of Sociology* 110, 6: 1764–1802.

Pontusson, Jonas. 1994. Sweden: After the Golden Age. In Perry Anderson and Patrick Camiller, eds., *Mapping the West European Left.* London: Verso.

Potrafke, Niklas. 2013. Minority Positions in the German Council of Economic Experts: A Political Economic Analysis. *European Journal of Political Economy* 31: 180–187.

Powell, David. 1986. The New Liberalism and the Rise of Labour, 1886–1906. *Historical Journal* 29, 2 (June): 369–393.

Power, Michael. 2011. Foucault and Sociology. *Annual Review of Sociology* 37: 35–56.

Prasad, Monica. 2006. *The Politics of Free Markets: The Rise of Neoliberal Economic Policies in Britain, France, Germany and the United States*. Chicago: University of Chicago Press.

Przeworski, Adam, and John Sprague. 1988. *Paper Stones: A History of Electoral Socialism*. Chicago: University of Chicago Press.

Przeworski, Adam, and Henry Teune. 1970. *The Logic of Comparative Social Inquiry*. New York: Wiley-Interscience.

Pugh, Patricia. 1984. *Educate, Agitate, Organise: 100 Years of Fabian Socialism*. London: Methuen.

Quinn, Dennis P. 2003. Capital Account Liberalization and Financial Globalization, 1890–1999: A Synoptic View. *International Journal of Finance and Economics* 8: 189–204.

Reichley, A. James. 1992. *The Life of the Parties: A History of American Political Parties*. New York: Free Press.

Reid, Alastair J. 2000. Labour and the Trade Unions. Pp. 221–247 in Duncan Tanner, Pat Thane, and Nick Tiratsoo, eds., *Labour's First Century*. Cambridge: Cambridge University Press.

Riddell, Neil. 2002. Walter Citrine and the British Labour Movement, 1925–1935. *History* 85, 278: 285–306.

Ringer, Fritz K. 1969. *The Decline of the German Mandarins: The German Academic Community, 1890–1933*. Cambridge, MA: Harvard University Press.

Rodgers, Daniel. 1998. *Atlantic Crossings*. Cambridge, MA: Belknap Press of Harvard University Press.

Roll, Eric. 1968. *The World After Keynes: An Examination of the Economic Order*. New York: Frederick A. Praeger.

Roosevelt, Theodore. 1912 [2007]. Introduction. Pp. vii–xi in Charles McCarthy, *The Wisconsin Idea*. Charleston, South Carolina: BiblioLife, LLC.

Roth, Guenther. 1963. *The Social Democrats in Imperial Germany: A Study in Working-Class Isolation and National Integration*. Totowa, NJ: Bedminster Press.

Rothschild, Kurt W. 1972. Stagflation and Intensified Inflation. A Primitive Hypothesis. *The Economic Journal* 82, 328: 1383–1387.

Rothstein, Bo. 1991. State Structure and Variations in Corporatism: The Swedish Case. *Scandinavian Political Studies* 14, 2: 149–171.

Rueschemeyer, Dietrich, and Theda Skocpol, eds. 1996. *States, Social Knowledge, and the Origins of Modern Social Policies*. Princeton, NJ: Princeton University Press.

Rueschemeyer, Dietrich, and Roman Von Rossem. 1996. The Verein für Socialpolitik and the Fabian Society. Pp. 117–162 in Dietrich Rueschemeyer and Theda Skocpol, eds., *States, Social Knowledge and the Origins of Modern Social Policies*. Princeton, NJ: Princeton University Press.

Ruggie, John. 1982. International Regimes, Transactions, and Change: Embedded Liberalism in the Postwar Economic Order. *International Organization* 36, 2: 379–415.

Ryner, Magnus. 1994. Assessing SAP's Economic Policy in the 1980s: The "Third Way," the Swedish Model and the Transition from Fordism to Post-Fordism. *Economic and Industrial Democracy* 15: 385–428.

Sabato, Larry. 1981. *The Rise of Political Consultants: New Ways of Winning Elections*. New York: Basic Books.

Sabato, Larry. 1988. *The Party's Just Begun: Shaping Political Parties for America's Future*. Glenview, IL: Scott, Foresman/Little, Brown College Division.

Salant, Walter. 1989. The Spread of Keynesian Doctrines and Practices in the United States. Pp. 27–52, in Peter Hall, ed., *The Political Power of Economic Ideas: Keynesianism across Nations*. Princeton, NJ: Princeton University Press.

Sandelin, Bo, Nikias Sarafoglou, and Ann Veiderpass. 2000. The Post-1945 Development of Economics and Economists in Sweden. Pp. 42–66 in A. W. B. Coats, ed., *The Development of Economics in Western Europe since 1945*. Routledge Studies in the History of Economics. London: Routledge.

Sassoon, Donald. 1996. *One Hundred Years of Socialism: The West European Left in the Twentieth Century*. London: I. B. Tauris.

Sassoon, Donald. 1997. *Looking Left: European Socialism after the Cold War*. London: I. B. Tauris in association with the Gramsci Foundation, Rome.

Scanlon, Christopher. 2001. A Step to the Left? Or Just a Jump to the Right? Making Sense of the Third Way on Government and Governance. *Australian Journal of Political Science* 36: 481–98.

Schattschneider, E. E. 1942. *Party Government*. New York: Holt, Rinehart and Winston.

Schellenger, Harold K., Jr. 1968. *The S.P.D. in the Bonn Republic: A Socialist Party Modernizes*. The Hague: Martinus Nijhoff.

Schick, Allen. 1970. The Budget Bureau That Was: Thoughts on the Rise, Decline, and Future of a Presidential Agency. *Law and Contemporary Problems* 35, 3: 519–539.

Schmidtke, Oliver, ed. 2002. *The Third Way Transformation of Social Democracy: Normative Claims and Policy Initiatives in the 21st Century*. Hampshire, UK: Ashgate.

Schudson, Michael. 1998. *The Good Citizen: A History of American Civic Life*. New York: Free Press.

Schwarz, Jordan A., 1993. *The New Dealers: Power Politics in the Age of Roosevelt.* New York: Vintage.

Scott, James C. 1998. *Seeing Like a State: How Certain Schemes to Improve the Human Condition Have Failed.* New Haven: Yale University Press.

Senior, N. W. 1878. *Conversations with M. Thiers, M. Guizot and Other Distinguished Persons, During the Second Empire.* London: Hurst and Blackett.

Sewell, William H. 1980 [1989]. *Work and Revolution in France: The Language of Labor from the Old Regime to 1848.* Cambridge: Cambridge University Press.

Shapin, Steven, and Simon Schaffer. 1985 [2011]. *Leviathan and the Air-Pump: Hobbes, Boyle and the Experimental Life.* Princeton, NJ: Princeton University Press.

Shell, Kurt L. 1970. Extraparliamentary Opposition in Postwar Germany. In West German Election of 1969, special issue, *Comparative Politics* 2, 4: 653–680.

Shils, Edward. 1955 [1968]. The End of Ideology? Pp. 49–63 in Chaim I. Waxman, ed., *The End of Ideology Debate.* New York: Simon and Schuster.

Shils, Edward. 1968 [1955]. The End of Ideology. *Encounter* 5, 5: 52–58.

Shonfield, Andrew. 1958. British Economic Policy since the War. Harmondsworth, UK: Penguin.

Silvia, Stephen I., and Michel Vale. 1992. The Forward Retreat: Labor and Social Democracy in Germany, 1982–1992. *International Journal of Political Economy* 22, 4: 37–52.

Skocpol, Theda. 1992. *Protecting Soldiers and Mothers: Political Origins of Social Policy in the United States.* Cambridge, MA: Belknap Press of Harvard University.

Skowronek, Stephen. 1982. *Building a New American State: The Expansion of National Administrative Capacities, 1877–1920.* New York: Cambridge University Press.

Small, Albion W. 1924. Some Contributions to the History of Sociology. *American Journal of Sociology* 29, 6: 707–725.

Sombart, Werner. 1906 [1976]. *Why Is There No Socialism in the United States?* White Plains, NY: International Arts and Sciences Press.

Sorauf, Frank J. 1972. Party Politics in America. 2nd ed. Boston: Little, Brown.

Southwell, Priscilla L. 2012. A Backroom without the Smoke? Superdelegates and the 2008 Democratic Nomination Process. *Party Politics* 18: 267–283.

Sperber, Jonathan. 2013. *Karl Marx: A Nineteenth-Century Life.* New York: Liveright.

Speth, Rudolf. 2004. Die politischen Strategien der Initiative Neue Soziale Marktwirtschaft. Düsseldorf: Hans-Böckler-Stiftung.

Stampnitzky, Lisa. 2014. *Disciplining Terror: How Experts Invented "Terrorism."* New York: Cambridge University Press.

Starr, Joseph R. 1937. Research Activities of British Political Parties. *Public Opinion Quarterly* 1, 4: 99–107.

Stein, Herbert. 1996. *The Fiscal Revolution in America: Policy in Pursuit of Reality.* Washington, DC: American Enterprise Institute Press.

Steinmetz, George. 2007. *The Devil's Handwriting: Precoloniality and the German Colonial State in Qingdao, Samoa, and Southwest Africa.* Chicago: University of Chicago Press.

Steinmetz, George. 2008. The Colonial State as a Social Field. *American Sociological Review* 73, 4: 589–612.

Steinmo, Sven. 1988. Social Democracy vs. Socialism: Goal Adaptation in Social Democratic Sweden. *Politics and Society* 16: 403–446.

Stern, Charlotta. 2009. European Professors as Public Intellectuals. *Society* 46: 110–118.

Stockman, David. 1986 [2013]. *The Triumph of Politics: Why the Reagan Revolution Failed.* London: Harper and Row.

Stokes, Melvyn. 1983. American Progressives and the European Left. *Journal of American Studies* 17, 1: 5–28.

Sturm, Daniel Friedrich. 2009. *Wohin Geht die SPD?* Munich: Deutscher Taschenbuch Verlag.

Sundquist, James. 1983. *Dynamics of the Party System.* Washington, DC. Brookings. Institution.

Sundström, Göran. 2008. "He Who Decides": Swedish Social Democratic Governments from a Presidentialisation Perspective. *Scandinavian Political Studies* 32, 2: 143–170.

Swedberg, Richard. 1999. Civil Courage ("Zivilcourage"): The Case of Knut Wicksell. *Theory and Society* 28, 4: 501–528.

Sweezy, Alan. 1972. The Keynesians and Government Policy, 1933–1939. *American Economic Review* 62, 1–2: 116–124.

Tanzi, Vito, and Ludger Schuknecht. 1997. Reconsidering the Fiscal Role of Government: The International Perspective. *American Economic Review* 87, 2: 164–168.

Tanzi, Vito, and Ludger Schuknecht. 2000. *Public Spending in the 20th Century. A Global Perspective.* Cambridge: Cambridge University Press.

Taylor, Robert. 1989. Nordic Conference: Sweden Promises New Rules to Open Doors for Foreign Banking. World Trade News, *Financial Times.*

Teles, Steven M. 2008. *The Rise of the Conservative Legal Movement: The Battle for Control of the Law.* Princeton, NJ: Princeton University Press.

Thomas-Symonds, Nicklaus. 2010. *Attlee: A Life in Politics*. London: I. B. Tauris.

Thompson, Dorothy. 1939. On the Record: Want to Bet on It? *Washington Post*, May 26.

Thompson, Noel. 1996. *Political Economy and the Labour Party: The Economics of Democratic Socialism 1884–2005*. London: Routledge.

Thorpe, Andrew. 1996. The Industrial Meaning of "Gradualism": The Labour Party and Industry, 1918–1931. *Journal of British Studies* 35, 1: 84–113.

Thorpe, Andrew. 1997 [2008]. *A History of the British Labour Party*. New York: Palgrave Macmillan.

Thunert, Martin. 2000. Players beyond Borders? German Think Tanks as Catalysts of Internationalisation. *Global Society* 14, 2: 191–211.

Thunert, Martin. 2004. Think Tanks in Germany. Pp. 71–88 in Diane Stone and Andrew Denham, eds., *Think Tank Traditions: Policy Research and the Politics of Ideas*. Manchester: Manchester University Press.

Tilly, Charles. 1984. *Big Structures, Large Processes, Huge Comparisons*. New York: Russell Sage Foundation.

Tilton, Timothy A. 1979. A Swedish Road to Socialism: Ernst Wigforss and the Ideological Foundations of Swedish Social Democracy. *American Political Science Review* 73, 2: 505–520.

Tingsten, Herbert. 1941 [1973]. *The Swedish Social Democrats: Their Ideological Development*. Totowa, NJ: Bedminster Press.

Tomasson, Richard F. 1941 [1973]. Introduction. Pp. vii–xxxii in Herbert Tingsten, *The Swedish Social Democrats: Their Ideological Development*. Totowa, NJ: Bedminster Press.

Tomkin, Shelley Lynne. 1998. *Inside OMB: Politics and Process in the President's Budget Office*. New York: M. E. Sharpe.

Tomlinson, Jim. 1981. Why Was There Never a "Keynesian Revolution" in Economic Policy? *Economy and Society* 10, 1: 72–87.

Tomlinson, Jim. 2005. Managing the Economy, Managing the People: Britain c. 1931–70. *Economic History Review*, New Series, 58, 3 (August): 555–585.

Tomlinson, Jim. 2009. Balanced Accounts? Constructing the Balance of Payments Problem in Post-War Britain. *English Historical Review* 124, 509: 863–884.

Tomlinson, Jim, 2014. British Government and Popular Understanding of Inflation in the Mid-1970s. *Economic History Review* 67, 3: 750-768.

Toye, Richard. 2003. *The Labour Party and the Planned Economy, 1931–1951*. Rochester, NY: Boydell Press.

Tucker, Robert C, ed. 1978 *The Marx-Engels Reader*. New York: W. W. Norton.

Valdés, Juan Gabriel. 1995. *Pinochet's Economists: The Chicago School in Chile*. Cambridge: Cambridge University Press.

Vincent, Andrew. 2009. *Modern Political Ideologies*. Chichester, UK: Wiley-Blackwell.

Volkens, Andrea. 2001. Quantifying the Election Programmes. Pp. 93110 in Ian Budge, Hans-Dieter Klingemann, Andrea Volkens, Judith Bara and Eric Tanenbaum, eds., *Mapping Policy Preferences: Estimates for Parties, Electors, and Governments 19451998*. Oxford: Oxford University Press.

Wacquant, Loïc. 2004. Habitus. Pp.315–319 in Jens Beckert and Milan Zafirovski, eds., *International Encyclopedia of Economic Sociology*. London: Routledge.

Wacquant, Loïc. 2012. Three Steps to a Historical Anthropology of Actually Existing Neoliberalism. *Social Anthropology* 20, 1: 66–79.

Wadbring, Ingela. 2003. A Paper for Its Time? Metro and the Swedish Newspaper Market. English summary of *En tidning i tiden? Metro och den svenska dagstidningsmarknaden*. PhD dissertation, Göteborg University. http://www.kommunikationsforum.dk/log/wadbring-summary .pdf.

Walker, Edward. 2014. *Grassroots for Hire: Public Affairs Consultants in American Democracy*. New York: Cambridge University Press.

Watrin, Christian. 1979. The Principles of the Social Market Economy—Its Origins and Early History. Currency and Economic Reform: West Germany after World War II: A Symposium, *Zeitschrift für die gesamte Staatswissenschaft/Journal of Institutional and Theoretical Economics* 135, 3 (September): 405–425.

Waxman, Chaim I., ed. 1968. *The End of Ideology Debate*. New York: Funk and Wagnalls.

Weber, Max. 1902 [2001]. *The Protestant Ethic and the Spirit of Capitalism*. London: Routledge.

Weber, Max. 1903–1917 [1949]. *The Methodology of the Social Sciences*. New York: Free Press.

Weber, Max. 1915 [1958]. Religious Rejections of the World and Their Directions. Pp. 323–359 in H. H. Gerth and C. Wright Mills, eds., *From Max Weber: Essays in Sociology*. New York: Oxford University Press.

Weber, Max. 1920 [1978]. *Economy and Society*, Vol. 2. (Guenther Roth and Claus Wittich, eds.). Berkeley: University of California Press.

Weber, Max. 1919 [1958]. Politics as a Vocation. Pp. 77–128 in H. H. Gerth and C. Wright Mills, eds., *From Max Weber: Essays in Sociology*. New York: Oxford University Press.

Weir, Margaret. 1992. *Politics and Jobs: The Boundaries of Employment Policy in the United States*. Princeton, NJ: Princeton University Press.

Wilentz, Sean. 2008. *The Age of Reagan: A History, 19742008*. New York: HarperCollins.

Williamson, Philip. 1984. A "Bankers' Ramp"? Financiers and the British Political Crisis of August 1931. *English Historical Review* 99, 393: 770–806.

Wilson, Nicholas Hoover. 2011. From Reflection to Refraction: State Administration in British India, circa 1770–1855. *American Journal of Sociology* 116, 5: 1437–1477.

Wittrock, Björn, and Peter Wagner. 1996. Social Science and the Building of the Early Welfare State: Toward a Comparison of Statist and Non-Statist Western Societies. Pp. 90–114 in Dietrich Rueschemeyer and Theda Skocpol, eds., *States, Social Knowledge and the Origins of Modern Social Policies*. Princeton, NJ: Princeton University Press.

Wörlund, Ingemar. 1992. The Swedish Parliamentary Election of September 1991. *Scandinavian Political Studies* 15, 2: 135–143.

Yonay, Yuval P. 1998. *The Struggle over the Soul of Economics: Institutionalist and Neoclassical Economists in America between the Wars*. Princeton, NJ: Princeton University Press.

Zaretsky, Eli. 2012. *Why America Needs a Left: A Historical Argument*. Cambridge, UK: Polity Press.

Zelizer, Julian E. 2000. The Forgotten Legacy of the New Deal: Fiscal Conservatism and the Roosevelt Administration, 1933–1938. *Presidential Studies Quarterly* 30, 2: 331–358.

Zelizer, Viviana A. 2003. Stephen Skowronek's *Building a New American State* and the Origins of American Political Development. *Social Science History* 27, 3: 425–441.

Zelizer, Viviana A. 2010. *Economic Lives: How Culture Shapes the Economy*. Princeton, NJ: Princeton University Press.

Index

Page numbers followed by *f* or *t* indicate figures or tables.